The Artist as Thinker

Rockefeller Memorial Chapel
The University of Chicago
See Appendix D

The Graduates' Window   *The Works of the Mind Window*

The Artist as Thinker

FROM SHAKESPEARE TO

JOYCE • *George Anastaplo*

Swallow Press
Chicago   Athens Ohio   London

George Anastaplo is
Lecturer in the Liberal Arts
at The University of Chicago,
Professor of Political Science and of Philosophy
at Rosary College,
and Visiting Professor of Law
at Loyola University of Chicago.

Swallow Press Books
are published by
Ohio University Press
Athens, Ohio 45701

Library of Congress Cataloging in Publication Data

Anastaplo, George.
    The artist as thinker.

    Bibliography: p.
    Includes index.
    1. English literature—History and criticism.
2. Philosophy in literature. 3. American fiction—
19th century—History and criticism. I. Title.
PR409.P48A5   820'.9   82–6502
ISBN 0-8040-0416-1   AACR2
ISBN 0-8040-0417-x

To

MY WIFE

Artist and Mother of Artists

who

a quarter of a century ago

ventured to sing:

Ariadne at Naxos

If I could be the world! I would explode
Then smash the dust itself to bits
So I could murder you.

Was it for this I doomed my brother,
Tricked my father, grieved my mother,
And chose your ugly, black-sailed ship?
Coward! Safe, you are fool enough to think
You could have solved the labyrinth,
Killed, and lived—without my help?

I only slept; I was not dead
In Naxos on this rocky bed,
Drowsy with his love and child.
I woke: dear Theseus was gone!
Oh, better to be dead at home,
Where only pity made me wild.

Lucky, high-browed Athens, be ruled by a knave,
A common sacrifice, garbage for the grave.
I deserve the shame of an unroyal choice.
You immortals know my better
Mind. Send my sweet love a letter
For me, in this wise:

I am still the princess of the royal house of Crete.
I will not, like a peasant woman, weep, rave and sweat!
With salt water, I shall wash away salt tears;
And, relentless, comb the tangles from my stringing hair.
Then I will wait. Dionysus will come.
He is a god, and handsomer than you.

Contents

Preface

Rubek:
    You have no conception, really, of the way
    an artist's mind works.
Maya (smiles and shakes her head):
    Good heavens. I don't even have any concep-
    tion of the way my own mind works.

        —Henrik Ibsen, *When We Dead Awaken,* II

THE BEAUTIFUL beckons us, not only to enjoy it but also to imitate it in our lives and to grasp it in our thoughts. Some of the beautiful things that artists have made are looked at in this book. This is, in effect, a book on how to read—on how to read certain kinds of "books" a little better. My aim is to be useful both to the general reader and to the specialist in English literature.

My first book, *The Constitutionalist: Notes on the First Amendment,* was devoted to "a consideration of American institutions and circumstances and what we can learn from them about both the human being and the citizen." That inquiry was pursued further in my next book, *Human Being and Citizen: Essays on Virtue, Freedom and the Common Good:*

> The human being is essentially unconcerned about his immediate circumstances: he reaches out to those virtuous men in other times and at other places who have thought as he has—to those, that is, who have thought. The citizen, on the other hand, is always rooted in a particular place: to him circumstances very much matter, as does the good of the country he chances to serve and for which he is prepared to sacrifice himself.

> One can see, in the relation of human being to citizen, something of the relation of general to particular, of abstract to concrete. But one sees there also something other than the relation of whole to part— for in some ways the human being and the citizen are quite different people, oftentimes in tension with if not even mortally opposed to one another.

The artist, too, is rooted in particularity. Is the artist related to the philosopher (and not only in this respect) somewhat as the citizen is to the human being?

Artists have a profound influence (and not only as guardians of our language and of our imagination) in shaping people, perhaps even more so today than formerly, since the influence among us of the family, of religion, and of sound political associations has been dangerously abridged. Consider, for example, the uses to which art has been put by our all-pervasive television, extending even to the "staging" of Presidential "debates" and inaugurations.

An artist in my family has made the following provocative suggestions about what art is:

In its broadest definition, an artistic thing is that thing whose essence resides outside itself. In contrast, a natural thing exists in itself and is answerable only to itself. Its reason for being is in itself. A tree grows, a stone falls, people have children. These are, in certain critical respects, natural occurrences; they can happen on their own. But a thing cannot be called artistic until it is considered in the context of human intent.

Except as it is seen in the context of a human mind, a thing has no artistic integrity. A bench is in itself just a pile of wood. It acquires artistic import—is called a bench—only when it is seen as something to sit on, when it is seen relative to people who have designs on its use. Similarly, a statue is in itself just a battered stone. It is called a statue only when a human turns the stone into an intended shape and other people see it and can say, "Oh, yes, that's a dog," or, more simply, "Oh, yes, that's a fine shape." Consider a statue forgotten in an overgrown garden. Whoever may happen upon it would call it a dog but, separated from how people regard it, it just sits there in the weeds like any other stone.

The broad sense of "artistic" I have been using is somewhat archaic. Nowadays, made things which are put to use, such as a bench, are more likely to be called "artifacts" than "art." What we now mean by "art" is independent of a corporeal use. When we say "art" we probably do not mean something to sit on, to hold liquids in, or to fix our chariots with. What we call "art" are those made things which enter the mind and cause a change.

For us a work of art is usually some sort of reproduction of the world, some sort of distillation, which causes a motion in the beholder's soul so as to recall or illuminate the world.

A painting, for instance, is often a distillation of a visual experience into a set, two-dimensional plane. It reminds the viewer of that experience. Similarly, music is often a distillation of thought, emotion, inclination, character, or relation into a succession of sounds. Viewers, listeners, and readers come in contact with works of art and are caused to cast their minds back upon what they know, have seen, or perhaps have dreamt. Much art, then, is some sort of image which reflects, and causes a reflection in, the mind. The effect of much art is to recall the world. The effect of great art is to recall the world in a deep way.

Good art is evocative. Every work of art has many non-artistic but yet necessary aspects, if it is to exist—aspects which are somehow separate from that which is primarily responsible for its evocative power. It is contained by various limitations. Thus, it is made of and with some material, be it paper, a musical instrument, or a dancer's body. If it is written, it is in some language. It is a product of its maker's efforts.

Someone studying a work of art can concentrate on any number of concerns. One could read the *Iliad,* for example, for its clues about the development of language, for its religious, social, or nutritional implications, or even for what it reveals about the personality of its maker.

My obvious concern in this book is with the most important of the "non-artistic but yet necessary aspects" of art. I consider primarily the artist as thinker. Even so, I must respect the mystical tie of art to the divine—that mysterious gift which permits the artist to have an effect and a significance he would not have if he confined himself to writing such prosaic treatises as uninspired thinkers produce when *they* talk about love, mortality, prudence, and the relation of virtue to happiness. Thus, it is not possible to consider properly the artist as thinker without drawing upon those "artistic" aspects of art that are vital to the unique "evocative" effect of each work of art.

The works of art I consider here are approached in their insistent particularity. Still, what is said about one work in this book can throw light on another. There should be evident throughout this book, therefore, the principles and ends upon which genuine thinking depends and to which serious thinking repeatedly directs us.

These principles and ends, which help make sense of what the artist intends to say, include moral and political standards rooted in nature and discernible by reason. Thus, these pervasive principles and ends should be kept in mind if one is truly to see what an artist's characters are doing. These principles and ends are discussed at length in the Prologue, Epilogue, and Appendixes; they are touched upon again and again throughout this book. One reader of this book has been so bold as to suggest that it "establishes a genre of literary interpretation, in which the critic judges the development of the action primarily in the light of what the actors should have done."

My academic duties have helped determine which English-language artists I happen to draw upon here. I continue to profit from my regular courses at Rosary College and the University of Chicago and from my annual seminars at the Clearing and the University of Dallas. Also instructive have been my seminars in recent years at Ohio University, Memphis State University and the University of Illinois at Chicago Circle.

I continue to profit as well from the suggestions by generous readers, such as those provided by Sara Maria Anastaplo and J. Harvey Lomax (who have read the text, not the notes, of my thirteen chapters). George Malcolm Davidson Anastaplo, Theodora McShan Anastaplo, Andrew Patner, and Robert L. Stone have helped prepare this book for the press, as have Despina M. Damolaris and Judith M. Davies (both of Rosary College) and Jo Ann Preston. Frontispiece sketches were prepared for this book by Harold Haydon from photographs by Patricia Evans (Mrs. James Kalven). The cover design is by Irving Perkins, using a color photo by John Rosenthal.

Acknowledgments are also due to my earliest teachers in the humanities: to Fred K.A. Lingle and Georgia Campbell Lingle of Carterville (Illinois) Community High School and to Henry Rago of the College of the University of Chicago. They can be understood to have advanced Samuel Johnson's proposition that "the chief glory of every people arises from its authours."

The works of art I venture to comment upon invite us to contemplate them. One is sometimes privileged to discover vital things in these works that the artists themselves did not recognize. Emphasis *is* placed in this book, as I have indicated, upon looking at each work somewhat on its own. This is least so, perhaps, with respect to my discussions in Chapter I, Part Two, in Chapter II, and in Chapter III. What is said there about regimes, human rights, nature, law, and justice is intended to be useful in reading the remaining chapters. In these remaining chapters one can see manifestations of the modern movement from public to private "priorities" in human affairs. (I make considerable use of "the personal element" in my own work, if only to "engage" and perhaps restrain readers who are anything but austere themselves.)

The chapters of this book (as is true of the works of art commented upon) need not be considered in the order presented here, once the Prologue and Chapter 1, Part One, have been read. The virtual independence of each chapter means that some repetition is inevitable as I offer fresh guidance to what are, for the most part, quite familiar works of art (indeed, often the masterpieces of the artists considered). As Alexis de Tocqueville put it in his *Democracy in America,* "I prefer to repeat myself sometimes rather than not to be understood, and I would rather the author suffered than the subject." It is my hope that my readers will be encouraged by what I say here to return to the enduring works I consider—and to do so with renewed interest, enhanced competence, and deepened pleasure because of what is suggested in this book about old-fashioned moral and political sensibilities rooted in human rationality and in the very nature of things.

Do not the better works indicate to the imaginative reader, who must be to some degree an artist himself, the way each of them should be considered? I trust that what I say, here and elsewhere, about various artists as thinkers always remains aware of the massive fact that such thinkers do tend to be gifted ministers in the service of the beautiful.

George Anastaplo

Hyde Park
Chicago, Illinois

SOCRATES WAS the son of Sophroniscus, a sculptor, and of Phaenarete, a midwife, as we read in the *Theaetetus* of Plato; he was a citizen of Athens and belonged to the deme Alopece. It was thought that he helped Euripides to make his plays...Duris makes him out to have been a slave and to have been employed on stonework, and the draped figures of the Graces on the Acropolis have by some been attributed to him.

Diogenes Laertius

FROM THE very start me and Tom allowed that there was somebody sick in the state-room next to ourn, because the meals was always toted in there by the waiters. By-and-by we asked about it—Tom did—and the waiter said it was a man, but he didn't look sick. . . .

It was always nuts for Tom Sawyer—a mystery was. If you'd lay out a mystery and a pie before me and him, you wouldn't have to say take your choice; it was a thing that would regulate itself. Because in my nature I have always run to pie, whilst in his nature he has always run to mystery. People are made different. And it is the best way. Tom says to the waiter:

"What's the man's name?"

"Phillips."

"Where'd he come aboard?"

"I think he got aboard at Elexandria, up on the Iowa line."

"What do you reckon he's a-playing?"

"I hain't any notion—I never thought of it."

I says to myself, here's another one that runs to pie.

Huckleberry Finn

HE TOOK care to pronounce the word sea [*thálassa*] so clearly that all the dolphins within it might shine.

Odysseus Elytis

Prologue: THE ARTIST AS THINKER

> *The primary objects [of appetite and of thought]*
> *are the same. For the object of desire is that*
> *which appears to be noble, whereas the primary*
> *object of rational wish is noble. Appetite is con-*
> *sequent upon opinion rather than opinion upon*
> *appetite. For thinking is the starting-point.*
>
> —Aristotle, *Metaphysics* 1072a27–30

i

I CONFINE myself for the most part in this book to the verbal arts, although what I have to say can be applied to some (if not all) of the other arts as well. What is meant by "art" and "artist" has been anticipated in the Preface and is further indicated throughout this book and its Appendixes.

By and large, art both instructs and entertains us. It instructs us partly by entertaining us; it entertains us partly by instructing us. We are likely to learn from that which amuses us; we are likely to enjoy that which seems to teach us something.

This Prologue is divided into three parts. The first section is intended to entertain the reader and, thereby, to put him in a receptive (or, at least, benevolently patient) mood for what follows thereafter. The second section is intended to instruct him. This may (I admit) tax his patience here and there—but he can console himself not only with the hope that it may be good for him but also with my promise that a change of pace awaits him. The third section of this Prologue is intended (by challenging the reader) both to entertain and to instruct him. First, then, to the preliminary entertainment:

Once upon a time, there was a young comedian who was believed to do excellent imitations of the hard-boiled actor Humphrey Bogart. Arrangements were made to bring the actor in to watch himself thus imitated. When asked to comment on the performance he had just observed, Humphrey Bogart was heard to remark, "One of us stinks."

The reader is urged, as with my other publications, to begin by reading the text without reference to the notes at the back of this book.

1

If this story is told right, clever people should chuckle. However that may be, the story does turn in upon itself in a peculiar, even fascinating, manner. One may get from it a "taste" of infinity or at least of infinite regress.[1]

My next story is a story about a story. To be more precise, it is a story about a story about a story. A psychoanalyst I know becomes peeved with me (albeit in a jocular sort of way) whenever he recalls something I once did to him. In fact, *I* had forgotten I had done it until he reminded me of it in a moment of unprofessional (but becomingly human) exasperation. (One might even conjecture that *he* is obsessed with this episode and that *I*, for some peculiar reason, have repressed it. Be that as it may, I have had to consult him to make sure I remember correctly the episode I am about to describe: it is important to get the facts right.)

It seems that this psychoanalyst was once telling a group of us a story with profound implications about the social dimensions of suicide—about what the suicidal person is trying to say and whom he is "relating to." His story turned around the fact that in almost all of the many instances of suicide from San Francisco's Golden Gate Bridge, the victim jumps from the side of the bridge facing *toward the city* rather than from the side of the bridge facing away from the city.

It also seems that I asked on that occasion a simple-minded question that stopped my storyteller dead in his tracks and the recollection of which continues to annoy him: "Which side of the Golden Gate Bridge is the sidewalk on?" He did not know—nor did I. But we both sensed that the import of his story depended in part on the answer to my rather prosaic question. Indeed, do not many moving stories depend—if we are to understand them—upon what is done with the most obvious facts?

Of course, the suggestion has been made, there may be sidewalks on both sides of the Golden Gate Bridge. (Is that likely? Would that be an economical use of valuable space, considering how relatively few people can be expected to walk across a long bridge? Even so, that possibility cannot be ruled out.) Of course, also, there may not be any sidewalks at all on that bridge or, if there is only one sidewalk, it may not matter which side it is on since the would-be suicide *could* cross the bridge *to* the side from which he wants to jump. Our analyst has come up with these suggestions in an effort to salvage his story. But, one is tempted to point out in response to such suggestions, to walk on a busy bridge which has no sidewalk or to cross from one side of such a bridge to the other can get a man killed.

My third (and last) story in the first section of this Prologue is even shorter than my first one, to which it does bear some resemblance. But this one is even more profound, one may say, as well as even more subtle. This "story" consists of some sober advice, which my readers should take to heart: "When on the cage of an elephant you see the inscription 'buffalo,' don't believe your eyes."[2]

ii

THE NEXT section of this Prologue may seem unduly prosaic, especially by contrast with the first section, unless what I have to say should seem so absurd as to be ludicrous. But that is a risk—the risk of being either boring or outrageous—which one must run in the interest of the arts and of science. Besides, more stories do await the reader in the final section of this Prologue.

I begin this section with the prediction that most readers will remember one or more of the three stories I have just told—about Humphrey Bogart, about the Golden Gate Bridge, and about the elephant (or is it the buffalo?) in the cage—long after they have forgotten what I am now about to say.

Why should this be so? The hold that stories have upon us and the effects they achieve suggest something about the nature of art: seeds can be deftly planted and effortlessly absorbed, and they can produce bountiful harvests. A great deal can be summed up aptly and most economically in a few words—in an ambiguous play on words, in a reminder of the obvious, or in studied incongruity. A story, a work of art, seems somehow to be "real," to be drawn from life, to be meaningful and immediate, not merely "academic" and formal. And, at the very least, a story assures us that we do understand something—perhaps without having to work at thinking—and allows us to enjoy ourselves in the process.

But, we also know, art does deal in illusions—and one of its profoundest illusions may be that one can truly understand without thinking. Does this illusion appeal to our awareness of a lack of preparation (if not our laziness), to our vulnerability (or apprehensiveness), or to a certain innate conservatism? The artist may attract us *to* his work by holding out the illusion of easy access, but the thoughtful viewer (or reader or listener) does not permit himself to be satisfied with superficial impressions and responses. He recognizes, for example, when he comes upon a fine piece of art, that something deep *is* stirred in him, something inviting, even requiring, serious reflection. He may also see that such stirring has been induced by a craftsman who somehow knows what he is doing.

Homer could be called by his countrymen "the wisest of all the Greeks."[3] When one carefully examines Homer's poems, one can begin to understand why many considered him wise. There are to be found in his poems detailed and sophisticated arrangements which cannot be understood as the work only of "inspiration" or of "the unconscious." Consider, for example, in Book Two of the *Iliad,* "The Catalogue of Ships," that meticulous and, to most readers, uninteresting account of the various contingents of Achaeans who came to besiege Troy under the command of Agamemnon. In this inventory of contingents, one can notice upon stopping to count, the contingent of the prudent Odysseus is central to the array of Achaean ships, and the contingents of the two great rivals, Agamemnon and Achilles (each with his special claim to preeminence) are at an equal distance (in terms of numbers of contingents) on either side of the unifying Odysseus. It is the quarrel of Agamemnon and Achilles, the reader will remember, that is said to be largely responsible for what happens in the *Iliad*. (See the end of Chapter XIII, below.)

Are not such facts, based upon simple calculations, suggestive about Homer? Should they put us on notice about much of what he says (and not only about the relation of Achilles and Agamemnon)? Should they alert us not to underestimate the subtlety or carefulness of a great artist? But one does not make such calculations as these unless one is moved to read with the greatest care. (I touch, in the Epilogue to this book, upon that which may inspire one to read thus.)

Many (perhaps most) scholars argue that Homer merely picked up such passages as "The Catalogue of Ships" from his bardic predecessors, that he was "obliged" to retain extended traditional accounts long after the time they were necessary or even useful to his story. It is not, however, what one picks up from one's predecessors that is critical—it is instructive sometimes to compare Shakespeare's sources with his own versions of various stories—but rather what one does with what is picked up.

That which is merely suggested in "The Catalogue of Ships" about Odysseus and his prudence, and which is evident elsewhere in the *Iliad* as well, is developed even more in the *Odyssey*. Thus, central to the *Odyssey* is the concluding episode in the very long tale told by Odysseus in the Phaeacian court of Alcinous. The centrality in the *Odyssey* of this episode should become apparent to anyone who consults the number of pages in any standard edition of the *Odyssey*. (This episode is to be found at the end of Book Twelve of the twenty-four-book poem. The divisions into books are not Homer's, it seems, but they were evidently made by someone who was sensitive to the obvious articulations in the poem.) One can see in this central episode of the *Odyssey* that one's character and hence conduct do matter, that one chooses meaningfully—that is, it matters what one chooses. (This proposition is developed in my discussion in Chapter I, below, of prudence and mortality in Shakespeare's tragedies and is thereafter repeatedly drawn upon in this book.)

The central episode of the *Odyssey* is about the slaughter of the herd of the Sun and the effect of that sacrilegious slaughter on Odysseus's men. Only *he* survives the ensuing storm at sea—because, we are given to understand, only he restrained himself and chose properly. That is, only he refrained from killing and eating the cattle of the Sun, although he was as hungry as his men. Is it only retroactively that Odysseus attributes his men's destruction to their sacrilege? This raises a deeper question: what "really happened" on that occasion? Are we to understand that Odysseus is only making up all this to entertain his royal audience? Is all this his fantasy (a kind of dream), designed to appeal to his pious audience, whose help he needs, explaining why it is that only he has survived to invoke their aid? Yet Homer does seem, in the opening lines of the *Odyssey,* to ratify the story about the herd of the Sun. (Odysseus himself reveals how his curiosity, if not his greed, had led to the deadly encounter with the Cyclops.)

It has always been suspected by some that Odysseus made up much of what he reports in the court of Alcinous. (Such an argument proceeds, of course, on the assumption that Homer intends the overall story told by the *Odyssey,* as distinguished from the stories told by Odysseus, to be about things that do or can happen among human beings. See the end of Chapter XII, below.) Even so, whether or not the tale told by Odysseus in the court of Alcinous "really happened," the account does reflect the character of Odysseus—of wily Odysseus (or of an Odysseus-like Homer)—and, as such, it is both revealing and appropriate. We can see, in either understanding, why it is that Odysseus does prevail: he is a prudent man able to restrain himself; he is a man of considerable rhetorical gifts.

We are, I believe, meant by Homer to see this. And, if so, we again are obliged to recognize that he is far more than a gifted story-teller reworking old stories. We thus return, if we are to understand what permits art to have its enduring effect, to the need not to under-estimate the disciplined intelligence of the better artists. Behind whatever inspiration or beneath whatever unconscious Homer drew upon, a surpassing intelligence may be discerned, an intelligence which grasps the nature of things, human and non-human alike. Is it not prudent to assume that the intelligence evident in the works of the greatest artists is not simply that of imaginative critics but rather that of the artists themselves—and that their greatness consists, in part, in their ability to see and to describe what *is*, or (to use an old-fashioned phrase) to imitate nature?

To see and to describe—ay, there's the rub! To see and to describe does *not* mean to express oneself, to let oneself go. Self-expression is not worth much if the self being expressed is shallow or contorted or misguided. The only self truly worth expressing is that which under-stands what is. To the extent that it does understand what is, how-ever, it is not an individual, private self but rather one very much like other souls which have understood the most important things, not only now but always, not only here but everywhere.

There is, of course, a risk run when there is too much so-called art around—when (as with our voracious entertainment industry) a lot must be produced to supply a great (even unnaturally great) commercial demand. If much must be supplied, unprecedented inno-vation is promoted—and hence a good deal of foolishness, to say nothing of perversity and irresponsibility. The natural tendency of would-be artists *is* toward novelty, toward something which distin-guishes each of them from his competitors. To place a premium (as we often do) upon novelty is to legitimate self-expression and experi-

mentation at the expense both of discipline and of enduring standards
—and this means that the idiosyncracies of particular souls are made
much of and hence stimulated to excess.

When art becomes preoccupied with what we call feelings, both
excessive sensibility and moral obtuseness tend to result. Carelessness,
self-centeredness, and thoughtlessness are likely to be promoted when
there is a marked expansion and heightening of what passes for aesthetic experience. "Expansion" and "heightening," it should go without saying, are not the same as "deepening."

I have referred to the true artist's ability *to see* and to describe
accurately what he sees. I have also suggested that a precondition of
proper seeing is a well-developed understanding. Thus, an ancient
Greek once observed, "Eyes and ears are bad witnesses to men having
barbarian souls." Or, to put this insight in the American idiom, we
have the observation from Mark Twain's Connecticut Yankee, "You
can't depend on your eyes when your imagination is out of focus."[4]

To see and to describe human beings, one must be able to discern *what is going on.* To be able to discern properly and fully, one
must see what is right and wrong among the things that *are* going on.
(One encounters this in every work discussed in this book as well as
in everyday life.) It is not enough to regard a deed in a "neutral"
fashion: one must determine whether the deed is good or bad, sensible or senseless, noble or base. To describe human things without
taking these vital characteristics into account is to be shallow and to
distort and to mislead. The neglect of these characteristics cuts one
loose from one's roots in the best and condemns one to live with the
impoverished soul one thereby happens to have.

Of course, a moral judgment may be implied in one's descriptions, whether or not one is aware of it. But unless one *is* aware of
one's moral judgment, one cannot question properly that judgment
and understand it and, if need be, refine and elevate it. The greatest art, I should add, reflects an awareness of the *limits* of both the
good and the noble. It reflects an awareness of the tension there can
be between the good (such as the just) and the noble, to say nothing
of the beautiful.

But we can leave that tension and its resolution for another
occasion. It suffices for the moment to be reminded, for example,
that there *is* something to be said, in Sophocles' *Antigone,* both for

Antigone and for Creon the king: she stands for a family-based nobility at the expense of the city; he stands for a city-based justice at the
expense of the family. She neglects the city; he neglects the family.
Each is critically (indeed, naturally) vulnerable in and through that
which is imprudently neglected.

It will be said by some that it is all very well to talk about the
need of the artist and his public to know what it means to be good,
sensible, and noble, but do we not all know *now* that these things
(goodness, sensibleness, nobility) are but matters of taste, that they
are conventions which happen to have evolved one way here, another
way there? What can be said in response to this criticism made by the
sophisticated social scientist?

I have referred to art as an imitation of nature. Does not the true
artist help us see what nature is like? And does he not, when he depicts
human things, show us what nature calls for? Does he not thereby
awaken and inform in us that which nature provides and prescribes?
If that is so, then the artist can help us see both how our conventions
appear in the light of nature and why conventions *must be*. Indeed,
one can come to see that conventions are imperfect responses (but
responses, nevertheless, they *are*) to what nature prescribes. Thus,
for example, although languages may be in large part shaped by conventions, it is not conventional but rather natural that men should
have language.

I have also referred to the recourse of the artist to illusions.
Conventions, too, are a kind of illusion. The more alert artist is aware
of the social usefulness of salutary illusions—illusions which he addresses himself to and questions only in the most guarded manner.
He is aware that not everyone can be as thoughtful or as secure as he
is—and so he proceeds responsibly even when he probes to the very
roots of things.

Some, I have said, will argue (in response to what I have said)
that conventions and arbitrary tastes, not nature, are what move us.
I have addressed myself (here and in Appendixes A and C) to their
criticism, at least in a preliminary way. But others will invoke nature
herself in arguing against what I say about the guides provided by
nature to the thoughtful man. That is, some will argue that man is so
constituted that he cannot help but be moved by his passions, the
passions with which nature has endowed him. Particularly demanding upon us, one may be told, is the passion of love.

Love is a very strange and powerful thing indeed, and artists (certainly modern artists) do make a lot of it. However, there is about love one feature which is not generally appreciated and which, especially among the young, may be at first difficult even to notice: one can have a surprising amount to say about *whether* one will fall in love on any particular occasion. Consider the following exchange between two of Henry James's characters as they discuss a not-quite-respectable (but nevertheless fetching) American woman and the most respectable English aristocrat who is entangled with her:[5]

> *A:*   It [would not be] a proper marriage, at any rate.
> *B:*   Why not, if he loves her?
> *A:*   Oh, if that's all you want! Would you marry her yourself?
> *B:*   Certainly, if I were in love with her.
> *A:*   You took care not to be that.
> *B:*   Yes, I did—and so [Sir Arthur] had better have done.
>   But since he's bitten—!

If one *is* in love, one is moved to do certain things, many strange, even wild, things. But it is believed by James's characters—and does not experience bear this out?—that one may have considerable control over whether one falls in love. Of course, once one's "bitten," things may get somewhat out of hand.

Is not love (or any other passion, such as the desire for glory or the desire for revenge) essentially like drunkenness in this respect? Consider what Aristotle indicates in response to the argument by someone who tried to excuse his own misconduct by explaining that he had been drunk and hence could not control himself. Aristotle grants that this man might not have been able to control himself once drunk, but he *had* been able to control whether he would become drunk in the first place. That is to say, everyone of mature years knows, from his own experiences and those of others, what may happen when certain restraints are removed or when certain passions are unleashed—and thus he is responsible for his "liberating" self-indulgence and its consequences.

There is, in practice, a reciprocal relation between what we know and how we feel, between our understanding and our passions. Art does help shape and, if need be, purge the passions. Thinking about art also helps: it helps correct and direct the artist when his own passions lead him astray; it helps train a people's response to the art they see.[6] Standing behind and above both the makings of artists and the thinkings of critics is what nature shows us about what the human being is and should be.

I leave it to my readers to think of examples which test what I have said about the moral judgments one has to make before one can adequately describe what is going on, whether in the humanities or in the social sciences (and sometimes even in the physical sciences). I have already mentioned Sophocles' *Antigone.* I can mention as well other widely known works (which I discuss in this book): Shakespeare's *Hamlet,* Charles Dickens's *Christmas Carol,* and Mark Twain's *Adventures of Huckleberry Finn.* Is it not impossible to understand fully what any of the principal characters in these stories is *doing* unless one thinks about, and arrives at, a judicious opinion about how that character *should* act in the circumstances in which he happens to find himself?

For example—to anticipate our discussion in the first chapter of this book—one *can* try to concern oneself only with what Prince Hamlet's response to his father's command to kill King Claudius shows about Hamlet's indecisiveness. But one moves to an even more serious inquiry, and one which better illuminates Hamlet's character and conduct, when one asks whether he *should* have respected a ghost's command to kill the king. Shakespeare surely had an opinion about this. What *is* that opinion? And what would Shakespeare say in support of his opinion? Or rather, what *does* Shakespeare say in support of his opinion? For is not the play as a whole a reflection of Shakespeare's opinion about the soundness of the things Hamlet believed, felt, and did?

I have, in what I have said and particularly in the illustrations I have used, drawn upon the verbal arts. But must we not think as well about what the greatest practitioners of the nonverbal arts are doing and saying? Thus, I am reminded of Raphael's *School of Athens,* which requires days (if not months and years) of careful study if one is truly to *see* it and its companion frescoes. I am reminded also of the daring commentary on the relation between gods and men to be seen in the sculpture of the Parthenon. I am reminded as well of the mathematical genius which (I have heard) is at the foundations of the greatest music.[7]

Much of what I have said here may apply only to genuine art. That is, much of what *passes* for art is, no doubt, mere passing fancy.

We need not concern ourselves with many of the artistic experiments we encounter, except as momentary diversions—unless they become so pervasive or so debasing as to corrupt our passions, eventually our understanding, and then even more our passions. It is upon arriving at a sound understanding of genuine art that one comes to see—and here I sum up much of what I have said thus far in the second section of this Prologue—one sees that an artist thinks; one sees that an artist passes moral judgment; one sees that thinking is required if one *is* to be able to pass moral judgment; one sees that moral judgment is required if one is fully to think, if one is fully to understand what is going on; and one sees that art may be a convenient, perhaps the most salutary if not an indispensable, way to instill or to preserve in a community at large the thought (including the moral standards and sound judgment) of the best men.

At the very least, then, art should help shape our passions, not just permit us to express and indulge and hence intensify and degrade them. It should teach us that there is an intimate connection between character and fate—that is, between the kind of human being one is and what happens to one. It should also teach us that reason is central to any effort to live the best possible life.

The right kind of art teaches the young to be tough-minded, to see and to judge things as they are, to understand how they should be—in short, to be wary of both sentimentality and callousness. (One not altogether unattractive problem with youth—especially with the best or most noble youth—is its tendency toward excessive generosity, even toward generosity on principle without regard for consequences.) Thus, the right kind of art—that is, again, genuine art—discovers the sense of the universe and man's place in it, if only by reminding us of and refining the enduring questions, including questions both about what it means to know and about what is truly knowable.

I conclude this stage of the Prologue with the reminder that those whom the ancient Israelites called "prophets," the equally ancient Greeks called "poets."

iii

I RETURN, in the final section of this Prologue (and in the Epilogue to this book), to that *practice* of art (amateurish though it may be) with which I opened—that is, to the telling of stories that are, I trust, not inappropriate for illustrating what I have to say. I began with three stories. The reader has earned a double measure of additional stories by enduring the perhaps prosaic comments I have made (in several different ways) on the nature of art and on the relation of art to thought, including moral judgments.

And so I conjure up here a half dozen more stories, but stories which are (so to speak) informed by what I have thus far said about art. The stories I now tell, all quite short, are instructive diversions. The reader is challenged to think about them, about the relations among them, and how they fit into what I have said. But, first of all, and necessarily first if these stories *are* to interest and challenge him, the reader should consider what each of them (like each of the chapters in this book) says on its own. They are (I should warn) problems and puzzles even more than they are stories: they are, so to speak, stories in an interrogative mode. Each reader should find at least one upon which he will be tempted to reflect from time to time.

Which of these stories particularly intrigues one will no doubt depend somewhat upon one's temperament—just as this selection, and its arrangement, may depend somewhat on my temperament and experiences, including the books I have happened to come across. Even so, these stories, as here set forth, may help us see something about the problem of justice and its attainment, about the relation of the permanent to the impermanent, about the relation of mind to matter, and about what can and cannot be in (and be known about) the very nature of things. I hope it is also evident that all these stories assume and say something about what human nature, including the nature of thinking, is like.

But I am reverting to the terms and tones of the prosaic second section of this Prologue—and I *have* promised stories, albeit puzzling stories. Well, here they are—for the reader's amusement and diversion, as well as instruction. The reader may well have heard one or two of these before.

The first story I should like to leave with readers goes like this: If the rich could hire other people to die for them, the poor could make a wonderful living.[8]

My second puzzle is a very ancient one. Indeed, it is said to have stumped Homer himself, who was told by some boys who were (unknown to him) killing lice in their clothes, "All that we catch we leave behind, and all that we do not catch we carry home."[9]

Next: I heard, during my first months in law school more than thirty years ago, of a flower in the South Seas which was of a quite remarkable color except when someone looked at it.

Next: Democritus, the philosopher, used to live in the cemetery of his town. It was very quiet there—and he could study. One midnight the mischievous boys of the town tried to frighten him with ghostlike noises. When at the dead hour, intent on his studies, he heard strange sounds, he did not so much as move his eyes from his page, but simply said, "Boys, little boys, go home. This is no place for you. You will catch cold here."[10]

Next: I once heard of an incantation which permits one to turn whatever one chooses into gold, so long as one does not while invoking it think of elephants. There may also be, for all I know, another such incantation which depends upon one's not thinking of buffaloes while invoking it.[11]

Next: We return to the peculiar psychology of suicide. It is reported by Thomas Hobbes that there was once an epidemic of suicides among romantic young women in a city of ancient Greece. The resourceful rulers of the city announced that the body of any future suicide of this kind would be stripped and exposed to public view. This dramatic threat to the women's perverse desire for honor, it seems, promptly put a stop to the epidemic (which Hobbes called "a fit of madness").[12]

My final puzzle for readers is one that could have served as the inspiration for the Humphrey Bogart story with which I began this Prologue. It is taken from the first book of Plato's *Republic;* its theme can even be thought of as having been developed throughout that dialogue. It seems that a man from the insignificant island of Seriphus once abused the Athenian leader, Themistocles, saying that Themistocles was famous, not thanks to himself, but thanks to his city, Athens. To this Themistocles replied that if he had been a Seriphian he would not have made a name for himself, nor would this Seriphian have made a name for *him*self had he been an Athenian. Or, put another way, Themistocles can be taken to have said, "If you had been an Athenian and I had been a Seriphian, neither of us would have been famous."

I introduced these half dozen puzzles by calling them stories. But, the reader will agree, they are not quite stories but rather dramatized mysteries or riddles around which an intelligent man of imaginative talent—that is to say, an artist—could indeed weave engaging stories, each of which would say something significant about human relations, about human thought, and even about the nature of things.

What artistic endeavors point to and what can be made of them depend on careful study of each piece of art which results—that is, on the study of the work itself much more than on the study either of the artist himself or of the artistic "process" by which the work is produced. And such a study, I repeat, means that one must *think* about what one sees and hears: one must ask the questions and make the judgments which help bring to light the sense and sensibleness of what appears to be there.

Of course, even without thinking and questioning—even without the informed seeing which the artist expects from the best of the community which he serves—there is manifest in genuine art a beauty which can please one and all, even when it is not explicitly recognized that such beauty is, first and foremost, a material reflection of an enduring excellence (including the excellence of an understanding mind) and, with respect to human things, a promise of virtue.

I have been speaking in much of this Prologue in more general terms than I usually do in the chapters that follow, where some thirty-nine works of art are discussed (for the most part) in their particularity. (Respect for the particular and the concrete is essential to the artist and hence to the respectful critic as well.) I reserve for the Epilogue and the Appendixes a more extended indication of the presuppositions and "method" relied on in this book.

I begin my survey of English-language artists with Shakespeare, the founder (since he is the early peak) of our literary tradition. The things (and especially the thinking) we notice in his work should be evident as well (if only, in some instances, by way of contrast) in the other artists touched upon in this book.[13]

I. WILLIAM SHAKESPEARE

(1564-1616)

PART ONE

> *For a happy life, the first requisite is neither to act unjustly to others nor to be treated unjustly by others. Of this pair, the former is not very difficult, but it is wholly difficult to secure immunity from being unjustly treated; indeed, it is impossible to gain this completely, except by being completely good.*
>
> —Plato, *Laws* 829A

i

IT HAS been reported of the 1939 Munich conference between Neville Chamberlain and Adolph Hitler that "when the time [came] to sign the final Agreements, it [was] found that the ink pot into which Herr Hitler dipped his pen was empty."[14]

We are not surprised when a poet notices such details. One is reminded, for example, of a woman in Ovid's *Metamorphoses* who stumbles as she goes to an incestuous liaison.[15]

But what are we to make of the fact that a sober historian transmitting this report about Munich can call the ink-pot detail "ominous"? Does not such an assessment, drawing on what is known to have happened *after* Munich, assume that the great is mirrored in the trivial, that even the fall of a sparrow is not without significance?

Do not men fasten upon such details as a poetic way of making sense of the wholeness of things?

ii

What, indeed, is the whole like? What does tragedy (or, more precisely for our purposes, Shakespearean tragedy) assume and say about the whole?

All citations in the text of this chapter to the works of William Shakespeare are to them as they appear in *The Complete Pelican Shakespeare*. Alfred Harbage, ed. (Baltimore: Penguin Books, 1969).

How do we begin to understand the whole? Perhaps by understanding what goes on in a tragedy and what the characters are like to whom happens what does happen. But *can* one understand these characters and what happens to them without understanding what should have happened, what they should have done?[16]

One cannot understand an organ of a living body or the operation of a useful machine if one does not know what the organ or machine is supposed to be like at its best. Is not the same true in any effort to understand the deeds of men? But such understanding implies standards and ends and, perhaps in principle, an awareness of what the best possible ordering of human life would be.

We are obliged, in order to understand the characters and actions depicted in a tragedy, to ask such questions as: What is called for? What is the right thing for a man to do in this situation? It does help, in describing someone, to say of him (if it is indeed so) that he did not act as he should have. Is it not important to see about a man that he, in critical circumstances, could not see or do what was right?

Of course, there would not be a tragedy (in the classical sense of the term) if people did not act other than they should have. But it does not truly help us, if we are to understand what did happen, to speak as some do of "dramatic necessities." Rather, one must see *why* a man of a certain character acted thus and so. If the dominant character in a story knows what he should do, and is able to do it, there can be no tragedy. Indeed, there may be little of serious dramatic interest, except to the extent that it occurs in a play like *The Tempest*—and even there, past error is to be corrected, thereby providing fuel for current dramatic interest.

In order to be able to choose correctly, one must be *prudent*. No simple formula suffices. Thus, as we shall see in *Macbeth*, Duncan trusts too much; Macbeth does not trust enough, neither time nor fate nor his underlings. Prudence tends to lead us to moderation, both personal and communal: the good for man and the common good are kept in view. We are taught by the tragedies, just as by life itself, that it is hard to be sure about the application of general principles to particular cases; so one should be careful.

If one is moderate, the chances of going astray are markedly reduced; recovery and correction are easier.

iii

SHAKESPEARE IS a literary constitutionalist.[17] He helps us see, as do the prophets and the other great poets, what generally accepted standards of right and wrong, of good and bad, mean in practice. He helps us see the difficulty of implementing such standards, the particular problems encountered, and the passions affected or aroused.

The prudent man has learned that misjudgments hurt. It is a world in which this *is* so, to which one might usefully say, "Thank Heaven!" Are not misjudgments worse, in some ways, than obvious vices? The obviously vicious is likely to be resented and hence to be guarded against. On the other hand, a man prone to misjudgment may be well intentioned and hence tolerated.

In the tragedies of Shakespeare, critical misjudgments, as well as vices, are marked by (in a sense, they are deserving of) death. All tragedy can be said to be, in part, an effort to come to terms with death, with the mortality and hence the vulnerability of man. But, in addition, death seems to be, at least for a tragedian such as Shakespeare, a kind of convention, an indication that something has gone seriously wrong. This is not to say, of course, that the instrument of death is himself necessarily faultless. Indeed, he is often worse than his victim.[18]

Although not all serious misjudgments are marked by death, death might come so close to the imprudent as to blight his life forever. Friar Lawrence, in *Romeo and Juliet,* comes to mind. We do not need his death to recognize that he has destroyed himself: his fear ("a noise did scare me from the tomb" [V, iii, 262]) suffices to repudiate him. He may not be "worth" killing. *Othello*'s Iago seems a special case: he is still alive when the play ends, as befits one of diabolical character. But, it should be noticed, he *is* silenced. This silence is a kind of death for one who has lived as has Iago (a dramatist of sorts) through the use of words. (His silence seems to reflect his mortification.) Virtue, for him, is the successful use of one's skills, however they happen to be employed.[19]

But it is not enough to say that prudence is life-serving.[20] Nor is it enough to say that there is no major character in Shakespeare's tragedies whose premature death is "not fitting" or "completely undeserved." The fittingness of such deaths may be sensed by the

audience—the death, say, of a Hamlet or a Desdemona or even a
Cordelia—but it takes much more than the immediate dramatic effect
for us to understand precisely how the character went wrong. Let us
look, then, at some who have died in the tragedies of Shakespeare to
see what these deaths may tell us about what the world is like, about
the nature of prudence, and about how men should live—as well as
about how the greatest artists think.

                                  iv

MY POINT of departure, in this review of good people (not of vicious
people such as Macbeth and Iago), is to see how they should have
conducted themselves. That is, how are they to be understood? I will
assume among my readers knowledge of the half dozen plots on which
I now draw for my examples as we examine, in the tragedies of
Shakespeare, the relation of prudence to mortality.

  1) *Hamlet.* Prince Hamlet is generally diagnosed as having suffered from a fatal indecisiveness in that he did not do promptly what
his father had commanded him to do. Why did he hesitate? Partly
because he wanted to test the genuineness of the Ghost, to make
sure it was not diabolical. (II, ii, 583-91) Perhaps a sound instinct
was a work here. *Should* he have done at all what his father commanded, at least so long as his own life or the welfare of Denmark
was not endangered?

  That is, did the deceased King Hamlet know what he was doing
when he ordered his son to kill King Claudius? The stage is unnaturally littered with corpses at the end of the play; Ophelia and her father
have already died because of Prince Hamlet's activities. Not only that,
but a Norwegian claimant, the hereditary enemy of the Danish royal
house, is about to take over the country. Should the Ghost be satisfied *now?* Whom can he now urge to action for the good of Denmark?

  We must wonder whether the Ghost had all this in contemplation.
If he did, did he care? If he did not, what does that say about *his*
judgment? One does not lightly set out to kill a king: the "ideal"
moments to do so are rare and the consequences are unpredictable.
(III, iii, 9-23) Did King Hamlet—was he behaving then as a *king*—did
the Ghost care what happened either to his son or to his country?

  What, then, should Prince Hamlet have done? An otherworldly
command does not suffice, for it *can* be diabolical as well as divine

in origin. What distinguishes the divine? At least some sensibleness, some concern for the good? What would have been sensible for the prince to do? Does it not depend somewhat on how Claudius had been conducting himself *as king* and whether Hamlet could reasonably expect to control the consequences of an assassination attempt? Was not Hamlet himself due to succeed Claudius as king? If so, could not Claudius be repudiated in good time? What was the hurry?

We are obliged to wonder what King Hamlet had been like in his time. He, like Macbeth's King Duncan, had been killed in his sleep, unaware of perfidy in those close to him. Should we suspect that King Hamlet had been, in life, a man who could be, after death, as blindly impassioned as he is here shown to be? We hear of an "angry parle" in which he had engaged (I, i, 62), and he *is* in armor, as one at war (perhaps with the world, or at least with Claudius, if not with Denmark?). He acts as if Claudius would live forever if he is not killed by Prince Hamlet.

Are we not also obliged to wonder what use King Hamlet's revenge is? Claudius had not killed out of revenge, but for something more sensible, a throne, perhaps also a woman. Indeed, one might say that Claudius is exhibited as having a more serious interest in Denmark than has King Hamlet. The older Hamlet comes forward now as a completely private man, not as a king, not even as a father: he ruthlessly exploits what he was in order to get what he wants.

Hamlet is his father's son in one fatal respect: just like his father, he does not confine his actions to the realm in which he happens to be. Thus, he does not kill Claudius at prayers (when the opportunity to do so presents itself) because he wants to attain, by what he does here and now, a decisive effect in eternity as well: he wants to send Claudius' soul to hell as well as to deprive him of life on earth. Shakespeare would have us notice that if Hamlet *had* killed Claudius "at prayers," Claudius would not have (according to the current orthodoxy) been spared from eternal damnation. That is, *we* learn that Claudius had not been able to pray, after all. (III, iii, 36–98)[21]

Had Hamlet killed Claudius at prayers, most of the bad consequences of the pursuit of revenge would have been avoided. In this sense, Hamlet *was* fatally indecisive—or rather, he was decisive here, but wrong. One gets few such "perfect" chances as Prince Hamlet had—and King Hamlet should not have counted on *that*. He seems not to have cared, however, so long as he got what he felt he wanted.

But misguided and misguiding as King Hamlet was, Prince Hamlet too was at fault. He should have known that, bad as things were, they could be made worse. One must sometimes leave bad enough alone.

2) *Othello*. Othello, too, listened to the wrong advisor. But there is not, for our immediate purposes, much of a problem about that, nor about why Othello should suffer from his folly, a folly based upon his desires and his illusions.

But what about Desdemona? Some see her death as undeserved, as a sacrifice to so-called dramatic necessities, in order that we may see what Othello has become. Her death, we are told, does not make sense. But, we should remember, she did deceive and, in effect, destroy her father in contracting a marriage with Othello, thereby stripping herself of the guidance that elders can provide an impressionable girl. (Her habit of deception and its consequences caught up with her in the episode of the lost handkerchief. [III, iv, 51-102])

In addition, she is rather gullible—a failing made worse by her separation from the family. This gullibility, evident in her response to the outlandish stories Othello told her (I, iii, 128-66), leads finally to her failure to judge Othello properly. (III, iv, 25f) Thus, she does not take reasonable precautions when she sees him unduly agitated: Emilia should have been kept with her. (IV, iii, 10-19) Desdemona is, in a sense, too self-forgetting, and ours is not the kind of world in which such disregard for one's welfare is healthy.

Emilia, too, had failed to judge properly the man she had lived with so long. (Desdemona had not had the advantage of a long marriage, and her conduct had deprived her of the counsel of experienced people who cared for her, that counsel which is the natural substitute for the experience and mature self-knowledge one can hope to acquire in due time. [IV, iii, 82; IV, ii, 134]) Emilia served Iago's devious schemes once too often. (III, iv, 100-106) One cannot do this repeatedly with impunity. Finally, Emilia was mistaken to reveal the truth about Iago—however strong, ultimately, her respect for the truth may have been (a respect which the chronically deceitful Iago could not anticipate?). That is, she was mistaken to reveal the truth about Iago in his presence while he was armed: a word to the appropriate officials afterwards would have sufficed. There was no longer any need for hurry.

Thus Emilia had delayed too long in judging Iago properly; she did not delay long enough in revealing what she knew about him. Such errors can be fatal.

3) *Romeo and Juliet.* These young lovers also acted as if they had no families. Can one thus cut away one's roots without serious, even traumatic, consequences? We never learn the ultimate cause of the family feud: is its origin as obscure as the causes of love? In any event, the feud had in the course of years settled into a kind of order. To disregard the feud was to go against something almost natural in its effects.

Since the feud was an old one, it had tended to become somewhat benign. At least, the fathers were not altogether harsh. (I, i, 73–77, 102; I, ii, 1–5; I, iv, 54–92; III, i, 17–84; V, iii, 291–305) Should not an effort have been made to consult the parents before the marriage? In any event, Romeo would have done better to have gone to the duke for help, rather than to Friar Lawrence. To proceed as Romeo and Juliet did was to run the risks which come from entering "privately" into marriage, a relation which is critically dependent, in some respects, upon the public as well as upon the family.

Of course, the friar hoped to use the marriage to reconcile the feuding families. (II, iii, 90–92) But he (unlike Prospero of *The Tempest?*) was foolish in his plan, a plan which may have relied too much on faith. Indeed, should he not be understood to have usurped the duke's powers in the community? We hear of the lovers having been "star-crossed." (Prologue, 6; V, iii, 261, 293–95) We hear much of accident and misadventure. But is not accident likely, even natural, when people conduct themselves as these people did? When one needs many things to go right in order to be able to execute a dangerous scheme, one is asking for trouble.

For a man who should not care for this life, the friar proves unduly fearful of death. Perhaps, indeed, death is too good for him.

4) *Macbeth.* Good King Duncan first comes to view putting down a rebellion. He had, it seems, trusted the wrong people. He soon steps wrong again in bestowing his trust on Macbeth. This naïveté is, in a king, a disturbing trait, one which is dangerous both to him and to his people.

His son Malcolm, we see, is far more cautious than his father and lives to survive the action of the play. Thus, he rigorously tests

Macduff before he accepts his proffer of help. (IV, iii, 1–139) Earlier, he had fled Macbeth's dangerous castle immediately upon learning of his father's death. (Macbeth, on the other hand, is too suspicious. Was the murder of Fleance botched because Macbeth did not leave the murder to the first two murderers he had commissioned?) I assume, by the way, that an unprepared Malcolm would have resisted any Ghost of Duncan who demanded, in the manner of King Hamlet, an immediate assault upon Macbeth.

But what about Banquo's death? Had *he* not failed in his duty to his king in not reporting what he had heard on the heath from the witches? And was it not foolish of him to proceed as he did, after the death of Duncan and the accession to the throne of Macbeth, knowing that Macbeth knew what he did of the prophecy about Banquo's line? Banquo had been put "on notice": one warning suffices a sensible man.

Lady Macduff's death may seem harder to understand. But that is only because we do not appreciate that the relevant "natural" units here are the family and the country. She is *Lady* Macduff: she had benefitted, presumably, from her association with Macduff; it is inevitable that she suffer from his shortcomings. Just as Banquo had been unduly silent, Macduff had been unduly open in his opinions about Macbeth. He had even refused to go to Scone to see Macbeth crowned. Thereafter, he misjudged how fierce and unreasonable Macbeth could be. (IV, iii, 25–28) The prophecy that Macbeth need fear no man of woman born points up Macduff's radical patriotism. Who is Macduff's true mother? Scotland.

Only someone willing to dedicate himself completely to Scotland can destroy such a ruthless tyrant as Macbeth. This dedication includes the sacrifice of one's own family. Such men are not even able to ask whether the price is worth it: they cannot help themselves.

5) *Julius Caesar*. Julius Caesar is flattered to death. Perhaps he was willing to settle for the immortal glory (also a kind of flattery?) which survived him.

Either the conspirators should not have made the effort they did to restore republican institutions, or they should have organized themselves better. The condition of Rome is such that Brutus and Cassius, properly blended, would have made an old-style Roman of the nature needed to suppress a Caesar. Cassius knew what was needed —the killing of Antony, the use of Cicero—but he did not have the moral confidence to oppose the somewhat pretentious (but nevertheless necessary) Brutus. Brutus again and again gets his way. But unless one is clear about what is needed and is prepared to be guided by serious deliberation, one had better not contend for power in perilous times.[22]

But what about Cicero himself? Why should he have gone to his death? The oratorical talent and general reputation for which Cassius evidently wanted him probably led to his proscription by the Triumvirate. Cicero should have known he would be vulnerable. Was he not partly responsible for the condition of things in Rome, including the tendency of the leading republicans to misjudge what was possible or how it could be achieved? Was it not the duty of Rome's greatest orator to contribute his services to the preservation of the Republic, or to a transition to a humane alternative if the Republic was not salvageable, even if he could not do so in the leading capacity he was accustomed to?[23]

Indeed, should someone like Cicero have waited on someone like Cassius to recruit him? What was he waiting on? Death?

6) *Coriolanus.* Rome needed Cicero, and Cicero needed Rome. Perhaps the same is true of Coriolanus.

Did Tullus Aufidius know better than Coriolanus how much even the superior warrior depends upon others? Aufidius' final word, the closing word of the play, is the simple request, "Assist." Even with Coriolanus dead, Aufidius needs help in handling him.

Coriolanus is aware of his dependence upon the city, but he does not always act upon this awareness. An awareness of his dependence may be detected in his final words, before he is killed by Aufidius' men.

> O that I had him,
> With six Aufidiuses, or more, his tribe,
> To use my lawful sword!
> [V, vi, 126-28]

However much he is moved by pride and a desire for glory, Coriolanus does recognize that his sword is but mere force if it is not a "lawful sword." One's sword is legitimated by some city.

The family, too, we are again reminded, is legitimated by the city; otherwise, there is mere sexual congress. Coriolanus' mother recognizes that her family aspirations are ultimately keyed to the city. Coriolanus, on the other hand, steps outside the city and thus ex-

poses himself to destruction. He does not recognize in time what his
mother never forgets, that to be a citizen of the world (to be cosmo-
politan) is to be a citizen nowhere, and that it is unnatural *not* to be
a citizen somewhere.[24]

Coriolanus' mother never allows family feeling to overcome her
perceptions and duties as a citizen. And so she survives, perhaps to
see her fierce grandson properly dedicated to public service.

7) *King Lear.* King Lear, unlike Coriolanus' mother, did allow
parental feelings to overcome his perceptions and duties as a citizen,
as the first citizen of the kingdom. It was foolish of him not to have
long recognized Goneril and Regan for what they were. It was also
foolish of him, assuming that his plan to divide the kingdom (if only
temporarily) had been well conceived, to allow himself to be diverted
by Cordelia's reluctance to speak in the desired fashion. Indeed, he
could well have *said* that her reticence obviously reflected a deep love,
whatever he may have believed.

Had his plan been well conceived? Did it not depend ultimately
on his desire to provide specially for Cordelia? Was it not improper
for a king to allow parental desire to divide, or to seem to divide,
what had been a united kingdom? The opening lines of the play record Gloucester and Kent observing that the king had always preferred the Duke of Albany to the Duke of Cornwall. It is further
convenient that Albany, who turns out to be both decent and effective, should have been the oldest daughter's husband. Should not
Lear have provided from the outset for the eventual transfer of the
crown to Albany? Is this not what his royal duty called for? Should
not Cordelia have been destined from the outset for a foreign marriage, with no share of her father's power?

However all this may be, Cordelia's failure to go along with her
father's plan was not based on a considered opinion about the political improprieties involved. Rather, she could not bring herself to say
what an old man wanted to hear. She is noble and attractive—and yet
is she not wrong? How should one act in the face of folly, especially
folly by someone whom one loves and toward whom one naturally
owes a duty? She should have seen that something dreadful might
come if she continued in her silence (a kind of incivility). Should she
not have made even more of an effort to say something of what she
felt? Should not a princess be able to flatter when the common good
or the good of her royal father requires it?

In marked contrast to Cordelia is the legitimate son of the Duke of Gloucester. He readily assumes one disguise after another in his successful effort to serve his father and to save himself. He is able to use deception justly and effectively—and he is in a position to call to account his unjust half-brother (Edmund) when the opportunity comes and thereafter to assist the Duke of Albany in the governance of the country (or, as some critics would have it, to succeed to the throne himself).

There remains for our consideration here what has been called "one of the most difficult problems in the interpretation of *King Lear*"—a problem which one critic described as the "apparent wantonness of the gods in permitting the deaths of Cordelia and Lear." This critic has observed: "It has been cited as a fundamental defect of the dramatic structure that these deaths do not follow as a result of the necessities of the action, as in the cases of Macbeth, Othello, Hamlet, Brutus and other tragic heroes. It has been held that the poet's theme became too gigantic even for his colossal powers and that, although dramatic fitness required the deaths of the hero and heroine, he knew no way of effecting these deaths but by chance."[25]

Thus, it is not the death of Cordelia or of Lear which is troublesome—I have already suggested something about the fittingness of those deaths—but *the way* Cordelia's death comes about. For, this critic goes on to say, "One of the puzzles of the last scene is the apparently inexplicable delay of the dying Edmund, from line 200 [in V, iii], where he promises to 'do good,' until line 245, where he finally tells of his order for the death of Cordelia. The delay might even conceivably be traced back to line 163, where Edmund already appears to show remorse...."[26] This critic then suggests that Edmund, in his delay in revealing the order for Cordelia's death, might have deliberately served the cause of justice: Cordelia's death will facilitate the transmission of a unified kingdom to the Duke of Albany.

Certainly that is one *effect* of her death. And there is, as I have recognized, something appropriate in Cordelia's death: she had helped set in motion destructive forces which could thus catch up with her also. But Edmund's motivation is another matter. Shakespeare's justice, it should be noted, is not the same as Edmund's; Shakespeare is competent to do justice, but Edmund is not. If Edmund is an instrument of justice, he is an inadvertent instrument. It is one thing to want to "do good"; it is quite another thing to know what the good is and to be able to control events for the good—that is, to reorder events after one has woefully disordered them.

One has to know much more than Edmund does, and to be habituated more to justice than Edmund can ever be now, in order truly to "do good." Neither good intentions nor mere intelligence can be enough.

v

ONE CAN observe in the difficulty Edmund has in trying to "do good" the problem of the relation of virtue to knowledge. This problem bears on what I have said about the sensibleness of the way things work out in the tragedies. Such sensibleness, however, may seem questionable to the inspired artist as well as to the enraptured aesthete. Thus, Graham Greene has confessed to "the suspicion of something cold and prudent in [Shakespeare's] nature...."[27] And when *he* says "prudent" here, he does not intend it to be praiseworthy.

Is the moral universe of Shakespearean tragedy cold and forbidding?[28] Shakespeare suggests to us what prudence calls for in various circumstances. Is this not reassuring rather than threatening? Is this not a more sensible world than unexamined common experience, as well as much of modern drama, might make it seem to be? Are we not instructed, through the tragedies, about the many (albeit interesting) ways that men may go wrong? Are we not encouraged by the tragedies, properly understood, to believe that men need not be simply victims of caprice and irrationality?

But, some would say, the Shakespearean universe I have charted is devoid of the poetic or, at least, of the tragic. For, they would say, there is something subversive of the tragic—there may even be something essentially comic—in the interpretations suggested in this chapter. I have acknowledged that if people did act as I have said that Shakespeare implies they should act, there would be no tragedy. But is there any "danger" that we will be deprived of diverting stories about serious misjudgments among us? Rather than worry about so unlikely a deprivation, should we not try to understand precisely how misjudgment leads to the aberrations which tragedy makes use of?

Is there not some such moral calculation as I have suggested at the core of Shakespeare's understanding of his characters and of their passionate follies?

vi

THERE IS, it has long been recognized, something fundamentally illusory about art. The artist does make use of the material consequences of actions; he does make use of death, when the tragic form is employed, to point up the serious shortcomings of characters and to suggest the implications of significant human types.

We know that death does not always "work" as the tragedian represents it. But then, death is not needed (off the stage) to make the tragedian's point. For, we have been taught and sometimes come to see, bad men cannot truly hurt a good man, nor need anything happen to a bad man at the hands of others in order that he should suffer the worst consequences of his badness. That is, it is punishment enough for the bad man to be what he is. We should not need to see Macbeth killed to understand that he has ruined himself.

But art does drive lessons home, making things appear much more clear-cut than they are. Virtue is thus made to appear more attractive, vice and folly more questionable, than they might otherwise appear to many. There is in the poetic a more *obvious* connection between cause and effect than is visible in everyday life—and citizens are consequently trained to respect, perhaps even to pursue, the good. People feel the moral thrust of a great play, even when they do not understand it, even when they do no more than sense what is at work in it and on them. Nature is thereby reaffirmed in Shakespearean tragedies and sentimentality is minimized.

In this way the passions of men are purged and moderation is encouraged.

vii

IT SHOULD be recognized that the thoughtful man is not likely to be moved by the things which move the typical audience, even when he is addressed by the greatest playwrights. But he *will* be interested.[29]

The thoughtful man will wonder, for instance, about the passions dealt with and ministered to in the moving of audiences. He will wonder as well about the condition of the soul in which the tragedian plans to leave his audience.

The thoughtful man will notice that most of the audience does not care as he does about understanding for its own sake. He will notice as well that few in the audience care to address themselves to anything but the poetic components and effects of plays and thus only to particulars.

The thoughtful man will wonder, of course, whether the playwright is ultimately one of the few or one of the many. He will wonder, that is, whether he is mistaken in discerning in the better playwrights an authoritative judgment and hence (among other things) a serious political purpose which both indicates and invites serious thought. He cannot help but notice that a great playwright can so "say" the things we have surveyed—if indeed this is what he intends to say—as to shape a community in a way that few other thinkers can hope to do.

But, again, the thoughtful man must wonder whether even the better playwright has an opinion about good and bad that guides him not only in what he says in a particular play but also in determining both *whether* plays should be made public and *what* kinds of plays are needed in various circumstances.

Or are we to insist that one cannot help being a playwright, that it is a matter of life and death?[30]

PART TWO

*[I]t is pleasant to see great works in their semi-
nal state, pregnant with latent possibilities of
excellence; nor could there be any more delightful entertainment than to trace their gradual
growth and expansion. . . .*

—Samuel Johnson, *Life of John Milton*

i

I HAVE drawn thus far in my commentary on Shakespeare upon his
great tragedies. I turn now to what is generally regarded as one of his
worst plays, *The Most Lamentable Romaine Tragedie of Titus
Andronicus*, and thereafter to his early poem, *The Rape of Lucrece*.
One can see in these works, too, how the artist can think about political problems, particularly the question of the regime, as well as about
that relation of prudence to mortality examined in Part One of this
chapter.

T. S. Eliot called *Titus Andronicus* "one of the stupidest and
most uninspired plays ever written."[31] Indeed, the editor of one recent edition begins his introduction to the play: *"Titus Andronicus*
is a ridiculous play. This gallimaufry of murders, rape, lopped limbs,
and heads baked in a pie, lavishly served with the rich purple sauce
of rhetoric, may have been to the taste of the Elizabethans, but what
is one to make of it to-day?" This editor also observes: "[T]he view
has been [ingeniously] put forward that the obvious absurdities of
plot and diction prove that it was part of Shakespeare's conscious
intention to burlesque the conventional excesses of the then popular
'tragedy of blood'. . . ." And he adds, "The continuing debate attests
to the widespread feeling that the play calls for some sort of apology."[32]

Criticisms of the play cut even deeper than those I have already
mentioned. It is seen as "an exercise in woe and wonder," a play
which (alone of Shakespeare's tragedies) "does not raise profound
questions about the nature of man and his relationship to the universe, nor does it, except in half-hearted fashion, ask us to consider
the nature of justice."[33] "The play's failure to arouse any of the
emotions usually associated with the tragic experience must be

29

attributed largely to the lack of that frame of moral reference, so clearly and unequivocally established in Shakespeare's major tragedies.... Without this moral framework the play is little more than an horrific entertainment, an empty exercise in revenge tragedy...."[34]

Scholarly apology on Shakespeare's behalf, with respect to *Titus,* has gone so far as to induce "many editors [to] refuse to believe in its authenticity."[35] Some say Shakespeare never had anything to do with it; others, that he merely did parts of it; still others, that he did no more than revise here and there the work of another playwright. But the authoritative scholarly opinion now is that Shakespeare did have a great deal to do with the play, that it must be recognized as one of his first efforts for the stage. Thus one scholar has conceded: "If we could acquit Shakespeare of being an accomplice in *Titus,* we should all be glad to do so. But it is attributed to him by close colleagues who presumably knew Shakespeare well enough to be aware of what they were doing. At any rate they knew him much better than we do. All the tests of affinities, parallels, resemblances, and methods of technique point definitely to Shakespeare. No convincing evidence has been brought forward which could connect *Titus* with any other dramatist." This apologist goes on to say: "The horrors of the play are undeniable. But if scholars would refrain from still harping upon these horrors and would instead consider the play on its merits as an excellent piece of stagecraft, they might see in it something not unworthy of the young Shakespeare."[36]

The youth of the playwright has been emphasized by apologists. Thus, one of them writes: "Despite [its] glaring faults, it must be conceded that *Titus Andronicus* anticipates, in a way which other early tragedies of blood do not, later and better works in the genre, including Shakespeare's own. It has a kind of savage energy and exuberance that carry it successfully over the rough places to its bloody conclusion. Through its imperfections we catch a glimpse of the kind of play it might have been, written ten years later by a more mature and practiced playwright." He adds: "Reading *Titus Andronicus,* one is constantly reminded of what was to come. None of these tremendous possibilities are realized in the play, yet they are unmistakably there; no other early revenge play has such powerful stuff in it."[37]

Perhaps we can go even further, recalling the observation by one commentator on *Julius Caesar,* "Those passages at which our

tastes most stick are perhaps most revealing of what we do not know
and need to learn."[38]

ii

THE MOST plausible justification for dwelling upon *Titus* is that it
is "interpenetrated by 'reminiscences' of Shakespeare's early plays
and by 'fore-shadowings' of what was to come."[39] Thus, it has been
said, "*Titus Andronicus* may be the least satisfactory of Shakespeare's
plays, but as the work that marks the beginning of the road that leads
to *Macbeth, Othello* and *King Lear,* it is by no means the least significant."[40] Another scholar suggests that "in the character of Titus we
have strong suggestions of no less than three of the great male characters of [Shakespeare's] acknowledged masterpieces, namely, Lear,
Coriolanus, and Hamlet."[41] This scholar adds, "[F]urther, we have
in Tamora [the Gothic queen who becomes Titus' enemy] an early
study for at least two of Shakespeare's great women characters—
Lady Macbeth and Cleopatra."[42] The anticipation of Lear can be seen
in this comment (on *Titus,* I, i, 286): "Titus, like Lear, will brook
no opposition, and promptly slays one son and disowns the others
when they oppose his will. Like Lear, he cannot realize that he has
really divested himself of power. By his own rash and unwise actions
he has now made a deadly enemy of Tamora, a treacherous and ungrateful one in Saturninus, an indignant one in Bassianus, and outraged the feelings of all his family, including Marcus, his admiring
brother. He is now left almost isolated to feel his impotency and
regret his ill-judged action."[43]

Not only do we see "in the raw," so to speak, characters and
passions which will be refined later, but this play is instructive in
other respects as well. Its flaws matter less than one anticipates during a first reading, once one begins to study the play, especially in
conjunction with the other Roman works of Shakespeare. For certain
serious purposes, it does not matter whether Shakespeare wrote the
play: it suffices that he worked on it and was familiar with it. It does
reflect his (and some of his more thoughtful contemporaries') view
of Rome and its significance—and about this I will have much more
to say.

The craftsmanship of the play, we have seen, has been noticed.
Thus, it has been suggested: "For young students *Titus* forms the

best introduction to Elizabethan tragedy. There is perhaps no single play which contains so many different tricks of technique."[44] Thus, also, it has been said about a passage in the play: "What *Titus* here lacks is spiritual depth and imaginative significance, not (or at least not so much) constructional competence."[45] Elsewhere this editor observed: "The sense [in the play] that errors and crimes alike spring from the same personality strikes me as already particularly Shakespearian."[46] This sense of the fitness of things and the craftsmanship displayed induced this editor to conclude that "the author of *Titus* was obviously going *somewhere....*"[47]

Even so, the action in this play may be so unlikely and the characters so unreal that one is encouraged to consider primarily the political and moral opinions that are dealt with. Thus, this may be a play more to be thought about than to be experienced, particularly since Shakespeare's understanding is not concealed here behind his dramatic art as much as it is later. Studying a play (if by a very intelligent man) that is dramatically inferior may be peculiarly instructive: one is not beguiled by the art or the ornamentation; one finds it easier to *think* about the play, to consider its premises and principles. Besides, one could again add, the thoughtful man does tend to see plays stripped of the characteristics which *move* men.

Titus Andronicus, then, can be said to be a play more easily seen much as philosophers see plays. It is a play presented somewhat as the Socrates of the *Republic* would present the story of actions which move men—that is, presented in such a way as to emphasize their "intellectual" content.[48] Might one dare go so far as to suggest that this may well be, therefore, the most instructive play written by Shakespeare? This may seem to those of my readers who have actually endured the play on the stage a rather perverse conclusion. But, then, it may be a peculiarly fitting conclusion in that it reflects the perverse character of the play itself. Also fitting, I trust, is the imposition upon the reader of many extended quotations, and not only to suggest the manifest roughness and complications of this play.

iii

LET US turn now to an examination of this remarkable play, a play written when Shakespeare was some thirty years old. It would be useful to have before us a conventional synopsis of the play (which I take, although it is not altogether accurate, from the Cambridge edition):

> Even in the supreme hour of his triumph as he receives the acclamations of the cheering Roman populace upon his return from the Gothic wars with Tamora, Queen of the Goths, and her three sons as captives, the victorious general, Titus Andronicus, mourns the death of his twenty-one sons, [slain in several campaigns over many years,] and vengefully demands, as a fiery sacrifice to appease their souls, [Alarbus,] the eldest son of the conquered Queen who pleads tearfully but in vain for his life.

> His sons buried, Titus turns to affairs of state and, although offered the Roman crown, he upholds in strict justice the claim of Saturninus, elder son of the late Emperor, who disputes the inheritance with his brother Bassianus. Through the general's influence, the treacherous Saturninus ascends the throne, offering to wed Titus' daughter Lavinia, though the Gothic queen had already caught his fancy. Bassianus wrathfully declares that Lavinia is betrothed to him, and with the support of her brothers [Titus' four surviving sons] abducts and marries her. Enraged at this open breach of faith to the new Emperor, Titus starts in pursuit of his daughter, and finding his way blocked by one of his [four surviving] sons he kills him. Saturninus seizes the opportunity to choose Tamora for his bride and to disgrace the noble Titus, but the wily Queen urges him publicly to restore the general and his sons to his favor and forgive Bassianus, while in secret she ruthlessly plans with the Emperor and her foul Moorish lover Aaron the destruction of the entire Andronicus family in revenge for the death of her son.

> During a royal hunt in the forest Aaron hears Tamora's evil sons, Chiron and Demetrius, quarreling over the prospect of possessing Lavinia whom they both desire, and he incites the bestial pair to ravish her in turn and to insure secrecy by tearing out her tongue and cutting off her hands. Straying through the wood while the hunt is in progress, Bassianus and Lavinia discover the love affair of Tamora and Aaron, and, fearing their disclosures, Tamora calls her sons, telling them that her brother-in-law and his wife [Bassianus and Lavinia] have insulted her and threatened her with torture. The sons kill Bassianus, throw his body into a deep pit, and drag Lavinia away to defilement and mutilation as she begs them for death. Aaron, enticing two of Titus' [three surviving] sons to the pit into which they fall

on top of Bassianus' body, quickly summons Saturninus, points to the young men struggling to escape, produces a falsely incriminating letter arranging for the payment of the murder, and discloses a bag of gold which he had previously placed near the spot.

The Emperor accuses [these two sons of Titus Andronicus] of his brother's death, and, regardless of Titus' pleadings, they are sentenced to death, but before the execution the lying Aaron brings word that their lives will be spared if either Lucius, the [remaining] son, or Marcus, his uncle [Titus' brother] will chop off one of his hands and send it to the Emperor as a token of good faith. With Aaron's vicious help, the old father [Titus] forestalls the others and sends his own hand, which is later scornfully returned with the heads of his two sons. [In the meantime, the mutilated Lavinia is discovered by her family.]

Titus, Marcus and Lucius vow a terrible requital [for all that has happened to them], and Lucius, whom the Emperor has just banished [for having tried to rescue his brothers], is instructed [by Titus] to raise an invading army among the Goths. Lavinia contrives to fasten the crime of ravishment and mutilation on Chiron and Demetrius by turning the pages of Ovid's *Metamorphoses* with the stumps of her arms until she reaches the tragic tale of Philomena, and, with a staff held in her mouth and guided by her arms, writing in the sand the names of her assaulters. Pretending to be mad, Titus sends presents to Chiron and Demetrius and shoots arrows into the Roman streets and the palace, all of which bear messages to the gods proclaiming his wrongs.

Meanwhile, Tamora gives birth to a black child, of which Aaron is father, and her sons try to kill it, but Aaron takes possession of it, kills the nurse and midwife to prevent gossip, and has a white baby substituted in his child's place as the Emperor's son. Taking the infant away to be brought up by the Goths, Aaron is captured by a soldier in the army of Lucius and exultingly relates to the general [Lucius] the full story of his crimes after extracting a promise for his child's protection. Saturninus, knowing the popularity of Lucius, is greatly disturbed when news reaches him of the huge forces drawing near the city, and he endeavors to arrange a banquet and parley at Titus' house where Tamora will separate the general from his army and stir up enmity between them.

To win the support of the supposedly insane Titus, Tamora goes to him disguised as Revenge, stating that her great desire is to avenge

his wrongs at the banquet, and Titus promises to send for Lucius. She
returns in glee to the Emperor to make ready for the feast, leaving
her two sons at the home of Titus. He has them overpowered, cuts
their throats, as Lavinia holds a basin [between the stumps of her
arms] to catch their blood, and, grinding their bodies to a pulp,
bakes [them] in a pie which, in the costume of a cook, he serves
to Tamora. Titus informs Saturninus of the crime of Chiron and
Demetrius, and tells Tamora she has just eaten their bodies in the
pie. He kills Lavinia to put an end to her shame, and stabs Tamora.
Saturninus kills Titus, and is himself killed by Lucius. Lucius tells
the Roman people the complete story of his father's tragedy, and is
proclaimed Emperor. Aaron is condemned to death by torture.[49]

This, then, is an account of some of the deeds and misdeeds to
be found in this rather lively play. I remind the reader, before I proceed to comment upon all this, of certain critical decisions by Titus
in the first long scene of the play. He shows himself merciless in the
sacrifice of Tamora's son; he is foolish, in the selection of a new
emperor, in his preference for Saturninus over Bassianus; he is unnaturally violent in defense of his honor, even killing one of his four
surviving sons, when his sons support Bassianus' prior claim to
Lavinia; and he is naive in his failure to anticipate that Tamora will
always hate him and his family for the sacrifice of her son. These
decisions and attitudes can be seen to be generated by Titus' character and experiences. Thus, he can be described by one scholar in
this fashion:

> Titus is an old man who retains the strength but has lost the elasticity
> of youth.... As with many soldiers, the religion of Titus is a firm and
> somewhat naive acceptance of the usages consecrated by tradition.
> He kills Alarbus [Tamora's son] not so much out of cruelty, but be-
> cause the traditional rites of religion demand it. He makes Saturninus
> Emperor for much the same reason. Sacred tradition requires that
> the eldest son of the Emperor should succeed. He stabs his son Mutius
> in wrath but also as a soldier exacting that same obedience which is
> the rule of his own life.... Surely in all the blunders of Titus we see
> the corruption of the best turned to the worst, qualities fine in them-
> selves producing disaster because of Titus's devotion to a false ideal.
> Further, Titus's habit of loyalty keeps him blind to the dangers that
> threaten him. His own probity makes it difficult for him to suspect

duplicity in others. When the emperor proves false, his world breaks down, and he begins to go mad.[50]

Titus' madness, such as it is, is heralded by his laughter upon learning, after he had cut off his hand to save them, that two (of his three surviving) sons have nevertheless been executed. (III, i, 264) The worst things have now happened to him—and the rest of the play is devoted to his revenge. A scholar has put this development thus:

> This terrible laughter of Titus is startlingly dramatic, and a sudden change of mood and a new departure (almost what Aristotle would call a "discovery") in the action. Almost simultaneously Titus' bitter sorrow is transformed into the fiercest lust of revenge, and he seems at once to conceive the whole terrible scheme of vengeance which the rest of the play is occupied in displaying. He shakes off his despair, and with it the feebleness of age. His old instinct of command re-asserts itself, and he at once takes the lead and despatches to bring a Gothic army to their rescue.[51]

Lucius, and of course Titus as well, I will say more about. But more should be said now by way of introducing the other principal characters, Tamora the Queen and Aaron the Moor.

Tamora first comes to view in her plea to Titus for the life of her son about to be sacrificed in the burial ceremony for Titus' sons. (I, i, 107) It has been said of her speech on that occasion:

> No one can fail to be struck by the extraordinary resemblance between these lines and the famous eulogy of mercy in Portia's speech in the *Merchant of Venice*. Inferior as they are to the celebrated passage, they seem to contain the germs of it, and also to exhibit that kind of moral or religious anachronism into which Shakespeare so frequently falls in this and other plays. For the pagan gods were not merciful gods, whatever they were, and mercy as a divine attribute has come to us entirely from Judaism through Christianity, and indeed in Judaism itself it was a comparatively late development, except in the narrow sense of special favour shown to a tribe or person. Tamora's speech here is to my thinking very fine indeed, and not unworthy of Shakespeare at any time of his career. It is the rejection of her noble appeal to Titus that brings the first and fatal elements of tragedy into the play, and turns her into a fury.[52]

I shall say more in due time about mercy and the divine. The problem
of the divine itself is anticipated in our introduction to Aaron, who
is told (by Lucius), "[T]hou believest no god." (V, i, 71) And thus a
scholar notes: "This author makes his villain an atheist, whereas Mar-
lowe and others themselves gave expression to sentiments regarded as
atheistical. Shakespeare never does."[53] This same scholar has also
noted, "The union [in Aaron] of unmatched effrontery and cruelty
with natural paternal feeling is one which only Shakespeare could
have carried out so triumphantly."[54]

Finally, by way of introduction to the principal characters, we
have this scholar's observation about our playwright's art: "It is highly
characteristic of Shakespeare's irony to put his fine speeches into the
mouths of his bad or inferior characters. So, in this play, Tamora and
Aaron have all the best of the poetic rhetoric."[55]

iv

WHY DO things happen as they do in this play? A sufficient answer
has been implied in what has already been said about Titus' mistakes
and about his character. One critical mistake, related to his sacrifice
of Tamora's son, can be traced back to his rigid piety. Titus is spoken
of by his brother, in the first reference to him in the play, as "Andronicus, surnamèd Pius." (I, i, 23) Titus, when he makes his appearance,
is hailed by an anonymous Roman captain (who expresses what can
be considered the official view of the general):

> Romans, make way. The good Andronicus,
> Patron of virtue, Rome's best champion,
> Successful in the battles that he fights,
> With honour and with fortune is returned
> From where he circumscribèd with his sword
> And brought to yoke the enemies of Rome.
> [I, i, 68]

This play is, at least in part, a study of piety and civic virtue gone
monstrous.

Piety aims, many believe, at godlikeness. And Tamora, in her
plea for her son, addresses herself to this aim:

> *Wilt thou draw near the nature of the gods?*
> *Draw near them then in being merciful.*
> [I, i, 120]

Is godlikeness what all the Roman heroes had aspired to?[56] Of course, the question remains, What *are* the gods like upon whom men might pattern themselves? Titus' response to Tamora suggests *his* answer to this question:

> *Patient yourself, madam, and pardon me.*
> *These are their brethren whom your Goths beheld*
> *Alive and dead, and for their brethren slain*
> *Religiously they ask a sacrifice:*
> *To this your son is marked, and die he must,*
> *T'appease their groaning shadows that are gone.*
> [I, i, 124]

"Religiously they ask a sacrifice," Titus has said. "O cruel irreligious piety!" Tamora says in response. (I, i, 133) And insofar as these *are* "Roman rites" (I, i, 146), there does seem to be something wrong with Rome and with Romans such as Titus.

Titus' gross affront to Tamora is compounded by his unwarranted trust in her good will toward him thereafter. When the queen captured by Titus becomes the wife of the emperor selected by Titus, Titus naïvely asks his brother: "Is she not then beholding to the man/ That brought her for this high good turn so far?/ Yes, and will nobly him remunerate." (I, i, 399. See, also, II, ii, 11–13.) What he does not appreciate—and this is partly because he (until his eyes are opened) takes everything at face value, assuming that others view the fortunes of war as he does and that everyone is as frank and open as he is—is that *she* has a quite different view from him as to what a noble remuneration would be.

The remuneration *she* will consider appropriate is anticipated in what had been said in the first scene about the sacrifice of Tamora's son. The first speech by Lucius, the son of Titus who will eventually become emperor, opens with this request of his father:

> *Give us the proudest prisoner of the Goths,*
> *That we may hew his limbs [for the sacrifice].*
> [I, i, 99]

The hewing of limbs is emphasized again as Lucius prepares to take Tamora's son off for the sacrifice (after the mother's plea had failed). Lucius says:

> *Away with him, and make a fire straight,*
> *And with our swords, upon a pile of wood,*
> *Let's hew his limbs till they be clean consumed.*
>
> *[I, i, 130]*

And when Lucius returns, he announces:

> *See, lord and father, how we have performed*
> *Our Roman rites. Alarbus' limbs are lopped*
> *And entrails feed the sacrificing fire...*
>
> *[I, i, 145]*

All this, I suggest, anticipated the "remuneration" Tamora considers appropriate: for later on, of course, we see that Lavinia's limbs are lopped off, that they too are hewn. (II, iv, 17) We should not be surprised to learn, thereafter, that Titus should consider it *his* duty in turn to hew the limbs of Tamora's surviving sons. He carries matters further (as we have seen) by thereafter feeding her sons to her rather than, as had happened with her first son, "feeding" them to the gods. (V, ii, 166–205; V, iii, 60–63)

Thus, one thing does lead to another. These Roman rites—if Roman they be—have gotten out of control. How is such harsh piety —if piety it be—to be curtailed? Does not such piety depend upon virtuous rulers if it is to be kept within bounds and not destroy those who practice it? The last ruler of Rome, Titus reports, held upright the scepter which controls the world. (I, i, 203) But which of that ruler's sons should be chosen to succeed him? Why not Titus himself? He declines, arguing that he is too old, that he could be chosen today and die tomorrow—thereby requiring them to choose still another ruler. Instead, he will settle for a "staff of honour for [his] age." (I, i, 201) Is he primarily self-centered in this decision?

Does self-centeredness characterize any overwhelming concern about honor? Consider what Titus says, in the final scene, when he kills the ravished, mutilated Lavinia. He addresses Saturninus:

My lord the emperor, resolve me this:
Was it well done of rash Virginius
To slay his daughter with his own right hand,
Because she was enforced, stained, and deflow'red?
                                        [V, iii, 35]

The emperor answers that Virginius had done well, explaining:

Because the girl should not survive her shame,
And by her presence still renew his sorrows.
                                        [V, iii, 41]

Whereupon Titus kills Lavinia (and this begins a series of killings in the last scene which immediately include Tamora, Titus himself, and Saturninus). In the original story, however, Virginius had killed his daughter to protect her *from* being ravished.[57] The version of the Virginius story put forward by Titus and accepted by Saturninus permits a father to be at least as much the beneficiary of such a killing as his daughter.

But whatever may be the influence of self-centeredness, is it not clear that Titus should have chosen Bassianus emperor rather than Saturninus? Indeed, is it not odd that Titus should choose as he does after he hears how both Saturninus and Bassianus address him (and knowing as well Bassianus' regard for Lavinia, who seems to have been promised to him)?

The play opens with the contending claims of Saturninus and Bassianus, claims which pit the evidently accepted way in Rome against a way which pays more heed to merit. Perhaps the critical problem with Rome, at this time, is in large part that there is such a gap between convention and merit. Consider the Saturninus speech with which the play opens:

Noble patricians, patrons of my right,
Defend the justice of my cause with arms,
And, countrymen, my loving followers,
Plead my successive title with your swords.
I am his first-born son that was the last
That ware the imperial diadem of Rome.

Then let my father's honours live in me,
Nor wrong mine age with this indignity.
[I, i, 1]

This is immediately followed by Bassianus' speech:

Romans, friends, followers, favourers of my right,
If ever Bassianus, Caesar's son,
Were gracious in the eyes of royal Rome,
Keep then this passage to the Capitol;
And suffer not dishonour to approach
The imperial seat, to virtue consecrate,
To justice, continence, and nobility;
But let desert in pure election shine;
And, Romans, fight for freedom in your choice.
[I, i, 9]

Saturninus and Bassianus are both said (by Marcus) to be princes who "strive by factions and by friends/ Ambitiously for rules and empery." (I, i, 18)[58] An editor's note on this opening passage observes:

It is well to note how carefully the characters of the two brothers are distinguished from the first, and the different style of their address to their followers. Bassianus speaks in that strain of aristocratic republicanism which we find both in *Julius Caesar* and *Coriolanus.* Saturninus, a despicable character throughout, appeals merely to his right by primogeniture.[59]

Lavinia did not help matters by her own conduct. Her acquiescence to the marriage with Saturninus (which leads to trouble in the first scene) and her later rebuke (with Bassianus) of Tamora in the woods (letting flow her suspicions about Tamora's relations with Aaron and threatening to expose her to the emperor) are not the conduct of a prudent woman. One editor—one of those who doubt Shakespeare's authorship of the play—has this to say about the sudden rearrangement of marriages in the opening scene:

It was pity to part a couple who seem to have corresponded in disposition so exactly as Saturninus and Lavinia. Saturninus, who has just

promised to espouse her, already wishes he [could] choose again; and
she who was engaged to Bassianus (whom she afterwards marries)
expresses no reluctance when her father gives her to Saturninus. Her
subsequent railery to Tamora is of so coarse a nature, that if her
tongue had been all she was condemned to lose, perhaps the author
(whoever he was) might have escaped censure on the score of poetick
justice.[60]

And so in the opening act the stage is set, primarily by Titus
and his family, for the horrors which follow. An editor observes that
"it is curious, to say the least, that Aaron, the demonic force behind
most of the action of the play, should be silent during the entire first
act [and a quite long act, at that]."[61] This may not have been good
theater, but does it not make sense? "Demonic forces" are always
waiting for the opportunities provided them by men's follies. Among
those follies (as we of the twentieth century well know) is the selection, by communities, of tyrannical rulers.

Once unleashed, an Aaron runs wild. Thus, Aaron exults upon
having deceived Titus, who cuts off his hand to save his sons:

> ... *O, how this villainy*
> *Doth fat me with the very thoughts of it!*
> *Let fools do good, and fair men call for grace,*
> *Aaron will have his soul black like his face.*
>   *[III, i, 202]*

Again and again, Aaron parades his misdeeds, seeking in them a certain distinction. He boasts, for example:

> *But I have done a thousand dreadful things*
> *As willingly as one would kill a fly,*
> *And nothing grieves me heartily indeed*
> *But that I cannot do ten thousand more.*
>   *[V, i, 141]*

In such an appetite for notoriety is there not a perverse image of the
Roman appetite for honor?

Once evil men are unleashed, and even given royal support, monstrosities appear. The mutilitated Lavinia is bad enough, but then
there is the scene when the mutilated Titus organizes an exit with

the heads of his two sons and with his own severed hand. There are not enough hands for everything, he says, and so Lavinia must carry her father's severed hand in her teeth! At one point, Titus can characterize as "monstrous" Saturninus' ungrateful reproach of him. (I, i, 311. See also, I, i, 450; IV, iii, 17, 33; IV, iv, 58–59) Has not Rome reached the stage where she "naturally" brings forth monsters? (Why this should be I shall say something about later.) Thus, there is unintended irony in the concern Lucius had had, in the opening speeches of the play, to sacrifice a prisoner at his brothers' funeral:

> *That so the shadows be not unappeased,*
> *Nor we disturbed with prodigies on earth.*
> *[I, i, 103]*

The conduct of the Andronicus family in this opening scene helps produce far more disturbing prodigies than they had feared.

This conduct, as we have seen, was condemned by Tamora as a "cruel irreligious piety." (I, i, 133) One of her sons observes that Scythia—the part of Russia which was notorious for its savagery—was never "half so barbarous." (I, i, 134) At one point, Marcus (in his effort to persuade Titus to permit the burial in the family tomb of the son Titus had killed [in the course of Bassianus' seizure of Lavinia] says to Titus, "Thou art a Roman, be not barbarous." (I, i, 381) Critical to this play is the evident barbarization of Rome. Rome has become "but a wilderness of tigers" (III, i, 54); life in Rome has become a "fearful slumber." (III, i, 252)

This is not the Rome of the Republic (nor, for that matter, the Rome of the better emperors). A scholar's characterization of Shakespeare's handling of the Romans suggests how things have changed:

> ... Shakespeare portrays the Romans as a people of rugged simplicity, "pious," loyal, brave, without much imagination or subtlety, "religiously" observing the customs handed down to them from their fathers. "Continence" is the virtue which he makes the good Romans value above all. In Titus himself he has shown the excellence and the defects of the Roman character. It is typical of Shakespeare to show that the excess of a good quality in Titus, his "piety," is his chief defect. Furthermore Shakespeare brings out the peculiarities of the Romans by setting up Aaron and the Goths in contrast. The

Romans are everything the Goths are not, the Goths are everything
the Romans are not.[62]

When the Romans become barbaric, they become worse than the
barbarians in certain respects. Or, at least, the effect of their corruption is more serious. Do not "lilies that fester smell far worse
than weeds"?[63]

The play is replete with classical allusions, but the times are
nevertheless barbarian. The chaotic character of Roman life "now"
can be said to be mirrored in the structure of the play itself and in
its relative crudeness. There is no grace, no central meaning which
obviously informs everything. Consider Lavinia's last speech (before
she is assaulted and loses her tongue). This is her final plea to Tamora:

> *No grace? no womanhood? Ah, beastly creature,*
> *The blot and enemy to our general name!*
> *Confusion fall—*
>
> *[II, iii, 182]*

She is not permitted to finish her sentence: "Confusion fall—." And
the next thing she says, when she writes with a staff in the sand, is
"Stuprum [Defilement, Disgrace]" (with the names of her assailants
—barbarians who, by the way, have Greek names, again indicating
what has happened to the "culture" of the day). (IV, i, 78)

How did things get into this sad condition? Perhaps Rome's
almost constant wars have had something to do with its sorry state.
Titus has been forty years a soldier. (I, i, 196) The present wars, it
seems, have been going on for ten years:

> *... Five times he hath returned*
> *Bleeding to Rome, bearing his valiant sons*
> *In coffins from the field...*
>
> *[I, i, 33]*

Have men become much more brutal because of the constant killing?
And yet is there not also about all this killing the quality of a game?
Perhaps this state of continual war bears on Titus' naive expectations

with respect to Tamora: he expects her to take in her stride the fortunes of war, just as he does, and this means that one does not hold grudges for losses openly inflicted, that one is prepared to shift alliances as circumstances change, that one proceeds according to rituals and "the drill."[64]

Continual war has also placed Rome in extended contact with her enemies. One does tend, in war, to become like one's enemy—or, perhaps, both tend to sink to a lower, "effective" common denominator of conduct. The barbarians pick up Greek names and Latin literature. And the Romans pick up barbarian ways. It is significant, as one editor has noticed, that "the excessively artificial diction [in this play] contrasts oddly with the violence of the events."[65]

It is not surprising in these circumstances that something should be wrong with Titus. What seems wrong with him cannot (it seems to me) be accounted for as one scholar did who suggested:

> *Titus Andronicus* is in a way a drama concerning a man born out of his time, if not place; and much of the often-remarked absurdity of the piece comes from the fact of Titus Andronicus's attempt to act like an old Roman gentleman among barbarians.[66]

It is hard to imagine Brutus or Cassius, or Julius Caesar (who *was* known for magnanimity), acting *at any time* like Titus does again and again in the play. Titus does things no *gentleman* would do. And some of the things he does are simply mad. He recognizes that others think him mad (V, ii, 21, 185), but what he does not recognize is that he is not as sane as he believes, and certainly not when he is "in control" of the plot against Tamora and the sons on whom she will feast.

It is probably a sign of the times that, at the end of the play, Lucius and Marcus seem to endorse (or, at least, do not repudiate) what Titus has done in baking Tamora's sons into a pie. And this is the Marcus who is capable of well-wrought rhetorical exercises.[67] This is also the Marcus of whom a scholar has said, not without some justification: "In a world of hard, fierce, revengeful men, he alone is given to gentleness and moderation.... Frequently scholars declare that characters thus marked off are the 'mouthpiece' of Shakespeare."[68] (See III, i, 214f)

Rome is now such that even the temperamentally moderate Marcus is led astray into sanctioning horrendous violence. What Rome is like—and not Titus alone—is suggested by a scholar's response to the concluding scene:

> It is not only that Titus is cruel; it is more, he is cruel to the end. He is not a Lear who grows in stature as the play proceeds and whose sufferings purge his character of its baser elements until he emerges as a man entirely good. Titus alone of Shakespeare's tragic heroes never arrives at healing self-knowledge. At the beginning of the play we hope that Titus will succeed against his enemies: at the end we wish that he had not.... [A Senecan revenge play] leaves no room for change of character.... Roughly speaking, Lear is a Titus who becomes a Marcus, but a revenge-play necessarily precluded this type of development.[69]

But, although there may be no change of character, there *is* in Titus the development of a somewhat better recognition (not a full recognition) of who *some* of the worst evildoers in the world are.

Not only is Titus cruel to the end, but the play is also. That is, the play's last words have much to do with further afflictions to be visited upon the enemies of the Andronici. More should be said about this ending, in which reconciliation is hardly to be seen. But, first, let us briefly consider Shakespeare's *Rape of Lucrece:* that story of the rape which led to the founding of the Roman republic should help us in our efforts to understand *Titus Andronicus* and the political thought of Shakespeare.

V

TITUS ANDRONICUS and *The Rape of Lucrece* were evidently written within a few years of each other. Most scholars put *Lucrece* first; a few put *Titus* first. One of the latter does so in terms which are instructive about the relation of *Titus* to *Lucrece*, a poem of 1,855 lines:

> The similarities between [*Titus*] and *Lucrece* have led Sir Sidney Lee to suggest that they occupied Shakespeare's atttention at the same period. If we go further and conjecture that it was his work upon the play which first gave to Shakespeare the definite suggestion

of a poem on the story of Lucrece, it will follow that Shakespeare
did not begin with *Lucrece* until late in the autumn of 1593.[70]

Another scholar, describing the relation between the play and
the poem, introduces us to the action of the poem:

> Shakespeare in his dedication [of *Lucrece*] calls it a "pamphlet."
> This is a sufficiently nondescript category.... With just a slight effort,
> Shakespeare could have pushed *The Rape of Lucrece* into a "lament-
> able tragedy of a chaste Roman lady, with the revenge of Collatine
> upon the wicked Tarquin." It is significant that just at the time he
> produced this "pamphlet," he was working on the revision of a play
> on Roman history, full of rage and brutality and revenge. That play,
> *Titus Andronicus,* is hardly more of a play from the modern point
> of view than *Lucrece*. Both pieces of work carry the burden of a violent
> story. Tucked into the interstices of these stories are rhetorical pas-
> sages of incitement to violence and reflection upon it. Such passages
> bulk large. In the "pamphlet" Shakespeare puts the preliminary stages
> of the action in a prose "Argument" of twenty-six lines. There is in
> this "Argument" the stuff of some excellent stage scenes.... Because
> Shakespeare is creating a dramatic poem and not a poetic drama, he
> passes this material over. He opens his story where Tarquin, already
> having seen the beautiful Lucrece and having listened to her husband
> extolling her faithfulness and chastity, suddenly is possessed to visit
> her alone and win her.[71]

Here is a summary of the passage from the Roman historian
Livy upon which the Elizabethans evidently drew for information
about the rape of Lucrece:

> Sextus Tarquinius, son of the King of Rome, having heard Lucrece's
> husband, Collatinus, boast of his wife's beauty and unassailable chas-
> tity, develops a wild passion for her. He leaves a siege at which he and
> Collatinus were fellow soldiers and goes to visit Lucrece in her palace.
> She receives him in the hospitable manner that is his due and assigns
> him a room in the wing of the building as remote as possible from
> her own quarters. In the dead of night Tarquinius steals along the cor-
> ridors until he reaches her chamber. Once there, deaf to her appeals,
> he stifles her cries with the bedclothes and rapes her. The frantic
> Lucrece at once summons her father and husband, tells them what
> has happened and then stabs herself to death.[72]

And, as we are reminded by the Argument, this led to an uprising which drove the Tarquin family out of Rome, whereupon the Republic was established for centuries to come.

The Argument, or preface to the poem (supplied by Shakespeare), which was published with the poem in 1594, is provided here in its entirety:

Lucius Tarquinius (for his excessive pride surnamed Superbus), after he had caused his own father-in-law Servius Tullius to be cruelly murdered, and, contrary to the Roman laws and customs, not requiring or staying for the people's suffrages, had possessed himself of the kingdom, went, accompanied with his sons and other noblemen of Rome, to besiege Ardea; during which siege the principal men of the army meeting one evening at the tent of Sextus Tarquinius, the King's son, in their discourses after supper every one commended the virtues of his own wife; among whom Collatinus extolled the incomparable chastity of his wife Lucretia. In that pleasant humor they all posted to Rome; and intending by their secret and sudden arrival to make trial of that which every one had before avouched, only Collatinus finds his wife (though it were late in the night) spinning amongst her maids; the other ladies were all found dancing and revelling, or in several disports. Whereupon the noblemen yielded Collatinus the victory, and his wife the fame. At that time Sextus Tarquinius being inflamed with Lucrece's beauty, yet smothering his passion for the present, departed with the rest back to the camp; from whence he shortly after privily withdrew himself, and was (according to his estate) royally entertained and lodged by Lucrece at Collatium. The same night he treacherously stealeth into her chamber, violently ravished her, and early in the morning speedeth away. Lucrece, in this lamentable plight, hastily dispatcheth messengers, one to Rome for her father, another to the camp for Collatine. They came, the one accompanied with Junius Brutus, the other with Publius Valerius; and finding Lucrece attired in mourning habit, demanded the cause of her sorrow. She, first taking an oath of them for her revenge, revealed the actor and whole manner of his dealing, and withal suddenly stabbed herself. Which done, with one consent they all vowed to root out the whole hated family of the Tarquins; and bearing the dead body to Rome, Brutus acquainted the people with the doer and manner of the vile deed, with a bitter invective against the tyranny of the King; wherewith the people were so moved that with one consent and a general acclamation the Tarquins were all exiled, and the state government changed from kings to consuls.

The poem, as has already been indicated, starts later than does the Argument. On the other hand, certain critical things in the poem are left out of the Argument: for example, an extended exchange between Sextus Tarquinius and Lucrece (in which she does most of the talking) and an extended set of reflections by Lucrece on a painting of the fall of Troy (about which more later). It does seem that the artist assumed that the reader of *Lucrece* would know much more than is related here. And is not the same true about the Roman plays? That is, is not elementary general information about Rome assumed to be known by readers of all the Roman works of Shakespeare?

Collatine's folly—in the form of vanity (a form of the desire for honor?) with respect to his wife's virtues (10, 29f, 78f)—contributes to disaster. That folly is critical to unleashing Tarquin's lust upon his family. (And, it should be remembered, Lucrece *did* choose to marry such a man, thereby enjoying the privileges of this alliance and risking its liabilities.) Once Collatine, Lucrece, and Tarquin do their part, it should be added, Junius Brutus does his! For it is he, a patriotic Roman, who seizes upon this as an opportunity for driving out of Rome the king and kingship itself (which, as we saw in the Argument, he calls "tyranny").

It is instructive, in thinking about *Titus Andronicus,* to consider how *The Rape of Lucrece* can be interpreted with a view to what it says about the role of the divine in the universe. Thus, one commentator has made the following observations:

Lucrece is indeed the poet's first great theodicy, a justification of God in relation to the existence of evil in the world.... [Lucrece's] fate as represented by Shakespeare is an indictment of the Divinity. Irreproachable in her moral attitude and without a shadow of personal guilt, indeed as a very consequence of the purity and guilelessness of her thought, which makes her incapable of detecting evil creeping upon her and of protecting herself against it, she falls victim to Tarquin.... This is the result of a deity not concerned with the protection of the weak; therefore freedom, man's power to control his destiny, is an empty word. Man can never secure to himself the fruits of his moral striving.... Finally, from the quietness and narrowness of private life we are transported by a sudden turn into the very midst of the struggles of the political life of nations, in order that we may view their effects on the happiness of mankind. This is in fact the reason for the introduction of the Fall of Troy [depicted

in a painting to which Lucrece turns] ... which to Shakespeare, as
to his whole time-period, stood as a symbol of all great political
catastrophe. ... He conceives of [the] catastrophe [of Troy] as one of
those political events led up to by the guilt of individual persons. ...
In [the] picture [presented in *Lucrece*] human life is entirely responsible for itself; no God intervenes for the protection of the weak; it is a
self-sufficient organism which contains its own center of gravity. ...
This view, carried almost to the starkness of atheism, Shakespeare
makes the basis for his vindication of the system. ... How did Lucrece's
misfortune come upon her? According to Shakespeare, Collatine,
who as her husband was her natural protector, failed her. ... A wom-
anish soul, characterless good nature, a lack of seriousness in [Priam's]
conception of the duties of the royal office were, as Shakespeare
shows, more responsible for the fall of Troy than was the hostile
violence of evil. ... Both Priam and Collatine are—not men who face
life with a full consciousness of its seriousness, but women who allow
themselves to be guided by the impulses of their changing emotions,
their vanity, and their weakness.[73]

A couple of my several reservations respecting this comment
upon *The Rape of Lucrece* bear also on my reading of *Titus Andronicus*. Is it truly virtuous for a mature person, male or female, to be
guileless, to be unaware of the evil that men are capable of? (Should
not Lucrece have had a maid or two spend the night with her?) Besides, was not Lucrece unduly moved by considerations of honor in
what she did, both in acquiescing in Tarquin's attack and in killing
herself? That is, if she thought death preferable to the attack, why
did she not die in resisting the rape? Primarily, it seems, because
Tarquin made the ultimate threat to her:

> *"Lucrece," quoth he, "this night I must enjoy thee.*
> *If thou deny, then force must work my way;*
> *For in thy bed I purpose to destroy thee.*
> *That done, some worthless slave of thine I'll slay,*
> *To kill thine honour with thy life's decay;*
>   *And in thy dead arms do I mean to place him,*
>   *Swearing I slew him, seeing thee embrace him.*
>
> *"So thy surviving husband shall remain*
> *The scornful mark of every open eye;*
> *Thy kinsmen hang their heads at this disdain,*

Thy issue blurred with nameless bastardy;
And thou, the author of their obloquy,
Shalt have thy trespass cited up in rhymes
And sung by children in succeeding times."
                                    [512f]

This means, does it not, that honor—hers and her husband's—matters
not only more than life itself but also more than virtue for its own
sake?

Tarquin's threat to honor is emphasized by Shakespeare in the
poem. Is this not related to the poet's understanding of Rome? What
should Lucrece have done? Could she—should she—have remained
silent altogether, once she had been forced to acquiesce?[74] Or should
she have revealed what happened, but without killing herself? It depends, does it not, upon what mattered most to her, upon what she
was after? The most she explicitly asks for is "revenge on him that
made [her] stop [her] breath." (1180) She is driven to link her fate
(and, in effect, Rome's) to that of Troy, saying of her fall before
Tarquin, "So my Troy did perish." (1547) The personal is seen in
terms of the political: but it *is* the personal that is emphasized, with
the political (at least on the surface) little more than the personal
writ large. It is left to the resourceful Junius Brutus to transform
the personal disaster into a public good.[75]

                                    vi

I HAVE suggested that an interpretation of *The Rape of Lucrece* can
help us see—can reinforce for us what we see in—*Titus Andronicus.* I
have mentioned several considerations which support the proposition
that these two works have a special affinity. A few more points, briefly
made, should further support this proposition.

Similar language can be found in the two works; similar allusions
are used, including the important allusions to the story of Philomel
(upon which the story of the mutilation of the ravished Lavinia is
based). (*Titus,* II, iii, 43; II, iv, 26-27, 38-43; IV, i, 47-48, 52; V, ii,
194-95; *Lucrece* 1079, 1128, 1134. Compare *Sonnet 102; A Midsummer Night's Dream,* II, ii, 13; *Cymbeline,* II, ii, 44-46.) Oaths
very much matter in the two works; so does the feigning of madness
by a critical opponent of the ruler (Junius Brutus in *Lucrece,* Titus

in *Titus Andronicus*—this is also seen later, of course, in *Hamlet* and in *King Lear*). In *Titus Andronicus,* Marcus (the brother of Titus) can, at the end of the play, imitate Junius Brutus (V, iii, 67f), and, throughout the play, the story of Lucrece is referred to (by villains and heroes alike). (II, i, 108; III, i, 298; IV, i, 63-64, 91)

Many of the similarities between these two works can no doubt be attributed to the time of their composition. But, I suggest, these similarities have something to do as well with an opinion about the "nature" of Rome which guides what Shakespeare is saying about Roman developments.

vii

WHAT *DOES* Rome mean? Rome was obviously an important political possibility for Shakespeare and his contemporaries (just as were Venice, perhaps Greece and, of course, England). That Rome should be important is understandable to Americans: consider the effect of the memory of Rome on the United States in the early days of the Republic. Indeed, one might even dare to suggest that the American founding fathers were the last of the Romans (but "Romans" with a somewhat more moderate view than their prototypes of the relation of family honor to political action).

One cannot begin to address the question of what Rome means, however, without addressing as well the question of what it is that Rome is a response to in the nature of man and in the nature of things. In addressing this question, one must consider various things I have already touched upon—such things as piety; the relation of honor and chastity; the gods; monarchy; and, of course, the nature and cause of evil. Thus, for example, *are* the gods relied upon? Do prayers to them matter? How are they understood to respond both to prayers and to human events? (We return to these questions in Chapters II and III of this book.)

What is said in these Roman works about the natural order? Is not evil shown to have a self-defeating character? Are not the wicked shown, in their selfishness, to be improvident? At times it seems that nature is set up in opposition to honor—and perhaps that is as it should be, since honor does so much depend on the opinions which happen to be in vogue at a particular time and place. At times, also, it seems that the gods themselves are reduced to manifestations of the natural order—however salutary it may be not to make much of this in the public doctrines of a regime.[76]

Such are the matters about which one is obliged to wonder in considering what is said by Shakespeare about the Roman regime. We are also obliged to wonder whether Shakespeare had essentially the same opinions about these matters, insofar as they relate to Rome, throughout his career as a playwright—opinions which can be traced back to his temperament, to his experience, and especially to his thought.

viii

AMONG THE opinions Shakespeare might well have had, and which would affect his treatment of Rome, is that there is a kind of natural history of regimes, perhaps even natural life spans for regimes. Certainly, it is the life span of Rome that these two works, *The Rape of Lucrece* and *Titus Andronicus,* can be understood virtually to have frame. Titus speaks of a family tomb which is five hundred years old. (I, i, 353) Are there not indications that this family has been what it is only under the Empire?[77] Certainly, it is as a family under the Empire that *we* know the Andronici. Is not the action of the play, then, well into the fourth century, if not the fifth century? (No dates are referred to in the play; no emperors, of recent rule, are referred to by name.) Would not Shakespeare and his contemporaries have taken five centuries or so to have been the extent of the Republic established after the Tarquins were expelled? If so, we can see here a span of some one thousand years for the Roman regime: five hundred years under the Republic; five hundred years under the Empire (starting with the careers of Julius Caesar and perhaps his immediate predecessors).

In any event, there is, both at the beginning of the first five centuries referred to and at the end of the second five centuries, a rape. In both cases, the woman's name begins with *L*. One rape leads to the establishment of the Republic; the other rape leads to mere revenge and to a change in emperors (but almost accidentally so), not to a change in regime. Thus, in the second instance—in *Titus*—the emphasis seems more on the private (which happens to have some public consequences). Lucrece, too, had spoken of a private revenge—but Junius Brutus, at least, had other ideas, and they were not limited to replacing one king with another. Lucius, who is off with the Goths, does lead an army against Rome, for private revenge and perhaps for a change in rulers, but not for a change of regime.

The name of Lavinia, in *Titus Andronicus,* reminds us of that vital Roman history *before* the rape of Lucrece and the founding of the Republic—that history (drawn upon, but not made explicit, in *The Rape of Lucrece*) which goes back to Aeneas' war for the hand of Lavinia (in order to establish himself and his fellow Trojan refugees in Italy).[78] This reference to Aeneas reminds us as well of Dido—and the references in *Titus* by Tamora and Marcus to Aeneas' dalliance with that queen. (II, iii, 10-29; V, iii, 80-84) We are further reminded that Romans and their supposed Trojan ancestors had always had the problem of arranging for their women, of reconciling their sexual desires with political necessities. This problem is evident in the perennial difficulty the Romans seem to have had, as Shakespeare sees them, of establishing a proper relation of the honorable and the erotic to one another and to the political. Even if we consider Shakespeare immature at this stage of his career—the stage of *Lucrece* and *Titus*— is not the opinion he holds in these plays his enduring opinion of Rome, an opinion that may have deepened as he matured but that he retained, in its essentials, throughout his career?

ix

I HAVE argued that these two works—*Lucrece* and *Titus*—fittingly bracket much of Roman history. We find three plays within the "poetic" frame thereby provided—*Coriolanus, Julius Caesar,* and *Antony and Cleopatra.* I have touched upon two of these plays in Part One of this chapter. I add only a few words about each here, to indicate how they fit in to what I have been suggesting about Shakespeare's general opinion of Rome.

We see in *Coriolanus* a crisis of the Republic in which family ties and patriotism collaborate to reconstitute and to save the Republic. Coriolanus finally sacrifices himself to Rome, at the instigation of his mother. Although Lucius, in *Titus,* is likened to Coriolanus (IV, iv, 67), there is one critical difference (among others) between Lucius and Coriolanus: the common people love Lucius. Are we supposed to suspect, for this and other reasons, Lucius's passions? (See *Titus,* V, iii, 113-18.)

We see in *Julius Caesar* the fall of the Republic: the would-be saviors of the Republic prove ineffectual. Why should this have been so? Brutus and Cassius, we have seen, are only parts of a Roman: together they would make the complete old-style Roman, who is no longer available (except perhaps in the "divine" but somehow too self-centered Julius Caesar).

And we see in *Antony and Cleopatra* the final establishment of the Empire (almost a century in the making?)—the revival of kingship under a new name (with intense, all-sacrificing personal love, not republican virtue, as the only alternative to kingship). The mechanical man, the organization man, so to speak, asserts himself in a public capacity: he prevails over the self-indulgent, but at the price of his humanity. (This sacrifice of humanity we see carried to its extreme in *Titus*.)

Somehow or other, there comes (over the centuries) a corruption of the erotic, a rigid piety, and a callous political order which make Rome the place where monstrosities of all kinds are to be found.

                                    X

THE SEEDS of the Roman development can be said to have been implicit in the story of *Lucrece,* with *Titus Andronicus* the penultimate stage. The ultimate stage will see the barbarians finally prevail. They come close in *Titus,* but they overreach themselves *this* time. Just as *Titus* presents the second stage from the end, *Lucrece* presents the second stage from the beginning. The first stage (anticipated in *Troilus and Cressida?*) is available in the story of Aeneas told by Virgil.

Thus there are seven stages in Shakespeare's thoughtful account of Rome (as I have reconstructed it): the career of Aeneas, his predecessors, his contemporaries, and his successors (including Romulus and Remus?); the establishment of the Republic (at the time of Lucrece); the crisis of the Republic under people such as Coriolanus; the fall of the Republic with Julius Caesar and the response to him providing the final push; the establishment of the Empire (at the time of Antony and Cleopatra); the crisis of the Empire under Titus Andronicus and his contemporaries; the fall of Rome to the barbarians and their successors.

Under this interpretation, *Lucrece* can be seen to exhibit both the nobility of Rome and certain of its inherent defects. Did Rome peak early? Did it try to set too high a standard for itself in certain respects? For example, in the future, no woman could be raped without killing herself (or she might be suspected of complicity)? Does this make too much of chastity and of honor and not enough of chance and of prudence? Such an attitude *can* lead to excesses of all kinds, as we see in *Titus*. The duty in these matters of leaders who know how to hold public passions in check should be obvious.

Junius Brutus, we have noticed, was able to convert a personal wrong to a political use. (He does observe that Lucrece, in her suicide, killed the wrong person. [1826-27] Thus, Brutus is a Roman who exploits the personal, or family, sense of honor for public purposes. We notice that if there had been a reliable ruler in Rome, Lucrece's family would probably have been willing to go to him for a redress of grievances.) But conditions being what they were, if it had not been Lucrece's mistreatment, would not something else have been exploited by Brutus? Still, it may very much matter, and matter for a long time (indeed, for ten centuries?), that the occasion for the decisive revolution in Rome should have been sex-linked.[79] It affects, among other things, the status thereafter of family relations and the very tone of community opinions about honor and erotic things.

Other interrelated features of Roman life evident in, or influenced by, the Lucrece story should be briefly noted: the taste for rhetoric, the role of dramatic self-sacrifice, the importance of spectacle, and the constant recourse to war. Thus, it sometimes seems that the only solution Titus Andronicus has for problems is to *kill*, whether his victims be foreign enemies, his son, his daughter, or domestic enemies.

xi.

WHAT, THEN, about the future of Rome after the time of Titus Andronicus? I have suggested that the threat of barbarization, perhaps as much from within as from abroad, lies ahead.

Titus Andronicus ends with Lucius in command. The last speech is his. At the beginning of this millennium (in Shakespeare's account), it will be recalled, there is another Lucius—for the Argument published at the head of *The Rape of Lucrece* begins with the name, Lucius. This is Lucius Tarquinius, the king who is the father of the man who raped Lucrece. (Did Shakespeare know and choose to ignore the first name of Lucius Junius Brutus?) Thus, the series of Roman stories in

Shakespeare begins with a Lucius who is the father of the critical male
character (Sextus Tarquinius); the series ends with a Lucius (also a
ruler) who is the son of the critical male character (Titus Andronicus).
Such symmetry also supports the proposition that Shakespeare did
think of these works as a grand whole. (I suggest in passing that it is
not, as many believe, careless of Shakespeare to have Saturninus several times referred to in *Titus* as "king," not only as "emperor": we
are, in some respects, back in the days of the tyrannical Tarquins.
[See I, i, 250–51; II, iii, 87, 259; III, i, 154; IV, iv, 80. See, also,
IV, iii, 19.])

What, in any event, is to be expected from Lucius, the new emperor? It should not be forgotten, however much the immediate effects of the theater do depend upon such forgettings, that Lucius was
one of the originators of the troubles the Andronici have in this play.
It was he who first asked for the sacrifice of Tamora's son at the funeral of his brothers. (I, i, 99–104)[80] He does exhibit mercy toward
Aaron's infant—but this is on the basis of a contract sealed by a solemn
oath: this was the only way he could learn what the well-informed
Aaron knew. (V, i, 69–86) Such mercy is not exhibited toward Aaron
himself. (Indeed, Aaron is to be treated somewhat like Lucifer is in
the very depths of Dante's Inferno—he is to be buried to his waist
[V, iii, 179] —but with this vital difference: no paradise lies obviously
ahead for anyone.) Nowhere in the play does one see mercy shown
for its own sake, even though it is several times begged for.

The closing lines of the play are harsh. Aaron is to be starved to
death; Tamora's body is to be left to the birds and beasts. Lucius
then concludes the play, in the generally accepted version:

> *See justice done on Aaron, that damned Moor,*
> *By whom our heavy haps had their beginning.*
> *Then, afterwards, to order well the state,*
> *That like events may ne'er it ruinate.*
>
> *[V, iii, 201]*

Thus, there is no indication here of any recognition by Lucius that his
father and he had made one critical mistake after another in what we
know as the first act of the play, that act in which Aaron says not a
word. (See V, i, 151.) One would be more hopeful for the future of
Rome if one could believe that there is in this closing statement by

the emperor Lucius a kind of noble lie, an effort to let bygones be bygones in putting everything on Aaron as scapegoat. But the progeny of Aaron does live on (to be raised in Rome?)—and one must wonder what that bodes for the future.

xii

IS THERE something of a return here, at least in some particulars, to the *Lucrece* resolution? Has Rome been brought back to some of its original principles, but (even if so) too late? Are the times wrong for the *Lucrece* approach to the governance of Rome? Is something else needed, something to tame Rome since barbarism has become so important there?

Whatever may be needed, is not Christianity due to emerge among the Romans? This would be a new regime with its own strengths and liabilities, one in which piety and love and sacrifice would be redirected. One must wonder, especially in the light of the chronology I have suggested, whether there are any traces of an incipient Christianity in the story. We are encouraged to so wonder, of course, when we recall that students as diverse as Augustine, Dante, and Gibbon saw the Roman polity as the seedbed of the Church. (Christianity was not irrevocably established in the Roman Empire until the end of the fourth century, if not later. See, for example, the epigraph to Appendix E, below.)

Among the traces of an incipient Christianity to be taken into account are the "anachronistic" references (too easily dismissed by scholars as carelessness on Shakespeare's part) to "popish" things, to a "monastery" (where Aaron and his child had been captured by Lucius' army), and to "christening" Aaron's child with a sword (that is, killing it). (See V, i, 76; IV, ii, 70; V, i, 21. See also, I, i, 210, 326; III, i, 149; III, ii, 41; IV, iii, 49; IV, iv, 42, 47; V, i, 40; V, ii, 146; V, ii, 86-90, 144; V, iii, 5.) Central to the array of allusions to the Christianity which threatens to spill over into this play can be said to be the oaths by the martyred messenger. (IV, iv, 42, 47)

The significance of Aaron's curiously influential infant, of dubious parentage, bears thinking about in this connection. So does Aaron's very name, of course: one should wonder, for instance, who plays Moses to the Moor's Aaron—perhaps Titus with his forty years as a soldier?

Indeed, there is about the Aaron type, with its single-minded dedication to evil for its own sake, something which is not unrelated (if only by distortion, just as witchcraft is) to the Christian view of the world and of human nature. The reflections on piety prompted by this play suggest problems with the Christian regime as well. Does it, too, fail to be flexible enough in its own way, perhaps in its considerable emphasis upon mercy? What should its life span be expected to be? Had it had *its* "thousand years" of sovereignty by Shakespeare's time?

In any event, the seeming insistence by Lucrece, and later by the family of Lavinia, on chastity at all costs does fit in with a Christian view of the world. (Is it clear that Lucrece's family fully agreed with her? The Andronici may be more extreme about chastity than those around Lucrece, perhaps even more extreme than Lucrece herself [who *can* be understood to have preferred honor to chastity]. Certainly, Lucrece's family would *not* have killed her in order to kill her shame. Compare *Titus,* V, iii, 46–47.)

However all this may be, it can be deduced that Shakespeare recognized that an ascetic Christianity was, by the beginning of the fifth century and despite its own limitations, the way of the future for profligate Rome in the desperate straits depicted in *Titus.*

That, then, would be a new way out for Rome.

xiii

AN OLD way out also seems to be indicated—but it is less likely than Christianity to be resorted to in these desperate circumstances. This "way out" starts from the recognition that folly *is* likely to lead to disaster, irrespective of what the gods do. (Here I draw on Part One of this chapter.) Such folly can be either of the heart or of the mind: of the heart, as seen in the fierce passions of Titus and Lucius which lead to the sacrifice of Tamora's son (and as seen in Collatine's vanity about Lucrece's virtue); of the mind, as seen in the misjudgments by Titus with respect both to Saturninus as emperor and to Tamora as friend (once her son had been sacrificed).

To speak thus of folly is again to remind ourselves of the role of prudence in human affairs, a role that is treated with respect by Shakespeare in all his plays. Ulysses is seen as a model of such prudence in *The Rape of Lucrece,* as well as in *Titus Andronicus.* Lucrece notices him in the painting of the fall of Troy: "sly Ulysses," who exhibits in a "mild glance . . . deep regard and smiling government." (1399–1400) That is, Ulysses considers matters carefully and has a confident, even relaxed, self-control. He is thus praised by someone who considers herself a descendant of the Trojans, even though he was a critical factor in the fall of Troy. And Lucrece's assessment is made in circumstances that contrast Ulysses to Ajax, his rival, whose eyes exhibit "blunt rage and rigour." (1398) It is also in connection with Ajax that Ulysses is invoked in *Titus* as a man able to put aside personal animosity and ask his fellow Greeks to permit the burial of Ajax. (I, i, 383)[81] This is recalled by Marcus in his plea to Titus, "[A]nd wise Laertes' son,/ Did graciously plead for [Ajax's] funerals." (It is only after this speech that Titus agrees to allow the son he had rashly killed to be buried in the family tomb.)

Was there not something of Ulysses in Junius Brutus as well, the man who had concealed by a show of folly his opposition to the Tarquins but who was able to take advantage of Lucrece's death? Thus, it is said in *Lucrece:*

> Brutus, who plucked the knife from Lucrece's side,
> Seeing such emulation in their woe,
> Began to clothe his wit in state and pride,
> Burying in Lucrece' wound his folly's show.
>
> *[1807]*

We should take care, however, not to consider Ulysses an endorsement of mere duplicity. There is duplicity enough in *Titus.* Aaron, with his talk of "policy," shows what happens when someone pursues duplicity for its own sake. (II, i, 104; IV, ii, 149. Compare *Lucrece* 1814–15.) On the other hand, Titus himself (as well as Lucrece earlier) shows what happens when one is so lacking in duplicity as not to anticipate it in others. When Titus does become duplicitous, it is while he is mad—and this leads to monstrosities which no civilized people can tolerate or long live with or by.[82]

I trust I have said enough, however tentative and even outlandish some of my observations may have had to be, to support the suggestion that *Titus Andronicus* is, properly conceived, not the least instructive play associated with the name and genius of Shakespeare.

It is fitting that we close this chapter with questions (prompted by this play) which lead us to our next two chapters: What are the conditions of civilization? What, in the effort to produce both a civilized community *and* men of godlike virtue, are the advantages and liabilities of Rome? What, in short, are justice, human perfection, and the common good?

II. JOHN MILTON (1608-1674)

> *Consequently we must say that the natural
> law, as to general principles, is the same for all,
> both as to rectitude and as to knowledge. But
> as to certain matters of detail, which are con-
> clusions, as it were, of these general principles,
> it is the same for all in the majority of cases,
> both as to rectitude and as to knowledge; and
> yet in some few cases it may fail, both as to
> rectitude, by reason of certain obstacles (just
> as natures subject to generation and corruption
> fail in some few cases on account of some ob-
> stacle), and as to knowledge, since in some the
> reason is perverted by passion, or evil habit, or
> an evil disposition of nature; thus formerly,
> theft, although it is expressly contrary to the
> natural law, was not considered wrong among
> the Germans, as Julius Caesar relates....*

> --Thomas Aquinas, *Treatise on Law*, Q. 97, A. 4

i

JOHN MILTON'S sonnet, "On the Late Massacre in Piedmont," has
been called "the most elevated and passionate" of all his shorter poems,
"perhaps the greatest [sonnet] in the English language," and "easily
the most powerful sonnet ever written."[83] Although several of Shakespeare's sonnets do seem to me to be better, Milton's is certainly
worthy of serious consideration. Of special interest for us in Milton's
poem, as well as in the work considered in the next chapter, is the
greater reliance by the artist on Christian sentiments than is evident
in the work of Shakespeare. What is the relation of such reliance to
that prudence which, I have suggested, is one critical aspect of the
thinking that the artist does?

One of the earliest, perhaps the earliest, international invocations
of human rights may well be Milton's Piedmont Massacre sonnet of
1653. In thinking about this sonnet, it can be instructive to remind
ourselves of what human rights have come to mean, what they presuppose, and what their consequences can be.

ii

THE PRESIDENT of the United States, who had declared himself an
advocate of human rights, was welcomed to Venezuela in 1978 as a
"champion of universal democracy."[84] We are thereby reminded of
an assumption, rarely made explicit, of any systematic, worldwide
advocacy of human rights—the assumption of a particular kind of
regime. Is not one kind of democracy presupposed—a democracy that
is international in scope and that calls into question the particular
political allegiances men are accustomed to?

But, we have been taught (and I have, in effect, argued in the
first chapter of this book), the regime appropriate to a country depends on circumstances. Some of those circumstances are changing
or changeable; others are more or less permanent. Is it prudent to
proceed on the assumption that democracy is good, and called for, in
all the countries of the world today? Does not such an assumption
tend to undermine decent nondemocratic regimes where they are
appropriate? Indeed, does it not undermine the idea of democracy
itself? Democracy can be seen to make matters worse if it should be
insisted upon where it cannot work well, if at all.

And yet, do not some of the human rights that we hear invoked
presuppose or encourage the establishment of democratic regimes?
Consider, for example, how freedom of speech and of the press and,
perhaps also, the right to property and the right of religious liberty
are spoken of. Are *all* of these rights always essential to a decent regime? Is it always desirable that these rights be emphasized? Are not
these and other such rights somehow different from the right (if it
should be called that) to be spared various atrocities? Thus, the condemnation of torture is appropriate in nondemocratic as well as in
democratic regimes, as is the condemnation of lawless killing. But
surely there can be, depending on circumstances, decent regimes that
do not permit a press as free as ours or that do provide for an established religion. Human rights, insofar as they can be universalized,
should recognize divergences in the circumstances and capacities of
peoples.

Or to put what I have said another way, care should be taken, in
any international advocacy of human rights, lest the advocacy become
little more than a glittering form of partisan nationalism. Such advo-

cacy can simply become another way, temporarily fashionable, of advancing a case which may be grounded in other, perhaps cruder, differences.

I do not mean to suggest that there are no standards by which regimes, and their appropriateness, can be judged. The traditional natural right doctrines, as well as what we otherwise know about justice, can provide a basis for assessing regimes. But "imperialism," in the form of *self-righteous* "interference in another country's domestic affairs," should be guarded against.

Thus, prudence is needed in applying the standards we do have and in suggesting modifications of the regimes we confront. Otherwise, matters can be made worse—and conflict is likely to be promoted. Peace *usually* serves human rights, as well as national security, better than war. When war starts, or is threatened, a people are usually willing to take more risks—or are more likely to allow their leaders to do terrible things. It should be remembered that the Nazis could not do their worst even in Germany itself until war began in Europe.

In any event, criticisms of the domestic affairs of another country have to be made with care. We must take care, that is, neither to undermine useful national associations nor to make world opinion seem irresponsible or otherwise irrelevant. Mere indignation, and especially uninformed indignation, should be guarded against.

iii

NOTHING COMES to mind from either ancient Greece or republican Rome comparable to the human rights appeal in Milton's Piedmont Massacre sonnet. (Perhaps medieval papal condemnations of what was happening elsewhere could be found, but they would not be quite comparable, in that they would not have been addressed to misdeeds in *another* jurisdiction. The same may be said of imperial condemnations in ancient Rome.) The Greeks did speak of differences in regimes, and of the different practices in other countries—see, for example, Pericles' funeral address—but they do not seem to have been disposed to comment, *with a view to immediate action,* on particular episodes in other countries unless their own citizens were involved. Has a worldwide communications network reinforced the tendency in recent centuries to monitor the doings of other countires?

The event about which Milton wrote, and his activities in response to it, have been described in this fashion:

> The outrage of the slaughter [by] the Piedmontese, by order of the Duke of Savoy on April 24, 1653, had shocked all Protestants. In their eyes, the Vaudois, or Waldensians, living quietly apart in an isolated section of the Alps, were true primitive Christians who for hundreds of years had kept alive the spirit of the teaching of Christ. Without warning they were set upon and slaughtered with every kind of barbarity. It is estimated that 1,712 men, women and children were killed. The few fugitives who escaped over the wild and desolate snow-covered mountains carried word of the massacre to Paris, begging the protection of Protestants.
>
> In his capacity as Latin Secretary, Milton, acting for [Oliver] Cromwell, wrote an official protest to the Duke of Savoy, followed by letters of state to the kings of Denmark, Sweden, to the Dutch Republic, and the Swiss Protestant cantons, urging them to join the British Commonwealth in protest. Similar appeals were sent to Cardinal Mazarin and to the King of France. Cromwell also sent a special ambassador to Savoy to protest the persecution and to indicate that Cromwell was willing to go to war if necessary. From his state papers which, though firm and outspoken, nevertheless had to be restrained within the limits of international diplomacy, Milton turned to poetry for release of his profound emotion. In structure, style, and intensity of feeling, this is Milton's greatest "trumpet."[85]

Milton's "trumpet" took the form of this poem (printed here with somewhat modernized spelling):

ON THE LATE MASSACRE IN PIEDMONT

> *Avenge O Lord thy slaughter'd Saints, whose bones*
> *Lie scatter'd on the Alpine mountains cold,*
> *Ev'n them who kept thy truth so pure of old*
> *When all our Fathers worship't Stocks and Stones,*
> *Forget not: in thy book record their groanes*   5
> *Who were thy Sheep and in their antient Fold*
> *Slayn by the bloody Piemontese that roll'd*
> *Mother with Infant down the Rocks. Their moans*
> *The Vales redoubl'd to the Hills, and they*
> *To Heav'n. Their martyr'd blood and ashes sow*   10

> *O're all th'Italian fields where still doth sway*
> *The triple Tyrant: that from these may grow*
> *A hunder'd-fold, who having learnt thy way*
> *Early may fly the Babylonian woe.*

The scholar from whom I have drawn an account of the event goes on to introduce the sonnet with comments which suggest something about both its structure and its biblical sources:

> Even Milton never so surpassed himself in keeping within the limits of a form yet in releasing that form from the narrow restrictions it might have imposed. There is no line, with the possible exception of the second, at the end of which we pause as we read the sonnet aloud. Inevitably we are carried on through the first quatrain to find the governing verb, "Forget not." We cannot be sure whether the sestet begins in the eighth line with "Their moans" or in the tenth, with "Their martyred blood and ashes," nor does it matter, since octave and sestet are magnificently welded into one masterly whole.
>
> In *Lycidas* alone has Milton so far achieved such majestic control over sound, meaning, and structure. [This is said just before the scholar turns to consider "The Major Poems," such as *Paradise Lost.*] ... The [Waldensians] had been the original sheep of the Good Shepherd; they had followed His gospel while our rude ancestors were still worshipping stocks and stones. As from the dragon's teeth once sprang up armed men, so from the martyred blood and ashes strewn over the fields of Italy will come retribution upon the "triple Tyrant." We cannot break this sonnet into artificial distinction of two themes, one in octave, another in sestet. It is all one great invective, calling for vengeance, from "Avenge, O Lord" to "Babylonian woe," the destruction foretold in the Apocalypse. In its compelling resonance (the sonnet must be read aloud) Milton continues the "dread voice" of the Old Testament, "Vengeance is mine" with the "loud voice" of Revelation, at the opening of the fifth seal, "How long, O Lord, holy and true, dost thou not judge and avenge our blood on them that dwell on the earth."[86]

A few more points should perhaps be mentioned before we consider somewhat systematically the sonnet itself. Commentators have suggested that the sowing image draws upon both the parable of the sower, in *Matthew* 13: 3–9, and (as we have seen) the Greek story of the warriors who sprang from the dragon's teeth (sowed by Cadmus at Thebes). The parable of the sower finds the seed, when it "fell into good ground," bringing "forth fruit . . . an hundredfold."[87] Also drawn upon here, we are told, is Tertullian's saying, "The blood of the martyrs is the seed of the Church."[88] Furthermore, various commentators have identified "the triple Tyrant" as the pope, who wears the triple crown and claims the keys of earth, heaven, and hell.

iv

NOW THAT we have touched upon the historical setting of the sonnet, upon Milton's circumstances, and upon the sonnet's sources, we turn to the poem proper.

The sonnet is made of three sentences: the first and third sentences are long and complicated (the first extends across eight lines; the third, across five); the second sentence runs less than two lines. The first sentence deals, for the most part, with the past—with the history of the victims and with what has just happened to them; the third sentence deals, for the most part, with the expected divine response to what has happened. The second sentence provides a transition—between past and future, between earth and heaven: the moans which announce what has happened in the Alpine mountains make their way to heaven and somehow affect what happens thereafter.

The central lines of the poem, lines 7 and 8, find the victims:

Slayn by the bloody Piemontese that roll'd
Mother with Infant down the Rocks.

We can see here the extreme atrocity: mothers and infants, not only men, are killed, and killed in such a way as to have them treated like rocks to be rolled down the mountain side.[89] Differences in condition seem to matter. Following upon these central lines, which show bodies rolling *down,* there are the decisive moans—in a reversal of the dominant motion—making their way *up* to heaven, gathering strength as they rise, just as falling bodies accelerate.

Are these moans decisive in moving heaven? Certainly, they are intended to move humanity as well as the Lord, especially when put into the form of this poem. Why is the Lord told, "Forget not"? Indeed, why is the Lord told anything at all? Does He not already know all? How is one to understand the Lord's willingness to permit the massacre? Why should He be asked to avenge what He did not choose to prevent? Besides, why should He have to be *asked:* does He not already realize what is good, what is called for?

The narrator seems sure of what is needed. Is the Lord being implicitly chided for His shortcomings? Or is this only the narrator's effort to determine (or to reassure himself about) what kind of a world this is? Perhaps, indeed, we should recognize that this poem is not addressed to the Lord. Thus, we are reminded of an old question about the nature of prayer. Is prayer the way that men remind each other, and themselves, of what the divine is, of what the truly good calls for? After all, some would ask, how else does the Lord act but through men—through men invoking and implementing the divine, appealing to and depending upon the openness in men to the divine?

The primary concern in the poem is, ostensibly, with what happens in Italy. And yet, since the poem is written in English (not in the Latin Milton used for some poems), its readers are going to be (for the most part) the poet's countrymen, not Italians or even the Roman Catholic Church. Is this poem an effort to influence Englishmen with respect to religion, especially with respect to Roman Catholicism? What is being said about the Roman Church? Is it intrinsically Babylonian in its mode? Or is it corrupt at some times, not at others? Is its continued and permanent (even if not reformed) existence assumed? It is far from clear what the relation is between "the bloody Piemontese" and the Roman Church. Is it because they believed in the doctrines of "the triple Tyrant" that the Piedmontese did the terrible things they did? Or did they act as they did, not because of the precise doctrines they believed, but simply because they believed *differently?* It is no more than suggested, if even that, that the order to kill came directly from Rome. I will say more later about what Rome stands for.

What is invoked in this poem? Certain fundamental rights, or a sense of humanity and decency? Relatively little is indicated about the doctrines which divide the contending sects. The victims have kept, we are told, "thy truth so pure of old," a truth which led them to worship rightly "when all our Fathers worship't Stocks and Stones." What is the relation of the old to the good? The old is not intrinsically good, since even older than the victims' pure worship, it seems, is the worship of "Stocks and Stones," a worship indulged in by pagans and perhaps continued (it is suggested?) by contemporary image—or icon—worship. On the other hand, the Lord, it should be presumed, is even

older than the oldest form of worship—but is it that His goodness does
not depend on His oldness, but rather that His oldness (or eternality)
reflects and ratifies His goodness? (Do human rights advocates today
invoke something ancient [and pure] or something new [a new world]?)

In any event, little is said in the sonnet about the orthodox doctrines of the day, except in what is indicated about idol worship and
about the triple claims of a church suffering from Babylonian corruption. But does it matter to *us* what the orthodox doctrines were? Does
the sonnet's effect depend upon that? If the doctrines really matter,
then the poem might be seriously flawed, for one could argue that
not enough respect is shown Roman Catholic ways. Of course, the
conjuring up of the Babylonian image—of the corruption and of the
inevitable destruction of Babylon—would be sufficient for the reader
of Milton's day to suggest all that is wrong with the Church. But it
should be recognized that thoughtful and pious Roman Catholics
have plausible arguments for the use of images and altars and for the
other sacred objects and claims of their Church. All somehow try to
come to God. What *is* needed by and for a people, especially in large
numbers, over centuries? Must the purity of old be limited to a few,
and those unnamed few living in primitive and isolated conditions?[90]

The "triple Tyrant" brings to mind an established church, or at
least the elaborate institutions of an old church—and this can mean
traditions and reliance on error-laden precedents (or the old) in preference to a simple reliance on Scriptures (or the new, which is the
enduring truth). Recourse to the Scriptures, and not to the traditions
of interpretation of those Scriptures—this was a distinction that Milton
made again and again in his writings—such recourse to the Scriptures
by each generation, by each man, is critical to Christian liberty. But,
one must wonder, does not such liberating recourse endanger human
community? May it not deprive men of the accumulated wisdom, or
at least the sustained moderation, of the ages? It is no accident that
the Roman Catholic Church does retain an informed (even though
sometimes distorted) respect for natural right, a respect that humane
non-Catholics today not only should recognize but should take advantage of.[91]

The enduring effect of this sonnet, I suggest, does not depend
upon the aptness of the narrator's opinion about "the triple Tyrant."
The truths that matter, insofar as they are relied upon in this sonnet,
are threefold:

1. The killing of innocent people is wicked.
2. The Lord works things out to right wrongs.
3. This righting of wrongs consists not of more killing, but of conversion—this is the true divine "revenge."

It is important to *record* what has happened and thereby to *sow* (that is, to use the record effectively). Only then will justice prevail. The narrator wants an effect in this world, not "just" at the Day of Reckoning. What happens in this world is, it seems, vital. What does this say about God, about religion, about politics?

The sonnet, we have noticed, is addressed primarily to Englishmen. Perhaps it is a prudent way of reconciling *them* to what has happened. That is, the poem's statement sounds, at the outset, much more forceful (in the ordinary sense) than it is. It opens with a call for vengeance—and the reader expects to hear a call for blood—but it closes with a reliance on having others see the truth. Does this not tend to moderate the desire for physical revenge, that desire which had caused English leaders to talk about war? Thus, Cromwell had indicated to European Protestants that "although they differ[ed] among themselves in some things of little Consequence, [their Cause was] nevertheless the same in general and united in one common Interest."[92]

But war or a punitive expedition should have had to consider costs. And it should also have had to consider more particulars of the episode. No reasons are given here why blood was spilled on this occasion, what the killers were thinking of (what motives, including fears, had guided them), or what the victims had done to provoke the massacre.[93] Perhaps the narrator senses that more needs to be learned— or, at least, that moderation is called for, even though the tone of immoderation is retained. Indeed, one must wonder, does not poetry itself (with its disciplined use of language) *tend* to be intrinsically moderating?

In any event, there is a movement in the sonnet from the avenging God associated with the Old Testament to the converting God associated with the New Testament, the God who sows and thereby makes possible a different kind of revenge. In this movement, the moans to heaven are critical, the moans of victims whose treatment should not be forgotten: does effective *sowing* depend upon a lively recollection of the alternative of old-fashioned *avenging?* What *does* move men to listen to reason, to give reason a chance to make itself heard?

Thus, this is a prayer not for revenge of the victims but for the redemption of the offenders (or, at least, of their descendants). The true victims are the killers, not those killed (who are now in heaven— or, at least, who are now to have their position vindicated). Is this not a prudent way to reconcile decent, spirited men to what has happened? But how far does prudence extend here? What of the evident assumption that the sowing of the martyrs' blood will yield a harvest of truth? "[T]hat from these may grow a hunder'd-fold" could be taken to suggest a natural process. The truth will eventually win out, as seems to be suggested by Milton's *Areopagitica* as well? Is the important thing about these martyrs, not what they happened to believe in, but that they died for those beliefs? That opinion hardly seems the thrust of the poem, but it may well be the opinion accepted by those who (long after the doctrinal struggle it reflects is subdued) continue to be moved by this poem. (One qualification would be generally recognized: to sacrifice oneself for a diabolical creed should not arouse admiration.)

In any event, is Milton's effort to be seen as a struggle for men's minds? Does the truth win out, or tend to win out, if there are genuine artists available to champion it? Does truth tend to enlist the nobler souls among us? How are the more talented to be trained? Does not proper shaping depend on particular communities, where one can know others and be well known? But does the "better" modern opinion, which Milton can be seen to have anticipated, depreciate the particular (and somewhat irrational) allegiances of men, allegiances which should, and eventually will, be surmounted as men ascend toward a "universal democracy"?

v

ONE WAY, then, in which the Piedmont Massacre controversy bears on the international advocacy today of human rights may be seen in how Milton subjected the passions of his day to the discipline of poetry. It would have been easy for the poem to have become prosaic and hence temporary in its effect. It *can* be reduced to pedestrian

terms: the dead should be avenged, the "memory" of nameless victims should be used to overthrow a tyranny. But the considerable
technical ability evident in this sonnet assures us that *a mind* is at
work, a mind of remarkable power. Thus, the rhyme patterns are an
outward assurance of discipline; the involved and intricate verbal
maneuvering, with sounds playing against sounds throughout the
poem, testifies to an extraordinary skill.

Does not such discipline assure us that passions are not only
being restrained but that they are being refined? (The danger of an
autonomous indignation in such matters *is* always to be guarded
against.) Is not the sense of humanity heightened when there is disciplined writing? A higher level of culture is revealed and reinforced
by disciplined writing than by writing that appeals to mere slogans
(which appeals are a kind of force in words). Such discipline (which
reminds us that the artist *is* a thinker) permits, if it does not require
and promote, serious thought. A suggestion of the thinking that
went into this poem is the "coincidence" which finds its hundredth
word to be "hunder'd-fold."[94]

The disciplined poet—the true artist—takes over from the sectar-
ian. (This means, among other things, that the devout Roman Catholic could endorse what is sought in this sonnet.) Such a use of poetry
is a responsible way of invoking, or talking about, universals without
losing sight of vital particulars—a way which takes account of the circumstances, and hence limitations, of mankind.

vi

ONE CONSEQUENCE of the diverse circumstances of mankind is
that people are all too open to the excitement and assurances of self-
righteous indignation. Partisanship, especially when a good cause is
invoked, should be watched—not eliminated. Its elimination could
lead to a demoralizing and unseemly (if not dangerous) apathy. But
partisanship should certainly be watched.

It *is* difficult, however, to keep an invocation of human rights
from becoming partisan. Such an invocation can, I have suggested,
very easily become part of a continuing struggle which finds sides
chosen on the basis of something other than attitudes toward human
rights. When that happens, is humanity respected—or only combativeness, which in turn promotes a destructive defensiveness? Is it not
better to be firm about principles while recognizing how circum-

stances can affect the application of those principles? The classic case for Americans has been Abraham Lincoln's response to the status of slavery in the South. A contemporary case of considerable interest is that posed by Aleksandr Solzhenitsyn. One should be careful, even in one's responses to gross misconduct elsewhere, not to become doctrinaire: one's political judgments are apt to be dubious whenever indignation, even an understandable indignation, overwhelms one. One should also be careful, in championing the cause of victims, not to misuse them once again, thereby further victimizing them.

Whenever possible, the best in the offenders should be appealed to; in this way, they may be raised up—and, if that fails, at least the critic is not brought down to their level. Thus, an academician under Stalin could say, in 1942, in the course of what he referred to as "the most tremendous battle of all history," that Shakespeare "is a part of the culture we are fighting to defend." Questionable regimes—whether in Eastern Europe, Latin America, China, Southern Africa, or Southeast Asia—tacitly acknowledge common standards of humanity by concealing their misconduct.[95]

It is heartening to notice that "the triple Tyrant" against which Milton wrote *is* today generally on the side of decency and liberty. Perhaps, indeed, it was always inclined in that direction, whatever aberrations it may have been subject to from time to time. The teachings it rested upon encouraged correction from within, especially when the implications of those teachings as well as the implications of aberrations were pointed to from without. Can the same be said of, and done for and to, our contemporary tyrannies?

vii

DOES THE call today for human rights unduly emphasize the opinion that everyday life is what matters most? Does such emphasis upon the here and now tend to undermine that sense of the eternal upon which an enduring humanity depends?

What rights should be emphasized today? Which are truly universal? Which depend on local political institutions, on a particular way of life, and hence on variable circumstances? With these questions we return to the beginning of this chapter.

Can the truth be depended upon to prevail? Milton's contemporaries invoked God on behalf of the true way and the faithful. But, we have seen, the problem arises of how God is to be understood to work among men. Of particular interest is the role of *nature* for Milton: he *did* invoke it in his efforts to restrain those who, in the name of a power grounded in revelation, would control religion and politics.

Is there in everyone, or at least in most men, a sense of natural justice? Does sustained persecution require a rationale, so much so that exposure and argument can often have a salutary effect? On the other hand, can single-minded invocations of transcendent standards and ends be resorted to without undermining respect for all earthly communities and regimes? This question, among others, is addressed in the next chapter.

III. J O H N B U N Y A N (1628-1688)

> *If one shall say, "A people is the association of*
> *a multitude of rational beings united by a com-*
> *mon agreement on the objects of their love,"*
> *then it follows that to observe the character of*
> *a particular people we must examine the objects*
> *of its love.... And obviously, the better the*
> *objects [of this love], the better the people;*
> *the worse the objects of this love, the worse*
> *the people.*

> —Augustine, *The City of God,* XIX, xxiv

i

BERNARD SHAW, in a review entitled "Better than Shakespeare,"
argues for the clear superiority of John Bunyan to William Shakespeare. He grants Shakespeare's "extraordinary artistic powers,"
but immediately adds, "he understood nothing and believed nothing."
Shaw then goes on to say:

> Thirty-six big plays in five blank verse acts, and (as Mr. Ruskin, I
> think, once pointed out) not a single hero! Only one man in them all
> who believes in life, enjoys life, thinks life worth living, and has a
> sincere, unrhetorical tear dropped over his deathbed, and that man—
> Falstaff! What a crew they are—these Saturday to Monday athletic
> stock-broker Orlandos, these villains, fools, clowns, drunkards, cow-
> ards, intriguers, fighters, lovers, patriots, hypochondriacs who mistake
> themselves (and are mistaken by the author) for philosophers, princes
> without any sense of public duty, futile pessimists who imagine they
> are confronting a barren and unmeaning world when they are only con-
> templating their own worthlessness, self-seekers of all kinds, keenly
> observed and masterfully drawn from the romantic-commercial point
> of view.... But search for statesmanship, or even citizenship, or any
> sense of the commonwealth, material or spiritual, and you will not
> find the making of a decent vestryman or curate in the whole horde.
> As to faith, hope, courage, conviction, or any of the true heroic qual-
> ities, you find nothing but death made sensational, despair made

---

All citations in the text of this chapter to *The Pilgrim's Progress* are to the Penguin
Books edition (Baltimore, 1965).

stage-sublime, sex made romantic, and barrenness covered up by
sentimentality and the mechanical lift of blank verse.[96]

I have already suggested the role in Shakespeare's tragedy of
prudence (and hence of "statesmanship, or even citizenship"). There
is no need to repeat here what I have said in the first chapter of this
book. Rather, it is (by way of instructive contrast) the citizenship
and statesmanship depicted by Bunyan which will be our immediate
concern. For Shaw argues in his review:

> All that you miss in Shakespeare you find in Bunyan, to whom the
> true heroic came quite obviously and naturally. The world was to
> him a more terrible place than it was to Shakespeare; but he saw
> through it a path at the end of which a man might look not only
> forward to the Celestial City, but back on his life and say: "Tho'
> with great difficulty I am got hither, yet now I do not repent me
> of all the trouble I have been at to arrive where I am. My sword I
> give to him that shall succeed me in my pilgrimage, and my courage
> and skill to him that can get them." [p. 370] The heart vibrates
> like a bell to such utterances as this....[97]

Shaw then continues with additional disparaging remarks about
Shakespeare, that great predecessor whom Shaw always recognized as
the artist he had to surpass (one way or another) in order to be recognized in his own pretensions. This led Shaw to say a number of silly
things. But it is Bunyan, not Shakespeare or even Shaw, with whom
we *are* primarily concerned in this chapter. Of interest, particularly,
are the implications of Shaw's suggestions about Bunyan's "statesmanship" to which I have referred.

To speak of statesmanship is to speak not only of prudence but
also of that sense of justice, or of the common good, by which the
prudent statesman takes his bearing. To assess properly the statesmanship (and indeed the very story) of *The Pilgrim's Progress,* therefore, we must consider the nature of justice. By proceeding thus, we
return, of course, to questions touched upon in the first two chapters
of this book, and we anticipate questions we will be concerned with
in later chapters. For, we should notice, one of the principal subjects
artists think about, when they do think, is justice.

Justice, we are told, is derived from *jus* (that is to say, right or law). The intimate relation between law and what we commonly know as justice is indicated in that we designate as "courts of justice" the places where laws are interpreted and applied. Although we know there may be bad laws, unjust laws, even laws which should not be obeyed, there is certainly a presumption among us in favor of being law-abiding. We look with suspicion upon anyone who makes a habit of breaking the law; it is difficult to regard him as a just man.

Why is there this presumption in favor of obeying laws—in favor, that is, of the rules laid down by the community prescribing our conduct? Several reasons come to mind:

1. We recognize (when we ourselves are not personally involved) that one does tend to overestimate both one's own worth and one's own pains and pleasures. This is evident in the tendency of parents to regard their children as exceptional—judgments which, in most cases, everyone else can easily see are anything but sound.

2. We recognize that it is good to support the law itself, whenever possible, if general respect for law is not to be undermined, especially since we cannot depend on others to be as refined and as restrained as we are in judiciously setting aside the law.

3. We recognize that a sincere effort is usually made by the community in developing through the law the best way (or, at least, a decent way) for handling matters in need of regulation.

4. We recognize that the community is often more open to argument and correction when its determination has been faulty, than are men pursuing their private interests.

5. We recognize that in many circumstances it is more important to have a known and respected rule to follow than to have the very best rule possible.[98]

6. We recognize that it may not be because most men are corrupt that law is required. Indeed, men may have to be restrained in their pursuit of good as they see it: they have to be brought around to see much as others do both the good and how it should be pursued.[99]

7. We recognize, especially when our best intentions are thwarted and when community interests are stressed, why justice has been at times disparaged as "another's good." We usually do not require a law to induce us to do what we "want" to do. Justice *can* be seen as onerous, as a problem. Yet it does not take much imagination for us

to see that general lawlessness is usually far worse[100] than life in a community that again and again restrains us in what we would have or in what we would do.

Even so, it has always been more difficult to justify or make attractive the virtue of justice than it has been to justify the other cardinal virtues, the private advantages of which are far more evident. Intemperance *is* likely to wreck one's body or, at least, to produce hours of acute discomfort; cowardice *is* likely to make one miserable with fear; ignorance often *does* leave one with an uncomfortable sense of inadequacy, or at least one suffers from the practical consequences of uninformed judgments. In none of these cases is the affliction accompanying the vice soothed much by the assurance that one is not known to have the vice but rather may even be thought to be fully virtuous. The unjust man, on the other hand, may revel in his illgotten gains, perhaps all the more so if he derives pleasure from having successfully deceived others about his character.

Here, then, we have one problem of justice, the problem of discounting the attractions of "successful" (that is, undetected) injustice. The attractions result, it would often seem, from the desire to minister to oneself, to do what one can do for oneself. When there is this desire, along with the inclination to take oneself more seriously than others generally do, there is what we know as selfishness.

Consider the forms selfishness—a considerable emphasis upon self—can take; some are rather base, others rather elevated. Selfishness is most obvious in any effort, for the sake of personal gratification, to take or keep that which belongs to another. It is fairly evident that something is wrong when one takes (or keeps) that which is known to belong to another.[101] Thus, few acknowledge to themselves that they are indeed taking or keeping that which belongs to another. Rather than live under the strain of such a recognition (which may threaten as well one's sense of security with respect to that which one has oneself), a redefinition of terms may serve the occasion. One such redefinition is with respect to what "taking" or "keeping" means. Thus, one may "borrow," or one may simply "use," or one may "take from another before one is taken from," or one may "recover" or "replace" what had previously been taken from one.

An even more interesting redefinition occurs in the meaning of "belongs to another." Something is clearly wrong with a man when he is ignorant of what belongs to another. But something may be *seriously* wrong with him when he is always ignorant "in the same direction." Take the shopkeeper who is "bad with figures" and who, consequently, often makes mistakes in adding up your bill. You cannot help but wonder about him, however, when the mistakes are always in his favor. You suspect that his desires have somehow influenced his genuine ineptness with figures. (I rather enjoyed correcting daily such a chronically miscalculating—that is, calculating—shopkeeper when we lived on the Avenue Ledru Rollin in Paris in 1955.)

There may well be, of course, an arbitrary element in determinations of what does belong to others. It is often necessary to have an allocation of the economic goods of the world, to have them allocated in a known or knowable fashion, if they are to be used somewhat efficiently. Indeed, the common good and hence efficiency may require the sacrifice of precision and of the most refined standards in making and preserving such allocations. The determination of an appropriate basis for allocation (whether rough or refined) can be troublesome: it depends on what is expected, on what has been done before, on what is treasured by the community.

ii

EVEN MORE significant than ignorance about what belongs to another, in leading one to take or keep that which is another's, may be an exaggerated notion of what is due to oneself. This rests, in turn, partly on a notion of a self independent of community and partly on a notion of what lies ahead and hence what should be done with a view to what lies ahead.

Consider, first, the notion of the *self* as independent of the community. It may be assumed (as many do today) that a man is, and can be, himself without any significant contribution from the community making him what he is. Does not this assumption rest in the faith that one is free to choose the kind of person one will be? The difficulties with this assumption begin to become apparent when one notices that even the definition (or awareness) of alternatives and the thinking involved in any choosing depend on language—on something that is virtually impossible to acquire without community. Other difficulties should become apparent to anyone who troubles to consider what his self could possibly mean independent of some formative association, be it political, religious, academic, or familial.

I have referred to a second cause of an exaggerated opinion of what is due to oneself, a cause which draws upon a vivid opinion of what lies ahead for man. If life here is but a moment and we are but vulnerable sojourners on this earth, then it is only sensible that we guide ourselves, not by the demands of this moment (however many other people we may be joined with or however they may be joined together), but by considerations of the truly long run in which three score years and ten are but an instant.[102]

We are now confronted by an emphasis upon self that becomes eminently respectable (indeed, even "pious") at the same time that it becomes destructive of justice in the everyday sense of the word—destructive because it induces the "high-minded" to disparage and ignore everyday concerns. What counts, then, is that one does (or believes) "the right thing." Certainty about what is right can, for such people, mean a lack of concern for worldly consequences. This kind of certainty (with its disregard for ordinary prudence) may be made possible because of a legitimated unconcern about immediate consequences or because of a firm belief about eventual consequences.[103]

What is at the root of such an emphasis upon self among us? For the answer to this we may need to go back (even in this secular age) to the pervasive influence of Christianity (at least as practiced in Western Europe). And so we are obliged to consider what self, community, and hence justice mean for the Believer who does see life here on earth as but a moment, so much so that he regards men here as no more than pilgrims who are making their way to another, better, and, indeed, the only real world.

The classic statement of this position in the English-speaking world may well be *The Pilgrim's Progress*.[104] Part One of Bunyan's allegory is a particularly vivid account both of the hazards confronted by the pilgrim and of his attempts to overcome them in order to make his way through life and death to the Celestial City. His story of challenges, trials, and successes has been well known among us for three centuries.

What are the implications of this story for contemporary considerations of justice and the community? What does the story reveal, upon examination, about what is taken for granted with respect to these matters? For one thing, we see the overriding concern for self to which I have referred. Everything else—literally everything else:

body, health, life, family, country—can and should be sacrificed to the salvation of the self (that is, the soul).

Thus, Christian is asked whether he ever thinks of the country from which he came. He draws on *Hebrews* 11: 15–16 in his reply:

> Yes, but with much shame and detestation; *Truly, if I had been mind-ful of that country from whence I came out, I might have had opportunity to have returned; but now I desire a better country; that is, an heavenly.* [p. 82]

He has abandoned his wife and their four small children. Of course, his wife had had an opportunity to accompany him. (pp. 39–41) In the second part of the book, written some years later than the first, she does change her mind and follow after him (with the children) on pilgrimage. (p. 222) But Bunyan had already shown Christian cutting himself off completely from his family in the successful effort to save himself.

The children are not of an age to choose for themselves. The mother is permitted to choose for them, it seems—and Christian is willing (even, the reader might suspect, eager) to leave the care of them to his wife as he makes his private journey to the Celestial City. (pp. 41, 219, 371) He is truly on his own. Is it not evident that he is (and always will be) essentially independent of family and country, whatever may be anticipated about his joy upon welcoming his wife and children to the Celestial City? Even that joy is said to rank below "the joy of seeing himself there." (p. 351)

In *The Pilgrim's Progress,* then, the concerns of this world are displayed as trivial, if not corrupting. Activities which cannot be seen as serving the pilgrimage are regarded as frivolous. Life here is disparaged: it is no more than an opportunity; what truly counts is beyond the Black River, among the angels and with God. There is a way laid out for the pilgrim—and he is obliged to follow that way, and no other, at the risk of eternal damnation. Thus, it is reported of Christian (in one of the most vivid passages in English literature): "Now he had not run far from his own door, but his wife and children perceiving it began to cry after him to return: but the man put his fingers in his ears, and ran on crying, 'Life, life, eternal life.'" (p. 41. See, also, pp. 43, 75, 80, 83–84, 90, 190–91, 302f. See, as well, p. 98.)

iii

ONE FINDS in Bunyan's book little concern about justice (in the ordinary sense of that virtue). When it does appear, it is likely to be put in terms of "righteousness"—in terms, that is, of obedience to divine command (which *is* a kind of law). (pp. 258–60) There is, however, neither a basis nor a need for passing judgment on, or for trying to understand, divine commands; it suffices to obey them. Thus, a pilgrim who is offered a dish of apples asks, "May we eat apples, since they were such by and with which the Serpent beguiled our first mother?" He is assured:

> *Apples were they with which we were beguiled,*
> *Yet sin, not apples hath our souls defiled.*
> *Apples forbid, if eat, corrupts the blood:*
> *To eat such, when commanded, does us good.*
> *Drink of his flagons then, thou, Church, his dove,*
> *And eat his apples, who are sick of love.*
>   *[p. 317]*

It cannot be emphasized too strongly how trivial earthly life is. This bears on the relative lack of concern in the book for justice as ordinarily understood, since justice does depend in large part (as we have seen) on the interests of the community, on what serves others as well as oneself. Men on pilgrimage are expected to care primarily, if not exclusively, for themselves—although goodhearted pilgrims do try to help one another, when they can do so without jeopardizing their own salvation.

The neglect of earthly justice can be seen most critically, perhaps, in what is indicated in *The Pilgrim's Progress* about the possibility of just regimes on earth. It almost goes without saying that the best regime is not here: it is beyond the river of death. But, then, the "best regime" has always been regarded (by political philosophy) as difficult of attainment. What is significant in *The Pilgrim's Progress*, however, is the total absence (perhaps even the implicit denial of the possibility) of *any* just regime on earth.

Justice among men is effectively repudiated by the denial of the possibility that any earthly regime could, to any significant degree, embody that virtue. Since justice is that which makes for health and harmony in communities, we can see why political thinkers have expressed reservations from time to time about the effect of Christianity upon citizenship and upon citizen-virtue. Vital to justice is dedication to the community.

Reservations have often been directed at the pacifism of Christianity—but *that* is not the difficulty in *The Pilgrim's Progress*. Martial efforts are plentiful in the course of this pilgrimage. Christian himself does not mind fighting. Indeed, some of his fellow pilgrims are eager both to fight and to describe their battles. No doubt, the struggles described should be considered as allegorical. Even so, the accounts (such as the following one by Valiant-for-Truth) do nourish combativeness:

> I fought till my sword did cleave to my hand, and when they were joined together, as if a sword grew out of my arm, and when the blood run through my fingers, then I fought with most courage. [p. 349]

(See also, pp. 12, 94.)

The fundamental problem for citizenship in the attitude of pilgrims, I have suggested, is the lack of caring for the community as community. The earthly community is not taken seriously: no sacrifices, certainly no sacrifice of the most precious things, are made *or are expected to be made* on behalf of the community. (pp. 90–91) It is not the community which gives meaning to life; it is not in the community that fulfillment is to be found for most men. Rather, the pilgrim's true life is elsewhere: in the Celestial City, where there will be no bodies, hence no needs and no question of the allocation of resources. There will be there (or, I should say, then) no communal effort, no occasion for human justice, especially since all souls will be blended with (or at least will be completely subservient to) God.

We see in the pilgrim, therefore, the ultimate elevation and legitimation of selfishness. It is fortunate (or providential?), of course, that this kind of selfishness has had dictated to it conduct which is, to a considerable extent, consistent with earthly justice, even when it is not critically concerned about it.[105]

We should notice further that since the welfare of the earthly community is of no serious concern in determining how men should act towards one another, there is no need for the pilgrim to make a study of justice. The relation of reason (and hence wisdom) to justice may safely be ignored. There is no need to apply reason seriously to human affairs, except, perhaps, to make certain that the course one follows is indeed in accordance with the known commands of God.[106]

Neither intelligence nor education seems to be needed to guide men to their salvation.[107] An essential equality "by nature" among men is assumed with respect to the most important things. But nature herself is suspect. (pp. 186–87, 337) Each man is on his own: he stands or falls according to the "choice" *he* makes in "the wilderness of this world." (p. 39)[108]

Yet we do find in the second part of *The Pilgrim's Progress* a less austere—or, we can say, a less self-centered—account of the soul's progress. (pp. 22–23) The woman's pilgrimage is described: children have to be fed, housed, instructed, nursed in illness, and eventually married off. (pp. 315, 319, 325–34) The party stops for extended visits along the way: there are games, music, pleasant conversation, even riddles, conviviality, food and drink—in short, a kind of community. (pp. 334, 340) True, everything is done with one eye on the grave—but at times the pilgrimage seems to be forgotten, something that would have been unthinkable in the first part. Only in the final scene, as members of the community go to their deaths, is the mood of the first part revived to any sustained degree.

Does not this preoccupation with communal affairs in the second part have something to do with the peculiar interests (as well as vulnerabilities), and hence the practical sense, of women and of the world of women?[109] Are men more apt to be irresponsible? Are they better equipped by nature to cut themselves off from community, or at least from the family which is itself the nucleus of the community?

We are reminded by these inquiries that Christian must (in his youth) have required nourishment and instruction, to say nothing of exposure to language: he did not start immediately from the cradle upon his pilgrimage.[110] The usefulness, if not the absolute necessity, of such an instructing institution as the church becomes evident, if only to teach men what their spiritual choices are—if only to provide men both authoritative writings (revelation) and the examples of earlier pilgrims to emulate and to be fortified by. (pp. 346–47)

When the church is formed—when men and women gather together on earth in worshiping communities—requirements and obligations become apparent which the solitary pilgrim is able to ignore.

Standards are needed and insisted upon so as to permit useful cooperation. The practical requirements of community make themselves
felt: men, in spite of themselves, begin to consider (if only to make
their associations mutually profitable) what they must concede to
the demands of others, that is, *to the good of others*. Rules are established and enforced that ratify and guarantee such concessions.

It has long been known that even a band of robbers needs some
justice to keep itself together, to permit it to function with some efficiency and to serve the apparent interests of its robber-members.
We have seen that this may be true as well for a band of saints, so
long as they remain in their bodies. Thus, we have returned to law as
that which attempts to establish justice among men and as that which
justice relies upon for its implementation, if not for its definition. We
have returned, that is, to the intimate relation between justice and a
concern for a viable community.

We also return, if only briefly, to that sense of fairness which is
somewhat independent of, and which passes judgment upon, both
law and the requirements of community. It is a sense of fairness, perhaps that very sense of fairness drawn upon by what is known as
righteousness, that permeates justice. It is righteousness without concern for consequences, which is perhaps reflected in Christian doctrine and which may be seen also in the maxim, "Let justice be done,
though the heavens fall."[111]

Is this maxim primarily a salutary sentiment needed to restrain
and edify men when they are tempted (as they often are) by self-
interest (and in the name of prudence) to extend deference, beyond
what is absolutely needed, to what are conveniently identified as communal necessities and consequences? What is there in the hearts of
men that can be appealed to by such an imprudent maxim? Should
not this single-minded maxim particularly appeal to the Christian of
the first part of *The Pilgrim's Progress?* But is the maxim not called
into question by the work of Shakespeare with its considerable respect (Shaw to the contrary notwithstanding) for statesmanship and
citizenship?[112]

What, in short, *is* justice and what is it good for?

IV. J A N E A U S T E N (1775-1817)

> *... We are in need of a second education in order
> to accustom our eyes to the noble reserve and
> the quiet grandeur of the classics. Xenophon as
> it were limited himself to cultivating exclusively
> that character of classical writing which is wholly
> foreign to the modern reader [who has been
> brought up on the brutal and sentimental liter-
> ature of the last five generations]. No wonder
> that he is today despised or ignored. An un-
> known ancient critic, who must have been a
> man of uncommon discernment, called him
> most bashful. Those modern readers who are so
> fortunate as to have a natural preference for
> Jane Austen rather than for Dostoievski, in
> particular, have an easier access to Xenophon
> than others might have; to understand Xeno-
> phon, they have only to combine the love of
> philosophy with their natural preference.
> In the words of Xenophon, "it is both noble
> and just, and pious and more pleasant to remem-
> ber the good things rather than the bad ones."*

> —Leo Strauss, *What Is
> Political Philosophy?* pp. 103-4

i

IN THEIR quiet worldliness, Jane Austen's novels are in marked contrast to John Bunyan's *Pilgrim's Progress*. The reader returns, in her
novels, to Shakespeare's prudence and openness to nature—but in the
household rather than among generals, kings, and other rulers.

What is the relevance of the work of Austen—the embroidery of
a late eighteenth century (and early nineteenth century) English spin-
ster—to our time and place, especially since her work is set forth in
language (and is about a class of people) quite unfamiliar, if not even
tedious, to us? How can her opinions be of any interest to moderns,
to people who are coming to believe that truth may be found only

---

All citations in the text of this chapter to the novels of Jane Austen are to *The Complete Novels of Jane Austen* (New York: Modern Library, 193-).

in tempests of the soul, in self-exhibitions of the most revealing kind, not in the restraints and sense of decorum of the early 1800s?

Joseph Conrad described in 1910 (in *Heart of Darkness*) the response of a sophisticated European to the wild yelling from natives gathered on the shores of an African river watching the white man's boat go by:

> It was unearthly, and the men were—No, they were not inhuman. Well, you know, that was the worst of it—this suspicion of their not being inhuman. It would come slowly to one. They howled and leaped, and spun, and made horrid faces; but what thrilled you was just the thought of their humanity—like yours—the thought of your remote kinship with this wild and passionate uproar. Ugly. Yes, it was ugly enough; but if you were man enough you would admit to yourself that there was in you just the faintest trace of a response to the terrible frankness of that noise, a dim suspicion of there being a meaning in it which you—you so remote from the night of first ages—could comprehend. And why not? The mind of man is capable of anything —because everything is in it, all the past as well as all the future. What was there after all? Joy, fear, sorrow, devotion, valor, rage—who can tell?—but truth—truth stripped of its cloak of time. Let the fool gape and shudder—the man knows and can look on without a wink. But he must at least be as much of a man as these on the shore. He must meet that truth with his own true stuff—with his own inborn strength.[113]

Conrad's narrator speaks of "just the faintest trace of a response [in us] to the terrible frankness of that noise." Indeed, have we not come to see in such "terrible frankness," if not the royal road, at least the modern "liberated" man's path, to "fulfillment"?

Compare, in Austen's *Mansfield Park,* a sensitive man's comment about a woman he had perhaps loved:

> No, hers is not a cruel nature. I do not consider her as meaning to wound my feelings. The evil lies yet deeper; in her total ignorance, unsuspiciousness of there being such feelings; in a perversion of mind which made it natural to her to treat the subject as she did. She was speaking only as she had been used to hear others speak, as she imagined everybody else would speak. Hers are not faults of temper. She would not voluntarily give unnecessary pain to anyone, and though I may deceive myself, I cannot but think that for me, for my feelings

she would—Hers are faults of principle, Fanny; of blunted delicacy
and a corrupted, vitiated mind. Perhaps it is best for me, since it leaves
me so little to regret. Not so, however. Gladly would I submit to all
the increased pain of losing her, rather than have to think of her as
I do. I told her so. [p. 749]

Conrad's (and our?) "terrible frankness" should be contrasted with
this condemnation of someone who spoke "only as she had been used
to hear others speak, as she imagined everybody else would speak."
We have seen our terrible frankness transformed into something even
more ominous, that which prompted Sigmund Freud (writing in Vi-
enna in the late 1930s) to observe:

> We live in very remarkable times. We find with astonishment that
> progress has concluded an alliance with barbarism.[114]

This observation refers to Stalin's Russia. Even worse for him must
have been what he observed in Nazi Germany, the recognition "that
retrogression into all but prehistoric barbarism can come to pass independently of any progressive ideas."[115] It is when we confront the
barbarism of our time—or the substitute for it in prosperous vulgarity
on a continental scale—that the restraints of the late eighteenth and
early nineteenth centuries may again come to have an appeal for us.

ii

HOW MEASURED life is in the drawing rooms and on the garden
paths of Austen's novels. The rare exceptions to this calm—a sometimes lively calm, to be sure—only point up the typical scene, exceptions such as:

1. war in the distance (pp. 612, 860);
2. references to the slave trade (pp. 588, 946);
3. the disordered natural family of Fanny Price in Portsmouth
    (pp. 467f, 699f, 733);
4. elopements, with and without benefit of marriage (pp. 393f,
    738–39, 740f);
5. gypsies who create disturbances (pp. 956–66);

6.   divorces (pp. 122–23, 753);

7.   the providentially useful chicken thieves at the end of *Emma* (p. 1060).

I do not recall a single act of spontaneous violence (occurring in England) of one man against another portrayed (or even referred to) in any of the four novels I will be drawing upon here.[116] There are, on a couple of occasions, references to a duel ("Elinor sighed over the fancied necessity of this") or to the possibility of a duel. (pp. 125–26, 402, 406)

The author is charitable: we see no thoroughly evil men, but only impulsive or selfish people. Do the social conventions of the day eliminate or at least moderate the very worst? Villains speak with some sensitivity and understanding (as may be seen in a Willoughby or a Crawford [even, as on page 281 in Wickham, when he is lying]). It is as if the forms of social intercourse restrain and shape men despite themselves. (See, for example, pp. 108, 199, 227, 755f.)

iii

THESE STORIES (a general familiarity with which I assume among my readers) are told from a woman's point of view.[117] It has been noticed that the author never portrays men speaking to one another without a woman present: she writes, that is, only about that which she knows.[118]

Austen's novels are stories of the domestic world, the world of the household. They are not stories of the world of business or politics or high adventure. Austen portrays, most of the time, the lives and concerns of most human beings (however exclusive, stylized, or otherwise limited the people in her novels may be). Of all the concerns of men and nations, Austen chooses to deal with those which immediately affect household relations. Perhaps one can even see these stories as attempts to show what reason and something like nobility look like in the household. One *is* reminded of Xenophon.

What *would* we be primarily concerned with if our political, including our economic and international, problems could be put to one side? Aldous Huxley's *Brave New World* suggests one contemporary answer to this question. Jane Austen suggests a different answer, as she describes to us "all those little matters on which the daily happiness of private life depends." (p. 834) The descriptions *are* a woman's—in tone, in sensibility, in information and concern, in a delicate exploration of the subtleties of the human soul. Indeed, Mr Knightley forebears giving Emma a detailed account of a certain incident:

> Your friend Harriet will make a much longer history when you see her. She will give you all the minute particulars, which only woman's language can make interesting. In our communications we [men] deal only in the great. [p. 1052]

iv

WHAT IS truly instructive for us is not how the people of that time lived but rather their opinion of what a virtuous human being (not a citizen) is and what makes one thus. The objective is to lead a rational life, a life guided by reason in which one enjoys sensible pleasures. One does one's duty to one's own (including the particular poor toward whom one happens to have an obligation); one is sensitive to the concerns of others; one avoids inflicting upon another unnecessary pain by either word or deed. There is also the duty to preserve and pass on to the next generation that which has been handed down to one. One should take pleasure only in what one ought: the properly trained man does not have to restrain himself from misdeeds; he does not even enjoy contemplating doing what he should not do.

Rationality is critical. Is it not reason which sees "how wretched, and how unpardonable, how hopeless, and how wicked it [is], to marry without affection"? (p. 665) That is, the reason knows what the human soul is like, and what the conditions for reasoning *and* for enduring pleasure are. (p. 291) Consider, for instance, this report about Emma:

> Their conversation was soon afterwards closed by the entrance of her father. She was not sorry. She wanted to be alone. Her mind was in a state of flutter and wonder, which made it impossible for her to be collected. She was in dancing, singing, exclaiming spirits; and till she had moved about, and talked to herself, and laughed and reflected, she could be fit for nothing rational. [p. 1054]

But however much is made of rationality, is it not sensible to recognize that some do not "deserve the compliment of rational opposition"? (p. 150. See, also, pp. 73, 94, 347, 507.)

What makes one virtuous—that is, what leads one to be guided by reason as one should be? One's circumstances are important, circumstances which permit leisure and exposure to the proper training and influences. (See, for example, pp. 667, 686, 718.) But circumstances are not sufficient, as indicated by the many instances in which one member of a household is exemplary while others are not. One's nature, or what is called one's "temper," is important. (See, for example, pp. 76, 82, 710–11, 1046.) One must have principles. (See, for example, pp. 753, 759.) One's habituation must be of a certain kind, and preferably under a single guiding mind and set of forms. But forms are not sufficient, for they do not bring the necessary enjoyment in doing one's duty—and, without this enjoyment, trouble is likely. Pleasure should reinforce a sense of obligation if freedom is to be used properly. This means, of course, that there must be an understanding not only of what the rules are but also of *why* they are and why they should be. There must be, that is, a sound awareness of what one is doing if one is to be the very best.[119]

Society helps keep men in check. But anyone who goes only by what society permits will eventually go astray. He will not be of the very best. The best know what is right and they do it, however they may err sometimes because of erroneous information. Men and women of good natures and good inclinations learn by their mistakes and by the mistakes of others.

Foolish people can be charming, even delightful—and their novelty makes them attractive—but do they not depend too much on chance and the good judgment of others to save them from their follies? The truly best are, in this respect, self-sufficient.

Thus, we see it suggested in these novels that a good life based on rational principles is possible, that it can be planned for and deliberately preserved, that it is not merely a product of chance.

We do not see, except in *Mansfield Park,* just how the young are trained, but we are given indications of that training throughout the novels. One should try to be mistress of oneself. (pp. 23, 49, 214) This means that one should make a serious effort to know oneself. And, it should be emphasized, there is for the good little struggle.

Self-control means control even of the passions one has. The references in Austen to "conscience" are not critical: to make much of
conscience means that one part of oneself is struggling against another
part—and would it not be even better if all parts should be in harmony? (See pp. 145-46, 194, 197, 209, 225, 481, 443, 564, 862,
1019, 1021. See, also, pp. 11-12, 721, 964.)

v

YET, IT *is* recognized by Austen that the truly good and happy are
rare. It is recognized that it takes a lot to produce and preserve the
very best. The uses of discipline are evident. Manners (however limited
in value) *are* important, for they are the outward sign of true civility.
of that serious regard one should have for the sensibilities and claims
of others. Compare the concern about amateur play-acting, in which
one would say certain things to another that one should not.[120]

Discipline means that one has the informed desire to forego
immediate gratification. Only the disciplined can control their passions and use properly their reason and sensitivity (just as an army
is more effective than a mob, however much more formidable the
mob may appear to the untrained eye). Only the disciplined can be
perceptive about their passions. (See p. 182.) Only if one is calm
enough to see, and only if one is equipped to know what to look for,
may one grasp, develop, and enjoy the best in oneself.

It is not enough to be brought up in the right family. The influence of the community is necessary, if only to keep families in line
(even though community opinion is not the highest standard). (p. 56)
Some communities are better than others: the country is better than
London. (See, for example, pp. 101, 197, 251, 255-56, 503-4, 524,
734.) The community on which the people of Austen's novels rely is
substantial and self-confident and influential—but is it not subject to
the deadly threats of urbanization and war, threats which are just on
the fringes of the scenes the novelist brings on stage?[121]

vi

WE TODAY are less confident than were our eighteenth century coun-
terparts about what the good is and how it should be developed. We
are, consequently, less likely (than we might otherwise be) to produce

refined human beings, since we leave so much more to chance than other peoples have. We are, in this respect, far less prudent than is Austen: things are, for us, less in our deliberate control.[122]

Furthermore, modern "mass culture" and our mobility require and promote insensitivity as well as irresponsibility. The lowest among us is not only appealed to but all too often seems authoritative (especially when it is called "the market"). Another result of mobility is a "natural" recourse to quick friendships and a depreciation of enduring intimacy. (Symptomatic of the decline of traditional civility among us is the insistence that people of different generations or of different stations in life should be on a first-name basis with one another. And so, "confusion fall—.")

Vulgarity, too, easily follows from quick prosperity. Only the violent and the emphatic (or the most private and personal) can move us: the sensational becomes attractive. (One sees in *Mansfield Park* a hint of what much of our press has come to be like. [p. 738]) We seek novelty and hence excitement. But, Austen teaches us, civilized life is that life in which what is usually called excitement is minimized. The more one knows and controls, the fewer surprises there can be, the less suspense there can be. (Suspense *is* acceptable during courtship?) Modernity is opposed to this approach: it favors the attitudes of the immature Marianne of *Sense and Sensibility*. (See pp. 3, 10f, 49, 62, 73, 93, 199. Compare pp. 206–8, 227.)

To know and to control, one must be able to see. But we are less likely in our cities to be able to *see* people today, to learn from them and hence about ourselves, than one would have been in the towns and estates Austen describes. This development, one may say, is unavoidable. But, then, one must also say with Austen, the circumstances are against us for production of the best. It is only prudent to recognize this—and for this recognition she is most relevant to us.

vii

BUT THERE are deeper questions here than the relevance of Jane Austen today. One must wonder whether she is right in what she discerns about the moral universe.

Notice how things "work out" in her novels: good, generally, comes to the good (and this can be presented without the impression of sentimentality). Why is this? Is it providence, nature, or chance which is primarily responsible for the way things do work out? (There is, in the novels, little reliance on prayer.) It *is* suggested by one decent man, "We were all disposed to wonder, but it seems to have been the merciful appointment of Providence that the heart which knew no guile should not suffer." (p. 748)

Things seem to develop in conformity with the character of people: the ignorant and those of bad tendencies do come to grief; the worst punishment is to *be* the way one is, if one is not as one should be. A series of observations drawn from Austen's novels indicates a reliable "moral physics" at work in human affairs:

> Lady Middleton was equally pleased with Mrs. Dashwood. There was a kind of coldhearted selfishness on both sides, which mutually attracted them; and they sympathised with each other in an insipid propriety of demeanour, and a general want of understanding. [p. 137]

> Her thoughts were silently fixed on the irreparable injury which too early an independence and its consequent habits of idleness, dissipation, and luxury, had made in the mind, the character, the happiness, of a man who, to every advantage of person and talents, united a disposition naturally open and honest, and a feeling, affectionate temper. The world had made him extravagant and vain; extravagance and vanity had made him cold-hearted and selfish. Vanity, while seeking its own guilty triumph at the expense of another, had involved him in a real attachment, which extravagance, or at least its offspring necessity, had required to be sacrificed. Each faulty propensity, in leading him to evil, had led him likewise to punishment. The attachment from which against honour, against feeling, against every better interest he had outwardly torn himself, now, when no longer allowable, governed every thought; and the connection, for the sake of which he had, with little scruple, left her sister to misery, was likely to prove a source of unhappiness to himself of a far more incurable nature. [p. 198]

> "One observation may, I think, be fairly drawn from the whole of the story—that all Willoughby's difficulties have arisen from the first offence against virtue, in his behaviour to Eliza Williams. That crime has been the origin of every lesser one, and of all his present discontents." [p. 210]

> Had Elizabeth's opinion been all drawn from her own family, she could not have formed a very pleasing picture of conjugal felicity

or domestic comfort. Her father, captivated by youth and beauty, and that appearance of good humour which youth and beauty generally give, had married a woman whose weak understanding and illiberal mind had very early in their marriage put an end to all real affection for her. Respect, esteem, and confidence had vanished for ever; and all his views of domestic happiness were overthrown. But Mr. Bennet was not of a disposition to seek comfort for the disappointment which his own imprudence had brought on, in any of those pleasures which too often console the unfortunate for their folly or their vice. He was fond of the country and of books; and from these tastes had arisen his principal enjoyments. To his wife he was very little otherwise indebted, than as her ignorance and folly had contributed to his amusement.... Elizabeth, however, had never been blind to the impropriety of her father's behaviour as a husband. She had always seen it with pain; but respecting his abilities, and grateful for his affectionate treatment of herself, she endeavoured to forget what she could not overlook, and to banish from her thoughts that continual breach of conjugal obligation and decorum which, in exposing his wife to the contempt of her own children, was so highly reprehensible. But she had never felt so strongly as now the disadvantages which must attend the children of so unsuitable a marriage, nor ever been so fully aware of the evils arising from so ill-judged a direction of talents; talents, which, rightly used, might at least have preserved the respectability of his daughters, even if incapable of enlarging the mind of his wife. [pp. 372–73. See, also, pp. 458, 752.]

That punishment, the public punishment of disgrace, should in a just measure attend his share of the offence is, we know, not one of the barriers which society gives to virtue. In this world the penalty is less equal than could be wished; *but without presuming to look forward to a juster appointment hereafter,* we may fairly consider a man of sense, like Henry Crawford, to be providing for himself no small portion of vexation and regret; vexation that must rise sometimes to self-reproach, and regret to wretchedness, in having so requited hospitality, so injured family peace, so forfeited his best, most estimable, and endeared acquaintance, and so lost the woman whom he had rationally as well as passionately loved. [p. 756; italics added.]

I purposely abstain from dates on this occasion, that everyone may be at liberty to fix their own, aware that the cure of unconquerable passions, and the transfer of unchanging attachments, must vary much as to time in different people. I only entreat everybody to believe that exactly at the time when it was quite natural that it should be so, and not a week earlier, Edmund did cease to care about Miss Crawford, and became as anxious to marry Fanny as Fanny herself could desire. [p. 757]

One natural consequence of the evil she had involved herself in, she said, was that of making her *unreasonable.* The consciousness of having done amiss had exposed her to a thousand inquietudes, and made her captious and irritable to a degree that must have been—that had been—hard for him to bear. [pp. 1019–20]

Many more such observations are found in Austen's novels, observations which assure us that it is natural that the best should happen to the best. Certainly, the best of heroines get the best of husbands. Certainly, also, the best depend least on chance to make their way in the world.

Does not such an expectation rest on stability, on a community in which constant changes take place within a fairly steady framework?[123] Not everything is "up for grabs" or open to question. This stability is reflected in, and reinforced by, the longstanding property institutions of the community, those institutions around which families move and by which families are influenced. Financial circumstances are usually indicated early in each of Austen's novels: these are matters that need to be understood at the outset of any proper story, she seems to say. (See pp. 2f, 231–32, 235, 246, 469, 763. See, also, pp. 21, 29, 54, 115, 191, 221, 224, 225, 305, 307–8, 312–13, 323–24, 338, 355, 456, 491–92, 598.)

This approach to social relations can appear mercenary and materialist to more romantic sensibilities, but it may only be sensible, a recognition of the conditions necessary for the emergence of the best. It is because of a stability grounded in established property arrangements that the fate of "ordinary" people (not just the fate of, say, an Achilles or an Odysseus) can be generated by their character. Thus, the reader can often work out quite early what is going to happen to Austen's people. In other novels, such "working out" *would* be sentimental. But in Austen, it is merely a deduction from the things which are "given" (including, but not limited to, property arrangements). She is, in this respect, the Euclid of modern domesticity.

And it may be because of the importance of this property-grounded stability of families that courtship is as vital as it is in her novels. One's duty throughout one's life is clear if one is a good (that is, a reasonable) man or woman. One's circumstances indicate what one must consider and do.

But a serious question remains open, for which one's training cannot lay down definite guides: whom should one marry? Marriage is the threshold to a new world, to new circumstances. (Consider, for example, all the relations one immediately acquires.) Chance, unfortunately, can play a critical part here. (See, for example, pp. 148, 754, 990-91.) There are better and worse ways of proceeding in these matters (as we saw, in our first chapter, in the consideration of Shakespeare's *Othello* and *Romeo and Juliet*).

Thus, the community is partially reshaped every generation. This reshaping, as well as that which leads up to it, is decisive for determining what the future is likely to be. It means, among other things, new property relations, new opportunities or new disabilities. Thus, as the self-centered Mr. Woodhouse lamented, matrimony is "the origin of change." (p. 764)

viii

IT IS courtship alone, then, which can be (in time of peace) the scene of a troublesome uncertainty for the good woman or man in private life. There is much about intimate relations with another—perhaps the most vital things—that one finds difficult (if not impossible) to know before entering into them. (See, for example, pp. 67, 372-73, 458, 495-96.) This is where chance seems most important: one has to be very careful in taking one's leap into the dark. The most prudent lovers *can* make sensible choices—but such choices are not easy. It is difficult for love to be clear-sighted.[124]

What one's life should be like after marriage is prescribed. There is no need (Austen seems to say) to examine *that*: one does one's duty and enjoys one's legitimate pleasures. (See p. 219.) And one prepares one's children for *their* great leap into the dark—into that most attractive even though threatening darkness.

It is when one reflects upon that darkness that one is reminded of another threshold in the life of man, but a threshold which Austen virtually ignores. That is, not much is made of death in her novels. One is not invited to contemplate "the awesome, unfathomable experience of death, of the death of one near and dear to us."[125] Is this because death is so little a part of the life with which she is primarily concerned, that life of courtship in which neither infants nor the elderly (the most vulnerable physically among us) figure much?

Still, does not our mortality—and our attempts to come to terms with it—color our virtues and intensify our vices? Even so, perhaps Austen believes there is little she can say about death that would be useful, little to add to what religion (which, except perhaps in *Mansfield Park*, does not figure much in her stories) teaches and provides.[126]

Perhaps, indeed, Austen sees nothing at that final threshold to be rationally troubled by—nothing that a reasonable man can know well enough to be specially concerned about or to deal with.[127] Or perhaps she even believes that "death is terrible, terrifying, but we cannot live as human beings if this terror grips us to the point of corroding our core"[128] —and so she shields us from something she cannot help us with.

Which of these responses to death is hers? Certainly, one must— or at least one learns to—"carry on," to get on with the business of life. Nature permits this and, we sense, reason requires it.

ix

REASON ALSO requires, or at least encourages, us to consider what life is "all about."

Mr. Bennett reminds Elizabeth of his answer to this question: "For what do we live, but to make sport for our neighbours, and laugh at them in our turn?" (p. 450) The author herself improves upon this remark somewhat, observing that time is forever producing considerable changes in the opinions of mortals, "for their own instruction, and their neighbours' entertainment." (p. 758) That is, *she* seems to say, we live not only to laugh and to be laughed at, but also to learn. (See pp. 356, 453, 1012-16, 1022, 1024, 1054.)

Consider, also, the Xenophonic statement by the author. "Let other pens dwell on guilt and misery. I quit such odious subjects as soon as I can, impatient to restore everybody, not greatly in fault themselves, to tolerable comfort, and to have done with all the rest." (p. 751) Is it not likely, therefore, that it is Austen's desire to be both entertaining and instructive, rather than any unbecoming fear, that permits her to help us avert our eyes (if not her own) from the solemn spectacle of, and unproductive speculations about, death?

All this supports the proposition, "This world is a comedy to those that think, a tragedy to those who feel!"[129] Life seen as Jane Austen sees it is for the most part a comedy, not a tragedy. But it does seem important to her that the comedy not be frivolous, that the play be well acted. Every dedicated actor respects his obligation to the playgoers—just as for Euclid it was important that the playful sketches men and women conjure up should be well demonstrated, even if they have all been demonstrated innumerable times before.

V. MARY WOLLSTONECRAFT SHELLEY (1797-1851)

A good book is the precious life blood of a
master spirit embalmed and treasured up on
purpose to a life beyond life.

—John Milton, *Areopagitica*

i

WE MOVE, in this and the next two chapters, from the Age of Reason to an age of "monsters." Thereafter we consider various attempts to escape the monstrous. First, we encounter one of the favorite monsters of our time, the one found in Mary Wollstonecraft Shelley's *Frankenstein.*

One should forget, if only for the moment, the movie versions of Shelley's book if one is to see her story in itself. I say "for the moment," since the movie versions do help us notice (if only by distortion and omission) what is indeed in the original book. (See pp. xxxiv–xxxv.)

The book was, at the time of publication, summed up most succinctly in *Gentlemen's Magazine* (April 1818) in these terms:

> In the pride of Science, the Hero of the Tale presumes to take upon himself the structure of a human being; in which, though in some degree he is supposed to have succeeded, he forfeits every comfort of life, and finally even life itself.[130]

A half century later, upon the issuance of a Boston edition of the book, a local newspaper observed, "The principal moral to be derived by Harvard boys from this book is that dangerous proficiency in chemistry should be carefully avoided."[131]

Frankenstein opens with four letters by Robert Walton, a twenty-eight-year-old Englishman of independent means, written to his married sister back in England. He describes his efforts to launch an unprecedented voyage to the North Pole. (pp. 9–16) In the fourth of

---

All citations in the text of this chapter to *Frankenstein* are to the Bobbs-Merrill Company edition (Indianapolis, 1974).

these letters (written on board his ship, which is in the Arctic regions) Walton reports that a dog sledge has been sighted moving north across the snow carrying "a being which had the shape of a man, but apparently of gigantic stature..." (p. 17) The following day, an exhausted man on another sledge (pulled by only one dog) was found alongside the ship; he consented to be rescued only after he had been assured that the ship was also heading north. (pp. 18, 20)

When the "rescued" man, Victor Frankenstein, recovers somewhat, he tells Walton a story to account for his pursuit of the "man" they had seen earlier. (p. 24f) Frankenstein is a native of Geneva; he had gone to Ingolstadt, to study. (pp. 27, 38f) He became obsessed there with the ambition of creating the progenitor of a new race, using parts of human corpses. (p. 46f) He succeeded in doing so, but was repelled by the eight-foot-tall being as soon as it came to life. (pp. 52–53) Frankenstein abandoned the monster he had made, suffered a nervous breakdown, and took a long time to recover (under the care of his old and intimate friend, Henry Clerval, who happened to arrive the very morning the monster was brought to life; Clerval was never told of the monster). (pp. 53–58)

It was not until Frankenstein recovered that news came (from Switzerland) that his younger brother (a beautiful child of tender years) had been strangled. (pp. 66–68) (The brother could not be killed, it almost seems, until Frankenstein had recovered: one step at a time, it would seem.) He returned home for the trial of the nursemaid, Justine Moritz, who had been accused of the murder. (p. 74f) On the outskirts of Geneva, upon visiting the site of his brother's murder, Frankenstein saw the monster lurking and suspected that *it* was the murderer. (pp. 70–73) But the nursemaid was found guilty, condemned to death, and executed. (pp. 80–85) Deemed conclusive of her guilt was a locket found on her, a locket last seen in the possession of the murdered child (but, we learn later, planted on Justine by the monster). (pp. 78, 140)

The execution of Justine upset Frankenstein again, and he was taken on a tour to recuperate. (p. 85f) There he met the monster, which told him its story since its creation (p. 94f): how it had had to live; how it had been rejected everywhere because of its ugliness (pp. 100–101); how it came to learn to speak and read (by observing at close range, but without being observed itself, the attractive De Lacey family who were themselves refugees in Germany from France) (p.

107f); how it was spurned by that family when it dared to approach them (pp. 128-31); how it saved a little girl from drowning, only to be shot by her companion (who had misunderstood what had happened) (p. 137); how, in a subsequent rage, it killed Frankenstein's brother (whom it had met while looking for Frankenstein himself); how the killing came as it tried to silence the boy, who was denouncing the monster as an ogre. (pp. 138-39)

The "solitary and detested" monster (p. 126) had a demand to make of Frankenstein: it must have a female made for it, or else it would wreak further vengeance on Frankenstein's family. (pp. 140-42) (It had given up hope of establishing normal relations with human beings.) The monster's faith in Frankenstein was touching. He was moved by the monster's story—and agreed to provide the female, with whom the monster promised to go to the wilds of South America and not to be heard of again among men. (pp. 142-44)

Thereafter, Frankenstein went to Great Britain with Clerval, doing a good deal of sightseeing on the way. (p. 150f) Frankenstein eventually hid himself in the Orkneys, where he worked on the promised female. (p. 161f) (Why should production of a female have required even greater secrecy than had been necessary for production of a male? Or was it that Frankenstein had come to recognize the folly of his original project?) As he was about to finish, he reflected on the danger to mankind from a race of monsters—and (in spite of the risk to himself) destroyed the monster's mate. (pp. 163-64) The monster, which had been following closely his work, was enraged—and vowed vengeance, singling out Frankenstein's wedding night. (pp. 164-66) But first, it went to kill Clerval, in circumstances which led to the temporary imprisonment of Frankenstein himself as the murderer. (pp. 170-80)

Frankenstein did manage to return home to marry his childhood sweetheart, Elizabeth Lavenza. (p. 189) But his bride was killed by the monster on their wedding night. (pp. 192-94) Thereafter, Frankenstein's father died of a broken heart (pp. 195-96), and Frankenstein began a determined pursuit of the monster across the earth (and was told by it that all this, including the pursuit, was part of the monster's revenge). (pp. 197-205) (This pursuit can well have influenced Herman Melville's *Moby Dick.* [p. xxxi])

The pursuit eventually took them across Russia and into Arctic regions. By the time Frankenstein finished his tale—a tale which lasted a week in the telling—he was exhausted and dying. (pp. 207, 211) He was concerned to the end of his life that Walton continue the chase if Frankenstein himself should not be able to do so.

Walton returns to the letter to his sister (in which this tale is enclosed). (p. 206) He reports on the troubles his ship is having moving through the ice; on his men's exacting from him the promise to return home if an opening to the south should become available (and this despite Frankenstein's exhortation to the men that they continue their adventure) (pp. 211-13); on the decline and death of Frankenstein (pp. 214-16); on the monster's appearance, in Walton's cabin, to mourn over Frankenstein's body (pp. 216-17); on the monster's account of what it had done and how wretched it had felt (pp. 217-19); on the monster's announcement that it would continue to the North Pole where it would prepare a funeral pyre on which it would meet its death. (pp. 220-21) The monster is last seen by Walton, borne away from the ship on its sledge. (p. 221) This concludes the letter by Walton (who is on his way back to England). (p. 213) It also concludes the book.

The events of the book take place in about seven years. (They begin shortly after the premature death of Frankenstein's mother.) That is, the work Frankenstein did on the monster took a couple of years (p. 52), and, according to my calculations, the monster was about five years old when it died. (The story seems much shorter than it is, due to its highly dramatic [even melodramatic] character.) It should also be noted that the monster is not the clumsy, inarticulate being portrayed in the movies, but rather quite agile and articulate. This is not to say that the monster is not grotesque—but it is the grotesqueness, combined with gracefulness, which can sometimes be seen in the histrionic efforts by a gifted conductor to induce an orchestra to express "the inexpressible."

ii

WE HAVE, in Shelley's *Frankenstein,* a rare opportunity to watch the artistic temperament at work. The novel was called (in 1882), "one of the most extraordinary accidents in literature."[132] The romance of the novel extended even to the account of how it came to be written.

"Everyone knows" about the challenge to write ghost stories which presented itself to an intimate circle of English writers (Lord Byron, Percy Shelley, and his eighteen-year-old wife, Mary Shelley) that fateful summer of 1816 in Switzerland. (p. 224f) (It has been called by some, because of the literature generated among these artists, the most fruitful summer in the history of English literature.) Mary Shelley's own account (in her preface to the 1831 edition) of what happened on that occasion shows the effect of art: episodes may have been considerably rearranged by her, but by doing so, she has illustrated how an artist (deliberately or unconsciously) fashions (or refashions) the given material in order to make sense of it (or at least to make it interesting).

Her 1831 preface includes the observation:

> Invention, it must be humbly admitted, does not consist in creating out of void, but out of chaos; the materials must, in the first place, be afforded: it can give form to dark, shapeless substances, but cannot bring into being the substance itself. In all matters of discovery and invention, even of those that appertain to the imagination, we are continually reminded of the story of Columbus and his egg. Invention consists in the capacity of seizing on the capabilities of a subject, and in the power of moulding and fashioning ideas suggested to it. [p. 226]

Thus, as in this case, the artist so organizes the available matter as to hit home. The book has not been out of print since it was first published in 1818; it has been translated into many languages, and it is currently available, in English, in a half dozen editions. That it "hit home" may be seen in the fact that even grossly distorted movie versions continue to appeal to large audiences—with dozens of versions now available. Or, as was observed a few years ago, "Mary Shelley hit an exposed nerve in the human psyche with [*Frankenstein*] and we're still feeling it tingle today."[133] Indeed, perhaps it can be said, there is something of Frankenstein or of his monster or of both in all of us: after all, the death of the monster (at the end of Mary Shelley's story) is not reported but only anticipated.

I will return to the problem of whatever "exposed nerve in the human psyche" that this story may somehow stimulate. But first, we can notice how this story can be taken to address (or at least to illuminate) contemporary issues. Thus, in British parliamentary debates (in 1824), *Frankenstein* was used (without the story or its author being mentioned by name) to support an argument against the emancipation of Negro slaves:

> To turn [the Negro] loose in the manhood of his physical strength, in the maturity of his physical passions, but in the infancy of his uninstructed reason, would be to raise up a creature resembling the splendid fiction of a recent romance; the hero of which constructs a human form, with all the corporeal capabilities of man, and with the thews and sinews of a giant; but being unable to impart to the work of his hands a perception of right and wrong, he finds too late that he has only created a more than mortal power of doing mischief, and himself recoils from the monster which he has made.[134]

(It is not so, however, that the monster has no "perception of right and wrong.")

Another issue, which has received considerable attention in recent decades, concerns the relation of scientific research to moral responsibility. On such issues, Shelley's story is felt by many to throw a useful light. How useful a light—how deep and enduring the insight to be provided—may depend on just what the artist is doing in this story.

iii

CONSIDER HOW Shelley tells, in 1831, the story of her story. There had been much talk, in her circle, of animating principles and of science. She herself, she recalls, had been the least successful, among those in the group, in devising a ghost story—and this, she also recalls, had been the cause for her of some discomfort. But then there came one fateful night of stimulating talk:

> Night waned upon this talk, and even the witching hour had gone by, before we retired to rest. When I placed my head on my pillow, I did not sleep, nor could I be said to think. My imagination, unbidden, possessed and guided me, gifting the successive images that arose in my mind with a vividness far beyond the usual bounds of reverie. I saw—with shut eyes, but acute mental vision,—I saw the pale student of unhallowed arts kneeling beside the thing he had put together. I saw the hideous phantasm of a man stretched out, and then, on the working of some powerful engine, show signs of life, and stir with an uneasy, half vital motion. Frightful must it be; for supremely frightful would be the effect of any human endeavour to mock the stupendous mechanism of the Creator of the world. His success would terrify the artist; he would rush away from his odious handywork, horror-striken.

He would hope that, left to itself, the slight spark of life which he had communicated would fade; that this thing, which had received such imperfect animation, would subside into dead matter; and he might sleep in the belief that the silence of the grave would quench for ever the transient existence of the hideous corpse which he had looked upon as the cradle of life. He sleeps; but he is awakened; he opens his eyes; behold the horrid thing stands at his bedside, opening his curtains, and looking on him with yellow, watery, but speculative eyes.

I opened mine in terror. The idea so possessed my mind, that a thrill of fear ran through me, and I wished to exchange the ghastly image of my fancy for the realities around. I see them still; the very room, the dark *parquet,* the closed shutters, with the moonlight struggling through, and the sense I had that the glassy lake and white high Alps were beyond. I could not so easily get rid of my hideous phantom; still it haunted me. I must try to think of something else. I recurred to my ghost story,—my tiresome unlucky ghost story! O! if I could only contrive one which would frighten my reader as I myself had been frightened that night!

Swift as light and as cheering was the idea that broke in upon me. "I have found it! What terrified me will terrify others; and I need only describe the spectre which had haunted my midnight pillow." On the morrow I announced that I had *thought of a story.* I began that day with the words, *It was on a dreary night of November,* making only a transcript of the grim terrors of my waking dream.

At first I thought but of a few pages—of a short tale; but [Percy] Shelley urged me to develop the idea at greater length. [pp. 227–29]

It is likely, is it not, that what was in effect a dream caught, reflected, and perhaps developed various notions that had been in the air (so to speak), notions that Mary Shelley had been exposed to, had perhaps been bothered by, and somehow or other had mulled over? The words she first set down to paper (which she italicized here, along with "thought of a story") may be found at the beginning of the fifth chapter (in the 1831 edition; at the beginning of the fourth chapter in the 1818 edition). (p. 52) The dream, as she recalled it a decade and a half later, occupies no more than a couple of pages in the final story. Does the terror that Shelley felt, in her dream, ever come through to us? Perhaps it does in the monster's account of William's death (p. 139), or when Frankenstein tears the female monster to pieces (p. 164), and (of course) when the monster first comes to life (which draws directly on the original dream itself). (pp. 52-53)

This dream, it would seem, is the true heart of the story. It is that which pumps life into the entire body of the tale.[135] All else is extrapolation and explanation (including the imaginative consideration of what the monster itself felt). This helps account, perhaps, for the fact that the book is rather labored in parts.[136] Everything radiates from—echoes from, depends upon—the dream material. The further away from that material this artist if obliged to move, the more rational (that is, the more calculating and, hence, sometimes the more contrived) she runs the risk of becoming.

To the extent she succeeds as a storyteller, it may be in large part because the author allows the terror of her dream to dominate the entire book. A dream's tone can, we all know, affect one all day, long after the details of one's dream are forgotten. This is reflected in lines taken from a poem by Percy Shelley which the monster quotes to Frankenstein:

> *We rest; a dream has power to poison sleep.*
> *We rise; one wand'ring thought pollutes the day.*
> *[p. 93]*

Mary Shelley seems to have sensed that she had somehow captured a mood—and so she was reluctant to change anything once written.[137]

No other book of hers has been as effective as this one. (Some say *The Last Man* is her best book—but the public has not agreed.) No other book of hers, it seems, drew as deeply on the psyche revealed in the dream. In some way, perhaps, her dream took the place of sustained poetic inspiration.[138] Insofar as Shelley was successful thereafter, it was because there was in all her work the spirit of *Frankenstein;* there was, it seems, little else that was truly inspired in her other work.[139]

Not only is this a story based on a dream (real or feigned)—a dream or a fantasy responsible for tremors which reverberate through the entire novel—but it is a story in which the principal character himself can be considered acting out, or acting in, a dream. It is, in a sense, a story *about* dreaming. Thus, Frankenstein reported (after he had destroyed the monster's mate) that he was, in his effort to escape retribution, "overcome by the sensation of helplessness, so often felt in frightful dreams." (p. 164) Earlier, after Clerval's death and his own arrest and subsequent release, he could say, "The past appeared to me in the light of a frightful dream..." (pp. 180–81)

The quality of dream-life may be seen as well in how events are organized around (and, in a sense, *by*) Frankenstein. He is aware of more than he explicitly recognizes. Thus, is he not somehow aware that Clerval is to be the next victim of the monster (after the destruction of the monster's mate)? (pp. 160, 166) He may even be aware that Elizabeth will be the victim thereafter: "the whole truth" rushed into his mind when he heard her scream. (p. 193) But perhaps even more revealing is how Frankenstein goes down to wait for the arrival of the passenger coach after he has fled from his newly created monster: he expects (that is, arranges for?) Clerval to come unexpectedly to take care of him! (pp. 54–55) This accounts, I suspect, for various of the "strange coincidences" in the book (p. 173): they are due neither to providence nor to chance—but rather to the order imposed (in effect) by Frankenstein's (or, from another perspective, by Shelley's) vivid mind.[140]

Frankenstein does argue, in telling his story to a skeptical Swiss magistrate (pp. 196–97), "The story is too connected to be mistaken for a dream..." It may be true that dreams are not as well connected as waking life—but they certainly can give one the impression (if only temporarily) that they *are*. Of course, there are documents available here to attest to "reality," and Walton reports that he sees the monster. But is not the tenor of all this still that of the dream from which it originally issued?

To make as much as I do of the origins of this story suggests that there may be considerably more to it than its author suspected. It also suggests that there may be in this story much more of the personality of the artist than is appropriate for the greatest art. Does not nature seem more evident—more ministered to or better imitated—in those works where the artist is least evident?[141] Still, one can learn from the work of a talented *young* artist: the usually hidden workings of the artistic impulse can sometimes be exposed to view, especially if (as we saw in *Titus Andronicus*) the work should be flawed in revealing ways.

iv

I REMIND my readers of the plot of *Frankenstein* by repeating one editor's summary:

> *Frankenstein* is constructed of three concentric layers, one within the other. In the outermost layer, Robert Walton, in his letters to his sister, describes his voyage towards the North Pole and his encounter with Victor Frankenstein. In the main, middle layer, Frankenstein tells Walton how he created the monster and abandoned it in disgust, how it revenged itself by murdering all those he loved and how he finally turned and pursued it. In the very centre, the monster himself describes the development of his mind after the flight from the laboratory and his bitterness when men reject him. In spite of her inexperience, Mary Shelley uses this concentric structure with considerable subtlety.[142]

Some critics, however, consider "the most glaring fault" in *Frankenstein* the addition of prefatory chapters to the initial draft.[143] That is, they prefer to see Frankenstein's own account begin with the vitalization of the monster (on that "dreary night of November"). (p. 52) Others see as a fault the use of Walton's letters (at the beginning and end of the book). But both of these criticisms may rest on a failure to see how the parts do fit together. May not the letter-writing Walton, for example, be (in his highminded adventurousness) somehow worthy of the story about the monster? Other principals see the monster at a distance or only as a threat. Walton is privileged to see it close up, even to talk with it, and yet live. I shall return to the significance of the mild-mannered Walton and his letters.

The original laboratory scene does not suffice: one has to be told (if only by flashbacks) how it all happened; the character of the creator is important. (He is shown—even when dealing with the monster which has murdered his brother—to exhibit both curiosity and compassion.) (p. 97) The setting of the experiments is important: it is not in staid Geneva, but rather at a university in that land of learning, Germany. But, it should at once be added, Frankenstein (however scientific in appearance) retains the ambitions of the medieval alchemist. (pp. 32–35, 40–43) Few details about his methods are given: those are not as interesting (or important) as the human problems encountered. Frankenstein is moved by a desire for glory as the

discoverer of the means of banishing disease and making man invulnerable to any but a violent death. (p. 34) Someone who can "create"
life may be able to preserve it indefinitely, for such a man will have
learned the secrets of life itself—so Frankenstein seems to believe.

The secrets of life, we are given to understand, have little to do
(at least for people such as Frankenstein) with the prospects of an
immortal soul. Indeed, the book was thought by some of its contemporary readers to be impious. This assessment may be, in part, a
response to the evident replacement of the biblical God by Frankenstein as creator of life.[144] Christianity itself is explicitly mentioned
on several occasions. There is a confessor who advises an innocent
Justine to confess William's murder; earlier, there is another confessor,
who rebukes Justine's mother for her treatment of Justine. (pp. 82,
61. See, also, p. 119.) Justine, on the eve of her execution, does say
she expects to see the murdered William soon in heaven. (p. 82) Earlier, Frankenstein's mother had expressed, on her deathbed, the expectation of being reunited with her loved ones in heaven. (p. 38. See,
also, p. 69.) Frankenstein, however, does not seem to express unequivocally any such hope (for example, with respect to Clerval). (p. 154)
Consider, also, the final sentiment of the monster (p. 221): "My spirit
will sleep in peace; or if it thinks, it will not surely think thus."[145]

Even when Frankenstein is most moved—upon anticipating a
visit to him by the monster while he is imprisoned for Clerval's murder ("For God's sake" [p. 177]) and upon fully comprehending that
the monster had all the time planned to murder Elizabeth ("Great
God!" [pp. 188, 193])—even in these circumstances, his invocations
of the Deity leave open the question of what can be expected of divinity and of what happens to the souls of the dead. (See, also, pp.
52, 74.) Thus, Frankenstein (at the cemetery, after Elizabeth's death,
in pledging himself to pursuit of the monster) can swear also by the
shades that wander near him, by the deep and eternal grief he feels,
and by night and the spirits that preside over night. (p. 199) Later,
he can invoke the spirits of the dead and the wandering ministers of
justice. (p. 200) Earlier, in talking to his father (while attempting to
identify himself as the true murderer of those close to him), he swears
by "the sun and the heavens." (p. 183) This echoes the oath that had
been taken by the monster, which had sought from him a mate, "I
swear by the sun, and by the blue sky of heaven, that if you grant
my prayer, while they exist you shall never behold me again." (p.
144)[146]

It is difficult to know how such things should be taken—for that depends, in part, upon how disciplined and hence careful the author is. It does seem to be suggested that Frankenstein is someone who has been nurtured on Christian expectations of immortality but who can no longer take comfort in any prospect of life after death. And so he looks to immortal fame and, even better, as a victory over mortality, to the conquest of disease. Perhaps this can be taken as a worldly form of the Christian concern to be victorious in the struggle against the flesh (or, at least, against the lusts of the flesh).[147] Such a struggle, when it takes the form seen in Frankenstein's grand experiment, can be condemned as radically presumptuous.

V

BUT THERE may be something perverse as well about Victor Frankenstein's struggle against the flesh. This perversity may be seen when one examines the role played in this book by his marriage.

Consider, first, how chastely Frankenstein can speak of sexual relations: "Even if [the monster and its mate] were to leave Europe, and inhabit the deserts of the new world, yet one of the first results of *those sympathies for which the daemon thirsted* would be children, and a race of devils would be propagated upon the earth, who might make the very existence of the species of man a condition precarious and full of terror." (p. 163; italics added) Consider, next, how Frankenstein likes to regard his prospective marriage to Elizabeth: he dares whisper to himself, in thinking upon her, "paradisaical dreams of love and joy." (p. 186)

Seven premature deaths, we calculate, can be attributed to the monster, the seventh being that of the monster itself (if and when it kills itself).[148] Central to these is the death of Elizabeth. Indeed, she is the last one (except for itself) whom the monster kills directly. Her importance may be seen as well in what Frankenstein can say after he describes her death to Walton: "But why should I dwell upon the incidents that followed this last overwhelming event. Mine has been a tale of horrors; I have reached their *acme* [that is, *nadir* or *crisis*], and what I must now relate can but be tedious to you." (p. 195) He then goes on to mention his father's death and to anticipate his own.

Be that as it may, there *is* something odd in Frankenstein's relationship with Elizabeth. Indeed, one can see in it—or, rather, in his response to it—the hesitations of an incestuous affair. Again and again,

Frankenstein seems to regard her as a sister (and she seems to recip-
rocate: thus, she virtually identifies herself as a sister to the murdered
William [p. 79]). (See pp. 29, 148.) This relationship is not as evident
in the 1831 edition as in the 1818 edition, for Mary Shelley made
changes in the origins of Elizabeth. (In 1831, she becomes an Italian
foundling—daughter of a nobleman; in 1818, she had been Frankenstein's cousin, the only daughter of his father's deceased sister). The
author's changes may suggest she herself did sense some of the psychic
implications of her story, but the changes did not alter its tenor. One
must wonder whether Frankenstein protests too much by insisting
that he really wants to marry Elizabeth. (pp. 148–49)[149]

But the fear of incest may go even deeper than I have already
suggested. Elizabeth is, it is indicated in various ways in this book,
a substitute for Victor Frankenstein's much beloved mother, who
died quite young. It is Elizabeth's scarlet fever which kills the mother.
(p. 37) But there are other indications as well of displacement or
substitution. (See, for example, p. 39.) Most vivid is a passage which
was inserted into the very pages Shelley originally wrote to record
her vivid dream. (p. 53) This is when Frankenstein lies down, exhausted, after having fled his newly vitalized monster:

> ... I slept indeed, but I was disturbed by the wildest dreams. I thought
> I saw Elizabeth, in the bloom of health, walking in the streets of In-
> golstadt. Delighted and surprised, I embraced her; but as I imprinted
> the first kiss on her lips, they became livid with the hue of death; her
> features appeared to change, and I thought that I held the corpse of
> my dead mother in my arms; a shroud enveloped her form, and I saw
> the grave-worms crawling in the folds of the flannel. I started from
> my sleep with horror ... [p. 53]

And when he awoke, he saw the monster holding up the curtain of
the bed and looking at him! Thus, there may be an intimate relation
between, on the one hand, what both the monster and his mother
mean to (or do for) Frankenstein and, on the other, his desire (such
as it is) for Elizabeth. Does he regard that desire as somehow monstrous?

The last summer that Frankenstein labored on the construction
of his monster was a beautiful season. But, he said, his eyes were
"insensible to the charms of nature." (p. 50) Nature cannot attract

him, it seems. In fact, he proposes to supplant the natural order of things. Is this because sexual relations threaten him? Or do the causes go even deeper, having something to do with the desire to conquer nature and thereby make oneself invulnerable? Or does he propose to supplant the natural order of things in order to serve as a benefactor for all mankind, if not even in order to know?[150]

Let us return to the array of the monster's seven victims. We should notice, among other things, that the first and last in this list are William and the monster. Do they not share a kind of youthfulness? (The monster, after all, is only four or five years old.) They are both youthful in being quite dependent on others and in their need for love and care. We have noticed, already, that Elizabeth is central to this list. Immediately on either side of her are Clerval and Frankenstein's father. Both are paternal in the care of Victor Frankenstein. This leaves, in this list, Justine and Frankenstein himself to be accounted for—the second and the next-to-last people in the list. They share the experience of being accused of murder of a loved one. Notice, also, that every other person in this list (the second, the fourth, and the sixth) is a female—*if,* that is, the sixth, Victor Frankenstein, is so recognized. And may it not be appropriate so to recognize, in some respects, *the* "parent" of the monster? Does Shelley intend him to be so recognized? But then, does she herself recognize everything that she has gathered together in this very revealing story?

We should also notice, in considering this list of victims, that no one outside the intimate circle of the Frankenstein family is killed by the monster. It does frighten others, perhaps many others, but it does not attack (with murderous intention) anyone else. (See, for example, p. 201.) This suggests that this book is primarily about family, or personal, problems, not about social problems, not even about the problem of the social control of science. It is for this reason, perhaps, that the great scientific achievement of Frankenstein can be ignored while its personal consequences can be made so much of.

Notice as well that the monster's principal concern throughout most of the book is to try to find a substitute family. It pins its hopes on the De Laceys (the family it had secretly observed and learned much from). Unfortunately, that is a family which knows nothing about the monster and owes it nothing. So the monster has to go back to the family which rejected it, that which Frankenstein represents. Frankenstein, however, will not give the monster what he himself could not have (or handle), a usable female. (Frankenstein is too self-centered to recognize explicitly that the wedding-night threat does not apply only to him personally.)

One can say that the murderous monster stands for life, at least in a primitive sense. Its primitiveness (a kind of naturalness) may be seen in the ways it kills and is itself to die. William, Clerval, and Eliza-beth—the people it kills directly—it kills with its bare hands (stran-gling or breaking the neck). (Justine also dies, on the scaffold, by the neck. [See p. 246.]) And when the monster itself comes to die, it announces, it will die by fire. It will not fall on a sword. (Franken-stein, a man of science, had urged Walton to use a sword on the monster.)

vi

THIS IS, I have suggested, a story about "family" problems. Perhaps it is this theme which appeals to us, to most people. *Is* there such a monster in us all with which each of us must come to terms?[151]

Certainly, it can be argued that there is a monster in Franken-stein, that *the* monster is somehow a part of Frankenstein. (It is a re-vealing mistake that the monster often has been given, in the public mind, the name of its creator.) The monster is nameless in the story: is this partly because it is so elemental as not to require a name? Is this also because it *is* part of Frankenstein and hence needs no other name? (We notice that Victor Frankenstein is first addressed by his family name in the story only after he had made the monster live. It is used by Clerval. [p. 55. See p. 32.])

The intimate correspondence of the monster to Frankenstein is indicated in various ways. Each intends to die after the other does. (p. 210) They quote from the same poems by John Milton and Percy Shelley. (pp. 124, 132, 201) Frankenstein can observe of the monster, "I do not doubt that he hovers near the spot which I inhabit." (p. 197) They often seem to talk the same way. (Does this do no more than reflect the limitations of Shelley when she presses for effect?) Frankenstein can feel for the monster something of the desire that he feels for Elizabeth (with the same ineffectiveness in both cases, it should at once be added). He speaks of the "ecstasy" of joining his dead Elizabeth (it is not clear whether he anticipates meeting her in death or merely being dead like her [see p. 202]), and he utters "a wild cry of ecstasy" when he sees the monster he has been pursuing. (p. 205) This parallel suggests that the monster (like Elizabeth) is both something he very much wants to possess or control and something he is very much threatened by.

Where do all these characters come from? We are told by editors that the social doctrines in the story come, in part, from the teachings of Mary Shelley's father, William Godwin (the author to whom the book is dedicated). The women in the story are, by and large, abandoned early (one way or another) by their parents, especially by their fathers. All this reminds us of the lonely childhood of the author herself. Hers was a loneliness only partly alleviated, it seems, by the marriage to Percy Shelley. For is she not saying something about that marriage and about Shelley himself in this story? Was he not in some ways like Frankenstein, in other ways, like the monster? (See pp. xviii–xxi.)

Perhaps this story is too personal. If it were less so, the monster could be more like Prospero's Caliban; Frankenstein, more like Goethe's Faust. That is, Mary Shelley's family connections and the resulting psychic conditions might well have distorted things. (One suspects that there are here glimpses also of Percy Shelley's relations with women, including with his first wife as well as with Mary Shelley.) Mary Shelley seems to have been the most sober person in the company she kept—and this sobriety became evident in how she conducted her affairs after she was widowed (at an early age, not long after the publication of *Frankenstein*).

I emphasize the extent to which she in effect commented here upon what the geniuses around her (her father, Shelley, and Byron) were doing. I say what I do partly in opposition to what is said about her in the *Dictionary of National Biography*:

> Nothing but an absolute magnetizing of her brain by Shelley's can account for her having risen so far above her usual self as in 'Frankenstein.'[152]

No doubt, Percy Shelley influenced her—but perhaps not simply in the way indicated here by her biographer. (See p. xviii.) The death of her husband must have relaxed the need (as well as the encouragement) to express herself as she had.[153]

vii

TO POINT up the correspondence of the monster to Frankenstein is not to imply that each cannot be assessed somewhat apart from the other, however dependent each may have been on the other.

I have spoken about Frankenstein's psychic failings. His refusal to take responsibility for what he did was evident from the outset. In this, he can be distinguished from Prometheus, to whom (it would seem) he is likened by Mary Shelley. He can be distinguished also in that Prometheus was *not* punished by those whom he benefited (or, if he is considered as the maker of men, by those whom he created). Nor did Prometheus regret what he did. Rather, he could foresee and accept what happened—and *he* was eventually redeemed. Frankenstein, on the other hand, seems selfish and self-centered in what he does. Indeed, there *is* about what he does something deeply presumptuous.[154] The secrecy in which he works suggests the dubiousness of his venture. (Walton's project, on the other hand, is quite public.)

The monster, too, is aware of the dubiousness of much of what *it* does. It seems to be a creature whose somewhat primitive nature is responsible for a certain childishness in its attitudes. But, it should at once be added, the monster should know better. One can say—considering the remarkably high quality of the books happened upon and read by the monster (Goethe's *Sorrows of Werther;* a volume of Plutarch's *Lives;* Milton's *Paradise Lost* [p. 123])—one can say that the monster's career suggests the limits of liberal education. Should it not have learned, from the books it read, to behave better than it did?

The monster stands for the doctrine that misery breeds vice. Thus, its first words to Frankenstein are: "I expected this reception. All men hate the wretched..." (p. 94) But should it not sense that it is hated more for its wickedness than for its wretchedness? After all, it *is* the murderer of a child and of an innocent nursemaid. Insofar as the monster is shunned because of its ugliness, it can be added, is it not because ugliness does remind us of evil, beauty of goodness?[155] The monster sees another (Safie, the Christian Arab), who lacks the language of the De Lacey family, win acceptance—partly, no doubt, because she is beautiful.

Frankenstein sees on the monster's face, when the monster and he first talk, "bitter anguish, combined with disdain and malignity." (p. 94. See, also, p. 164.) The monster explains, "[M]isery made me a fiend..." (p. 95) Make me happy, it can say, and I will be virtuous. (See, also, pp. 97, 141.) This is a doctrine we are familiar with: we expect people in slums to have high crime rates; we expect people brutalized in prisons to be even worse than they would have been. The elderly De Lacey observes that to be driven from society and human sympathy makes men desperate. (p. 130) Frankenstein himself observes that the suffering of the people in the Orkneys had blunted even their coarser sensations. (p. 161)

But are these not likely to be the tolerant assessments of men with some goodness already in themselves? Is it "unrealistic" to present the monster as having benevolent inclinations at the outset?[156] Is the author unclear as to what *is* to be understood about the monster? Are the contradictions—the monster is presented at times as almost devilish and yet as something rather simple and affecting in its desire to be loved—the result of Shelley's immature effort to make the story interesting?

Frankenstein's own youth, we should remember, was passed most happily. (pp. 31-32) If the monster is correct, Frankenstein should have been quite virtuous. But his shortcomings are evident. Even he recognizes that his overpowering desire for revenge is a vice. (See p. 198. Compare p. 204 ["the eternal sentiment of a just retribution"].) Felix De Lacey, on the other hand, has been subjected to considerable deprivation—and yet he acts, by and large, better than does Frankenstein. Consider how each responds to flagrant cases of official injustice: Frankenstein is curiously ineffectual in the case of Justine; Felix De Lacey is vigorous in the cases both of Safie's father and of his own family's imprisonment. (pp. 75f, 118f) Still, Frankenstein does become someone who is "wretched beyond expression" (p. 96); he is not made vicious, whatever his shortcomings.

But perhaps the monster's doctrine should be limited to the consequences of one's formative years. Once a man has been properly raised—and this includes a healthy exposure to a loving family (not just to good literature)—we should expect his virtues to make him happy, or at least to make any outward misery imposed upon him more easily borne.[157] Otherwise, happiness becomes a mere matter of chance—since one's circumstances (and hence misery or happiness) are in large part beyond one's control.

Or, to put all this another way, one is taught by the better books that it is finer to suffer than to do injustice. But, I am afraid, the monster learned the wrong things from each of the three great authors

it studied. Thus, it takes *Paradise Lost* as its guide to spiritual rebellion: that book provided models for resentment.[158] It sees itself both
as the fallen Adam and as the rebellious Satan, appropriating from
the latter the motto, "Evil thenceforth become my good." (p. 218.
See p. 125; compare p. 127.) (Should one not know that if the virtuous and the divine do appear to be in conflict, one's understanding
of one or the other, or of both, is likely to be faulty?) *Werther* legitimated for the monster both sentimentality and self-destructiveness.[159]
The stories of Plutarch happened upon by the monster were lives of
founders—that is, men who won acclaim by breaking with the ways
of their respective pasts.[160]

One can also question whether these books, and others like them,
were read properly by the Shelleys, their contemporaries, and hence
their literary characters. (But impressive *is* the amount of reading
people [including poets such as Percy Shelley] did, and of the best
literature.) Certainly, it is not from Plutarch that the monster derived
the teaching, which one sees the effect of again and again in the monster's career, that more should be made of the rights one can exact
from the community than of the duties one owes to it.

All of the male principals in the book expose their self-centeredness in the emphasis they place upon fame (least so, perhaps, the
monster [compare p. 219], except in the form of progeny). And all
of them are very much concerned to explain themselves, in the effort,
evidently, to make (or save) a name for themselves. All of them, it
seems, would have been better served if they had been taught that
virtue should be pursued primarily for its own sake. Frankenstein, in
any event, does achieve the distinction of being (in his eyes, at least)
"the most wretched of human beings." (p. 70)

An emphasis upon glory may provide some sense of purpose for
existence. But if there is a serious question about the meaning of existence, why would a sense of purpose be infused into one's life by
creating still another race of *mortal* beings whose existence would
raise the same question with respect to purpose—a race whose critical
capacities are no greater than man's? Is there about what Frankenstein
tried to do something intrinsically thoughtless—with its distortion and
ugliness evident upon examination? (Should this be evident to anyone who may have an imagination like Mary Shelley's? That is, there
is nothing accidental about the monster's problems and character?
The monster does share with Frankenstein the opinion that such
beings as the monster should not be created again. [p. 220])

Yet the dying Frankenstein justifies his life: he does not find it "blameable." (p. 214) His last words, "yet another may succeed," suggest that he has not learned what all this had to teach. (p. 215) Still, one can say that he indeed succeeded in the harder task (making life) and that he failed to perform the easier task (training the monster properly). But, I have suggested, an even greater task awaited him (and us all?), that of investigating the meaning of human existence.

viii

ST. AUGUSTINE speaks of the terrifying abyss of ignorance which is the source of all error; this he sees to be related to the evils belonging to all men since Adam.[161] What is to be done for the misery (in this life) of the multitudes of mankind? Philosophy, Augustine recognized, is available only to a few (whatever it may do for those few).[162]

A concern for the multitudes—a worldly concern which replaces the mission of the pious Christian?—may be seen in the language both of Frankenstein and of Walton. They both picture themselves as seeking that glory which comes to benefactors. (They, too, it would seem, read only the founders' lives in Plutarch.) Frankenstein's benefaction may consist, ultimately, in developing means of preserving men from every threat to life but violent death (and a well-ordered community will protect one against violence?). Walton's benefaction, which presumably is to follow from his expedition to the North Pole, is not made clear. (But see p. 10.) Is all mankind somehow bettered as some men come to understand more and more?

Be that as it may, one cannot help but notice that Frankenstein's and the monster's tales *are* put in the setting provided by Walton's letters home to England—to a sober England, not to the Continent with its Romantic inclinations. (Walton's sister is not only married, she also has children. [p. 210]) That was the England that the Shelleys could not bear—and that could not bear the style of life of the Shelleys and their most intimate associates. (See Chapter XIII, below. Compare Chapter VIII, below.)

The letters not only provide a setting for these monstrous tales but also serve to place a welcome distance between us and the careers of Frankenstein and his progeny. Thus, what is unbearable in Frankenstein and his monster becomes bearable (even "enjoyable") through the mediation of Walton. This is a phenomenon we are all familiar with in our response to tragedies. (It took a week for Frankenstein to tell his story, and he personally corrected the transcript of the account made by Walton. [p. 207] That passage of time was good for Walton, providing *him* some distance as well.)

Why should pain-filled stories give us pleasure? The "distance" may be a condition for the pleasure we derive. But perhaps even more important may be that we do learn from such stories: the nature of things is revealed (including the relation between prudence and mortality). One learns that man can somehow master the pains and fears he encounters from time to time. Thus, art can tame (make bearable, perhaps even elevate) the terrible (especially when a man's misery can plausibly be seen as resulting from his faults).[163]

The artistic transformation of the terrible may be seen, in its reassuring effects, in Mary Shelley's personal response to her terrifying nightmare. That nightmare became "cheering" when she recognized that it could be converted to artistic purposes. (p. 228) She must have been relieved, if not even delighted, by her recognition that she had somehow taken command of the passions that threatened to engulf her. As an observer of the artistic, one is both "involved" and "safe."

Shelley could report (in 1831) that she had a certain "affection" for her "hideous progeny." (p. 229) In a sense, of course, she is Frankenstein and this book is her monster, but a monster that is more or less tamed by her. That is, she somehow (if only instinctively) comes to terms with what is disturbing her.

ix

WE NOTICE that Walton can be appealed to by his men: *he* can be induced to return home, rather than continue what had turned virtually into a suicidal mission. The mutiny he dreads from sailors oppressed by ice and cold seems once again to testify to the relation between misery and vice. (p. 211)

Walton *can* turn back—even though he castigates his men as cowardly, and even though he sympathizes with an unrepentant Frankenstein. He does know, at the end, what Frankenstein did not learn before he died, that the monster says it intends to kill itself shortly. But this may not be the decisive consideration: for Walton never seems to adopt Frankenstein's mission against the monster. The only problem for Walton is whether he should continue his own mission to the North Pole (a mission which the monster assumes *it* will be able to accomplish).

Thus, Walton can be said to have been moderated by the story he has heard, a story of grand ambition at almost all costs. (See pp. 24, 48.) Is not Walton's ambition, like that of Frankenstein, rooted ultimately in curiosity, in the desire to be (not just to be known as?) a great discoverer? (p. 12) But Frankenstein, however much he continues to be moved by a lust for revenge, did explicitly disavow the promptings of curiosity. (p. 20: "idle curiosity", p. 207: "senseless curiosity") Did not Frankenstein, in abandoning curiosity for revenge, sacrifice something essential to his humanity?

Does not Walton call off his mission because of a respect for humanity? There are raised here, for Walton to consider, contending arguments as to what justice calls for. Questions are raised throughout the book about justice and its administration. (Consider what happens to Justine and to the De Lacey family.) Even the monster can report that its blood boils at the injustice done it. (p. 219)[164]

The securing of justice may depend, ultimately, on the ordering of regimes. The Frankenstein family is well established politically in Geneva. (p. 27) What *is* the status of Geneva in this era of revolutionary change?[165] (One can notice, in passing, that Victor Frankenstein's brother, Ernest, does seem to survive, presumably to marry and continue the line. But this is left implicit: it would adversely affect the tone of the story to make anything more of this explicit.[166])

The anxious sailors put their pleas to Walton in terms of justice. What they consider justice is set against Walton's desire for achievement. (p. 211) (Frankenstein lectures the men about fortitude and benefiting mankind and glory. [p. 212]) Walton, in turn, considers what they demand to be "injustice." (p. 213) But, he explains to Frankenstein, "I cannot resist their demands." (p. 214) After all, Walton's mission requires considerable cooperation from other men; Frankenstein's had not, and perhaps he suffered because of that, since he had not had to make a case before others for what he wanted to do. (Frankenstein's isolation is seen in his inability to get any help from the magistrate for pursuit of the monster. Indeed, one can regard the monster's loneliness as a projection, or intensification, of Frankenstein's essential isolation. See, in this respect also, Chapter VIII and Chapter XIII, below.)

Was it shameful (as Walton felt) for the mission to turn back in these circumstances? What, after all, is the role of prudence not only in doing justice but also in pursuing the truth? Walton had insisted he was a prudent fellow. (pp. 15, 17) Prudence may have helped him learn from his encounter with Frankenstein—perhaps even more from Frankenstein's deeds (and fate) than from his words.

It can also be said that the story of Frankenstein and his destructive monster bestows a life-preserving influence on the ambitious.[167] Frankenstein's ambition was, in a sense, unnatural, in that he (a male) wanted to combine in himself the roles of both male and female in producing a new life.[168]

Frankenstein's presumptuous enterprise covers (as we have seen) some seven years. On the other hand, Walton's enterprise—the period covered by his letters home about this mission—takes some nine months. Thus, the Frankenstein story is set in the frame of that nine-month experience of the narrator. One is reminded, of course, of the normal gestation period for bringing forth new human life.

This correspondence seems not to have been noticed by critics, evidently because they do not take seriously the framework provided by the author. This artist as thinker has not been sufficiently appreciated by them. (It should also be noticed that there was, of course, for Frankenstein, a quicker, and more pleasant, way of accomplishing his purpose, narrowly conceived. Would not Frankenstein be involved today in tedious cloning experiments?) It can be said, therefore, that the nine-month frame of the story is a tacit reaffirmation of the female principle in human relations. It is, indeed, a reaffirmation of nature and the nature of things.

Mary Shelley's story—an account of a series of couplings of careers, the careers of Frankenstein and the monster, of Frankenstein and Walton, of Walton and the monster—can be understood, then, as constructive "creativity." This creativity is more pleasurable, less presumptuous, certainly more successful than that attempted by Victor Frankenstein.

Perhaps even more pleasurable is the story of still another monster, the hero of Charles Dickens's *Christmas Carol*. He is, to be sure, a less threatening monster (at least in appearance), although he can be identified (toward the end of Stave Three of that story, in a Christmas-Day game) as "an animal, a live animal, rather a disagreeable animal, a savage animal, an animal that growled and grunted sometimes, and talked sometimes, and lived in London, and walked about the streets..." It is to him and his timely conversion that we now turn.

VI. CHARLES DICKENS

(1812-1870)

> Macbeth:
>> One cried 'God bless us!' and 'Amen!' the
>> other,
>> As they had seen me with these hangman's
>> hands,
>> List'ning their fear, I could not say 'Amen!'
>> When they did say 'God bless us!'
> Lady Macbeth:
>> Consider it not so deeply.
> Macbeth:
>> But wherefore could not I pronounce
>> 'Amen'?
>> I had most need of blessing, and 'Amen'
>> Stuck in my throat.
>
> —William Shakespeare, *Macbeth*, II, ii

i

A CLASSICAL scholar, in assessing the Greek dramatists, has remarked on the "extraordinary creative power that [Aeschylus] shares with Shakespeare and Dickens." An *Encyclopaedia Britannica* authority reports that Charles Dickens stands second only to Shakespeare in English literature, that he is "[g]enerally regarded as the greatest English novelist." Thus, one finds again and again, in critical discussions, elevations of Dickens to the most exalted heights.[169]

Whatever reservations one may have about the ultimate soundness of these assessments, no English author ever enjoyed during his lifetime the popular acclaim which came to Charles Dickens. Only Shakespeare and Lewis Carroll created so many characters who (either in their names or in now familiar quotations) have taken on a life of their own.

Among Dickens's memorable characters is Ebenezer Scrooge, the hero of that 1843 tale, *A Christmas Carol,* one of the author's

---

All citations in the text of this chapter to *A Christmas Carol* are to the story as published in *The Christmas Books of Charles Dickens*, Michael Slater, ed. (Baltimore: Penguin Books, 1971).

best-known books. No Christmas among us is complete without its representation on stage, radio, and television, as well as in the home. Indeed, for many people, there are only two Christmas stories of note, that of the New Testament and that written by the 31-year-old Charles Dickens. It has even been said that Dickens has made the modern Christmas what it is, a time for feasting and good cheer, "a good time: a kind, forgiving, charitable, pleasant time." (p. 49)

The story of the conversion of Scrooge is familiar. It is the story of the instructive "haunt[ing] by Three Spirits" of "a squeezing, wrenching, grasping, scraping, clutching, covetous old sinner," a man who was "[h]ard and sharp as flint, from which no steel had ever struck out generous fire; secret, and self-contained, and solitary as an oyster." (pp. 63, 46) We first see our hero (on Christmas Eve) disparaging the Christmas spirit in the approaches to him (in turn) of his good-natured nephew, of two gentlemen soliciting for the poor, of a little boy who tries to sing him a Christmas carol, and of Bob Cratchit (his clerk) whom he reluctantly gives the next day as a holiday with pay (but not without the parting injunction, "Be here all the earlier next morning!" [p. 53]).

Within a few pages, one has a lively (and permanent) awareness of the kind of man Scrooge is. One is not yet aware, however, of anything in him that could lead to his famous conversion, a conversion that follows upon the visitation to Scrooge of the ghost of his deceased partner, Jacob Marley, and thereafter of Three Spirits, the Ghost of Christmas Past, the Ghost of Christmas Present, and the Ghost of Christmas Yet to Come.

Marley's Ghost (who is almost as chilling as the sombre Ghost of Christmas Yet to Come) is anticipated for Scrooge by what he experiences when he returns home after "his melancholy dinner," an experience which so startles him "that his blood was ... conscious of a terrible sensation to which it had been a stranger from infancy." (pp. 53, 55) Since it is this "rejuvenating" experience that proves to be the apparent threshold for Scrooge to everything else of note in the remainder of the story, it would be useful to recall the narrator's account of it:

> Now, it is a fact, that there was nothing at all particular about the knocker on the door, except that it was very large. It is also a fact, that Scrooge had seen it night and morning during his whole resi-

dence in that place; also that Scrooge had as little of what is called
fancy about him as any man in the City of London.... Let it also be
borne in mind that Scrooge had not bestowed one thought on Marley,
since his last mention of his seven-years' dead partner that afternoon.
And then let any man explain to me, if he can, how it happened that
Scrooge, having his key in the lock of the door, saw in the knocker,
without its undergoing any intermediate process of change: not a
knocker, but Marley's face.

Marley's face. It was not in impenetrable shadow as the other objects
in the yard were, but had a dismal light about it, like a bad lobster
in a dark cellar. It was not angry or ferocious, but looked at Scrooge
as Marley used to look: with ghostly spectacles turned up upon its
ghostly forehead. The hair was curiously stirred, as if by breath or
hot-air; and though the eyes were wide open, they were perfectly
motionless. That, and its livid colour, made it horrible; but its horror
seemed to be, in spite of the face and beyond its control, rather than
a part of its own expression. [pp. 54–55]

Dickens, in this passage, lays down for us an instructive challenge
when he says, "And then let any man explain to me, if he can, how it
happened that Scrooge ... saw in the knocker ... not a knocker, but
Marley's face." (p. 54) This challenge—how it happened that Scrooge
saw not only Marley's face but also, if I may expand it, Marley's Ghost
and thereafter three more ghosts—this challenge is what provides us
an opportunity to discuss a great novelist and his art by examining
one of that artist's favorite stories. An opportunity is also provided
thereby to develop further what we may know about how to read a
book.

A simple explanation of the extraordinary manifestations in *A
Christmas Carol* is, it can be said, implied by Dickens himself in the
way he presents this story. Cannot everything that happens after
Scrooge "took his melancholy dinner in his usual tavern" (pp. 53–
54) be understood as an extended dream by Scrooge? (This understanding may not be essential to my interpretation of the book—but
it does add at least a diverting, and perhaps instructive, grace note to
my composition.)

An early hint of a dream may be provided us in the observation
that Scrooge, after "having read all the newspapers [in his tavern]
and beguiled the rest of the evening with his banker's-book, went

home to bed." (p. 54) It is only after this is reported by the narrator—only after Scrooge is said to have gone "home to bed"—that
Scrooge is described as "actually" walking up to his door, encoun-
tering the transformed knocker and then other strange sights and
noises as he ascends to and settles into his chambers.

But to suggest that all this is essentially a remarkably productive dream is only a preliminary explanation in response to Dicken's
challenge. We have still to consider how this dream "works" and
what it says about Scrooge and, indeed, about human beings generally. How did it happen that Scrooge had this revolutionary experience, whether or not in the form of a dream? After all, this Christmas
was spent in his usual melancholy manner. Why was this night different from all other nights?[170]

ii

A CHRISTMAS Carol begins with the stark observation, "Marley was
dead." (p. 45) And a few paragraphs further on, the narrator emphasizes this by saying: "There is no doubt that Marley was dead. This
must be distinctly understood, or nothing wonderful can come of the
story I am going to relate." (p. 45) Scrooge's counting-house, we are
told, still bears the sign, "Scrooge and Marley":

> Scrooge never painted out Old Marley's name. There it stood, years
> afterwards, above the warehouse door: Scrooge and Marley. The
> firm was known as Scrooge and Marley. Sometimes people new to
> the business called Scrooge Scrooge, and sometimes Marley, but he
> answered to both names: it was all the same to him. [p. 46]

Death looms large throughout *A Christmas Carol*, and not only
emphatically in its very beginning. All of the Third Spirit's visitation,
for example, turns around two future deaths, that of Tiny Tim and
that of Scrooge himself, a death (in the latter case) which is grim,
lonely, and an occasion for jesting if not even "serious delight" on
the part of others. (pp 119–20) But, in a manner of speaking, Scrooge
had already died—at least insofar as he is interchangeable with Marley
(in whose chambers he now lives [p. 54]). Scrooge has seen someone
very much like himself, with his own interests and resources, come

to die. He was reminded of Marley's death, when he was obliged to inform the charitable gentlemen, "Mr. Marley has been dead these seven years. He died seven years ago, this very night." (p. 50)

A few minutes earlier, Scrooge had had an encounter with his well-wishing nephew—in the course of which the nephew had defended Christmas as

> the only time I know of, in the long calendar of the year, when men and women seem by one consent to open their shut-up hearts freely, and to think of people below them as if they really were fellow-passengers to the grave, and not another race of creatures bound on other journeys. [p. 49]

Scrooge does seem to consider himself one of those "creatures bound on other journeys"—one of those who have somehow transcended their mortality. *His* journey is in a substantial chariot fashioned of silver and gold—but the recollection of Marley, who had died this very night, can be said to have reminded him that the rich man's journey is at best but a slight detour on the route to the grave.

Perhaps Scrooge also senses—and this the nephew's liveliness may have impressed upon him—that there is something deadly about his own way of life. He may sense, that is, that he has cut himself off from genuine human contact, from a life of breadth and meaning. He may even sense, especially at a season of the year when so much is made of a Birth and of rebirth, that he has somehow hastened for himself the death that (it is evident throughout the book) he dreads. In short, he has, in his desperate efforts to preserve himself, made himself more vulnerable.

iii

TO SPEAK of vulnerability and of preservation is to direct our attention (if only briefly) to what it is that really moves a miser such as Scrooge. After all, what do the avaricious seek?

Avarice is a determined attempt to fence oneself off from death and from any lesser, related vulnerability. It is an attempt to save one's life by providing oneself the means to deal with whatever may threaten one. It is an attempt to be self-sufficient rather than to have to rely upon someone else in a critical moment.[171]

The helplessness that the miserly Scrooge is concerned to avoid lies just below his veneer of worldly wisdom and everyday competence. The first episode that Scrooge recollects, under the aegis of the Ghost of Christmas Past, is of himself as a schoolboy who is abandoned at Christmas time, left alone in his miserable boarding school, when all the other boys have gone home. (pp. 70–73) Is there not about this experience something traumatic, so much so that it is only natural that the scarred adult might make every effort not to permit himself ever to become helpless again? (The plight of a vulnerable child means a great deal to Dickens also, as is evident in the first [and best] part [which is autobiographical] of *David Copperfield*.)

Scrooge as a child (again, it seems, like Dickens before him) suffered from the callousness of his father. The second episode shown to Scrooge by the Ghost of Christmas Past once again displays a child abandoned at Christmas time—but, on that occasion, he is rescued from his loneliness by his sister, who had interceded with their father. (pp. 73–75) Scrooge repeats before us, in a more dramatic form, the conversion evidently experienced by his father, who (for an unstated reason) changed suddenly from a harsh parent to a kind one. Indeed, Scrooge can be thought of, at the beginning of *A Christmas Carol,* as subject still to the harsh father in himself. His rescue on the reader's Christmas Eve is again contributed to (in effect) by his now-dead sister. She acts this time through her son, the nephew who had insisted upon bringing Christmas cheer to his formidable uncle.

The nephew's seemingly unwelcome visit on Christmas Eve to Scrooge's counting-house begins a series of recollections which can be said to have naturally brought to the surface of Scrooge's consciousness a reexamination of the kind of life he had resorted to.

iv

THE PROBLEM with Scrooge's kind of life is pointed up in one critical exchange he has with his nephew. Scrooge responds to his nephew's opening greeting, "A merry Christmas, uncle! God save you!", with his now notorious, "Bah! Humbug!" The disgruntled uncle goes on to say, "Merry Christmas! What right have you to be merry? what reason have you to be merry? You're poor enough." To which the nephew replies gaily: "Come, then. What right have you to be dismal? what reason have you to be morose? You're rich enough." And, the narrator adds, "Scrooge having no better answer ready on the spur of the moment, said, 'Bah!' again; and followed it up with 'Humbug'." (pp. 47–48)

It is significant that Scrooge does *not* have here a ready answer (something which he does have in dealing immediately thereafter with the two solicitors and with Bob Cratchit). He had himself invoked right and reason in challenging the appropriateness of merriment in his poor nephew: he had thereby indicated the standards by which he judged others and was prepared to be judged himself. He evidently cannot deny that he is dismal and morose—and this despite his wealth. That is, he tacitly concedes, when it is implicitly pointed out to him, that his wealth has not insulated him from childlike misery, from that vulnerability of which death is the most dramatic form. Scrooge is practically dead in the way he lives—and this the nephew's argument brings home to his not unperceptive uncle.[172]

This may be brought home as well by the aborted Christmas carol sung to Scrooge through his keyhole by the little boy whom he drives off:

> *God bless you merry gentlemen!*
> *May nothing you dismay!*
> *[p. 53]*

This has been said by the editor of the *Oxford Book of Carols* to be "the most popular of Christmas carols." The version usually sung in London streets in the time of Dickens has been changed in this story from "God rest you" to "God bless you." "Rest," which means (in this context) "keep," would be inappropriate for Scrooge. He cannot be *kept* merry. "Bless," however, has the connotation of being made something, of being changed into something, of having something done for one. The boy can be considered providential in making this vital change (as well as other appropriate changes) in what he sings. Perhaps he (or whoever is responsible for the boy's intervention) senses what Scrooge is in need of.

"May nothing you dismay!" It is dismay—or dismalness or moroseness (to use the nephew's language)—which Scrooge has somehow accumulated *with* (not necessarily *because of*) his wealth. And, being

an eminently practical man of considerable intelligence, he is aware
that his state of affairs does not make sense. This awareness is put
together, in an imaginative and hence instructive manner, by the visitations he conjures up this Christmas Eve.[173]

V

CRITICAL TO one's understanding of what does happen to Scrooge
is how the nephew regards his Christmas Eve encounter with his uncle.
The nephew's opinion is shown to Scrooge by the Ghost of Christmas
Present, when he hears the nephew explain to his Christmas Day
guests what had happened the evening before upon visiting his uncle's
counting-house:

> [T]he consequence of his taking a dislike to us, and not making
> merry with us [today], is, as I think, that he loses some pleasant
> moments, which could do him no harm. I am sure he loses pleasanter
> companions than he can find in his own thoughts, either in his mouldy
> old office, or his dusty chambers. I mean to give him the same chance
> every year, whether he likes it or not, *for I pity him.* He may rail at
> Christmas *till he dies,* but he can't help thinking better of it—I defy
> him—if he finds me going there, in good temper, year after year, and
> saying Uncle Scrooge, how are you? If it only puts him in the vein
> to leave his poor clerk fifty pounds, *that's* something; and I think I
> shook him yesterday. [pp. 103–4; all but the final italics added]

The narrator then adds:

> It was their turn to laugh now, at the notion of his shaking Scrooge.
> But being thoroughly good-natured, and not much caring what they
> laughed at, so that they laughed at any rate, he [Scrooge's nephew]
> encouraged them in their merriment, and passed the bottle, joyously.
> [p. 104]

Such willingness to be laughed at anticipates (in the nephew)
that which happens (at the very end of the story) to Scrooge himself:

> Some people laughed to see the alteration in him, but he let them
> laugh, and little heeded them; for he was wise enough to know that
> nothing ever happened on this globe, for good, at which some people

did not have their fill of laughter in the outset; and knowing that such as these would be blind anyway, he thought it quite as well that they should wrinkle up their eyes in grins, as have the malady in less attractive forms. His own heart laughed: and that was quite enough for him. [p. 134]

Thus, both uncle and nephew are revealed to be more perceptive, more discerning, and hence perhaps wiser than most of their associates. Is the nephew correct in believing that Scrooge "can't help thinking better" of Christmas if he finds the nephew visiting him, "in good temper, year after year"? How often has the nephew gone there before? We are not told. Even so, the compassionate nephew does stand for the gentlemanly proposition that one should persist in doing what one believes to be right, without being much concerned about the likely futility of one's efforts.

The central question in our analysis of this story may well relate to the observation by the nephew which had moved the guests to laugh, "I think I shook him, yesterday." I have already suggested what it was that may have shaken Scrooge, the nephew's meeting him on his own ground with respect to the supposed correlation of poverty to misery and of wealth to happiness. We have noticed that Scrooge had been at a loss for words in response to his nephew's deadly query, "What right have you to be dismal? what reason have you to be morose? You're rich enough." (p. 48)

More significant, perhaps, than the nephew's effectiveness in checking Scrooge's attack on Christmas merriment is that the nephew *noticed* that Scrooge had indeed been checked, that he had been shaken. But even more significant, however, is that Scrooge himself may have noticed that the nephew had noticed that Scrooge had been shaken. For, I have suggested, this narrative may best be understood as Scrooge's dream—an introspective reverie in which Scrooge is able to step back and see what he has been up to all his life.

The central question in our analysis of the story is, then, What is there about Scrooge in his circumstances which accounts for, perhaps even justifies, his conversion? Critical to his salvation, I have also suggested, was his perceptiveness, his awareness of what his life past and present meant and what that life was tending to. It was no accident nor simply due to the ministrations of Jacob Marley (for what, after all, moved or permitted Marley to intervene?) that salvation came to Scrooge, but rather as the result of efforts on the part of others (such as his nephew). These efforts prompted Scrooge to face up to what had become of the vulnerable child abandoned decades before in a lonely schoolroom.

There is about this view of the matter something hopeful and reassuring, for it rests on the proposition (does it not?) that virtue is somehow dependent upon wisdom, that one can somehow learn to be good. Thus, cause and effect can be discerned and relied upon in the moral as in the physical universe: the conversion and salvation of Scrooge are, therefore, not mere happenstance. But, one might wonder, was Scrooge truly capable of the kind of perceptive soul-searching I have conjured up here?

It *is* said by the narrator, in his account of the transformation of the knocker into Marley's face, that "Scrooge had as little of what is called fancy about him as any man in the City of London." (p. 54) Does not "fancy" refer, as in the words of one dictionary, to a capricious or delusive sort of imagination? Such imagination is one thing— and Scrooge is *not* subject to that. But an imagination informed by an awareness of things, and of the implications or tendency of one's life, is quite another matter. (pp. 117, 124, 126)

That Scrooge is not simply *un*imaginative by nature is attested to in the course of the first episode presented in Christmas Past. As real in Scrooge's recollection as his former schoolmates are the images of characters in books he read as a neglected child, characters who came to him *then* (for his solace) as Marley and the other ghosts come to him *now* (for his "reclamation" [p. 69]). Notice how Scrooge recalls those storybook characters of Christmas Past:

> The Spirit touched him on the arm, and pointed to his younger self, intent upon his reading. Suddenly a man, in foreign garments: wonderfully real and distinct to look at: stood outside the window, with an axe stuck in his belt, and leading an ass laden with wood by the bridle.
>
> "Why, it's Ali Baba!" Scrooge exclaimed in ecstasy. "It's dear old honest Ali Baba! Yes, yes, I know! One Christmas time, when yonder solitary child was left here all alone, he *did* come, for the first time, just like that. Poor boy! And Valentine," said Scrooge, "and his wild brother, Orson; there they go! And what's his name, who was put down in his drawers, asleep, at the Gate of Damascus; don't you see

him! And the Sultan's Groom turned upside-down by the Genii; there
he is upon his head! Serve him right. I'm glad of it. What business
had *he* to be married to the Princess!"

To hear Scrooge expending all the earnestness of his nature on such
subjects, in a most extraordinary voice between laughing and crying;
and to see his heightened and excited face; would have been a surprise
to his business friends in the city, indeed.

"There's the Parrot!" cried Scrooge. "Green body and yellow tail,
with a thing like a lettuce growing out of the top of his head; there
he is! Poor Robin Crusoe, he called him, when he came home again
after sailing around the island. 'Poor Robin Crusoe, where have you
been, Robin Crusoe?' The man thought he was dreaming, but he
wasn't. It was the Parrot, you know. There goes Friday, running for
his life to the little creek! Halloa! Hoop! Halloo!"

Then, with a rapidity of transition very foreign to his usual character,
[Scrooge] said, *in pity* for his former self, "Poor boy!" and cried
again. [pp. 72–73; final italics added]

Scrooge is much moved by "yonder solitary child...left here
all alone": twice in the course of this recollection of storybook characters, he says, "in pity for his former self, 'Poor boy!'" This recollection, which has the effect of reviving that "former self" buried
deep within the single-minded businessman, moves Scrooge to tears:

"I wish," Scrooge muttered, putting his hand in his pocket, and
looking about him, after drying his eyes with his cuff: "but it's too
late now."

"What is the matter?" asked the Spirit.

"Nothing," said Scrooge. "Nothing. There was a boy singing a Christmas Carol at my door last night. I should like to have given him
something: that's all." [p. 73]

This is, in the book, Scrooge's first articulation of a desire to reform his former way of life. It is his first explicit repudiation of past
conduct—and it consists in the identification by him of one boy with
another, the identification of the abandoned child in the schoolroom
at Christmas time many years before with the chased-off singer of a
Christmas carol the evening before. Scrooge expresses the wish to act

more kindly to such a child as the caroler. Should he not be taken as now wanting to reenact toward that child (and to other children) the role long ago of the converted father toward the youthful Scrooge himself? (The first act of generosity on Scrooge's part, the Christmas morning after his fateful night, is toward still another little boy, the youngster whom he rewards liberally for serving as a messenger to the Poulterer's from whom the turkey will be purchased for the Cratchit family. [p. 129])

The importance of the revived child in Scrooge, a battered child so to speak, is attested to by the emphasis given in the book to Tiny Tim. I dare say that Scrooge feels more deeply about that rather trying youngster than many readers—but then, Scrooge may see in the crippled child something of himself. We return to Scrooge's relation to his mysterious father when we notice the report that Scrooge became "a second father" to Tiny Tim (p. 134), a child saved thereby from impending death of the body just as Scrooge himself is saved from impending death of the spirit.

I return for a moment to Scrooge's first expression of repentance, the desire to have given something to his Christmas Eve caroler. The narrator then adds, "The Ghost smiled thoughtfully, and waved its hand: saying as it did so, 'Let us see another Christmas!'" (p. 73)

This is the episode already referred to, of an older (but still youthful) Scrooge again abandoned at school. Things are even worse than the time before. "He was not reading now, but walking up and down despairingly." (p. 73) Scrooge watches the scene "with a mournful shaking of his head, glanc[ing] anxiously towards the door." (p. 73) Scrooge knows whence his deliverance will come, even as he feels deeply for the despairing boy, the schoolboy so burdened by dismay that he no longer takes refuge in imaginative reading. In this way, too, the Scrooge of the reader's Christmas Eve has within him both the moroseness noted by his nephew and the deliverance begun by his nephew—thereby repeating the pattern of that Christmas episode when the nephew's mother (Scrooge's sister) came to release her despairing brother from his holiday bondage.

There is prefigured, then, in these two schoolroom scenes, essentially what happens to the "mature" Scrooge we come to know. When he is moved to repent for his treatment of the youthful caroler, his redemption is decisively on its way.

vi

THE FIRST steps in Scrooge's conversion are the hardest, just as they might be in any sincere repentance. Indeed, Scrooge's night of intense soul-searching can be considered equivalent to a program of thoroughgoing therapy, all compressed into one long session. He is obliged to unearth, put together, and face up to diverse elements of his life, an enterprise initiated by the self-awareness pressed upon his consciousness by his Christmas Eve conversations.

Scrooge, in going back to childhood, becomes again as a child—in order to be "born again," an appropriate enough motif at Christmas time. (pp. 55, 128) He has to become helpless again, in order to see whether he can adopt a course different from that adopted by him the first time around. That course is suggested to him by the third episode presented by the Ghost of Christmas Past, the episode with Mr. Fezziwig, an employer of Scrooge's youth who does well by his associates, especially at Christmas. (pp. 75-77) Mr. Fezziwig's course is the one Scrooge does pursue upon his conversion: he throws himself into his nephew's party (as old Fezziwig had done); he becomes a generous employer of Bob Cratchit.

But Scrooge had not taken Fezziwig's generous route the first time around—and the reason is given in the next episode, that in which the parting of the ways is shown between Scrooge and his fiancée, Belle. The narrator reports of Scrooge:

> He was older now; a man in the prime of life. His face had not the harsh and rigid lines of later years; but it had begun to wear the signs of care and avarice. There was an eager, greedy, restless motion in the eye, which showed the passion that had taken root, and where the shadow of the growing tree would fall. [p. 79]

Belle tells him that a golden idol had displaced her. And she says to him in a benevolent spirit, "[I] f it can cheer and comfort you in time to come, as I would have tried to do, I have no just cause to grieve." (p. 79) Scrooge justifies his acquisitiveness in this fashion: "This is the even-handed dealing of the world! There is nothing on which it is so hard as poverty; and there is nothing it professes to condemn with such severity as the pursuit of wealth!" Her reply is:

You fear the world too much. All your other hopes have merged into
the hope of being beyond the chance of its sordid reproach. I have
seen your nobler aspirations fall off one by one, until the master-
passion, Gain, engrosses you. Have I not? [p. 79]

That which the girl had tried to tell him in her gentle way, experience has moved Scrooge to learn the hard way: the fruitlessness
of the approach he had taken out of fear of the world and in his effort
to avoid the helplessness of poverty. At this point in his recollections,
there is an exchange between Scrooge and the Ghost:

"Spirit!" said Scrooge, "show me no more! Conduct me home. Why
do you delight to torture me?"

"One shadow more!" exclaimed the Ghost.

"No more!" cried Scrooge. "No more. I don't wish to see it. Show
me no more!"

But the relentless Ghost pinioned him in both his arms, and forced
him to observe what happened next. [p. 81]

What he is next shown is an episode of seven years before, the
night Jacob Marley had died. For Scrooge, Marley had become Belle's
replacement—and Scrooge sat alone in his office as his partner died.
(p. 83) But the episode shown him is neither about himself nor about
Marley's death but about the happy, fruitful life enjoyed by Belle
and the man fortunate enough to have married her. This is an episode
Scrooge had never previously witnessed but which (it would seem) he
had come to sense that he could not bear to contemplate. The narrator reports:

And now Scrooge looked on more attentively than ever, when the
master of the house, having his daughter leaning fondly on him, sat
down with her and her mother at his own fireside; and when he
thought that such another creature, quite as graceful and full of
promise, might have called him father, and been a spring-time in the
haggard winter of his life, his sight grew very dim indeed. [p. 82]

Had not Scrooge, a man with an ability to calculate, come to the
recognition that he had gotten the worst of the bargain in his effort
to protect himself against the vagaries of life? Seven years before, he

was (as he has Belle's husband report to her) already "[q]uite alone in the world." (p. 83) It is at this point that Scrooge insists to the Ghost, "Remove me! I cannot bear it!" And, as is usually true of dreamers, he controls the duration of his dream—this part of his dream—as he seizes an extinguisher-cap and presses it down upon the head of the Ghost of Christmas Past in an effort to hide the light illuminating a past which he had come to see the misery of.

Once Scrooge has come to terms with his past, by recognizing it for what it is, he can then bear to consider the present and, even more formidable, the future. He can, among other things, face up to the kind of death—the death of himself and the death of others—which his present course of life leads to. Having so faced up to death (that death which he dreads as the extreme of helplessness), he is prepared for a radical reclamation. The most difficult task before Scrooge, when he returns to the world of the living, is to go to his nephew's house on Christmas Day: "He passed the door a dozen times, before he had the courage to go up and knock. But he made a dash, and did it . . ." (p. 131) It had proved far easier to be generous to the messenger-boy sent to the Poulterer's and to make amends to the gentlemen who had solicited money for the poor the evening before, and it was to prove far easier (the following morning) to reform his relations with Bob Cratchit.

Perhaps Scrooge's marked hesitation before the visit to his nephew's house confirms what I have suggested about the importance of his encounter with his nephew in the counting-house the evening before. It had been in that encounter, more than anywhere else, that Scrooge had had to face up to the fact that his way of life, of which he had been so confident, had not produced for him the results he had bargained for. It had been the nephew, in his comment on Scrooge (as presented by the Ghost of Christmas Present), who had made the decisive assessment of Scrooge's way of life:

> He's a comical old fellow, that's the truth: and not so pleasant as he might be. However, his offences carry their own punishment, and I have nothing to say against him. [p. 102]

And, the nephew had gone on to say (echoing his decisive exchange with his uncle the evening before): "His wealth is of no use to him. He don't do any good with it. He don't make himself comfortable with it. He hasn't the satisfaction of thinking—ha, ha, ha!—that he is ever going to benefit Us with it." (pp. 102-3)

To speak thus is to account not only for Scrooge's deliverance but also for the form it takes. Otherwise, that deliverance may seem mysterious, perhaps even unjust (in that he is permitted to escape the misery he deserves). This, then, is not a miraculous deliverance but one rooted in Scrooge's character, in his understanding of the world and in his calculations concerning what he fears and what he longs for. No doubt, the appearance of a miraculous rebirth contributes to the engaging nature of this story, which has delighted multitudes for more than a century. But even more interesting is to see how the dramatic miracle works—and also how an artist of genius works and what he understands about the movements of the human soul, waking and dreaming alike. Indeed, it is because the artist senses what souls are like, thereby striking a responsive chord in soulful readers, that works such as this have an enduring effect.[174]

vii

BUT TO say that an artist has an enduring effect is not to say, of course, that what he does should never be questioned.

It may be somewhat a matter of chance whether a presentation such as Dickens's becomes sentimental. At times, some will think—particularly in the treatment of the Cratchit family, especially of Tiny Tim—Dickens goes too far. But the unduly pathetic is corrected, or at least moderated, by the humor employed—much of it exaggerated, some of it fairly subtle, all of it good-natured. It is corrected as well by the reader's tendency to remember Scrooge more as a rogue than as a saint. We are given very little of the converted Scrooge—just a few pages. After all, what is there to say about him then? There is not much variety, and hence dramatic interest, in thoroughgoing goodness.

A question should be raised, if only in passing, about the status of death in the stories of Dickens. Is not Scrooge's terror of death made too much of and, in effect, legitimated by this story? Does not this legitimation reflect the modern attitude—an attitude of deep-rooted anxiety in the face of that death which threatens the continuation of the self, of the individuality, we make so much of today? This considerable concern about death, which Dickens repeatedly puts to dramatic use, may be seen as well in the remarkable role assigned to food and drink in this and other Christmas-season tales by Dickens. The virtue of liberality is endorsed—but at the cost of at least the virtue of temperance—so much so that Dickens's accounts do remain the most exuberant accounts of what Christmas feasting should be like.

Does not glorying in food and drink assert, in a crude way, that one is truly alive? May it not be for many, and perhaps even for Dickens himself, an effort to repress the terrors of death?

There may be, in short, something corrosive and corrupting in Dickens's attitude toward death.[175]

viii

I HAVE been touching upon the question of what Dickens considers a truly good man. Virtues such as temperance sometimes seem to be sacrificed by him to the fellow-feeling evident in an enthusiastic liberality.

One should pose the question of the status for Dickens of still another virtue, that of justice. This naturally leads, in turn, to the question of what Dickens considers a good community.

. One effect of Scrooge's avarice, it can be argued, is that he does accumulate the wealth required for effective charity. It can also be argued that the thrift practiced by Scrooge is desirable, if not even necessary, if there is to be available as well the capital required for steady industrial development and thereby a systematic alleviation of old-fashioned poverty.

Scrooge does have (before his conversion) that ability which many of the poor, it seems, simply do not have, the ability to defer gratification of ordinary desires. "[D]arkness is cheap, and Scrooge liked it." (p. 55) "External heat and cold had little influence on Scrooge." (p. 46) He can live a simple life and be satisfied with it— or, at least, be reconciled to it. He can be depended upon to live up to his bargains, to deliver what he promises to deliver, to pay what he promises to pay. (pp. 45, 133) He believes in minding his own business—and, it turns out, he is open to reconsideration of what is truly one's business. (pp. 51, 62, 115)

Scrooge is, in his way, a reliable man—and we depend on the likes of him for the remarkably high economic standard of living to which we are accustomed. The unconverted Scrooge places an emphasis upon social reforms, upon political efforts, to deal (as efficiently

as a sound economy permits) with the inevitable ills of modern industrial life. (pp. 51, 108–9) Dickens himself, if not also Scrooge after
his conversion, seems to have been skeptical about the usefulness of
political endeavor. He may have come to political endeavor from
too low a level to appreciate its genuine scope. (p. 49) He much preferred, in dealing with problems of the day, to rely upon personal
influence. (This may help account for the dependence of Dickens's
stories upon remarkable coincidences to make things work out
right.)

To say as we often do that commercial industrialization may be
the most efficient way to organize the economic exploitation of natural and human resources is not to deny that the characters of many
of the people caught up in such an impersonal enterprise may be
stunted. Such a life easily degenerates into a frantic pursuit of private
pleasures, into a more and more desperate concern about one's self.
Dickens's remarkably popular melodrama about Ebenezer Scrooge, a
modern-day Faust of the marketplace, can provide a corrective.

Among the salutary efforts made by Dickens are his repeated
endorsements of festivals, particularly Christmas, which prompt privileged men to commune from time to time with their "fellow-passengers
to the grave," to establish a humanizing contact with others in a highly
mobile society that ordinarily tends toward anonymous isolation.
Dickens makes a great deal of festivals associated with family life,
however, perhaps inadvertently reinforcing thereby the tendency of
modern men to make too much of personal existence (and hence of
death?). That is, the festivals he promotes are not primarily patriotic
occasions.

Even so, Dickens does condemn self-centeredness. The self-
centered are characterized by a lack of grace and of graciousness.
They are too much concerned with themselves, especially with what
they take to be their preservation, to be open to or to care for others.
A Christmas Carol should promote among a commercial people good-
natured compassion and a useful cheerfulness—and may help guard
against that patriotism which degenerates into a ruthless, death-defying
nationalism.

ix

ITS GRAPHIC descriptions of London and of English life in the middle of the nineteenth century no doubt contribute to the enduring

charm of *A Christmas Carol.* So does the simple fact that Dickens *can* write. Besides, his heart is, as we say, in the right place in his appeals to children and to the childlike in us.

That Dickens can write well is suggested, as we saw at the outset of these remarks, by the high praise he has again and again received during the past century. I return to the comparison of Dickens with Aeschylus and Shakespeare provided us (providentially enough) by a classical scholar.

The best known stories of redemption and rehabilitation by Aeschylus and Shakespeare may well be *The Oresteia* and *The Tempest.* In both of these tales redemption can be understood to depend ultimately upon political (including divine) rearrangements, not upon family circumstances or personal inclinations. In Dickens's stories, on the other hand, virtues, misconduct, and remedies are of a tamer, or more domestic, variety.

The move, then, from Aeschylus and Shakespeare to authors such as Dickens may reflect a shift from political concerns to private concerns, from a concern with justice to a concern with personal salvation. One finds that the petty and the common often do interest moderns more than the grandiose and the noble. (This shift is central to this book, as we move from Shakespeare to Joyce.)

Are we to understand that the deep-rooted concerns of, say, *The Oresteia* have been taken care of, once and for all—so much so that we can safely devote ourselves to promoting benevolence and charity? Or have those once all-consuming concerns merely been concealed from view, only to erupt in ever more destructive forms from time to time because they have not been properly tended to by moderns dedicated to a determined pursuit of private happiness?

Dickens *is* more sentimental, and otherwise more limited, than Aeschylus and Shakespeare were—or were permitted by their more discerning publics to become. Yet, cannot much be said *among us* for the generous festival of Christmas as Dickens fostered it? If that *is* the case, we should not permit "unhallowed hands" (p. 45) to mishandle the salutary parable with which he has endowed us.

VII. HERMAN MELVILLE

(1819-1891)

> *"At least," said Latimer, "he died by violence.*
> *That is something very like justice."*
> *"Ah!" The Colonel leaned forward. "There*
> *is the writer speaking. Everything must be tidy,*
> *artistic, like a* roman policier.*"*
>
> —Eric Ambler, *A Coffin for Dimitrios,* chap. II

i

A VITAL question for the reader of *Moby Dick* is why it is that Ishmael survives.

The artist could have presented the thought and sentiments of someone such as Ishmael—of an Ishmael who perishes with his shipmates—had he desired to do so. To assume there would have been no story except by having Ishmael survive, or that the interior motions of characters could not have been otherwise presented, is to cast doubt upon the artist's capacity. Shakespeare, for example, shows in his plays profound movements of the soul without any narrator. Ishmael himself gets behind the public faces of various of the characters he presents. (See, for example, pp. 166–67, 196–201, 210–13, 471.)

Nor does it seem that Ishmael's survival is dictated by the Christian parallel upon which his story, if not the book as a whole, draws. The voyage of the *Pequod* does begin on Christmas day, the day of a celebrated birth; it ends with the survival, even in a sense the resurrection, of Ishmael after a fateful three days of deadly struggle. Indeed, he comes to life, returns to life (so to speak) riding a coffin. But we must wonder, granting the Christian parallel, why it is that this particular character should be the one "resurrected." (See p. 228.)

That is, what *sense* does it make that Ishmael survives? And sense there must be (I argue in this book) if things are to be interesting and worthy of study. Chance does not make sense. Is that not what chance means, a senseless occurrence? Chance developments are not truly

---

All citations in the text of this chapter to *Moby Dick* are to the Modern Library edition (New York, 1926).

instructive, morally or otherwise, except to the extent that they may point up the fragility and limitations of human life. Accidents do happen, of course, including the accident of various illnesses. But accidents are not usually matters of regret and self-recrimination in the way that misjudgment and moral inadequacy are.

There exists in literature an instructive relation between an "unnatural" death and folly. We have seen that this relation is exhibited, and counted upon, by the greatest artists. Is it not reassuring to be reminded that folly is dangerous? Does that not make it worthwhile for us to try to be sensible? Is there not indicated thereby a path to spiritual salvation if not physical safety?[176]

But before addressing directly the appropriateness of Ishmael's survival, let us briefly consider a related illuminating question. Is not the destruction of the *Pequod* fitting? Is it not "realistic," and hence satisfying, however sobering it may also be, that the *Pequod* should go down with all hands? Does not this "disaster" make sense, so much so that it is highly instructive? Does it not reflect the nature of things —and the finer that reflection, the better the book?

The *Pequod* disaster is not merely a matter of "dramatic necessity." This is not to say, however, that the participants do not in any way act for the sake of a story: there *is* here a dramatic challenge (and hence a story) which catches them up and shapes their fate. This challenge may be, in part, a matter of chance. Captain Ahab *is* special —and he lays before them a prospect which this particular crew cannot resist. (pp. 161–65, 176, 414, 501)

It is indicated many times during the story that the *Pequod* is destined for destruction. (See, for example, pp. 91–94, 104, 105–6, 119, 145, 186, 209–10.) These intimations are proper: if an outcome does follow from the nature of things, it should not come as a surprise. The very name of the ship is proper, also pointing up as it does the wholeness (or oneness) of things: it is the name of an ancient, extinct Indian tribe. (p. 68) When things are just right—that is, when chance is not decisive—do not the appearance, the substance, and the name of a thing reinforce one another?

We do not become sentimental about the ship's destruction; lamentation is not called for. One might even say (despite the regret one might have about the fate of such men as the equivocating First Mate, Starbuck) that the crew earned the end they were awarded.

They were worthy of such a fate: they had to work at it, to persevere through many difficulties to achieve it. Their fate is better than that of most whalers. But then, most whaling captains are not moved as Ahab was by the great white whale, that monster which the monstrous Ahab somehow sees as the embodiment of all the evil in the universe. (See, for example, pp. 162, 186.)

It is the gift of the artist which can help us see, through graphic particulars, that which is universal. We need not be familiar with whales and whaling to be able to assess the various responses to the whale encountered among the whaling ships in this book—the responses of fear or skepticism or prudence or regret or Ahabian single-mindedness.[177] The story of the chase of the white whale by the *Pequod* is the story of the lives and deaths of men determined to come to terms with what they consider a hostile, or at least a dangerous, world.

There is no question that Ahab risks all and that he is entitled to the dignity of a fitting end. Ahab *is* a man of action, and he sees every death as due to the blow of an enemy, not as a natural event to be accepted gracefully. (p. 499) It would not do for the aging Ahab to die of pneumonia, or for his crew to give up after only a couple days of the final chase. The reader knows that the *Pequod* crew had gone along with its captain; it had ratified his perhaps mad or blasphemous purpose. Otherwise, the reader might be tempted to conclude that the universe is presented as malign, in that all are destroyed, regardless of their quality and deeds. There *is* about the *Pequod* something which can be considered self-annihilative—something which can remind one of, say, the noble (but not necessarily just) Antigone of Sophocles.[178]

No doubt, there are significant responses to something such as the great white whale other than those of the *Pequod* and its captain. There is, for example, the response of a Socrates, who would find the whale curious and an occasion for calm study. (p. 50) But *most* of the responses among the other whalers, as we have noticed, are hardly Socratic. Rather, they too are self-annihilative, but of a tamer sort, of a sort which is not worthy of extended telling and reflection. "To produce a mighty book, you must choose a mighty theme. No great and enduring volume can be written on the flea, though many there be who have tried it." (p. 452) (Consider, in this connection, what Franz Kafka attempted to do with "a gigantic insect" in *The Metamorphosis*. Consider, as well, Ovid's *Metamorphoses*.)

ii

THE SURVIVAL of Ishmael suggests that a certain discrimination guides the ordering of things.

Of course, Ishmael too had endorsed Ahab's bold project. He is swept along by Ahab, but not permanently, not in the deepest part of his soul. He does see himself joining the crew as it is moved by Ahab. But to *see* oneself thus is not fully to join? Thus, the narrator can begin Chapter 41 with the observation, "I, Ishmael, was one of that crew; my shouts had gone up with the rest; my oath had been welded with theirs..." But he immediately adds, "[A]nd stronger I shouted, and more did I hammer and clinch my oath, because of the dread in my soul." (p. 176)

Ishmael concludes this chapter with these observations:

> Here, then, was this grey-headed, ungodly old man, chasing with curses a Job's whale round the world, at the head of a crew, too, chiefly made up of mongrel renegades, and castaways, and cannibals —morally enfeebled also, by the incompetence of mere unaided virtue or right-mindedness in Starbuck, the invulnerable jollity of indifference and recklessness in Stubb, and the pervading mediocrity in Flask. Such a crew, so officered, seemed specially picked and packed by some infernal fatality to help him to his monomaniac revenge. How it was that they so aboundingly responded to the old man's ire—by what evil magic their souls were possessed, that at times his hate seemed almost theirs; the White Whale as much their insufferable foe as his; how all this came to be—what the White Whale was to them, or how to their unconscious understandings, also, in some dim, unsuspected way, he might have seemed the gliding great demon of the seas of life,—all this to explain, would be to dive deeper than Ishmael can go. The subterranean miner that works in us all, how can one tell whither leads his shaft by the ever shifting, muffled sound of his pick? Who does not feel the irresistible arm drag? What skiff in tow of a seventy-four can stand still? For one, I gave myself up to the abandonment of the time and the place; but while yet all a-rush to encounter the whale, could see naught in that brute but the deadliest ill. [p. 186]

Ishmael's reservations are evident throughout. What the crew had abandoned themselves to, he had indicated earlier, was Ahab's "audacious, immitigable, and supernatural revenge." (p. 186)

It can even be said that only Ahab and Ishmael took the whale seriously. Ishmael can begin the following chapter (Chapter 42), "What the white male was to Ahab, has been hinted; what, at times, he was to me, as yet remains unsaid." Thus, Ishmael can both feel and observe. A mere observer would be "dead," in a way different from physical destruction—and yet Ishmael is not fully "engaged." Thus, he is watching himself, even in his passion.

Moby Dick opens with the celebrated introduction, "Call me Ishmael." That is, "Call me Outcast" (or outsider), not "Call me Survivor." Survival is not critical. Indeed, is not he who is concerned primarily with survival most apt to perish? (Did we not see this in Ebenezer Scrooge?) An outcast is on the fringes of the action—and Ishmael remains an outcast (or castaway) to the very end. "Orphan" is what he calls himself as he is buoyed up by the coffin. It is the last word in the book.

Very little is told about Ishmael's family circumstances. An unfriendly stepmother is recalled. (pp. 25–26) Are we not meant to recall Sarah and her harsh treatment of the original cast-out Ishmael? Ishmael tells few of his personal experiences, once he is on the ship: the sense of self is subdued. He is, somehow, a perennial innocent. He is never fully engaged for long; he accepts various impositions and innovations, even a fierce-looking savage and his idol, with an open mind. (Do we not meet this receptive innocent again in *Huckleberry Finn?*)

Ishmael escapes the fate of the others because he can move off to one side and watch. Unlike officers such as Starbuck, he has neither the opportunity nor the obligation to stop Ahab in what he is trying to do. One might even say that all that happens in *Moby Dick* is, in some sense, done *for* Ishmael: he (and perhaps he alone) recognizes the sense of all this; most do not see all that he sees. Like Jonah, he is destined to survive and to deliver his message about how things are.[179]

How Ishmael knows all that he narrates remains a nice question. A good deal he observed himself, of course; some things he may have been told; other things he perhaps figured out. He has been whaling many times (p. 289)—but since the voyage on the *Pequod* was his first on a whaler, he must have gone out often thereafter. He seems to have kept looking for something (if not Moby Dick), a search which makes him somewhat sympathetic to Ahab himself. (But Ahab is the captain, and Ishmael is among the lowest of the common sailors. Do they ever talk to one another?)

Perhaps Ishmael's survival rests in part, as I have indicated, upon his refusal to make primary either survival or Ahab's passion or the prospect of gain (which is another way of talking about survival?). Consider, as indicative of his cast of mind, his reflections on the dangers of the whale-lines, which can sweep men out of the whale-boat and drag them into the depths of the sea:

> All men live enveloped in whale-lines. All are born with halters round their necks; but it is only when caught in the swift, sudden turn of death, that mortals realize the silent, subtle, everpresent perils of life. And if you be a philosopher, though seated in the whale-boat, you would not at heart feel one whit more of terror, than though seated before your evening fire with a poker, and not a harpoon, by your side. [p. 282]

Our Democritus of the cemetery comes to mind. (See Prologue, Section iii, above. See, also, pp. 112, 156–57, 564.)

Ishmael as outcast—and hence as survivor—is revealed by the manner of his escape from the fate of his fellow crewmen. The artist could have placed him on another ship (if only temporarily) or otherwise provided for his safety. Rather, he has Ishmael thrown from one of the whale-boats and left at a distance from the final, fatal encounter with Moby Dick. (pp. 562, 565) Thus, Ishmael is literally cast out, left on the fringes of the action: close enough to observe and to be threatened, yet distant enough to escape with his life and with his story.

iii

THE ADVANTAGES of being cast out may be quickly noticed. Survival does follow from it, but it is not for the sake of survival alone that it should be prized. Although survival cannot become the end-all of existence, it *is* critical to certain vital developments in man. Still, unless survival is defined as the full development of what is best in man, it should not become one's central concern. The danger is, of course, that without the proper attitude toward survival one might become either wastefully reckless or unduly cautious, so reckless as to destroy oneself prematurely or so cautious as to become nothing and thus perish ignobly.

To be an outcast—to be on the fringe of the action—may mean that one is shirking one's duty. Or it may mean—and here we are talking of Ishmael, of the artist—that one may properly stand aside and watch. One is thereby able to observe and judge what partisans cannot. One may even be obliged, as well as encouraged, to examine what others take for granted. One may be better able, thereby, to see the universe as a whole.[180] The outcast steps back from the universe, so to speak; but when stationed where Ishmael is, he is also inside, looking out, experiencing and feeling what others do.

The advantages of being cast out can be summed up: As an outcast the sensitive Ishmael is permitted to bring this tale to our attention. He has his art: he can both learn and relate what he has learned. Art makes (or, as we have seen, finds) the sense in things. Compare Ahab. He cannot come to terms with the great whale in any other way than by attacking it: it does not suffice for him to observe, to try to understand, and thereafter to relate what he has observed and understood. His temperament, unlike Ishmael's, is very much engaged in the voyage and its doings. (pp. 4, 560)

Ishmael can step out of himself and watch. As an observer, he is invulnerable: after all, is it not true that it is only the "self" in one which can be destroyed?[181]

But an undue emphasis upon the advantages of being an outcast leads to a confusion of art with mere bohemianism. And this is what has become of much so-called art today: artists today seem bohemian to a degree, or in a way, that was not true of the Greek dramatists or of Shakespeare or even of the exiled Dante.

This bohemian emphasis leads to an indulgence in self-expression, not only on the part of artists but among intellectuals generally. But artists are even more dependent than intellectuals are on nature—and so this indulgence in the self leads to distortion and a lack of disciplined storytelling, so much so that poets lose their popular appeal.[182]

Indulgence in self-expression often leads to arrogance and even inhumanity. Certainly, irresponsibility results from the depreciation of tradition, of community, and, as I have said, of nature. One comes to believe that rebelliousness is good for its own sake: growth is seen to consist in striking out against whatever is established, rather than in rising above the city which has made possible the development of one's talents. And all this, in turn, can lead to the weakening of serious personal ties, to a deep loneliness, even to that dreadful abyss which is said to be awaiting us on either side of the uncertain path (discovered by reason) along which men are said to be groping.

Thus, the very separatism which contributes to the useful detachment of the artist can be his *and our* undoing. Art should be at least salutary. Deadly truths—if, indeed, the truth is deadly—should be carefully dealt with if art is not to be either paralyzed (and paralyzing) or otherwise irresponsible in doing what it (and perhaps only it) can do by trying to make human beings out of most citizens.

It is not accidental that Ishmael is a schoolmaster on land. The typical schoolmaster is, to some degree, a citizen, one who is concerned to transmit from one generation to another what he and others have learned.

Whatever the limitations of citizenship—of that partisanship which conceals from view both one's own faults and one's enemies' virtues—the city can make available traditions, skills, and opportunities critical to the development and use of those outcasts who do happen to have artistic gifts.

We turn now, in the chapters that follow, to a series of outcasts (voluntary exiles, for the most part) who have made a variety of intriguing efforts (characteristic of moderns?) to escape the prosaic everyday world of change and chance, of prudence and morality.

VIII. MATTHEW ARNOLD

(1822-1888)

> *In a few words, most reports are false, and the
> timidity of men gives fresh force to lies and un-
> truths. As a general rule, everyone is more in-
> clined to believe the bad than the good. Every-
> one is inclined to magnify the bad in some
> measure, and although the perils thus reported
> subside like the waves of the sea, yet like them
> they rise again without any apparent cause. Firm
> in reliance on his own better convictions, the
> leader must stand fast like the rock on which
> the wave breaks. The role is not an easy one; he
> who is not by nature of a buoyant disposition
> or has not been trained and his judgment streng-
> thened by experience in war may let it be his
> rule to do violence to his own inner conviction,
> and incline from the side of fear to the side of
> hope. Only by that means will he be able to
> maintain a true balance.*
>
> —Karl von Clausewitz, *On War*, I, vi

i

MATTHEW ARNOLD'S "Dover Beach" is said to be "the most widely
reprinted poem in the [English] language."[183] It has also been said to
be Arnold's one great poem.[184] Certainly, it is his best poem, published
quite late in his career as a poet (when he was in his late forties) but
written almost two decades earlier.[185] Arnold lived two more decades
after this publication, devoting himself to criticism and essays, rather
than to poetry, while he worked as a quite influential inspector of
schools.

"Dover Beach" is a poem which has moved men deeply—and
continues to do so, including men considered tough and confident.
Even those who "do not in the least agree with it" hear in it "a ma-
jestic music."[186] Algernon Swinburne said of it, upon its publication,
"[I]t has a grand choral cadence as of steady surges, regular in reso-
nance, not fitful or gusty, but antiphonal and reverberate."[187] Pre-

cisely how Arnold achieved his effects has been suggested by critics who have analyzed his use of sounds and meanings, his use of open vowels,[188] his use of rhyme patterns and rhythms which somehow suggest the movement of the sea.[189]

I once heard that the French consider "cellar door" perhaps the most beautiful set of sounds in the English language. Who knows what arrangements of sounds affect us, why and how? I am inclined, therefore, to leave to others the no doubt useful study of the technical make-up of poems. Besides, we have it on the authority of T.S. Eliot —whose disillusioned *Waste Land* has been said to have been anticipated by "Dover Beach"[190] —that Arnold's poetry has "little technical interest."[191]

I proceed (here as elsewhere in this book) on the assumption that an enduring artistic effect in literature rests ultimately upon thoughts of some significance, that there is an intimate relation between the form of a work and the truth it attempts to present. It seems particularly appropriate to proceed as I do in talking about a poem which itself makes an argument about the relation of appearance and reality. What, then, does "Dover Beach" say?

There are three kinds of answers one can make to this question. The first answer is simply this:

DOVER BEACH

The sea is calm tonight.
The tide is full, the moon lies fair
Upon the straits;—on the French coast the light
Gleams and is gone; the cliffs of England stand,
Glimmering and vast, out in the tranquil bay.   5
Come to the window, sweet is the night-air!
Only, from the long line of spray
Where the sea meets the moon-blanched land,
Listen! you hear the grating roar
Of pebbles which the waves draw back, and fling,   10
At their return, up the high strand,
Begin and cease, and then again begin
With tremulous cadence slow, and bring
The eternal note of sadness in.

Sophocles long ago   15
Heard it on the Aegean, and it brought
Into his mind the turbid ebb and flow

Of human misery; we
Find also in the sound a thought,
Hearing it by this distant northern sea.   20

The Sea of Faith
Was once, too, at the full, and round earth's shore
Lay like folds of a bright girdle furled.
But now I only hear
Its melancholy, long, withdrawing roar,   25
Retreating, to the breath
Of the night-wind, down the vast edges drear
And naked shingles of the world.

Ah, love, let us be true
To one another! for the world, which seems   30
To lie before us like a land of dreams,
So various, so beautiful, so new,
Hath really neither joy, nor love, nor light,
Nor certitude, nor peace, nor help for pain;
And we are here as on a darkling plain   35
Swept with confused alarms of struggle and flight,
Where ignorant armies clash by night.

Except where there is a serious problem with the text of a poem,[192]
it is satisfying to let a poem speak thus for itself.

ii

THIS ANSWER alone does not promote discussion, except, perhaps, discussion about how various lines are to be read. This sometimes depends, of course, upon how they should be understood. Indeed, it can be argued, one's first reading is tentative, serving as an
aid to understanding what is truly being said.

The second answer to the question, What does this poem say?,
consists of a paraphrase of the thought of the poem. By suggesting
and restating, a paraphrase can, perhaps, guide one in one's readings,
especially if the paraphrase recognizes what is supplied to the meaning of a poem by its form. What, then, does "Dover Beach" say?

There are in this poem thirty-seven lines distributed among four
stanzas. It is convenient to divide the poem into three parts: the first
part consists of the first stanza of fourteen lines; the second part con-

sists of the second and third stanzas totaling fourteen lines also; the
third part consists of the final stanza of nine lines.

The first part (lines 1–14) presents a seaside setting, an idyllic
setting. The narrator describes the scene; he calls someone (his beloved, we learn later) to the window to share with him the sweet night
air and, perhaps, the scene of calm sea, full tide, and massive cliffs in
the moonlight. But there are at least two threats to the idyllic. One
threat, the unsteady light on the French coast, suggests change, even
deterioration, and uncertainty. The other threat is conveyed by "the
grating roar/ Of pebbles which the waves draw back, and fling." There
is heard, in this "tremulous cadence slow," "the eternal note of sadness." Perhaps these threats had been anticipated by the final word
in the first line, "The sea is calm tonight." Perhaps, indeed, that "tonight" should have put us on notice that what seems true of the sea,
and of whatever the sea stands for, is true only for the moment: it has
not been calm before; it will not be calm after. Is this too didactic?
But, then, this *is* a rather didactic poem—one of the most moving
didactic poems in the English language.

That "eternal note of sadness" invites the two sets of recollections found in the next part of the poem (lines 15–28). The narrator
recalls that Sophocles heard in the movement of the sea "the turbid
ebb and flow of human misery." That recollection leads to "a thought"
about what is heard by the narrator in the sound of the sea, a thought
about what is happening to the once-full Sea of Faith and about how
the world is stripped to the sound of the "melancholy, long, withdrawing roar" of the retreating sea.[193]

What the ebbing of the Sea of Faith means is developed further
in the concluding part of the poem (lines 29–37): the hopes of the
day are said to be illusory; the reality is that of a dismal chaos. This
concluding description of the world is introduced by the resolution
that the narrator and his beloved should "be true to one another."
The images conjured up at the end are not of the sea but of armies
clashing on "a darkling plain." Is this plain the land left after the Sea
of Faith receded, a ready ground for purposeless struggle? Is this the
new land, reclaimed land so to speak, which had been promised by
those who had ventured to push back the Sea of Faith? We notice
that nothing is added to the description of the scene at Dover once
the reflections begin at line 13. One might also wonder what reflections might be induced when the narrator truly looks at his beloved.

With these last remarks, however, we have moved from paraphrase to commentary. Still, it should be further noticed, even a paraphrase is not possible without some implicit commentary, some overriding opinion about what is happening and what is important. Even so, our paraphrase has been rather restrained, since some points that might have been included in it have been reserved for the commentary that follows. But repetitions cannot be avoided in this chapter.

iii

A COMMENTARY is included in the third answer one can make to the question, What does this poem say? Any serious effort to set forth what anything says must include an assessment of the soundness of the opinions which are assumed or set forth. After all, as we have seen, one of the most critical things that can be known about any statement is whether it is true.

We can begin to assess the narrator's statement by considering, first, the distant history that he uses to reinforce, if not even to validate, his recent survey of the Sea of Faith. To proceed thus may seem to exhibit an unpoetic turn of mind. However, does not the narrator himself feel and say what he does because of what he believes himself to *know* about the past? Is not the effect of the poem achieved, in large part, because of the theory of history it incorporates? Ever since the Greeks, it seems to say, thoughtful men of a sensitive bent of mind—that is to say, artists—have known certain things about human existence. Without such an invocation of history, the poem expresses no more than a fleeting personal mood.

What, then, *did* Sophocles, and people like him, believe? Did *he* see the life of man primarily in terms of the ebb and flow of human misery? Is there not in Sophocles' work—in the seven plays we have, and which (I believe) Arnold also had before him—something of the heroic, of the moments of grandeur in life, as well as of the rise and fall of misery? One can see the heroic even in Sophocles' last play, in which the blind and battered Oedipus, on the edge of the grave, fiercely justifies himself before he is transfigured into something almost divine.

The narrator's second excursion into history finds him lamenting the retreat of the Sea of Faith: but are we not meant to understand that there was a time—since Sophocles, of course—when man enjoyed a full faith? That time, presumably, was not a time of misery.

But if not a time of misery, was it a condition for mankind that the narrator's Sophocles did not anticipate?

It is important that the narrator invokes Sophocles. Various Stoics could have been recollected as having seen life in terms of an ebb and flow of human misery. Or the narrator could have invoked an ancient historian. (In his closing lines the narrator does seem to have drawn upon a famous description by Thucydides of a nocturnal battle during the Peloponnesian War. Thucydides' history *is* permeated by a note of noble sadness. It is not a sadness, however, in which the personal predominates.) The narrator seems to want the authority of a poet in order to be as persuasive as he is.

Sophocles *can* be understood to stand for classical antiquity. But the lesson of the classics seems to me somewhat different from the lesson learned by the narrator. The tragic poets drew upon the heroic and the grand; the classical philosphers endorsed the urbane, the witty, and the great-souled. Certainly, the student of the classics is encouraged not to take himself too seriously, while the lover, especially the modern lover, cannot help but make much of himself. Indeed, one can add, the classic emphasis upon self-sufficiency makes the modern emphasis on love dubious.[194]

Does this narrator suffer from knowing too much—or from not knowing enough? He takes a long view of human history; he is consequently disheartened with what he believes others to have seen. But his problem may be that he does not take a long enough view or a deep enough look.[195] Is the narrator serious about trying to understand things? He does invoke terms ("faith" and "true" and "ignorant") that point to understanding as eminently desirable. Sophocles evidently derived solace from seeing how things really are. Is the narrator that kind of man?

In any event, it can be a serious mistake to read the classics through our eyes rather than truly learning from them.[196] This can be worse than *not* reading them at all: a misreading can suppress or distort the promptings of nature by which we might otherwise be guided.

iv

BUT, THE modern will immediately respond, the promptings of nature point to the importance of love, love as ordinarily conceived, in human affairs. And it is upon the invocation of love that the poem can be felt to turn. Although very little is said explicitly about love—only a line and a half—love is very much relied upon. Is love one of those things about which the less said, the better—especially if what is said is put in the form of systematic examination rather than in the form of the soulful (but not threatening) repetition of stock sentiments heard, say, in popular music? We must venture, nevertheless, to say something about the place of love in this poem.

Curiously little *is* said about love, even though love is critical to the resolution of the narrator's problem. What is love here? Love is emphasized as ministering to need. But is it really love, if one has to argue, from desperate need, "[L]et us be true to one another"? Has love thus become a crutch, or a device, used to conceal from oneself (or, at least, to permit one to bear) unpleasant facts? Do true lovers need to have reasons to be true to one another? Do they not have a natural desire to do so? Is there not in love a joy that makes love worthy of choice for its own sake?

But, it would seem, there is no "joy" left in the world. Still, to advertise love as relief—notice the regret that there is not generally available any "help for pain"—is, in effect, to make too much of neediness and dependence, if not even of sickliness and death. To see love as a kind of nursing may not be a healthy view of love.

Still, one must wonder why love is as important as it is in this poem. Is it because of the Faith which continues to influence us even though it has receded? That Faith, which seems related to Christianity, had made much of love. Has it inclined men to expect a great deal from love? Is this reliance on love an afterglow of that great Faith?[197]

Is love the new faith? If so, it is narrower than the communal faith it replaces: fewer factors have to be taken into account by this new faith; it rests more on *will* than it does on evidence. Such love can envelop one as faith once did the earth. Love does give the impression that it can be all-providing, that it can serve to fulfill us completely, that nothing else matters. What does being "true" to one another mean? Is it not a way of *avoiding* the truth about things—including the truth about the mortality of oneself and of one's beloved? Thus, love may offer a *sense* of completion—or a concealment which permits one to consider oneself safe and, in a way, complete—not the understanding that some have thought love promotes. In any event, we are very much on our own, and fidelity is desperately sought for. (Curiously enough, Arnold's narrator tends here to side, in effect, with the Aristophanes of Plato's *Symposium* as against Socrates.)

What does it mean to say that we are on our own? Or, put another way, what is the relation of community to love? (Communities are hinted at in the references to England and France as well as in the references to armies.) Can clinging to one another suffice? After all, how do we come to be the way we are? How have we been shaped to be the kind of people we are, the kind of people *worth* clinging to? Is love depended upon in the poem to provide the companionship and support that are naturally provided by a community grounded in a common faith?

The love invoked in this poem seems to rest on the expectation that two can somehow become one. (Preferable to such blending is, I repeat, that each should become as good as possible.) Can *these* two share fully? Indeed, does the beloved of the poem hear what is recorded in the second and third stanzas? Those are the more introspective, less conversational, lines of the poem. Even if she does hear everything, she may not understand what the narrator does. What *is* his beloved like? She does seem available; she is responsive: she *does* come to the window, it seems. He tells her how things truly are—and she listens. He expects her to be moved somewhat as he is, and hence to be inclined (out of self-defense also?) to be true. But is she as depressed as he seems to be? We cannot know; we do not know *her* temperament, or how the sight and sound of the sea affect *her*.

He seems to be the assertive one here. There are three exclamation marks in the poem—and all three are found in the only sentences where the narrator asks something of his beloved. (lines 6, 9, 30) Do these exclamation marks reinforce the new faith, an insistence on the sanctity or sanctuary of personal relations? Since all else is in retreat or disorder is it only in these personal relations that the narrator can assert himself, at least for the moment?

There may even be something immediately defensive in this assertiveness. Did the woman's approach to him, in compliance with his first sign of assertiveness, move him in turn to "distance" himself by talking of history? He is, perhaps, ambivalent in his attitude toward her? Perhaps he is testing her and himself in what he says about the uncertainty of things—testing to see how they respond to each other in "the worst case."

Perhaps, indeed, all that matters to the narrator is what is said in the final stanza. His primary concern may not be with the state of the world but with the relation between himself and his beloved—and not because of the state of the world either. Evidence is available which suggests that the fourth stanza of this poem was written earlier than the others. Certainly, the love sought in the final stanza is to some extent independent of everything else in the poem. This independence reflects the position of the narrator, which *is* very much the modern position, that love can be separated from everything else in life, that it can stand by itself, that lovers together can be self-sufficient.[198]

Such reliance upon love is enticing. But do not sensitive people sense the futility of such single-minded reliance? Even if lovers should be worthy of being clung to, their love, too, can ebb and flow. If the lovely scene in the opening lines of the first stanza can produce melancholy, why not love also, especially since love is not likely to be as tranquil as a calm sea? Is not mortality, or uncontrollable change, the problem here—a problem that the recourse to love can, at most, only temporarily conceal?[199]

Does it not say something about the temper of our times that the last stanza of this poem *is* taken to affirm something, that people can invoke it in moments of despair? (Whether such invocation leaves them worse off, once the immediate spell is dissipated, is another question.) It says more, perhaps, about the sense men have of eventual dissolution than it does about what love has to offer. Is there not something pretentious about *this* invocation of love—as well as something desperate? Is it not unduly self-centered—as if everything will somehow be all right if you and I love each other? At least, everything will be as good as it can be? Should one take oneself as seriously as the narrator does? Or is this self-indulgence, along with love, a necessary step toward self-confidence and thus toward a healthy trust in oneself and in others?

Is it good for the narrator, for his beloved, or for us that he should make as much as he does of his melancholy? After all, does not ebb imply flow, does not the night by which the armies are clashing imply (even for this narrator) an inevitable dawn by which men of good will can take their bearings once again?

A good night's sleep can sometimes do wonders.

V

TO SPEAK (as the narrator does) of ebb and flow in these matters, as if there were a movement somehow natural or in accordance with established patterns, may not be sensible. *Are* there natural cycles in human affairs, independent of chance dreams and promises (or opinions)?

That is, is the narrator justified in the view he takes of the world and its history? How critical is that view to the meaning and to the effect of the poem? What does that view tend toward? Does it discourage a moderate approach to things? In some circumstances it might do so, just as in others it can be salutary in counteracting reliance upon an expectation of unlimited and unambiguous progress.

In any event, one is obliged to ask what the character of human life is. Are not theories of history dubious enterprises? If the future is indeed indeterminable, it makes sense to have recourse to political action or (if matters are so uncertain as to make political organization difficult) to personal integrity.

Even so, a crisis of confidence does seem to have emerged during the past century—with Arnold's poem anticipating that crisis. What is the cause of that crisis? The momentary gleam of light reported by the narrator *is* from France; the cliffs of England, to the narrator's back, seem steadier. Dover *is* a well-known connecting point between England and the Continent. And the Continent means, among other things, the Enlightenment and its French Revolution—the Enlightenment and its "land of dreams." Promises have been held out in the form of dreams, dreams perhaps of liberation from the social and personal effects of the old (presumably Christian) faith.

Of course, the narrator is himself an "Enlightener" of sorts: he shows his beloved what the tranquil sea and the lovely scene truly mean. He sees intrinsic to what looks good, a bad result (whereas the Enlightenment, in exposing as it does the bad, holds out unprecedented promises of the good). For the narrator, nightmares, in the form of nocturnal battles for example, replace dreams. Does the poem offer a dreamlike love? Is not the poem itself dreamlike, as if to replace the shattered dream upon which so much reliance had been placed?

How bad *are* things? Should we be melancholy? Is the breakdown of Faith a cause—or an effect? Have expectations built up by the Faith been disappointed—or was that faith more practical, so far as life on earth was concerned, than the Enlightenment which has undermined it? The narrator insists, while he and his beloved are at the window to enjoy the night—when they come to see and feel what is obvious—they cannot help but hear in the sea questions about how things truly are. England is not enough, it would seem; its tranquillity is deceptive.

Have expectations been healthy—the expectations both of the Faith and of the Dream which has replaced that faith? Have people been led to expect too much of (or the wrong things from) life, either life here or with a view of eternity? May not a proper study of the classics contribute to moderation, helping modern man to learn the truth about history and "forces" and life itself? In any event, there seems something prescient in what the narrator says: it bears on our understanding of the struggles of the twentieth century, especially that catastrophic folly known as the First World War.[200]

The Faith and the Dream may be gone. But have they not left behind certain patterns of longing? Is love the new faith partly because it was so critical to the old faith? Did the old faith magnify the place of love in life? To be "true to one another" is to be "faithful to one another"? Is it a fidelity to which even the truth may have to be sacrificed at times? But can such fidelity replace a prevailing, communal faith, with its confident opinion about how things are and about how men should conduct themselves? Does the modern longing promote a constant struggle, with no steady idea held by anyone as to what is going on, as to who is doing what to whom, as to what should be done?

Much depends, that is, upon whether the narrator's reading of history, or of "the historical process," is correct. It affects both our understanding of how things are and our determination of what we should do.

vi

INDIVIDUAL TEMPERAMENT, we suspect, can also affect how one responds to the intellectual and social forces one encounters. The narrator's temperament may be critical, a temperament which keeps a middle-class Englishman from enjoying a lovely night by the sea with his beloved.

Of course, temperament can be affected by opinions. But it may also be somewhat independent of one's opinion. After all, what would this narrator see in a storm? Suppose the poem had opened, "The sea is rough tonight." The scene in "Dover Beach" is intrinsically calming:

consider how other narrators (that is, in other poems) have responded
to such a setting.

We suspect also that this narrator may *want* to see happen what
he talks about. He reads the sound of the waves a certain way, a way
perhaps anticipated in the gleam of light. There is a considerable personal element here; the narrator must deal with his beloved, with
whom he is evidently alone. Consider the use of "girdle" in line 23.
Is this related to the "naked" element in line 28? Is the earth, like
his beloved, female? Perhaps he is not sure of what is going to come
of their intimate relationship—and he takes refuge in seeing it in universal terms?[201]

But to recognize the role of temperament here is not to eliminate altogether the role of opinion, for opinions can be critical in
moving, if not even in shaping, one's temperament. Certainly, opinions
are critical in this account: the *heard* things are presented as being
more influential than the seen things. The seen and felt things noted
at the outset affect what is "heard" at the end. The central lines of
the poem show the relation of sound to thought. Thus, the heard
things are indicated to be much more important than the seen things.
Is not this true of the receding faith, as well as of the promises of a
new world?

Is not what we understand about things critical in shaping what
we *do* hear in the noises of the earth? And is not personal temperament—that which lies within us (or the peculiar bent of one's community)—rather than the nature of things, the principal cause of error?[202]
In a sense, then, it is the narrator's "sea" which has receded, perhaps
never to return. How much has that recession been influenced by the
general loss of faith? The narrator does not seem to be able to stand
alone in proclaiming his own faith for others to adopt (if new) or to
return to (if old). He is left high and dry—or, worse, in shallow waters.
When the general faiths go, one suspects, faith-needing men are driven
to improvise personal creeds (with a dedication to "love" being one
such).

Does the narrator's happiness come from feeling somewhat miserable? He cannot stand prosperity? Is he childish in thus scaring
himself? Is the narrator perverse *not* to stop with lines 1–6, especially
when he is in a lovely place alone with his beloved? Does he sense that
life may have peaked for him, that it may all be downhill from here?
Or is his foreboding a way of adding to the intensity of the love-rela-

tion, to justify the desired intimacy? Is this a new love? Is he unsure of himself? Is he even guilt-ridden?

Certainly, the narrator is impressionable; he is subject to moods, to chance stimuli. Should not one be able to moderate such movements in oneself (just as one should be able to control somewhat whom one loves and how)? What had the narrator been like just before the poem opens?[203] Had he been troubled? He had then been calmed, before being troubled again? And may the calming sea reassert itself at the end, once he has expressed his gloom (not merely "gotten it out of his system," but given it its momentary due)?

We can see mirrored in the narrator's passions (or moods) the ebb and flow not only of the soul, but also of mankind and the world.

vii

THUS, THE narrator falls back on his own. There is no general faith; there is no world-community at peace. (Civilization itself is a problem?) Instead, there is England. England is to his back—and further back, as a second home, the Aegean beach. France (or whatever France stands for) is uncertainly, perhaps even threateningly, in the future. There is also his beloved.

What is his relation to his beloved to be? An enduring one, it seems to be hoped. This is, in a sense, a marriage proposal. But a marriage is something other than a reliance on love, whatever role love may play in its genesis. Marriage has a considerable social element to reinforce and sustain it and does not depend merely upon an unnatural reliance on unchanging love. It should be noticed that the proponents both of the old faith and of the new dreams were, in a sense, civic-minded, whereas this narrator holds out hope only for a personal solution, not a social one. No missionaries are to be sent out to the world by the narrator (as distinguished from the poet who does publish this poem). (See the end of Chapter XII, below.)

What should we expect to come of this love, this marriage? We are told that Arnold's own marriage was a happy one. And we know that he wrote little poetry after the publication, in 1867, of the collection in which "Dover Beach" appears. Had poems such as "Dover Beach" helped him come to terms with his wife, with himself, with the world? (See the poem on my dedication page.)

But we must distinguish the artist (who *may* be something of a missionary) from the narrator. This narrator is only one of Arnold's "characters," albeit, perhaps, a character to whom the artist is particularly drawn. Indeed, in principle, an artist knows (or at least senses) what we do about his narrator—and stands back from him.

We wonder what Sophocles, with his greater talent, his greater mind, would think of all this. What *he* thought has to be worked out from what he shows about what his characters think and about what happens to them and why.

I conclude my commentary on "Dover Beach," and indicate the ground to be covered in the second half of this book, by restating (and applying to this poem) various principles of interpretation introduced in my Preface and Prologue:

Arnold's narrator (who had invoked Sophocles) may be saying far more than he recognizes. (This may be true, as well, of an artist, of course, especially an artist who is caught up by his characters.) We see here the role of inspiration. We can study a poem the way we study a tree or an animal embryo: such things *are* in ways they themselves do not understand, and there are intrinsic to them developments and connections which are of interest, even instructive, both about them and about the world. Consider how the narrator, perhaps without recognizing it, anticipates from the outset the fitfulness of the conclusion. Thus, the light on the French coast gleams and is gone, whereas the cliffs of England stand glimmering and vast. (Is this glimmering a constant gleaming?) The uncertain light from across the Channel forecasts what is to follow?[204]

England, it would seem, stands for something solid and reliable. But it does not suffice—and so recourse is had to an intense personal relation. The title of the poem reminds us that it could have been called "The Cliffs of Dover." But that would have changed the poem's perspective. Would this title have meant looking toward England rather than outward? The title *is* critical to the meaning of the poem. But is not that the artist's choice, not the narrator's?[205]

Does this artist recognize the limits of his narrator? Does he recognize, as we do, that love may not be enough, that it can become a means of avoiding the truth? Even so, love is vulnerable to reflection, just as the calm sea was. Certain things are there for all detached observers to see and to learn from. That is, nature is one as is the truth about nature, whereas circumstances can lead to different perspectives (and to obstructed views).

An artist can outgrow a stage of development; his dramatic character, if well conceived, is not likely to do so if he is an adult. Arnold had fifteen years between the poem's composition and its publication. It is likely the artist did not feel the same by the time he did publish this poem as he felt when he first wrote it. His "creative" days are over when he does publish it, as are also, it seems, his days of anxiety (perhaps also the sense of impending anarchy). Has the nonpoetic part of his mind taken complete control, permitting Arnold to become a successful school inspector dedicated to a practical dream?[206]

Art brings reason to bear in novel ways on concrete situations, making sense (or, at least, seeming to make sense) of what may otherwise appear to be governed by chance. Some artists (we have seen) are better able than others to disengage themselves from the circumstances or narrators they present. Some artists are more aware than others of what is going on. (Does this not depend partly on their temperament?) This narrator puts an emphasis on the ebbing of things, whereas the artist does seem more aware of the cyclical character of it all. (Of course, ebbing is not always bad—for example, the ebbing of hate or anger. But in this poem the ebbing provokes anxiety.) It depends on the artist where in the cycle an account (or poem) ends: it depends, for example, on the mood the artist wants to establish, the immediate stage he wants to deal with, the impression he wants to leave of the narrator's view of things. Still, how good a poem is depends, in part, on how sound the thought is which the poetry attempts to illuminate (by recourse to descriptions of particulars). What *is* life like?

One further question here may be, What *is* poetry like? That is, to what extent does truth depend upon particulars, upon the concrete? Poets do believe in telling stories: the concrete is vital to their general insight, even in didactic poems, as well as to their effect. But are poets all too often more concerned with the effect achieved than either with the thought behind or with the consequences (social and personal) of that effect? Thus, a poet can be self-contradictory or thoughtless (with respect to ideas) or irresponsible (with respect to consequences). In this poem, "Sophocles long ago" is invoked to lend support to what is observed on this occasion: both the old and the new, we are told, point in the same direction.

It is significant that poetry (by its use of sounds and images, for example) can have a profound effect even when its thought is confused. Certain sounds, like the sounds heard by the seaside narrator, suggest things to us, depending on our susceptibility. Does not this poem restore the calmness of the opening lines, even though, at the ends, armies sweep the land like the tide sweeps the sea?

One critic suggests that "Dover Beach" calms by offering "a heavy massive set of defenses."[207] But may not the calming also come, in part, from the assurance (or, at least the satisfaction) one can derive from a grasp of the whole? Does not the practiced artist—by instinct, by thought, by inspiration, or by all of these— somehow understand the narrator and sense his limitations? The artist as artist may sense what we (the artist as reader?) do. May not both the artist and the reader sense that the narrator's dependence upon love is forced, if not even desperate?

Should the narrator's intellectual curiosity and intellect be challenged by what he encounters on this occasion? Or is he tired, defeated? Does the artist somehow sense this without being tired or defeated himself? And so the artist can indeed understand things that the narrator cannot.

It has been noticed that one derives "a pleasing melancholy" from "Dover Beach."[208] The discipline and beauty of the lines relieve somewhat the sense of anarchy and of gloom they portray. Also, the discovery of parallels in the past is somehow reassuring. The discipline, regularity, and affirmations of art can thus moderate the despair it might describe—just as it can restrain ecstasy as well? (It does seem fitting, in any event, that a didactic poem should elicit a didactic commentary.)

This, then, has been one escape story. We turn now to another, under the guidance of an artist who sensed (perhaps too acutely?) that it is most difficult for two people to "be true to one another" when one or the other is yet immature or is otherwise subject to chance and change.

IX. LEWIS CARROLL (1832-1898)

*The fair illusion of the dream sphere, in the
production of which every man proves himself
an accomplished artist, is a precondition not
only of all plastic art, but even, as we shall pres-
ently see, of a wide range of poetry. Here we
enjoy an immediate apprehension of forms, all
shapes speak to us directly, nothing seems indifferent or redundant. Despite the high intensity with which these dream realities exist for
us, we still have a residual sensation that they
are illusions. . . . Men of philosophical disposition
are known for their constant premonition that
our everyday reality, too, is an illusion, hiding
another, totally different kind of reality. . . .
The person who is responsive to the stimuli of
art behaves toward the reality of dreams much
the way the philosopher behaves toward the
reality of existence: he observes exactly and
enjoys his observations, for it is by these images
that he interprets life, by these processes that
he rehearses it.*

—Friedrich Nietzsche, *The Birth of Tragedy,* I

i

IT HAS been said that Lewis Carroll is, except for William Shakespeare, quoted more in Great Britain than any other English author.

There can be no doubt about the artistic effectiveness of Carroll's
extraordinarily popular books about what happened to a seven-year-
old girl in her dreams, *Alice's Adventures in Wonderland* and *Through
the Looking-Glass, and What Alice Found There.* His imagination,
good will, and style captivate us. One is inspired to imitate him, if
only as a respectful critic.

It should be conceded that subjecting stories such as these to
careful scrutiny might do one's reader the disservice of subverting
their magic. But we dare to take this chance, since such scrutiny can

---

All citations in the text of this chapter to the *Alice* books are to *The Annotated
Alice,* Martin Gardner, ed. (New York: World Publishing Co., 1971).

contribute to our ability to read other books, perhaps can even help us understand the very best works of the mind. In addition, our pleasure and profit in reading Lewis Carroll himself may be enhanced— especially if we should happen to notice aspects of his stories which have been neglected in earlier readings.

What is the principle of order in these stories? We should not be surprised to learn that a professional mathematician such as Charles Dodgson, an Oxford don and a churchman of sorts, should (as Lewis Carroll) produce texts which exhibit and exploit certain proportions. Does not such organization acknowledge an intelligent, and intelligible, grasp of things? Are not numbers, and the stability and symmetry they may reflect, essential to the ordering of things literary as well as physical?

Artists are, I have noticed in this book, obviously thoughtful beings—and the better the artist, generally, the more thoughtful. The use of numbers by poets is evident in their recourse to meter, to rhyme patterns, and to quantities and arrangements of lines. Inspiration is, of course, vital to any successful artistic endeavor. But it surely is not enough. It must be disciplined, or at least supported by discipline, thereby permitting the finest artistic effect to be achieved and preserved.[209]

I assume in what I say here that the reader is somewhat familiar with Lewis Carroll's *Alice* stories.

ii

CHAPTER DIVISIONS and chapter headings are provided by Carroll for his *Alice* books, books which appear at first reading as chaotic or haphazard as dreams are apt to. Each of the two books has a dozen chapters: an effort seems to have been made to make them similar in this respect. This formal organization by chapters provides convenient guideposts for the inexperienced reader.

An even more instructive principle of organization emerges if one divides each book according to its action or development. The difference in the principal form of change in the two books makes a considerable difference in the overall meaning and effect of the two stories. In *Wonderland,* Alice does move around, but the moving around (important as it is) is overshadowed by her changes in size. These changes in size are what permit her to get into and out of places.

Her primary purpose, to which she refers on several occasions, is to be where she longs to be—in the Garden. In *Looking-Glass,* on the other hand, it seems that Alice remains constant in size, but her changes in location are critical—for they are what permit her to become that which she desires to be: a queen.

There are, according to my calculations, twelve different size changes explicitly referred to in *Wonderland,* including Alice's gradual return to her natural size at the end of the dream. Twelve size changes mean thirteen different stages in the career of Alice in *Wonderland,* with each stage set off by size changes. The first stage is before the first size change occurs in the dream—that stage which is itself preceded by the natural growth we have as human beings. The last stage, in which the dream ends, is followed by Alice's natural growth, the growth into womanhood that her older sister anticipates.

Of the thirteen stages in *Wonderland,* the central one (Stage VII) is critical in certain respects. Alice acquires, toward the end of the preceding stage, the secret of the power to control her size. That is, she learns from the Caterpillar that eating from "one side" of the mushroom can make her grow taller, and eating from "the other side" of the mushroom can make her grow shorter. She has to experiment, however, to learn which is which. (p. 73)

Alice's first and second uses of the mushroom tightly bracket what I am inspired to identify as Stage VII of her career in *Wonderland:*

> "And now which is which?" she said to herself, and nibbled a little of the right-hand bit to try the effect. The next moment she felt a violent blow underneath her chin: it had struck her foot!
>
> She was a good deal frightened by this very sudden change, but she felt that there was no time to be lost, as she was shrinking rapidly: so she set to work at once to eat some of the other bit. Her chin was pressed so closely against her foot, that there was hardly room to open her mouth; but she did it at last, and managed to swallow a morsel of the left-hand bit. [pp. 73–74]

She soon finds herself, upon eating of "the left-hand bit," with a terribly elongated neck, extending high above the trees. (pp. 74–77) This growth (in Stage VIII) brings on problems of its own, but at least she has been saved from extinction.

Stage VII is the shortest in the book, only a dozen lines in all. On the other hand, Stage VIII, with Alice at her tallest, is *not* the longest in the book: there is no conformity *there* between form and content. Does the reinforcement in Stage VII of content by form further indicate that this stage is particularly significant?

Indeed, Stage VII can be thought of as *the* crisis for Alice in *Wonderland*. She must confront other difficulties, of course, but nothing so frightening as this grotesquely violent threat to her very existence. She now recognizes the power she has managed to acquire. Her experiments permit her to harness that power by Stage IX. Thereafter she controls her size, as circumstances require, until she finds herself somehow growing to her normal size in bringing these adventures to an end.[210]

We can say, therefore, that Stages I through VI of *Wonderland* are stages of exploration, inquiry, and experimentation, stages of challenge and even frustration. Then, by the end of Stage VI, Alice is starting to come into full control of her size, mastering such control by Stage IX. She then goes on to Stage X with the Duchess and the Cheshire Cat, Stage XI with the Mad Tea Party, and Stage XII where she finally enters the longed-for Garden. Stage XII is, by far, the longest stage in the book, for the Garden leads on, eventually, to the final Trial scene. The entire book has been, in a sense, a preparation for Stage XII, to which one-third of the book is devoted.

We can also say that the turning of the story around Stage VII depended on Alice's *doing* something, on her making a sensible choice. *She* had to make a determined effort to save herself from extinction. If she had not been able to cope with the challenge she had set herself, she would probably have awakened—and the experience would have been remembered as a nightmare.

We need not decide whether the artist deliberately devised what I describe here. It has long been known that an artist may instinctively arrange things, without quite knowing what he is doing, in order to achieve the desired effect. Carroll did try out earlier versions of these stories on children—and he must have perceived what combination of difficulty and success for Alice was required to hold the interest of children and, perhaps above all, what the turning point should be in Alice's progress toward what young readers would accept as a satisfactory control of her destiny.

All this raises the question, to which I will return, Why did these things happen to Alice especially? A preliminary answer is that Lewis

Carroll did know and like someone like Alice (and of that name), a girl who was evidently quite remarkable (as recorded, for example, in John Ruskin's impressions of her). Be that as it may, is not the reader made to sense that the Alice of this story has somehow earned her way to the ability she acquires to get into the Garden?

Is the Garden really worth all the trouble? One might as well ask: Is adulthood worth the trouble of getting there? Does the Garden represent an instinctive desire to return to the Garden of Eden— or to a Golden Age? Perhaps the former, with its bountiful innocence —since there seem to be relatively few traces of classical imagery and language in Carroll.

It suffices for the moment to notice, with respect to the intrinsic worth of the Garden, that the first thing Alice sees upon entering "the beautiful garden" are three workmen painting the roses to conform with the Queen's expectations. Thereafter she observes sporadic attempts at tyranny. And this part of her juvenile adventures ends, as does the dream itself, with her rebellion against unjust judicial proceedings in the famous trial of the Knave of Hearts.

iii

CHESS PROVIDES the model for the action in *Looking-Glass*. It seems that Alice has recourse to a dream partly in order to come to terms with the defeat she has just suffered in a game of chess.

She moves, in *Looking-Glass,* from the status of pawn to that of queen. There are, in addition to the preliminary and concluding accounts—that is, the accounts before and after the "chess game" is "played"—seven stages in Alice's journeying across the chessboardlike terrain. (A pawn starts from the second row and can move to the eighth row and become a queen.) These seven stages are one-half of the thirteen stages found in *Wonderland*.[211]

Why are there only half as many stages in *Looking-Glass* as in *Wonderland?* In a "looking-glass" world, the "missing half" can be seen as "reflected"—as turning around Stage VII of *Looking-Glass,* and thereby implied. This missing half can be thought of as Alice's adult life, her career as a "queen." Carroll does not choose to—perhaps he cannot—show us *that.* Alice's adult career may be prefigured in the affectionate way she mothers the kittens. (We notice, by the way, that Dinah, her cat, is a determined mother in *Looking-Glass;*

she had been spoken of primarily as a successful huntress in *Wonder-land*.)

A "program" is given Alice in Stage I of *Looking-Glass:* she is told what to expect in each of the squares she will pass through. Five moves will suffice to get her from the second row to the eighth row. That program is provided for Alice by the Red Queen in these words:

> A pawn goes two squares in its first move, you know. So you'll go *very* quickly through the Third Square—by railway, I should think—and you'll find yourself in the Fourth Square in no time. Well, *that* square belongs to Tweedledum and Tweedledee—the Fifth is mostly water—the Sixth belongs to Humpty Dumpty....
>
> ... The Seventh Square is all forest—however, one of the Knights will show you the way—and in the Eighth Square we shall be Queens together, and it's all feasting and fun! [p. 212]

Central to the seven stages in *Looking-Glass* is Stage IV (or the Fifth Square), described by the Red Queen as "mostly water." There are various indications that this is the turning point of the book (just as Stage VII, the final stage in *Looking-Glass,* is the turning point of Alice's life, as she moves from childhood into adulthood): on either side of Stage IV, in the Red Queen's program, are the only characters in the program with proper names, Tweedledum and Tweedledee (in Stage III) and Humpty Dumpty (in Stage V); the Queen had said that each of those squares "belongs" to those she named. In the descriptions of Alice's activity in the squares two rows away on either side of Stage IV, there is an emphasis on movement: thus it is said of Stage II that she will move through it "by rail*way*," and it is said of Stage VI that a knight "will show [her] the *way*." Finally, only in the squares three rows away on either side of Stage IV (that is, Stages I and VII, the first and last stages in the *Looking-Glass* "chess game") are Alice and the Red Queen together.

What is special about Stage IV (the central Fifth Square) that so much should turn upon it in *Looking-Glass?* The movements within the stage are most dreamlike. Alice observes that "things flow about so here" (and she soon finds herself on water, the only time in this book, I believe). (pp. 253–58) She says what she does about things flowing because it is hard for her eyes to focus on anything in the shop in which she first finds herself: each shelf she looks directly at is empty, although all other shelves around it are filled. Does this not emphasize the difficulty of grasping dream-things?

Also, it is dark in the shop: it is hard to see. In fact, is it not harder to see here than anywhere else in *Looking-Glass?* Is not the competent and self-reliant Alice least herself, here, as a seeing and hence controlling being? Her powers of comprehension and direction shrink to a minimum, just as had happened to her physical stature in the central stage of *Wonderland*.

Matters are complicated by the internal fluidity of the scene: first Alice is in a shop; then she finds herself rowing in a boat; then suddenly she is back in the shop. The shop attendant's knitting needles (the shop attendant had been a white queen; she now looks very much like a sheep)—her knitting needles turn into oars, and it is hard rowing for Alice. Even her attempts to pick rushes are frustrating: the best ones keep getting away, and the ones picked quickly fade and even melt. It is from this stage alone that the crossing over into the next stage is not shown as either being done by Alice or being ratified by her (as when on the railway): she is somehow across the brook bordering this square without knowing what is happening. (p. 259)

Is not Stage IV the nadir of Alice's experiences in *Looking-Glass?* Is not she here the most passive, the least royal? Both the stage immediately before and the stage immediately after find her recollecting verses—about Tweedledee and Tweedledum (in Stage III), about Humpty Dumpty and about the Unicorn and the Lion (in Stage V)— verses which permit her (in the way of an artist) to anticipate, and thus, in effect, to control the action.

I have likened the central stage in *Looking-Glass* to that in *Wonderland*. There, Alice moved desperately, but effectively, to save herself from extinction. Does Alice do anything to resume control of her career here? She does manage, despite all the uncertainty in the shop, to buy something from the difficult shopkeeper. Her choice of an egg manages to lead her into the Humpty-Dumpty stage. Did she not somehow draw upon what the Red Queen had told her at the outset about her program, that the next square belonged to (the egglike) Humpty Dumpty? She then conformed to, even though she did not yet understand, the shopkeeper's announcement: "I never put things into people's hands—that would never do—you must get it for yourself." (p. 259)

Alice thus insists upon sticking to the course originally plotted for her, a course which she very much wants to pursue, despite the distractions and frustrations of the maturation which the journey across the squares represents. She keeps her wits about her and earns thereby (should we not say?) the right to continue. And she continues on to the end, until she wakes, having tested herself and gotten where she wants to be.

iv

THE DECISIVE test may seem to some to lie beyond Stage IV of *Looking-Glass,* for Alice must still work out her relations with a character who resembles the artist himself, in the next-to-last stage of this journey. But Stage VI does not seem to me to pose for her the difficulties the central stage did: she has, by that time, become quite sure of herself, very much in control of what is happening, and eager to make the final crossing into queenhood.

Indeed, the critical problem remaining after Stage IV is not Alice's but rather Dodgson-Carroll's. More than with any other work of stature I know (with the possible exceptions of Marcel Proust's and James Joyce's), the "personality" of the author can, perhaps should, figure in the reader's understanding of the *Alice* books. Compare, for example, Shakespeare's work: we need know nothing of *his* life in order to understand his plays. One indication of this is that all kinds of theories have been propounded as to who actually wrote those plays. The serious reader of Shakespeare need not concern himself with these contending theories. It is quite a different matter, however, when one turns to the *Alice* books.

We see Carroll as fairly sure of himself in *Wonderland:* the Oxford child he works from there is still quite young. Her eventual maturation does not yet pose a threat to him (although that maturation is anticipated in the sister's soliloquy at the end of that book). At one point we are told about the Dodo, which had appeared in *Wonderland,* ". . . the Dodo could not answer without a great deal of thought, and it stood for a long time with one finger pressed upon its forehead, (the position in which you usually see Shakespeare, in the pictures of him). . . ." (p. 48) It seems to be generally known that "Dodo" was a nickname for Dodgson. (p. 44) (We also see the Dodo invent and organize a game, just as Dodgson is known to have done on many occasions.)

Does not Carroll quietly recognize himself here as a kind of Shakespeare, as doing for children or with the child's world what Shakespeare had done for and with adults? Are we not again reminded ("one finger pressed upon its forehead") that the greatest artists do not rely on inspiration alone, that intelligence and thought are critical in what they do? One can see here a self-conscious artist, someone who recognizes and appreciates what he is doing, but not without some self-mockery.

All this is merely to be glimpsed in *Wonderland.* In *Looking-Glass,* published six years later, the artist is much more explicit about his state of mind, perhaps because he is more threatened as a human being by the maturation of the girl who has meant so much to him.[212] Alice must pass through the forest in Stage VI (the next-to-last stage) of her journey to queenhood. A knight must help her along. It has been noticed by commentators that the White Knight who comes to help Alice very much resembles Dodgson physically; it has also been noticed that he is one of the few characters, in the all-too-often threatening world of the two books, who seems truly fond of Alice.

But I do not believe it has been noticed that the White Knight is presented at his most confident in the role of artist. In the course of this forest episode, he falls off of his horse some thirteen times. He is an awful rider—and even the compassionate Alice cannot always restrain her mirth at his ingenious incompetence. But while he recites his poem, a longish poem in which an old man (like himself?) gives three accounts of his life, he sits securely in his saddle, without even holding the reins. The White Knight resumes falling off his horse after he serves as poet. (pp. 306–14)

Perhaps this is indeed the story of Dodgson-Carroll's life. The White Knight knows that Alice must grow up, but he cannot bear the sight of her leaving him; he must have it seem that he leaves her. She readily agrees to see *him* off (no reason is given—it is simply understood between them?—why he makes this request) before she crosses the final brook. (pp. 314–15)

The artist does not seem to think much of what lies ahead for Alice. At the outset, the Red Queen had promised "feasting and fun" in the Eighth Square—but life in that square (just as in the Garden of

Wonderland) turns out to be far less pleasant than had been anticipated. Dodgson-Carroll evidently did not see adulthood as an attractive (however inevitable) successor to childhood—and this may have
helped him to see life as a dream, as something to be diverted (if not
even enriched) by ingenious play with children. But Alice will not be
denied: one may even say nature will not be denied, however much
this artist would arrest this development.

There is about this the poignancy expressed in the sister's reflections at the end of *Wonderland* and restated in the poem appended
to *Looking-Glass*. But there is, for the artist, some self-knowledge as
well. When not an artist, Dodgson stumbles along. Did he sense this
would be especially true of himself as a lover (or as a father)? But as
a dreamer (or artist), Carroll can assert himself and touch the child in
us all, thereby reviving our "vanish'd summer glory." (p. 174)[213]

V

A RECOURSE to play and dream—to the kind of playful dreaming
which is drawn upon for both of these books—is a respectable escape
for the adult to whom everyday life has never become attractive. Is
there not about all this something ultimately questionable? It is not,
in the final analysis, serious. But in an artist of genius it can be great
fun, and instructive, especially when (as here) there is a piquant mixture of old–fashioned propriety, casual whimsy, and modern science.

One valuable lesson for us older readers of the *Alice* books is
what a sensitive observer such as Carroll can teach us about the nature
of dreams. Or rather, we can confirm a good deal of what we all already know, and perhaps have always known, about dreams. By thus
making explicit and examining further what we know, we may add
to our awareness not only of dreams but also of art and the mind of
the human being.

One can catalogue dozens of instances in the *Alice* books that
depend upon Carroll's awareness of the nature of dreams, an awareness which may be as informed and perceptive as any found in modern literature. A few examples must suffice here: in dreams one casually accepts the incongruous as routine; one can do all sorts of dangerous things without injury; one can wish for a way out of a predica-
ment—and miraculous means somehow become available; one is

unexpectedly called upon to produce "prizes" and finds them in one's pocket, with just enough for everyone; one has a frustrating inability to do the simplest things and an exhilarating ability to do the most difficult; one moves in scenes that flow easily into one another, as one knows just where to look for what one wants; one can pass on to something different when one's interest in or ability to cope with a situation fades.

Is not everything in a dream "known" by the dreamer throughout the dream (except, perhaps, when outside stimuli suddenly intrude)? Is not a dreamer in control from the outset, anticipating what is to come, somehow handling all that comes along in a manner which had been originally "planned" by the dreamer? And are not the *Alice* books sound, so far as they go, in thus presenting the dreams of their heroine—dreams in which each memorable character has a part of the dreamer in it?

Throughout a dream the dreamer knows what she is doing—or, at least, is aware of much of what she knows in her waking state. She incorporates into her dream what she has experienced theretofore, what is happening around her, what she believes to be good, what she happens to want, and what she has imagined. All this permits her (especially if she has a well-ordered soul) to understand better, and thus to accept with more grace and perhaps even wisdom, the sometimes harsh necessities of what Nietzsche called "everyday reality."

The dreamer usually controls the length of her dream. In both books, Alice *breaks* out of the dream world, thereby reasserting her dedication to waking life and the standards and aspirations she has been taught. When she awakens in *Looking-Glass,* Alice can confidently bring the two worlds together, the waking and the dreaming, by connecting "people" and incidents in the dream to her everyday experiences and acquaintances.[214]

It is significant, I believe, that Alice recalls her immortal dreams as "wonderful" and "nice." Does she not thereby ratify, and reinforce, the kind of human being she is?

vi

I HAVE suggested that the experience, character, and aspirations of the dreamer are critical in determining the content and tone of a dream. Can these, however, be Alice's dreams? Of course, Lewis Carroll imagined all this—but *is* he sound in what he attributes to Alice?

By and large, it can be argued, nothing is presented but what Alice herself observes. Carroll does slip when he presents details that Alice does not, perhaps could not, notice. This flaw is difficult to avoid, especially since the artist always does know more than even his principal character, if only because he knows the whole story from the outset and in a way that a character, in the progress of a story, cannot. But then, I have argued, Alice as dreamer also knows the whole story in advance.

A truly serious artistic flaw would be to present dreams that simply are not consistent with the character and experience of the supposed dreamer. Some sophisticated devotees of the *Alice* books consider Alice herself as essentially irrelevant to the story, as merely a foil for Carroll's wit. For such readers, far more important than Alice are the other characters in the stories, the episodes, the commentaries on human affairs, the logical games, and the paradoxes.

There is a surface plausibility to the belief that Alice does not matter. Consider, however, what I have suggested about the decisions Alice (as dream-character) does make, about the relation between the ways she conducts herself and the outcomes of the two books. I suspect that the decisive role of Alice, which may become fully evident only to the reader who plots the developments in each book, is instinctively sensed by the sympathetic child in the reader—and adds to the charm and interest of the books for young and old alike.

But we still have the problem of whether a child's mind can be as subtle as Carroll depicts it in the *Alice* books (whether or not he is aware of what he has done). It is a mind that can, for instance, sense the White Knight's ambivalence about the pawn's impending elevation to queenhood, and that can sense as well the decency of allowing the White Knight to leave her rather than for her to leave him. Does not the sensitive and kind woman in Alice recognize and respect the signals transmitted by the vulnerable Dodgson?

How subtle, indeed, is a child's mind? Do we not underestimate the complexity of the souls of children? After all, what do Platonic suggestions about the innateness and pervasiveness of "the ideas," and about the nature of recollection, teach us about what is some-

how imbedded in every human soul? Thus, for example, may not the
alert, intelligent child intuitively grasp and rework what is implied in
the folklore, morality, and history (and hence language) of her people?

Who *is* the Alice who dreams the dreams recorded in Lewis
Carroll's narratives? She does have the form of a nicely courteous
girl of some seven years, an imaginative, good-natured, and sensible
explorer. But there is about this curious girl something eternal as
well—and this truly engaging part of her may be divined in the soul
she shares with the aging artist who has proved to be her benevolently
perceptive spokesman. (The decisive egg she chooses in *Looking-Glass*
testifies to a female potency that will not be denied?)

vii

OUR UNDERSTANDING of human things, which art is dedicated to
helping us with, cannot rest only on such books as these. If sense is
to be made of the whole of things, we need also to learn more about
what an Alice would be like as a woman, as well as about the male
side of humanity (both among children and among adults), and about
the tragic dimension of life.

To make sense—or should we again say, to discover the sense?—
of the whole depends, therefore, upon a thorough exploration of
nature, an examination of the status of nature in human affairs. What
does nature mean to Carroll? Is not he (or a part of him) threatened
by it? Nature does mean, among other things, growth and dissolution,
whereas Carroll yearns, in a childlike way, to deny change and death
and hence life itself.

But is it not also childlike—and Carroll respects this in Alice—to
want to grow, to take one's chances with life, to try to become the
complete adult to which one is drawn by nature, however forbidding
this prospect may at times seem to the immature? And does not nature
try to teach child and adult alike that virtue is somehow rewarded,
that prudence and self-restraint make sense?

We have advanced our inquiry into what sense there is to artistic
accounts of human things by noticing how the *Alice* stories (which in
this respect imitate nature) are put together, what helps make them
"work" as deservedly popular stories, and why it is that our maturing
heroine can entrust herself with—and interest us in—the adventures
she dares to dream.[215]

$X.$ MARK TWAIN (1835-1910)

> *He awoke towards dawn, as the cocks were*
> *crowing; and immediately he saw that all the*
> *company were either sleeping or gone, except*
> *Agathon, Aristophanes, and Socrates, who alone*
> *remained awake and were drinking out of a large*
> *vessel, from left to right; and Socrates was argu-*
> *ing with them. As to most of the talk, Aristo-*
> *demus had no recollection, for he had missed*
> *the beginning and was also rather drowsy; but*
> *the substance of it was, he said, that Socrates*
> *was driving them to the admission that the same*
> *man could have the knowledge required for*
> *writing comedy and tragedy—that the fully*
> *skilled tragedian could be a comedian as well.*
> *While they were being driven to this, and were*
> *but feebly following it, they began to nod; first*
> *Aristophanes dropped into a slumber, and then,*
> *as day began to dawn, Agathon also. When*
> *Socrates had seen them comfortable, he rose*
> *and went away . . .*

> —Plato, *Symposium* 223C–D

i

STILL ANOTHER outcast—this one on a Mississippi-River raft—is found in Mark Twain's *Adventures of Huckleberry Finn.* His is a quite different escape route from the one resorted to by Lewis Carroll in his effort to avoid love and other entanglements. (Both of these authors do share a protective device, the use of a pen name.)

Huckleberry Finn is a puzzling book. It is often a very funny book, sometimes a hilariously funny book for the typical reader. And yet one finds in it some of the most pathetic scenes in American literature, scenes of brutality and violence presented with great skill and remarkable effect. How is this unusual combination to be under-

---

All citations in the text of this chapter to *The Adventures of Huckleberry Finn* are to the Chandler Publishing Company facsimile edition (New York, 1962).

179

stood? Does it not point to an even more critical tension in Mark Twain's work—or among the people he portrays?

In 1891, seven years after the original publication of *Huckleberry Finn*, Andrew Lang described the book:

> It is the story of the flight down the Mississippi of a white boy and a runaway slave. The stream takes them through the fringes of life on the riverside; they pass feuds and murders of men, and towns full of homicidal loafers, and are intermingled with the affairs of families, and meet friends whom they would wish to be friends always. But the current carries them on: they leave the murders unavenged, the lovers in full flight; the friends they lose for ever; we do not know, any more than in reality we would know, "what became of them all." They do not return, as in novels, and narrate their later adventures.
>
> As to the truth of the life described, the life in little innocent towns, the religion, the Southern lawlessness, the feuds, the lynchings, only persons who have known this changed world can say if it be truly painted, but it looks like the very truth, like an historical document. ... The drawing of character seems to be admirable, unsurpassed in its kind. By putting the tale in the mouth of the chief actor, Huck, Mark Twain was enabled to give it *a seriousness not common in his work,* and to abstain from comment. Nothing can be more true and more humorous than the narrative of this outcast boy, with a heart naturally good, with a conscience torn between the teachings of his world about slavery and the promptings of his nature. ...
>
> The casual characters met on the way are masterly: the woman who detects Huck in a girl's dress; the fighting families of Shepherdson and Grangerford; the homicidal Colonel Sherburn, who cruelly shoots old Boggs, and superbly quells the mob of would-be lynchers; the various old aunts and uncles; the negro Jim; the two wandering imposters [the duke and the king] ; the hateful father of Huck himself. ...
>
> No novel has better touches of natural description: the starlit nights on the great river, the storms, the whole landscape, the sketches of little rotting towns, of the woods, of the cotton-fields, are simple, natural, and visible to the mind's eye. The story, to be sure, ends by lapsing into burlesque, when Tom Sawyer insists on freeing the slave whom he knows to be free already, in a manner accordant with "the best authorities." But even the burlesque is redeemed by Tom's real unconscious heroism. There are defects of taste, or passages that to

us seem deficient in taste, but the book remains a nearly flawless
gem of romance and of humour. [Italics added][216]

The story, as Andrew Lang put it, is that "of the flight down
the Mississippi of a white boy and a runaway slave." The slave flees
from being sold in New Orleans and thus separated from his family;
the white boy flees from a harsh father who threatens his life. Both
are fleeing violence, one the steady violence of slavery, the other the
erratic violence of family life. All around them, too, is violence: it *is*
a violent society they move through, whether seen in the overt violence of guns and ropes or in the subdued violence of fraud and dem-
agoguery. It is such a society Mark Twain must deal with—and since
the people and shortcomings he deals with tend to be low (even though
at times deadly), it is comedy he resorts to—but a comedy which, in
its faithfulness to what is around him, includes accounts of the most
sober episodes. Perhaps Mark Twain (the one-time journalist) describes
so well what he sees in order to hold our attention for the implicit
commentary he makes, a commentary on the individual sense of
honor and on the public opinion that both make and keep society
as violent as he sees it to be.

ii

CRITICAL TO the entire book, spanning its central chapters, is the
episode referred to by Lang in which "the homicidal Colonel Sherburn . . . cruelly shoots old Boggs, and superbly quells the mob of
would-be lynchers."

This episode takes place after the duke and the king have moved
in on Huck and Jim—and have, in fact, taken over the raft. (pp. 109f,
160f, 290-92) Each of the frauds has "established" his noble blood—
and has proceeded to "work" the towns along the river. In one town,
the king imposes upon a camp meeting, where he collects a goodly
sum for the conversion of his supposed fellow-pirates in the Indian
Ocean; the duke occupies a temporarily empty print shop and exploits
it. (pp. 171-75) All the while, the pair rehearse a series of Shakespearean scenes that culminates in the medley of quotations called "Hamlet's Immortal Soliloquy." (pp. 179, 181) This medley is a gross, and
hence comical, distortion of the problem of death confronted in the

original soliloquy. Death is to become far more immediate in the book—and soon. (Compare p. 18.)

The shooting of Boggs takes place in a shabby Arkansas town on circus-day, a town in which, when we first see it, loafers are wheedling "chaws" of tobacco from one another. We encounter the sophomoric, even cruel, humor of these people who delight in "putting turpentine on a stray dog and setting fire to him, or tying a tin pan to his tail and see him run himself to death." (p. 183) The shooting of Boggs is described in this way:

> The nearer it got to noon that day, the thicker and thicker was the wagons and horses in the streets, and more coming all the time. Families fetched their dinners with them, from the country, and eat them in the wagons. There was considerable whiskey drinking going on, and I seen three fights. By-and-by somebody sings out—

> "Here comes old Boggs!—in from the country for his little old monthly drunk—here he comes, boys!"

> All the loafers looked glad—I reckoned they was used to having fun out of Boggs. One of them says—

> "Wonder who he's gwyne to chaw up this time. If he'd a chawed up all the men he's ben a gwyne to chaw up in the last twenty years, he'd have a considerable reputation, now."

> Another one says, "I wisht old Boggs 'd threaten me, 'cuz then I'd know I warn't gwyne to die for a thousan' year."

> Boggs comes a-tearing along on his horse, whooping and yelling like an Injun, and singing out—

> "Cler the track, thar. I'm on the waw-path, and the price uv coffins is a gwyne to raise."

> He was drunk, and weaving about in his saddle; he was over fifty years old, and had a very red face. Everybody yelled at him, and laughed at him, and sassed him, and he sassed back, and said he'd attend to them and lay them out in their regular turns, but he couldn't wait now, because he'd come to town to kill old Colonel Sherburn, and his motto was "meat first, and spoon vittles to top off on."

> He sees me, and rode up and says—

> "Whar'd you come f'm, boy? You prepared to die?"

Then he rode on. I was scared; but a man says—

"He don't mean nothing; he's always a carryin' on like that, when he's drunk. He's the best-naturedest old fool in Arkansaw—never hurt nobody, drunk nor sober."

Boggs rode up before the biggest store in town and bent his head down so he could see under the curtain of the awning, and yells—

"Come out here, Sherburn! Come out and meet the man you've swindled. You're the houn' I'm after, and I'm a gwyne to have you, too!"

And so he went on, calling Sherburn everything he could lay his tongue to, and the whole street packed with people listening and laughing and going on. By-and-by a proud-looking man about fifty-five—and he was a heap the best dressed man in that town, too—steps out of the store, and the crowd drops back on each side to let him come. He says to Boggs, mighty ca'm and slow—he says:

"I'm tired of this; but I'll endure it till one o'clock. Till one o'clock, mind—no longer. If you open your mouth against me only once, after that time, you can't travel so far but I will find you."

Then he turns and goes in. The crowd looked mighty sober; nobody stirred, and there warn't no more laughing. Boggs rode off blackguard-ing Sherburn as loud as he could yell, all down the street; and pretty soon back he comes and stops before the store, still keeping it up. Some men crowded around him and tried to get him to shut up, but he wouldn't; they told him it would be one o'clock in about fifteen minutes, and so he *must* go home—he must go right away. But it didn't do no good. He cussed away, with all his might, and throwed his hat down in the mud and rode over it, and pretty soon away he went a-raging down the street again, with his gray hair a-flying. Every-body that could get a chance at him tried their best to coax him off of his horse so they could lock him up and get him sober; but it warn't no use—up the street he would tear again, and give Sherburn another cussing. By-and-by somebody says—

"Go for his daughter!—quick, go for his daughter; sometimes he'll listen to her. If anybody can persuade him, she can."

So somebody started on a run. I walked down street a ways, and stopped. In about five or ten minutes, here comes Boggs again—but not on his horse. He was a-reeling across the street towards me, bare-headed, with a friend on both sides of him aholt of his arms and

hurrying him along. He was quiet, and looked uneasy; and he warn't
hanging back any, but was doing some of the hurrying himself. Somebody sings out—

"Boggs!"

I looked over there to see who said it, and it was that Colonel Sherburn. He was standing perfectly still, in the street, and had a pistol
raised in his right hand—not aiming it, but holding it out with the
barrel tilted up towards the sky. The same second I see a young girl
coming on the run, and two men with her. Boggs and the men turned
round, to see who called him, and when they see the pistol the men
jumped to one side, and the pistol barrel come down slow and steady
to a level—both barrels cocked. Boggs throws up both of his hands,
and says, "O Lord, don't shoot!" Bang! goes the first shot, and he
staggers back clawing at the air—bang! goes the second one, and he
tumbles backwards onto the ground, heavy and solid, with his arms
spread out. That young girl screamed out, and comes rushing, and
down she throws herself on her father, crying, and saying, "Oh, he's
killed him, he's killed him!" The crowd closed up around them, and
shouldered and jammed one another, with their necks stretched,
trying to see, and people on the inside trying to shove them back,
and shouting, "Back, back! give him air, give him air!"

Colonel Sherburn he tossed his pistol onto the ground, and turned
around on his heels and walked off.

They took Boggs to a little drug store, the crowd pressing around,
just the same, and the whole town following, and I rushed and got a
good place at the window, where I was close to him and could see in.
They laid him on the floor, and put one large Bible under his head,
and opened another one and spread it on his breast—but they tore
open his shirt first, and I seen where one of the bullets went in. He
made about a dozen long gasps, his breast lifting the Bible up when
he drawed in his breath, and letting it down again when he breathed
it out—and after that he laid still; he was dead. Then they pulled his
daughter away from him, screaming and crying, and took her off.
She was about sixteen, and very sweet and gentle-looking, but awful
pale and scared. [pp. 184–87]

This is, as the reader has seen for himself, a graphic scene, drawing at the end (it seems) on something the author had witnessed in his
childhood back in Hannibal. This scene is quite believable—and sticks

with the reader, who tends to sympathize with Boggs, or at least with the family of Boggs.

There is then a short interlude which permits the change of mood for the next appearance of Colonel Sherburn. That appearance is anticipated by this report:

> Well, by-and-by somebody said Sherburn ought to be lynched. In about a minute everybody was saying it; so away they went, mad and yelling and snatching down every clothes-line they come to, to do the hanging with. [p. 188]

Huck then describes what happens at the colonel's house:

> They swarmed up in front of Sherburn's palings [before his house] as thick as they could jam together, and you couldn't hear yourself think for the noise. It was a little twenty-foot yard. Some sung out "Tear down the fence! tear down the fence!" Then there was a racket of ripping and tearing and smashing, and down she goes, and the front wall of the crowd begins to roll in like a wave.
>
> Just then Sherburn steps out on the roof of his little front porch, with a double-barrel gun in his hand, and takes his stand, perfectly ca'm and deliberate, not saying a word. The racket stopped, and the wave sucked back.
>
> Sherburn never said a word—just stood there, looking down. The stillness was awful creepy and uncomfortable. Sherburn run his eye slow along the crowd; and wherever it struck, the people tried to outgaze him, but they couldn't; they dropped their eyes and looked sneaky. Then pretty soon Sherburn sort of laughed; not the pleasant kind, but the kind that makes you feel like when you are eating bread that's got sand in it.
>
> Then he says, slow and scornful:
>
> "The idea of you lynching anybody! It's amusing. The idea of you thinking you had pluck enough to lynch a man! Because you're brave enough to tar and feather poor friendless cast-out women that come along here, did that make you think you had grit enough to lay your hands on a man? Why, a man's safe in the hands of ten thousand of your kind—as long as it's day-time and you're not behind him.
>
> "Do I know you? I know you clear through. I was born and raised in the South, and I've lived in the North; so I know the average all

around. The average man's a coward. In the North he lets anybody walk over him that wants to, and goes home and prays for a humble spirit to bear it. In the South, one man, all by himself, has stopped a stage full of men, in the day-time, and robbed the lot. Your newspapers call you a brave people so much that you think you *are* braver than any other people—whereas you're just *as* brave, and no braver. Why don't your juries hang murderers? Because they're afraid the man's friends will shoot them in the back, in the dark—and it's just what they *would* do.

"So they always acquit: and then a *man* goes in the night, with a hundred masked cowards at his back, and lynches the rascal. Your mistake is, that you didn't bring a man with you; that's one mistake, and the other is that you didn't come in the dark, and fetch your masks. You brought *part* of a man—Buck Harkness, there—and if you hadn't had him to start you, you'd a taken it out in blowing.

"You didn't want to come. The average man don't like trouble and danger. *You* don't like trouble and danger. But if only *half* a man—like Buck Harkness, there—shouts 'Lynch him, lynch him!' you're afraid to back down—afraid you'll be found out to be what you are—*cowards*—and so you raise a yell, and hang yourselves onto that half-a-man's coat tail, and come raging up here, swearing what big things you're going to do. The pitifulest thing out is a mob; that's what an army is—a mob; they don't fight with courage that's born in them, but with courage that's borrowed from their mass, and from their officers. But a mob without any *man* at the head of it, is *beneath* pitifulness. Now the thing for *you* to do, is to droop your tails and go home and crawl in a hole. If any real lynching's going to be done, it will be done in the dark, Southern fashion; and when they come they'll bring their masks, and fetch a *man* along. Now *leave*—and take your half-a-man with you"—tossing his gun up across his left arm and cocking it when he says this.

The crowd washed back sudden, and then broke all apart and went tearing off every which way, and Buck Harkness he heeled it after them, looking tolerable cheap. I could a staid, if I'd a wanted to, but I didn't want to. [pp. 189–91]

iii

ONE SENSES in the Boggs-Sherburn episode (right at the heart of the book) a deep-rooted flaw in Mark Twain's understanding of hu-

man things. Is not the reader intended to see the shooting as despicable *and* the facing down of the mob as magnificent? The author
does seem to intend both of these effects. In the shooting one can
see Mark Twain's resentment of the "aristocrat"; in the mob scene
one can see his contempt for the democrat, "the average man." That
is, Mark Twain emphasizes the worst of each.[217]

It is, I suggest, not *fitting* that a man who has acted as the colonel has against Boggs should be able to conduct himself as the colonel
does against the mob. The man who could speak as the colonel does,
and mean it, should not (indeed would not) have shot down in cold
blood a defenseless drunk who was pleading for mercy. Is there not
about the combination Mark Twain presents something unnatural
(although not impossible), something which reflects a curious twist,
if not even perversity, in the order of things?

The man who acts and speaks before the mob as the colonel
does should be, *if anyone,* a sheriff, an officer who would, at the
same time, take the colonel in for trial.[218] I have emphasized "if
anyone"—for there may be no one in this town to stop in this way
(that is, with such *words*) the outraged (and, one can add, the properly outraged) mob.

A proper sheriff would blend democratic opinion, expressed in
an election, and aristocracy, exhibited in the merits of the man selected for office. But Mark Twain does not see such legitimate authority at work very often along the river (or perhaps in any community).[219]

This book is laid in pre–Civil War America, in an America which
was unable to settle peacefully the problem of Negro slavery. This
fact should be emphasized even though this is one episode in which
Negroes barely figure at all.

iv

WHEN I suggest that it is not fitting that a man who has acted as
the colonel has against Boggs should be able thereafter to conduct himself *and speak* as the colonel does against the mob, I am suggesting
not only that the virtues are dependent upon one another but also
(and perhaps more important) that there is an intimate relation between virtue and knowledge. (This proposition—in its authoritative
formulation by Shakespeare for the English-speaking peoples—has

been examined in the first chapter of this book.) (See pp. 100 and 310 of *Huckleberry Finn.*)

Mark Twain seems to deny there *is* such an intimate relation— and so he can display Huck and Jim, in their ignorance, as morally superior to virtually everyone they encounter along the river. He seems to believe that there is a natural goodness in the untrained (and hence uncorrupted) human soul. (Notice that the colonel spoke to the mob of the "courage that's born" in men.) Whether this is so must be challenged, especially by those who believe that what is truly natural (and hence the best) in a man depends on the full development of his reason. That is, one must challenge the suspicions about civilization expressed in Mark Twain's work. Of course what often *passes* for civilization must itself be challenged, but on the basis of a refined understanding, not in the name of a return to an untutored consciousness. (After all, why should Huck happen to be different from his uneducated father? What difference should it make if we read this book?)

Does not much of Mark Twain's humor depend for its effectiveness on a misunderstanding—a misunderstanding easily pandered to in a democratic age—of the relation of virtue to knowledge, a relation which ordinarily bears the taint of aristocratic associations? And yet, in spite of his somewhat egalitarian doctrines, Mark Twain has an awareness of what the truly aristocratic means, even though he perverts this awareness when he gives it artistic form in various of his stories. Thus, in a 1901 essay, "The United States of Lyncherdom," Mark Twain recalls the childhood experience he evidently drew upon in portraying Colonel Sherburn's defiance of the mob:

> A Savonarola can quell and scatter a mob of lynchers with a mere glance of his eye: so can a Merrill or a Beloat. For no mob has any sand in the presence of a man known to be splendidly brave. Besides, a lynching mob would *like* to be scattered, for of a certainty there are never ten men in it who would not prefer to be somewhere else— and would be, if they had but the courage to go. When I was a boy I saw a brave gentleman deride and insult a mob and drive it away....[220]

Mark Twain himself provides notes to this passage which identify Merrill and Beloat as *sheriffs,* one in Georgia, the other in Indiana. He adds, "By that formidable power which lies in an established repu-

tation for cold pluck they faced lynching mobs and securely held
the field against them." As I have indicated, this kind of talk and
action makes sense, even in "real life." But Mark Twain's art failed
here to imitate—that is to say, to respect and learn from—nature,
unless "real life" *is* to be seen as "schizophrenic" in his day.

We also notice that Mark Twain says nothing in this 1901 passage about the "brave gentleman" (who had derided and insulted a
mob) having been a cowardly murderer. And this induces us further
to notice that Colonel Sherburn, in his masterful speech to the mob,
does not refer *at all* to what he has done to Boggs. Indeed, it is as if
another man were speaking. Is this not symptomatic of the spiritual
tension at the heart of Mark Twain's work?

We are left to believe that Colonel Sherburn escapes altogether
the consequences of his murder of Boggs. Is it indeed that kind of
world? This, we have been prepared to believe, will never do!

V

WHAT *DOES* follow the shooting of Boggs? One of three responses
is likely among an organized people: a just response, a comic response,
or a tragic response.

We have seen that there is no just response: that is, there is
neither the formal justice of a trial nor the informal justice of a perhaps not inappropriate lynching. The colonel speaks with contempt
of what usually happens at trials—and he himself thwarts the lynching.

A "tragic" response of sorts may be seen in the immediate sequel
to the shooting of Boggs. After Boggs is shot, he is taken into the
drugstore and the crowd presses around to watch him die. Huck's
description continues:

> Well, pretty soon the whole town was there, squirming and scroug-
> ing and pushing and shoving to get at the window and have a look,
> but people that had the places wouldn't give them up, and folks
> behind them was saying all the time, "Say, now, you've looked
> enough, you fellows; 'tain't right and 'taint fair, for you to stay
> thar all the time, and never give nobody a chance; other folks has
> their rights as well as you."

> There was considerable jawing back, so I slid out, thinking maybe
> there was going to be trouble. The streets was full, and everybody

was excited. Everybody that seen the shooting was telling how it
happened, and there was a big crowd packed around each one of
these fellows, stretching their necks and listening. One long lanky
man, with long hair and a big white fur stove-pipe hat on the back
of his head, and a crooked-handled cane, marked out the places on
the ground where Boggs stood, and where Sherburn stood, and the
people following him around from one place to t'other and watching
everything he done, and bobbing their heads to show they understood, and stooping a little and resting their hands on their thighs
to watch him mark the places on the ground with his cane; and then
he stood up straight and stiff where Sherburn had stood, frowning
and having his hat-brim down over his eyes, and sung out, "Boggs!"
and then fetched his cane down slow to a level, and says "Bang!"
staggered backwards, says "Bang!" again, and fell down flat on his
back. The people that had seen the thing said he done it perfect;
said it was just exactly the way it happened. Then as much as a
dozen people got out their bottles and treated him. [pp. 187–88]

First the dying, then the dead, man is placed on exhibit, on the stage,
so to speak. Thereafter his shooting is reenacted and thus dramatized.
It immediately becomes historic, worthy of inclusion in a tour-guide's
repertory.

This "tragic" interlude provides a transition to the mob scene
at the colonel's house. Is there not something about this interlude
which puts much-needed distance between the shooting of Boggs
and the colonel's braving of the mob? (My exclusion of the interlude earlier deliberately put the two Sherburn episodes in stark contrast to one another, something Mark Twain did not want to face up
to?) The shooting has been transformed, in some way made less
immediate, less brutal, by the dramatization of it—and so the colonel
can more plausibly be presented facing down the mob.

The comic response to the shooting occurs at the circus. *Immediately* after the mob scene, which ends with Huck saying, "I could a
staid, if I'd a wanted to, but I didn't want to" (p. 191), Huck goes to
the circus. He "could a staid" if he had wanted to—that is, if he had
dared. But he did not care to, nor did he care to explicitly notice
that he too had been intimidated by the colonel.

For Huck the circus seems an immediate escape from the dreadful things he has witnessed. Perhaps it is an escape for others as well.
The circus does provide Huck a rare occasion (while in society) for

sustained enjoyment, perhaps as comic compensation for what has just happened. Certainly it provides relief from the oppressiveness of everyday life in the town:

> It was a real bully circus. It was the splendidest sight that ever was, when they all come riding in, two and two, a gentleman and lady, side by side, the men just in their drawers and under-shirts, and no shoes nor stirrups, and resting their hands on their thighs, easy and comfortable—there must a' been twenty of them—and every lady with a lovely complexion, and perfectly beautiful, and looking just like a gang of real sure-enough queens, and dressed in clothes that cost millions of dollars, and just littered with diamonds. It was a powerful fine sight; I never see anything so lovely. And then one by one they got up and stood, and went a-weaving around the ring so gentle and wavy and graceful, the men looking ever so tall and airy and straight, with their heads bobbing and skimming along, away up there under the tent-roof, and every lady's rose-leafy dress flapping soft and silky around her hips, and she looking like the most loveliest parasol.
>
> . . . Well, all through the circus they done the most astonishing things; and all the time that clown carried on so it most killed the people. The ring-master couldn't ever say a word to him but he was back at him quick as a wink with the funniest things a body ever said: and how he ever *could* think of so many of them, and so sudden and so pat, was what I couldn't noway understand. Why, I couldn't a thought of them in a year. And by-and-by a drunk man tried to get into the ring—said he wanted to ride; said he could ride as well as anybody that ever was. They argued and tried to keep him out, but he wouldn't listen, and the whole show come to a standstill. Then the people begun to holler at him and make fun of him, and that made him mad, and he begun to rip and tear; so that stirred up the people, and a lot of men begun to pile down off of the benches and swarm towards the ring, saying, "Knock him down! throw him out!" and one or two women begun to scream. So, then, the ring-master he made a little speech, and said he hoped there wouldn't be no disturbance, and if the man would promise he wouldn't make no more trouble, he would let him ride, if he thought he could stay on the horse. So everybody laughed and said all right, and the man got on. The minute he was on, the horse begun to rip and tear and jump and cavort around, with two circus men hanging onto his bridle trying to hold him, and the drunk man hanging onto his neck, and his heels

flying in the air every jump, and the whole crowd of people standing up shouting and laughing till the tears rolled down. And at last, sure enough, all the circus men could do, the horse broke loose, and away he went like the very nation, round and round the ring, with that sot laying down on him and hanging to his neck, with first one leg hanging most to the ground on one side, and then t'other one on t'other side, and the people just crazy. It warn't funny to me, though; I was all of a tremble to see his danger. But pretty soon he struggled up astraddle and grabbed the bridle, a-reeling this way and that; and the next minute he sprung up and dropped the bridle and stood! and the horse agoing like a house afire too. He just stood up there, a-sailing around as easy and comfortable as if he warn't ever drunk in his life —and then he begun to pull off his clothes and sling them. He shed them so thick they kind of clogged up the air, and altogether he shed seventeen suits. And then, there he was, slim and handsome, and dressed the gaudiest and prettiest you ever saw, and he lit into that horse with his whip and made him fairly hum—and finally skipped off, and made his bow and danced off to the dressing-room, and everybody just a-howling with pleasure and astonishment.

Then the ring-master he see how he had been fooled, and he *was* the sickest ring-master you ever see, I reckon. Why, it was one of his own men! He had got up that joke all out of his own head, and never let on to nobody. Well, I felt sheepish enough, to be took in so, but I wouldn't a been in that ring-master's place, not for a thousand dollars. I don't know; there may be bullier circuses than what that one was, but I never struck them yet. [pp. 192–94]

Huck's enjoyment of the circus depends on his ignorance as well as on his good will. He does not know that the exhibition of the drunk on horseback is prearranged; he sees much of what happens to be spontaneous, and all the richer for that. And what happens is all the more enjoyable for him because he (unlike many in the audience) does not want to see anyone hurt: he is pleased, not disappointed, that the drunk carries things off so well.

vi

THIS COMIC response provides a corrective to what had happened in the Boggs-Sherburn episode. It is a subtler, and hence safer, corrective than had been possible at the colonel's house. Is not the entire Boggs-

Sherburn episode duplicated at the circus, but in a critically altered manner? Once again Boggs confronts the colonel, the plebeian challenges the aristocrat: the "drunken spectator" challenges the lordly ringmaster. Indicative of the critical alteration is that, this time, the drunk begins on foot and ends up on horseback—and masterfully so. This time, the duel is won by Boggs, by a transformed Boggs—and the arrogant colonel is humiliated.[221]

Thus, the artist—the comic poet—in Mark Twain asserts himself, perhaps even against the ideologue in himself. Is the reader affected by this comic reversal of, or compensation for, the Boggs murder? Does this begin to correct what Mark Twain's doctrines have permitted to be done and said by the colonel? Does Mark Twain recognize the extent to which he has reenacted, but in a more humane and hence civilizing manner, the dreadful Boggs story? Artists, as we have seen, need not understand the fine things they achieve—and yet their work can have a civilizing effect, thereby gentling the life of man.

If Mark Twain had not had the instinct to provide comic reworkings of the more somber episodes in this novel, the book would not leave with most readers the sense of deep satisfaction that it does.

vii

BUT TO say "deep satisfaction" is *not* to say *complete* satisfaction. For there are problems about the ending of *Huckleberry Finn*. Thus, as Andrew Lang noticed: "The story ... ends by lapsing into burlesque when Tom Sawyer insists on freeing the slave whom he knows to be free already, in a manner accordant with 'the best authorities.'"

Some critics have argued that the concluding chapters fit well in the book as a whole. But this argument fails to adequately consider the dissatisfaction which has been felt for several generations now by the bulk of the book's readers. (See pp. xvi, xxi.)

To notice dissatisfaction, however, is not to say (with most critics) that the concluding chapters are simply inappropriate. It may be fitting that dissatisfaction be felt. There may have been no peaceful way to solve one critical underlying problem posed by this book: the problem of slavery. There may have been no solution consistent with the impotent Huck Finn's humanitarian instincts. (See pp. 166, 291–92.)

Thus, we have noticed, the unnaturalness of the "schizophrenic" combination in Colonel Sherburn of two quite different characters may be due not to flaws in Mark Twain's art but to conditions of American life in his time. It was a time when "prudential" accommodations to the cruel requirements of slave institutions had compromised the admirable principles of the regime invoked in the Declaration of Independence. Whether Mark Twain himself ever recognized in *Huckleberry Finn* what his art permits us to notice can be left an open question.

The resort to burlesque in the concluding chapters is, in effect, a concealment of an *impasse* from which violence may be the only escape. The deliberately adventurous Tom Sawyer is needed—with his heroics *and* heroism. It will be Tom Sawyer who will fight in the Civil War—on *which* side may depend upon chance?—Tom Sawyer, not Huck Finn (who is really a pacifist). Huck Finn intends "to light out for the Territory," away from "siviliz[ation]" and hence away from the demands and the atrocities (as well as the unrecognized achievements) of society. (pp. 17, 47, 366)

These atrocities, we are given to understand, are not limited to those of slavery. Other, less obviously violent but nevertheless pervasive, atrocities can be expected, especially in a society which is as ambitious, as mobile, as vital as this one.

Perhaps Mark Twain's comedy can help "sivilize" this people, but Mark Twain himself appears, at times, rather dubious about this. But *that* may be, as I have indicated, the doctrinaire ideologue, not the instinctive poet, or truly thoughtful artist, speaking.[222]

XI. WILLIAM S. GILBERT (1836-1911) AND ARTHUR SULLIVAN (1842-1900)

> *"So, Glaucon," [Socrates] said, "isn't this why the rearing in musik is most sovereign? Because rhythm and harmony most of all insinuate themselves into the inmost part of the soul and most vigorously lay hold of it in bringing grace with them; and they make a man graceful if he is correctly reared, if not, the opposite. Furthermore, it is sovereign because the man properly reared on rhythm and harmony would have the sharpest sense for what's been left out and what isn't a fine product of craft or what isn't a fine product of nature. And, due to his having the right kind of dislikes, he would praise the fine things; and, taking pleasure in them and receiving them into his soul, he would be reared on them and become a gentleman. He would blame and hate the ugly in the right way while he's still young, before he's able to grasp reasonable speech. And when reasonable speech comes, the man who's reared in this way would take most delight in it, recognizing it on account of its being akin?"*
>
> —Plato, *Republic* 401D–402A

i

LEOPOLD BLOOM, as he walks across Dublin one fateful June day in 1904, notices a squad of constables "marching in Indian file." He ruminates:

> Goose steps. Foodheated faces, sweating helmets, patting their truncheons. After their feed with a good load of fat soup under their belts.

All citations in the text of this chapter to the Gilbert and Sullivan operettas are to them as published in *The Complete Plays of Gilbert and Sullivan* (New York: Modern Library, 1936).

Policeman's lot is oft a happy one. They split up into groups and
scattered, saluting towards their beats. Let out to graze.[223]

A few pages later, in James Joyce's *Ulysses*, Bloom says (to himself)
of "one of those policemen sweating Irish stew into their shirts,"
that "you couldn't squeeze a line of poetry out of him."[224]

Bloom (or, if the reader will, Joyce) *had* squeezed a line of
poetry, evidently from Gilbert and Sullivan, to fit his impressions
of the just-fed policemen: "Policeman's lot is oft a happy one."
One is intended to recall the famous lines from *The Pirates of Penzance:*

> *When constabulary duty's to be done—*
> > *To be done,*
> *The policeman's lot is not a happy one.*
> > [p. 175]

A few more pages along, Bloom can recall "Three Purty Maids from
School,"[225] which seems an echo from *The Mikado*, with its song:

> *Three little maids from school are we,*
> *Pert as a school-girl well can be,*
> *Filled to the brim with girlish glee,*
> > *Three little maids from school!*
> > [p. 356]

Thus, Joyce would have us understand, Gilbert and Sullivan
were very much in the air for his Dublin hero a quarter-century after
the operettas had opened in London (*Pirates,* 1880; *Mikado,* 1885).
What was evident in Dublin in 1904 was probably so at that time,
and ever since, throughout the English-speaking world. (There was
a time when *H.M.S. Pinafore,* which had opened in London in 1878,
had a half dozen pirated versions playing simultaneously in New York
City.) Only Shakespeare, it seems, has been so frequently on view
among us.

Shakespeare ranges across human experience, in both tragedies
and comedies, in a manner which does suggest a comprehensive view
of things. Joyce, in his detailed account of a Dublin day in the lives

of several characters, draws on the accumulated memories of the West. In the cases of both Shakespeare and Joyce, one has the impression of minds at work—a working which manages to suggest what it means to be human. Cannot the same be said of Gilbert *and* Sullivan, that there is here too *a* mind, a mind with a career of its own? This and related questions should help us consider further what "inspiration" means, what the effects of all art are, and what the effects are of these particular plays.

ii

TO FULLY discuss these plays, one should include reflections upon the inestimable contribution made to the complete effect by the music of the operettas. There is here a remarkable blending of words and music. The words seem to come first, with the music reinforcing the sense of those words. Sullivan, it seems had a gift for fitting music to the words supplied by Gilbert, for bringing out the full flavor of those words, perhaps even to a degree that Gilbert could not have anticipated. On the other hand, Gilbert had a gift for devising language to which music *could* be fitted.

   One exception proves the rule which governed their collaboration. I was struck, upon studying the libretti of the operettas, by one of the songs, a duet by Elsie and Jack Point in *The Yeoman of the Guard,* which goes (in part) like this:

Elsie.	I have a song to sing, O!
Point.	What is your song, O?
Elsie.	It is sung with the ring

Of the songs maids sing
Who love with a love life-long, O!
It's the song of a merrymaid, peerly proud,
Who loved a lord and who laughed aloud
At the moan of the merryman, moping mum,
Whose soul was sad, and whose glance was glum,
Who sipped no sup, and who craved no crumb,
As he sighed for the love of a ladye.

[pp. 474–75, 516–17]

I was, as I have said, struck by this and even wrote in the margin of my copy, "How did Gilbert conceive of a song like this prior to the music?" The words seemed, even to someone as amusical as I am, fitted to some music, not the music to the words as one can consider most of Gilbert and Sullivan to have been. Martyn Green, the great Gilbert and Sullivan trouper, supplies an instructive annotation to this song in his edition of the play:

> This may well be put down [he says of the song] as the one number which Gilbert composed. Sullivan was completely stumped when he received the lyric. The rhythm was strange and unlike anything Gilbert had done before. Sullivan took the only course open to him and called [Gilbert], saying that it seemed apparent that he had had a tune in his mind when he wrote the lyric, and would he come over and hum whatever it was? Gilbert explained that he had heard some sailors (members of the crew of his own yacht) singing a chantey, the tune and form of which had haunted him, and that was what he had had in mind.... The style of the lyric is curious, and as Leslie Bailey says: "...one that is believed to be a corruption of an old Cornish carol."... He then goes on to say that Sullivan promptly wrote a new tune to Gilbert's words. Yes, new—and yet so old that the first time I heard it I was struck by its familiarity. So who did write it? It's hard to say, but without Gilbert, Sullivan would never have put this particular melody down on paper.[226]

Gilbert and Sullivan each did put a number of things to paper without the aid of the other. Indeed, they were famous in their day for things they did on their own. And on occasions, each collaborated with others. But it is evident that their principal claim to enduring fame comes from their collaborative production of the operettas—and in this joint enterprise they can best be understood as one mind at work. In thus thinking about their poetic enterprise, one engages in a form of interpretation which is itself a kind of poetic enterprise.

What poetry means to us is suggested in *The Pirates of Penzance:*

> *... For what, we ask, is life*
> *Without a touch of Poetry in it?*
>
> *Hail, Poetry, thou heaven-born maid!*
> *Thou gildest e'en the pirate's trade...*
>   [p. 160]

If my poetic interpretation in this chapter appears outlandish at times, I trust I will be forgiven: I merely emulate Gilbert and Sullivan in the lengths they go to to achieve *their* effects.

Gilbert and Sullivan produced their first play together in 1871, their fourteenth (and final) play, in 1896. Their best plays—a string of eight or nine plays—ran from *H.M.S. Pinafore* through *Yeoman of the Guard* (or perhaps *Gondoliers*), from, that is, 1878 through 1888 or 1889.

Their career could be what it was—given the peculiar talents of these two men (or three men, if one includes the invaluable D'Oyle Carte)—because it drew on a rich stage tradition, on the high-spiritedness of the British schoolboy, and on that form of high civilization known as the Victorian Age.[227] The stage tradition, musical as well as dramatic, disciplined Gilbert and Sullivan as to what words and music should go together. It also liberated them somewhat from conventional notions with respect to disparities in ages among would-be lovers and other deliberate incongruities in their plots. The enduring popular response to these plays suggests that they draw upon a rich vein of human inclinations and experience.

The thinking that Gilbert and Sullivan did as a pair was, one might say, often instinctive, just as, for example, a tree root seems to pursue a crack in a rock in its effort to find sustenance. That is, the artistic response, or approach, makes sense in the circumstances—circumstances which included, for Gilbert and Sullivan, the sophistication of their audiences, the theatrical tradition of their community, and the moral expectations and limitations of their times. Theirs is not the most profound thinking, one might concede, but neither is it without considerable merit. We can see for ourselves what this kind of thinking can mean by reflecting (still another time) upon what we know about our dreams, those unconscious adventures in arranging, and rearranging, the workings of our minds.

A remarkable account of dreams is presented in *Iolanthe* (by the Lord Chancellor): "such horrible dreams," he says. (pp. 275–78) The dreams reflect the misery of an official who wants to marry one of his wards and who senses that this cannot (or, at least, should not) be. In this account, incongruities are accepted by the dreamer; one thing slides somehow into another. A general state of discontent is evident; the futility of his enterprise seems to be evident to him—and he does "awake with a shudder despairing." The artists seem to have deliberately portrayed thus the unconscious struggle and despair of their subject. Perhaps the career of the artists can also be seen as unconscious yet similarly "structured." The artists remain thinkers, even in their reliance on dreams or on the unconscious. For these are the dreams and the unconscious, it should never be forgotten, of the rational animal.

The career of Gilbert and Sullivan reflected, I have suggested, a deep sense of the tradition and of the audience, of what was available to an artist and of what was expected of him. Regrets are heard from time to time about the quarrels that interrupted the fruitful partnership of these men and deprived us of several more operettas. But, I suspect, those quarrels were not the cause of interruptions, but rather symptoms of their awareness that they may have gone just about as far as they could go. The two plays produced after they resumed their collaboration—*Utopia, Limited* and *The Grand Duke*—are inferior to all the others, with the possible exception of the first two, *Thespis* and *Trial by Jury* (the latter being superior in what it *does* do but perhaps somewhat deficient in size). The last two plays before Gilbert and Sullivan's temporary break—*The Yeoman of the Guard* and *The Gondoliers*—represent a falling off from what they had done in their best days. *Gondoliers* tends to be somewhat flabby (however engaging its music can be); *Yeoman of the Guard* suffers from a defective moral vision. By the time *Gondoliers* comes along, the artists are pressing for their effects—and this must have disturbed relations between the collaborators.

The reader who is more attuned to Gilbert and Sullivan than I am can check against his own impressions and recollections the assessments I have just ventured to suggest about the first two and last four plays. No doubt, an artist need not be as explicit as I have been about what he is doing; he need only be "effective," and what is required for effectiveness he may often merely sense. But Gilbert and Sullivan could be unhappy even while they were most effective. A proper interpretation, or criticism, should have reassured them about the seriousness and enduring worth of what they *were* doing with their comedies.

At the very least, Gilbert and Sullivan held a mirror up to their community, reinforcing in it what was commendable, laughing at, and thereby refining, what was questionable.

iii

THE COMPLETENESS of their career, given their talents and circumstances, is suggested by an imaginative consideration of the shape
that career happened to take. Certain features of that shape should
now be noticed; other features will be noticed later.

There are, we have seen, fourteen plays produced by Gilbert and
Sullivan. The first and last plays are the only ones featuring troupes
of actors (with allusions to "long runs" and other theater talk); they
are also the only ones in which a substantial part (in the first, all of
the play; in the fourteenth, half of the play) is in ancient Greek dress.
And, it should be added, these two plays have been the least successful of the fourteen: they had the shortest first runs of any of the
plays—and they are rarely revived.

The first and last plays are, in a way, the most self-conscious of
the fourteen. They present troupes of actors trying to take over the
governance of things—of things spiritual and things temporal. Thus,
these two plays explore the relation of the stage to life, which means
(in effect) that the aspirations, or perhaps the pretensions, of drama
are recognized and dealt with.

I acknowledge that to dwell upon the first and last plays *is* to
concern oneself with inferior plays. I do examine these works, however, because they provide instruction about the meaning of the
artistic thinker in the career of Gilbert and Sullivan (just as *Titus
Andronicus* could be used with respect to Shakespeare). Besides, the
better plays much more obviously speak for themselves. In any
event, the magic—in music, in wit—the magic of the better plays
remains; I cannot deal properly with *that*. But I can reasonably
hope to deal somewhat with the more prosaic aspects of the plays,
such as the "frame" of the Gilbert and Sullivan corpus, the opening
and closing plays.[228]

In the first play, *Thespis, or The Gods Grown Old,* the rather
decrepit Greek gods are replaced by a troupe of actors while the gods
spend a year on earth in an effort to revitalize themselves. This direct
replacement of "religion" by "art" does not work. For one thing,
the surrogate gods do not do their work properly, with the result,
among others, that there are no intermittent wars (and hence no
peace) and no death (for Pluto's replacement is kindhearted). (pp.

26–27, 36) So the original gods have to return to chase out their inadequate surrogates.

I notice in passing that little is done explicitly with religion in the fourteen plays. References to Christianity are few and, except for *Sorcerer,* incidental. (Thus, Christmas boxes are mentioned in *Thespis*, a confessor in *Yeoman* [pp. 5, 471. See, also, pp. 17, 264, 622, 669].) A conflict between Wesleyan Methodism and Roman Catholicism is involved in the history of the action in *Gondoliers* (pp. 530–31), but there is no reference to creeds or to differences in creeds.

Nor is it indicated that Christianity has supplanted the Greek gods. In fact, again and again, the gods of antiquity (who, it can be argued, are the gods who "naturally" evolve) are taken for granted or are invoked in these plays. (See, for example, pp. 116, 127.) Thus, one must ask onself, as in *Pinafore*, "Oh, god of love, and god of reason, say,/ Which of you twain shall my poor heart obey!" (p. 125) And the pirates of Penzance can kneel as they hail Poetry as "thou heaven-born maid!" (p. 160) (Compare the epigraph to Part One of Chapter XIII, below.)

The theater, we see in the first play, does not suffice to replace the gods, even old gods. What the theater does do much better is to "idealize" the gods, making them appear more impressive to mortals. (pp. 17–18) The head of this troupe, for instance, plays a more credible Jupiter than Jupiter himself can do these days. (pp. 17–18) In addition, the troupe, when it takes over Mount Olympus for its long run, spruces up the ruins, if only by the use of stage props. (pp. 22, 34)

But the play does seem to suggest that the gods did do useful things. (pp. 26–27) That is, the divine has had, and continues to have, a place in human affairs—and its depreciation has serious consequences for men. *Thespis* ends with a condemnation of the troupe by Jupiter:

> *Enough, your reign is ended;*
> *Upon this sacred hill*
> *Let him be apprehended,*
> *And learn our awful will.*
> *Away to earth, contemptible comedians,*
> *And hear our curse, before we set you free;*
> *You shall all be eminent tragedians,*
> *Whom no one ever goes to see!*

[p. 39]

Perhaps Gilbert and Sullivan sensed that the more *obviously* serious approach to divine matters (which tragedy can be said to embody) no longer has a dramatic appeal. Tragedy, one might say, has indeed replaced the gods at times; perhaps, indeed, the gods have been most widely viewed through the eyes and efforts of tragedians. But comedians, such as Gilbert and Sullivan propose to be (for the most part), cannot take over divine functions or even properly present divinity; but they can comment upon, and thereby help correct, distortions in derivations from the divine.

A kind of faith, one might say—a faith with moral implications—is preached in the subsequent plays. In this way, drama continues to serve the divine. (Consider the correspondence, referred to at the end of Section ii of the Prologue, above, between Hebrew prophets and Greek poets.) There seems to be implicit in these plays a teaching as to the role either of chance or of providence in how things turn out, with respect shown for natural inclinations and affinities (especially in matters of love). Justice is dealt out, more or less, even though audiences *are* reminded that "virtue only triumphs at night from seven to ten" (that is, on the stage). (p. 14. See, also, pp. 389, 600.)[229]

Thus, it seems to me, *Yeoman of the Guard* is so troublesome a play because it disappoints expectations about theatrical conduct that Gilbert and Sullivan have induced audiences to have. In a sense, this play is an unsuccessful (or partial) effort to move into tragedy.

These comedies, in short—perhaps this can be said of much of drama—represent efforts to deal with the enduring tensions in human affairs between what is desired (in part by human nature) and what is ordained by law both human and divine.

iv

THESE TENSIONS are most effectively presented in the Gilbert and Sullivan plays by the repeated juxtaposition of determined innocence and worldly wisdom. Such a juxtaposition, which can be made plausible by invocations of the charms of language and music, may well be critical for the healthy community. If there is only worldly wisdom, there are no aspirations, no enduring sense of decency; if there is only determined innocence, there is no useful "realism," no reliable practical sense.

This juxtaposition of innocence and wisdom is made more interesting when it is seen, as in modern comedy, in the male-female relation—and in the concern for the fulfillment of ourselves through love. We are induced to wonder, as we see love arranging and rearranging people, "What is fair? What is seemly?" And this, it seems, is to ask, "What does *nature* suggest?"

Does not a kind of instinct—a natural sense of what would be fitting—usually move Gilbert and Sullivan's characters to work their way to the proper conclusions? Thus, it can be said in one play, "Art is wrong and Nature right." (p. 641) The troupe on Mount Olympus failed because of the changes it had made, or had allowed to be made, in the nature of things.

Nature means the reliable impulse of a heart. Nature means that naïve maids can also be shrewd in their exploitation of conventions. This does seem to be the result of instinct; we see it again and again. But, it should be added, it is natural for men to have conventions, however obstructive conventions may sometimes be to the workings of nature.

Love does tend to mitigate the effects of rank, but it cannot altogether remove them. Nor should it, even though social stratification may sometimes keep love from its natural course. Thus, Deadeye Dick, on the *H.M.S. Pinafore*, observes, "When people have to obey other people's orders, equality's out of the question." (p. 114) And, in *Gondoliers*, a nobleman observes:

> *In short, whoever you may be,*
> *To this conclusion you'll agree*
> *When every one is somebodee,*
> *Then no one's anybody!*
> [p. 565]

In *Sorcerer* the conventions that normally govern love are overturned when an entire village is surreptitiously supplied a love-potion. Each unmarried villager is thus induced to fall in love with the first unmarried person of the opposite sex he sees. This use of the potion (which produces, in effect, a novel convention) interferes with the help that conventions normally can give to love, to the control of the excesses of love. The potion drives maidens to insist upon broken-down old men. Chance thereby plays a greater role than under the former dispensation in determining the most intimate relations. Is not the natural order closely related, despite the theory of the man who introduces the love potion, to the familiar, conventional order and to ranks in society (p. 72)—at least when things are reasonably well ordered?[230]

The unavoidable dictates of nature are pointed up as well in *Princess Ida,* where women separate themselves from men to establish their own regime (a regime based on study). Aside from the natural inclination of some of the women toward the male invaders they are supposed to resist, two serious flaws appear: the women are simply not suited for the combat required to defend themselves; the women will not be able to perpetuate themselves if their isolation attempt proves successful. (p. 340) In short, there is a natural pairing of male and female which must be provided for. Although love is again and again seen in the plays to be changeable, it is also seen to be inexorable.[231]

Mikado illustrates what can happen when law attempts to ride roughshod over love, when it becomes a capital offense for men to flirt. In *Iolanthe,* on the other hand, there are problems with the natural promptings of love:

> My Lord [the young hero says to the Lord Chancellor], I know no Courts of Chancery; I go by Nature's Acts of Parliament. The bees—the breeze—the seas—the rooks—the brooks—the gales—the vales—the fountains and the mountains cry, "You love this maiden—take her, we command you!" 'Tis writ in heaven by the bright barbed dart that leaps forth into lurid light from each grim thundercloud. The very rain pours forth her sad and sodden sympathy! When chorused Nature bids me take my love, shall I reply, "Nay, but a certain Chancellor forbids it"? Sir, you are England's Lord High Chancellor, but are you Chancellor of birds and trees, King of the winds and Prince of thunderclouds? [p. 252]

This is a stirring challenge. But there seems merit as well in the Lord Chancellor's response to the question put to him:

> No. It's a nice point. I don't know that I ever met it before. But my difficulty is that at present there's no evidence before [this] Court that chorused Nature has interested herself in the matter. [p. 252]

Perhaps what we can hope for is a sensitivity to the attractions and equities of particular cases, of particular pairings, not an unvarying adherence to the conventions we happen to rely upon for the necessary ordering of our social relations. That sensitivity must include an awareness of the mysteries and subtleties of the human soul as nature (or love) contends with convention. A delightful illustration of this may be found in *Patience*, where the Lady Angela and Patience, a dairy maid, explore (at the lady's insistence) the love-life of the maid. Notice how the lady probes. Notice, also, the problems which rise as to how such matters should be interpreted. One can see here an anticipation of Freud as well as the Victorianism upon which Freud thrived:

> *Angela:*   Noble girl! But is it possible that you have never loved
> anybody?
> *Patience:*   Yes, one.
> *Angela:*   Ah! Whom?
> *Patience:*   My great-aunt—
> *Angela:*   Great-aunts don't count.
> *Patience:*   Then there's nobody. At least—no, nobody. Not since I
> was a baby. But *that* doesn't count, I suppose.
> *Angela:*   I don't know. Tell me all about it.
> *Patience:*   Long years ago—fourteen, maybe—
> When but a tiny babe of four,
> Another baby played with me,
> My elder by a year or more;
> A little child of beauty rare,
> With marvellous eyes and wondrous hair,
> Who, in my child-eyes, seemed to me
> All that a little child should be!
> Ah, how we loved, that child and I!
> How pure our baby joy!
> How true our love—and, by the by,
> *He* was a little boy!
> *Angela:*   Ah, old, old tale of Cupid's touch!
> I thought as much—I thought as much!
> He *was* a little boy!
> *Patience:*   Pray don't misconstrue what I say—
> (shocked)   Remember, pray—remember, pray,
> He was a *little* boy!

Angela: No doubt! Yet, spite of all your pains,
              The interesting fact remains—
              He was a little *boy!*

[pp. 202-3]

We see here, by the way, a typical plot element in Gilbert and Sullivan: a childhood love is somehow redeemed. Patience does end up with the male she had been enamored of at four; it requires considerable maneuvering, but she is worthy of her name, and so she manages!

But even more instructive for our immediate purposes is the masterful manner in which Gilbert and Sullivan handle the sentence, "He was a little boy!" The shifting of emphasis, with great effect, in four successive sentences is a remarkable display of linguistic power. Prudery (or naiveté) and suspicious curiosity contend with one another; each has its effect because of the force of the other; both elements are in the plays, and in Victorian life, and enliven what is said and done. And when a community is well ordered, there is a healthy dose of each element in it. Thus, something of that era, and of the charming power of Gilbert and Sullivan, may be seen in the handling of this simple sentence:

He was a little boy!
He *was* a little boy!
He was a *little* boy!
He was a little *boy!*

That is the lighter side of Gilbert and Sullivan. (See, also, p. 14.) But there is a darker side as well. It shows up in somewhat disturbing forms in the self-sacrifices in *Sorcerer* and in *Yeoman.* In the former, John Wellington Wells, the Sorcerer, sacrifices himself in order to counter the effects of the unfortunate love-potion. This is one place in the plays where Christian influences can be seen. This is a Christ-like sacrifice: to restore love to its proper place, someone must exhibit the greatest love, self-sacrifice. (See pp. 78, 961.) This insight is prompted, it seems, by the willingness of the love-smitten vicar to sacrifice himself, not by allowing himself to be killed, but by leaving the country at once. (p. 96) The vicar's proposed sacrifice seems to remind Wells of a way of countering the disastrous love-potion—and Wells becomes one of two men to die in a Gilbert and Sullivan play.

The other death (if death it be) is that of Jack Point in *Yeoman*. (p. 517) That death may not be as revealing of a darker side to the plays, however, as what happens to Phoebe, a girl (in the same play) who allows herself to be contracted for marriage with a loathsome executioner in order to save the life of the man she loves, a man who blithely goes off married with another woman who chanced upon the scene. (pp. 462, 482, 510–12) It is a troubling state of affairs— and may point (as I have anticipated) to the impending demise of the Gilbert and Sullivan genius.

Perhaps there is reflected in *Yeoman,* in a particularly grotesque form, a limitation that the Victorians may never have faced satisfactorily, that is, their tendency to see a conflict between pleasure and duty. (pp. 150, 152) Duty is not pleasurable. This is made explicit in *Patience*, where the dairy maid must maneuver and delude herself in order to get what she truly wants. (pp. 231–32)[232] Pains alone are true, we hear in *Princess Ida*. (p. 314) And, in *Iolanthe*, when the Queen of Fairies chastises her subjects for their attraction to mortal men, the fairies answer, "We know it's weakness, but the weakness is so strong!" (p. 271) Of course, to put the problem this way may not be to resolve it; but it does make it something one can laugh at and hence learn to live with. (The proposed self-sacrifice here, by Iolanthe, is treated somewhat more casually than it is in *Sorcerer* or in *Yeoman*.)

The underlying problem in these plays may concern what human life itself means, even what a life span means. Nanki-Poo and Yum-Yum are about to be married:

> Nanki-Poo: Yum-Yum in tears—and on her wedding morn!
> Yum-Yum: They've been reminding me that in a month you're
> (sobbing)   to be beheaded. *(Bursts into tears)*
>
> [p. 375]

Nanki-Poo says, aside, "Humph! Now, some bridegrooms would be depressed by this sort of thing!" Then aloud, "A month? Well, what's a month? Bah! These divisions of time are purely arbitrary. Who says twenty-four hours make a day?" Someone else interjects, "There's a popular impression to that effect." To which Nanki-Poo replies, "Then we'll efface it. We'll call each second a minute—each minute an hour—each hour a day—and each day a year. At that rate we've about thirty years of married happiness before us!"

The madrigal, sung thereafter by the party, includes these lines:

> Let us dry the ready tear,
>> Though the hours are surely creeping
>> Little need for woeful weeping,
> Till the sad sundown is near.
>> All must sip the cup of sorrow—
>> I to-day and thou to-morrow;
> This the close of every song—
>> Ding dong! Ding dong!
> What thou solemn shadows fall,
> Sooner, later, over all?
> Sing a merry madrigal—
>> A madrigal!

[p. 376]

After which everyone bursts into tears.

The closing moments of the *Mikado* find Yum-Yum and the reprieved Nanki-Poo, now happily married, singing:

> The threatened cloud has passed away,
> And brightly shines the dawning day;
> What though the night may come too soon,
> We've years and years of afternoon!

[p. 400]

Is one not moved to wonder, despite the beguiling resolution of the conflict of *this* play, how long a life *is* natural to man? Is satisfaction with even an ordinary length of life depicted as a self-deception? For what Nanki-Poo had argued so eloquently—that each minute can be regarded as an hour and each day as a year—cannot help but make the imaginative observer wonder (as, say, Marcus Aurelius did) whether each year should be regarded as a day and each hour as a minute.

However that may be, conventional love does offer the illusion of perpetual possession of the beloved. Is the audience not left with this illusion more or less intact as the play ends?

v

THERE *ARE* two sides to the Gilbert and Sullivan plays: perhaps this helps account for their liveliness, for their vitality over many decades. Unlike most comedy, which tends soon to be neglected as topical, the Gilbert and Sullivan plays *have* endured.

This career of fourteen plays reflects these two sides: the first half predominantly light, the second half predominantly dark. The central plays represent the transition from one side to the other. *Iolanthe,* the seventh play, is the last of the lighter love stories; *Princess Ida,* the eighth, is the first of the grimmer problem-plays.

One must wonder whether there was something grim in Gilbert's temperament—for this transition I suspect he is more responsible than his collaborator—which could not be contained any longer. There is something cruel, if not sadistic, in various of the *Bab Ballads* which he wrote, and was famous for, before the collaboration with Sullivan began. The ballad about Annie Protheroe is particularly grim (and it is drawn upon in *Yeoman of the Guard*). But, in the ballad at least, the loathsome executioner does not get the girl—but what she had been prepared to do gives one pause to think.[233] In the later plays we find—as in *Mikado* and in *Yeoman*—rather moving accounts of executions or of dreadful preparations for executions. (pp. 385–87, 498f) In *Ruddigore* we find excruciating torture exhibited on stage, as a young man is driven by his ancestors (in the manner of the Furies) to continue the family tradition of evil conduct. (pp. 445–46)

Dark secret forces sometimes appear at work beneath the gay surface of the Gilbert and Sullivan plays. These forces are perhaps most dramatically revealed in the phenomenon, seen again and again in the plays, of the older woman who is hostile to young love. (*Iolanthe* is an exception, for there the older woman supports the young lovers—but then, *that* older woman is an unaging fairy, one who looks even younger than her son.) Generally, the older woman is determined to have the young man for herself—but she has insuperable obstacles to overcome. Certainly, the old and the ugly and the handicapped do not get much sympathy from Gilbert and Sullivan. There is something both cruel and, as I have indicated, natural about this. Thus, in *Pirates,* the young hero says to the older woman who had been urging him to marry her and whom he can at last compare to younger women, "And now I see you're plain and old . . . your face is lined, your hair is grey." (p. 148) The ugly Deadeye Dick, in *Pinafore,* protests, "I ain't as bad as I seem" (p. 128)—but to no avail: his perceptiveness cannot compensate for his appearance. (See, also, pp. 85–86, 102–3.)

It is the persistence of the older woman as pursuer of the young —of the usually reluctant young man—which may be most revealing here. This scenario is repeated so many times in the plays that one cannot help but wonder what it conceals. Is it not, in effect, a comic treatment of the Oedipal problem?[234] One reads that Gilbert's relations with his mother were, to put it mildly, strained. But that is not explanation enough, for audiences too (made up of many with normal parental relations) seem to have accepted the Gilbertian attitude. Perhaps they still do, which also suggests something about the nature of things.

The Oedipal problem takes the form, in *Pinafore* (once ranks and relations are rearranged), of the captain's marriage to the woman who had nursed him, while his daughter marries someone old enough to be her father. (pp. 134–37) Although the artist does not make explicit these discrepancies in age, the discrepancies are there. "Things are seldom what they seem," we are shown again and again.

Nor does the artist make what might have been made of Ko-Ko's reluctant willingness (in *Mikado*) to save his own life by having his prospective bride married to another man for a month. (p. 366) It was left for a resident of Boston, in a letter to a local paper, to strip away the poetic disguise from this questionable transaction. This proper Bostonian considered *The Mikado* indecent, declaring that he would not take his wife and child to a performance wherein one of the characters was willing to sell the body of his fiancée to another man simply in order to save his own life.[235] Machiavelli's *Mandragola* comes to mind, with its radical questioning of established institutions for the sake of political adventure in the form of love.

Be all this as it may, the uneasy personal relations papered over by the Gilbert and Sullivan scripts seem to have troubled the artists to the very end of their collaboration—and no doubt contributed to the psychic energy put to such exuberant use in many of the plays.

vi

WE RETURN to the final play in the series, the other play (with the first play, *Thespis*), in which a troupe of actors gets very much involved in the action. This last play, *The Grand Duke*, had been anticipated, in a way, by the next-to-last play.

That is, Gilbert and Sullivan consider in this next-to-last play, *Utopia, Ltd.,* if only in passing, the way out of enduring human travail promised by radical reconstitution of the political order. The relatively minor ills of the community—such as dubious practices in the courts and in Parliament—could be treated by the theater: comedy can cut pretensions down to size and expose ordinary abuses to public view. But fundamental questions about the meaning of life are quite different.[236]

Utopia, Ltd. presents a reconstituted society. But life becomes rather drab, and party politics have to be introduced to liven things up, to induce the necessary inefficiency and hence challenge in life. (p. 645) The play itself drags; it does not, despite what we are led to expect from Bernard Shaw's (perverse) praise of it, carry off what it attempts to do. Perhaps the artists sensed that an even more radical effort was needed—and *The Grand Duke* emerged. In this play, a troupe of actors attempts a conspiracy that would place actors in the offices of state. (In a sense, Shaw's plays are a successor to this operetta.) But this effort proves as futile as the attempt, by another troupe in *Thespis,* to replace the gods.

The Grand Duke is a complicated play, which has recourse to a contrivance called a statutory duel to solve one problem after another: the drawing of cards is resorted to as a means of determining who is to "die" by a kind of legal fiction. (pp. 662–65) (One can see here, as elsewhere, Gilbert's considerable interest in and knowledge of law— and his repeated efforts to come to terms with the shortcomings of the law.) Death by a legal fiction conceals from view the fact that natural death continues. May not the stage itself be a way of softening death by substituting for it something which is somewhat contrived? A kind of immortality is thereby suggested?

The failure of this play—not only do the actors fail to carry off their conspiracy, but so do Gilbert and Sullivan—reflects the artists' awareness of the limits of the theater. It can also be said to reflect their awareness of the ultimate sovereignty of the theological-political order within which the theater, along with the other arts, is assigned its place.[237]

vii

THERE MAY have been divined, by the dark side of the Gilbert and Sullivan imagination, something of what was to happen to British society. Within a generation after the last operetta, the Great War began—that thirty-years war which was made more dreadful than it would otherwise have been by the unthinking massive sacrifices of a dedicated people nourished on the patriotic reassurances of the Victorian Age. Consider the self-congratulatory chorus at the end of *Utopia, Ltd.*:

> *There's a little group of isles beyond the wave—*
> *So tiny, you might almost wonder where it is—*
> *That nation is the bravest of the brave,*
> *And cowards are the rarest of all rarities.*
> *The proudest nations kneel at her command;*
> *She terrifies all foreign-born rapscallions;*
> *And holds the peace of Europe in her hand*
> *With half a score invincible battalions!*

> *Such, at least, is the tale*
> *Which is borne on the gale,*
> *From the island which dwells in the sea.*
> *Let us hope, for her sake,*
> *That she makes no mistake—*
> *That she's all she professes to be.*
>
> [pp. 645–46]

Well, a mistake *was* made—to enter into, and then to persist in, an unnecessary war of cataclysmic proportions.[238]

The last expression of the Gilbert and Sullivan mentality in British public life may well have been seen in the abdication of Edward VIII. There was about him, in his sacrifice of his royal prerogatives for the sake of love, something of Nanki-Poo, the son of the Mikado. But nothing intervened to make everything turn out right in Edward's case. (Perhaps his character was against him from the outset.)

And yet Gilbert and Sullivan have given us a good, long run for our money. Audiences on both sides of the Atlantic still derive satisfaction from these plays, plays very much dependent upon self-confident peoples who are aware of *some* of their shortcomings and who are prepared to laugh at them and hence at themselves. The English-speaking peoples are justifiably proud of their fairly reliable systems of law. And they enjoy seeing, and are reassured and instructed by, the community which *is* celebrated in these plays.

Besides, one should not, in the all-too-human effort to attain something even better, fail to appreciate what is good. Should the theater of the days of Gilbert and Sullivan have been able to anticipate and ward off the dark years ahead? Perhaps this is too much to ask for: is it not rather up to politics to try to deal with chance, with the inevitable declines and failures to which unforeseeable developments contribute?[239]

Art may, within its limited sphere, overcome chance. But whether art will have an opportunity to emerge, and to have whatever effect it *can* have, depends on where it happens to find itself. That is, art is dependent on chance, just as had been the happy collaboration of Gilbert and Sullivan. It was, I have suggested, a remarkably productive collaboration, one that ran its natural course and came to a somewhat fitting end.

At the core of their theatrical power is the gift of the artist who works with both words and melodies and who draws upon what happens to be available in his time and place. Consider, as I prepare to close my own run, the song of Nanki-Poo:

> *A wondering minstrel I—*
> *A thing of shreds and patches,*
> *Of ballads, songs and snatches,*
> *And dreamy lullaby!*
>
> *My catalogue is long,*
> *Through every passion ranging,*
> *And to your humours changing*
> *I tune my supple song!*
>
> [p. 346]

One might wonder whether the range of Gilbert and Sullivan is indeed "through every passion." However that may be, we do notice how supple are the lines of this "supple song." We notice also how one can hear the music intimately mated with these words. This mating once again reminds us of the collaborative art of Gilbert and Sullivan. It reminds us, that is, of how much I, in this chapter, have had to leave unsung.

We turn now to still another Victorian escape story, one which displays, in a curious way, a somber counterpart to the comic balancing of light and dark seen in the Gilbert and Sullivan plays.

XII. ROBERT LOUIS
STEVENSON (1850-1894)

> *Odysseus: ... Yet I pity*
> *His wretchedness, though he is my enemy,*
> *For the terrible yoke of blindness that is on*
> *   him,*
> *I think of him, yet also of myself;*
> *For I see the true state of all of us that live—*
> *We are dim shapes, no more, and weightless*
> *   shadows.*

—Sophocles, Ajax 121–26

i

THE STRANGE *Case of Dr. Jekyll and Mr. Hyde* made its thirty-six-year-old author famous overnight. The effect of the story was both electric and enduring, so much so that "Jekyll and Hyde" have become household names for well-regarded people in whom there is concealed an unsavory personality.

The story of Dr. Jekyll and Mr. Hyde is known by many who have never read it. That is, "everyone knows" the story of someone by the name of Jekyll who was a respectable, tolerably well-behaved chap who had hidden within him somebody by the name of Hyde who, when he was released, would act like a fiend. Not everyone may know that Jekyll was a doctor whose experimentation with drugs released Hyde, that the release included a physical transformation of Jekyll in facial appearance, in posture, even in stature, that after several such transformations Hyde took possession of Jekyll, so much so that Jekyll would sometimes find himself transformed, unawares, into the criminal Hyde (to the deadly peril of "both" of them, since Hyde came to be sought for a capital offense), and that the careers of Jekyll and Hyde ended with the suicide of a cornered Hyde who could not secure the drug necessary to return to the safety of Jekyll's appearance.

All citations in the text of this chapter to *The Strange Case of Dr. Jekyll and Mr. Hyde* are to the story as published in *The Works of Robert Louis Stevenson* (New York: P.F. Collier & Son Co., 1912), vol. 6, pp. 167–239.

215

Two quite different, yet perhaps related, questions are posed by this popular story:

1. Why has the story had the remarkable effect it has had?
2. What is said by the story about the nature of the human soul?

What the story says about the nature of the human soul could be mistaken, even though the story has had a remarkable effect. Such a book may be more significant for its effect (perhaps an inadvertent effect, or one which depends on transitory influences) than for what its author truly understands.

We begin, then, with a consideration of the effect of the story upon generations of readers. What *does* the story touch in us? (We should be reminded here of our discussion, in Chapter V, above, of Mary Shelley's *Frankenstein*, to which I shall return in this chapter.)

ii

STEVENSON'S STORY reflects the widespread opinion that there are in all men deep-seated passions of a dubious character, passions which lead to a desire for anonymous devilry. This opinion—which does seem to be the general opinion of the age, even though it may have distant sources—includes the awareness that we sometimes are not very confident about being able to handle such passions—and this partly because we may not fully want to handle them. Consider what is said—by Glaucon, it should be noticed, not by Socrates—in the second book of Plato's *Republic* (through the story of Gyges' ring of invisibility) about the dark yearnings lurking in every man, or at least in most men. (See p. 227 in Stevenson's story.)

Consider also a dream recently called to my attention—the dream of a mature, well-behaved man with a rather practical sense and with considerable understanding of himself. He dreamed of people digging around in a place where he had once buried, and buried deeply, someone whom he had killed. The digging threatened to bring to light a killing which he had covered up so well that he himself had almost forgotten about it, a killing so awful for him that he did not want ever to recall it. The dreamer awoke with this dangerous exposure threatening him; he could not bear it, and so he escaped from his dream to the waking state. But—and this is what I want to emphasize in thinking about the story of Dr. Jekyll and Mr. Hyde—this dream was so graphic that not only did it take several minutes for the man to comprehend that he had indeed been dreaming but it also took several days for him to become absolutely certain that he had never committed any murder or buried any body, that he had never submerged in his unconscious such a dreadful deed. That is, he had been moved by the dream to wonder whether he had, in fact, killed a man and hidden the body—and then repressed it all out of terror at being exposed.

Why was this dreamer so susceptible? What buried misdeeds—or, more likely, what suppressed passions—did the dream threaten to expose to *his* attention? Are there these passions in all of us? Do we not get glimpses of such passions in our dreams? We sometimes see what inebriation can bring out in a man, a side of him well concealed from view in his everyday life. (I recall observing the inhibition-lowering effect of oxygen-lack upon Air Cadets during our training in the use of flight-masks. Indeed, I recall seeing a sly and ugly passion exhibit itself in the makeup of one colleague on that occasion more than three decades ago that, it turned out, others lived to regret not having taken due notice of. Had those observers not been so young, "idealistic," and hence tolerant, a considerable amount of subsequent heartache could perhaps have been warded off. That is, one is not always prepared to believe what one chances to see.)

Does the story of Jekyll and Hyde remind us of submerged passions in us? Does it appeal thereby both to our hidden desires and to our hidden fears? As Dr. Jekyll's life draws to an end, it is observed of Jekyll and Hyde:

> Jekyll (who was composite) now with the most sensitive apprehensions, now with a greedy gusto, projected and shared in the pleasures and adventures of Hyde; but Hyde was indifferent to Jekyll, or but remembered him as the mountain bandit remembers the cavern in which he conceals himself from pursuit. [pp. 230–31]

Is everyday life—the respectable lives we live—the cavern in which our more undisciplined and licentious passions conceal themselves from pursuit? (See, also, p. 233.)

How seriously *is* the story to be taken as descriptive of the hidden excesses of the human soul and of the complexities of human motivations? Does it appeal to us because it *is* descriptive or only because, in its persuasive "realism," it appears to be?

iii

OTHER FEATURES of this story contribute to its appeal. These features can perhaps be summed up by the observation that this story combines, in a curious manner, both the very old and the very new—both witchcraft and science fiction.

Jekyll and Hyde is essentially the story of a respectable man who is able to conceal his shameful desires and his occasional escapades, but who is finally overcome by the wicked follies he permits himself. What would the effect of the story be if Dr. Jekyll had been remarkably good at disguises, with the role of Mr. Hyde one which permitted him to "express himself"?

This is a way of asking whether the use of the drug is essential. Does not its use contribute substantially to the dramatization of the moral risks of hypocrisy? Not just any drug would do, by the way, but one which changes not only the behavior but also the very appearance of the doctor. Perhaps even more sensational, the experiments with the drug lead to the inability of the doctor to recover himself. (pp. 205-6, 238) This incapacity makes the story particularly effective since (as we saw in Chapters I and V, above) most people, most of the time, may not believe that someone who misbehaves is truly hurt unless he is caught. Dr. Jekyll must get trapped in the person of Mr. Hyde to make his folly apparent to all.

The primary purpose of the drug must be to release Mr. Hyde in Dr. Jekyll, not the other way around. That is, most readers are interested in the evil lurking in us all, not in the good of which we may all be capable. (But consider the popular conversion of Scrooge, in Chapter VI, above.) Drugs which make us behave ourselves are suspect, but drugs which release the inner man, even a worse man, are interesting. This perverse interest is particularly strong when the experimenter is himself a scientist. Perhaps there is, for many of us, something intrinsically ambiguous about the scientist: he wields great power. Knowing what we do about our own secret yearnings, we fear that that power may be used as much for ill as for good—but some ills we are not altogether reluctant to watch someone experiment with.

Dr. Jekyll is the one character in the story who stands for research, for seeking out the truth at all costs. He broke with Dr. Lanyon because that old friend was skeptical about Dr. Jekyll's research. (pp. 175-76) Dr. Jekyll insisted upon pursuing "heretical" inquiries—inquiries which can invest mankind with unprecedented powers and opportunities. (p. 182) Do we not, as moderns, have a deeper affinity with Dr. Jekyll than with either Dr. Lanyon or Mr. Utterson, the old-fashioned lawyer of unquestioned probity? Do we not endorse Dr. Jekyll's openness to experiment and novelty, however much we may regret the excesses to which Mr. Hyde was inclined? (p. 224) Do we not, in the anonymity of our cities and with the marvels of modern technology, safely lead—are we not trapped in—the lives of "liberated" Dr. Jekylls?

iv

CENTRAL TO the story of Dr. Jekyll and Mr. Hyde is the episode in which Mr. Utterson is summoned to Dr. Jekyll's house, where he finds the household terrified. (p. 202f) He breaks down the door to the mysterious laboratory in which a harried man is known to be hiding. Once this happens, things begin to unravel. That is, the principal action ends when Mr. Hyde's body is found inside the laboratory. (p. 210)

All is over then, except for Mr. Utterson's reading (in his own home) of Dr. Lanyon's narrative and of Dr. Jekyll's confession, and except for Mr. Utterson's promised return to Dr. Jekyll's house before midnight when the police shall be called to deal with Mr. Hyde's body. (pp. 213f, 222f) (What *is* Mr. Utterson's midnight duty? What should he say about what has happened? He alone knows what has been going on. What duty does he owe to the community and to his client? [p. 213] There is Mr. Hyde's body: how is it to be buried, as Mr. Hyde or as Dr. Jekyll? Is Dr. Jekyll simply to be considered permanently missing?)

Thus, the first half of the story is action, rather strange action turning around the periodic appearances of Mr. Hyde, around the fluctuating public moods of Dr. Jekyll, and around the puzzling relation of one man to the other. The second half of the story is all explanation, the accounts by Dr. Lanyon and by Dr. Jekyll. We move, that is, from the outer life of Dr. Jekyll and Mr. Hyde to their inner life. Is not this inner life somehow to be regarded by readers as "the real thing''? We are not satisfied that the everyday conduct of men is the most critical thing about them, except as indications (but only indications) of what is hidden from sight.

And, it seems to be indicated by the story (or, at least, believed by us), that which is hidden from sight is more nearly genuine (or, as one hears today, "authentic"). It is that hidden version of ourselves that we are supposed to care about most: we move thereby from the outer to the inner story, from the seeming to the real.

It is the "real self," the true self, that we are to care about. But have we not been *shaped* to regard hidden desires as somehow the true self, as the self to be cared for? That true self, we have been taught by modern analysts, cannot be changed; it can only be controlled in the interest of personal utility and social harmony. Yet, are not these opinions about the real and the unchanging themselves quite changeable?

Be that as it may, Stevenson prefaced his story with a poem, addressed to a favorite cousin:

> *It's ill to loose the bands that God decreed to bind;*
> *Still we be the children of the heather and the wind.*
> *Far away from home, O it's still for you and me*
> *That the broom is blowing bonnie in the north countrie.*

"It's ill to loose the bands that God decreed to bind": this suggests that it was fatal folly for Dr. Jekyll to release the fiend hidden within him. Does this not also suggest that that fiend is something permanent, something unchangeable? It is natural, it seems to be suggested, that men be complicated, a mixture of impulses both benevolent and wicked.

Is not the story taken to suggest that the passions can only be inhibited, not trained?[240] A masterful restraint of passions is seen in Mr. Utterson, the faithful lawyer, but it seems to be at the expense of liveliness and even a vital curiosity. Or, put another way, Dr. Jekyll (it would seem to the modern reader) is the only one who tries to *live*. (p. 226) His attempt proves disastrous, but nevertheless interesting—and perhaps not altogether blameworthy?

The modern opinion about such matters depends on certain notions about the self and about what is good.

V

THE *SELF* is what emerges when much is made of what is called *individuality* among us. (Notice that we do use in this connection the term *self* more than the old-fashioned term, *soul*.) An emphasis upon individuality means, among other things, that we should attempt to intensify the experiences of the self. But, I suggest, if the emphasis is placed upon individuality and its expression, we are bound to have schisms of the soul; indeed, we *should* have such schisms, if only to give each part of the soul something of what it yearns for.

Individuality means, at least for many, no serious family ties; no community in which one is immersed; no religious or other "commitments" that are deep and enduring and independent of the inclinations one happens to have. Thus, none of the men in this story is married; it is a sexless society. (This may be seen, in a perverse form, in the trampling of the little girl by Mr. Hyde. [p. 169] [241]) Each man is largely on his own. Thus, Dr. Jekyll pushes to an extreme what may be implied in the lives of the other successful men in this large city. He says of his feelings, upon his first transformation into Mr. Hyde:

> There was something strange in my sensations, something indescribably new and, from its very novelty, incredibly sweet. I felt younger, lighter, happier in body; within I was conscious of a heady recklessness, a current of disordered sensual images running like a mill race in my fancy, a dissolution of the bonds of obligation, an unknown but not an innocent freedom of the soul. I knew myself, at the first breath of this new life, to be more wicked, tenfold more wicked, sold a slave to my original evil; and the thought, in that moment, braced and delighted me like wine. I stretched out my hands, exulting in the freshness of these sensations; and in the act, I was suddenly aware that I had lost in stature. [pp. 224–25]

Notice the identification here of novelty as "incredibly sweet." Is not this openness to novelty one feature, perhaps necessarily so, of a democratic age and its legitimation of everyone's self-expression? Notice, also, that Dr. Jekyll (and Robert Louis Stevenson) can still use *soul* where we would probably say *self*. In this, they are old-fashioned. (But see pp. 228, 232.)

Is not *soul* critically different from *self*? *Self,* as I have indicated, is somehow intimately related to individuality. *Soul,* on the other hand, points to what is common or general, to a principle, to a natural function, to a standard to be realized. The full development of the soul means a lessening of selfness, of individuality—a conformity of oneself to the very best. When one's soul is fully developed, one's childhood and personal history do not matter much. But would not such disciplined development be regarded by many moderns as a kind of death?

The drug employed by Dr. Jekyll empowered Mr. Hyde; it freed him both from moral restraints and from social control. But it did not do anything *for* Dr. Jekyll: he still had Mr. Hyde within him, wanting to get out. Does this affliction suggest, in still another way, that much of modern experimentation can only legitimate (or empower) the bad, not better equip the good? Or would we still say that this risk is worth running, that it is good to try to understand one's whole self, that it is "only human" and hence good to give all one's faculties full play?[242]

vi

MR. UTTERSON, the lawyer, is commendable but, alas, quite forgettable. (Indeed, of all the characters in this story, do only Dr. Jekyll and Mr. Hyde come alive?) To be forgotten is, in a way, to die.

But Mr. Utterson does prevail. Indeed, he inherits Dr. Jekyll's sizable estate. (p. 212) What accounts for that? He is *utterly* a *son* of his people, of the moral conventions of the day (and of his profession); he is integrity and loyalty personified. (pp. 183, 198) We depend upon such men—but we are not much interested in them. Even so, his name opens the book. (p. 167)

Dr. Lanyon does not prevail. Indeed, he is driven to his death even before Dr. Jekyll. What is his failing? At first, he is not openminded enough: perhaps he could have helped Dr. Jekyll at an earlier stage of his research if he had not been so skeptical. Later, he becomes too open-minded: perhaps he should not have been as curious as he was in his encounter with Mr. Hyde. (p. 220) What does the fatal shock come from? Surely not from seeing Mr. Hyde, since others had seen him (evil as he was) and lived, but rather from seeing the *change* itself (from Mr. Hyde to Dr. Jekyll). Should this be enough to kill an experienced doctor who has many times seen such profound changes as that from life to death? Is this shock an intellectual one, more than a moral one, an inability of Dr. Lanyon to face up to his error about what Dr. Jekyll or science was capable of? Can this shock be fatal?

Nor does Mr. Hyde prevail. He is, in a way, rather stupid in his evil, however calculating he might be.[243] Mr. Hyde is restrained only by his intense desire for self-preservation. We can see here how important an element *that* can be in promoting justice. (In this way, at least, the virtues tend to be helpful, to be good for one.) What would happen if every man could switch freely between the respectable, and the dissolute, parts of himself? Would only the foolish man do so, the one who does not appreciate that good is truly better than evil, even aside from public opinion and its consequences?

The descriptions of Mr. Hyde are instructive. He arouses an instinctive repulsion in those who see him. (pp. 170, 172, 179-80, 187, 189, 200, 208, 217-18, 225-26) This repulsion suggests, does it not, that man is naturally attuned to good and against evil? Evil, we again notice, is linked to ugliness—as the unattractive side of the soul is seen for what it is.[244] Evil truly disfigures, no matter what the misguided may suppose. Nature at large, it seems to be suggested, reflects the evil in the human world: atmospheric and other conditions mirror the moral action we happen to be interested in. Thus, *the world* (we are reassured) *is one*—with evil as "the lethal side of man." (p. 226) Evil is shown to be intrinsically self-defeating: the evil man, too, seeks a good (his good). That is, he, too, recognizes the primacy of goodness, however he may misapprehend it.

Mr. Hyde invokes God in his last words, as he pleads for mercy. (p. 40)

vii

I HAVE suggested that we are fully ourselves—fully expressing the most important part of our selves—when we *act* as we should. Perhaps this suggestion should now be amended to include the observation that we truly are fully developed souls when we *understand* how things are.

The story of Dr. Jekyll and Mr. Hyde does draw upon our desire to understand things, upon our interest in working things out. We enjoy seeing, especially in a second reading of this well-crafted story, how the clues fit together to make sense of the entire account. But the story itself makes more of action than of understanding. (Dr. Jekyll's efforts to understand certain things contribute to his downfall; the same may be said of Dr. Lanyon's.) Is it not assumed in the story that virtue rests more on *will* than on *understanding?* And is not understanding more related to the soul and will more related to the self? Understanding is more general, will is more particular?

The emphasis upon the self and upon the importance of the will, as well as the emphasis upon inevitable dark passions, may be a legacy of Christian teachings that survive (however transformed) into a skeptical age. Thus, Dr. Jekyll can speak of "the perennial war among my members." (p. 223)[245]

But, I have suggested, it may not be natural to believe that dark passions are inevitable in all men. This belief may be an opinion about the passions—an opinion as much subject to shaping as the passions themselves. I have also suggested that the modern opinion, which Stevenson so graphically supports, may be faulty: it regards schisms of the soul as inevitable—perhaps as signs of life—if not even as simply good. Does this modern opinion somehow make us, if only in self-defense, more permissive than we should be toward the psychic aberrations of others?[246]

Be all this as it may, the dramatic does appeal (in its concreteness) to the individual, even to the child in us. Stories are useful for teaching moral lessons which may otherwise seem dry and uninteresting. Whatever illusion it may be in his (and our) interest to produce and cherish, the perceptive artist understands that what he presents in dramatic form may not be simply true.

We notice, for example, that we cannot be sure, even within the terms of this story, that there ever were the vital transformations from Dr. Jekyll into Mr. Hyde around which the story turns. There is no "evidence" of this metamorphosis except for what Dr. Jekyll and Dr. Lanyon (both dying, perhaps desperate, men) say. Dr. Lanyon doubts his senses, and Dr. Jekyll may be disturbed when he writes. The narrator himself never says, in his own name, that such transformations do, or can, take place. (Compare p. 201.)

Why is the narrator so guarded? Why does he leave us only with the questionable testimony of Dr. Lanyon and of Dr. Jekyll? Does he remind us thereby that he has had recourse to a persuasive allegory because most people cannot see directly the self-defeating character of secret vices? Does the narrator insist upon thus recording the truth, if only for readers like himself, whatever it may be useful to induce others to believe?

In this manner, the truthful moralist (the killjoy, so to speak) can find sanctuary, in the manner of Mr. Hyde, in the form of the attractive storyteller who exploits for dramatic interest the dark yearnings we may have from time to time. In this manner, also, the artist (even when he himself is not fully aware of what he is saying) reveals to the thoughtful reader what he may think.

The reader has no doubt been reminded of Mary Shelley's *Frankenstein*; many things said in Chapter V, above, have been relevant here. But one critical difference should be emphasized. The world of Jekyll and Hyde is far less public, and less public-spirited, than that of Walton and Frankenstein: far more is made in Shelley's story of noble ambition and of great adventure; far less is made of personal gratification. (This shift is reflected in the reliance in Stevenson's story upon a narrator who is, as a lawyer, in the private service of the "hero.") We now move on to an even greater privatization, not only of the lives described but also of the very art developed to describe them.

XIII. JAMES JOYCE (1882–1941)

PART ONE

> *"Now," [said Socrates,] "if a man who is
> able by wisdom to become every sort of thing
> and to imitate all things should come to our
> city, wishing to make a display of himself and
> his poems, we would fall on our knees before
> him as a man sacred, wonderful, and pleasing;
> but we would say that there is no such man
> among us in the city, nor is it right for such a
> man to be born here. We would send him to
> another city, with myrrh poured over his head
> and crowned with wool, while we ourselves
> would use a more austere and less pleasing poet
> and teller of tales for our benefit, one who
> would imitate the style of the decent man and
> would say what he says in those models that we
> set down as laws at the beginning, when we
> undertook to educate the soldiers."*

— Plato, *Republic* 398A–B

i

WILLIAM BUTLER Yeats, in a letter to the Secretary of the Royal Literary Fund, spoke of the impecunious James Joyce as an artist with "a most beautiful gift."[247] He reports, in this letter, "I have read in a paper called *The Egoist* certain chapters of a new novel, a disguised autobiography, which increases my conviction that he is the most remarkable new talent in Ireland to-day." This tribute is to Joyce's *A Portrait of the Artist as a Young Man,* that sensitive account of the first two decades in the life of an aspiring poet, Stephen Dedalus, who would emerge, a couple years later in that life, as one of the principal characters in Joyce's *Ulysses.* (*Portrait* was finished in 1914; *Ulysses,* in 1921.)

All citations in the text of this chapter to *A Portrait of the Artist as a Young Man* are to the Viking Press edition (New York, 1957).

All citations in the text of this chapter to *Ulysses* are to the Modern Library edition (New York, 1942).

The opening pages of *Portrait* suggest the natural aptitude of Stephen Dedalus for the arts: his sensitivity to stories, to rhyming, and to play upon words is evident from his earliest years. (pp. 7-8, 9, 16) His father tells him stories (p. 7); the father is a singer, but one who recognizes other singers as superior (pp. 88-89); the entire family sings together, evidently well (p. 163); Stephen himself consciously imitates various poets (pp. 70, 252); Stephen's own gifts can be said to be evident quite early in the tale he relates, with success, to youthful fellow students of his bold visit to the rector, when he complains about unjust treatment at the hands of one of the school staff. (pp. 54f, 59, 72-73, 78, 156) Indeed, the hero's "strange name seemed to him a prophecy," hearkening back to that of the "fabulous artificer" of Greek antiquity. (pp. 25, 168, 225, 253) In short, Stephen Dedalus considers himself born to be an artist. (pp. 64-65, 169-70, 200-201, 221)

How, then, does the artist understand himself? He conceives it his "destiny," perhaps even his duty, "to be elusive of social or religious orders." (p. 162) "He was destined," he tells himself, "to learn his own wisdom apart from others or to learn the wisdom of others himself wandering among the snares of the world." (p. 162) Thus, he resists attachment to any established institution. (pp. 160, 201-2) Poetry is what matters: it is irrelevant if one's model (for example, Lord Byron, as against Lord Tennyson) is heretical or immoral. (pp. 70, 80-81) Dedalus is told by a patriot that a man's country comes first, that he can be a poet or mystic after. (p. 203) But Dedalus is not concerned with the affairs of the day or with such issues as world peace. (pp. 197-98) Instead, he very early separates himself from his fellows:

> The question of honour here raised was, like all such questions, trivial to him. While his mind had been pursuing its intangible phantoms and turning in irresolution from such pursuit he had heard about him the constant voices of his father and of his masters, urging him to be a gentleman above all things and urging him to be a good catholic above all things. The voices had now come to be hollowsounding in his ears. When the gymnasium had been opened he had heard another voice urging him to be strong and manly and healthy and when the movement towards national revival had begun to be felt in the college yet another voice had bidden him be true to his coun-

try and help to raise up her language and tradition. In the profane
world, as he foresaw, a worldly voice would bid him raise up his
father's fallen state by his labours and, meanwhile, the voice of his
school comrades urged him to be a decent fellow... And it was the
din of all these hollowsounding voices that made him halt irresolutely
in the pursuit of phantoms. He gave them ear only for a time but he
was happy only when he was far from them, beyond their call, alone
or in the company of phantasmal comrades. [pp. 83–84]

To be far from others, and from their admonitions and beguile-
ments, permits him to assert himself. Creativity is seen as essentially
the expression of one's soul, so much so that willfulness is virtually
transformed into art. (p. 203) Dedalus finds it difficult to remain in
Ireland. (pp. 38, 201–3, 225) He seeks a mode of life that permits
exercise of the spirit in "unfettered freedom." (pp. 245–46) The
ancient Daedalus is drawn upon as his model, not Homer or Orpheus:
for Daedalus, more than the others, was an *artificer*, someone who
did not express (or imitate) but rather overcame or harnessed nature.
Stephen Dedalus is not disposed to subordinate himself to *discovery*.
Rather, he must express himself: he must create, if possible, as God
had done in making the world from nothing (or from worthless stuff),
devising even his models and standards as he goes. (pp. 189–90, 215)
In this sense, it seems, Dedalus tries to identify his will with the will
of God. (p. 241)

Such identification of one's will with God's is obviously to be
understood not as humility but as self-assertion. It is not subservience
but rather revolt. (p. 247) It draws upon Lucifer's defiant *non serviam*
("I will not serve"). (pp. 117, 239, 247–48) We know this state of
mind as pride—and it is pride that is referred to again and again in
Portrait as vital to Dedalus's self-assertion. Thus, pride restrains him
from repentance, "pride in his own sin," "his barren pride." (pp.
103–4) The sin of pride, he is told, led to the fall of Lucifer. (pp.
117, 247; also, p. 133) Pride is reflected in his concern about where
he will confess his sins, when he does decide to confess. (pp. 126,
140) Pride is seen as intimately associated with all the vices. (p. 106)
It is even seen in the priest who tries to induce Dedalus to join the
Jesuits: it is "the greatest honour" to be called into the order by God,
he is told. (pp. 157–59, 161) Here, pride counters pride. (p. 158) On
another occasion Dedalus is told, "In your heart you are an Irishman

but your pride is too powerful." (p. 203. See, also, pp. 59, 134, 150, 153, 164-65, 168-69, 175-76.)

Dedalus is said by a colleague to be the only one among them with "an individual mind." (pp. 200-201) Sometime before, while Dedalus watched his father and two cronies drink to the memory of their past, he reflected:

> An abyss of fortune or of temperament sundered him from them. His mind seemed older than theirs: it shone coldly on their strifes and happiness and regrets like a moon upon a younger earth. No life or youth stirred in him as it had stirred in them. He had known neither the pleasure of companionship with others nor the vigour of rude male health nor filial piety. Nothing stirred within his soul but a cold and cruel and loveless lust. His childhood was dead or lost and with it his soul capable of simple joys and he was drifting amid life like the barren shell of the moon. [pp. 95-96]

Dedalus goes on to announce a credo, affirming the consequences of the aloneness he has long experienced. (p. 201) He informs a temporary companion:

> You have asked me what I would do and what I would not do. I will tell you what I will do and what I will not do. I will not serve that in which I no longer believe, whether it call itself my home, my fatherland, or my church: and I will try to express myself in some mode of life or art as freely as I can and as wholly as I can, using for my defence the only arms I allow myself to use—silence, exile, and cunning. [p. 247]

He then adds:

> I do not fear to be alone or to be spurned for another or to leave whatever I have to leave. And I am not afraid to make a mistake, even a great mistake, a lifelong mistake and perhaps as long as eternity too. [p. 247]

Thus, a principle has been made of standing alone, of being oneself, of expressing and thereby risking oneself. We are not surprised to notice that Percy Shelley, another gifted exile, can provide Dedalus comfort and guidance (pp. 96, 213), and that his patron saint should be the first Christian martyr. (p. 159)

ii

WHAT IS that soul like which is determined to express itself fully? A companion suggests that Dedalus is still "supersaturated with the religion" which he says he disbelieves. (p. 240) (Yeats observed, in a 1933 letter, that Joyce "never escapes from his Catholic sense of sin."[248]) Certainly, Dedalus will not trifle with the Roman Catholic communion service: he fears, at the least, "the chemical action which would be set up in [his] soul by a false homage to a symbol behind which are massed twenty centuries of authority and veneration." (p. 243. See pp. 46–47.) But his is also a soul which can confide to itself, in a diary, as Dedalus prepares to leave Ireland:

> Welcome, O life! I go to encounter for the millionth time the reality of experience and to forge in the smithy of my soul the uncreated conscience of my race. [p. 253]

To speak of forging something "in the smithy of [one's] soul" is to show the positive side of the artist's activity. He is obliged not only to strip himself of attachments and of crippling passions (such as anger [p. 82]); he is obliged also to *make* something. Dedalus regards the artist as one who "forg[es] anew in his workshop out of the sluggish matter of the earth a new soaring impalpable imperishable being." (p. 169) He insists that "he [will] create proudly out of the freedom and power of the soul, as the great artificer whose name he bore, a living thing, new and soaring and beautiful, impalpable, imperishable." (pp. 169–70) Central to *this* restatement of the attributes of the living thing he would create—new, soaring, beautiful, impalpable, imperishable—is, of course, beauty.

The dean of studies, a somewhat deferential priest, puts a problem to Dedalus in this way:

> You are an artist, are you not, Mr. Dedalus? The object of the artist is the creation of the beautiful. What the beautiful is is another question.... Can you solve that question now? [pp. 185–86]

Something is expected from Dedalus "on the esthetic question." (p. 186) He draws for his "esthetic philosophy" (p. 180) on Aquinas, "that is beautiful the apprehension of which pleases" (pp. 186, 207); on Plato, "beauty is the splendour of truth" (p. 208); and on Aristotle, with his invocation of pity and terror, which Dedalus attempts to define. (pp. 204–5) Dedalus then returns to Aquinas to explicate the proposition, "Three things are needed for beauty, wholeness, harmony and radiance." (p. 211) (I observe in passing that Lucifer had been spoken of as "a radiant and mighty angel" by the artful preacher during the boys' retreat. [p. 117])

We can profit from a consideration of Dedalus's reflections on the beautiful and the ugly. (See pp. 123, 129, 145, 176, 189–90, 206f, 251.) It may be enough for our immediate purpose to notice that Aquinas (himself a poet [p. 210]) suffices for Dedalus up to a point:

> McAlister would call my esthetic theory applied Aquinas. So far as this side of esthetic philosophy extends Aquinas will carry me all along the line. When we come to the phenomena of artistic conception, artistic gestation and artistic reproduction, I require a new terminology and a new personal experience. [p. 209]

That is, Aquinas (or, behind him, Aristotle?) suffices for Dedalus so long as the explicit concern is with the *object* to be created.

It is a different matter, however, when Dedalus turns to what sometimes seems to him (and to Joyce as well?) most absorbing: the self-consciousness of the artist as artist. For Aquinas, it would seem, the artist is primarily the servant of beauty; but Dedalus (as we have seen) insists that he will not serve; rather, he will assert himself. Beauty, then, must take a subordinate place in his artistic striving: perhaps it can even be said that for Joyce, as well as for Dedalus, beauty usually results (in an artist of talent) from uncompromising self-assertion in artistic matters. Beauty (a form of truth?) results from, but is not the primary object of, the self-assertion which characterizes artistic striving.

iii

ARTISTIC STRIVING cannot truly be an end in itself, whatever artists may say from time to time. Let us reconsider, then, Dedalus's attempt "to forge in the smithy of [his] soul the uncreated conscience of [his] race." (p. 253)

What does "race" refer to? It no doubt includes the Irish people (p. 203), but is it limited to that people? Does it include the English-speaking peoples, the peoples of the language in which Dedalus will write? (pp. 188–89, 252) Does it even extend to all the peoples of the West, all those who can be influenced by his writings, all those who trace their heritage and hence their interests back to Homer, Plato, Aristotle, and Aquinas?

And what of "the uncreated conscience"? Notice that Dedalus speaks of it as being *forged* by him. (See, also, pp. 169–70.) He does not regard the conscience he proposes to establish as requiring the discovery and reaffirmation of the best of his race, of his heritage.[249] But if it is to be "created" anew, what standards will be brought to bear by the artist in establishing standards? Are we to understand that the condition of *his* soul may well determine the standards laid down? And is not that condition likely to be a matter of chance?[250]

If the condition of the artist's soul should be decisive, then the private becomes critical, especially that part of the private rooted in one's childhood, a childhood which is not "dead or lost" (as the romantic Dedalus had wanted to believe) but rather buried alive and still quite potent. (pp. 95–96) Thus, art criticism tends to become biography. Is it not somehow fitting that the most rebellious modern artist—an artist who can even imply that Lucifer with his *non serviam* may be the patron saint of his calling (pp. 117, 247)—is it not fitting and proper that this most rebellious artist should prove the most tethered (even more so than Proust)? His greatest story, his master-piece, is limited to a compulsive account of one day in one town.[251]

This tethering, an almost instinctive tethering, can be regarded as a natural reaction, in an artist of genius, to an unprecedented (and threatening?) liberation from restraints long established both by his people and by his art. In Joyce's tethering himself to the Dublin of his youth, his own (his unwilled own) reasserts itself with a vengeance. Thus, convention and chance take on the appearance of nature. It is natural, of course, to be shaped by one's own, but it is natural also (in a sense, *more* natural) to look beyond one's own, with a view to what is simply the best (or, in matters of art, with a view to what is beautiful in its perfection).

The reader is obliged, in thinking about Joyce's notions and the modern addiction to experimentation he promoted, to consider the place of nature both in the beautiful and in that good of which beauty is the pleasure-including manifestation. Compare Dedalus, who in his definitions of pity and of terror draws upon that which is "grave and constant in human sufferings." (p. 204) Does eternal nature show herself for him only in that which is enduring in human misery? One can wonder if there was something about Joyce's upbringing, or about the Ireland of his day, that made nature suspect, perhaps even more suspect than it had become among intellectuals all over the West by the time Dedalus began to assert himself.[252]

One further consequence of Dedalus's self-assertion should be noticed. Once he has made or founded ("for the millionth time"? [p. 253]) the "uncreated conscience" of his race, others will be bound by what he has done, by what he has chosen to do, by what he has happened to *will*. That is, if this artist has his way, he will be the last free man of his race—until another self-centered rebel (perhaps generations, if not even centuries, hence) happens to find himself in conditions which permit *him,* in turn, to assert himself.

This kind of enduring subjugation, rooted in the (potentially tyrannical?) will, bears thinking about—especially since it appears in the form of a liberation from venerable aspirations which may have been more or less rooted in nature.

Thus, we see, an escape can be transformed into a new imprisonment. Is it always likely to be thus when that which is to be avoided is considered more vivid and more critical than that which is aspired to—when men (not so much Joyce as those who have provided the philosophic setting for his self-aggrandizement) take as their goals "not the perfection of man but those lower goals actually pursued by most men and most societies most of the time"?[253]

We can turn now to the books, *Ulysses* and *Finnegans Wake,* for which this portrait of the artist as a young man was a self-conscious preparation. This will conclude our episodic review of the more or less steady retreat from the grand public world of Shakespeare into the intense, intimate, the all too often disturbed private world of the modern artist—that private world in which neither old-fashioned nobility nor genuine philosophy nor the deepest piety can be taken seriously.

PART TWO

i

JAMES JOYCE'S *Ulysses* has won for itself a reputation which makes it plausible to hear it acclaimed as "a literary monument of our age."[254] It is reported that Joyce himself remarked to his wife, upon finishing *Ulysses,* that the only question in his mind was whether he was a greater writer than Shakespeare.[255]

On the other hand, a critic in *The Times Literary Supplement* recently singled out James Joyce as one "vastly overrated" writer of this century, labeling him as "arrogant, unpleasant, and above all, quite unreadable."[256] But it should be noticed, considering the difficulties Joyce once had getting his book past the censors, that even the most vigorous opponents of obscenity today have no quarrel with him on *that* score. Thus, one recent attack on certain newsstand publications included the insistence that a sensible community should be able to discriminate "between pornography and *Ulysses*."[257]

Whatever one may think of *Ulysses,* it may well be one of the most influential novels of the twentieth century. One critic has suggested that it has replaced Milton's *Paradise Lost* as "the book which all subsequent books in English take for granted."[258] Certainly, the influence of the book has been profound, just as the responses to it have been varied. The book is something of a touchstone, so varied have been the responses to it: how one responds to *Ulysses* is likely to say a good deal about one—about one's interests, standards, and sensibilities. Many of the achievements and failures of modern literature are suggested by this book.

The variety of responses to *Ulysses* may well point to serious problems in modern life. This may be one of those times when the very best—or an elaborate counterfeit of the best—is not generally recognized for what it is. Something is wrong, that is, when most people do not see obvious things pretty much as they are.

ii

ONE THING should be recognized at the outset of our consideration of *Ulysses:* there are many knowledgeable and sensitive people (such as Edmund Wilson and Malcolm P. Sharp) who are ardent admirers of the book. Whatever one's reservations about it may be, one must somehow account for the considerable appeal the book has for them.

One might not have to make such remarks if there were not many other equally well read and receptive readers who consider it very difficult. They find large sections of the book quite tedious and laborious. But for the prestige of the book and the prospect that it will "pick up" again, they would not continue to the end. Even among those who like the book very much, there can be considerable puzzlement about what is going on (not about how something is to be understood, but rather about just what is happening). This is a kind, and degree, of mystery that one does not have when one reads, say, Homer's *Odyssey* or Cervantes's *Don Quixote*—and this difference in accessibility is so even though we are much further from Homer's Mediterranean and Cervantes's Spain than we are from Joyce's Dublin. Many of the difficulties in this respect are not likely to be decreased (but rather increased) by the passage of time. These difficulties are intimately related, it would seem, to what Joyce is attempting to do in his book—and can be seen as resulting, in part, from the author's drawing upon a large fund of personal recollections to suggest the character of private life.

How puzzling the book can be—perhaps this says something important about the very nature of things?—may be seen in a passage taken from the account of a casual meeting among several men in a newspaper office:

> Pause. J.J. O'Molloy took out his cigarette case.
> False lull. Something quite ordinary.
> Messenger took out his matchbox thoughtfully and lit his cigar.
> I have often thought since on looking back over that strange time that it was that small act, trivial in itself, that striking of that match, that determined the whole aftercourse of both our lives. [p. 138]

I know of no one who has authoritatively explained what this passage means. Is it meant seriously? Is it ironic? Is it, perhaps, a playful reflection of Proust? Who is the "both" referred to? Indeed, who is the narrator here? There may well be clues elsewhere in *Ulysses* that illuminate this passage—but I have not happened upon them. This is one illustration of the many, many puzzling things in the book—an illustration that is particularly challenging because it *is* about something that is designated as overwhelmingly significant. (See, also, p. 268.)[259]

Ulysses was preceded by *Dubliners*, a collection of good short stories, and by *A Portrait of the Artist as a Young Man*. Difficulties in reading are not significant in those earlier books. The one major book published after *Ulysses*, however, makes child's play out of *Ulysses*, so difficult is *it* to read: one can read page upon page of *Finnegans Wake*—that is, pass one's eyes over its pages—and have no notion of what is going on. Thus, although the experimentation with language and style anticipated in the two earlier books does not usually cripple effective communication in *Ulysses*, it does get out of hand in *Finnegans Wake*—which is likely to be read all the way through only by professional students of English literature.

The most significant thing about *Finnegans Wake* may well be the light it throws back upon what Joyce did, or tried to do, in *Ulysses*. One is obliged to wonder what the purpose of art is—of that art which is shared with a public. We depend in part on our artists to see and to show us how things truly are. Can Joyce and his successors be depended upon to do that for the era of the common man? One should, in asking this question, recall that artists such as Shakespeare and Dickens did have great popular appeal during their own lifetimes: what they wrote had, at the least, a surface meaning immediately accessible to the English-speaking peoples.

Joyce's critical precedessors may not be Dickens and Shakespeare but rather such thinkers as Descartes, Rousseau, Sterne, and Stendhal —Stendhal, with his openness to spirited sensibility, Rousseau, with his emphasis on a "natural" individuality; and Descartes and Sterne, with their efforts to build the universal upon intimate details drawn from the here-and-now. And, whatever one may think of Joyce's art, there is to be found in *Ulysses* a character, one Leopold Bloom, who ranks in recognizability with the foremost literary characters of the twentieth century. (Saul Bellow's Herzog and Philip Roth's Portnoy are similarly familiar in this country. They are characters who can be said to have been inspired by James Joyce's Bloom, but in an even more Freudian "world" than Joyce took for granted.) This wanderer across Dublin is known to many who have never opened the book in which he tried to find a home.

iii

THAT BOOK *is* about the here-and-now—about what happens to certain Dubliners on June 16, 1904. It was on a June day, we are told, that Leopold Bloom began courting his future wife. (p. 370) And, we can learn from Joyce's letters, it was on a June 16 that Joyce himself began to court his own wife.[260] But how is this June 16 different from all other June 16s? It is the day, Bloom has correctly surmised, that his sexually attractive wife will be visited in his absence by a lusty bachelor, one Blazes Boylan. Bloom, in his guilt and gentleness, tacitly acquiesces in the arrangement made—and stays away all day and well into the night, indeed well past midnight, wandering around Dublin, doing good here and there and having little good done to himself. Various people seem to be aware of the connection between Boylan and Molly Bloom (see, for example, p. 91); certainly, Bloom himself is obsessed by Boylan, being reminded of him time and again throughout the day as he goes about his affairs.[261] His guilt is generated in part, it seems, by his impotence, at least with respect to his wife, which began with the death a decade before (after only eleven days of life) of their second child, their only son. (See pp. 743, 765.)

The first part of *Ulysses* is devoted to the morning adventures of Stephen Dedalus, a twenty-two-year-old poet. We see him in the quarters which he will abandon today (as Bloom temporarily does his own) to the companion from whom he has become estranged; then, at the school where he teaches, first in the classroom and thereafter talking to the head of the school; and then walking to meet others at lunch, musing on his circumstances. He is shown as a sensitive, bitter (even petulant) young man of talent who gets considerable respect from some of his elders. This sequence of scenes is, to repeat, the first part of the book, to which almost fifty pages are devoted.

The second part of the book, of some 540 pages, opens with the early morning hours in the Bloom household, where Molly is served breakfast in bed by her husband. He is then followed in his morning movements. He receives a letter from a woman he does not know, with whom he has been carrying on an amorous correspondence, and indulges in a visit to a bathhouse. At eleven o'clock, he is found in a carriage with others, including Stephen Dedalus's father, riding out to the graveyard for the burial of Paddy Dignam. (This episode, which reminds one of stories in *Dubliners*, is one of the best in the book.) All of these episodes, as well as the three in Part I, depend a great deal on the private musings of the principal characters (Dedalus in Part I; Bloom, thus far, in Part II). We hear what each happens to say to himself, or to notice, as he moves about the city. Much that would explain matters to us is left unsaid: characters do not say things for the sake of this narrator, who scrupulously records no more than what happens on such occasions. The same limitations are placed on reports of conversations. These limitations may be seen in the next episode, which is largely devoted to encounters among several men (including Stephen Dedalus) in a newspaper office and elsewhere. Bloom is flitting about outside during this episode, trying to sell advertisements. In the next episode he goes to lunch, abandoning a repellent restaurant for a more genteel one. Next, we find ourselves in a library: Bloom moves on the edge of this scene; it is dominated by Stephen Dedalus's discourse to his companions about the decisive relationship of Shakespeare's private life to his plays (especially *Hamlet*). The seventh episode, or section, in Part II, finds us moving across Dublin, following first a priest in his excursion and concluding with the governor general's cavalcade. We see Bloom and others going about their affairs. He, an intellectual of sorts, buys some trash for his wife at a book stall. The next episode is rather musical in its construction: some five dozen "notes," usually phrases or short sentences, are struck at the beginning. These notes anticipate various incidents, which occur, for the most part, in a pub. Among these incidents is the singing by Stephen Dedalus's father. The following episode also turns around a pub, but in circumstances where anger predominates—so much so that Leopold Bloom has to beat a hasty retreat after having antagonized a Jew-hating "citizen." He finds solace, in the next episode (which occurs at about sunset), on a beach where he and a young girl flirt with each other at a safe distance, providing each other with an opportunity for fantasy and some sexual satisfaction (to the accompaniment of a nearby church service). Bloom is reluctant to return home—although it is now well past the time of Boylan's assignation with Molly. He goes, instead, to a maternity hospital to make a sympathy call on a woman who had been in labor three days. As far as the style is concerned, this is one of the more obscure episodes in the book. In fact, its styles vary; one is obliged to labor through it (perhaps like the woman?), as the language is developed (gestated?) from its earliest to its most recent forms. The next (and final) episode of Part II finds Bloom and others (medical students and Stephen Dedalus, who had been in the hospital) visiting a low-life district of Dublin. Here, too, it is often difficult for the reader to figure out what is happening, as the fantasies of various characters are "acted out" before us (particularly the fantasies of Bloom and, to a lesser degree, of Stephen Dedalus, who had disappointed his dying mother by his rejection of the Church). Dedalus, after having been knocked down by a soldier, is rescued by Bloom. This rescue of (and establishment of an intimacy with) someone half his age permits the fortyish Bloom the final fantasy of this episode, the appearance of his dead son, now an idealized eleven-year-old.

Part III, like Part I, consists of three episodes (some 170 pages altogether). The first episode occurs, for the most part, in a cabstand where Bloom tries to bring Dedalus back to complete consciousness (and where a sailor tells tall tales). The second consists of a long series of questions and answers which inform us of Bloom's postmidnight return home with Dedalus in tow, of their conversation and Bloom's thoughts about many subjects, of Dedalus's departure and of Bloom's retirement to his wife's bed. The final episode consists of a long monologue (made up of eight extended sentences) by Molly Bloom who wonders about what her husband has been up to, who recalls her sexual encounters of the day before and of other days, and who perhaps reaffirms her marriage to the long-suffering and long-suffered Leopold Bloom (all this while he sleeps beside her, having uncharacteristically "ordered" her to serve him breakfast in bed in the morning[262]).

These stories—some 760 pages altogether—are presented in such detail and with such skill that we have the sense of having been there, of having also lived through that day. And, we are given to understand (because everything depends on the "consciousness") that one day can stand for the whole of time, and Dublin for the whole of the world. (See p. 377.) Thus, various recapitulations of events, in the course of the day, find us quite familiar with the principal characters and some of the minor ones. One of the recapitulations—Bloom's accounting to himself of his expenditures for the day (pp. 695–96)— reflects the petty character of the day's deeds. (See, also, pp. 373–74, 488, 713–14, 720.) The pettiness seems, in part, due to the malaise following upon the fall, in the preceding decade, of Charles Stewart Parnell and the consequent difficulties of the Irish struggle for independence.[263]

Bloom's troubles might seem independent of the political life of the Irish. Many men cannot understand why Molly ever married him. (See, for example, p. 105.) She is seen by them as eminently desirable. But in choosing him, and staying with him, she may be judging better than they do. Bloom, in turn, knows that he has been happier than he is now in his relations with his wife. (pp. 153, 165) He does not know what to do with or about her—and a legal separation is not foreclosed at the end. (pp. 637–718) It is important for Bloom that he has met Stephen. (pp. 444 [Kismet], 585f, 592, 645 [arm-in-arm]) He is reminded many times that day of his lost son, the son who might have given meaning to his life. Thus, Bloom, who is in some respects a weak and perhaps uninteresting man, tries to "find" himself by attaching himself to Stephen Dedalus. (See pp. 466, 721.)

Bloom finds Dedalus, however, at a time when the talented young man is determined to cut himself loose from all bonds—religious, familial, political. Dedalus is presented as more serious, as considering greater themes, perhaps as more heroic, than Bloom. Bloom is more of a muddler, who somehow stands for life itself. Even so, the genuine human contact provided Dedalus by this fleeting association with his benefactor may help him to write a book such as *Ulysses*.[264]

Critical to any description of this book may be an assessment of the characters portrayed, particularly as to what relations among them should have been. What, especially, should Bloom do about and for Molly? Is he as helpless as he tells himself he is to prevent what happens that day between Molly and Boylan? (p. 67) Does he somehow want it to happen? Is he motivated in part by pity for her? The answers to this line of questions bear on what we should think of him, on how seriously we should take Bloom (and perhaps Joyce

as well). What does Molly have to commend her? How should Bloom
(and we) regard *her?* Should we care about what happens to Bloom,
Molly, and the others? Are they worth the considerable space devoted
to them? Is there too much made of gentleness, not enough of firmness, in this book? Is this disproportion related to the political malaise to which I have referred? In any event, there is something inap-
propriately juvenile about Bloom's fantasies and about his approaches
to sexual gratification, however sophisticated some of his musings
may be. Indeed, one might even dare to ask whether such a book is
good for us, especially if its comic effects should not be decisive.[265]

iv

JOYCE IS absorbed in Bloom's Jewishness, in what distinguishes his
imagination and sentiments from those of Dedalus.[266] *Ulysses* is, a
sensitive Jewish lawyer has told me, a remarkable job of getting into
Bloom's skin. And, this well-read friend also tells me, he finds his
own thoughts similar to those of Bloom. It is, I take it, a major accomplishment to describe so well the mental life of this Jew—of
someone whom Joyce could see as an exile somewhat like himself.[267]

But, one might ask, is Bloom truly a Jew? The conventional
"legal" answer would be that he is not: his Jewish father (an immigrant from Hungary) converted to Protestantism; his mother was
Irish and Roman Catholic; he himself was baptized first a Protestant
and then (evidently upon his marriage to Molly) a Catholic. (pp. 666,
701) There is something comic about these conversions (less so in
the case of Bloom's father?). In any event, the conversions do not
"take."

Consider how Bloom thinks and acts. Instinctively, when musing
to himself, he refers to Christians (that is, most of the Irish) as "they."
(See, for example, pp. 79-81, 94-95, 102, 149.) He is intrigued by
various of *their* practices and religious opinions, but as an amateur
anthropologist. He is quite aware of his Jewish ancestry and may be
deeply disturbed by his abandonment of it. He recalls, often in a distorted way, Jewish words, holidays, and rituals. He even observes,
perhaps annually, his father's *yahrzeit.* (pp. 680, 732) Certainly, he
is different from the others—in sensitivity, in generosity, in moral

concern. One is reminded of the Talmudic account of the signs of the people of Israel: they are merciful, they are doers of kind deeds (such as visiting the sick and helping to bury the dead).[268]

Further—in our effort to identify Bloom—we notice that the others, the Irish with whom he associates, do consider him a Jew although he does not seem to associate with any practicing Jews or with any Jewish community. He has the vulnerability of a Jew in a Christian land, and so he is cautious. He is at his worst, perhaps, when he indulges in certain anti-Jewish remarks, in an effort to be "one of the boys." (pp. 93, 180) He is, of course, a pre-State-of-Israel Jew, but one who does not have the confidence and dignity that were possible even in his time.[269]

When Bloom is pressed—whatever he says at other times—he will identify himself as a Jew. His altercation with a "citizen" in a pub is triggered by his assailant's mistaken belief that Bloom has come into considerable money that day on a long shot which he won—and that Bloom is concealing his winnings in order not to have to buy drinks. (pp. 84, 176, 329, 335, 339, 522, 588, 632, 659–60, 702, 734) Bloom's honor is challenged by the anti-Jewish slurs directed against him, including the jeer, "Three cheers for Israel!" And so Bloom is moved to the following exchange as he is about to be carried away to safety by the pacific Martin Cunningham:

> And says he:
> —Mendelssohn was a jew and Karl Marx and Mercadante and Spinoza.
>   And the Saviour was a jew and his father was a jew. Your God.
> —He had no father, says Martin. That'll do now. Drive ahead.
> —Whose God? says the citizen.
> —Well, his uncle was a jew, says he. Your God was a jew. Christ was
>   a jew like me. [p. 336]

At this, the drunken citizen looks for something to throw at "that bloody jewman," who is being carted away by Cunningham. Bloom (not without exaggeration) recalls several times thereafter that day, with a certain pride, his rejoinders to the citizen (for example, pp. 373–74, 488, 627, 641, 713; compare p. 720)—rejoinders in which he recognizes Christianity as theirs and Judaism as somehow his.

It is no wonder, then, that the reader takes Leopold Bloom to be a Jew—a mixed-up Jew, to be sure, but a Jew nonetheless. He is, in fact, a Jewish intellectual of sorts, something of an intellectual magpie, vulnerable and yet, in certain critical respects, a man of integrity.[270]

V

JOYCE CAN be understood to suggest that Bloom stands for something that Ireland (if not mankind) needs—for charity and compassion, for a refusal to allow dogmas (whether political or religious) to take the place of a genuine regard for humanity. In this respect, Joyce (who helped Jewish refugees escape from Europe on the eve of the Second World War) is far superior to artists such as Ezra Pound and T. S. Eliot (the first, a blatant hater of Jews; the second, someone who was several times obliged to deny that he was an anti-Semite).

It is one of the better qualities of Molly Bloom that she does not care for anti-Jewishness. Not that she actively disapproves of it—rather, she is simply above (or, in a way, beneath) it. That is, in her sensuality, she is open to the humanity in another—and she recognizes in Bloom someone who is simply more decent than most of the men she has known (and, in many ways, superior to the brutal man who had occupied her that Thursday afternoon and whose return the following Monday she yearns for). (pp. 766–67)

One must wonder, in considering the circumstances of Leopold Bloom, whether a Jew is necessarily an outsider in most countries of the world.[271] Thus, the outbreak at the pub was preceded by this exchange:

> Bloom was talking and talking with John Wyse and he quite excited with his dunducketymudcoloured mug on him and his old plumeyes rolling about.
>
> —Persecution, says he, all the history of the world is full of it. Perpetuating national hatred among nations.
>
> —But do you know what a nation means? says John Wyse.
>
> —Yes, says Bloom.
>
> —What is it? says John Wyse.
>
> —A nation? says Bloom. A nation is the same people living in the same place.

—By God, then, says Ned, laughing, if that's so I'm a nation for I'm
   living in the same place for the past five years.
So of course everyone had a laugh at Bloom and says he, trying to
muck out of it:
—Or also living in different places.
—That covers my case, says Joe.
—What is your nation if I may ask, says the citizen.
—Ireland, says Bloom. I was born here, Ireland.
The citizen said nothing only cleared the spit out of his gullet and,
gob, he spat a Red bank oyster out of him right in the corner. [p. 325]

The citizen, it is evident, considers Bloom no more than born
in, but not *of,* Ireland. The narrator in this passage—a narrator who
is himself prone to anger and sarcasm—refers to Bloom's enemy as
"the citizen." This designation is probably meant to underline the
question of what the relation is of Jews to the communities in which
they happen to find themselves. There is evident in the book an affinity between the Jews and the Irish: the Irish, for instance, need a
Moses to liberate them from the British. (See, for example, pp. 140–
41.) But suspicion of the Jews is also there—and so the question can
be put to Bloom, "What is your nation if I may ask."

Most countries induce deep allegiances, including local religious
allegiances, which Jews are suspected to have reservations about. Thus,
it is not accidental that Bloom should be attacked by someone identified as a kind of professional patriot. Does patriotism inevitably
depend upon a certain narrowness? How much can this prejudice be
moderated by the gospel of love that Bloom depends upon?[272]

Or, to put the citizen's concern in a more civilized form than he
is capable of, it can be said that Jews, in most parts of the world,
carry their community with them. Indeed, is it not because many
Gentiles sense this that Jews are often regarded as outsiders? (I saw,
while stationed in Egypt with American forces at the end of the Second World War, the same thing, quite vividly, in the status of the
Greeks in Cairo and Alexandria, if not throughout the Middle East.
The same can be said of the Chinese outside China throughout the
Far East.) Such "outsiders" cannot be simply patriots; something
higher beckons (sometimes even commands) them. They can make
great, perhaps even irreplaceable, contributions to the communities
in which they live but with which they cannot fully identify them-

selves. Indeed, it may well be that they can make the contributions
they do—they can be as good as they are—because they *are* different
and, in critical respects, better.

vi

JOYCE COULD use Bloom as he did partly because he saw himself as
an outsider as well. He felt he could not do his work if he remained
in Ireland, an Ireland where family demands and religious influences
were too strong for him. And so he left Ireland in his late twenties,
never to return.

There was about his conception of the artist something romantic: bohemianism somehow seemed to him necessary. This view of
things meant a marriage with a woman far beneath his station (in
class and in education); it also meant life in places where he could
live as a foreigner on the fringes of society.[273] Thus, he did not have
to regard personal and social relations the way he would have had to
do in Ireland.

But, I suspect, these considerations (which Joyce explicitly
made so much of) were secondary in generating his extended self-
exile. May not that exile have had much more to do with the kind
of artist he wanted to be, rather than with the nature of art itself?
To do what he wanted to do—to write about the Dublin of his youth
(a city with which he had what is today called a love-hate relationship)—he had to get away from it, not only so that he could see it
from a distance, but also (and perhaps most important) so that it
could not imperceptibly change around him. In this respect his instincts may have been sound.

Why he should have wanted to devote himself to the details and
nuances of a particular time and place is another question, however.
There may have been in this a kind of arrested development, an effort
to come to terms with the Dublin of his youth, a youth which he,
despite all his talent, never could put behind him. Stephen Dedalus's
arguments about the relation of an artist's personal life to his art seem
to me rather farfetched, certainly when applied (as Dedalus does) to
Shakespeare. (pp. 183–95, 202) The greatest artists rise above their
origins.[274]

But Dedalus's theory does apply, it seems to me, to Joyce himself. Indeed, his art is so much dependent on his personal life that

many things in his best book cannot be understood unless one knows a good deal about the life of Joyce and his family.[275] The extent of Joyce's considerable accomplishment cannot be appreciated unless one becomes immersed in accounts of his time and place.

One consequence of Dedalus's theory is that, since research in time and place is necessarily limited (and to some extent arbitrary), one cannot fully appreciate what a great artist has done. Such inaccessibility is not a problem if an artist radically transcends his time—which suggests, if this does happen, that Joyce may not have understood either Shakespeare or Homer (despite his considerable reliance upon Homer in his construction of *Ulysses*).[276]

Another consequence of the Dedalus theory, to which Joyce does seem to subscribe, is that art can become radically personal in its statement. One can see this in the extreme to which Joyce goes in *Finnegans Wake*.

vii

JOYCE WAS perhaps fortunate in his time and place, considering his temperament and inclinations. He could indulge himself in his rebelliousness and still have his work well received—at first in the world at large and eventually in Ireland herself.

There is in his assessment of the Ireland of his day a distortion: Ireland simply was not as bad as he made it out to be. In fact, the reader today cannot help but notice that the Dublin Joyce describes is a civilized place and (when we consider the alternatives that have been thrust upon us in the twentieth century) is quite preferable to much else that men have since been subjected to.[277]

Joyce is, in this as in other respects, a child of the Enlightenment (as is the eminently curious Leopold Bloom). This means, among other things, that he may not have a proper respect for the limits of human community; he may not recognize that prejudice and parochialism are inevitable even in decent communities. Should not one take care when criticizing any community that there not be subverted the community itself, provincial as it may be in some respects—the community which makes possible the development of standards and sensibilities that empower one to see what is wrong with one's own (and most) communities?[278]

viii

DUBLIN IS civilized in many respects. (See pp. 217, 222–23.) Even
its cruelty is restrained.

There has been since Joyce's time, I have argued, a considerable
deterioration in communities and in the finest products of communities (products such as language and "modes and orders" and literature). How much have writers such as Joyce contributed to this
deterioration?

Joyce's work has helped make it legitimate to describe and discuss in public many matters which would once have been considered
deeply private. The restraints evident in Dublin in 1904 seem to have
been swept away. Has this liberated and elevated us or merely made
us subject, even more than formerly, to the lowest passions and to
chance?

Another (related) consequence of Joyce's work may be that
the old stories are much harder to read as originally intended: the
petty and mundane (including sexual routines) have come to be regarded as more meaningful than the heroic and the timeless. To put
Odysseus and his wanderings in Bloomian terms may make the lives
of people such as Bloom seem more significant than they are—but it
is to do this at the risk of losing sight of what people such as Achilles
and Socrates and Abraham (to say nothing of Lucrece and Odysseus
himself and Jane Austen's heroines) stand for. (See Appendix G,
below.)

ix

ALL THIS is not to suggest that Joyce's *Ulysses* is not worth serious
study. In fact, my own respect for the book has grown considerably
as I have come to know it better. One *is* drawn into it: one can come
to like, even, at times, to respect, Stephen Dedalus, Leopold Bloom,
and Molly Bloom, Also, one cannot fail to be affected by extended
lyrical passages in the book.

But reservations remain. Curiously enough, Joyce—the successor,
so to speak, to the spirited young man described in *A Portrait of the
Artist as a Young Man*—Joyce himself is too much the scholarly
thinker, not enough the inspired artist. There may be in *Ulysses* too

much calculation, not enough passion—that is, passion of the kind which should move the artist to say what needs to be said if men are to be shown how things truly are.

The inspired artist is quite evident, of course, in the Homer whose stories Joyce brings down to earth. A tantalizing glimpse of Homer is provided by a response supposedly made by the Delphic Oracle to an inquiry put by the Emperor Hadrian about Homer's birthplace and parents. The response—ingenious, if not truly inspired—was, "His residence was Ithaca; Telemachus was his father and Epicaste Nestor's daughter was his mother, who bore him to be a very wise man." This suggests, among other things, that the mature Homer, as Odysseus' grandchild, took an old man's recollections of the adventures of his youth and put them in an "idealized" form which has permitted ready communication and constant instruction across millennia.

Joyce's difficulty in communication culminates naturally, I have suggested, in *Finnegans Wake.* But even *Ulysses,* I have also suggested, has serious problems in this respect: one can see there an abuse of language and literature—an abuse that may contribute to what we have seen in this century, the straining of the West's deep ties to a long and thoughtful tradition. In short, the self and self-expression (personal as well as literary) seem to be made too much of in Joyce's work. Truth and tolerance are also made much of, but in such a way that a debilitating relativism and an amoral permissiveness tend to be encouraged, so much so that we have become accustomed to monsters both political and personal.

I close my survey of English-language artists with a story from Plutarch that suggests something about how James Joyce and all too many modern artists fit into our vital theological-political order:

> [Those Spartans who remained bachelors] were denied the respect and observance which the younger men paid their elders. No man, for example, found fault with what was said to Dercyllidas, though so eminent a commander: upon his approach one day, a young man, instead of rising, retained his seat, remarking, "No child of yours will make room for me."[279]

This is not to deny, of course, that there is much in the work of these artists worth thinking about. Dercyllidas *was,* in his time, an eminent commander—even though his blood had no future.

Epilogue: THE THINKER AS ARTIST

Once there was in the city a beautiful woman named Theodoté, who was ready to keep company with anyone who prevailed upon her. One of the bystanders mentioned her, declaring that the beauty of the woman defied words and adding that artists visited her to paint her and to them she showed as much as was fitting. Socrates said, "We must go see for ourselves: whatever defies words can't very well be learned by hearsay." "Come with me at once," replied his informant. So off they went to Theodoté's house, where they found her posing before an artist, and they looked on.

—Xenophon, *Memorabilia,* III, xi, 1–2

i

WORKS OF art, like other things of beauty, seem to defy words. Must not one simply go to look at them, as well as think about them, if one is fully to know them? They do seem to await all comers.

Of course, one can be helped to find one's way by the guidance that bystanders provide—bystanders who report the existence of a particular work, or who have noticed interesting features about it, or who can locate it with reference to other works. But the work itself—if it is indeed a work worth serious attention—must be permitted to exercise its magic. And so my readers are urged to search out, perhaps in most cases to return to, various of the works I have sketched—and thereby to see for themselves what is to be thought of the features I happen to have noticed.

The critic, like any thinker, is to some extent an artist, adapting his "method" and his ideas to the circumstances—that is, to the work at hand and to those whom he is addressing. In each chapter of this book, the suppositions I have relied upon and the method I have employed have been, for the most part, evoked by the particular work under consideration.

But a more general exposition of principles may be fitting here.[280] An *indication* of the suppositions and methods I have drawn upon is

249

provided by what I have had occasion to say about one of my teachers at the University of Chicago. In this case, too, the serious student would have to go to look at *his* works. Even so, one is more likely to be induced to go see for oneself if the reports brought to one are intriguing. My somewhat personal report, on the beauty of a remarkable mind at work (and at play), first appeared in the *University of Chicago Magazine*. It was originally addressed to fellow alumni of the university under the title, "On Leo Strauss: A Yahrzeit Remembrance." That 1974 article follows in Sections ii–viii of this Epilogue:[281]

ii

THERE CAME to my attention, during my first twenty-six years in the University of Chicago community, two men of an extraordinary eminence, Enrico Fermi and Leo Strauss.

This has been an eminence accorded them by their immediate associates. That is, a number of men of obvious talent have recognized each of them as somehow of a different order from other intellectual leaders they have known at the university and, indeed, anywhere else in their respective professions, physics and political science.

My primary concern on this occasion is with Mr. Strauss, particularly as approached from his years at the university. But it will be useful, in thinking about Mr. Strauss, to glance at Mr. Fermi and his career. The significance of modern physics for modern life, including for politics and political science, is no doubt generally appreciated. Physics can be seen as attempting to provide us that comprehensive view of things once expected by most men from Revelation.

Mr. Fermi was born in Italy on September 29, 1901. He came to the United States in 1939, to the University of Chicago with the Manhattan Project in 1942, and became an American citizen in 1944. He died in Chicago on November 30, 1954, in the fifty-fourth year of his life.

Mr. Strauss was born in Germany on September 20, 1899. He came to the United States from England in 1939, became an American citizen in 1944, and came to the University of Chicago from the New School for Social Research in 1949. He died in Annapolis, Maryland, on October 18, 1973, in the seventy-fifth year of his life.

Mr. Fermi—by the time I came to the university in 1947 upon completing my service as an Air Force flying officer—was already a figure of international renown. He had been awarded the Nobel Prize for physics in 1938 "for his identification of new radioactive elements produced by neutron bombardment and his discovery, made in connection with this work, of nuclear reactions effected by slow neutrons." He had been in charge of the successful military efforts (at the University of Chicago) to achieve "the first self-sustaining chain reaction and thereby initiated the controlled release of nuclear energy." He would be pointed out to new students as a campus institution. I recall sitting in on lectures of his, where an exceptionally vital mind could be observed in action. It is upon talking to former colleagues and students of his—mature men who are themselves obviously talented in their own right—that the outsider can really get some idea of how remarkable Mr. Fermi must have been, ranking just below Albert Einstein in their estimation.

Mr. Strauss, on the other hand, worked in a field (that of political philosophy) where excellence is less readily recognized today than it is in physics. Even so, I had heard enough about him to want to sit in on classes of his while I was still in the Law School. But it was not until after it became unlikely that I would ever practice law and that I should go ahead for my doctorate while I was employed at the university (this was after 1951), that I began to follow his courses steadily—something I was to do for his final thirteen years at the university.

That which was said of Mr. Fermi by a fellow physicist can be said as well of Mr. Strauss: "[His] most striking trait was his simplicity and realism, his willingness to accept facts and men as they were. He disliked complicated theories and avoided them as much as possible." Each man was, as I have indicated, distinguished by the caliber of the men who regarded him as their master. Mr. Fermi's admirers included the scientists who had harnessed the atom; Mr. Strauss's included much-traveled veterans of the Second World War. Both investigators shared as well, but in different ways of course, a reliance upon numbers and numbering as an indispensable key to the things most worth studying: in physics, such reliance is generally recognized to be required; in political science—in the reading of the books of the greatest minds—counting (as distinguished from quantifying) has long been regarded with suspicion because of its cabalistic connotations.

The successes of Mr. Fermi's discipline, ratified in recent centuries by noteworthy technological feats, make more difficult today the proper recognition of Mr. Strauss's old-fashioned political science. What physics and the method generated by mathematical physics (along with Darwinism) have done to the idea of "nature," as well as to our understanding of "knowing," very much affects the status, standards, and methods of the social sciences. All this has been complicated by the understandable inclination of university administrations to be fashionable, to go along with the opinions and judgments of the discipline to which each department is devoted. In this way, universities become essentially derivative, and hence unimaginative if not even irresponsible, in their assessments.

In the case of Mr. Fermi, of course, such institutional timidity did not matter. A scientist who had won the awards he had, and who was eventually to have an element named after him, was bound to be recognized by any university which he served. Thus, we have on campus (right across Ellis Avenue from the site of the famous Stagg Field experiment, now marked by Henry Moore's ominous death-head helmet) the Enrico Fermi Institute for Nuclear Studies. Mr. Strauss did become a Distinguished Service Professor at the university in 1959. But he remained controversial (and, one may even say, generally suspect) to the end of his days here: his students were enthusiastic but always a minority even in his own department, and they expected to remain that in the political science profession.

A few more comments on modern physics can serve to illuminate what will be said on this occasion about Mr. Strauss's career. What seems to be missing in the current scientific enterprise is a systematic inquiry into its presuppositions and purposes. That is, the limits of modern science do not seem to be properly recognized. Bertrand Russell has been quoted as saying, "Physics is mathematical not because we know so much about the physical world, but because we know so little: it is only its mathematical properties that we can discover." But the significance of this observation is not generally appreciated—as one learns upon trying to persuade competent physicists to join one in presenting a course devoted to a careful reading of Aristotle's *Physics*.

Is there any reason to doubt that physicists will, if they continue as they have in the twentieth century, achieve, again and again, "decisive breakthroughs" in dividing subatomic "particles"? But what future, or genuine understanding, is there in *that*? I believe it would be fruitful for physicists—that is, for a few of the more imaginative among them—to consider seriously the nature of what we can call the "ultron." What must this ultimate particle be like (if, indeed, it is a particle and not an idea or a principle)? For is not an "ultron" implied by the endeavors of our physicists, by their recourse to more and more ingenious (and expensive) equipment and experiments? Or are we to assume an infinite regress (sometimes called progress) and no standing place or starting point? Or, to put this question still another way, what is it that permits the universe to be and to be (if it is) intelligible? To ask such questions is to raise fundamental questions about what Mr. Strauss called "the modern project."

It was one of Mr. Strauss's accomplishments that he recognized there were several long-standing philosophical questions, taken by contemporary intellectuals to be settled, which had merely been bypassed in recent centuries. His work consists, in large part, in reviving such fundamental questions, in demonstrating that they have not really been answered, in demonstrating also that they very much need to be addressed today, He had no ready answers himself—and indeed he *can* be thought of as having no answers at all—but he was confident (and he managed to instill that confidence in others) that the truly important questions had been most usefully addressed (and sometimes forgotten) long before the twentieth century. Even so, he also recognized that modern science has kept alive a tradition of inquiry, a respect for reason and for the truth.

This is not the occasion to try to develop Mr. Strauss's thought, even though that is the essential part of him. Rather, I shall provide here a few notes toward a memoir, notes about the "human side" of Mr. Strauss which may be useful for those who will try some day to write at length about him. These notes, in addition to being an introduction of him to the larger University of Chicago community served by this magazine, also hold a mirror up to both the university and contemporary scholarship.

The human side of Mr. Strauss may have been easier to observe while he was at the University of Chicago than at any other stage of his career, for he was here for a generation and thus long enough to share with a settled community the full range of human experience—to have opportunities to respond to both joy and sadness, to birth and death, to triumphs and disasters, to the wholeness of life.

Such wholeness, with its proper mixing of gravity and levity, is suggested by what he wrote in his *Thoughts on Machiavelli:*

Other contemporary readers are reminded by Machiavelli's teaching of Thucydides; they find in both authors the same "realism," i.e., the same denial of the power of the gods or of justice and the same sensitivity to harsh necessity and elusive chance. Yet Thucydides never calls in question the intrinsic superiority of nobility to baseness, a superiority that shines forth particularly when the noble is destroyed by the base. Therefore Thucydides' *History* arouses in the reader a sadness which is never aroused by Machiavelli's books. In Machiavelli we find comedies, parodies, and satires but nothing reminding of tragedy. One half of humanity remains outside of his thought. There is no tragedy in Machiavelli because he has no sense of the sacredness of "the common."

iii

MY LIMITATIONS, even as the mere reporter I here try to be, should be acknowledged at the outset of these recollections: I was a quarter century Leo Strauss's junior; I was never an intimate of his; and I am neither Jewish nor conventionally conservative, both of which conditions did tend to promote intimacy with him. In fact, I was probably the most, at times the only, "liberal" of the students associated with him, at least among those I know well. He was to identify, and hence tolerate, me as someone "unique," as "a conservative libertarian."[282]

The last time I talked to Mr. Strauss was in a hospital room in Annapolis. (He had, upon retiring from the university in 1967, settled in as Scholar in Residence at St. John's College after a trial interlude at a Southern California college.) I had then the impression that I was intruding upon a dying man. It was at his insistence that I did not simply pay my respects and leave him to his nurses and their ministrations. There then followed what happened with his students during other hospital visits over the years, a revival of his spirits and his strength as he talked. And so we had an hour and a half of good conversation, even though he had begun by saying that the day before had been the worst day of his life.

I had the sense, on this occasion, that various "accounts" between us were being settled, that he felt that certain things should be said by him "for the record." Much of our talk was about the Univer-

sity of Chicago, partly because he no doubt recalled my inclination
on other occasions to say what could be said on its behalf. Certain
memories had at last been softened for him.

I encouraged him to dwell upon the better aspects of his days
on the Midway. Thus, he could volunteer and enjoy the recollection
of having had three good political science department chairmen
(whom he named) and of having been able to teach classes of enduring worth. He wryly recognized as well, in accounting for the difficulties he had had in his last years at the university, that he had been
so imprudent as to show his contempt for certain colleagues and
administrators.

Mr. Strauss indicated, in the course of this "settling of accounts,"
that he had recently been obliged, by the considerate competence
shown him by his nurses during intermittent hospital visits, to move
closer than he had been to the "liberal" position on American race
relations. He was particularly impressed, in this connection, by the
sacrifices he had learned one of the hospital scrubbing women to
have been making in order to send her children to college.

He was, in these as in other respects, a man always open to new
experiences and to reconsiderations of both the old and the new. Such
reconsiderations, we can assume, must take into account his caution
(in the preface to his *Spinoza* book), "It is safer to try to understand the low in the light of the high than the high in the light of the
low. In doing the latter one necessarily distorts the high, whereas
in doing the former one does not deprive the low of the freedom to
reveal itself fully as what it is."

Mr. Strauss was, during the last twenty years of his life, a man
who was often seriously ill and in pain. (He expressed, during our last
conversation, amazement and not a little pleasure that he had somehow managed to live longer than his father, a far stronger man, it
seems.) Students who met him for the first time in his final decade
could be impressed most of all by how ill he was. Yet there was
throughout this period, however much he dramatized and even exploited his afflictions, a steady dedication to his work. Despite the
general decrepitude of his body, heralded by a massive heart attack
in (I believe) 1956, he was able to do a quite considerable amount of
fine writing after leaving the university. Through one medical disaster
after another, the mind kept working steadily—and he seemed to the

end clearly superior to even his best students both in depth of insight and in literary productivity.

Mr. Strauss was small, markedly small, of delicate features and bones, at times quite frail. His hands were especially delicate and most expressive. His manner was gentle and courteous, yet sometimes so firmly efficient as to border on a callous selfishness. He could remind one of Socrates—not in his body, for evidently Socrates was robust and took care of himself (or at least did not abuse his body)—but in the majesty of his head, a very large head, made to appear even larger by the smallness of the body which supported it. He had, as well, a very small voice—and a congenital incapacity to make proper use of a microphone or of a telephone, especially when he warmed up to his subject. He sported, with charming casualness, a beret, a cigarette holder, American slang, and an acute sense of propriety.

For years students at the university (many from outside his department) packed his classes, classes which would routinely run double the ninety minutes allotted to them in the time schedule. I believe that personal contact was critical to the effect Mr. Strauss achieved. I do not believe that his intellectual common sense, his instructive playfulness, and the range of his scholarship and memory are as evident in his writing as they were in conversation (of which one can get some notion from the transcripts which have been preserved of his courses). Nor do I believe that his writings alone would have produced the personal devotion which has contributed so much to his influence among thoughtful political scientists in this country and abroad. Certainly, it was largely a matter of chance that most of us got to know him—for I doubt that his writings alone would have induced us to *go* to him.

The University of Chicago was, I believe, the right place for him to be in this country. Things of the mind mattered here, even in such "practical" departments as political science, not the delusion by which certain other schools are dominated that "we are going to run the country some day." I pointed out to him, at a time when he was considering leaving the university even earlier than he did, that many, perhaps most, of his best students since the war had been of the kind who would normally be attracted to the university, who had come here for other purposes, and who had been "captured" by him. But it soon became evident to me that this consideration did not matter for him as it might have a decade earlier. He would, in his declining years, establish few intimate ties of the kind established earlier. He once pointed out to me that a man of fifty could establish relations with twenty-five-year-old graduate students that a man of sixty-five simply could not.

He was never, upon leaving Chicago, to teach as he had here. The old-style conversations (with considerable good-humored give-and-take) came to be reserved for the most part for those whom he had come to know earlier. He did continue to work hard, of course, but he was less open and relaxed in class, less inclined to consider at length the questions which students raised. (In addition, the students were younger and less informed professionally than the Chicago graduate students he had gotten used to.) He was all too conscious that time was running out—and he had a sense of much to do. And yet, he once explained to me, he had done far more than he had ever "planned" to do. Thus, he considered his last books as "bonuses."

The significance of the University of Chicago in Mr. Strauss's life can be suggested in still another way. Two anthologies have been published in which there is reflected his influence on others, a history of political philosophy (which he coedited) and a *Festschrift* (on the occasion of his sixty-fifth birthday). Of the three dozen different contributors to these two volumes, about three-fourths have been associated in some capacity with the university. Thus there developed a "Chicago school," generated by one man, which the university has not yet been able to acknowledge properly.

Even if the University of Chicago was the right place for Mr. Strauss to have been in this country, the question remains whether it was good for him to have been in this country at all. I believe he could accomplish in American universities what he could never have done in Europe. It was in a sense fortunate for him (as well as for us) that he had been obliged to leave German academic life and become exposed for so long to the English and American communities—communities in which political common sense was much more important than it had been on the Continent for at least a century.

In fact, I suspect that our political sobriety, implicit in the very language which we shape and are in turn shaped by, is needed to permit one to deal properly with the metaphysical excesses of the Germans who have dominated philosophical endeavors of the past two centuries. This suspicion is supported by Mr. Strauss's note, in one of his last writings, that he had relied for an interpretation of one of

Edmund Husserl's essays upon the English translation as well as upon the German original. Or, put another way, it was good that someone dedicated as he was to political philosophy should have spent so much of his academic career in a country where politics are fairly sensible, decent, and stable.

This is not to say that Mr. Strauss allowed himself to get caught up in American political life, however alert he might have been to what was happening here. He was always interested primarily in the books produced by the greatest minds, in articulating each book strictly in its own terms and getting to the nerve of its argument. What he did was referred to by him as "interpretation." What this meant for him *is* a problem. Thus, a classical scholar has found Mr. Strauss's book on Aristophanes' plays one of the strangest books he has ever read. It first appeared to him only a paraphrase of the plots of various comedies—mere summaries. Then, as he reconsidered the book, he changed his mind and decided that it was not about Aristophanes at all but was entirely a construction by Mr. Strauss himself.[283]

Be that as it may, Mr. Strauss's primary concern *was* to understand books in their own terms—and this permitted and required him to take the classics seriously. (There was about this approach something which could be recognized as Talmudic or rabbinic in character. Of course, sectarianism can result from such an approach, especially when "reading between the lines" is made as much of as Mr. Strauss was obliged to do.) Although his comments on the moderns are valuable, it is probably his restoration of interest among political scientists in the classics which remains his greatest achievement. Xenophon has been resurrected by him, and this may be thought of as his distinctive contribution to conventional scholarship. Even so, Plato was his acknowledged philosophical master.

The competent authoritativeness of Mr. Strauss's mind remained evident to the end. One of my children remarked upon the uncompromising thoroughness with which Mr. Strauss would approach a text in his weekly seminar at St. John's College. He did not make big, spectacular points (I was reminded by this account of what I had myself observed a generation earlier) but rather accumulated, as he moved along, a considerable aggregate of many points (any one of which, it sometimes seemed, other scholars might have made). Mr. Strauss somehow managed to keep all these points in mind, all of

them together, as he subjected the text to a deeper and deeper interpretation week after week.

This youngster, who had been imbued with the salutary St.
John's College modesty in the face of the greatest authors, once
listened in silent wonder when we visited the Strauss apartment. It is
unusual for a St. John's student to hear someone speak as familiarly
as did Mr. Strauss about the authors touched upon during that conversation. Particularly memorable for the student that afternoon was
a comment Mr. Strauss made about Friedrich Nietzsche: he always
found Nietzsche interesting in his masterful generalizations, but he
often found him simply wrong in the details which he could check
out for himself. It was somehow evident that this magisterial assessment was not presumptuous on Mr. Strauss's part.

One almost always had the impression in Mr. Strauss of a mind
at work, a mind in which the reason was in charge, not what we call
the esthetic element. He had little to do with the plastic arts. Nor did
he have an ear for music, except (I believe he once told me) for military marches and synagogue music. These, I take it, were legacies of
his childhood—as was, in a different way, the political Zionism to
which he was passionately devoted as a young man. All that was put
behind him as he sat down at his well-ordered desk for a half-century
of truly serious inquiry.

One of his former students now on the faculty of the university,
who regards Mr. Strauss's reading of books as "somewhat doctrinaire"
and who is dubious about the discipleship he "permitted" among
students, continues to stand in awe of his "electrifying seriousness."
And a former university colleague can remember him, despite their
profound differences, as "a man of extraordinary mental power with
a kind of fantasy of the intellect, creative, almost like a poet...He
cared about thoughts and their life and their relation to books and
to the world with a white-hot intensity."

iv

THESE REMARKS have been, at times, more intimate than might
have properly been made public in Mr. Strauss's lifetime. How he
seemed to some of us then, insofar as that *could* be expressed in his
presence, may be seen in the introduction I delivered December 1,
1967, when he lectured at the Downtown Center of the university:

Heretofore it has been sufficient upon Mr. Strauss's annual appearance on these premises merely to call the meeting to order. It is obvious from the size of this audience tonight that on this occasion, too, no introduction is required.

But it is also obvious that since this is the last public appearance of Mr. Strauss as a member of this university, something in the way of a valedictory prologue is called for. As Mr. Strauss himself once advised me in circumstances far sadder than these, propriety requires that certain ceremonies be prolonged, that it is better in such cases to err on the side of excess than of deficiency.

The lecture tonight is sponsored by the political science department of the University of Chicago and by the university's Basic Program of Liberal Education for Adults. Mr. Strauss—who has been for two decades a distinguished member of the political science department—has had a significant influence on the Basic Program. He has been, for at least a decade, not only a regular lecturer at the Downtown Center of the university but also a teacher on the Quadrangles of Basic Program teachers. His lectures have included examinations of the *Book of Genesis,* of Aristophanes' *Clouds,* of Plato's *Republic,* of Lucretius's *On the Nature of Things,* of Machiavelli's *Prince,* of Hobbes's *Leviathan,* and of liberal education.

These lectures (which reflect his wide-ranging work in political philosophy) have been particularly appropriate for Basic Program—that is, for adult—audiences, not only because of the quality of the books examined, but even more because of the rigorous yet imaginative way Mr. Strauss examines them. His way of reading, informed as it is by an abiding respect for nature and hence for the whole of things, takes very seriously (if only as a beginning) the surface, the obvious meaning, of a great book, the appearance of the book as it first comes to view not to the learned scholar but to the interested adult. He utilizes, in his quest for the eternal, that which common sense discovers.

Mr. Strauss shares with the layman the all-too-human desire to make sense of the world and thus to master it. This yearning is nicely suggested by an observation made by a former prison inmate who happened some years ago to talk with members of the political science department of this university. The ex-convict was thereafter asked for his impressions of various members of the department. Yes, he did recall Mr. Strauss. In fact, he was moved to describe him by drawing upon his prison experience: "He reminds me of a con about to make a break." It was not, we trust, any incipient criminality which was detected by that observer—for Mr. Strauss is (despite his playfulness) obviously the most law-abiding and, some might even say, the most pious of men—but rather there must have been divined in Mr. Strauss the single-minded and even consuming purpose, the self-confident yet cautious daring, and the disciplined but infectious excitement which have characterized his constant wondering about the things that truly matter.

An even more fitting description of him, however, is one spoken not in the accent of American prison life but comes rather from the ghettos of Eastern Europe, where it would be said of a rare kind of man, "He knows how to learn." Mr. Strauss, too, is a man who knows how to learn. It is sad to realize that he is about to succeed, at last, in making a break from our community by escaping to those Elysian Fields men believe California to be. But how much sadder still we of this university would have reason to be if fortune had not afforded us the opportunity all these years to observe through him what it means to know how to learn.

Mr. Strauss is a man who knows also how to speak for himself—and this we can now permit him to do, now that our spiritual debt is acknowledged and our ceremonial duty is discharged. His subject for his occasion, "The Socratic Question," is most fitting and proper, reminding us once again of Mr. Strauss's lifelong eagerness to examine, with all who desire to know, "the treasures of the wise men of old."

Mr. Strauss departed Chicago shortly after this lecture. He came back to the city only once more, on the train which took him from California to Annapolis in 1969. A spontaneous champagne party greeted him, his wife, adopted daughter (an orphaned niece), and son-in-law at the railroad station between trains.

It is fitting that his last book—on Plato's *Laws*—should be published by the University of Chicago Press.

v

MR. STRAUSS'S seriousness was no doubt evident to all. There was about him no foolishness, even though there was often considerable comedy in what he had to say. Indeed, it was a joy to see him truly amused. He did like to joke, but usually with a point to be made in the process.

Even my 1967 introduction of him could not be delivered without the risk of provoking some playfulness on his part. His spontaneous response on that occasion is revealing, reminding us in passing of what he had learned about enthymemes, about America from hours of relaxation in front of the television set, and about the significant exotericism which moderns have lost sight of:

> I must say a few words about the remarks of Mr. Anastaplo. If one may compare a lofty thing with a thing that is not so lofty, Mr. Anastaplo's remarks reminded me of a verse which some of you may have heard: "If you're out of Schlitz, you're out of beer." That is an exaggeration. We all know there is Pabst and Budweiser and Lowenbrau and quite a few others. Someone might say, "But it was Schlitz that made Milwaukee famous." To which I would reply, "There are other brands which made other places famous—for example, Berkeley and Harvard and some other places."
>
> But to speak somewhat more seriously, it is an embarrassing situation. If I agree with Mr. Anastaplo—then I would be justly accused of lack of modesty. If I disagree with him, I accuse him tacitly of lack of judgment and not only him but, in a way, even the University of Chicago—and this would seem to show lack of civility.
>
> What then should one do? Now, some of my teachers—they were Islamic philosophers in the twelfth century or thereabouts—found a way out of a comparable, although not identical, dilemma. They began their books in about this manner: "After the praise of Allah, I say that it is my intention to explain the intention of Aristotle's science of prior analytics."
>
> So I will say, "After my thanks to Mr. Anastaplo, I say that it is my intention to explain the Socratic question."

Mr. Strauss then turned immediately to his lecture.

I trust I had in mind, as I prepared my introduction of him (which I later learned he spoke well of in private), the story Mr. Strauss liked to tell about the public reception accorded a prominent official by an obsequious subordinate who punctuated virtually every sentence with "Your Excellency." To this reception the great man eventually responded, "'Your excellency,' yes, but only now and then."

Such playfulness as Mr. Strauss could exhibit was, I suspect, inherited, for another story he liked to tell was of a prank played by his father upon a traveling businessman who used to stop in their

German town. The traveler was known as a prodigious eater—and among his feats was that of feasting upon an omelet of a dozen eggs. On one occasion, the elder Strauss paid the innkeeper to put, unannounced, *two* dozen eggs in the omelet. The traveler ate and ate and ate but simply could not finish what had been served him. He was heard to lament, as he pushed his plate away, "I am not the man I was."

The man Mr. Strauss always was may be seen in a story he told a decade or so ago on his "closest friend," a friendly rival of a half-century who had always had an "idiosyncratic abhorrence of publicity—of anything which even remotely reminds of the limelight." I make a few minor adjustments in Mr. Strauss's story for publication:

> I always found that Mr. —— went somewhat too far in this but all too justified abhorrence of publicity. When we were in our twenties we worked every day during a longish period for some hours in the Prussian State Library in Berlin, and we relaxed from our work in a coffee house close by the library. There we sat together for many hours with a number of other young men and talked about everything which came to our mind—mixing gravity and levity in the proportion in which youth is likely to mix them. As far as Mr. —— was concerned, there was, I am tempted to say, only one limit: we must not appear to the public as young men cultivating their minds; let us avoid at all costs—this was his silent maxim—the appearance that we are anything other than idle and inefficient young men of business or of the lucrative professions or any other kind of drones. On such occasions I derived enjoyment from suddenly exclaiming as loudly as I could something such as "Nietzsche!" and from watching the anticipated wincing of Mr. ——.

Mr. Strauss, it was evident to all who knew him well, not only had eccentricities but was not unaware of them. He did get some reassurance as well as pleasure, however, from a story he told of an exchange with one of his nurses in Annapolis: He had had occasion to apologize to her for a series of impositions. "I'm a queer man in some ways....No doubt you've noticed." "No, Mr. Strauss," she replied, "you're not queer; you're real!"

Some would consider even more eccentric what he said on another occasion to one of his students. "I'm aware of the fact that the wholeness of a part does not preclude a plural: there is barely a moment in my waking life when I do not think of dogs and donkeys." However that may have been, he did delight in the exuberance of puppies and the braying of donkeys.

One of his finest jests took the form of the pious insistence, opportunely resorted to when it suited his convenience, that he was "always respectful of authority."

vi

SOCRATES WAS, for Mr. Strauss, always a question, a riddle, not an authority. He devoted himself in his last years to a search for the meaning of Socrates, relying on the guidance provided by Aristophanes, Plato, and Xenophon and testing thereby the seductive prescriptions of Nietzsche. He had prepared himself for this quest by delving for many years into the moderns, into the men who claim to have superseded the ancients.

The "Socratic question" includes an inquiry into how it was that philosophy and political philosophy emerged when they did, into what the relation is among poetry, philosophy, and revelation (or "physics"), and into what it was that Socrates sought and did. There were about Mr. Strauss several features which could be said to be Socratic. He had a certain immoderation, an uncanny single-mindedness, with respect to the things of the mind. His probing into the very foundations of things could and did threaten established scholars: since he did try to go to the root of things, he could not help but call into question much of what passes today for academic accomplishment. (He could say that there may have been one or two of Plato's dialogues which he completely understood. Such modesty could threaten those conventional scholars who believe themselves to know virtually all there is worth knowing about the classics.)

In Mr. Strauss's hands the "value-free" social sciences (and many of the humanities as well) either were exposed as childish or were supplied a setting which made some sense of them. Neither contribution made him popular with his academic peers. Secondary sources became superfluous as he encouraged his students to approach directly the texts most worth reading. But he also encouraged them to practice the prudence he saw in the greatest writers, a prudence which reflects an awareness of the tenuous position both of philosophy in the cities of men and of the rule of law in every community.

Mr. Strauss attracted the students he did because deep thinking was obviously the major part of his life. Students could see how close he was to the life of great minds, how much that kind of life mattered to him, and what he could do for and with it. He managed to face, and to seem to face, the great questions more directly than the other scholars one encountered. But not all serious questions occupied him, it should be noted, or at least not all of them to the same extent: he had more to say (at least explicitly) about *anthropos* and nature than about *nous* and the cosmos. (These *can* be considered parallel inquiries, but with different emphases.)

One of his students—a student who was for many years very close to him—spoke at the St. John's College memorial meeting for Mr. Strauss "about the themes of his investigations":

Philosophy and science come into the world, according to Strauss, with the discovery of nature, and the fundamental intraphilosophic issue, the issue between the ancients and the moderns, concerns their different understandings of nature and nature's status. Mr. Strauss concentrated especially on the study of human nature. This is not the place to go into how the study of human nature is complicated by the rediscovery of exotericism, except perhaps to remark that the study of what most of the greatest writers prior to Kant mean by human nature is inseparable from the study of the implications of their rhetoric. The connection between nature and human nature becomes evident by questions such as these: Are we correct to speak of what is good for man by nature? Are we equipped by nature to understand nature, to understand what is good by nature? Or is nature indifferent or hostile to man's highest aspirations? Is it naive to think that the human intellect is constituted by nature so as to understand nature, that nature is so constituted as to be understood by the human intellect? If it is naive, as the moderns argue, is not nature rather to be studied with a view to its ultimate conquest, with a view to its intellectual conquest by means of the art of symbolic mathematics and experiment and its physical conquest by the technological arts concomitant with mathematical physics? Is nature then to be studied with a view to the ultimate triumph of human art? But if nature cannot provide us with standards, how are we to determine the purposes to which that art is to be put? The dilemmas, not to speak of horrors, consequent upon the modern project require a careful tracing back of our steps, the rediscovery of the fundamental notions and assumptions that brought us to this impasse. That means, to speak in the broadest outline, the rediscovery of the fundamental notions and assumptions that underlie the modern understanding of nature, the rediscovery of the fundamental notions and assumptions of the classical understanding of nature which the moderns reject and thereby presuppose that they understand. And lastly it means the rediscovery of the basic insights and assumptions that underlie the original discovery of nature, the original discovery of philosophy and science. This last task brings us face to face with the alternatives to philosophy.

Mr. Strauss was so compelling and so alive (and hence truly human) because he took seriously the possibility of philosophy. He *did* question even this, in that he took seriously as well "the alternatives to philosophy," including the recourse to living-according-to-nature (a radical rejection of civilization) and the recourse to an all-consuming political (or religious) life. What he had to say, especially in his Herculean revival of the ancients among political scientists, was like a light in the dark. He was thus able to appeal to and challenge the best in students, especially the young and the young in heart.

It would be both foolhardy and superfluous of me to attempt to say more than I have already about "the Socratic question" to which Mr. Strauss addressed himself. His writings are, of course, available to the interested reader. Different kinds of introductions to Mr. Strauss's thought (including his "method," the most careful reading) are provided by three of his books, *On Tyranny, The City and Man,* and *Natural Right and History* and by four of his articles, "Persecution and the Art of Writing," "Preface to Spinoza's *Critique of Religion*," "What is Political Philosophy?" and "What Is Liberal Education?"

Something more might usefully be recorded, as a guide for those who come to write some day of Mr. Strauss's career, about the perhaps inevitable effects of his Socratic ways upon those in the community who (for one reason or another) could not be expected to understand his thought. Thus, the sensitive wife of one of his students could write years afterwards of the teacher who had come to mean so much to the graduate students she had known at the university:

Mr. Strauss was a man's man. This was instantly obvious to any woman who met him. Whatever exists in a man's personality to interest a woman or to be interested in her was lacking in him. I believe he could respond to feminine admiration; in fact, I rather suspect he thought it was his due, and he could talk to women without discomfort for short periods of time. But the bridge that forms quickly between some minds of opposite sexes would never form with him.

Mr. Strauss was both over-anxious and indifferent to the conditions of the material world. He had no sense of measure. He ignored things while he worked until "nature struck back" and he had to rely on others to salvage the situation. Although he could judge which way the wind was blowing, he was not quite sure what to do about it.

He could be a delightful companion and, I hear, an ardent pursuer of ideas. However, much of his personality was childlike. He could sum up the world at a distance in writing and words, but one had the feeling that somehow he had never really grown to be a man.

A kind of impracticality, a not-caring, about the things of this world may be detected in this sketch of Mr. Strauss, the sort of aloofness from the cares of the world (with its sometimes disastrous effects on family life) which one detects as well in the complaints about Socrates. (One recalls, in this connection, Socrates's long-suffering, and long-suffered, wife. One recalls as well Callicles' rebuke to Socrates: "Grow up!") Also Socratic is the dedication to philosophy of the erotic part of the soul which may be detected in this sketch (which blithely contradicts in its closing words what had been said in its opening words).

It should at once be added that Mr. Strauss did not have that contempt for death which one also associates with Socrates. He was through much of his life a physically timid man, perhaps unduly so; certainly, curiously so. (I am reminded in this respect both of Cicero and of Hobbes.) But bodily existence did become a dreadful burden for him—and he could finally ask to be allowed to die. This was a long way from the man who could once be intimidated by thunder and lightning. (See Aulus Gellius, *Attic Nights*, XIX, i.)

However that may be, it would have been unthinkable for Mr. Strauss, while in good health, to go to his death as willingly as Socrates seems to have gone. He always felt vulnerable, physically and

financially, even while most confident about his ability to think and
to write.

But, on the other hand, Socrates did have his "daemonic thing"
to help protect him from a premature death, thereby permitting him
through a long life to do good both for himself and for others.

vii

MR. STRAUSS'S curious sense of vulnerability (which he himself
never seemed to treat as a serious defect) has not kept several of his
most intimate, and perhaps best, students from publicly pronouncing
him to have been a philosopher. He, it should be noticed, never called
himself a philosopher. That was a term he carefully reserved for the
rare man, perhaps one or two a century at best. He did call himself
a scholar. Perhaps we can dare to expand that appellation at least
into Plutarch's phrase, "philosophical companion." (See, e.g., Plutarch, *Cicero*, XX, 2.)

To regard Mr. Strauss as simply a philosopher would mean
(among other things) that one had come to terms with the Judaism
which seems to have meant so much to him. Of course, one could
simply say that what Judaism really meant to him can be inferred
from the fact that he *was* a philosopher—but this, it seems to me,
would not take due account of the reservoir of passion in him upon
which "Jewish" issues drew. (His occasional references to the medieval "Islamic philosophers" should also be considered.) Did his Judaism, with its dedication to a wise righteousness, permit him to ignore
to the extent he did the cosmology of modern science? But must not
philosophy come to terms with physics, ancient or modern? (See
Cicero, *Republic*, I, x, 15–16; Diogenes Laertius, *Lives* ["Socrates"],
II, 45. Cf. Plato, *Phaedo* 96D sq.; *Deuteronomy* 4:6. See, also, Philo,
On the Account of the World's Creation Given by Moses. Cf., also,
Philo, *On the Eternity of the World;* Maimonides, *The Guide of the
Perplexed*, II, 13 sq.)

Socrates, we suspect, did not really recognize the traditional
gods of his people. No such public charge was ever leveled against
Mr. Strauss, even though he was not (in the conventional sense) an
observant Jew. Indeed, it may have been his Judaism, including its
tradition of careful reading of the most exalted texts, which permitted a man of his extraordinary talents to remain open to philosophy

by keeping him from certain contemporary excesses—excesses associated with the Enlightenment and Cosmopolitanism and their infatuation with the idea of progress, with modern science and its technology, and with individuality.

I have heard it said that Mr. Strauss's Judaic studies alone would
have made a name for him in the scholarly world. One could see him
at Hillel House, helping a particularly astute rabbi and his conscientious successor make Judaism intellectually respectable for sophisticated young Jews. Mr. Strauss showed them, as well as their Gentile
fellow travelers, that there was indeed much in Jewish faith and tradition to be respected and salvaged. There was, perhaps above all for
him, an obligation for every Jew (mindful of family feeling, honor,
and gratitude) to stand firm with his people around the world and
through the ages. (See Plato, *Apology* 34D.)

If there is any "false step" among Mr. Strauss's writings it may
have been occasioned by his dedication to this noble obligation to
defend the respectable post in which one happens to have been stationed by one's birth. That is, he observed in one of his last essays:

> In order to understand Heidegger's thought and therefore in particu-
> lar his posture toward politics and political philosophy, one must
> not neglect the work of his teacher Husserl. The access to Husserl is
> not rendered difficult by any false step like those taken by Heidegger
> in 1933 and 1953. [The reference here is, of course, to Heidegger's
> Nazi experiment in 1933, which was never repudiated by him and
> which he tacitly reaffirmed in 1953.] I have heard it said that the
> Husserlian equivalent was his conversion, not proceeding from con-
> viction, to Christianity. If this were proven to be the case, it would
> become a task for a casuist of exceptional gifts to consider the dis-
> similarities and similarities of the two kinds of acts and to weigh
> their respective demerits and merits.

I suspect that this kind of "weighing" would not really be much of a
problem for a *Gentile* casuist appalled by Martin Heidegger's gross
misconduct, misconduct which leaves him exposed as the Macbeth
of philosophy.[284]

Be that as it may, the serious student of Mr. Strauss must certainly come to terms with what Judaism meant for him and why.
He did travel to Israel. I do not believe he ever made it to Athens
and its Acropolis. He did get as far as the Piraeus, on a voyage be-

tween Israel and the United States. But he was too ill to travel up to the city and had to settle for a view of Athens from its port. Was Jerusalem necessarily for him more a thing of the body than was Athens, something to be seen close-up rather than from a distance?

Mr. Strauss did walk the streets of Jerusalem and feel at home there. Fellow Jews can remember him standing in front of his apartment at 7:30 in the morning, with his fuel can in hand, waiting for his regular allotment of *neft* from a horse-drawn wagon. This was a physical discipline which he seems to have looked forward to and which it would have been unthinkable to expect of him in the Chicago that served as his Athens.

viii

IT SHOULD be evident, when I speak of Mr. Strauss and Judaism, that I do presume to speak of matters which I can glimpse only at a distance, if at all. Even so, as I have indicated, the outsider can recognize that there is something here to be investigated by a competent student. Thus, Mr. Strauss could acknowledge publicly that there was a disproportion between the "primitive feelings" he always retained from his Orthodox upbringing and the "rational judgment" guided in him by philosophy.

Perhaps nothing can serve as well as certain remarks made thirteen years ago by Mr. Strauss himself both to put the trespassing Gentile on notice here and to challege the thoughtful Jew. One can see in these remarks, made by Mr. Strauss on December 6, 1961, at the funeral in Chicago of a thirty-two-year-old graduate student, the solace which Judaism can provide mankind in the face of death, especially an untimely death:

> We are struck by the awesome, unfathomable experience of death, of the death of one near and dear to us. We are grieved particularly because our friend died so young—when he was about to come into his own, to enter on a career which would have made him esteemed beyond the circle of his friends here and elsewhere and his pupils in the Liberal Arts Program. It is not given to me to say words of comfort of my own. I can only try to say what, I believe, Jason Aronson had come to know. I saw him for the last time about three weeks ago in my office. He knew where he stood. He jokingly reminded

me of an old joke: all men are mortal but some more than others. He decided bravely and wisely to continue his study of Shaftesbury. At his suggestion we agreed that we would read the Bible together, starting from the beginning.

Death is terrible, terrifying, but we cannot live as human beings if this terror grips us to the point of corroding our core. Jason Aronson had two experiences which protected him against this corrosive as well as its kin. The one is to come to grips with the corrosives, to face them, to think them through, to understand the ineluctable necessities, and to understand that without them no life, no human life, no good life, is possible. Slowly, step by step, but with ever greater sureness and awakeness did he begin to become a philosopher. I do not know whether he knew the word of a man of old: may my soul die the death of the philosophers, but young as he was he died that death.

The other experience which gave him strength and depth was his realizing ever more clearly and profoundly what it means to be a son of the Jewish people—of the *'am 'olam*—to have one's roots deep in the oldest past and to be committed to a future beyond all futures.

He did not permit his mind to stifle the voice of his heart nor his heart to give commands to his mind.

I apply to his life the daring, gay, and noble motto: *courte et bonne* —his life was short and good. We shall not forget him and for what he stood.

I address to his wife, his mother, and brother, and his sister the traditional Jewish formula: "May God comfort you among the others who mourn for Zion and Jerusalem."

Thus ends my remembrance for this occasion of a most remarkable man, an intrepid stepson of the University of Chicago and its determined benefactor. Even if I should be destined to remain in this university community another twenty-six years, I for one do not expect to happen upon his like again.

ix

THIS, THEN, was my 1974 report on Leo Strauss, a teacher of extraordinary powers and influence.[285]

Of course, much more can be said about Mr. Strauss than I have provided here.[286] But this article (set forth in Sections ii–viii of this Epilogue) does indicate what he, and hence some of his students, considered important in choosing the things worthy of the greatest care and in settling upon the proper way to read such things.

The proper way to read depends not only upon a "method" of reading but perhaps even more upon the suppositions about the good, about prudence, and about human nature on which the soundest reading rests. Particularly instructive for readers of this book should be the comment by the scholar who remembered Mr. Strauss as "a man of extraordinary mental power with a kind of fantasy of the intellect, creative, almost like a poet.... He cared about thoughts and their life and their relation to books and to the world with a white-hot intensity."[287] Here, indeed, we catch much more than a glimpse of the thinker as artist.

Critical to an understanding both of the artist and of the thinker is a sense of the general order of things—that sense which is the proper subject of philosophy and (with respect to human things) of political philosophy.[288] Mr. Strauss drew upon his studies of political philosophy, as well as upon his lifelong dedication to Jewish studies, to reassure his students that there *are* standards by which moral precepts and opinions about the common good can be defended and refined. Such a reassurance, I have argued in this book, is vital to sensible readings of most of the works of the better artists.

But what I have done in this book will probably stand or fall, not on the basis of any "theory" I have drawn upon or developed, but rather on the basis of the "practice" I have exhibited—a practice which consists of bringing to one text after another appropriate observations and questions for illuminating one's reading of each particular text. If I have succeeded in sharing with patient readers what I have discovered (or, in most cases, rediscovered) about a variety of familiar yet still challenging books, plays, and poems, I may be entitled to say with Socrates:

> Just as others are pleased by a good horse or dog or bird, I myself am pleased to an even higher degree by good friends.... And the treasures of the wise men of old which they left behind by writing them in books, I unfold and go through them together with my friends, and if we see something good, we pick it out and regard it as a great gain if we thus become useful to one another.[289]

Appendixes: ON ART, NATURE, AND PRINCIPLES OF INTERPRETATION

Appendix A. A PRIMER ON THE GOOD, THE TRUE, AND THE BEAUTIFUL

> Hector:
>> ... What merit's in that reason which denies
>> The yielding of [Helen] up?
>
> Troilus:
>> ... Nay, if we talk of reason,
>> Let's shut our gates and sleep. Manhood and
>> honor
>> Should have hare-hearts, would they but fat
>> their thoughts
>> With this crammed reason. Reason and respect
>> Make livers pale and lustihood deject.
>
> Hector:
>> Brother, she is not worth what she doth cost
>> The keeping.
>
> Troilus:
>> What's aught but as 'tis valued?
>
> Hector:
>> But value dwells not in particular will;
>> It holds his estimate and dignity
>> As well wherein 'tis precious of itself
>> As in the prizer. 'Tis mad idolatry
>> To make the service greater than the god;
>> And the will dotes that is attributive
>> To what infectiously itself affects,
>> Without some image of th' affected merit.
>
> —William Shakespeare, *Troilus and Cressida*, II, ii

i

WE MAKE much today of something called open-mindedness. But should we not take care lest a civilized willingness to hear out arguments become nothing more than a perverse mindlessness?

This memorandum was prepared in 1976 for students in my political science and philosophy classes at Rosary College. An abridged version of this memorandum was published in 26 *DePaul Law Review* 801–5 (1977).

275

One is asked again and again by liberated intellectuals, especially when serious matters are under discussion, "Who is to say who is right?" This tiresome rhetorical question usually implies that one is entitled to do no more than express the preferences one happens to have. To pass judgment on another—to speak of right and wrong—is considered provincial, if not even bigoted.

"Right" and "wrong," as well as "good" and "bad," are explained away by the liberated as merely conventional ways of indicating one's preferences, the preferences determined (for the most part, if not altogether) by one's environment. Indeed, these advanced thinkers are incapable of any sustained argument, independent of "arbitrary" religious and legal prohibitions, against even such a practice (to take an extreme case) as a routine indulgence in cannibalism.

Such open-minded people (who, of course, happen personally to abhor cannibalism and other such social aberrations) do consider themselves *thinkers*. That is, the old-fashioned respect—perhaps an almost instinctive respect—for man's nature continues to assert itself in their implicit assumption that thinking is both possible and desirable. Thus, it is assumed proper, if not necessary, for men and women to attempt to think. Is it not also assumed that there are correct and incorrect conclusions following from the thinking one might attempt?

ii

MANY OPEN-MINDED people do have decided opinions critical of social injustice, of bigotry, and (perhaps above all) of those who are not open-minded. But why should one bother to complain about what others are (or are not) doing or saying if right and wrong are but matters of opinion, if men have no defensible basis for the choices they make about the good and the bad? Why should one bother to try to "improve" things if one's preferences cannot be other than a matter of chance?

A matter of chance? If one's preferences are decisively determined by one's environment, and if one's environment and hence upbringing are essentially matters of chance, what basis *is* there for preferring or promoting one environment over another, for preferring one set of preferences over another? Will not whatever we change into be as much subject to chance (with *its* successor eventually becoming as appealing to some partisans) as whatever we may now happen to be? So, again, why bother to change things?

Why bother, if there is not something in the nature of man which demands (or at least permits) an ordering of alternatives, which suggests a hierarchy of better and worse ways of shaping, developing, and preserving both men and their communities? What sense does it make to speak of "progress" if men do not have some sense—if only a dim awareness—of what the very best would be for human beings?

Perhaps, then, we ought to replace open-mindedness by simple-mindedness. The paralyzing open-mindedness criticized here depends upon and reinforces a determined, if not suicidal, thoughtlessness. A certain simple-mindedness, on the other hand, may at least have the merit of acknowledging the primacy of mind, and hence of thinking, in human affairs.

iii

WHO *IS* to say who is right? The simple-minded answer is, "Whoever knows what is right." But, it should at once be recognized, there are all kinds of foolish people who *believe* themselves to know what is right. Is not this, however, a reflection of man's natural yearning for, and perhaps openness to, goodness and truth? (Beauty, it can be suggested in passing, may be the pleasure-inducing manifestation, often in corporeal form, of the good or of the true.)

We must distinguish, therefore, between those who know what is right and those who mistakenly believe themselves to know. It is one thing to recognize that it is often difficult to know what is right or good; it is quite another to conclude from this long-familiar difficulty that it is always impossible to know what is right or good.

To recognize this vital distinction, as well as the perils of unexamined dogmatism, is to give ourselves an opportunity to begin to understand what can indeed be known and done about human beings. Such understanding, to which serious education should be directed, rests upon:

1. an array of refined intellectual skills (as well as psychic maturity);

2. a body of carefully sifted information (including information about the obvious and the self-evident, as well as about the apparently self-evident);

3. an awareness of the fundamental questions thoughtful human beings have always recognized to be worthy of repeated investigation.

Appendix B. CITIZENSHIP, PRUDENCE, AND THE CLASSICS

Gentlemen, the condition of our nature is such,
that we buy our blessings at a price.

—Edmund Burke, *Works*, III, 19

i

YESTERDAY YOUR colleague Gunnar Myrdal graciously assured me, upon reading my paper on the Emancipation Proclamation, that the view I take there of Abraham Lincoln's policy toward slavery and emancipation is essentially that which sensible men (including men such as W. E. B. Du Bois) have always taken. And he indicated that the disposition among some today to dismiss Lincoln as a racist or as a mere opportunist is ill-founded.

If Mr. Myrdal is correct—and it would be imprudent of me to question, with respect to American race relations, the judgment of someone who has for so long been an acknowledged authority in the field—if he is correct, there may be nothing critical for us to discuss in my paper. That is, we as "sensible men" can be taken to be in essential agreement, at least with respect to the general argument of my paper—an argument which shows Lincoln deliberately displaying himself as working so long and so conscientiously within constitutional limits as to permit him to move with assurance and with the

---

This talk opened a discussion on June 19, 1974, of my paper, "The Instructive Prudence of Abraham Lincoln's Emancipation Proclamation," at the Center for the Study of Democratic Institutions, Santa Barbara, California. The commentary on the Emancipation Proclamation set forth in that paper has been published in *Constitutional Government in America*, Ronald K.L. Collins, ed. (Durham: Carolina Academic Press, 1980).

The epilogue to this talk is adapted from pages 78 and 81 of the Center transcript of the discussion which followed the talk. It was observed in the course of that discussion by Joseph J. Schwab (Visiting Fellow at the Center, from the University of Chicago), "... Since prudence always involves the weighing of goods, the weighing of the present circumstances, the problems of rhetoric, the responses and reactions of friends and enemies, almost every prudential situation tempts us to be more prudent (in the crude sense) the next time, and still more prudent the third time, until we end up as opportunists. And I think that every man of character knows this."

vital support of his fellow-citizens when he did take his radically decisive action against the institution of slavery in this country.

But we are scheduled this morning to discuss *something*. I suspect, from what I have seen of the publications of this Center, that a difference of opinion between us does remain to be developed, not with respect to Lincoln's policy, but rather with respect to whether one can profitably study democratic (or any other) institutions by relying as much as I do here and elsewhere on particular texts, upon the very careful reading of primary texts.

I suspect, that is, that some of you, perhaps most of you, would not consider it economical to devote yourselves at length to such texts—to the organization and details of the texts themselves, not to what scholars have said about them and their influence or about their authors or about the times in which they happen to have been written. If my suspicion is unfounded, what I am about to say will at least lend support to our common effort against those who do not take seriously the careful reading of the most important works of the mind.

What I am about to say can also be taken as a tribute to Robert Maynard Hutchins, upon his recent retirement as presiding officer of this institution—for it was in the college he championed at the University of Chicago that I was first instructed, a quarter of a century ago, about the importance of the classics.

ii

PERMIT ME to begin my argument with what may seem a truism: one can truly think about—one can know—only the knowable. One cannot know substantially the irrational or the accidental or, for that matter, the historical.

A carefully thought-out text—that is, a text written by a man who knows what he is saying—invites and permits serious interpretation. It draws upon, requires, and nourishes the very best in us. Such texts *are* rare. But they are not as rare as we today, with the supposition that we are somehow superior to the great men of old, generally tend to believe. Perhaps our inability to take seriously our predecessors is due in part to our recognition that the writings *we* produce are usually meant to be read on the run—and when we "naturally" read *their* writings thus, they often do appear naive and superseded.

A commentary on a carefully wrought text can serve to instruct (or, at least, to reassure) us that there are, indeed, minds superior to ours. Careful reading is a salutary discipline, a discipline which is especially important at a time when self-expression is made so much of and when a concern with the topical, especially if one can be "original" in one's approach, tends to make one feel useful—and may thereby contribute to that sense of self-gratification which self-expression usually serves.

On the other hand, such self-centeredness can feed and induce an appetite for the shocking instead of the sober. The shocking has the added advantage, in its uprooting of well-established opinions, of allowing one to believe not only that one *is* profoundly concerned with the topical but also that one is even in the vanguard of an intellectual revolution in the service of a general enlightenment.

But, I should at once add, it is difficult, if not impossible, to maintain a constitutional regime if the desire for self-gratification *should* become dominant among a people. Constitutionalism depends upon a critical self-restraint, such restraint as may be seen, for example, in Lincoln's careful delineation of where the Emancipation Proclamation did and *did not* apply. The self-restraint I refer to is the mark of *the citizen,* of the man who puts the interest of his community above that of himself. Indeed, the man who indulges himself in self-gratification is not, strictly speaking, a citizen.

The citizen is, perhaps above all, *a prudent man* in the service of his country. Prudence may depend, ultimately, on a vital awareness of *the nature of things.* Such an awareness rests upon an opinion of the whole which, in turn, suggests standards to be applied to our lively topical concerns, to the always pressing and sometimes intriguing problems of the day.

An inquiry into the nature of things leads, in its political manifestation, to a development, if only in thought, of "the best city." Such thinking provides the only reliable touchstone by which the unaided reason of man can determine what prudence truly calls for in exceptional circumstances. In ordinary times (and even in times such as ours), the well-established rules, tastes, and language of a people should be respected, especially by sophisticated intellectuals. This is one of the things prudence teaches us.

It can be asked about Lincoln (as perhaps about almost every remarkable political man), "What does *he* take to be the best regime?"

Or, indeed, "Does he have an opinion of whether any regime would, in the proper circumstances, be by nature the very best?" Or, put still another way, "Is Lincoln too much dependent on his constitutional and historical circumstances (and not enough on nature) to be able to address himself explicitly to the question of the best regime?" Are not political men—men who dedicate their lives and talents to the community—necessarily thus circumscribed? And yet, as prudent men, is not some opinion of the best regime tacitly held by them? And should not they be supported in this opinion?

iii

I HAVE suggested that a proper awareness of the best regime, and of its conditions, permits us to deal sensibly with the problems of the day—permits us to recognize what would be an improvement, what would be a deterioration, and what could well be settled for in various circumstances.

Thus, for example, we might observe that the size of a country, and its consequent diversity, could preclude the emergence there of the very best community (whatever may happen there to particular men of extraordinary talent). In countries of very large scale, therefore, it may indeed be sensible to settle for the decent and the stable, thereby encouraging and permitting people to weave their lives and expectations around reliable institutions. In continental empires such as ours, where superficial change is so easily induced (and not only by men who seek the gratification of profitable enterprises), should not novelty be firmly discouraged? That is, the more influential one is, the more sober one should appear to be—and this, I believe, President Lincoln, as an eminently prudent man, understood.

If what I have said about all this *is* sensible, then I have merely restated what you as sensible men have no doubt long known—and so we are right back where we started from, reassuring one another about the soundness of our opinions.

EPILOGUE

...I must say, as we draw near the end of this two-hour discussion, that it must have been some god who inspired me to say what I did at the beginning of this discussion today about the problem of reading the classics. One has to struggle, with vigor and vigilance, against the fashionable notion that one must know a lot about the historical setting of a text and about the life of its author in order to understand what is said in any of the greatest books. If the authors we study are indeed men of the first rank, they themselves can be trusted to provide us the information we need to understand what they are saying, especially if they intend their works to be read for years to come "in states unborn and accents yet unknown."

   . . . In conclusion, one can sum up my answer to the concern expressed this morning by many of you about whether prudence can be "a threat to character": prudence is a virtue; one cannot by the exercise of a virtue become less virtuous.

Appendix C. WHAT IS A CLASSIC?

The books speak to us in more than one way. In raising the persisting human questions, they lend themselves to different interpretations that reveal a variety of independent and yet complementary meanings. And, while seeking the truth, they please us as works of art with a clarity and a beauty that reflects their intrinsic intelligibility.

—Statement of the St. John's College Program, 1974–1975

i

WE ARE all familiar with the term *classic,* using it and hearing it used in a wide variety of circumstances. Thus, an automobile can be advertised by its manufacturer as a "contemporary classic"; the exuberant manager of a pennant-winning baseball team can proclaim, "We're in the fall classic, we're right where we belong," in referring to the World Series; and a relieved professional football coach can explain, after a ragged victory, "We found a way to win. Our special team blocked that punt for a touchdown. It wasn't a classic. We needed a few breaks. But we won."

A literary use of the term may be found in a statement by Somerset Maugham in his comment on Jane Austen's *Pride and Prejudice:* "What makes a classic is not that it is praised by critics, expounded by professors and studied in college classes, but that the great mass of readers, generation after generation, have found pleasure and spiritual profit in reading it." Another account of *classic,* which directs itself more to the thing itself than to its supposed effect, is found in James Russell Lowell: "[A] classic is properly a book which maintains itself by virtue of that happy coalescence of matter and style, that innate and exquisite sympathy between the thought that gives life and the form that consents to every mood of grace and dignity, which

---

This talk was given in the Works of the Mind Lecture Series, The Basic Program of Liberal Education for Adults, The University of Chicago, October 22, 1978. The 1982–1983 reading list of the Basic Program is appended to this talk.

can be simple without being vulgar, elevated without being distant, and which is something neither ancient nor modern, always new and incapable of growing old." And thus, I have had occasion to speak of the best teachers as "those few books every century which constitute both the seed and the flowering of our civilization."

There are "classics." And there is something we know as "classical education." This has been described by the *Encyclopaedia Britannica* as "the study of anciently revered authors or of the language (or languages) in which they wrote. In Europe and countries settled by Europeans, the study of Latin and often of Greek authors long formed the core of the traditional school curriculum. In India, classical education has centered on the Vedas and Sanskrit; in China, it has been based on Confucian and other ancient writings."

ii

THE REFERENCE in this last quotation to the study of the ancients reminds us of the origins of the word *classic*. It has been suggested that the root meaning of the Latin word *classicus*, "of the first class," "of the highest order," is best captured by our slang expression, "classy."

Thus, the *Century Dictionary* defined *classic*, when used as a noun, as "An author of the first rank; a writer whose style is pure and correct, and whose works serve as a standard or model; primarily and specifically, a Greek or Roman author of this character, but also a writer of like character in any nation." And, we are also told by this dictionary, the root term, *classicus*, relates "to the classes or census divisions into which the Roman people were anciently divided, and in particular pertaining to the first or highest class, who were often spoken of as *classici* (hence the use of the word to note writers of the first rank)."

Thus, there is among us, traditionally, an emphasis upon Greek and Roman authors of the first rank when we refer to *classical*. For the English-speaking peoples, those ancient sources are usefully drawn upon in the work of Shakespeare (who is concerned with, among other things, the problems posed by the allegiances in the West to biblical faiths). And, as it has often been said, we are the beneficiaries of the great conversation which has been conducted for centuries, if not even millennia, among "writers of the first rank."

All this bears, of course, on the Basic Program—and what we purport to do by way of liberal education in our classes and through the Works of the Mind Lecture Series. Indeed, as we shall see, even to speak of "works of the mind" implies that there *are* classics, works that are superior to the general run of books and that repay repeated attention.

iii

OUR PRIMARY concern on this occasion is not to attempt to identify the classics. The true classics available to us tend to identify themselves.

Rather, our primary question today is whether we should continue to take the classics seriously—for doubts are expressed from time to time about the supposed attributes and role among us of the classics, doubts suggested even by those who have been themselves decisively shaped by the classics. I respond on this occasion to the instructive challenge laid down last spring by our Basic Program graduation speaker, the dean of the college of this university, who said, in effect, that we take our texts too much for granted and that we should examine what we are doing.

There are, with respect to our reliance upon the classics, a half-dozen objections which can themselves be designated as classic, so enduring and critical are they. Some of these objections can be traced back to antiquity—as may be seen, for example, in Callicles' assault on Socrates in the *Gorgias* (in which Socrates is told to "grow up") and in the eristic argument made by Socrates' principal companion in the *Meno*.

We shall consider each of these half-dozen objections in turn. After all, something *has* led to a depreciation of the classics today, so much so as to have contributed to a marked lowering of the level of serious thought among us. If the classics did serve the purpose they were once thought to serve, and if they should have been repudiated by influential intellectuals among us, a lowering of the level of discourse is not surprising, however regrettable that may be.

The purpose the classics were once believed to serve is suggested by still another passage from James Russell Lowell where he spoke of the education available to young men in this country in the late eighteenth century: "The amount of Latin and Greek imparted to the students of that day was not very great. They were carried through Horace, Sallust, and the *De Oratoribus* of Cicero, and read portions of Livy, Xenophon, and Homer. Yet the chief end of classical studies was perhaps as often reached then as now, in giving young men a love for something apart from and above the more vulgar associations of life."

In the course of considering our half dozen objections to reliance upon the classics, we will draw upon and develop further what we have already indicated a classic to be. Since, as we shall see, a significant aspect of what a classic is depends upon how it is regarded and used, our consideration of these objections should help remind us of what a classic indeed is.

iv

THE FIRST of the objections to be considered—and one that has considerable immediate impact today—is that any extended study of the classics is impractical. It is often said that the classics, emanating as they do from a remote and (some would insist) dead past, cannot help us *live*.

Is this opinion about the impracticality of the classics, at least for anyone beyond secondary school, a *cause* of the decline in the importance of the classics? Or is it an *effect* of the decline? That there has been a decline in the importance attributed to the classics in education is evident in the fact that many good students manage to spend four years in many "good" colleges without being obliged to study any of the writers once considered classics.

This (our first) objection, which is put in terms of everyday usefulness, links the "practical" to a set of authoritative doctrines, such as those found in Sigmund Freud, or in a revealed religion, or in *Das Kapital;* or it links the "practical" to science (and to the technology produced therefrom, such as in medicine and in engineering); or it links the "practical" to the personal, the individual, the spontaneous. We shall consider the objections which further develop each of these notions of what the practical is linked to.

A key question in considering objections based on practicality is, of course, What *is* practical? It should be noticed that what the practical is, and what is good about it, remain problems for those who link the practical to technology or to the immediately personal.

The *goodness* of the practical *is* assumed by those who link the practical to an authoritative set of doctrines. But that good tends to be an unexamined good.

In considering what is practical, then, we are obliged to consider what life is, how it should be lived, and what (if anything) is real and enduring. That is, an objection to the classics based only on considerations of practicality may not be truly practical. Practicality makes sense only when seen as instrumental to something else, to an end beyond itself.

V

THE SECOND objection to the classics—and one that the practicality objection sometimes draws upon—is made in the name of science, that is to say, the modern physical sciences. Only science, it is said, can be depended upon to provide what *is* sought, not the outmoded classics.

What *is* sought? An apostle of science might answer, "What men seek is a reliable basis for life (the relief of man's estate; a better conduct of their affairs, etc.), or the truth simply, or both. And for these purposes, the sciences, kept up-to-date, are required, not the classics of a bygone age."

A key question in considering any objection to the classics based on modern science is, Does science understand itself? Upon what *does* science depend for its very being? Upon what does it depend, not just "historically" but even to this day, for its principles and standards? What does science take for granted about the world that science itself cannot establish or even be clear about? What does it assume about the nature of truth?

Of course, there are classics in the physical sciences, but these too are said to be outmoded, having been superseded by many, many discoveries and advances. But it is all too often in those outmoded works, especially those responsible for the foundations of their respective sciences, in which one can see laid bare the presuppositions, methods, and purposes of science.

Even so, modern science (despite its need of the classics for a sound examination of its ends and means) has contributed to further reservations about the classics among us. Marvelous, and hence fascinating, as it is, should not science be kept in its proper place? What *is* that place?

vi

IT IS due, at least in part, to science (in the form of archaeology, astronomy, economic history, evolutionary biology, and psychology) —it is due to modern science that the classics can be objected to as essentially derivative. This third objection in our series rests on the discovery that the classics are preceded by many very old works, some of which remain lost or are not even known. The classical writers, it is pointed out, were unaware of the origins of their works in the past, or in the hidden depths of the psyche, or in material circumstances. Nor were they aware, it is argued, how big things are—on earth and in the universe. In addition, they have provincially ignored the work (classics or otherwise) of other lands and peoples.

A key question here, however, is, What *is* the quality of the works prior to our classics? We can recognize the classics of Athens and of Jerusalem to be superior to what we know of the many works they were perhaps derived from and superior as well to the even greater number of works derived in turn from them. That is, *we* recognize differences and gradations, and it is evident that the classical authors did also. Thus, the Greeks of the classical period knew there had been a long past, which they respected; they knew that many cities had risen and fallen. They also knew, from Herodotus and from others, how diverse the peoples of the earth could be. And yet, the classical Greeks could see something special, perhaps even unprecedented, in what they were doing. The same can be said, can it not, of the experience of the Israelites, who were all too aware of the many forms of worship around them? Indeed, one can understand—upon comparing with the remnants we have of their supposed predecessors the works that come down to us from Athens and from Jerusalem—why Athens and Jerusalem have not only survived but have for so long prevailed.

As for the classics of other lands—particularly those of China and of India—should it not be recognized that they have gone their way, and we have gone ours? Is it possible for one way truly to understand the other? Is it desirable that quite diverse ways be somehow amalgamated? I shall return to these questions.

Notice one set of implications of the objection based on derivation. Is it not assumed that the judgment of superior and inferior requires the learning of more than can ever be learned? Is it not assumed, in effect, that there can never be enough of anything available for us

to judge by? Is it not assumed that there is no natural sense of suffi-
ciency, indeed of perfection, which entitles one to judge without
being obliged to see "everything"? Does not this approach lead to a
radically skeptical relativism—and leave us suspended over the abyss
which lies beneath the denial of nature? To these questions, too, I
shall return.

vii

THE NEXT objection to the classics follows closely upon those we
have already considered: the designations of classics made by us,
among the many things available, are simply arbitrary. It is objected
that the classical authors are "special" because they happen to have
been chosen, not chosen because they are intrinsically special. Obviously, this is not what we *mean* when we speak of the classics, as
is evident in the recognition of a work as "a much-neglected classic."
Even so, what is there to this objection, which is perhaps central to
the modern depreciation of the classics?

A key question here, and perhaps with respect to all the objections I collect on this occasion, is, Can one, in any way or to any significant degree, come to know oneself, so much so that such self-
knower can be aware of the best? The role of common sense, and
hence of a sense of the natural, may be critical here. Is not the role
of common sense, if not its very possibility, denied by the objection
that any designation of a classic is arbitrary?

Notice that it is assumed by the objection we are now considering that it would be *good* for critical choices (such as of the classics)
not to be *arbitrary*. Where do notions of order (and hence of the
arbitrary) and of the good come from? What standards are being invoked, and how do we come to be aware of them? If there are standards which permit us to recognize and prefer the orderly and the
good, and to repudiate arbitrariness, chance, and the bad, why should
they not also be available to permit us to recognize certain works as
truly superior?

Should we not also recognize that all times are not equal, that
there can be for a people a period of exploration, then a period of
ripening, and then perhaps a period of maturity when a peak is reached
which is evident to all as indeed a peak? We do recognize that certain
men have great talents. Some of them do have great opportunities—

and hence are able to see things more clearly than others. We recognize, that is, that there *are* times when one can see the alternatives clearly—and one can then establish a way which will be followed for generations, perhaps even for centuries. Thus, we do have an awareness of the better and the worse: indeed, we all know from personal experience that we have done and can do better and worse, that fatigue or physical conditions or training or persistence or even natural talent can affect our work. Some days, we know, we are not at our best. If we can thus judge ourselves, why cannot we judge others as well?

All that I have said about the conditions for the emergence of the best reminds us of the effect of political influences on the highest human endeavours. It is particularly fitting that the Latin word from which *classic* is derived *should* draw upon Roman political institutions. But to recognize a role here for the political *is* to recognize as well that there can be in these matters chance developments. Chance can affect what survives; chance can affect who develops fully. Still, this is not to say that it is a matter of chance what persistently seems to be the very best to mature men who are reasonably well informed. Is not the very best somehow independent of time and place?

I have suggested that the fact that we can, to some degree, come to know ourselves means that we can have (at least in uncorrupted ages) a reliable awareness of the best, that what we settle upon as the very best need not be arbitrary. Such self-knowing—that is, soul-knowing—is reflected in how one reads the true classics. One finds oneself trying to understand what the author does; one does not tend to dwell upon the "personality" of the author as author; one looks up to the author, reaching to attain something of what he knows; one does not look down upon him, accounting for his movements. This is, it seems to me, a sensible response in the face of the truth—and thus one is always open to learn from the greatest works of the mind.

viii

THE NEXT objection to the classics is one which suggests a different way of reading them from that which I have just argued is appropriate. Some would say that the genuine achievement, that which has made the classics what they are, is the considerable corpus of commentary generated over the centuries by the works which happen to have been designated as classics. This objection sees the commentary tradition as more interesting, important, and decisive than the work commented upon. It is easy to see—especially when one looks through the mammoth commentary on, say, the Bible—why this can be said. The work evident there *is* monumental.

A key question here is, What is the source of the principles used in developing the commentaries which inspire admiration? Do not these impressive commentaries draw upon the principles which pervade the way of life, a way which has been decisively shaped by the very classics being commented upon? These principles may be reflected even in the rules applied in correcting readings of classical texts: a view of the whole is implied. Consider, also, the suggestion sometimes made that there were available for inclusion in the canon of the Bible other books as good as some of those selected. Is not this suggestion itself dependent upon a critical sense, or a sensibility, somehow shaped by the pervasive biblical teaching and attitude? Is there not something which we are all aware of which transcends particular books of the Bible and which guides (and perhaps even inspires) much biblical commentary?

Do not commentators upon a classic assume they have before them something which they are somehow aware of as humanly possible, a work of integrity and intelligence? Or, rather, is not this assumption there at the outset—and may it not be undermined by certain kinds of commentaries? When commentaries are unduly "informed" by the doings of other "cultures" or of psyches (James Fraser and, again, Sigmund Freud come to mind), they are apt to become more concerned with psychology, with forms, or with the material causes of thought than with what is said and whether what is said is true. This leads, ultimately, to the pronouncement that it is only in our time that we can be liberated by the scholarly disciplines based on various sciences—liberated to see things as they really are. That is, it is only now that we can see that men do not really think.

And yet, do not the greatest works somehow escape their generally unreflective, even pedantic, commentators? The respectful reader is always reaching for more, reaching beyond the commentary to the text itself, to that which has animated the commentary tradition.

It can even be observed that nature thereby asserts herself. Indeed, there are a few writers who have such a range and depth that they compel us to suspect that nature is speaking through them.

ix

STILL ANOTHER objection to the traditional emphasis upon the classics recognizes that nature points to the brotherhood of man. The classics, it is objected, have been shortsighted; we should have, instead, a world culture, a culture that is properly rooted in the markedly diverse experiences of all peoples and which is self-conscious (in the modern sense). Thus, we can hear expectations voiced, as the dean of our college has done, respecting "our yet to be realized global culture." Such a culture, it would seem, would have as its cardinal principles one or more of those opinions upon which the objections I have already considered are based—opinions about the need to be practical, about the preeminent value of the physical sciences, about the arbitrary or derivative character of various provincial classics, and about the importance of the commentary tradition, especially to the extent that commentaries bring together the classics of various cultures.

A key question here is, Is it possible to have a genuine and meaningful community on a world basis? Indeed, we must sometimes wonder, is it possible to have it even in a large city today, to say nothing of continental North America? What kind of a whole is possible in these matters? What, and how much, can people regard as truly their own? No doubt, there is a good deal of the accidental in any determination of one's own. But is there not an obligation to respect one's own and to care for it? Is there not even something enduring to be seen and celebrated in respect for what happens to be one's own? *Can* any "global culture" be one's own?

I have already suggested that it may be virtually impossible for people in one "civilization" to understand those of another. It is hard enough for us, descendants, so to speak, of the ancient Athenians and Israelites, to understand either the Greeks or the Bible. Can we reliably know what the Chinese or the Indian or the Egyptian classics have said? It does seem that each had some notion of the best, and of order and of community. Do we get (because of profound differences in language) little more than mere glimpses of what they discovered about these things? And do not those glimpses suggest that what they have indeed discovered may be more reliably available to *us* in our own classics, especially if the very nature of things is thereby being drawn upon?

Of course, it can be said that a global culture is not only possible, but that it is already emerging. But is not that which *is* emerging to be found at a much lower level than the best of what has already been achieved among us (and perhaps among the ancient Chinese and others as well)? Is not this necessarily so, if it is to be something which can transcend limitations of language, of traditions, and of "provincial" influences? We know from our experience in this country the sacrifices that have to be made in subtlety and depth in order to make comprehensible to large audiences what a few have carefully worked out. There is, of course, no limit to how many can share the highest thoughts of mankind, but *that* "many" is made up of a few here and there, joined together across oceans and centuries in the common enterprise of serious reflection on the nature of things.

The apostles of a global culture preach against provincialism. But any global culture which does take hold will tend to be Western, will it not, if only because of the natural attractiveness of modern science and technology for men (including the appeal that science makes to intellectuals as a means of liberating men from local superstitions and prejudices)? This can be seen also in the appeal in many lands of Marxism, which is, after all, Western in its origins. It can be seen as well in the worldwide appeal of the Western standard of living (which includes our remarkable array of devices for both curing and killing one another).

I suspect that any global culture which takes hold of mankind will tend to be suicidal (or at least tyrannical) in its effects, if not in its intentions. Certainly, the best in us will have been suppressed if the classics should come to be regarded as mere relics of an unenlightened (and provincial) past.

X

A PROPERLY constituted global culture, a tenacious critic of the classics might object, would not have to concern itself with the "community" I speak for. Such culture would place greater emphasis than any writer in antiquity does (except, perhaps, in some books of the New Testament) on self, on spontaneity, on each generation "doing

its own thing." Each generation, indeed, each person, should be relieved of the grip of the dead hand of the past; even the family is
suspect. The classics, it is objected, have tended to deny life, or at
least life on this earth, in their dedication to a cold perfection, to a
passionless understanding.

Thus, a radical equality among the generations is insisted upon,
as is the freedom of each generation, if not of each individual, to act
as should happen to be deemed good. This new way is the really practical one, it is said with particular emphasis on such things as caring,
sharing, and "experience" (or, as one sometimes hears, "really living").
This is an approach which promotes experimentation, novelty, and
revisionism, not self-sacrificing patriotism, "unnatural" restraint, and
disciplined understanding.

This new way appeals to us as less "rigid" than that laid down
by the classics. It reflects a reluctance to subject each other and our
selves to the disciplined learning of what the best ("the old-fashioned")
have learned. Rather, it seems now to be fashionable for all too many
intellectuals to proclaim that one should not be bound by higher
laws, certainly not by divine laws. The classics are particularly suspect, it sometimes seems, because of the attitudes seen among them
with respect to the divine: the classical writers either "believe in" the
divine or at least regard a general belief in the divine as useful, if not
even necessary. Thus, the classical writers can be suspected of being
either superstitious or hypocritical.

A key question here, in considering this final objection to the
classics—an objection which does sense that the truly liberated self
cares more for the truth than for anything else—a key question here
is, May not the intellectuals making this objection fail to see what
the classics saw about the limitations of human communities and of
most human beings and in failing to see this, do not modern intellectuals permit a few to indulge themselves at the expense of the many,
at the expense of the community and ultimately at the expense of
themselves (since they too, as intellectuals, depend upon an enduring,
decent community)?

xi

OF COURSE, no single critic of the classics is likely to make all of
the half-dozen objections I have gathered together on this occasion.
No doubt, also, other objections can be conjured up, or at least vari-

ations of those I have surveyed here. But objections such as these, in whatever form they appear, have sufficed to undermine the place of the classics in the West. The traditional liberal education upon which we have depended to produce the best citizens and the most highly developed human beings is thereby lost sight of.

The physical sciences with all their wonders have, I have indicated, been critical to the replacement of the classics in education, a replacement which has led to a faith in global culture, a determined rationalism, a sort of equality, and a "principled" immoderation (or enthusiasm)—in short, it has led to that modernity which draws to it bright young people. But the physical sciences, we cannot too often be reminded, face serious limitations: they are quite limited in what they describe and in how they look at what they *can* deal with. For one thing, as I have also indicated, science depends on much that is prescientific, that is itself not subject to science, and that is more important than that which science does deal with. Modern science *is* "universal," but that is partly because it is descriptive of a narrow range of things, and even that range can be surveyed only in a special way which abstracts from "reality" in significant respects. This is not to deny that useful things can be learned from the study of the trivial and the transitory—even, for example, from the study of comic strips and the sports pages—but a useful study of trivial things depends on something important, firm, and persistent by which to see and judge. And it is this that the classics, and perhaps only the classics, can provide.

The classics of the West permit us to stand back and survey how things are—things both natural and conventional—without wrecking what we have. Modern science is itself distinctively Western in that it comes from our great tradition (rooted in the classics) of a recognition of, and concern with, nature. But, then, the objections to the classics that I have examined today are also distinctively Western: the kind of exploration and experimentation that these objections represent and encourage are somehow permitted by what the West has developed. There is in the West, and perhaps only in the West, an openness to, and a systematic pursuit of, the truth, for its own sake. In a sense, then, the West carries within itself the seeds of its own destruction. Would we have it otherwise?

This does not mean, however, that we should not be prudent in using the considerable freedom we are privileged to have. We should recognize, for example, that communities *are* fragile, that they are grounded in something other than open-mindedness, even when they make much of it. We can afford to experiment with such things as relativism, positivism, and historicism, but only after, and only so long as, our foundations, those foundations provided us by the classics, are secure. Thus, no other civilization, so far as we know, has been able to question as we have the ultimate worth of its own. Thus, also, the series of objections I have surveyed on this occasion—a series of objections to our classics, and hence to our way of life—comes only out of the West, directly or indirectly.

I have suggested that only the Western way of life is apt, even though in a somewhat degraded form, to serve as a global culture. In this form, man has become the measure of all things and a much diminished man at that. I say "much diminished," speaking again from the perspective of the Western classics.

Even so, there *is* that in the classics which makes plausible the desire for, and the possibility of, globalness: there is in the West, that is, that profound concern with, and dedication to, nature which embraces all men, without regard to boundaries, and calls out to all men who think. Even the West's decisive revelation has tended to be universal, proclaiming the oneness of God.

xii

I HAVE also suggested that the West carries within itself the seeds of its own destruction, that a critical divisiveness may be at its heart, but that we have learned to live with (perhaps even to profit from) this tension. Is not all this due in part to the obligation we have had to balance (for millennia now) the somewhat contending claims of Jerusalem and Athens? I say "somewhat contending," since it is evident that each has very much influenced the other among us, each pressing the other to examine itself and to determine what each truly means. Whatever the differences between these two approaches to understanding, to community, and to human action—differences that are profound, but which should be left for another occasion—whatever the differences between Athens and Jerusalem, it is evident that they share much in confrontation with the modernity for which they are, in some ways, jointly responsible.

We can see here the familiar contest of ancients versus moderns. Timing *can* be important. There *is* an advantage to a certain kind of firstness. If the reason is mature and somewhat unencumbered, it should be able to work out early *what is*. It should also come fairly early to an awareness of what cannot be known—just as, for example, Euclid sensed what could and could not be demonstrated about parallel lines. Timing can mean that one is obliged, as well as able, to *see* what is there. This is why Plato and Aristotle, on one hand, and the most inspired poets and prophets, on the other, give us an impression of comprehensiveness and authority, almost as if reason or wisdom are therein enshrined. We are consistently challenged by them to unfold what is there and what is thereby in us.

Not all our great texts, even those from antiquity, come directly from Jerusalem or Athens. But they are intimately related, one way or another, to Athens and Jerusalem, if only in how they have become available to us. It is not accidental, I suggest, that we *can* conveniently refer to the Greek and the biblical as "Athens and Jerusalem." In both cases, a way of life is presupposed, a way of life dependent upon, and decisively shaped by, the political. Does not a viable political regime tend to be intimately related to a "religion"—to a somewhat parochial view of the whole and of the eternal? Once again we can see how and why the classics can be seen to be in opposition to a science-based global culture, perhaps to any culture which denies the inevitability and power of local passions and allegiances.

xiii

THE WESTERN classics, I have suggested, make possible an education (what we know as liberal education) that permits one to grasp the best in such a way as to provide one as well with a reliable grasp of the mundane things of this world. Thus, classical poetry takes the variety of human passions and deals with them authoritatively in one form or another. Thus, also, the classics inform and arrange, and make sense of, much that we "experience." There is seen in them an abiding respect for common sense, as well as an awareness of its limitations.

It can be said, therefore, that Mind may be seen at work in *our* classics, Mind investigating *what is*. That is to say, there is to be seen in the classics a constant inquiry into nature, but with appropriate adaptations to circumstances and with due appreciation of elevated opinions concerning the divine. When we talk of the classics, then, are we not talking to a significant degree of that most human yearning and most human pleasure which philosophy represents in its most disciplined and productive form?

We cannot help but be grateful to iconoclastic critics of the classics, since they do challenge us to recognize and thereby to reaffirm the best in ourselves. Thus, we have been obliged, in our responses to a variety of objections to the traditional reliance upon the classics, to develop our awareness of what a classic must be—and an awareness, as well, of enduring questions to be pursued on other occasions.

We reaffirm the classics on the basis of what the classics have taught us: they equip us to make and to appreciate appropriate defenses of them. And they warn us against the obstacles placed in the way of true understanding and genuine morality, including that most formidable obstacle evident in the pampered Meno's attitude, "Let us not bother to think!"

The classics, we are told, exhibit a "happy coalescence of matter and style." Critical to style is the sense of when one has said enough for the occasion.*

---

*Still another way of suggesting what a classic may be is to display a number of them. The faculty of the Basic Program of Liberal Education for Adults, The University of Chicago, has developed over the years a list of classics and near-classics for the four-year course of study in the program (which was founded in 1946). (See Appendix E, below.) This list is reviewed thoroughly every spring by the Basic Program faculty of some dozen members. (There are about two hundred active students each term.)

Basic Program classes meet eleven times each quarter, three hours each time. Half of the time at each of these weekly meetings is devoted to the "seminar" and the other half to the "tutorial" (which has one or two works studied intensively, or for about seventeen hours, throughout the eleven weeks of the quarter).

The 1982-1983 reading list for the four years of the Basic Program is set forth below, with the numbers in parentheses indicating the weeks of the term during which each work is to be discussed. Three-fourths of the fifty or so works studied in the program are read in their entirety. Some of these works could no doubt be replaced by other works of at least comparable worth and "teachability." In the art of refining an effective reading list, trial and error can be important. The Basic Program reading list follows:

First Year

Fall Quarter. Seminar: (1) Introduction; (2-3) Sophocles, ANTIGONE; (4-6) Plato, APOLOGY, CRITO; (7-8) Tolstoy, THE DEATH OF IVAN ILYCH; (9-11) Dostoevsky, CRIME AND PUNISHMENT.
   Tutorial: (1-11) Plato, MENO.

Winter Quarter. Seminar: (1-3) BIBLE: GENESIS, JOB, MATTHEW; (4-7) Plato, REPUBLIC, I-IV; (8-11) Freud, INTRODUCTORY LECTURES ON PSYCHOANALYSIS.
   Tutorial: (1-11) Shakespeare, KING LEAR (or HAMLET or MACBETH or OTHELLO).

Spring Quarter. Seminar: (1-3) Machiavelli, THE PRINCE; (4-6) Hobbes, LEVIATHAN, I-II; (7-8) Rousseau, DISCOURSE ON THE ORIGIN AND FOUNDATIONS OF INEQUALITY; (9-11) Stendhal, THE RED AND THE BLACK.
   Tutorial: (1-11) Aristotle, NICOMACHEAN ETHICS.

Second Year

Fall Quarter. Seminar: (1–7) Plato, REPUBLIC; (8–9) Joyce, PORTRAIT OF THE ARTIST AS A YOUNG MAN; (10–11) Shakespeare, THE TEMPEST.

Tutorial: (1–11) Homer, THE ILIAD.

Winter Quarter. Seminar: (1–2) Thomas Aquinas, TREATISE ON LAW; (3–5) Locke, SECOND TREATISE OF GOVERNMENT; (6–8) Hume, AN INQUIRY CONCERNING THE PRINCIPLES OF MORALS; (9–11) Kant, THE FUNDAMENTAL PRINCIPLES OF THE METAPHYSICS OF MORALS (selections).

Tutorial: (1–11) LYRIC POETRY.

Spring Quarter. Seminar: (1–7) Sophocles, OEDIPUS THE TYRANT and Aristotle, POETICS; (8–10) Mark Twain, THE ADVENTURES OF HUCKLEBERRY FINN; (11) Conrad, HEART OF DARKNESS.

Tutorial: (1–11) Euclid, GEOMETRY, and Newton, PRINCIPIA (selections).

Third Year

Fall Quarter. Seminar: (1–4) Homer, ODYSSEY; (5–7) Aristotle, RHETORIC; (8–9) Plutarch, LYCURGUS, NUMA POMPILIUS, ALCIBIADES, ALEXANDER, CAESAR; (10–11) Shakespeare, JULIUS CAESAR.

Tutorial: (1–11) Thucydides, THE PELOPONNESIAN WAR.

Winter Quarter. Seminar: (1–3) Gibbon, THE DECLINE AND FALL OF THE ROMAN EMPIRE, I, i–v, xv–xvi; (4–6) St. Augustine, CONFESSIONS; (7–9) Dante, INFERNO; (10–11) Chaucer, THE CANTERBURY TALES (selections).

Tutorial: (1–11) Aeschylus, ORESTEIA.

Spring Quarter. Seminar: (1–4) Plato, SYMPOSIUM; (5–6) Tacitus, HISTORY; (7–8) Pascal, PENSÉES; (9–11) Nietzsche, BEYOND GOOD AND EVIL.

Tutorial: (1–11) Melville, MOBY DICK.

Fourth Year

Fall Quarter. Seminar: (1–3) Herodotus, THE PERSIAN WARS, I, VII; (4–5) Montaigne, ESSAYS, I; (6–8) Swift, GULLIVER'S TRAVELS; (9–11) Austen, PRIDE AND PREJUDICE.

Tutorial: (1–11) Descartes, DISCOURSE ON METHOD.

Winter Quarter. Seminar: (1–3) Aristotle, POLITICS, I, III; (4–7) Smith, THE WEALTH OF NATIONS (selections); (8–11) Marx, COMMUNIST MANIFESTO and CAPITAL (selections).

Tutorial: (1–11) Lucretius, ON THE NATURE OF THINGS.

Spring Quarter. Seminar: (1–4) THE DECLARATION OF INDEPENDENCE, THE CONSTITUTION OF THE UNITED STATES, THE FEDERALIST (selections); (5–6) Burke, REFLECTIONS ON THE REVOLUTION IN FRANCE (selections); (7–9) Tocqueville, THE OLD REGIME AND THE FRENCH REVOLUTION; (10) Dostoevsky, NOTES FROM THE UNDERGROUND; (11) Xenophon, HIERO.

Tutorial: (1–11) Plato, PHAEDO.

Appendix D. ART, CRAFTSMANSHIP, AND COMMUNITY

> *If someone wishes to construct an equilateral triangle out of wood, it is not enough for him to know what Euclid said in the beginning of his book on the construction of the equilateral triangle, without joining to this the craft of carpentry.*

> —Averroes, *On Plato's Republic*, 76.17

PART ONE

THE LAST Sunday morning in January saw the regular service at Rockefeller Memorial Chapel, at the University of Chicago, devoted to the dedication of the ten "Creation Windows" which had been made and installed during the preceding year.

These stained-glass windows are contributions to the chapel by members of the University community, three dozen of us ranging in ages from an eight-year-old child to a retired professor. We were introduced to the stained-glass craft by art professor Harold Haydon, director of the Midway Studios at the University (and Chicago *Sun-Times* art critic), who designed the windows and patiently supervised our execution of them in the chapel basement on Wednesday nights and weekends.

E. Spencer Parsons, dean of the chapel since 1965, had long believed that stained glass would add warmth and color to the austere beauty of the building. Permission was secured by him to have Mr. Haydon supply designs for the ten 53-by-10-inch window slits which line the long east and west aisle walls of the chapel just above eye level. It is believed to be the first time the board of trustees of the university has allowed amateurs to play so critical a role in mak-

---

This article was published, in an edited form, in *Midwest Magazine, Chicago Sun-Times*, March 11, 1973, p. 12, under the title, "Shedding light on the elements: Harold Haydon and friends put their thoughts into the abstract of stained glass." Color photographs of seven of the ten windows discussed were printed with the article.

See the Frontispiece to this book.

301

ing a change in the chapel. (No doubt amateurs had to be used in making the windows for the European cathedrals as well.)

Mr. Haydon's designs are devoted on the east side to The Heavens, Air, Water, Earth, and Fire—that is, to the elements long associated with the very foundations of things. On the west side there may be found the living things of this world: Plants, Animals, Man, Woman, and Works of the Mind—the last a representation of great discoveries capped by the reminder within a phoenix of the first controlled release of nuclear energy in 1942 at the University of Chicago.

Our own noteworthy discovery as the executants of Mr. Haydon's designs was that we could, despite the initial hours of frustration and bleeding fingers, come to work in glass with surprising precision. The materials and instruments we worked with were essentially those in use since medieval Europeans first began to work with stained glass. These were the sheets of colored glass (imported for us from France, England, and Germany), the double-channel lead strips (called "came") which must be fitted around each piece of cut glass; soldering wire; a sealing material made of tile grout, carbon and linseed oil; a knife for cutting the came; an ordinary glass cutter (first devised in the sixteenth century); hammer and nails; a wooden lathekin used to press came against glass; and a soldering iron (which was, in our case, heated electrically rather than in a brazier).

We developed, over the year, techniques and instruments which we found, upon research, that our many predecessors had used centuries ago. Research also indicated that it will take years of weathering to transform our windows from their present brilliance to the deep mellowness one associates with stained glass.

In a typical window there are more than 150 pieces of glass. It has been estimated that we devoted at least 200 man-hours of work to each window. Six tables, of four or five people, were each responsible for a window. A few tables were able to go on to make a second window, as was the case, for instance, at my own table from which there emerged several suggestions Mr. Haydon could use in the Works of the Mind design which we executed. (The reader is challenged to see how many of the dozen great discoveries of the Western world he can detect in that design. [See the Frontispiece to this book. See, also, Part Three of this Appendix.])

Mr. Haydon's design on heavy paper, indicating the shapes and colors of the pieces (there were seventeen colors from which he could choose), would be placed on the work table. Glass and came would then be cut to shape, working first along the border at the top and on one side, thereafter fitting in pieces in the body of the design from top to bottom, and finally closing in the border on the other side and at the bottom. Glass and came would usually be soldered in place after sections of ten or so pieces had been fitted snugly into place with the aid of a lathekin. The entire assemblage would then be reversed carefully for soldering the other side before the window could be sealed for installation. (There are more than 400 joints soldered in each window.) Installation, too, proved to be a demanding craft; two university maintenance men employed techniques which permitted them to fit a window firmly into place in only half a day.

It is particularly appropriate that the chapel, a magnificent frame for such work, should have been thus adorned by a sustained community effort. The chapel is the building on the Midway which dominates the architecture of the university campus and from which come every quarter-hour of the day the chimes which can be heard across much of Hyde Park. It is also the building in which, since it was built in 1928, the most solemn convocations in the community have been held, ranging from graduations and memorial services to grand weddings and town meetings.

Just as a university faculty reaches back across centuries to colleagues in many lands, so did the executants of these community windows join, in the work of their hands, with the legion of craftsmen across Europe who have also left visible testimony of their dedication to an enduring community of the spirit. And just as a university community has to be known from the inside to be judged properly, so does stained glass have to be viewed from within its building if the richness of its colors and the subtlety of its designs are to be apparent.

Rockefeller Chapel is open daily from 9 a.m. to 4:45 p.m.

PART TWO
by Harold Haydon

I BELIEVE I speak for all who participated in the making of the windows when I say that it was a privilege and an honor to contribute to

---

These remarks, by Harold Haydon, were made at the dedication of the "Creation Windows," Rockefeller Chapel, The University of Chicago, January 28, 1973. Mr. Haydon was then professor of art and director of the Midway Studios, The University of Chicago.

His remarks are published here with his permission.

the enhancement of this building, rich in symbolism. We can hope that the ten windows now installed will add to the voices with which the chapel speaks—speaks to and speaks for the university community. It was, as some of us know, a long-standing project of the dean of the chapel to add color, and to add color wedded to significance, to this chapel—something which he first thought of and first considered before he accepted his position here, and which over the years came into realization, first, most spectacularly, with the banners that you find constantly on view and rotated, and now with the small stained-glass windows.

The making of the windows was conceived from the beginning as a university community project, to be executed by workers, young—some younger than you would think—and older workers, both laymen and professional artists and craftsmen. Some, perhaps all of them, learned this craft as they worked. They were subjected to the discipline of the building and of its fabric, and it was no mean discipline to meet the requirements of the stone of the building, and then of the glass and the lead. The discipline began with the shape of the windows, dictating what might be put in them, and was continued, as the dean has said, with the nature of glass and what it can do, should do, will do, may do, will suffer having done to it in being cut and placed, and with the nature of lead, its strength and its weaknesses, culminating in the fitting of the finished windows to the building, when the expert craftsmen who managed that part had to cope with the vagaries of the building itself, a handcrafted building in which not all parts fit exactly.

We who participated in this making will have long memories of the work space—deep underground, out of sight—where for a year the tables and tools and materials could stay untouched except when people came to work on Wednesday evenings and on the Saturdays and Sundays when they also worked. It was a year of Wednesday evenings and more than that.

The material was English and French and German so-called antique glass of the best quality we could find, in rich, translucent colors, transmitting light, as bright, I find, on a dull day, or brighter, than on a day of sunlight, when the outside light comes in and, for a while at least, throws patterns of colors on the walls, on the framing of the windows and on the floors—something to see as it changes through a day.

We were dealing with an old craft—lead came, wheel glass cutters still used in the same fashion as they were centuries ago, lathekins, and stopping knives—echoes of the past. Those who are curious about this will have an opportunity at the end of the service to talk with some of the workers who are here, to see some of the materials and, I am told, to cut some glass and participate in a vicarious way in the experience which, in the long run, turned out to be envied by many. To this day I hear people saying, "I wish I had known. I would like to have joined that group."

We chose materials that were congenial to the building, despite the temptations of the "new." In this day and age that's a very strong temptation, to use different materials, new materials, new methods, new approaches. Instead, we accepted the discipline of simple, old-fashioned leaded glass, replacing plain squares of slightly tinted glass with the richer and more variegated shapes that you now see.

A program was devised, in consultation with the dean. That program listed the order and names of windows, reading clockwise from the northeast window (as we know them now): Heavens, Air, Water, Earth, Fire, Plants, Animals, Man, Woman, and Works of the Mind. These names may change, we expect will change with usage, and indeed already have changed: Is it Galaxies, Cosmos, or Heavens? Is it Eve or Woman?

But this was a program expressed in words that then had to be translated into visual imagery, a process that went on over a full five-month period, during which I am sure there must have been some evolution. We'll leave it to the scholars and the historians to detect the order in which the ten windows were designed. But I am aware that there *is* an evolution. There was change, there was development, as the windows were completed, and partially completed, and as the time passed and new ideas came in.

The borders were invented, in large part, by the workers, introducing a curious "irrational" and, I think, important element of chance, in all except two of them (the second and the tenth) where the people involved had an imagination that called for, in one window, the rainbow or a spectrum and, in another window, the "golden section" proportion, Plato's "divided line," for the borders, both stemming from the same mind that suggested themes for the tenth and last window called the Works of the Mind, originally thought of as Creativity. I refer to George Anastaplo, who contributed some very important intellectual elements to that development. [See the frontispiece to this book. See, also, Part Three of this Appendix.]

I have been asked—asked by George, asked by others—to describe the style of these windows and all I can say is that they have no style, in the sense of Frank Lloyd Wright's remarks that "style is no style." These windows have no particular style, yet they are abstract, not in the technical contemporary meaning of abstract, but in a profounder sense, I think. Simply, they are drawn out of—removed from—particular things. They are not pictures of, they are abstractions from—abstractions, and abstract figurations, existing in a unifying ambiance of color, based on quite specific ideas, such as water in all its forms, the patterns of earth's structures, and biological beginnings. They are meant to be read, not to be regarded as decorations, although decorations they must be, too. They are meant to be read, but not to be read at a glance. They were designed with deliberate multiplicity and ambiguity to reward study and refresh repeated encounters so that they may not be used up or worn out in a single viewing.

Furthermore, they are not intended to mean "just anything" to "just anybody," and yet to leave some scope for imagination. Already, in one curious instance, I have heard the accusation of male chauvinism, when the figure 2 was discovered buried mysteriously in the figure of Woman. And it was not intended and not seen by anyone until an imaginative feminist came along.

As designer of the windows and as supervisor of their execution, I can report that they were done with devotion and quite a lot of self-sacrifice on the part of the window makers. Many hours, including summer afternoons, were given over to this work in the not-very-comfortable basement of the chapel, time taken from other activities and taken from pleasure for this other kind of pleasure. The windows were executed by friends and neighbors who made their own individual contributions—subtle but very certain: subtle in that you might have to examine the kind of soldering, the details of craftsmanship—but always done with magnificent care. The discipline of this building said, "It has to be so; it must fit these windows," and that discipline was respected. "It must be done well enough to last a hundred years," was said more than once, and this expressed the spirit of the craftsmen.

I could feel among the group a sense of joy in working with others as an important part of this project, and also a mutual trust. They had to trust me as the designer. I had to trust them as the executants of the designs. They could not really know the effect of the windows when the windows were lying flat on the tables. It was impossible to imagine the effect of the glass, which looks one way in that position and quite another way up against the light, and so artist and workers together were engaged in a mutual exchange of trust with surprise, pleasure, excitement in the outcome and a legitimate pride in accomplishment. They took these half-formed materials—the glass (colored, sheet, blown by hand) and the lead (extruded, shaped to the came form), which might be regarded as half-formed materials. Out of this semichaos they gave order; they gave meaning; they brought significance to humble materials.

The windows were designed and made to speak of fundamental things as coherently, simply, and universally as possible, in visual language of this time, with the hope that they will speak to generations yet to come.

PART THREE

THE WORKS of the Mind window in Rockefeller Chapel at the University of Chicago (see Frontispiece) exhibits a balance of "hot" and "cool" colors. (See, for indications of the colors in this stained-glass window, the dustjacket for this book; *Midwest Magazine, Chicago Sun-Times*, March 11, 1973, p. 12. See, also, John Forwalter, *Hyde Park Herald*, Chicago, Ill., May 9, 1973, p. 24. See, for an account of our making of still another window for the chapel, Judith Barnard, *Chicago Tribune Magazine*, Nov. 12, 1978, p. 56.)

The Works of the Mind panel incorporates a series of noteworthy discoveries which are susceptible of visual representation. Mounting from the bottom are the Pythagorean theorem, the slave boy demonstration in Plato's *Meno*, an illustration taken from Galileo, Kepler's third law of planetary motions, the geodesics in hyperboloid geometry, and a lemma from Newton.

The series is capped by the phoenix, which appears on the seal of the university. The phoenix has as its body the Henry Moore "Nuclear Energy" sculpture which marks, on the campus of the university, the site of the first self-sustaining chain reaction devised and controlled by man. (See Epilogue, Section ii, above.)

The designer, when he came to weave together these half dozen discoveries, found that the colors and lines he chose to use (as well as

the discoveries themselves) invited departures from a strict chrono-
logical order in the vertical arrangement of the discoveries.

Included in the upper half of the panel (in the Newton segment)
are the Tablets of the Law; included in the lower half of the panel
(spanning the Galileo and Plato segments) are a Madonna and Child.
Other discoveries have been found, by ingenious students, to be depicted in this window.

The phoenix, whose wings suggest the hands of God, rests in a
nest of flames. These flames may also be seen at the bottom of the
panel.

The borders of this window are related to the themes of the
panel. The upper border suggests celestial light and colors; the lower
border suggests the earth. The side borders run repeatedly through
the spectrum, with clear glass indicating the proportions of "the
divided line" in the sixth book of Plato's *Republic.* (The four segments in each side border are forty-five centimeters, thirty centimeters, thirty centimeters, and twenty centimeters, respectively. There
are thirteen pieces of glass in the first segment and seven pieces of
glass in each of the other three segments.)

Since Socrates does not say which of the four segments in his
divided line is the longest, the right border places the longest segment
at the top, the left border places the longest segment at the bottom.
The entire window is thus framed by a question which is left open.

The designer of the window was Harold Haydon. The executants
of this window were Sara Maria Anastaplo, Virginia A. Smith, and to
a lesser extent, Theodora McShan Anastaplo, Susan H. Smith, Grace
Tress, and Mildred Tress. I suggested the overall design for this window and helped with its execution.* This window is fifty-three
inches by ten inches.

---

*I also suggested the design for the Graduates' Window, which was also made in 1972.
(See frontispiece.)

This stained-glass window, which is on the stairs from the basement of Rockefeller
Chapel, is seen by students as they file upstairs for the graduation ceremony. Depicted in
this window is the Möbius Band: the opinion is thereby expressed in the window that the
pursuit upon which students embark as members of the University community is unending.
(At the conclusion of the ceremony, those receiving bachelor's degrees are welcomed by the
President of the University to "the fellowship of educated men and women," and those receiving advanced degrees to "the ancient and honorable company of scholars." The designer
of the Graduates' Window was Harold Haydon and the executant, Sara Maria Anastaplo.
This window is twenty-seven inches by five inches.

The name of this window was suggested by our familiarity with the long-established Works of the Mind Lecture Series sponsored annually by the Basic Program of Liberal Education for Adults, The University of Chicago. (See Appendix C, above, Appendix E and Appendix G, below.)

Appendix E. ART AND
MORTALITY

When I heard of the misfortune,
that Myres was dead,
I paid a visit to his house, though I avoid
going into the homes of the Christians,
especially in times of mournings and feasts....

—Constantine Cavafy,
"Myres: Alexandria, A.D. 340"

PROLOGUE

WE CELEBRATE on this occasion the accomplishments of some seventy students who have successfully completed their course of study with the University of Chicago's Basic Program of Liberal Education for Adults. And we celebrate as well the completion of the thirty-fifth year of the Basic Program.

That the Basic Program is (once again) under a cloud is known to everyone associated with it. Questions have been raised, properly enough, as to whether this program should be supported much longer by a university whose generosity must be reconsidered in the face of the continuing financial crisis in higher education in this country today.

Whatever the ultimate fate of the Basic Program, we are entitled and obliged to celebrate its achievements. Whatever happens, we have its accomplishments to remember and to continue to profit from.

Since I am finishing this year a quarter-century with the Basic Program, I have been asked to speak on behalf of the staff. I can think of nothing better to do on this occasion than to continue the kind of discussions we have in our classes.

I draw for this purpose upon an ancient Greek text—the first new text I myself studied (this was in a Greek class with the late John Hawthorne) when I came to the University of Chicago the very year that the Basic Program was founded. This thirty-five year period, I

This talk was given at the Thirty-second Annual Awarding of Certificates to Graduates of the Basic Program of Liberal Education for Adults, The University of Chicago. See the note at the end of Appendix C, above, for the Basic Program reading list.

notice in passing, is more than one third the life of this university. I think it fitting and proper, if I am indeed reaching the end of my association as student and teacher with the university, to go back to my beginnings here by considering with you the "Heraclitus" poem by Callimachus.

This poem, which some of you have perhaps discussed in our lyric poetry tutorials, marks, appropriately enough, both the conclusion and the reaffirmation of a career. And, also appropriately enough, we in assessing the Basic Program, like Callimachus in assessing his friend Heraclitus, must take account of somber rumors of a demise.

Still, we like Callimachus, should try to make the best of the situation. No life worth living is altogether free of challenges.

i

WHO, THEN, is Callimachus? He has been described in these terms in a Loeb Classical Library collection of his poems:

> Very little is known about the life of Callimachus either from his own writings, or from other sources. The available information, however, enables us to trace a bare outline.

> The family of Callimachus came from Cyrene, and in fact the poet claimed to be descended from Battos, the founder of the city. [Cyrene, a Greek colony in North Africa about five hundred miles west of Alexandria, was founded about 630 B.C. Callimachus' forebears established at that time a dynasty which ruled the city for the next two centuries.] [Callimachus'] parents were called Battos and Megatime, and he himself was named after his grandfather, a Cyrenean general. According to Suidas, [Callimachus] married the daughter of a Syracusan called Euphraios, but her name is not given, and we are not told whether any children resulted from the marriage.

> The date of the poet's birth is not known, and the only information about his arrival and establishment at Alexandria [where he spent most of his career] is that it took place during the reign of Ptolemy II (285–247 B.C.). He must have reached the capital of the Ptolemies poor, for he worked as a school teacher—a proverbially poor profession—before he was introduced to the court. We do not know when, or by whom, he was brought into contact with the court circle, but his life seems to have changed completely after that. He was com-

missioned to prepare the *Pinakes,* the great catalogue of the books of the Alexandrian library; his later court poetry betrays a close intimacy with the royal family.

Many modern scholars have seen Callimachus as the most characteristic representative of Alexandrian poetry, in fact the man "who personified in the purest manner the Hellenistic spirit."

It is said that Callimachus lived, by and large, an uneventful life. Yet it can also be said of him, "Certainly in general [he] lived up to his name 'Glory in battle.'" The epitaph he wrote for his father includes this observation, "I am son and father of Callimachus of Cyrene... One commanded his country's armies: the other wrote poems beyond envy's reach ..." Callimachus did come to be regarded, especially by some Romans, as the first of the elegiac poets, as *the* writer of epigrammatic verses. Some consider him surpassed in this capacity only by Plato.

ii

THE GREATEST of Callimachus' epigrammatic poems which have come down to us is his "Heraclitus." The most famous translation into English of this six-line poem is one which is (as it has been said) "extravagant where Callimachus is economical, and effusive where Callimachus is restrained." Even so, this nineteenth century translation (by William Johnson Cory) is deservedly famous, despite its limitations. It goes like this:

> They told me, Heraclitus, they told me you were dead,
> They brought me bitter news to hear and bitter tears to shed.
> I wept as I remembered how often you and I
> Had tired the sun with talking and sent him down the sky.
>
> And now that thou art lying, my dear old Carian guest,
> A handful of grey ashes, long, long ago at rest,
> Still are thy pleasant voices, thy nightingales, awake:
> For Death, he taketh all away, but them he cannot take.

The complaint has been made of this translator that he says everything twice. But that may not be a bad thing for us, as we begin to come to grips with the thought of this poem. Thus, we are told that the narrator laments on learning of the death of an old friend, someone whom he had once talked much with through many a long day and well past sunset. Yet, we are also told, the narrator is consoled by believing that Heraclitus' "nightingales" live on, that they are beyond the grasp of Death (or, as in the Greek, Hades). What precisely those nightingales are needs to be considered further.

iii

BUT WE require a much more nearly literal translation for any further consideration of what is said in this poem. I suggest the following:

> Someone told me, Heraclitus, of your death and brought me to tears,
> as I remembered how often we talked the sun down. Somewhere,
> Halicarnassian friend, you are ages ashes. Yet your nightingales live;
> on them, Hades, who plunders everything, shall not lay hand.

One of the achievements of *this* translation, I note in passing, is that it employs only a few words more than the original Greek with its forty words), whereas the much more musical Cory translation has twice the number of the original Greek. I notice also that what I have given as "you are ages ashes" is literally, "you are fourpastly ashes" (or, "long, long, long, long ago ashes").

Our poem opens, "Someone told me." The informant is not named; he does not seem to matter. Also uncertain are *when* Heraclitus died—ages ago, it seems—or *where:* "somewhere." Of course, these uncertainties may be such as to make one wonder whether Heraclitus is indeed dead. Could it not be a false report? But if he is not dead yet, then later he will be, for death itself is inevitable. In fact, it may not even matter whether Heraclitus ever lived: is not something being said about mortality and about the proper human response to it, a response which affirms and thus reestablishes life?

We can sum up our preliminary impressions of the poem with a pair of questions and answers:

> *Is* Heraclitus dead?
> It does not matter: for he is certainly dead now.
>
> *Did* Heraclitus ever live?
> It does not matter: he certainly lives now.

iv

IF WE pursue these questions further we can recognize that for friends
to be long separated is like being dead to one another—especially if it
is not likely that they will ever meet again. Do we not all know people we have cared for and who are still alive, but whom we do not
expect ever to see again? And if we do not remain in touch, how does
that differ from death? If one must learn of another's death as the
narrator did, that other is not fully alive to one.

   There is no indication that Heraclitus' death was anything but
natural. That is, there is no indication that the narrator could have
done anything to save or prolong the life of his friend. Consider also
the disparity between the immediacy of the news about Heraclitus'
death and the considerable span of time since that death. It had not
mattered for a long time to the narrator, in his ignorance, that Heraclitus was dead: so why should the news of something that had happened some time ago and that was inevitable—why should such news,
when it does catch up with him, matter?

   Conceivably, the news might never have reached the narrator
during his lifetime. It is not like someone dying in the neighborhood.
So, again we can wonder, why should one become exercised by such
news when it does come?

   I have suggested that a permanent separation between friends is,
in some respects, like the death of one to the other. I now suggest
that it can also be said that a friend who dies at a distance is like
someone who lives on. But does *such* living on mean anything? Is it
like being praised or blamed without being aware of it? One may
even wonder what the worth of posthumous glory is? Certainly, one
can be unmoved to learn that someone, who had been silent for so
many years, had really admired one all the time—especially if one
learns of the admiration at a time when it is no longer supportive or
otherwise useful. Does not all this point to the need for self-sufficiency,
to knowing what is truly good and dedicating oneself to *that*, irrespective of what others say, are, or do?

                                  v

WHO, THEN, is the poem for? It *is* addressed to Heraclitus, as if he
were still living. Does this reflect an initial refusal by the narrator to

accept the truth? Certainly, it cannot be expected that Heraclitus (or even his relatives) will ever hear the poem, or hear of it—or be otherwise benefitted "personally" by it? Of course, one can enjoy in anticipation what others will someday say of one—or is it enough to recognize what *should* be said of one? But, again, does one need the assessment of others, if one's own assessment (of oneself) is sound?

Do we see in this poem, then, an effort by the narrator to come to terms with his own death? Thus to be prepared to die is one condition for truly living. Is the narrator trying to reassure himself, to reconcile himself with human mortality generally? Indeed, are there not suggested here highlights of the narrator's own life? The tears that are shed are intimately related to memories of his own activities (albeit with Heraclitus)—and the tears turn into a poem.

vi

WHAT *IS* being said in this poem about death (or Hades, the personification of death)? Hades tries to grasp everything. One translator speaks of him as a burglar. He is seen as an enemy.

But, it should be noticed, Hades is not omnipotent, however grasping he is. He cannot seize everything. Thus, he is not a birdcatcher: at least, he cannot readily catch nightingales. And, one must wonder, how important *is* that (whatever it is) which has turned to ashes, when nightingales can still survive?

Nightingales, it has been suggested, refer to poems. In other lines, Callimachus speaks of his own poems as "nightingales." In advocating short poems, he observed that "Nightingales sing sweetest being small." It has even been suggested that Heraclitus' collection of poems may even have been entitled "Nightingales." However this may be, Heraclitus' poems do not survive him: at least, they have not been found to date. But, then, perhaps the nightingales the narrator was thinking of are the memories of Heraclitus found in *this* poem. Heraclitus, we can see, was the sort of man who could have a friend such as the narrator, a friend who is affected in this way upon learning of Heraclitus' death. In any event, Callimachus, too, is remembered primarily for this poem. It remains to be seen what those recollections are worth which depend on the song of any particular nightingale.

vii

SHOULD IT matter if there are any nightingales at all surviving—that is, any particular nightingales, whose fates do depend to a considerable extent on chance? Whether one thinks of nightingales as birds or as the memories of one's friends or as poems, are they not rooted in nature? Do they not somehow attempt to express perfection?

Certainly, that which art aims at has its own rationale. This is true as well of other works of the mind, which are always there to be rediscovered. Is it not because there are things good in themselves, and an enduring nature which can be again and again discovered and imitated, that poetry is possible?

There are things which *are* and which are worthwhile on their own, things which are choice-worthy for their own sake—and they do not depend on memories or on poetry. But it is natural to resort to art on certain occasions, to celebrate the existence, or the apparent passing, of such things. One of the tendencies of poetry is to make us forget that it may be a matter of chance that any particular, cherished manifestation of things does exist. Or a poem may dwell upon the transitory character of particular things—and such impermanence can be a cause of regret or melancholy. But does not that which stands behind the particular persevere? Whether this or that particular (such as a friendship) exists may be accidental; but is it not necessary (that is, inevitable) that there be such things?

Art in its highest form, then, recognizes (and celebrates) the goodness of existence. It points up the very existence of the best itself, *not* the length of any existence, as that which counts most. Some things are to be treasured for having *been,* simply because they are good: they are choice-worthy for their own sake, not for the sake of honor or utility or mere pleasure.

Art, then, and philosophy (which, among other things, interprets art in its fullness, which the artist himself often cannot do)—art and philosophy can help us recognize what *is.* Among the things which are, in a sense, is Hades, or death itself: it, too, must partake of existence (a life, of sorts) if *it* is to be effective.

Be that as it may, art deals with what is, and is worthwhile, in particular manifestations. It works with the concrete—particulars are made much of, but they do point to universals. Philosophy is much more direct about *its* concern with universals. Even so, it too depends, although in a different way, on particulars (such as communities and the leisure and education they make possible) if it is to attain the flowering *it* is capable of. A full flowering, at least among human beings in this life, seems to require a certain intimacy, or friendship.

Friendship, in turn, is keyed to conversation, long leisurely talk, talk which is oblivious of time, which "masters" the cycles or demands of the sun—or, as Callimachus put it, "how often we talked the sun down." Friendship and the talk which is vital to it point to the highest association and activity: the working of minds, sharing with each other and contemplating what they have discovered, including the perpetually intriguing questions for which men may never have final answers.

This kind of pleasurable activity, rooted in the confidence that things are not without meaning, may be reflected in our conversations on various occasions in the Basic Program—as well as in the conversations that Heraclitus' friend recalls. But, of course, Heraclitus and his friend were not the first talkers—and we (more than two thousand years later) are not the last. There are many before and after them and us. *We* understand—we have experienced—such talk, without ever knowing *theirs*. This once again reminds us of enduring things which exist independently of particular manifestations.

viii

BUT I am not licensed this afternoon to talk the sun down. Still, our subject does require that two more points be at least identified, for future discussion, before we proceed to the award of certificates.

The survival of this particular poem by Callimachus is itself due to chance. There was some seventeen hundred years ago an energetic (and, to my mind, a considerably underrated) biographer of eminent philosophers, Diogenes Laertius. One of his subjects was Heraclitus—not Callimachus' Heraclitus but a much more eminent one, the great student of nature from Ephesus who lived three centuries earlier (flourishing about 500 B.C.).

Diogenes Laertius, at the end of his account of Heraclitus the philosopher, did what he often does: he collected the names of various people of some note who had had the same name as his subject. Thus he concludes:

> Five men have borne the name of Heraclitus: first, our subject; second, a lyric poet, who wrote a hymn of praise to the twelve gods;

third, an elegiac poet of Halicarnassus [on whom Callimachus wrote];
fourth, a Lesbian who wrote a history of Macedonia; fifth, a jester
who, after having been a musician, became that.

Central to this array of the five names is, of course, *our* Heraclitus,
the man memorialized by Callimachus—and when Laertius lists his
name he does something quite unusual (not altogether unprecedented,
but rare): he quotes poetry about *him*. Thus we have had saved for
us Callimachus' poem.

I suggest that this list of five names represents a tacit comment
by Laertius on Heraclitus' doctrines. I glance briefly at this comment
now, primarily as still another way of considering Callimachus' poem.

Laertius had opened his account of the life of the great Heraclitus
with that philosopher's criticism of various poets (including Homer).
Perhaps, then, there is a reason for Laertius' making as much as he
does of art at the end of this biography, correcting as this does the
anti-artistic (or austere) line taken by Heraclitus.

The second Heraclitus listed, we notice, wrote primarily about
the gods. This reminds us that there is nothing said in the Callimachus
poem about the gods, about the divine, or about any immortal soul.

The great Heraclitus had made much of fire and change. All
things are composed of fire, he taught, and into fire they are again
resolved. We recall that the Heraclitus of Callimachus' poem is reduced to ashes, to the dust of cremation (it would seem)—but the
narrator insists (we have seen) that there is more to such a friend than
that which is subject to fire. Does Laertius, in using Callimachus'
poem as he does, call into question the great Heraclitus' emphasis
on fire? How *do* mind and personality come from matter, from the
workings of an all-encompassing fire (or energy?)?

We recall also that the last of the Heraclitus namesakes was a man
who had become a jester after having been a musician (or artist?).
The account of the jester, as well as the Heraclitus biography as a
whole, ends with the word *eidos* (idea). Does Laertius thereby suggest that there may be something foolish about the doctrines of the
great Heraclitus, that those doctrines may not take due account of
the ideas, of beings that exist independent of bodies and energy?
Does not the art Heraclitus disparaged testify to such beings, for all
to see? (Is Heraclitus the Lesbian historian used as "filler"?)

We can see, when we pursue the suggestions made both by Callimachus' poem and by the diligent scholar who preserved it for us,

that questions dear to philosophy remain. These questions are always
there to be revived. But is the key bird-image (for philosophy, as distinguished from poetry) not that of the nightingale (of which there
are many) but rather that of the phoenix, of which there is only one
and which (although consumed by fire) rises again and again? For one
philosopher, it can be said, is in his perfection like any other philosopher, whether or not he knows, or even knows of, others of like mind.

Artists, on the other hand, can be said to live in and through,
and depend more on, others. The great Heraclitus, Laertius tells us,
was not a friendly fellow. Perhaps Diogenes Laertius, by tacking on
to his biography of Heraclitus this marvelous poem on friendship, is
saying something as well about the limitations of the great Heraclitus'
austere way of life. It is a way of life—this life of the philosopher—
that seems to promote isolation, if not even a harsh aloofness.

ix

THE POLITICAL alienation of the great Heraclitus calls our attention to the final feature we will notice in Callimachus' poem.

We can see in this poem that nothing is made either of the political order or of the family as substitutes for the immortality of the
soul and the divine. Thus, no family is indicated for Heraclitus: no
patronymic is given; nothing is said about children.

Callimachus and his friend Heraclitus come from different cities,
almost a thousand miles apart. Indeed, the fact that Heraclitus is
from a different city (in the Caria of Asia Minor) is indicated at the
very heart of the poem. The poem virtually turns around the phrase,
"Halicarnassian friend." One must wonder if the deepest friendship,
as friendship is ordinarily understood, *can* be shared between men of
different countries. Would the poem have been different if Heraclitus
had been a cherished neighbor or relative whom one saw often and
upon whom one depended? Certainly, news of *his* death would not
have come thus. Friendship, as I have indicated, does depend on
proximity, if it is to endure in most cases. The fact that Heraclitus
has been absent from him (both at the beginning and at the end of
his life) may make it easier for the narrator to distance himself from
the personal sorrow one would ordinarily expect at the news of the
death of an old friend.

A friend from another country is not quite the friend that someone from one's own country, of otherwise similar interests, can be.

Whatever illusions one may have about one's own country as some-how special, if not immortal, it is difficult to take another's country with the same seriousness and reverence that he does. We are reminded by all this that Callimachus himself is from Cyrene, that he is a Greek in Egypt, really a foreigner, however well established he may have become. Once again, we may see (as is often the case in eulogies), this poem of lamentation is as much about the speaker as it is about the deceased.

It is a poem of defiance as well. Certainly, it ends on that note: Hades, who plunders all, shall not lay a hand on Heraclitus' (or are they Callimachus'?) nightingales. But however immune nightingales may be, countries are not: death reminds us of the limits of human associations (whatever peoples may believe). Indeed, we could say that we are all citizens of Hades, on leave of absence, so to speak. Or is it, as Callimachus teaches, that the best in us never dies? Does Hades claim only the corruptible part of us? But that corruptible, or change-able, part—including countries and families and other associations—does seem to be necessary now and then if anyone is to appreciate, enjoy and perpetuate an understanding of the very best.

Both art and philosophy help us become aware of the best in us, which does have to do with the reason somehow understanding things. But philosophy, as well as poetry, depends on language and that in turn is rooted in some community, in some family.

EPILOGUE

AND SO we have returned, in celebrating the specialness (if not the immortality) of someone such as Callimachus and his Heraclitus—we have returned to a recognition that human associations are needed if the very best is to be able to manifest itself.

Two associations are immediately precious for us here today, the adult education program which has for more than three decades now provided thoughtful men and women in northern Illinois an opportunity to discuss together questions of enduring significance, and the university whose generosity and reputation have made the Basic Program possible (that university which, by the way, displays the phoenix on its seal).

We, too, are defiant—or, better still, resolute—as we face old challenges once again. But we are also aware of what we have accom-plished, no matter what may happen now. For no matter what does happen, we can insist, it has all been worthwhile so long as it has lasted.

Indeed, this is like a good life itself, something to be desired for itself so long as one is privileged to enjoy it. We have not learned what the greatest books can teach us if we cannot learn further from our adversities, if we cannot rise above them (as we endure them properly)—if we cannot recognize and celebrate excellence when we do happen to encounter it. Excellence, even if its manifestations come and go, does exist in a way different from essentially temporary things.

Mortality (seen in the beginnings and endings of things)—mortality will have its due, from institutions as well as from human beings. But if Callimachus is correct—if we are correct about what we see in Callimachus' poem—mortality is itself dependent on something enduring if it is to be. Change itself depends on that which truly endures, on that life beyond everyday life.

Certainly, no matter what does happen to the Basic Program and the University of Chicago, we need not (so long as we live) stop doing what we consider most truly human, discussing among ourselves matters of importance and the questions to which they give rise.

The students who are now to receive their certificates are to be congratulated—and to be thanked, for having helped to provide all of us (students and faculty alike) years of opportunity to inquire together into those matters that thoughtful men and women concern themselves with always.*

---

*The President and the Council of the Faculty Senate of The University of Chicago delivered, during the summer and fall after this talk, unprecedented ringing endorsements of the Basic Program of Liberal Education for Adults. No doubt, the merits of the Basic Program became generally apparent in the university community when an enthusiastic former student in the Program, Edwin A. Bergman, was elected Chairman of the Board of Trustees of The University of Chicago. "It was through their participation in the Basic Program of Liberal Education for Adults, which is administered by University Extension, that the Bergmans discovered an interest in art. They are now avid art collectors, and own a superb collection of Surrealist and contemporary art." University of Chicago Magazine, Winter 1982, p. 26. Thus, Mr. Bergman has been quoted as saying, "I really feel that I owe a great deal to the University, not just for the education I received here [as an undergraduate], but also for the Basic Program experience, which took us into the art world and changed our lives dramatically." Ibid., p. 26. Or, as I believe Louis Pasteur put it, "Chance favors the prepared mind." See notes 7 and 279, above.

Indeed, it can be said, it is in part because of the Basic Program that the University of Chicago was privileged to acquire its Bergman Gallery and thereafter Mr. Bergman as the chairman of its board of trustees. These developments alone, it can also be said, have more than repaid the University of Chicago for its acceptance over the years of the modest annual deficit incurred by the Basic Program.

Appendix F. ART AND POLITICS

> *We think of [Demetrius] today only as a man*
> *of polished elegance of style, and not as one*
> *who left in the minds of those who heard him*
> *thorns along with the roses, as Eupolis says*
> *Pericles did.*

> —Cicero, *Brutus*, IX

THIS TALK was prepared for the discussion following a viewing of the Columbia Pictures film, *The Front* (directed by Martin Ritt). This discussion was part of a freshman orientation program at the University of Chicago, September 27, 1976. (The other members of the panel were Malcolm P. Sharp, Bernard Weisberg, and Stanley A. Kaplan.)

The plot of the film is indicated in the review which appeared in *Time,* October 11, 1976:

> In a certain sense, *The Front* is an easy movie to criticize; almost everything it does could have been done better. On the other hand, it is a very difficult movie to judge because it takes up a previously forbidden subject—the blacklisting of showfolk suspected of Communist leanings during the early '50s—and has the nerve, and grace, to take an absurdist view of that deplorable era. For that, and for Woody Allen's fine performance (against his usual comic grain) in the title role, it deserves respectful attention.

> Allen plays a politically innocent but street-shrewd cashier in a bar and grill, whose old high school friend (Michael Murphy) is a blacklisted TV writer suddenly in need of someone to sign his scripts for him, cash his checks and show up for rehearsals pretending he wrote the thing. The friend is gifted, the network execs are pleased, and Allen (who takes a percentage for his services) soon finds himself prospering and enjoying his demi-celebrity. But of course, a tweed jacket and a book-lined pad do not an author make. *The Front's* best comic moments occur as Allen, whose character is just barely literate, tries to act the role of author. His worst moment (and one of the film's best comic scenes): an attempt at an on-set rewrite of one of his client's scripts.

> Before long, Allen is fronting for more than one talented writer. Then come the investigators. The witch-hunters just cannot believe

that a scriptwriter this skillful has not committed an investigatable
offense. Along the way Allen becomes involved with a comic named
Hecky Brown (Zero Mostel), whose career is destroyed by the witch-
hunters and who then destroys himself. Allen's consciousness (and
his conscience) have been steadily expanding. In the end, he hero-
ically—and funnily—defies the congressional committee that tries
to pry from him at least a few suspect names.

It bears on my discussion of the film to notice here that the last spoken words of the film are Mr. Allen's defiance of the congressional
committee, "You can all go —— yourselves!" (The expletive deleted
here is excluded as well from *Webster's Third New International Dictionary,* p. 917. Cf. James Joyce, *Ulysses* [New York: Modern Library,
1942], pp. 580, 739, 765. Cf., also, *Cohen* v. *California,* 403 U.S.
15, 16 [1971]. But see Plato, *Republic* 439E–440A. See, also, notes
248 and 257, below. See, on moving pictures, note 7 above.)
    My 1976 talk follows:

i

PERMIT ME to seem somewhat old-fashioned in my response to the
movie we have just seen by commenting first on the last words hurled
by the hero at the congressional committee and at us, an ending which
is intended (according to a studio release) to bring the story to "an
unexpected and dramatic conclusion."
    It does not do, it seems to me—it is not fitting and proper—to
reduce a serious issue, and what can be noble resistance, to an obscene epithet. At the very least, it reflects poverty of imagination;
at its worse, it is not only a calculated insult to the sensibilities of
decent people, but it is also a substitute for recourse to serious political and legal alternatives and a cheapening of the sacrifices and aspirations of men of integrity. And yet, it is evident that a gifted troupe
has built up the action to this outburst at the end. How is this, as well
as my old-fashioned reservations, to be understood?

ii

THE FRONT is in some ways a useful movie, especially if one guards
against its limitations and pitfalls. It is also, if one can judge from the
immediate response of this college audience, an entertaining movie.

There is no need, on this occasion, to inventory the movie's merits, but rather to recognize limitations which might not be noticed, especially by an audience of students.

This movie's limitations are partly its own, partly those of film generally (including television productions). For one thing, film has a tendency to flatten things out, to simplify them unduly, to be peculiarly shallow—even as it conveys the impression, more so than do most other art forms, that *it* is showing things as they truly are, and even as it requires less effort by audiences. Sentimentality is thereby promoted.

Not the least of the shortcomings of film (which tends toward inarticulateness) is that it diverts attention and hence talent away from the finest use of language, from that extended discourse in which humanity ultimately resides.

It is almost inevitable, then, from the very nature of this medium, that it should distort what it portrays—and thereby cripple the community which comes to depend on it. Even so, it is almost impossible for modern communities not to be beguiled into such dependence.

The shortcomings of film—shortcomings which have come (because of the influence of film) to affect other art forms as well—include the almost necessary emphasis by it on "personality," on the intimate and the private. People tend to be cut down to size (except perhaps in old-time Westerns), with the principal virtues becoming dedication to a vague sense of decency and an insistence upon self-expression. It is the expression of personality—a kind of self-expression—which is found in the concluding expletive of this film.

iii

ONE LIKELY result of this medium, I have suggested, is oversimplification—and that may be seen in various forms in this film. Thus, there is far too crude a distinction between the good guys and the bad, with the bad guys (whether professional investigators, television producers, or ambitious congressmen) being nothing but opportunists, when they are not sadists.

This oversimplification is at the cost of realism, if you should want to call it that. After all, those ferreting out "subversives" could do what they did as long as they did because there was genuine fear abroad in this land, and in other lands as well, about the intentions

and prospects of Stalinist Russia. It did not help then to exaggerate
the threat of Russia, just as it does not help now to disregard what
that threat meant, a threat not unrelated to far more ruthless repression of dissenting opinion in Russia and in Russian-occupied lands
than anything visited in this country upon those thought to be sym-
pathizers of Stalin's regime.

One should insist upon this, that there were not just straw men
(or simply opportunists) among the inquisitors, lest one not be able
to deal properly with such aberrations in the future. For when such
things do happen, there *is* all too often something to be said for "the
other side"—and if one expects the issue to be as clear-cut as it is
presented here (and in most films), one will be unwary, as well as
unable to enlist reliable allies. Consider what will happen among us,
despite our experiences of the 1950s, when terrorist organizations
come to be generally believed to have access either to portable nuclear
weapons or to the deadliest gases.

The problem, as it emerged in the late 1940s and the early 1950s,
concerned what liberties should be guaranteed to people who were
identified (sometimes with justification) as apologists for (if not advocates of) a tyrannical ideology. Consider an item from the *New
York Times* of June 27, 1976, entitled "Posthumous Reinstatement":

> The American Civil Liberties Union has had a change of mind on a
> 36-year-old issue. It has decided 12 years after the death of Elizabeth
> Gurley Flynn, a militant leftist, that it made a mistake in expelling
> her from its board of directors in 1940. Miss Flynn, who was a union
> organizer at the age of 15 and one of the founders of the civil liberties
> organization, was dismissed for being a member of the Communist
> Party. The resolution repealing the expulsion stated that it "was not
> consonant with the basic principles on which the A.C.L.U. was
> founded."

The intention of the A.C.L.U. and other such organizations
(labor unions readily come to mind) had evidently been to beat po-
tential tyrants to the punch by excluding from influence people who
would some day (it was feared) do the same to others if they should
come to power. This was a sort of preemptive strike. It is no wonder
that the materialistic entertainment industry, always peculiarly
sensitive to public opinion, should have been at least as cautious in
those days as the idealistic A.C.L.U.

To say all this is not to condone what was done by Joseph McCarthy and the like. Nor is it to deny that considerable damage, not only to individual citizens but also to the community at large, followed upon this kind of repression and the fear it both reflected and promoted. The damage included our follies of the past decade in Indochina. But we would be damaged even more if we should not assess these matters properly, if we should not see how they came to be. I have already referred to the special circumstances of the Cold War, but there were also the passions of the Second World War—and the sense of frustration, if not even betrayal, when that war did not bring (to a people previously traumatized by the Great Depression) the security which had been sacrificed for and anticipated.

iv

THE MOVIE we have just seen is misleading in another respect, it seems to me, and that is in the fate of its hero. People who were packed off to jail in those days did not go with the kind of jolly send-off depicted here. It was far grimmer business than that, not the glamorous, all-together-now business shown us at the end of this film. There is about this ending something of the 1930s and the romanticism of the class struggle, American-style. Certainly, it is highly unlikely that vulnerable men, such as the three blacklisted writers, would have shown up to take bows (so to speak) when a victim was about to be sacrified. Far more likely, however foolish in its consequences, was the response of Morton Sobell (of the *Rosenberg* case) who took off for Mexico in 1950 when he learned that a relative of an old acquaintance had been arrested for espionage.

On the other hand, it should also be said that it must have been rare to have had people jailed for what the hero of this movie is shown to have done. I myself doubt that an indictable offense is depicted here. Certainly, it should be said, however bad things got to be, people simply were not imprisoned for criticism alone, not even when they showed contempt (in the most literal, not the legal, sense) for congressional committees. There were throughout that period people who were consistent and open in their criticism of government and of redbaiting—and there was for them little danger of indictment, to say nothing of conviction and imprisonment.

Furthermore, an invocation of the Fifth Amendment by the
hero would have sufficed to have protected him from legal sanctions
—and in the circumstances, there was no point in not invoking it,
even as he told the committee what he thought of them. Certainly,
such a precautionary invocation would have been consistent with the
not highly principled character presented throughout the film by
Woody Allen. But this would have deprived the film—the film, more
than the hero—of the "dramatic conclusion" which is offered as a
substitute for informed and organized opposition to what the committee and the entertainment industry were doing.

It should also be noticed, in considering the fates of the victims
of what came to be known as McCarthyism, that one problem with
the people who were blacklisted—one reason they were so vulnerable
—was that they had gotten used to living well. There was something
sad, if not even silly, about artists (supposed students of the human
soul) allowing themselves to be paralyzed to the extent they were.
After all, they were, for the most part, talented people who were far
from helpless. Indeed, one sometimes suspects that this government-
induced obligation to reconsider and reorder their way of life may
have been for some of those people a blessing in disguise. For one
thing, it should have made them reconsider what Hollywood meant,
what it exacted of those whom it pampered.

In any event, it is best in such circumstances not to exaggerate
the obstacles one faces if one is to do one's best in attempting to hurdle them. Certainly, something is to be said for saving one's money
in times of prosperity—in anticipation of the return of the bad old
days, which may be just around the corner. It is important to recognize that one need not be destroyed if one resists, that one *can* do
something.

V

MY REFERENCE a moment ago to Hollywood brings us to still another distortion of this movie: its primary concern is with the New
York television community rather than with the West Coast movie
colony. But the most famous blacklisting victims of that ugly period
were the so-called Hollywood Ten. Even the announcement distributed on this campus refers to this as a film "about blacklisting in

Hollywood during the 50s.'' The blacklisting depicted here is really Hollywood, even though it is put in terms of television and New York. Hollywood has always been both timid and shameless—and so it can avoid facing up openly now to what it did then. Not the least of the offenders, it should be added, was the movie studio which is distributing the film we have seen on this occasion.

A further distortion along this line is to have a blacklisted actor commit suicide (a suicide which does not fit in with the tone of the movie as a whole). But this actor is someone who is shown to have been popular in his nightclub act. This meant that he had work to do, since the stage, throughout that period, was more accessible to the politically vulnerable, even actors, than either the movies or network television. It is instructive to notice who *were* vulnerable in those days and why: government personnel, defense industries employees, teachers (but not, for example, janitors) in universities (the public universities more than the private, but the private—including this university—did not always conduct themselves well either), movie studio employees, and television network personnel. That is to say, particularly vulnerable were people associated with institutions that had something of a public character about them or were especially dependent on public opinion.

But, as one can see in the movie, scripts could be sold—and they were bought by producers who often knew from whom they were coming. The movie is misleading about this, just as it is in showing the nightclub operator as the one who ruthlessly chiseled the victimized actor. In practice, it was the movie studios, as well as television networks, who got "high quality" scripts for far less than they would otherwise have had to pay.

But more important to notice—and this the film does not appreciate the significance of—is that there *was* indeed a market in scripts. This should remind us of that wide range of activities which remained unaffected by the worst repression throughout that period, the many forms of ordinary moneymaking in this country. The ideologists who would have government assume comprehensive control of our economy should take note. To a remarkable extent, the existence of a free market—with all its faults, not the least of which is the promotion of self-gratification and hence softness—the existence of an extensive, free, and largely anonymous market remains a powerful influence toward the preservation of political freedom in the United States, including the freedom of dissent. For one thing, it *is* of great value to have people with property willing and able to finance the promulgation of opinions which call into question the orthodoxies of the day. Sometimes, indeed, access to property in the form of a mimeograph machine suffices.

vi

ONE ORTHODOXY of *our* day obliges us to condone, if not even to promote, unseemly public language. Such language is dubious in itself: the tenor of contemporary deterioration may be seen not only in what is now available on the stage, in movies, and on television but also in political discourse, where even candidates for the highest offices in the land have had their sensibilities blunted with respect to both what they are permitted to talk about in public and the language they should use. Such debasement is not only bad in itself, but it also harms us in what it deprives us of: the truly noble and high-minded is thereby submerged.

This submergence may be seen (to return to my opening remarks) in the movie's concluding expletive, which is no doubt intended to be enlisted in the cause of decency, but which usurps the place before the congressional committee of traditional constitutional principles and the legal procedures serving those principles. Restraints in language and style may seem restrictive of free expression, but such restraints discipline the bad man, the potentially tyrannical man, more than they deprive the good man of an opportunity to say what should be said.

vii

TRADITIONAL CONSTITUTIONAL language is a responsible way of talking about the just, and at times the noble, things—both substantive and procedural—that a community has been fortunate enough to have developed respect for. The natural artistic yearning for novelty should be held in check. Intellectuals should recognize their duty to be responsible, to respect the opinions (including the public language) upon which decent communities rest. Indeed, one bad effect of the

McCarthy period has been, by encouraging vigorous reaction against its blatant injustices, to give moderation and self-restraint a bad name.

In short, a good deal remains to be said for old-fashioned ways of addressing the challenges of one's day.

Appendix G. ART, COMMON SENSE, AND TYRANNY

> *And in examining their actions and life, one sees*
> *that fortune provided them with nothing other*
> *than the occasion which gave them the matter*
> *into which they could introduce whatever form*
> *they pleased; without that occasion their virtue*
> *of mind would have been extinguished, and*
> *without virtue the occasion would have come*
> *in vain.*
>
> *It was necessary, then, for Moses to find the*
> *people of Israel in Egypt, enslaved and oppressed*
> *by the Egyptians, so that they, in order to*
> *escape their servitude, would be disposed to*
> *follow him. . . . Theseus would have been un-*
> *able to demonstrate his virtue if he had not*
> *found the Athenians scattered. These occasions,*
> *therefore, made these men happy, and their*
> *excellent virtue made the occasions known;*
> *whence their fatherland was ennobled and*
> *became most happy.*
>
> —Niccolò Machiavelli, *The Prince,* vi

i

IT SEEMS to me fitting and proper, in talking about George Seferis—
a Greek poet who often relied, both in his poetry and in his tributes
to other men, upon personal reminiscences and impressions—to begin
with a few words about our contacts with one another in recent years
and hence about the genesis of this talk.

I came to know Mr. Seferis only after the Colonels took over
his country in 1967. I had, of course, known *of* him before and of

---

This talk, which takes its departure from the career of George Seferis, was given in
the Works of the Mind Lecture Series, The Basic Program of Liberal Education for Adults,
The University of Chicago, November 19, 1971.

Additional information about Greek poets, about Mr. Seferis himself, and about Greek
politics may be found in the epilogue appended to this talk in the form of a note.

331

the Nobel Prize awarded him. I came to know him personally—indeed,
I presumed to make an effort to meet him—only after I had talked
to several people in Athens who had received from him copies of
articles I had written critical of American policy in Greece toward
the Colonels. (He himself had originally received copies of my articles from someone I knew in the American Embassy.) He endorsed
and distributed my articles, I came to learn, long before he was obliged to make his single, dramatic public statement against the Colonels' regime in March 1969, two years after the Colonels seized power.

Our evening meetings in his home, in his book-filled study—
with him sitting for hours behind his desk—proved to be relaxed conversations. He displayed himself to me (as he had for years to many
others) as a gentle, cultivated man, very much a man of affairs as
well as of literature. He urged me, at our last meeting in September
1970, to plan on another long evening together during my visit to
Greece the following year (and even went so far as to suggest I should
let him know when I was coming, just in case he could do something
to help me if I should have trouble entering the country as I had had
earlier that month).

The considerable concern he expressed on that occasion might
be regarded by the poetic as a premonition of the difficulties we
would encounter in ever meeting again. Others would see such expression of concern as merely another indication of his gentlemanly
manner. However that may be, I was not permitted to return to
Greece this past summer, having been declared by the Colonels to
be *persona non grata* because of the articles that I have written about
American policy in Greece and that the Colonels have condemned as
"defaming Greece and distorting the truth concerning the country."
My decision to give this talk was made upon learning of Mr. Seferis's
death (on September 20). Such a talk, I then felt, would be in lieu
of the conversation that twin necessities had kept us from having
this year.

Americans cannot be expected to know Mr. Seferis's poetry,
which depends so much, of course, on the Greek language—a language
of which I know far too little to be a reliable guide to myself. What I do
venture to say about him, therefore, should be regarded primarily as
an attempt to discuss modern poetry, especially that poetry which
has been profoundly influenced (as Mr. Seferis himself was and as
much American poetry continues to be) by T.S. Eliot and his asso-

ciates. That is, even if I should be mistaken (as I may well be) about the work of George Seferis himself, my analysis and argument should still apply to art of the kind I take his to be.

ii

I CAN introduce you to Mr. Seferis by quoting the authoritative description of him found in the *Medieval and Modern Greek Poetry* anthology published by the Oxford University Press:

> George Seferis is the poet who introduced genuine symbolism into modern Greek poetry; the role played by the English symbolists, particularly T. S. Eliot, in his evolution is by no means negligible. The tragic fate of modern man constantly recurs in his poetry, and his deep artistic depth and wonderfully musical language have given us works like the *King of Asine* which in their own way are masterpieces.

Mr. Seferis came originally from the ill-fated Greek community in Asia Minor. He was for much of his life a professional diplomat pursuing a career which culminated in his assignment as the Greek ambassador to Great Britain from 1957 to 1962. He succeeded, pursuant to the code of the diplomatic corps, in steering clear of domestic political controversy through most of his life. But he was obliged in March 1969 to issue the declaration to which I have already referred, a declaration which resembled his poetry both in its terms and in its tone. Here is the version which appeared in *The Times* of London for March 29, 1969:

> Long ago I resolved to remain out of the country's internal politics. This did not mean—and on another occasion I tried to make the point clear—that I was indifferent to our political life. For years now I have in principle abstained from such matters. But what I said in print up to early 1967 and the stand that I have since taken (for since freedom was muzzled I have published nothing in Greece) showed clearly what my attitude was.

> Now for some months, however, I have felt, within me and around me, that more and more it is becoming imperative for me to speak out on our present situation. To put it as briefly as possible, this is what I would say:

It is almost two years since a regime was imposed upon us utterly contrary to the ideals for which our world—and so magnificently our people—fought in the last World War. It is a state of enforced torpor in which all the intellectual values that we have succeeded, with toil and effort, in keeping alive are being submerged in a swamp, in stagnant waters. I can well imagine that for some people these losses do not matter. Unfortunately this is not the only danger that threatens.

We have all learnt, we all know, that in dictatorial regimes the beginning may seem easy, yet tragedy waits at the end, inescapably. It is this tragic ending that consciously or unconsciously torments us, as in the ancient choruses of Aeschylus.

The longer the abnormal situation lasts, the greater the evil.

I am a man completely without political ties and I speak without fear and without passion. I see before us the precipice towards which the oppression that covers the land is leading us. This abnormality must come to an end. It is the nation's command.

Now I return to silence. I pray to God that never again may I find myself under such compulsion to speak.

With this statement Mr. Seferis made clear to all perceptive observers of Greek political life, whether at home or abroad, that the Colonels could not hope to get the sober, established men of the country to join them, that they were doomed to remain nothing more than armed opportunists without any serious pretense to legitimacy. Their recourse from the earliest days of their power to systematic and deliberate torture of political prisoners and resistance suspects indicates how abnormal their standing is. Mr. Seferis's statement came some six months after the Colonels had conducted (in September 1968) a one-sided campaign to have the country "ratify" their constitution (a constitution which is yet to be implemented). His statement said, in effect, that there was nothing good to be hoped for from the Colonels.

Had our people in the State Department been alert to *the fact* as well as to the spirit of Mr. Seferis's statement, they would have at once recognized that the Colonels were truly "finished," however long they might manage to stay in power. They would have recognized also that the Colonels cannot be depended upon to make any genuine reforms, or to keep the promises given the American government (in return for its military and moral support) to restore constitutional government to our NATO ally. Such a recognition would have saved the United States the disappointment and humiliation it has had to endure since then at the hands of the Colonels.

When I say "State Department," I do not mean everyone in it, for there has been from the beginning (or almost from the beginning) a minority of experts both in Washington and in our Athens Embassy who saw the Colonels for the barbarians in khaki that they are. One of our experts (a man of considerable experience in Greece) has provided me his eyewitness account of the funeral of George Seferis, a funeral which reflected the stature Mr. Seferis had come to have in opposition to the Colonels' regime:

> ... The whole ceremony was political. The procession consisted largely of young people. Some thirty thousand people were there at an awkward time—4 p.m. The funeral was 95 percent a political demonstration: *Freedom, Democracy, Immortal, We Shall Overcome, Down With the Junta* were some of the slogans. And the "mourners" sang some of Seferis's poems put to music by [Mikis] Theodorakis. By the columns of Olympian Zeus a group shouted "Out with the Colonels," but this slogan was smothered by the National Hymn, *Se gnorizo apo* [*tin kopsi*]. Soon after the slogan "Down with fascism" was heard. Promptly the police intervened to arrest fifteen youths, who were taken to the police station and soon released! I must say that the police were polite, careful, tolerant with the crowd. I never saw Greek police so well behaved! They had orders, apparently, not to provoke trouble. The song that was most moving came from Crete: *Omalos*—the Cretan war song—*to rizitiko tragoudi!* It came from the Cretan group in the procession. [Panayiotis] Kanellopoulos [who had been prime minister when the Colonels seized power in 1967] received most of the [hand] clappings as he entered and left the church. When Archbishop Ieronomous [who had collaborated with the Colonels] entered the church, people began a *xerovihas* [clearing their throats, a sign of disapproval]. The victory sign *V* would frequently pop up from the crowd. Some foreign ambassadors were there, but not [Henry] Tasca [the American ambassador to Greece].

> Impressive was the emotion in the atmosphere, the determined and yet helpless expression on people's faces. The youthful demonstration was frightening! It was restrained, but unrestrainable! I found little support in Greece for [George] Papadopoulos [the leader of the Colonels], but this is a long story....

The absence of the American ambassador was noticed by the Greeks also, of course, but merely as a confirmation of the bankruptcy of American policy in Greece since the Colonels came to power. (It should be added that I have other reports which indicate that some of the students arrested, either at the funeral procession or afterwards, were held overnight at the police station and severely beaten before they were released.) In any event, the report I have quoted from a conservative observer in the State Department should suffice to indicate the state of mind of those Greeks who will be shaping the opinions of the next generation in their country.

iii

THE SHAPING of opinion in one's country can be said to be one vital effect, if not even the principal purpose, of the serious poet. It is with this observation that we can turn to our necessarily limited consideration of the poetry of George Seferis.

One feature of Mr. Seferis's poetry is implied in the public statement by him that I have read: the importance for him of economy, of the most restrained statement. He can be called (it seems to me) *the poet of silence,* the poet of a most telling use of silence. He once observed that if a language had only one word in it, the poet would still be distinguishable from the nonpoet. Presumably, poets would know better than most others when to use and how to use effectively that one word—how to pronounce it, how often to use it, to whom to use it, and so forth. Consider, for example, a language in which *good* is the only word: consider, that is, the circumstances in which it could be used with effect.

It is an effective use of silence that may be seen even in connection with Mr. Seferis's March 1969 public declaration. His silence for two years, while the Colonels made their case, prepared the stage for his emergence; his subsequent public silence, for the two remaining years of his life, permitted the echoes of his voice from the wings of the political stage to have their full effect. His was the respectable, established voice of Greek culture *and of the bureaucracy,* a voice which the Colonels could neither outshout nor control, however they might attempt (as they did) to slander it.

What is the poetry of silence like? It is terse, careful about every word, relying a good deal upon allusions and implications. In Mr.

Seferis's case, the allusions are drawn from Greek literature and history of three thousand years; they are drawn as well from his private experiences, experiences that include years outside Greece on diplomatic duties and (during the Second World War) in exile.

The poetry of silence does tend, however, to be obscure. It can be, as is Mr. Seferis's, impressive and moving for someone who understands the language; the very sound of it has power. But, whether one knows the language, the meaning of the lines often remains dark. Scholarship is needed to work out their meaning, scholarship which sometimes has to extend to the personal life of the poet. But this necessity is not thought to matter: that is, what is said to be important, ultimately, is what is evoked in the reader. This, in turn, depends upon the personal experiences the reader has, the reading he happens to have done, the kind of man *he* is. Thus, poetry under this dispensation is like a tuning fork, inducing sympathetic vibrations in other tuning forks "in states unborn and accents yet unknown." The reader, too, becomes a kind of poet.

Does not this approach to poetry dominate the better, or at least the better known, poets of the middle of the twentieth century? Mr. Seferis was, in this respect, both modern and representative and hence worth (as I have said) our further consideration.

iv

WHAT ARE the consequences of this particular modern understanding—or should we say, feeling?—about poetry?

Should not a poem be reasonably complete in itself, available at the time it is written to any educated reader versed in the language in which it is written? Is a poem which must be accompanied by scholarly apparatus or by personal explanations simply not of the caliber of a poem which *can* stand alone?

Certainly, the greatest poets of the past continue to be effective (for anyone who knows their language) without necessary reliance upon scholarship. Cannot one still read and interpret most of Homer with enjoyment and profit without a single research note? Is not the same true for most of Shakespeare, for most of Donne, and for most of Keats? (The notes one may sometimes be obliged to consult merely reflect the lapse of time and its effect upon vocabulary, terminology, and once familiar topical information.) That is, one can read such poets (and even someone as mystical as Blake) and have a fairly good idea of what they are talking about most of the time, even at first reading. That is not possible with much of Mr. Seferis's poetry. It is not true, for instance, of such major poems as those in his *Three Secret Poems* collection (published in 1966). One can read them over and over again (either in Greek or in English translation) and still have but the vaguest notion of what he is saying.

We have become accustomed to such obscurity in contemporary poets—in the better contemporary poets. This is especially so among American poets today: much of what "the better poets" in this country say is virtually impossible for most of us to decipher or to enjoy. One goes to their poetry as one goes to the dentist. Such poetry, when it *is* pleasurable, is closer than it should be to music and to opera than it is to prose: the effects of the sounds seem to be more important than the meaning of the words. These sound effects need not depend on a common language, of course, or even a common tradition. In fact, that poetry may be regarded with suspicion which *can* be generally understood, on the ground that it does not mirror properly that fragmentation of community which is supposed to characterize the modern world. Each man is to be understood as radically on his own: to be Westerners today is to be cut loose from one another; the peak of our development is the emergence of autonomous selves cut off from communion with one another, each self adrift without serious purpose in a wasteland of many memories.

Poetry has tended to become, then, the expression and diagnosis of disintegration: it is no longer something which contributes directly to the making of a community. Mr. Seferis could recall old sailors he knew as a child who could weep as they recited for him long passages from a centuries-old Cretan poem (the *Erotokritos*). No Greek child tomorrow will hear such old men to whom the better poets today (who write as Mr. Seferis does) are so familiar (except when they do happen to be set to the music of a Theodorakis).

In this sense, the poet on the Aegean is European. He is not simply Greek. He talks, by and large, only to others like himself: his is not the language of a community, nor the meaning of common sense.

This is not to suggest that Mr. Seferis, as a man of affairs, was not a man of common sense. I once had occasion to mention to him that however difficult sanity may be to define, it is fairly easy for the sane man to distinguish the sane from the insane. Yes, he responded, it is like the obvious difference between activities so similar as going upstairs and doing downstairs. Is this not a poetic way of reaffirming the sovereignty of common sense in human affairs? (Compare Heraclitus' hardly commonsensical, however challenging, paradox, "The way up and the way down is one and the same.")

Common sense (a common sense which a generally comprehensible poetry *can* refine and protect) does help us determine whether things beyond our grasp are plausible, whether they are stated with rigor and in good faith, whether they are worthy of our attention and of our respect.

V

IT IS NOT only of modern *art* that the criticisms I have suggested thus far can be made.

I have for several years now been attending the Thursday afternoon physics colloquium on the campus of this university, a colloquium to which the best men in the field are brought from all over the world to describe to their colleagues and a couple hundred graduate students what they are doing. Much of the work described is "on the frontiers" of science. It has long been evident to me that I should know more than I do about what scientists say *and how they say it*. But I find much of modern science as obscure as much of modern poetry.

Still, repeated exposure to both science and poetry can be instructive. I have observed, for instance, that what appears to the layman to be happening in poetry appears to the layman to be happening in science as well. Thus, I have observed that just as poets today speak (when they are serious) almost exclusively to other poets and a handful of critics, so scientists today speak almost exclusively to other scientists. That was not always the case: the modern lay reader can still read with profit many of the most serious writings of the scientists, as well as of the poets, of earlier centuries.

It is clear that something coherent *is* being said in the physics lectures I have been attending, that some of the (predominantly male) audience understand and most of the audience enjoy them. Even I can occasionally get a feel for what the lecturer is saying and for what scientists and students of science are like and what they respect. Perhaps even more important, I am repeatedly reminded of what I do not know about things which seem to be knowable.

Why do I not get more than I do? Partly because of my limitations: considerable training, practice, and experience are assumed and required (as is true, we are told, if one is to grasp modern poetry). But there is much which is said that even many of the scientists present do not seem to grasp: this is partly because of the high degree of specialization that is taken for granted. The emphasis for the gifted researcher seems to be placed more on what *he* discovers than on the satisfaction which could come from learning or teaching whatever has already been discovered by others. The limitations (as well as the considerable accomplishments) of modern science are related to this emphasis on continual discovery and the self-expression it may represent.

Furthermore, much of science today is hypothetical. (Things in themselves are not being talked about, it seems to be agreed.) The phenomena which are the subjects of investigation—an investigation which very much relies upon quantification—these phenomena are quite distant from things as they appear to human beings in the everyday world. Indeed, one must wonder what *is* being talked about by modern scientists. Their considerable reliance upon mathematics, the indispensable tool for explanation, does have the merit of screening out students of limited natural talent and insufficient self-discipline. But mathematics also serves (as poetry all too often does today) to conceal from view the surface of things, that which is commonly observed and accepted and relied upon. That surface is quickly left behind by the professional investigator.

Communication, then, becomes very difficult. One wonders whether we are really being helped by our advanced thinkers (whether scientists or artists) to answer the questions which first take men to science and to art, such questions as, What is the nature of things? What is the nature of nature? What is the cause of things? What is the nature of cause? What is the nature of knowing about things, their natures, and their causes?

Of course, modern science does "work." Things can be controlled with remarkable effects: the eminently useful electric light switch is a monument to this fact. In an analogous way, it can be said, modern poetry "works": the poet can so speak as to move some men thus and so. In neither case may true understanding be required but rather adherence to a tested method in an accepted climate of opinion. In both cases, the highest activity is likely to be, in effect, "private": when scientists pause to think about what they are doing, they may borrow the observation associated with Immanuel Kant that each of us can do no more than construct his account of things, an account which cannot be guaranteed to conform to accounts by others. Indeed, scientists can sound here very much like modern poets, perhaps because poetry too has been shaped by the psychological revolution following upon the enthronement of the "Kantian" hypothesis.

But to say that the pronouncements of scientists and artists are disjointed and essentially unexamined (and perhaps, in their terms, unexaminable), is not to say that they have nothing to say or that they talk nonsense. One can perceive both artists and scientists to be intelligent men and women who have no desire to deceive themselves or to mislead others. One can also perceive—as one listens to them, *as one observes them listening and responding to one another,* as one notices the importance (and hence the discipline) for them of "style" and of the order in which things are said—one can perceive that they *are* saying something, that they *do* have hold of something.

Both modern science and modern art must obviously be regarded as serious enterprises. Both may be seen as affected by the "enlightened" way of seeing and doing things. This means that neither may be able to satisfy the enduring longings of most men. They leave to others the duty (as well as the profit and popularity) of providing satisfactory public accounts of how things are and should be and why. But do not modern art and science tend to draw into their private preserves the best souls among us, thereby leaving the guidance (and entertainment) of the community to the callous, the ambitious, and the bizarre?

Tyrannies of both the mind and the body threaten to engulf mankind, their advent having been prepared by an "enlightenment" that has discredited serious politics, old-fashioned philosophical inquiry, and serious religion.

vi

AMONG THE features that modern art and modern science share is the significance for them of *process,* process as distinguished from the traditional and natural end or purpose of serious activities. For the contemporary poet in particular, self-consciousness about that process is important: a good deal of what poets say today has to do with their efforts to understand their own poetizing. Again, a comparison with Homer is instructive. It is rare for *him* to devote any effort to describing how *he* comes to say this rather than that: for him, the subject itself seems to dictate what is said and how he says it; Homer is permanently concealed behind the poetic facade presented to his readers. The same can be said about Shakespeare, of course.

The contemporary poet (as well as the contemporary scientist, who has been critically affected by "Kantian" teachings) cannot leave himself out of the picture. It is not the world he is presenting, but rather the world as it happens to appear to him, as it is constructed by him; it is, that is, *his* world, not *the* world. How one comes to see and say the things one says is often of supreme interest to the poet today and since we are all infected to some degree by the same concern with process and with the self, it has become of interest to us as well.

Because of the kinds of things that are presented in art, the genesis of artistic productions in the soul of the artist *is* of general interest. Since self-expression is obviously important in art, and perhaps in science as well, it can be instructive to consider what stimulates this rather than that expression, what *moves* the artist to see and say this rather than that. But unless the critic restrains himself, the study of art can become little more than a branch of psychology. Far less is made, in these circumstances, of art as an effort to imitate and hence understand nature.

Psychology, including the psychology of artistic activity, is, of course, interesting. Consider, for instance, the beautiful bird heads sculpted out of white stone by a local artist, Cosmo Campoli. I once asked him how he came upon those shapes. He recalled walking down Fifty-third Street (here in Chicago) with his children and suddenly being struck by a Tastee-Freez sign, such a sign as all of us have seen many times. What we have not seen in it, but which he suddenly perceived on that occasion—something *he* was inspired to notice—was the bird's head stretched forth from the cone in the curlicue of cream jutting out of the cone. Those graceful lines came to dominate his work for several years.

The decisive stimulus can come from any source—a stimulus that moves the soul to one expression rather than another, that moves

the soul to make explicit and develop this rather than that observation or memory. The importance of dreams in the twentieth century
may be related to the importance attached to movements of the soul,
to the private, individual movements of the soul. One can see in how
dreams "work" something about the "dynamics of the creative process" of which so much is made today.

Consider, for instance, Mr. Seferis's description of a dream of
his own, in a short essay (published by him in 1970) on an ancient
student of dreams, Artemidorus of Daldiano. Mr. Seferis had returned
to Athens, he reports, after a long absence. He went up to the Acropolis, where he found considerable excitement among the other visi-
tors to that ancient shrine: the Parthenon was being auctioned off
to commercial bidders, thereby permitting the government to solve
for a generation its chronic budgetary crisis. The highest bidder, he
learned upon drawing nearer to the temple, was announced: it was
an American toothpaste company. Mr. Seferis woke up screaming in
protest against the scheme of the company to carve the columns of
the Parthenon into the shape of toothpaste tubes, a brilliant advertising scheme!

We again observe here the artistic imagination at work. The sensitive man, upon returning home from abroad (a position Mr. Seferis
often found himself in) is disturbed by the modernization of his
country, a country whose soul is rooted in antiquity but whose rising
standard of living depends on industrialization. That disturbance,
which may be expressed in more cultured forms in Mr. Seferis's poetry, is voiced more openly (and, in some ways, more effectively?) in
his dream. He recounted to me last year, not without some humor,
how outraged he had been in his dream upon seeing what was being
done to the Parthenon. And, he told me, he had come to see how it
happened that the dream had taken the form it did: he had recalled,
shortly before our conversation, that there had been an American
company which had displayed on its toothpaste box something which
looked like the columns of a temple. I do not recall now whether he
showed me the box or described it to me so well that I remember (or
believe I remember) having seen it: but that toothpaste advertisement
is as clear to me now as that provocative Tastee-Freez sign may be to
some of you on the basis of my reference to it a few minutes ago.

But however revealing such insights into the unconscious or for-
tuitous origins of works of art may be, the man of common sense
must immediately add, the effectiveness of an artistic endeavor does

not depend ultimately on the particular stimulus which happens to trigger the artistic sensibility. It is still the thing made which we sense to be important. I suspect that human instinct to be sound which leads us to believe that the thing in itself (despite whatever Kant may have meant) is being somehow touched upon and presented to view by the true artist (and, I might add, by the true scientist). But if so, then the contemporary emphasis upon the vagaries of particular selves is misplaced. The process may be important in determining what a particular self happens to present on a particular occasion, but something else is decisive in determining whether that which is presented is worthy of attention and respect, something other than that which is concerned primarily with the workings and satisfactions of the self.

Nature, that is, must be given her due.

vii

I ONCE heard a teacher of mine, Henry Rago, observe of his friend T. S. Eliot that he did not write poetry but rather poems. Each poem by Mr. Eliot (the same can be said of Mr. Seferis) was distinct; there were relatively few of them. To "write poetry," it was implied by Mr. Rago, is to write much, without sufficient attention to, and respect for, each particular emission of the soul. The apt Greek contrast to Mr. Seferis in this respect is Nikos Kazantzakis: from him pages upon pages poured forth; there was no stopping *him*. Everything Mr. Kazantzakis touched turned into a story, often into an arresting story infused with his special energy.

No doubt, both the meticulous construction and the pouring forth are appropriate to art, but it is difficult for us, who see in Donne and Shakespeare and Keats what poets *can* do, to regard the obviously disciplined and sometimes contrived (if not lifeless) productions of an Eliot the peak of poetic endeavour. Must there not be in the greatest poetry at least the appearance of spontaneity, of effortlessness, of the inspired, of the flow of that which is rich and without measure? Does not such an appearance add to the sense of naturalness, and hence to the apparent truthfulness, of a poetic account?

I do not mean to suggest that careful analysis and serious thought should be absent from a poet's work. Heaven forbid! But is not the contemporary approach, with its evident studied effort, somehow to deny the truly poetic? Is it not to make too much of the poet's self? That is, is not poetry today too self-conscious, too self-centered and hence unconvincing? On the other hand, does not Mr. Seferis's "wonderfully musical language" serve to validate what he says?

We should not conclude our discussion this evening without an indication of what Mr. Seferis does say in his poems. He once observed of himself that he was a stubborn man who said over and over again the same things, the same few things. These sayings turned upon the double-sidedness of things, upon the dislocations and exiles of our time, upon the modern trauma of the spirit which has shaken Western man. He drew into his statements the antiquities all about him, the Greek sun and sea, and a pervasive sense of melancholy. His poems give the impression of exposure to much suffering; their compactness and terseness and obscurity add to that effect. (To speak with the vitality of a Kazantzakis, on the other hand, is to play down the importance of pain and suffering even as one revels in it.)

It should suffice for us, considering Mr. Seferis's proclamation of himself as essentially repetitious, to settle on this occasion (in a further attempt to indicate what he says) upon one set of poems, those issued (in 1935) at what turned out to be the midpoint of his life, the *Mythistorema* series. I trust I will be permitted a poetic interpretation of these poems, so poetic in fact that I can be permitted as well to select three of them to stand for the whole. Is not such distillation of the very essence of poetry? Even so, since I do not discuss the *Mythistorema* collection as a whole, my comments on merely three poems in the collection *are* apt to be distorted. (Any examination of the entire collection should consider the parallels between its twenty-four poems and the twenty-four books of the *Odyssey*. Are the Odyssean adventures being reconsidered by the poet in the light of all Greek history and thought since Homer? Consider, also, in this connection, what Nikos Kazantzakis does in *The Odyssey: A Modern Sequel* and what James Joyce does in *Ulysses*.)

I draw for the poems I use here upon the translations prepared by Edmund Keeley and Philip Sherrard. Allowances should be made, in judging the poems I discuss, for the fact that the celebrated music of Mr. Seferis's language is never likely to be available to the English reader.

Our first poem (No. 14 in the *Mythistorema* series) reads:

> *Three red pigeons in the light*
> *inscribing our fate in the light*
> *with colors and gestures of people*
> *we have loved.*

These four lines seem to stand aloof from the others in the collection in which they are found, perhaps as do the pigeons described. Three pigeons might, as they move in the light, remind us of people we have loved and, by their movements and colors, suggest what our fate has been (or will be?).

This insight is but a glimpse, suggesting how things are related to one another, how even that which is most precious to us may be decisively reflected in how prosaic birds happen to move about. If there is such a relatedness among things, then the heroic can be visible in petty things, the future and past in the present. To insist, instead, upon enduring distinctions and fixed categories (or even upon a differentiation between "I" and "they"?) is to violate the order of things. Everything may be evident in one thing—even the truth in a lie?

One celebrated lie is that told by Orestes' elderly companion (in Sophocles' *Electra*), a lie evidently intended to induce Orestes' mother to relax her guard and thus permit Orestes more easily to kill her. She is told that Orestes has died in a chariot race (at Delphi). This episode is drawn upon, and transformed, by Mr. Seferis in our next poem (No. 16 in the *Mythistorema* series):

The name is Orestes

> *On the track, on the track again, on the track,*
> *how many times around, how many bloodied laps, how many black*
> *rows, the people who watch me,*
> *who watch me when, in the chariot,*
> *I raised my hand glorious, and they roared triumphantly.*
>
> *The froth of the horses strikes me, when will the horses tire?*
> *The axle creaks, the axle burns, when will the axle burst into flame?*
> *When will the reins break, when will the hooves*
> *tread flush on the ground*
> *on the soft grass, among the poppies*
> *where, in the spring, you picked a daisy.*
> *They were lovely, your eyes, but you didn't know where to look*
> *nor did I know where to look, I, without a country,*

I who go on struggling here how many times around?
and I feel my knees give way over the axle
over the wheels, over the wild track
knees buckle easily when the gods so will it,
no one can escape, there's no point in being strong, you can't
escape the sea that cradled you and that you search for
at this time of trial, with the horses panting,
with the reeds that used to sing in autumn to the Lydian mode
the sea you cannot find no matter how you run
no matter how you circle past the black, bored Eumenides,
unforgiven.

The lie is exploited by Mr. Seferis. Is it taken by him to be true? Sophocles' story is changed in other ways as well, perhaps showing thereby the influence of modernity. Does only what is perceived as happening to oneself count? Thus, Orestes is changed into the narrator of the story, imagining his own death on the track: he both anticipates and reports this, much as would a refugee from a Pirandello play. It all seems to have happened before (and the Furies are bored with it all, but they will try to do what is required of them). A longing for the sea, as a memory and as an escape, is added, as is, at the very heart of the account, a "love interest" (in place of the "hate interest" exhibited by Sophocles' Electra?). These changes serve, at the risk of sentimentality, to intensify the poignancy and the dreadfulness of what is happening to the young hero-lover?

Things are indeed related to one another: the pigeons to us; one moves from dread to love to dread; the lies of one generation become the verities of the next, perhaps even the deceptive clichés of the following. The ancients may have been able to see these challenges and triumphs and disasters fresh, but in doing so they did not see all that could be known about them; they did not see the variations waiting to be played upon the same themes, the way (for instance) in which the adventurous and the public are intrinsically blended with the personal and the submissive. Nor did they see fully that there is no beginning, no end: Apollo, purgation, and a permanent resolution seem to be left out of the Seferis version. (Still, one may wonder, what have we moderns learned about these matters that Aeschylus and Sophocles did not know?)

Finally, let us consider our third poem (No. 11 in the *Mythistorema* series):

Sometimes your blood froze like the moon
in the limitless night your blood
spread its white wings over
the black rocks, the shapes of trees and houses,
with a little light from our childhood years.

Since there is no beginning, no end, one can begin—indeed, one can-not help but begin—just anywhere: every account is fragmentary; every account begins in the middle of things. One is sometimes—is one always?—on one's own, doomed to a limitless voyage, dark and forbidding. One's blood may be chilled like the moon; if like the chilliest of moons, then it is white, covering the black rocks. Black rocks become trees and houses: they are caught up on the wings of imagination in the light that remains in the haunted adult from child-hood, perhaps even from the childhood of the race and of the lan-guage.

What more can be said on this occasion about the poetry of Mr. Seferis? There is, we seem to be shown, no maturity, no fulfillment, but merely constant yearning and a kind of suffering. We move from old harbors to new shipwrecks. Or, perhaps, there is the maturity which lies in the insistence that this is the way things are, that re-peated frustration is our hope-tinged lot. But is not this insistence rooted in the opinion that there can really be no understanding? We remain decisively alone and yet are unable to shake ourselves free from the multitudes who accompany us from the past and await us in the future. We know enough not to be satisfied with what we can get; we do not know enough not to want more than we can use.

Does the poet mean all these things? Perhaps not. But who is to say that he does not inspire them in the reader? *Is* each on his own, authorized to voyage wherever stimuli take him? Yet what if one is inspired to add that reason and argument must ultimately be decisive if man is not to settle for either a primitive consciousness or a waste-ful anarchy in which neither thoughtfulness nor prudence governs human nature?

Perhaps it suffices at this point to observe, in thinking about the nature of man, that Mr. Eliot does argue in one of his notes to *The Waste Land*, "The interior of St. Magnus Martyr is to my mind one of the finest among Wren's interiors." The dependence of the percep-tion of beauty, and hence the artistic, upon the rational is perhaps inadvertently revealed in Mr. Eliot's instinctive use of that time-honored phrase, "to my mind." And with this observation we should be moved to recognize that we have stumbled upon still another episode in the ancient quarrel between poetry and philosophy.

viii

POETS ARE correct to remind us (as they do from time to time) of the virtues of both economy and discipline: there is much to learn (and unlearn) and so little time.

How can we best use our time, that is to say, our energy, sensitivity, and intelligence? Do modern artists, for example, have as much to teach us as do their predecessors, poets and philosophers alike? Can we afford the disintegration of community that modern poetry both records and in a curious way even ratifies?

Poets have long been suspected of saying things which they do not understand. Consider, for example, what Socrates says about them in Plato's *Apology*. Is this a misrepresentation by him of the poets? No more so, but (if so) more consciously so, than what Mr. Seferis says in his "Thrush" about the Socrates of the *Apology* and *Crito,* making him out to be more of a patriot than he was.

Whether it is true of the greatest of poets that they do not understand what they are saying, however fine what they say is— whether this is true must remain for us, at least on this occasion, an open question. Have the modern poets taken too seriously the ancient philosophical suspicion of them? Have they attempted to turn away such suspicion not by inquiring further into what they do say but rather by denying they really have anything specific *to* say?

Mr. Seferis was once asked (he reports) what his world view was. He replied he had none, confronting his questioner, a professor in Thessalonika, with the question of what Homer's world view was. This silenced his questioner. But the problem remains whether the silencing was due to an inability of the questioner to answer or to a recognition by him that an endeavor to press his inquiry would, in the circumstances, be hopeless. Mr. Seferis himself touches upon what can be said to be the world view of his predecessors, when he says (for example) that Euripides believed that the veins of men were as a net fashioned by the gods to trap them like wild beasts. Does this not say something about the relations of gods and men, about the uses made by the gods of human passions, of human morality, and of the very vitality as well as mortality of man? Did not Mr. Seferis have some awareness of the way the modern world is, what its principal accomplishments, defects, and challenges are, what the prospects and pitfalls are for man in our time?

Surely Homer had something which is today called a world view: one can work out from his poems what he understood the world to be like, what (if anything) the gods were doing and how men were related to them. His view of what is important may be usefully compared with Mr. Seferis's treatment of Homeric characters in his own poems. The heroic is muted in Mr. Seferis's work: when an Odysseus is brought to view, it is *not* with an emphasis upon his grander moments; minor characters loom large, such as the king of Asine (from an allusion in the *Iliad*) or Elpenor (from an incident in the *Odyssey*); the concerns expressed are usually modern, that is, predominantly domestic and personal, and intensely so.

A considered judgment of how things are and why (which is what world view must mean) is necessary if we are to determine whether modern poetry is worth the extensive study often required to discover, even in a preliminary way, what the poet is talking about. "This is the way the world ends," Mr. Eliot wrote, "This is the way the world ends/ Not with a bang but a whimper." Does modern poetry make too much of whimpering? Does it not require a world view, and an examination and assessment of world views, to deal properly with this and similar questions?

If one denies that poets do or should have a world view, one is not likely (either as poet or as critic) to examine properly the view of the world one *does* have. Is not tragedy, for instance, impossible without a world view of which one is at least aware? May not the same be said as well of serious comedy? Do not both tragedy and comedy draw upon a considered judgment of where man stands in his community, before nature, and with respect to the divine?

ix

THE QUESTION remains whether modern poetry is a cause or an effect of what may be regarded as a marked lowering of our sights, of our standards, and of some of our expectations. The likely answer is (as I have already indicated) that it is both cause and effect, that modern poetry both reflects and reinforces certain critical deficiencies of modernity, a modernity which was itself inaugurated by profound intellectual revolutions several centuries ago.

The deterioration to which I refer may be seen in what has been happening to ordinary language, a deterioration to which the harnessing of science and the influence of commerce and advertising (including, of course, toothpaste ads) have contributed as has a related decline in serious education. Poets may no longer contribute much to that deterioration by what they say and how they say it, but they do not seem to do what they can to arrest, if not to reverse, the deterioration. That is, they no longer speak even to most educated people and hence cannot shape and preserve common sensibilities as did their predecessors. All too often they *do* legitimate a concern for the personal and the petty which can lead to a kind of mediocrity.

Fortunate and useful, then, may be the poet who is lifted by his circumstances out of the private world in which poetry today for the most part is confined (or into which it has retreated), who is permitted and required to speak as a patriot and hence to be generally understood. George Seferis was, of course, throughout his life, a man in public service, but as a diplomat, not as a poet. The advent of the Colonels in 1967 provided him the opportunity to *say* to his countrymen what the poetry to which he was dedicated made difficult to communicate. That is, the advent of tyranny permitted him—partly because of the prestige in a country such as Greece of the Nobel Prize, partly because the Colonels' tyranny is (with its dependence on American opinion) not as ruthless as it might yet become—the advent of tyranny permitted and summoned him to enlist as patriot-poet in the service of a decent regime without sacrificing the integrity of his art.

The question remains whether modern poetry must wait upon such contingencies to be able to affect directly the life of the community. *Is* the most prestigious modern poetry as radically alienated as I have suggested? Does it want to be? Need it be? What could be the causes of such alienation? Will it ever be possible for poetry (in communities of the scope and resources of ours) to address itself again, as a matter of course and in language and forms readily comprehended by most literate men of good will, to the questions all men face and for which the artist may be uniquely empowered to provide to mankind comfort and encouragement, if not instruction?

The ultimate dependence of love and of adventure, and hence even of the artistic, upon community and therefore upon a sound, political order is sensed by the inspired poet. Thus, the exiled hero-lover is made to say, in the central lines of Mr. Seferis's challenging Orestes poem:

> *They were lovely, your eyes, but you didn't know where to look*
> *nor did I know where to look, I, without a country,*
> *I who go on struggling here how many times around?*

Men "without a country"—that is, without a healthy community by which they can take their bearings—the poet seems to divine, cannot fully be themselves.

It is somewhat reassuring in these troubled times to remind ourselves that one of the poems by this much-traveled Greek artist which is particularly worthy of careful study should be "The Return of the Exile" (written in the dark days of 1938 in Athens).*

---

*George Seferis (1900–1971) was awarded the Nobel Prize for literature in 1963. Another Greek poet, Odysseus Elytis (b. 1911) was awarded the Nobel Prize in 1979. The best Greek-language poet of this century was probably Constantine Cavafy (1863–1933), who spent most of his life in Alexandria, Egypt. Other outstanding Greek poets in modern times have been Kostis Palamas (1859–1943), Nikos Kazantzakis (1883–1957), Angelos Sikelianos (1884–1951), and Yiannis Ritsos (b. 1909). The best collection of English translations of Greek poetry is that by Kimon Friar, published by Simon and Schuster.

See, on the death of Mr. Seferis, *New York Times,* Sept. 21, 1971; 117 *Congressional Record* 34586 (Oct. 1, 1971). See, also, my letter in the *Washington Post,* Oct. 5, 1971 (printed as well in the *St. Louis Post-Dispatch,* Oct. 3, 1971, and in the *International Herald-Tribune,* Paris, Oct. 5, 1971).

The best collections of Mr. Seferis's poems (in Greek and English) are those prepared by Edmund Keeley and Philip Sherrard, published by Princeton University Press. His *Three Secret Poems* volume has been published by Harvard University Press in a translation by Walter Kaiser.

See, for my discussions of the Colonels' regime in Greece (1967–1974), (1) the articles listed under my name in the *Congressional Record* Index (volumes 115–21 [1969–1975]); (2) *The Constitutionalist: Notes on the First Amendment* (Dallas: Southern Methodist University Press, 1971), p. 564f; (3) *Human Being and Citizen* (Chicago: Swallow Press, 1975), p. 3f. See, also, my article on Greece in the fifteenth edition of the *Encyclopedia Britannica.* See, as well, my reviews of works of Mikis Theodorakis, George Seferis, and Nikos Kazantzakis, *Chicago Sun-Times/Showcase,* March 4, 1973, Sept. 1, 1974, and Jan. 26, 1975.

My State Department correspondent, whose letter I quoted in Section ii of my Seferis talk, was the late Charilaos G. Lagoudakis. Robert Keeley was another sensible observer of the Colonels' regime in the State Department.

One result of the Colonels' disastrous policies was the loss of much of Cyprus to Turkey in 1974, which has created serious problems for Greeks, Americans and Turks ever since. See 120 *Congressional Record* 14371, 15597, and 26618 (May 13, May 20, and August 2, 1974).

I was excluded from Greece in 1970. In 1960 I had been expelled from the Soviet Union for "subverting public order." See Anastaplo, *Human Being and Citizen*, p. 226f. See, also, *ibid.*, p. 105f ("What's Really Wrong With George Anastaplo?").

Notes

Prologue: THE ARTIST AS THINKER

1.　　See, for this story, the article by Nathaniel Benchley on Humphrey Bogart, "Here's looking at you, kid," *Atlantic,* February 1975, p. 39.

　　Zeno's paradoxes come to mind, as does the Cretan's questionable assurance that all Cretans are liars. See Douglas R. Hofstadter, *Gödel, Escher, Bach: An Eternal Golden Braid* (New York: Basic Books, 1979), p. 17f. Consider, also, in A. Conan Doyle, *The Adventure of the Final Problem,* the limits of the abilities of Sherlock Holmes and Professor Moriarty to anticipate each other's moves. Consider, as well, the crocodile mystery in James Joyce, *A Portrait of the Artist as a Young Man* (New York: Viking Press, 1956), p. 250; the discussion in the Epilogue, Section ii, below, of infinite regress and something I have named the "ultron" (which raises the question, ultimately, of whether modern science is capable of genuine knowledge; see Appendix G, Sections v–vi, above).

　　The reader is urged, as with my other publications, to begin by reading the text without reference to the notes. Throughout this book, as elsewhere in my writings, "cf." means "compare" and indicates a qualification of or something different from what has just been said or cited. See note 280, below. See, also, notes 145 and 289, below.

2.　　See Alexandre Kojève, "The Emperor Julian and His Art of Writing," in Joseph Cropsey, ed., *Ancients and Moderns: Essays on the Tradition of Political Philosophy in Honor of Leo Strauss* (New York: Basic Books, 1964), p. 95. See, also, Hofstadter, *Gödel, Escher, Bach,* pp. 493–94, 700–702. See, as well, Cartoon, *New Yorker,* Sept. 22, 1975, p. 35; Cartoon, *New Yorker,* Aug. 31, 1981, p. 80.

　　I am reminded of the lines from an American Indian poet (B. Sainte-Marie):

> You think I have visions
> because I am an Indian.
> I have visions because
> there are visions to be seen.

Chicago Tribune, Dec. 21, 1977, sec. 5, p. 2 (from *Wassaja*). See, on "historicism" and the problem of the objectivity of truth, Leo Strauss, *Natural Right and History* (Chicago: University of Chicago Press, 1953), p. 9f. See, also, note 145 (end), below.

　　Consider David Hume, *An Enquiry Concerning Human Understanding,* sec. XI, pt. II:

Upon the whole, then, it appears, that no testimony for any kind of miracle has ever amounted to a probability, much less to a proof: ... [T]herefore we may establish it as a maxim, that no human testimony can have such force as to prove a miracle, and make it a just foundation for any such system of religion.

In short, "don't believe your eyes"?

Consider, as well, Sankara's caution in his commentary on the *Bhagavad Gita:*

If a hundred scriptures should declare that fire is cold or that it is dark, we would suppose that they intend quite a different meaning from the apparent one.

The Bhagavad Gita, ed. Juan Mascaro (London: Penguin Books, 1979), p. 26. See, also, Shakespeare, *Twelfth Night,* IV, ii, 20–54. Cf. Shakespeare, *The Taming of the Shrew,* IV, v, 1–48. (All citations to Shakespeare in this book are, unless otherwise indicated, to his works as they appear in *The Complete Pelican Shakespeare,* Alfred Harbage, ed. [Baltimore: Penguin Books, 1969].)

Alfred North Whitehead is reported to have said, "Sometimes we see an elephant, and sometimes we do not. The result is that an elephant, when present, is noticed." Joseph Epstein, ed., *Masters: Portraits of Great Teachers* (New York: Basic Books, 1980), p. 55.

3.   Heraclitus, Fr. 56. See, also, Xenophon, *Memorabilia,* I, iv, 2–3. Thus, Aeschylus could say, "We all feast off the banquet table of Homer."

See, on the *Iliad* and "The Catalogue of Ships," Aristotle, *Poetics* 1459a37; Seth Benardete, *Achilles and Homer: The Homeric Hero* (University of Chicago Ph.D. dissertation, 1955); Anastaplo, *The Constitutionalist: Notes on the First Amendment* (Dallas: Southern Methodist University Press, 1971), p. 807. (See for corrections of *The Constitutionalist,* note 13, below.) Cf. R. Hope Simpson and J.F. Lazenby, *The Catalogue of the Ships in Homer's Iliad* (Oxford: Clarendon Press, 1970), p. 158f (on "the independence of the Catalogue in relation to the rest of the *Iliad*").

See, on the *Odyssey,* Eva Brann, "The Poet of the Odyssey," St. John's College print (October 1972); also, note 81, below.

See, as indicative of a general opinion that poets have a kind of wisdom, Plato, *Theaetetus* 179E, 180D; Cicero, *On the Nature of the Gods,* I, xv, 41–42, xxi, 60; Alfred North Whitehead, *Science and the Modern World* (New York: The Free Press, 1967), p. 95. Cf. Plato, *Epinomis* 975C–D, 980C–D, 984D, 990A–B; Epigraph, Chapter XIII, Part One; note 145 (end).

That which is central to the *Odyssey* as a whole (the episode of the herd of the Sun) is at the end of Odysseus' story to the Phaeacians. (I comment on this further on in this Prologue.) Homer and Odysseus have different audiences and purposes. See, for the thinker behind the artist, the ordering of contestants and winners in the various contests in the fifth book of Virgil's *Aeneid.* See, for the respect shown to the middle place, Plutarch, *Cicero,* I, 1–2.

Homer, the first of the great poets in the West, is used by me in the text of this Prologue to suggest the thinker behind the artist (assuming that there *are* critical differences between "artist" and "thinker" as ordinarily understood). Our careful reading of a poem by a contemporary master should assure us that my suggestion is not limited to the poets of antiquity. (See, e.g., Appendix E, below.) Consider, therefore, how Edwin Muir, one of the best poets in English in this century (perhaps W.B. Yeats is superior), draws in "The Animals" upon both his Hebrew and Greek sources—the biblical and philosophical traditions which, together, have been used to shape what we know as Western civilization:

The Animals

They do not live in this world,
Are not in time and space.
From birth to death hurled
No word do they have, not one
To plant a foot upon,   5
Were never in any place.

For with names the world was called
Out of the empty air,
With names was built and walled,
Line and circle and square,   10
Dust and emerald;
Snatched from deceiving death
By the articulate breath.

But these have never trod
Twice the familiar track,   15
Never never turned back
Into the memoried day.
All is new and near
In the unchanging Here
Of the fifth great day of God,   20
That shall remain the same,
Never shall pass away.

On the sixth day we came.

Much is made in the poem of "they." Indeed, almost all of the poem is devoted to the unnamed and unspeaking "they." Only in the last line of the poem does someone other than "they" appear upon the scene: "On the sixth day we came." The narrator, it seems, is one of those who came on the sixth day.

Little is said explicitly about "we." But everything that has gone before is, to some extent, about "we" as well as about "they." We are the ones, for instance, who do live in the world, who do have access to the word, who make use of names and hence who know of and know death. Indeed, it can be said, we and only we are the ones who truly live. In saying this, however, I anticipate our careful reading of this poem.

Here, again, are the first two lines:

> They do not live in the world,
> Are not in time and space.

The subsequent twenty lines—that is, all the remaining lines but the last one—can be understood as an explication of these first two, a development of what is said here. When it is said that *they* do not live in the world, does that mean that they do not live at all? The "world" is referred to, not the "earth"; perhaps they *are* associated with the earth, something which may be less the product of thought, of consciousness, than is the world. Perhaps, also, time and space are dependent on intellect or perception. Does genuine living take time and require space?

To say that they do not live, however, is not to say that they have no existence at all. Existence, the barest of existence, is suggested in the next line:

> From birth to death hurled

There are a beginning and an end for these things—do they themselves perceive birth and death?—but there is for them no movement on their own, no order, no serenity, no moment for reflection. To be hurled suggests what happens to something inanimate, such as a rock. (See the text at note 89, below.)

> No word do they have, not one
> To plant a foot upon,
> Were never in any place.

They do not, it seems, stand or walk: they have no place to plant a foot upon. Perhaps they do not even have a foot. (Paws and hooves are not really feet?) Words, it seems, are critical for standing. Genuine existence —being somewhere and sometime—it also seems, depends on words. Without the understanding that words make possible, and stand for, there can be no meaningful existence.

This is spelled out in the seven lines which immediately follow. The first two lines of this most abstract stanza of the poem read:

> For with names the world was called
> Out of the empty air,

This takes us back to the first line: there is, without words—without names—no world for them to live in. *Genesis* seems to be drawn upon. Was the original Creation a kind of naming? Certainly, Adam's naming of his fellow creatures is called to mind. (Is to call something to mind to make it or only to discover it, to recognize it?) The world itself did not truly exist before there were names—names, those most potent of words, those words which permit identification and hence full being.

The potency of the name-words, in filling the empty air, is recognized in the next line:

> With names was built and walled,

That is to say, with names the world was built and walled—in this sense it was called out of the empty air. And what *the world* means here is indicated in the two following lines:

> Line and circle and square,
> Dust and emerald;

These are the things the world is made up of: circles and squares are variations of lines; emeralds are one variation of dust. These are the simple things and their most complex manifestations, things both immaterial and material, the forms and the matter out of which the world is made. To speak of dust and emerald—and not, say, of atoms—is to speak from a human (and natural?) rather than a scientific (and artificial?) perspective.

All this prepares us for the central line of the poem and its immediate aftermath:

> Snatched from deceiving death
> By the articulate breath.

What, one must wonder, is snatched from deceiving death? The world, it would seem, and the things in it. The articulate breath—words, especially names—does something about death. It may not simply abolish death, but it can nullify the deception of death, if only the deception (for the inarticulate) that death is like everything else, that there is nothing special about it. That is, it may be only the articulate, and hence the knowing, who recognize death for what it is—who recognize it—and who thereby truly live, if only for awhile. Thus, death, too, is named—and is seen for what it truly is. Perhaps, also, unexamined death promises rest. But may not only personal oblivion follow? Names may salvage something from such oblivion. Perhaps, as well, those who do not understand do not even know that they die: they are deceived as to—ignorant of—what becomes of them. One can somehow live only when one learns one dies? To become articulate is to have the breath of life, the spirit, added to one's material existence.

To know that one dies, and hence to live, can mean that both past and future have meaning. Consider, however, the plight of the inarticulate. Here we return to the "they" of the opening lines:

> But these have never trod
> Twice the familiar track,
> Never never turned back
> Into the memoried day.

There is for "these" no memory, nothing truly familiar—even though all they do is trod the familiar track, repeating themselves by a kind of instinct. Indeed, there may be for them no distinction between themselves and the track they trod, between themselves and others (whether other animate or even inanimate things). Or, put another way, they have no sense of identity, to say nothing of individuality or self-consciousness. Or, put still another way, they never recall what they have done, and they never knowingly repeat themselves, although they do little but repeat themselves.

They are all they will ever be when they begin: what they will be is intrinsic to them from the outset. It is this we call instinct. And it is this which seems to be reflected in the lines which follow:

> All is new and near
> In the unchanging Here
> Of the fifth great day of God,
> That shall remain the same,
> Never shall pass away.

"New and near" are the most they can partake of "time and space." There is for them no past, no future, only the "unchanging Here." Their day, their time, is such that (for them) it never changes, it never passes away. They may pass on, or seem to, but they are replaced imperceptively and unperceivingly by others like themselves. Perhaps (one can say) it is for them the same whether they emerge from sleep or from birth.

The "fifth great day" is not really theirs, even though they depend upon it. Indeed, there are for them no days at all. Certainly, there is for them no awareness of what has come before: all is always present before them. If they adapt to changing circumstances, it is not with any awareness of what or where they have been or of what lies ahead. Everything can change around them—but since they cannot make comparisons, nothing changes. Thus, they are in their changelessness God-like; but in an even more critical respect they are not God-like, for they do not understand at all.

Who "they" are is, of course, confirmed by the invocation of the fifth day. But, we should recall from the first chapter of *Genesis,* the creation of the fifth day extended into the sixth day. From the perspective of the unreasoning, however, there is no difference between the fifth and the sixth days: the fish and fowl are created on the fifth day, the land creatures on the sixth. For this reason, perhaps, it is called the "fifth *great* day of God": what is essential to that day's creation continues into the sixth day. (That the fish, fowl, and land creatures are to be considered together may be seen in the fact that it is three times said in *Genesis* that they are given under the dominion of man. These three kinds of mobile creatures share a wordless character.)

Although the land creatures came on the sixth day, things remained as they had been on the fifth day—until "we came." One price of eternity, of changelessness, it seems, is lack of development, of understanding, of what we now call "individuality." And with us came, among other things, names. We are the naming creatures. We can reason (with poetry a particularly intense, beguiling, and hence instructive form of naming). Not much has to be said about what happens with us: *we* can speak for ourselves. A sample of what and how we think may be found in the twenty-two lines of the poem which set the stage for the final (one-line) stanza:

On the sixth day we came.

It is at this point, and not before, that "they" can be named *by us.* That is, it is only for the entire poem that a name can be provided, "The Animals."

Men, it would seem, can be regarded as animals with a profound difference. Or, put another way, that which is most animalistic about men (and which the thoughtless man exhibits) can be attributed to the fifth day; that which is truly human can be attributed to the sixth day. (Does not the assignment of land creatures to the sixth day reflect the recognition that they among the animals are most susceptible to, even if they are not themselves capable of, the reasoning power of men?)

Only on the sixth day do there emerge creatures capable of self-consciousness and hence of full realization. Is it not in this sense that man can be said to have been created in the image of God? Only man can imitate, if only imperfectly, what God does with that uncovering (or discovery) of the nature of things which we call creation. (Is it not such uncovering that the more troublesome "invasions of privacy" attempt to imitate?)

The animals, on the other hand, are like rocks (whether dust or emerald) in one critical respect: they continue unaware, and hence unchanging, from beginning to end. This is not to say that the animals are of no consequence. Not only is animality vital to what is man, but this artist, as is evident in other poems of his, respects the animals, even preferring them in some ways to men. But there is not in animals more than the dimmest awareness of death—and hence there can be for them nothing poetic. A lively awareness of death makes a full life possible. Tragedy, one form of the poetic, helps make death endurable for most men.

I return to my remarks about the poet's use of his sources. The emphasis in this poem seems to be Greek, but within the framework provided by the Hebrew Bible. The Hebrew influence may be seen, of course, in the account of the Creation taken from *Genesis.* This account is restated, so to speak, in the opening lines of *The Gospel of John,* with its emphasis on the importance of the Word. This emphasis can be said to reflect the Greek understanding of things. Certainly, we can see upon examining this poem with some care, it was not only in antiquity that the artist was very much a thinker.

"The Animals" may be found in Edwin Muir, *Collected Poems 1921– 1951* (New York: Grove Press, 1953), p. 192. See, also, Anastaplo, *The Constitutionalist,* p. 556; "The Public Interest in Privacy: On Becoming and Being Human," 26 *DePaul Law Review* 767, nn. 30, 50 (1977) (where an earlier version of this analysis of "The Animals" appeared). See, on the relation of reason to revelation, Epilogue, Sections vi and viii, below; also, Appendix C, Section xii, below. (I was introduced to Muir's poetry by Thomas McDonald [at The Clearing] and studied it in a course I taught thereafter with Harry Kalven, Jr. [also at The Clearing]. Mr. McDonald was a colleague in the Basic Program of Liberal Education for Adults, The University of Chicago; Mr. Kalven had been a teacher of mine at the University of Chicago Law School. The Clearing is in Door County, Wisconsin. [See 117 *Congressional Record* 46881 (Dec. 14, 1971); 43 *University of Chicago Law Review* 13 (1975); Sid Telfer, *The Jens Jensen I Knew* (Ellison Bay, Wis., 1982), p. 80.])

To speak, as I have in concluding my commentary on "The Animals," of "the Greek understanding of things" is to bring to mind philosophy —and this, in turn, reminds us of the ancient struggle for supremacy between philosophy and poetry. One complaint lovers of poems, if not poets themselves, have is against those of philosophical inclinations who subject art to an inappropriate analysis, an analysis that draws too much on the rational and not enough on the instinctual—that draws too much (one might even suggest, speaking poetically) on the sixth day and not enough on the fifth. See Anastaplo, *Human Being and Citizen: Essays on Virtue, Freedom and the Common Good* (Chicago: Swallow Press, 1975), pp. 135–38; also, notes 29, 48, 145, 280, and 288, below. (See, for corrections of *Human Being and Citizen,* note 13, below.)

A *National Geographic* supplement, August 1979, concludes an account on bird migration, "How the migrants process these cues is a mystery. But the incredible facts remain: The birds know where they are, and they know where they're going." What is the sense of "know" used here? See Plato, *Apology* 22A–E. (The *Apology* is now available in a quite reliable English translation by Thomas G. West, published by the Cornell University Press. The quite reliable translation of Plato's *Republic,* drawn upon for the epigraphs for Chapter XI and Chapter XIII, Part One, below is by Allan Bloom; it is published by Basic Books.) See, also, Aristotle, *DeAnima* 413a19 sq., 414b20 sq., 420b5 sq., 421a20 sq., 430a22–25, 432a15 sq., 433a5 sq., 434b10 sq., 435b19 sq., *Metaphysics* 980a21–25. See, as well, *Aitareya Upanishad,* II, 3, 2. 5.

See, on what it means to know and on the relation of poetry to philosophy, Robert Sacks, "The Lion and the Ass: A Commentary on the Book of Genesis," 8 *Interpretation* 29 (May 1980). See, also, notes 29, 145 (end), and 164 (end), below. Compare Justice Harlan in *Cohen v. California,* 403 U.S. 15, 25 (1971): "[I]t is nevertheless often true that one man's vulgarity is another's lyric. Indeed, we think it is largely because governmental officials cannot make principled distinctions in this area that the Constitution leaves matters of taste and style so largely to the individual." Is it assumed here that there are no "principled distinctions" available to be made in these matters? Does not the understanding of certain things presuppose moral judgment? See Anastaplo, *The Constitutionalist,* pp. 121, 549–51, 733. See, also, Appendixes A and F, below. See, as well, note 288, below.

See, on poetry and science, Appendix G, and on death, Appendix E, below. See, on the divine as unchanging, Plato, *Epinomis,* 982C sq. See, on Homer, Chapter XIII, Part Two, Section ix, below.

4.   Heraclitus, Fr. 107; Mark Twain, *A Connecticut Yankee in King Arthur's Court* (Scranton: Chandler Publishing Co., 1963), p. 560 (chap. 43).

See, also, Heraclitus, Fr. 92; Plato, *Laws* 739C sq.; Shakespeare, *A Midsummer Night's Dream,* V, i, 208–15; A. Conan Doyle, *The Adventures of Sherlock Holmes* (New York: Schocken Books, 1976), p. 45; Whitehead, *Adventure of Ideas* (New York: Free Press, 1967), p. 221.

Consider, in this connection, Leo Strauss, *What is Political Philosophy?* (Glencoe: Free Press, 1959), p. 260:

> It was ultimately because he grasped the meaning of shame
> and awe that [Kurt] Riezler was a liberal, a lover of privacy. By
> invading men's privacy one does not come to know them better—
> one merely ceases to see them. For man's being is revealed by the
> broad character of his life, his deeds, his words, by what he
> esteems and reveres not in word but in deed—by the stars for
> which his soul longs if it longs for any stars. Not anguish but awe
> is "the fundamental mood" which discloses being as being. Be-
> cause he was animated by this spirit, he felt more at home in the
> thought of ancient Greece than in the thought of his time.

(See, on Mr. Strauss himself, Epilogue, below.) Consider, also, Hegel's
observation (*Chicago Tribune, Book World,* July 20, 1975, p. 3): "No
man is a hero to his *valet de chambre* [it is often said], but not because
the former is no hero, but because the latter is a valet." Similar sentiments may be found in Goethe and Carlyle. Cf. Plato, *Apology* 32A;
Plutarch, *Moralia* 360D.

See, on the primacy of sight, *Brihadaranya–Upanishad,* V, 14, 4;
Plato, *Timaeus* 47A–B; Aristotle, *Metaphysics* 980a25; Lucretius, *On
the Nature of Things,* bk IV; Strauss, *Natural Right and History,* p. 86f.
See, also, Chapter VIII, Section vi; Chapter XII, Section ii (end), below.

See, upon considering what "really happened" in a story, H.D.F.
Kitto, *Sophocles—Dramatist and Philosopher* (London: Oxford University Press, 1958), p. 14: "[The lying account in Sophocles' *Electra* of
Orestes' 'fatal' chariot race] bristles with convincing detail; it is as brilliant a narrative as anything one can find in Greek." (See Appendix G,
Section vii, below, for George Seferis's handling of this episode.) Here,
too, we have the prospect of "infinite regress"?

5. Henry James, *The Seige of London* (chap. 8), in Philip Rahv, ed., *The
    Great Short Novels of Henry James* (New York: Dial Press, 1944), p.
    295. Thus, the Emperor Napoleon said to his brother, at the height of
    the Marie Walewska affair, "Yes, I am in love, but always subordinate
    to my policy." *New Yorker,* Nov. 26, 1979, p. 224. Compare Shake-
    speare's *Romeo and Juliet* and *Antony and Cleopatra.*

    See, for samplings of opinions about the control one may have with
    respect to falling in love, Boccaccio, *The Decameron* (London: Every-
    man's Library, 1973), I, 42 ("wherefore, yielding to the dictates of
    prudence and honour, he was now as prompt to quench, as he had been
    inconsiderate in conceiving, his unfortunate passion for the lady . . ."),

II, 294 ("he knew very well that, if he took not care, he would grow
enamoured"), 296, 302, 305; Cervantes, *Don Quixote* (New York:
Viking Press, 1949), pp. 104 ("[N]ot all beauty inspires love, but
may sometimes delight the eye and leave the will intact. If it were
otherwise, no one would know what he wanted, but all would wander
vaguely and aimlessly with nothing upon which to settle their affections;
for the number of beautiful objects being infinite, desires similarly
would be boundless."), 298, 326, 791 ("for I would place a wall between my desires and my virtue"), 794; Shakespeare, *The Comedy of
Errors,* III, ii, 57 ("Gaze where you should, and that will clear your
sight."), *The Merchant of Venice,* I, ii, 26–33, *The Taming of the Shrew,*
I, i, 143f, *Two Gentlemen of Verona,* II, vi, 1f, *A Midsummer Night's
Dream,* I, i, 56–57 ("I would my father looked but with my eyes."
"Rather your eyes must with his judgment look."), 117–18, 233 ("Love
looks not with the eyes, but with the mind."), II, ii, 115, 130 ("And
yet, to say the truth, reason and love keep little company together
nowadays."), III, ii, 134, *As You Like It,* III, iv, 53 ("The sight of
lovers feedest those in love."), *Twelfth Night,* I, v, 294–95, *Henry VI,*
pt. 3, III, iii, 132–33 ("When I have heard your king's desert recounted,/
Mine ear hath tempted judgment to desire."); Goethe, *The Sorrows of
Young Werther* (New York: Vintage Books, 1971), pp. 38–40, 53–54;
The Washington Papers, Saul K. Padover, ed. (New York: Grosset &
Dunlap, 1955), p. 401 ("Love is said to be an involuntary passion, and
it is, therefore, contended that it cannot be resisted. This is true in part
only, for like all things else, when nourished and supplied plentifully
with aliment, it is rapid in its progress; but let these be withdrawn and it
may be stifled in its birth or much stinted in its growth."); Gilbert and
Sullivan, *Iolanthe,* II ("On fire that glows/ With heat intense/ I turn the
hose/ Of common sense,/ And out it goes/ At small expense!"); Doyle,
The Adventures of Sherlock Holmes, pp. 137 ("We can't command
our love, but we can our actions."), 153. See, for Agamemnon on the
prudence of Penelope, Homer, *Odyssey,* XI, 441–53. See note 194,
below.

See, on prudence, notes 27, 103, and 112, below.

See, on young love, Aristotle, *Nicomachean Ethics* 1156b1 sq. (which
can serve as one beginning of a commentary on Shakespeare's *Romeo
and Juliet*). See, also, notes 218 and 263, below.

6.   "By their clamorous approval and applause, the people mould the character of the poets according to their will—as if the public were some
great and wise master whose praise is all-sufficient. But when poets are
so highly extolled, what darkness they bring into the soul! What fears

they incite! What passions they enkindle!" Cicero, *On the Common-wealth* (Indianapolis: Bobbs-Merrill, 1976), p. 238 (*Republic,* IV, ix). Cf. Aristotle, *Politics* 1281b7–10.

See, also, Anastaplo, "Self-Government and the Mass Media: A Practical Man's Guide," in Harry M. Clor, ed., *The Mass Media and Modern Democracy* (Chicago: Rand McNally, 1974) (reprinted, in part, in Mary L. Pollingue, ed., *Readings in American Government,* 2d ed. [Dubuque: Kendall/Hunt Publishing Co., 1978]); Essay No. 10, "Obscenity and Common Sense," in *Human Being and Citizen.* See, as well, note 122, below. (In the last sentence of my "Mass Media" essay, "audiences" should be "spectators.")

Pittacus doubled the penalty for offenses committed when drunk. Diogenes Laertius, *Lives of Eminent Philosophers,* I, 76. See Aristotle, *Politics* 1274d18–23; *Nicomachean Ethics* 1110b24 sq., 1113b31 sq., 1114b30 sq.

7.   I touch, in Chapter XI, upon the music of Gilbert and Sullivan, in Appendix D, upon the making of stained-glass windows, and in Appendix F, upon films. Laurence Olivier has been quoted by Yousuf Karsh as having said, "In general the film is the director's medium, the theatre is the actor's medium." See, also, *Chicago Tribune,* Sept. 29, 1980, sec. 2, p. 8. Schopenhauer has been quoted by Nietzsche as having said, "Music is distinguished from all the other arts by the fact that it is not a copy of the phenomenon, or, more accurately, of the adequate objectivity of the will, but is an immediate copy of the will itself, and therefore complements everything physical in the world and every phenomenon by representing what is metaphysical, the thing in itself." *The Birth of Tragedy* (New York: Vintage Books, 1967), p. 102. See, on painting, Howard B. White, "Rembrandt and the Human Condition," 4 *Interpretation* 17, 34 (Winter 1974); Werner J. Dannhauser, *Nietzsche's View of Socrates* (Ithaca: Cornell University Press, 1974), p. 166, n. 50; Laurence Sterne, *Tristram Shandy* (New York: W.W. Norton & Co., 1980), p. 201 (IV, vii); Leo Steinberg, "The Line of Fate in Michelangelo's Painting." 6 *Critical Inquiry* 411 (1980). Still awaiting publication, I believe, are the very instructive lectures by Peter H. von Blanckenhagen on the Parthenon (delivered at the University of Chicago more than a decade ago). See, on both the Parthenon and Raphael, Anastaplo, *Brief on the Merits, In re Anastaplo* (366 U.S. 182 [1961]), p. 78, n. 56. See, on modern painting, notes 277 and 279 (end), below. See, also, Appendix G and the note at the end of Appendix E, below.

"Finally, our last reflection must be, that we have in the end come back to a version of the doctrine of old Pythagorus, from whom mathematics, and mathematical physics, took their rise. He discovered the importance of dealing with abstractions; and in particular directed attention to number as characterising the periodicities of notes of music. The importance of the abstract idea of periodicity was thus present at the very beginning both of mathematics and of European philosophy." Whitehead, *Science and the Modern World,* pp. 36–37. "Now David was a man highly skilled in songs, a man who loved the harmony of music. But David was not the ordinary man for whom music is merely for pleasure; for him it served the purpose of his faith. He used it in the service of his God, the true God, by giving a mystical prefiguration of a matter of high importance. For the concord of different sounds, controlled in due proportion, suggests the unity of a well-ordered city, welded together in harmonious variety." Augustine, *The City of God,* XVII, 14 (in the Penguin translation). Cf. Whitehead, *The Aims of Education* (New York: Free Press, 1967), p. 48: "Art exists that we may know the deliverances of our senses as good. It heightens the sense-world."

See, on music, Plato, *Timaeus* 47A sq., *Phaedo* 60C, *Laws* 700A sq. See, also, notes 145, 218, and 226, below.

The reference in this note to films reminds me that the reader should be put on notice, early in this book, that the history of my family with respect to assessments of the arts would not be considered by many an auspicious one. My father, when he was a young immigrant in St. Louis, was approached by the Skouras brothers to join them (fellow-immigrants from Greece) in a new nickelodeon venture. He declined and advised the Skouras brothers, who went on to fame and fortune in the movie industry, "Boys, there's no future in the entertainment business." Cf. Charles C. Moskos, Jr., *Greek Americans: Struggle and Success* (Englewood Cliffs, N.J.: Prentice-Hall, 1980), p. 45, n. 29. (In addition, I married someone from a family with a similar experience in the Southwest, but with another newly developed art. My wife's father, C.E. Prince, would recall from time to time his advice to "old man Tom Braniff" when Mr. Braniff suggested that they fly passengers between Oklahoma City and Tulsa, "There's no money in flying people around.") It is in part because of the unpredictable role of chance in "actual" human affairs that Aristotle could say, "Poetry is something more philosophical and serious than history, because poetry tends to present universals, while history presents particulars." *Poetics* 1451b5. See, on chance, Alexis de Tocqueville, *Democracy in America* (Garden City: Anchor Books, Doubleday & Co., 1969), p. 357. See, also, notes 124, 250, and 259, below. See, as well, note 145 (beginning), below; Epilogue, Section ii (end), below; the note at the end of Appendix E, below (for the Pasteur quotation).

See, on the intrinsic limitations of film, Appendix F, below. See, on the abolition of broadcast television in this country, note 122, below. The appeal of moving pictures is reflected in this testimony by a "Mafia infiltrator":

> Younger members of the crime syndicate were so impressed with 'The Godfather' movies that they revived old traditions such as kissing the hands of senior "family" members...

Chicago Tribune, Feb. 27, 1981, p. 1. See, also, "Life imitates art in copter escape by two gangsters," *Chicago Tribune,* Feb. 28, 1981, p. 1.

8. Sydney J. Harris, *Chicago Sun-Times,* June 23, 1979, p. 31. Out of the same tradition comes the related observation, "When a poor man eats a chicken, one of them is sick."

9. *Hesiod, The Homeric Hymns and Homerica* (Cambridge: Loeb Classical Library, 1914), p, 476. See, also, Joseph Fontenrose, *The Delphic Oracle* (Berkeley: University of California Press, 1978), pp. 83, 384–85. See, on the wisdom and antecedents of Homer, *ibid.,* pp. 263–64; Chapter XIII, Part Two, Section ix, below. Did Homer do for Odysseus (his instructive grandfather?) what Plato did for *his* teacher? "No treatise by Plato exists or will exist, but those which now bear his name belong to Socrates become fair and young." Plato, *Epistle* II, 334C. (Does *Macbeth* transform Malcolm even more, who may have been, in history, as bad as Shakespeare's Macbeth, or as bad as he warns Macduff he will be?)

10. Herman Melville, "The Apple-Tree Table," in *Selected Writings of Herman Melville* (New York: Modern Library, 1952), p. 422. See, also, the opening passage of David Hume's essay, *Of Suicide.* See, as well, the "whale-lines" passage in Chapter VII, Section ii, below.
    "Socrates used to call the beliefs of most people bogies to frighten children with." Marcus Aurelius, *Meditations*, XI, 23. But consider, in Mozart's opera, Giovanni's mistaken response when Leporello and he hear the Statue talking in the graveyard: "It must be someone outside having a joke on us." See notes 218 and 263, below.

11. See Anastaplo, *The Constitutionalist,* p. 772. See, also, Sterne, *Tristram Shandy,* pp. 352–58 (VII, xx–xxv). See, as well, Plato, *Charmides* 155E.

12. Hobbes, *Leviathan,* I, 8. Cf. Plato, *Phaedo,* where, on several occasions during his last conversation with his friends, Socrates exhibits a lack of concern about the disposition of the body after his death. Does Socrates' attitude not raise a question about Antigone's judgment? See Section ii

of this chapter, above, note 178, below. See, also, Appendix E, above.
(Not that how or where one is buried cannot be salutary for one's community. [See Plato, *Republic* 427B–C.] I, for example, believe it would
be useful for "me" to be buried in a military cemetery. See Anastaplo,
The Constitutionalist, pp. 381–82, 399–400. See, also, note 145 [end],
below.)

Hobbes's report on the suicide epidemic prompts me to observe that
if there *should* be sidewalks on both sides of the Golden Gate Bridge,
perhaps the one facing the city should be closed off, if at all possible.
That is, my psychiatric colleague's intuition should be given a trial run.
(Christian rulers, by the way, were able to use a different kind of stripping from that employed in Hobbes's Greek city—a spiritual stripping—
to deter suicides.) But, it should be added, the Golden Gate victims may
select the side toward San Francisco *not* in order to "relate" (or to
"say" something) to the survivors but rather because the city side is
more interesting or more beautiful or less threatening than the other
side. Consider an Associated Press report (*Chicago Sun-Times,* August
28, 1977, p. 55), "One side of the bridge offers a view of the Pacific
Ocean. The other side, the 'jumper's side,' looks on San Francisco, the
bay and the silver Bay Bridge running to Oakland. It's a view carried by
most jumpers as they step over the 3½-foot railing and plunge 200 feet
to the cold water below."

See note 159, below.

13.   Considerable use is made in these notes of two books of mine (*The Constitutionalist* and *Human Being and Citizen*) in which I have touched
upon a number of artists and upon moral and political questions bearing on the interpretation of their work.

Corrections of *The Constitutionalist* may be found in notes 3 and 4
of my "American Constitutionalism and the Virtue of Prudence: Philadelphia, Paris, Washington, Gettysburg," in Leo Paul S. de Alvarez, ed.,
*Abraham Lincoln, the Gettysburg Address and American Constitution-
alism* (Irving: University of Dallas Press, 1976). Additional corrections
can be noticed here: p. 23, l. 30: for "Congress", read "general government"; p. 213, l. 25: note 33 should be keyed to "respectable" in l. 26;
p. 261, l. 34: for "self-expression", read "liberty"; p. 450, l. 25; for
"chap. 6, n. 69", read "chap. 7, n. 69"; p. 547, l. 5: for "one", read
"he"; p. 625, l. 14: for "chap. 7, n. 77, below.", read "186, below.
See, also, chap. 7, nn. 23, 35, above."; p. 781, l. 55: for "*Republic*
357B", read "*Republic* 557B"; p. 639, l. 10: for "government's", read
"governments'"; p. 782: delete the first full paragraph on this page
(which is the last paragraph of note 8); p. 782: add to the first paragraph of note 9 the following citations: "See *Exodus* 3: 6. Cf. *Exodus*

34: 29–35"; p. 794, l. 35: for "chap. 8, n. 107", read "chap. 7, n. 107"; p. 807, l. 55; insert, before the parentheses, "Cf. Aristotle, *Metaphysics* 984a31." Furthermore, at p. xi, l. 15, "The circumstances of my permanent exclusion from the practice of law" should begin a new paragraph; and, it should be recorded, another appendix would have been inserted in the book, had space permitted. (I have found still other errors that are noted, for the time being, in my copy. See note 76, below.)

Reviews of *The Constitutionalist* are cited in my *Human Being and Citizen,* p. 223. An extended, obviously serious, and yet deeply flawed (and otherwise unhappy) comment on *The Constitutionalist* by Glen E. Thurow (of the University of Dallas) may be found in 8 *Interpretation* 188 (May 1980). He is evidently dubious about any attempt to bring constitutional sobriety and intellectual playfulness together in one volume (even though it *is* a very large volume). Mr. Thurow's distortions with respect to *The Constitutionalist* can be said to be thorough (see note 252, below), ranging from his tripling of the number of my already considerable notes (787 mysteriously becomes 2,787) to his insisting ("supported" by a dubious citation) that I presume to teach "that all men should try to be philosophic." (8 *Interpretation* 188, 199) Indeed, the opening paragraph of the very page cited here (*The Constitutionalist,* p. 11) is in direct opposition to what Mr. Thurow suggests to be my position:

> This inquiry is, as its subtitle [*Notes on the First Amendment*] suggests, an exploratory effort. The Constitutionalist—as may perhaps be true of anyone who takes political things seriously— is occasionally obliged to beg the question, to proceed as if there were more certainty and precision than there can be about such matters. If he knows what he is doing, he can serve his fellow citizens by fashioning a salutary lawyer's brief which tells "a likely story."

See, e.g., Plato, *Republic* 493E sq.; the text at notes 162 and 278, below, and notes 76, 78, 239, and 285, below. See, also, *The Constitutionalist,* pp. 278–81, 581 ("What's a millennium [or two?] among friends?"), 786–87 (on literary playfulness and discipline). See, as well, W.B. Yeats, *The Scholars*. An appropriate response by me to Mr. Thurow should be provided in volume 10 of the journal (note 285 [end], below). But see Aristotle, *Metaphysics* 984a3–4. (See, on *Interpretation* itself, note 283, below. Mr. Thurow is the author of *Abraham Lincoln and American Political Religion,* published by the State University of New York Press in 1976, a book that every serious student of Lincoln's thought should be familiar with.)

The following corrections should be made in *Human Being and Citizen:* p. xii, l. 22: for "the chairman," read "chairman"; p. 52, l. 16: insert "is" after "novelty"; p. 63, l. 18: for "The rulers", read "Rulers"; p. 71, l. 18: insert comma after "disturbed"; p. 97, l. 29: for "nor", read "or"; p. 230, l. 38: for "to believed", read "to be believed"; p. 248, l. 50: for "88 *Ethics*", read "84 *Ethics*"; p. 251, l. 8: for "1895", read "1859"; p. 254, running head: for "Pages 55–65", read "Pages 55–56"; p. 268, l. 20: for "below", read "above."; the passage quoted at the bottom of page 321 continues to the next page.

Notices and reviews of *Human Being and Citizen* may be found in, among other places, *Hellenic Times,* Jan. 15, 1976, p. 10; *Greek Press,* Feb. 13, 1976, p. 12; *Chicago Sun-Times, Book Week,* Feb. 15, 1976, p. 7; *Chicago Daily Law Bulletin,* March 2, 1976, p. 3; *Chicago Daily News, Panorama,* March 6–7, 1976, p. 6; *Christian Century,* March 10, 1976, p. 236; *Southern Illinoisan,* Carbondale, April 11, 1976, p. 4, April 14, 1976, p. 4; *Chicago Tribune, Book World,* April 11, 1976, sec. 7, p. 7; *Focus/Midwest,* vol. 11, no. 70, 1976, p. 29; *Hellenic Times,* April 22, 1976, p. 8; 72 *Booklist* 1220 (1976); 69 *Law Library Journal* 380 (1976); *Chicago Magazine,* Dec. 1976, p. 118; *Chicago Daily News, Panorama,* Dec. 18–19, 1976, p. 7; *University of Chicago Law Alumni Journal,* Fall 1976, p. 29; 8 *Southwestern University Law Review* 744 (1976); 1976 *Wisconsin Law Review* 712 (1976); 50 *Southern California Law Review* 337 (1976); 9 *Southwestern University Law Review* 283 (1977); *Religious Humanism,* Spring 1977, p. 96; *The Athenian,* May 1977, p. 40.

See, on Themistocles and the Seriphian, Plato, *Republic* 329E–330A. See, also, note 23, below. Cf. Herodotus, *History,* VIII, 125; Seth Benardete, *Herodotean Inquiries* (The Hague: Martinus Nijhoff, 1969), pp. 30–31. See, also, Diogenes Laertius, *Lives of Eminent Philosophers,* I, 104–5. See, on the provincialism of Seriphus, Cicero, *On the Nature of the Gods,* 1, 88. Consider, as well, the exchange between Alexander the Great and his advisor, Parmenio: "I would take that offer, if I were Alexander." "So would I, if I were Parmenio."

See, on the principles of interpretation drawn upon in this book, note 280, below.

I. WILLIAM SHAKESPEARE (1564–1616)

14.   Ian Colvin, *The Chamberlain Cabinet* (New York: Taplinger Publishing Co., 1971), p. 169.

15.   Ovid, *Metamorphoses,* X, 452. See, also, *ibid.,* X, 571–72; Shakespeare,
        Richard III, III, iv, 84–86; *Henry VI,* Pt. 2, III, ii, 82–93; *The Rape of
        Lucrece,* 316–36; *Romeo and Juliet,* V, iii, 121–22 ("How oft tonight
        have my old feet stumbled at graves!"); Goethe, *Elective Affinities*
        (Chicago: Henry Regnery Co., 1963), pp. 20, 108 ("It was a warning
        to him in a double sense; but he did not heed these accidental hints
        which some higher Being seems to give us."), 114.
            Consider, as well, the following recent newspaper reports: "When
        the President was ushered in, accompanied by an honor escort of sena-
        tors, he stumbled on a step leading to the well of the chamber. When
        Rockefeller followed Ford a minute later [for the installation of the
        former as Vice-President], he nearly stumbled on the same step."
        Chicago Daily News, December 20, 1974, p. 3. "The big concern of
        Ford aides is that his candidacy might detract from what they perceive
        as a national image of a strong and respected former President. They
        fear that he might again be pictured as a bumbling, stumbling, accident-
        prone politician—an image enhanced when he fell down the stairs of
        his plane in Austria and his frequent head-bumping in his helicopter."
        Chicago Tribune, March 11, 1979, sec. 2, p. 6. See A.A. Brill, ed., *The
        Basic Writings of Sigmund Freud* (New York: Modern Library, 1938),
        p. 163f (especially p. 165, on the stumbling Roman). Cf. Sigmund Freud,
        Introductory Lectures on Psychoanalysis (New York: Liveright Book;
        W.W. Norton & Co., 1977), pp. 58–59. Cf., on not warding off the
        effects of inauspicious auguries, Chapter XII, Section ii, below (the
        Air Cadets illustration; see Plato, *Laws* 645C sq., 649D sq.).
            See, on omens, Plutarch, *Fabius Maximus,* II, 5; *Crassus,* XVII, 6;
        Sulla, XI, 1–2; *Pericles,* VI, 2–3; XXXV, 1–2; *Nicias,* XXIII, 1–6;
        Aemilius Paulus, XVII, 4–6; *Lucullus,* XXVII, 7. See, also, Cicero, *On
        Divination; On the Nature of the Gods,* I, xxvi, 71 ("It is held to be a
        matter of amazement that one soothsayer can look at another sooth-
        sayer without laughing."); Leo Strauss, *Thoughts on Machiavelli* (Glen-
        coe, Ill.: Free Press, 1958), pp. 150f, 208, 220, 228–29. Compare the
        resourceful Roman general who, upon falling while disembarking for an
        African campaign, had the presence of mind (in full view of his troops)
        to take hold of the earth and to proclaim, "Thus I seize you, Africa!"
        See note 202, below. See, also, note 76, below.
            On the other hand, I have known (but not well) a remarkably unin-
        hibited woman who was confirmed in her most daring indiscretions
        because she did *not* stumble on her way to them! Cf. note 289, below.
        Cf., also, Tocqueville, *Democracy in America,* p. 535.

16.   This inquiry (first touched upon in the Preface and the Prologue) will

be raised in various ways in this book. Is it not critical to the reading
of most (if not all) of the works I consider here?

A tragedy (perhaps this can be said of most serious art) is a kind of
worship at the altar of reason and justice, with beauty serving as the
presiding priestess. We "confess" thereby that cause and effect, as well
as right and wrong, govern the moral universe. See note 229, below. See,
also, Epilogue, Section ii (end), below.

See, on the perils of that open-mindedness which denies objective
standards, Anastaplo, *Human Being and Citizen,* pp. xi–xiii; Appendix
A, below. See, also, note 29, below.

17.   See, on Shakespeare (who can be said to have made possible among us
a constitutional regime), Anastaplo, *The Constitutionalist,* e.g., pp. 30–
33, 278, 436–38, 479, 739, 755, 790–91. See, also, *The Complete Novels
of Jane Austen* (New York: Modern Library, 193–), p. 674: "But Shakespeare one gets acquainted with without knowing how. It is a part of
an Englishman's constitution." Cf. the text at note 120, below. See, as
well, Tocqueville, *Democracy in America,* p. 471: "The literary inspiration of Great Britain darts its beams into the depths of the forests of
the New World. There is hardly a pioneer's hut which does not contain
a few odd volumes of Shakespeare." (Cf. *ibid.,* p. 493: "The drama of
one age will never suit the next if an important revolution has changed
manners and laws." "The more we look at American life the more we
see that any social aspect takes its main sense from its democratic connections." Henry James, *The Speech and Manners of American Women*
[Lancaster, Pa.: Lancaster House Press, 1973], p. 16. See note 124,
below.)

The soundness of Shakespeare's public-spirited appeal (as compared
to the appeal of other gifted, but self-centered, artists, such as Oscar
Wilde) is suggested by an account of nineteenth century cowboys by
Philip Ashton Rollins:

> The Englishmen brought a lot of culture into the West. There
> were practically no books out there, but an Englishman always
> brought Shakespeare with him: it was the decent thing to do.
> And they read their books, read them aloud to the cowboys,
> many of whom never got any further in their schooling than the
> rudiments of reading and writing. I've seen a bunch of cowboys
> sitting on their spurs listening with absolute silence and concen-
> tration while somebody read aloud.... Once when something of
> Oscar Wilde's was being read, one of the cowboys got up and left
> the room. Later I asked him why, and he said, "I don't see no

beauty in watching a hog eat swill." And I remember once after we'd been listening to *Julius Caesar,* one of them said to me, "That Shakespeare is the only poet I've ever heard who was fed on raw meat." When I sold my ranch in Montana, I divided my books among the riders, and eighteen out of twenty-one wanted Shakespeare.

J. Frank Dobie, Introduction, in Charles A. Siringo, *A Texas Cowboy* (Lincoln: University of Nebraska Press, 1950), p. xxvi (citing 9 *Princeton University Library Chronicle* 189 [1948]). See Anastaplo, "Human Nature and the First Amendment," 40 *University of Pittsburgh Law Review* 661, 732, n. 79 (1979). (Part One of this chapter has appeared in that article; see note 30, below.) See, also, note 279, below.

18. "Woe unto the world because of offences! for it must needs be that offences come; but woe to that man by whom the offence cometh!" *Matthew* 18: 7 (quoted by Abraham Lincoln in his Second Inaugural Address).

Death in the history plays of Shakespeare seems to be somewhat different from what it is in his tragedies. See, for example, David Bevington, in *The Complete Pelican Shakespeare,* p. 438:

Indeed, Talbot [in *Henry VI,* Pt. 1] is the standard of patriotic right reason by which Shakespeare measures the decline in other characters. Talbot is the embodiment of firmness and yet fair play toward the French. . . . Neither unscrupulous in personal ambition like Winchester and York, nor timorous in commitment to the right cause like Henry VI, Talbot and his virtuous son are concerned that their name be remembered forever as a synonym for valor. This fame, along with their achieving heaven, compensates for the seeming injustice of their deaths. Yet Talbot is denied the sort of tragic experience in which a man discovers a causal relationship between his character and his fate. No flaw exists in Talbot to produce his fate. He is victimized rather than self-destroyed.

How much did Shakespeare, in this connection, truly make of "achieving heaven"? Cf. Augustine, *City of God,* I, 8f; XIX, 27; XX, 2, 28.

See, on death generally, Anastaplo, *Human Being and Citizen,* Essay No. 17. See, also, note 3, above, notes 127, 145, 175, and 237, below. See, as well, Epilogue, Section viii, below; Appendix E, below.

19. One is reminded of Plato's *Meno.* (See, on the *Meno,* Anastaplo, *Human Being and Citizen,* Essay No. 6. See, also, Book Review, 32 *Review of*

Metaphysics 773 [1979]. At p. 775, l. 7, "ll7b19 sq." should read, "1179b19 sq."; at p. 775, l. 34, "It is not true" should read "But is it not true".)

20.   I am reminded of Socrates' daemonic thing, especially as described in Plato's *Apology*. See note 167, below.

See, on the relation of virtue to happiness, Plato, *Theaetetus* 176-77, *Laches* 199D–E, *Gorgias* 473C, *Republic;* Homer, *Odyssey,* XIV, 84 ("Verily the blessed gods love not reckless deeds, but they honour justice and the righteous deeds of men."); Anastaplo, "The Declaration of Independence," 9 *St. Louis University Law Journal* 390, 407 (1965) (see, for corrections, Anastaplo, "American Constitutionalism and the Virtue of Prudence," n. 1). See, also, Aristotle, *Nicomachean Ethics,* bk. I; Anastaplo, "American Constitutionalism and the Virtue of Prudence," n. 26, p. 146, n. 30. Consider, as well, the remarks of Rome's Communist mayor to Pope John Paul II: "It is my duty to say that Rome is not a happy city and in its suffering has a thirst overall for justice and solidarity.... Notwithstanding the efforts to change its chronic condition, Rome still remains a city torn by social injustice, beggared by unemployment, the lack of houses, of social assistance and culture. Too often, this uncertainty propels youth into the illusions of drugs, crime, violence and terrorism." *Atlanta Constitution,* Nov. 13, 1978, p. 7-A. The Pope himself said, upon being angered by the sight of the slums of Rio de Janeiro: "A society that is not socially just and does not intend to be, puts its own future in danger. Only a just society has the right to be." *Chicago Tribune,* July 3, 1980, sec. 1, p. 2. See Anastaplo, *The Constitutionalist,* p. 675, n. 10. Consider J.S. Fuerst, "Bombing in Bologna may be rightist plot," *Chicago Tribune,* Sept. 6, 1980, sec. 1, p. 9:

> [T]he communist government in Bologna has been extremely successful. It has made great improvements in housing, transportation, education, and health, and has greatly democratized decision-making. It has the support not only of labor, agricultural workers, and the huge cooperative movement in Bologna, but of many small businessmen and professional people in the area. The communists, in fact, do not even meet with much opposition from big business. Men like Agnelli of Fiat or Benedetti of Olivetti can recognize good government when they see it.

Cf. note 277, below. See note 103, below.

Consider the text at note 155, below. Cf. Shakespeare, *Measure for Measure*, II, i, 38, "Some rise by sin, and some by virtue fall ..."

Cf. note 107, below.

21.   Should Prince Hamlet have known that Claudius would not be able truly to repent (that is, to give up all that he had improperly taken)? Sin is not forgiven until stolen goods are restored. William Langland, *Piers Plowman* (London: Sheed and Ward, 1935), V, 388–94. See, for the mistaken impression that Hamlet held off killing Claudius at his prayers out of respect for the right to sanctuary, *New Yorker*, May 26, 1980, p. 118. See the comments on this episode by Laurence Berns in the essay cited in note 129, below.

King Hamlet's command to his son is not merely a dying command; rather, it comes from the other world. We need not worry here about whether the ghost is "real." Shakespeare shows us that others saw a ghost before Hamlet did—just as he shows us a ghost appearing later only to a by then much-disturbed Hamlet. It is indeed the old (that is, the former) king who appeared (one way or another to his son) to get his revenge. See Anastaplo, *The Constitutionalist*, pp. 31, 437; *Human Being and Citizen*, p. 306, n. 2; the text at note 8, above.

Consider, also, Cicero's remarks to Casca in Shakespeare, *Julius Caesar*, I, iii; the text at note 11, above. Cf. Plutarch, *Cicero*, XXXII, 4–5.

22.   I am reminded of Pompey of *Antony and Cleopatra* who "had his chance" and lived to fall before less scrupulous enemies who knew what to do with *their* chance. (II, vii, 36–83) What *should* Pompey have done? Cf. Shakespeare, *Macbeth*, I, v, 36f, I, vii, 46f. Is not this question central to an understanding of Shakespeare's politics? See note 103, below.

See Michael Platt, *Rome and Romans According to Shakespeare* (Salzburg: Institut fur Englische Sprache und Literatur, 1976), p. 246.

See, also, John Alvis, "A Probable Platonic Allusion and Its Significance in Shakespeare's *Julius Caesar*," 2 *The Upstart Crow* 64 (1979).

23.   Compare (in Plutarch's *Aristides*, VIII, 2–6) the proffer of services by Aristides to his political enemy, Themistocles, as the Persians approached Athens, "If we have any discretion, Themistocles, laying aside at this time our vain and childish contention, let us enter upon a safe and honourable dispute, vying with each other for the preservation of Greece; you in the ruling and commanding, I in the subservient and advising part . . ." To which Themistocles replied, "I would not willingly, Aristides, be overcome by you on this occasion; and shall endeavour, in emulation of this good beginning, to outdo it in my actions." See Benardete, *Herodotean Inquiries*, p. 193, n. 16. But see Hegel, *The Philosophy of History* (New York: Dover Publications, 1956), pp. 311–13.

See, on what could be said against kingship and on behalf of the Republic, Cicero, *De Officiis*, III, xxi. See, also, Allan Bloom, *Shake-*

speare's Politics (New York: Basic Books, 1964); note 56, below. May not the deterioration of the Republic be seen in the fact that none of Brutus' associates condemns him as self-centered or foolish or simply wrong, except for Cassius and he too late?

24.   See Anastaplo, "Utopia or Tyranny: The Universal Declaration of Human Rights," in *Notes on the First Amendment to the Constitution of the United States* (University of Chicago doctoral dissertation, 1964), p. 790. See note 277, below. See, also, Appendix C, Section ix, below.

       Notice, in connection with the closing word of *Coriolanus* ("Assist."), the end of Plato's *Laws* ("I shall assist."). See, on the *Laws* and on Plato's political religion, Leo Strauss, *The Argument and the Action of Plato's Laws* (Chicago: University of Chicago Press, 1975) (reviewed by David Bolotin, 71 *American Political Science Review* 668 [1977]). See, also, Plato, *Republic* 427A sq., 461D sq., 470E. See, as well, note 76, below.

       A proper study of *Coriolanus* should consider what is indicated in the play about the merits of Coriolanus' insistence that only his assessment of the food supply in Rome is in the public interest. Does not the principle of distribution he advocates call into question the constitutional allocation of powers in Rome? See Chapter I, Part Two, Section x. See, also, Plato, *Laws* 691C–D; notes 79 and 166, below.

25.   Harry V. Jaffa, *The Conditions of Freedom: Essays in Political Philosophy* (Baltimore: Johns Hopkins University Press, 1975), p. 96, n. 36.

26.   *Ibid.* Cf. Anastaplo, *Human Being and Citizen*, p. 261, n. 4. (See, on Mr. Jaffa himself, note 285, below.)

       See, on *King Lear*, Laurence Berns, "Gratitude, Nature and Piety in *King Lear*," 3 *Interpretation* 27 (Autumn 1972). See, also, Anastaplo, *The Constitutionalist*, pp. 790–91; *Human Being and Citizen*, p. xi; notes 202 and 208, below. On commanding love, see Kant, *Fundamental Principles of the Metaphysics of Morals* (Indianapolis: Library of Liberal Arts, 1949), p. 17. See, on the *Lear* text, Thomas Clayton, "Old Light on the Text of *King Lear*," 78 *Modern Philology* 347, 362–363 (1981).

27.   *Observer Review*, London, December 24, 1972, p. 17. See, on prudence, Aristotle, *Nicomachean Ethics* 1140a24 sq. For a reminder of what prudence is *not*, consider the description of Stalin in Roy A. Medvedev, *Let History Judge* (New York: Alfred A. Knopf, 1972), p. 331: "Stalin was not simply crafty; he was a man of unusual hypocrisy. He achieved

a great deal by his ability to put on any mask." See, also, Anastaplo, "American Constitutionalism and the Virtue of Prudence," p. 139, n. 17. See, as well, notes 96, 103, 112, and 285, below; Appendix B, below.

See, on the related problem of "conscience" (and on Shakespeare as "postclassical" in some degree), *ibid.*, p. 162, n. 58. See, also, Shakespeare, *Titus Andronicus,* V, i, 74–75; James Joyce, *Ulysses* (New York: Modern Library, 1942), pp. 17, 187, 204, 240; Friedrich Nietzsche, *Beyond Good and Evil* (New York: Vintage Books, 1966), p. 129, n. 25; Anastaplo, *Human Being and Citizen,* p. 275, n. 39, p. 311, n. 14; note 249, below. Cf. note 28, below.

It would be useful, in assessing Graham Greene's "cold and prudent" language, to return to the problem confronting Emilia upon discovering what Iago had done. I have suggested that she was mistaken to reveal the truth about Iago in his presence while he was armed; and I added that a word to the appropriate officials afterwards would have sufficed. This was written some years ago—and it has found substantial support in an Associated Press report distributed as this book was going to press:

> A woman [in Mobile, Alabama] who was raped in her home ran next door seeking help—only to find that her neighbor was the man who had attacked her, she told police Wednesday.
>
> [A police sergeant] said the 55-year-old woman was awakened about 1:20 a.m. by an intruder wearing a stocking mask and armed with a knife. She was beaten, raped and bound with clothing, police said.
>
> After struggling free, they said, she ran to the neighbor's house and pleaded for him to call the police. It was then she realized that the neighbor bore a striking resemblance to her attacker, having the same physical build and similar tattoos.
>
> [The sergeant] said that while the neighbor phoned police, the rape victim kept her composure, even after seeing a knife in the man's pocket. When police arrived, she pointed to the man. Police arrested [him], 21, on charges of burglary and rape.

Chicago Sun-Times, June 3, 1982, p. 36. Emilia should have been as "cold and prudent"—and as effective in the cause of both justice and justified self-preservation—as this Mobile woman. See note 60, below.

28.   Consider how George Santayana could speak of Shakespeare:

> Shakespeare's world ... is only the world of human society. The cosmos eludes him; he does not seem to feel the need of framing that idea. He depicts human life in all its richness and variety, but

leaves that life without a setting, and consequently without a meaning. ... In contrast with such a luminous philosophy and so well-digested an experience [as may be found in Homer and Dante], the silence of Shakespeare and his philosophical incoherence have something in them that is still heathen; something that makes us wonder whether the northern mind, even in him, did not remain morose and barbarous at its inmost core.

Little Essays (Freeport: Books for Libraries Press, 1967), pp. 189–90. See the text at note 96, below. Cf. Frank Chapman Sharp, *Shakespeare's Portrayal of the Moral Life* (New York: Charles Scribner's Sons, 1902), p. 105, where it is observed that "Shakespeare is nature." Cf., also, John D. Sinclair, ed., *The Divine Comedy of Dante Alighieri: Purgatorio* (New York: Oxford University Press, 1961), p. 65: "But what Bagehot said of Shakespeare was as true of Dante, that he had 'an experiencing nature'. . . ." See Anastaplo, "American Constitutionalism and the Virtue of Prudence," pp. 161–62, n. 58. See, also, note 145, below.

29.   Even if the deeper thinking on which the playwright depends should elude the audience (if only because of the constant movement on the stage), that thinking may nevertheless have manifestations which somehow or other draw audiences.

Thus, the opinions (or prejudices) of the audience can be enlisted. See, for example, Nancy Mitford, *The Pursuit of Love* (New York: Popular Library, 1974), pp. 62–63:

> Uncle Mathew went with Aunt Sadie and Linda on one occasion to a Shakespeare play, *Romeo and Juliet.* It was not a success. He cried copiously, and went into a furious rage because it ended badly. "All the fault of that damned padre," he kept saying on the way home, still wiping his eyes. "That fella, what 'is name, Romeo, might have known a blasted papist would mess up the whole thing. Silly old fool of a nurse too, I bet she was an R.C., dismal old bitch."

Cf. note 91, below. See note 221, below.

Thus, the inner recesses of the psyche can be touched, on the stage and hence in the audience? Consider, for example, how Iago "gets to" Othello: it is not really by talking about *Cassio* and Desdemona but rather by reminding Othello of what goes on (or will go on) between *Othello* and Desdemona? Was Othello drawn to Desdemona as someone who would be permanently "pure"? The dying Desdemona, when asked who had "done this deed," responded, "Nobody—I myself." (*Othello,* V, ii, 125) Should "nobody" be understood as "no-body"? That is,

neither Othello nor she ever came to terms with *her* body? If there is
something to all this, then "all" Iago did was to speed up the inevitable
deterioration of relations between Othello and Desdemona? (I have
drawn here upon what I observed going on between two fellow-officers
in one of my Air Force flight crews some thirty-three years ago. It is
typical of such relations that neither of these men knew what was happening or could identify himself from what I have said. How much did
Iago know about what *he* was saying?)

Thus, as well, audiences can be reassured (by means of poetic delights) about the nature of things. Consider, for example, Oberon's
final blessing to the newlyweds in *A Midsummer Night's Dream* (V,
i, 390):

> Now, until the break of day,
> Through this house each fairy stray,
> To the best bride-bed will we,
> Which by us shall blessèd be;
> And the issue there create
> Ever shall be fortunate.
> So shall all the couples three
> Ever true in loving be;
> And the blots of Nature's hand
> Shall not in their issue stand.

Is it no more than an illusion (however salutary it can be, when skillfully employed) that things *can* be taken care of thus? Are "the blots
of Nature's hand" to be properly anticipated and taken care of only
by one who truly knows nature? In any event, the thoughtful man
remembers something that the charmed audience is not likely to want
to think about: *the* issue believed (in one version of the story) to have
come from the union of Theseus and Hippolyta is Hippolytus. Should
not Shakespeare be expected to be aware of this tradition, and of the
dreadful story of what happened a generation later among this father
(Theseus), this son (Hippolytus), and the father's subsequent love-
maddened young wife (Phaedra)? What does this say about what we
should think about the decision by Theseus to set aside civic and parental prerogatives (and duties?) on behalf of young love? Ibid., IV, i, 178.
See, on Hippolytus, Seth Benardete, "Euripides' *Hippolytus*," in *Essays
in Honor of Jacob Klein* (Annapolis, Md.: St. John's College Press, 1976),
p. 22. See, also, Wendy O'Flaherty, ed., *Hindu Myths* (London: Penguin
Books, 1978), p. 260; Miriam Lichtheim, ed., *Ancient Egyptian Literature* (Berkeley: University of California Press, 1976), II, 203f. See, as
well, note 164, below.

Do I, in what I say about the sensibleness of Shakespeare's world, merely restate one position in the old argument between philosophy and poetry? See Plato, *Republic* 607B. And in doing this, have I recruited Shakespeare for the cause of the philosophers, making him into primarily (or ultimately) a thinker? See Anastaplo, *Human Being and Citizen*, pp. 135–38. See, also, note 3, above; the text at note 48, below; notes 138, 145 (end), and 246, below. Cf. A.E. Housman, *Selected Prose,* ed. John Carter (Cambridge: University Press, 1961), pp. 176, 187 ("Poetry is not the thing said but a way of saying it. . . . Meaning is of the intellect, poetry is not."), 192 ("some region deeper than the mind"), 193 ("Poetry indeed seems to me more physical than intellectual. . . . The seat of this sensation [in response to poetry] is the pit of the stomach.").

Be all this as it may, it should be evident from what I have already said in this book that the best works of art certainly bear thinking about.

30.   See, for a useful collection of essays on Shakespeare, John Alvis and Thomas G. West, eds., *Shakespeare as Political Thinker* (Durham: Carolina Academic Press, 1982). The thoughtful introduction to that volume collects citations to many other useful works on Shakespeare. See note 129, below.

Part One of this chapter was originally prepared, as "Prudence and Mortality in Shakespeare's Tragedies," for inclusion in a volume to have been dedicated to the memory of Howard B. White (1912-1974). His works include a study of Shakespeare, *Copp'd Hills Toward Heaven: Shakespeare and the Classical Polity* (The Hague: Martinus Nijhoff, 1970). See note 17, above.

I hope to be able to consider Shakespearean comedy systematically on another occasion. (See, e.g., note 29, above, note 78, below.) Do things "come out as they should" in the tragedies because of nature, and in the comedies *more* because of Providence? Of course, much is indicated in the comedies about individual character, about nature, and about political influences—and we can figure out, from what we know about the tragedies, how the stories in the comedies might have gone but for things working out "against all odds." "The audience must be returned from [*Twelfth Night*] to its own less patterned world where the sea rarely disgorges siblings given up for lost, where mistaken marriages rarely turn out well, where Violas rarely catch Dukes, and where Malvolios too often rule households with disturbing propriety." Joseph H. Summers, "The Masks of *Twelfth Night*," in Walter N. King, ed., *Twentieth Century Interpretations of Twelfth Night* (Englewood Cliffs, N.J.: Prentice-Hall, 1968), p. 22.

Fame is pursued in Shakespeare's *Love's Labor's Lost* to counter "the disgrace of death." (I, i, 1–3) Death nevertheless asserts itself decisively in the play (which is uncharacteristic in Shakespearian comedy). (V, ii, 705f.) Would Shakespeare have written his comedies, with the partial view of the world therein indicated, if he had not been writing his tragedies as well? See, on comedy, Christopher A. Colmo, *Ancient Communism* (University of Chicago doctoral dissertation, 1979), pp. 35f, 115. See, also, the text at note 129, below. See, as well, note 183, below.

31. *The Complete Pelican Shakespeare,* p. 823. He has also referred to it as a farce. See *Arden Edition of the Works of William Shakespeare: Titus Andronicus,* J.C. Maxwell, ed. (London: Methuen & Co., 1961), p. xxxvii.

32. Gustav Cross, in *The Complete Pelican Shakespeare,* p. 823.

33. *Ibid.,* p. 825.

34. *Ibid.,* p. 823. See note 240, below.

35. *Shakespeare's Tragedies* (London: Everyman's Library, 1964), p. v.

36. H. T. Price, "The Authorship of 'Titus Andronicus,'" 42 *Journal of English and German Philology* 55, 80 (1943). Even so, he closes his apology, "[W]e must conclude, however regretfully, that Shakespeare was the author of *Titus Andronicus*." *Ibid.,* p. 81.

37. *The Complete Pelican Shakespeare,* p. 824.

38. Bloom, *Shakespeare's Politics,* p. 110. See, also, Kitto, *Sophocles— Dramatist and Philosopher,* pp. 22 ("a more modest critic [than the younger Wilamowitz] would have suspected that he had missed something of importance"), 27 (critics should "renounce the attempt to be clever"), 35 ("The criticism [that the final scenes of *Antigone* are weak] proves one thing conclusively, that the critic has not understood what the play is about."), 52 ("This shows what a service can be rendered to a dramatist and his readers by a sympathetic commentator: the commentator can put in, at his leisure, what the dramatist in his haste left out.").

39. Price, "The Authorship of 'Titus Andronicus,'" pp. 63–64.

40.   *The Complete Pelican Shakespeare*, p. 825.

41.   *The Works of Shakespeare... Titus Andronicus*, H. Bellyse Baildon, ed. (Indianapolis: Bobbs-Merrill Co., 190–), pp. xxxiii–xxxiv.

42.   *Ibid.*, p. xxxiii.

43.   *Ibid.*, p. 18.

44.   Price, "The Authorship of 'Titus Andronicus,'" pp. 58–59.

45.   *Arden Edition... Titus Andronicus*, p. xxxix. "Technically [Act I of *Titus*] is one of the finest first acts that Shakespeare wrote. It is full of incident and yet it is never confused. It announces the subject boldly and unmistakably." Price, "The Authorship of 'Titus Andronicus,'" p. 72.

46.   *Arden Edition... Titus Andronicus*, p. xl.

47.   *Ibid.*, p. xlii. This instructive editor is J.C. Maxwell.

48.   See Plato, *Republic* 393C sq. See, also, Plato, *Timaeus* 17B sq. See, as well, Aristotle, *Poetics,* chap. 17. It is well to keep the effects of such "summarizing" in mind, lest the "artistic" be lost sight of in the commentaries upon various works in this book. See notes 3 and 29, above, notes 145 (end) and 202, below.

49.   *Complete Works of William Shakespeare*, W.A. Wright, ed. (Philadelphia: Blakiston Co., 1944), pp. 181–82. Shakespeare, when he wrote *Titus Andronicus,* was about the age Lincoln was when he delivered his prophetic Lyceum Speech. See, on the Lyceum Speech, Harry V. Jaffa, *Crisis of the House Divided* (Garden City: Doubleday & Co., 1959), p. 181. See, also, O'Flaherty, ed., *Hindu Myths*, p. 139.
       That which Dostoevsky said of Pushkin we can say of Shakespeare:

       I repeat, there are no fixed divisions between the periods [of his career]. Some of the works of even the third period might have been written at the very beginning of the poet's artistic activity, for Pushkin was always a complete whole, as it were a perfect organism carrying within itself at once every one of its principles, not receiving them from beyond. The beyond only awakened in him that which was already in the depths of his soul.

Fyodor Dostoevsky, *The Dream of a Queer Fellow and The Pushkin Speech* (London: George Allen & Unwin, 1961), pp. 54–55. See note 202, below.

50. Price, "The Authorship of 'Titus Andronicus,'" p. 75.

51. Baildon, ed., *The Works of Shakespeare... Titus Andronicus,* p. 70.

52. *Ibid.,* p. 9. See note 69, below.

53. *Ibid.,* p. 103. See the text at note 73, below.

54. *Ibid.,* p. 85.

55. *Ibid.,* p. 28.

56. And does only Julius Caesar realize, in some significant measure, this aspiration? See Chapter V, Section iv, item 5, below. See, also, note 3, above (on what it is to be godlike). It is remarkable how many times, and in what ways, Coriolanus is associated with the divine. See note 79, below.

Consider how still another artist-founder saw Rome: "The tradition has it that Virgil, when he had finished (or almost finished) writing the *Aeneid,* wanted to burn all he had written. [The emperor] himself is said to have prevented this from happening. We may surmise that Virgil knew this much about his myth: its truth depended on the actual destiny of Rome. And, prophet that he was, he forsaw the future *pax romana,* the future Roman peace, more often than not immersed in a sea of corruption, of monstrous crimes and dismal anarchy...." Jacob Klein, "The Myth of Virgil's *Aeneid,*" 2 *Interpretation* 10, 20 (Summer 1971).

57. See, e.g., *Arden Edition... Titus Andronicus,* p. 120. See, also, *Steevens Edition, The Plays of Shakespeare* (London: T. Longman, 1793), XIII, 365; Cicero, *Republic,* II, xxxvii, 63.

58. Demetrius and Chiron, when they contend for possession of Lavinia, also have to consider the problem of the claims of the elder brother. *Titus,* II, i, 26f. Lavinia's revelation (*ibid.,* IV, i, 78) suggests that the younger brother violated her first, just as Bassianus had prevailed over Saturninus for her hand in marriage?

59. Baildon, ed., *The Works of Shakespeare... Titus Andronicus,* pp. 3–4.

60.   *Steevens Edition,* XIII, 265. Consider, also, the comment on Emilia's
        inopportune honesty in Chapter I, Part One, Section iv, above. Does
        Truth sometimes have to resort to deception in order to secure justice
        against Falsehood? See Lichtheim, ed., *Ancient Egyptian Literature,*
        II, 212; Plato, *Republic* 414B sq. See, also, Larry Arnhart, *Aristotle on
        Political Reasoning: A Commentary on the "Rhetoric"* (DeKalb: Nor-
        thern Illinois University Press, 1981), pp. 10-11, 19-21, 26-27, 32-34,
        68-69, 81-84, 168, 183f; Thomas G. West, "The Two Truths of
        Troilus and Cresida," in Alvis and West, eds., *Shakespeare as Political
        Thinker,* p. 136. See, as well, note 27, above.

61.   *The Complete Pelican Shakespeare,* p. 824.

62.   Price, "The Authorship of 'Titus Andronicus,'" p. 68.

63.   See Shakespeare, *Sonnet 94.* See, also, Xenophon, *Memorabilia,* IV, i. 3-4;
        Chapter XII, Section iii, below. See, as well, Aristotle, *Nicomachean
        Ethics* 1150al sq., 1160bl sq.; Strauss, *Thoughts on Machiavelli,* p. 254.
              Thus, Sherlock Holmes could observe, in A. Conan Doyle's *Adven-
        ture of the Speckled Band,* "Ah, me! it's a wicked world, and when a
        clever man turns his brains to crime it is the worst of all."; "When a
        doctor does go wrong, he is the first of criminals. He has nerve and he
        has knowledge." *Corruptio optimi, pessima.* Alfred North Whitehead,
        The Aims of Education and Other Essays, p. 2. See, also, Plato, *Repub-
        lic* 567D; Aristotle, *Nicomachean Ethics* 1150a 1-7, 1160b 9.

64.   Thus, we see here still another reminder of the danger of prolonging
        military commands. See Machiavelli, *Discourses,* III, xxiv; Strauss,
        Thoughts on Machiavelli, p. 246. See, also, Cicero, *De Officiis,* II, viii.
        See, as well, note 56, above, note 285, below.

65.   *The Complete Pelican Shakespeare,* p. 825.

66.   Bloom, *Shakespeare's Politics,* p. 68. "But to the fate of [Coriolanus] —
        in whom character is emphasized at the expense of personality, and
        whose all but single-minded devotion to Roman virtue recalls Titus
        Andronicus uncomfortably to mind—it is easy to be indifferent." T.H.
        Howard-Hill, Book Review, 30 *Shakespeare Quarterly* 424 (Summer
        1979). Cf. note 56, above.

67.   See Price, "The Authorship of 'Titus Andronicus,'" p. 78 (on *Titus
        Andronicus,* I, i, 18-45).

68.   Price, "The Authorship of 'Titus Andronicus,'" p. 71.

69.   *Ibid.,* p. 73. Consider, also, what is said by Christian of Moses, that "he spareth none, neither knoweth he how to show mercy to those that transgress the law." John Bunyan, *The Pilgrim's Progress* (Baltimore: Penguin Books, 1965), p. 106. Cf. *Letters of Maimonides,* Leon D. Stitskin, ed. (New Haven: Yeshiva University Press, 1977), p. 34f. See the text at note 52, above.

70.   *A New Variorum Edition of Shakespeare: The Poems,* H.E. Rollins, ed. (Philadelphia: J.P. Lippincott Co., 1938), p. 415.

71.   *Ibid.,* p. 521.

72.   Oscar James Campbell, ed., *The Sonnets, Songs & Poems of Shakespeare* (New York: Schocken Books, 1967), p. 277. See Livy, *History of Rome,* I, 57–60. Cf. Seneca, *Phaedra* 860 sq., 1177 sq.

73.   *A New Variorum Edition of Shakespeare: The Poems,* p. 488. See the text at note 53, above. See, on Lucrece's marriage, my comments on Lady Macduff, Chapter I, Part One, Section iv, item 4, above.

74.   Was there the possibility of offspring to be considered from this forced union? Thus, Tarquin refers to a "nameless bastardy." (*Lucrece* 522) See, on the "ultimate threat" made to her, *Lucrece* 512f, 667f, 1632f. In any event, the Republic can be said to have been produced by this forced union (with Junius Brutus as midwife for the delivery of its progeny).

75.   It is Brutus who makes a civic issue out of the affront to a family. *Lucrece* 1807f. See the text at note 82, below. See, also, Machiavelli, *Discourses,* III, ii–iii, xlviii; Strauss, *Thoughts on Machiavelli,* pp. 168, 275, 287; Harvey C. Mansfield, Jr., *Machiavelli's New Modes and Orders* (Ithaca: Cornell University Press, 1979), p. 305f.
       See, for comments on the story of Tarquin and Lucrece, Cicero, *Republic,* I, xxxvii, xl–xlii, II, xxiv sq., xxvi (on the banishment of Collatine); Machiavelli, *Discourses,* III, ii, v, xxvi; Strauss, *Thoughts on Machiavelli,* pp. 320, 343; Mansfield, *Machiavelli's New Modes and Orders,* pp. 391–92. (See, on the "historical" Malcolm, note 9, above.) See, on Lucrece's suicide, Augustine, *The City of God,* I, 19 sq.

76.   See Anastaplo, "The Declaration of Independence," pp. 404–5; Jaffa, *The Conditions of Freedom,* p. 153.

Cf. Hans Küng, *Freud and the Problem of God* (New Haven: Yale University Press, 1979), pp. 95–96:

> Freud rightly objects to the widespread attitude or philosophy of "as if," which means that the groundlessness, even the absurdity, of religious doctrines is perhaps appreciated, "but for a variety of practical reasons we have to behave 'as if' we believed in these fictions." We practice a religious conformism or opportunism mainly because of the incomparable importance of religion "for the maintenance of human society." To a person not corrupted by such a philosophy religion would seem to be disposed of as soon as its absurdity and irrationality have been recognized....

But see Tocqueville, *Democracy in America,* pp. 443–45, 448; Strauss, *Natural Right and History,* p. 169; Kitto, *Sophocles—Dramatist and Philosopher,* pp. 21f, 34, 47f; Richard Kennington, "Descartes and Mastery of Nature," in S.F. Spicker, ed., *Organism, Medicine, and Metaphysics* (Dordrecht: D. Reidel, 1978), pp. 201, 221–22. See, also, the text at note 105, below; Appendix C, Sections x and xii, below; notes 15 (end) and 24, above, notes 84, 98, 103, 104, 105, 108, and 145, below. See, as well, Epilogue, Section ii (end), below.

See, on standing by the religion one happens to be born into, Pierre Bayle, "Paul Weidnerus," *Historical and Critical Dictionary;* Etienne Gilson, *The Philosopher and Theology* (New York: Random House, 1962), pp. 136–37, 160–63, 166–67, 168 (on Henri Bergson); the text at note 284, below (on Edmund Husserl). It is reported that for Morris R. Cohen, as for George Santayana, piety was "reverence for the sources of one's origins." Epstein, ed., *Masters,* p. 45. May not similar sentiments be found in Plato, Aristotle and especially Xenophon? But see Appendix E, Section ix, below. Cf. note 202, below.

The uses of "philosophy" in the Küng passage (either by the author or by his translator) suggest that philosophy is not recognized for what it is: this means, among other things, that the community can be undermined by attempts to make all men philosophers. See note 13, above. See, also, Strauss, *Natural Right and History,* p. 143.

I plan, for my next book (*D.V.*), to collect my commentaries on various constitutional documents ranging from Magna Carta to the Emancipation Proclamation. It is likely to be entitled, *American Constitutionalism and the Virtue of Prudence: Documents and Commentary.* (I am also preparing for publication by Swallow Press the most careful translation into English yet made of Plato's *Meno,* working from the draft left by John Gormly.)

My discussion of the religion clauses of the First Amendment has been published in Volume 11 of the *Memphis State University Law*

Review (1981). (In note 154 of that article, "sin of community" should be "sense of community.")

See Benjamin Franklin, *Autobiography* (Indianapolis: Bobbs-Merrill Co., The Liberal Arts Press, 1952), pp. 79–80. See, also, *ibid.*, pp. 7–9, 16, 17, 22, 24, 37, 39, 43, 56–57, 90, 94, 97–98, 104–8, 110–11, 111–15, 120, 147. Cf. *Svetasvatra-Upanishad*, VI, 20: "Only when men shall roll up the sky like a hide, will there be an end of misery, unless God has first been known." See, as well, Plato, *Laws* 888A sq.; *Epinomis* 980C sq.

See note 288, below. See, also, Laurence Berns, "Aristotle on Dramatic Poetry, Music, and Politics: Catharsis in the *Poetics* and the *Politics*"; Anastaplo, "Aristotle on Law and Morality." (Both in *Proceedings*, 1982 Annual Convention, American Political Science Association. Also there is Sarah Thurow's "On *Twelfth Night*." See note 78, below.)

77.   See, on the abundance of classical allusions in *Titus Andronicus,* Price, "The Authorship of 'Titus Andronicus,'" p. 68; *Steevens Edition,* XIII, 257, 373, 376–77.

See, on Machiavelli and the natural life spans of regimes (including religious regimes), Machiavelli, *Discourses,* II, 5; Strauss, *Thoughts on Machiavelli,* pp. 32, 142, 170; Leo Strauss and Joseph Cropsey, eds., *History of Political Philosophy,* 2d ed. (Chicago: Rand McNally, 1972), p. 289; 3 *Political Theory* 396–97, 404 (1975) (item 15, note 286, below); Harry V. Jaffa, "The Unity of Tragedy, Comedy, and History," in Alvis and West, eds., *Shakespeare as Political Thinker,* pp. 302–303. Cf. Cicero, *Republic*, III, xxiii. See note 251, below.

78.   See, for a quite useful discussion of the poem and of the history upon which it draws, Platt, *Rome and Romans According to Shakespeare.* On Aeneas at Troy, see A.W.H. Adkins, "Art, Beliefs, and Values in the Later Books of the *Iliad*," 70 *Classical Philology* 239 (1975).

See, on the importance the initial letter of a name can have, Shakespeare, *Richard III,* I, i, 32–61.

The possible significance of all the letters in a name may be seen in Shakespeare's *Twelfth Night.* (This title alerts us to the significance of the Epiphany.) Two of the three principal women have names which use the same letters (with "Olivia" somewhat less tightly organized, or disciplined, than "Viola"?). (One of Shakespeare's possible sources had, instead, Olivia and Violetta. *The Complete Pelican Shakespeare,* p. 305.) Olivia is, in the play, a pursuing woman of well-established position; Viola, a pursued "man" as well as a desiring woman of uncertain means (I, ii, 41–44). Are elements of both genders needed for the complete

human being, at least with respect to the love matters that the wills
here are subordinated to? (V, i, 255) The better marriages provide for
useful blendings of male and female elements into "one flesh." See note
235, below. See, also, Mrs. Thurow's paper, note 76, above.

Malvolio's name, too, uses all the letters of the women's names, and
only one more letter besides, M—with which the *mal* is formed (to make
up the name, "ill-will," another form of that self-assertion indicated in
the subtitle of the play, *What You Will*). He is a baser (or comic) version
of the women with respect to love matters. (Perhaps the Duke is also,
in that he is in love with love: his will is directed, from the outset, toward love for its own sake.) But to suggest that Malviolio is baser is not
to deny his merits: thus, he nobly insists on his sanity in most trying
circumstances. (IV, ii, 20f. See note 2, above. Both Olivia and Malvolio
are defective, in different degrees, with respect to pride. I, v, 85–86, 236)

Malvolio does notice that the four cryptic letters in the forged Olivia
epistle are to be found in his name. (II, v, 127–30. We are thus assured
that Shakespeare is indeed noticing the letters used in the names here.
The obscenity Malvolio [inadvertently?] expresses [but is subconsciously
inclined to?] is a further reminder that the letters in names must be
watched. [II, v, 80–83; II, iii, 172] See *The Riverside Shakespeare* [Bos-
ton: Houghton Mifflin Co., 1974], p. 422. Cf. Eric Partridge, *Shakespeare's Bawdy* [New York: E.P. Dutton, 1960], p. 53: "*Twelfth Night*:
the cleanest comedy except *A Midsummer Night's Dream*.") But the
Malvolio letters in the forged epistle are mixed up, in anticipation perhaps of the planned derangement of him that he (because of his considerable self-assurance?) successfully resists. Does Malvolio need something
of the female element to moderate him?

Is the play somehow a return to problems associated with the Garden
of Eden? Is love eagerly sought as a remedy against death? (II, iv, 50f)
Thus, the acute clown (see, e.g., I, v. 24–26, I, v, 52–84, V, i, 359–66, III,
i, 58–66), in the concluding lines of the play, reminds us of the origins
of things: "A great while ago the world begun"—origins which make it
inevitable that rain will fall (no matter how nicely things can be worked
out for the moment?). (V, i, 378f) What *is* the status of Ilyria, the site
of the play? How is it related not only to Eden but to the island where
Prospero foregoes mere revenge and works his healing magic in *The
Tempest*?

The third principal woman in the play, Maria, is referred to as "Eve's
flesh." (I, v, 26) Her name brings to mind the second Eve, the Eve of
redemption. (See I, iii, 49.) Is it not fitting, then, that she should under-
take to humble Malvolio? But she is, despite the promise of her name,
devilish in her wit (II, v, 190): the last we hear from Malvolio is a vow for

revenge. (V, i, 367. See, also, II, iii, 140, V, i, 366.) Is this, in a man of ambition, a "natural" result of disappointed expectations and of reason-denying humiliations based upon a spurious revelation? (Nietzsche would both understand and redirect his passion?)

Maria, of course, gets what she wills, a marriage considerably above her station (cf. I, iii, 97–99, II, iv, 28–29), which *she* can be expected to exploit to the limit. We should not be surprised, therefore, that refer-ences to devils and madness abound in the play. Malvolio, for one, has no problem believing, it seems, that a supposed exorcist can mistake darkness for light. (IV, ii, 31f)

Underlying any consideration of the problem of madness is the ques-tion of the relation of the seeming to the true. (See, e.g., I, ii, 47f, III, iv, 339f.) A sign that the seeming and the true do match up is that names, the outward signs of things, are reliable: Viola is not truly Cesario: for example, she cannot fight as men do. Her brother may emulate another Sebastian in the faith he exhibits in giving himself up completely to Olivia, the lady of Lucrece-like chastity and peace. (See I, v, 52, 199–200, II, v, 86, 98, V, i, 289. Consider the relation indicated between an established faith and Cesarism. See note 235, below.) The lovesick Duke asks for music (I, i, 1f, II, iv, 1f) and, of course, he gets a Viola (see I, iii, 23), having anticipated that musical instrument perhaps in what he had had to say about violets (I, i, 6). (Is the Arion-like Sebastian, too, gifted in music? See I, ii, 15.)

To suggest that names, to say nothing of the letters in names, can be meaningful is to suggest that the whole is susceptible of comprehension. Thus, is it assumed, if things are to work out properly in this play, that there is a reason for, a cause of, everything? (A modern form of this faith is exhibited in Freud's accounting for slips of the tongue and of the pen.) The natural order is thereby affirmed and chance minimized, if not de-nied. In a sense, then, *Twelfth Night,* with its reduction even of names to their elements, may be the Shakespearean equivalent of Plato's *Cratylus.* (Consider, also, Lucretius on the significance of letters as elements. Consider, as well, Plato, *Thaeatetus* 202 sq.)

One must proceed beyond these preliminary observations about the play, of course, if one is to understand what Shakespeare *is* indicating here about mankind and its prospects, as well as about the spiritual his-tory of the West (even as he seems to give audiences what *they* will in the form of a very popular play). Thus, for example, are the unholy trio of the Clown, Sir Toby, and Sir Andrew comic versions, respectively, of the reasoning, appetitive and spirited parts of the soul? See note 30, above. See, also, note 76, above, the text at note 91, below.

See, on the male and female in the complete human soul, Plato *Symposium* 189C sq.; *Svetasvatara-Upanishad*, V, 10; *Genesis* 2: 18-24, 3: 1-6. See, also, the text at note 168, below, notes 109, 215 and 230, below. Consider, on the comprehensiveness of the soul, Aristotle, *De Anima* 431b19: "[T]he soul is in a way all existing things, for existing things are either sensible or knowable..." Consider, as well, Appendix G, Section v, below (on the "Kantian" hypothesis); Plato, *Theaetetus* 152A sq., 160B sq., 165E sq., 170A sq., 178B sq.

It has been noticed that "to a conscientious scholar" certain arguments "are really distasteful for the very sake of their ingenuity." *The Upanishads,* F. Max Muller, ed. (New York: Dover Publications, n.d.), II, xxxiii. Cf., on the playfulness of Johann Sebastian Bach with respect to the letters of *his* name, Hofstadter, *Gödel, Escher, Bach,* pp. 79-81, 719. Cf., also, Anastaplo, *The Constitutionalist,* p. 581; note 13, above (on a 1980 reviewer who plays Malvolio to my Clown).

I have found useful the notions with respect to Shakespeare derived from conversations I have had with Christopher A. Colmo, a Rosary College colleague, and from seminars I have had with teachers in the University of Chicago Laboratory Schools.

79. See *ibid.,* p. 17f. See, also Machiavelli, *Discourses,* III, xxvi ("How states are ruined on account of women"). See, as well, Cicero, *Republic,* II, vii. See, for another opinion as to what Junius Brutus would have settled for, Mansfield, *Machiavelli's New Modes and Orders,* p. 316.

Titus Andronicus comes to recognize that the man he chose as emperor has become a tyrant. *Titus,* IV, iii, 19.

The deterioration of Rome "this time around" may be seen in the difference between an early and a late Cornelia. *Titus,* IV, i, 12; IV, ii, 141, 166f. See, on the future of Rome, note 82, below (the quotation from the *Christian Science Monitor* review).

A full understanding of Junius Brutus should take into account Shakespeare's *Coriolanus,* where he (as a tribune) appears rather devious, if not even cowardly. (This is some twenty years after the expulsion of Tarquin.) But the Republic *is* preserved from the consequences of the unmanageable passions of a noble warrior (with royal, if not even divine, aspirations?) who cannot bear to see the non-martial people have any share of the power (or of the food) of Rome. See note 24, above. Consider, also, how Junius Brutus is remembered in Shakespeare's *Julius Caesar* (I, ii, 158-161): "O, you and I have heard our fathers say/ There was a Brutus once that would have brooked/ Th' eternal devil to keep his state in Rome/ As easily as a king." See note 56, above.

80. Compare the summary at note 49 in the text, above (where Titus is said to have demanded the sacrifice of Tamora's son). Questions have been raised by scholars about the placement of lines 35–38 in *Titus* I, i.

81. See, on Odysseus in Sophocles' *Ajax,* Epigraph, Chapter XII, below; also, Laurence Berns, "Aristotle's *Poetics,*" in Cropsey, ed., *Ancients and Moderns,* p. 83. See, on Odysseus in Homer's *Iliad,* Prologue, Section ii, above. (Some corrections for Mr. Berns's *Poetics* article may be found in note 27 of his article on *King Lear.* See note 26, above.)

    Also instructive with respect to the *Odyssey* are lectures delivered by Eva T.H. Brann (at St. John's College) and by Amy A. Kass (at the University of Chicago). See, as well, notes 163 and 279, below.

    Does Lucrece sense that the much-buffeted Odysseus came to identify himself with the Trojan women upon the fall of their city? See Homer, *Odyssey,* VIII, 521–31.

82. See note 75, above. See, in Part One of this chapter, the comments on *Macbeth* and *King Lear* (and the cautiousness resorted to by those aware of their vulnerability, such as Malcolm).

    "*Titus* is a political play, and Shakespeare is the most political of all dramatists. His work excited the admiration of statesmen like Gladstone and Bismarck, who both wondered how he managed to penetrate so many secrets of their profession. Shakespeare's political interest shows itself in various ways. He likes to connect his heroes with an action involving the fortunes of the state, he is skillful in tracing the course of political intrigue, and he delights in exposing those kinks of character or intellect which unfit even men of action for political life...." Price, "The Authorship of 'Titus Andronicus,'" pp. 72–73. See note 117, below.

    We should not leave *Titus Andronicus* before noticing that its production proved one of the highlights of the 1980 season at Stratford, Ontario. The following excerpts from reviews bear on various points touched upon in this chapter. (These reviews have been provided me through the courtesy of Elliott Krick, a University of Chicago colleague.)

    > In the historic Peter Brook production of the mid 1950's, in which Laurence Olivier [at the Old Vic] gave one of his most brilliant performances, the scene [of Tamora having her sons served up to her in a pie] was played for its exquisite terror. I will never forget Olivier as he waited breathlessly for Tamora to begin her banquet; it was the diabolical culmination of all the play's insidious intrigues. [*New York Times,* June 14, 1980]

When Jon Jory adapted *Titus Andronicus* for Actors Theatre of Louisville, he created a musical extravaganza that laughed away much of the play's horrors. Stratford does not so glibly condescend to *Titus*. It plays it straight, piling murderous act on murderous act. [*Louisville Courier-Journal,* July 27, 1980]

[Brian] Bedford [in the 1980 Stratford production] deliberately keeps the play's gaudy excesses, its murders, mutilations, violent sexual abuses and cannibalism under steely handed control out of obvious respect for the sensibilities of his audience. The result is a skillfully guided tour *around* the evening's goriest aspects. The alternative would have been to have had one's nose rubbed into them in a needless pursuit of a so-called authenticity. [*Montreal Sunday Express*, June 22, 1980]

Mr. Bedford directed *Titus Andronicus* two years back. This revival features mostly the same cast. He has chosen to take this most violent, bloody, and ghoulish of Shakespearean plays and highlight the motivations for that gore, rather than the gore itself. Even when Titus cuts off his hand and carries off the head of his son, it is discreet, though still grisly. Bedford has pruned here and there—in one or two instances with too much gusto—and he has dropped the original ending entirely to graft on a quotation from the Sibylline oracle predicting the demise of Rome ["Inexorable wrath shall fall on Rome; a time of blood and wretched life shall come."] This device runs counter to Shakespeare. [*Christian Science Monitor,* June 28, 1980]

Although actor [William] Hutt [as Titus] shows clearly how much of King Lear there is in the enraged Roman warrior, the play is still pretty much a mindless revenge drama. The excesses of rape, murder and mutilation are toned down as much as possible. Director Bedford does not mean for us to wallow in gore. He looks for the Shakespeare we know in the play and occasionally finds him. [*Philadelphia Inquirer,* July 6, 1980]

No one regrets a murderous act even as he condemns the homicide of others.... Vengeance follows vengeance until the stage is blighted with corpses—a record 35 by the count of the Polish critic Jay Kott. [*New York Times,* June 14, 1980]

This *Titus Andronicus* is destined to be one of the blockbuster items in the current Stratford season.... The centrepiece remains William Hutt's powerful and impeccably judged characterization of Titus, the doomed general whose rejection of the emperorship

of Rome in favor of the power-mad Saturninus plunges his own
life and the empire into chaos. The role is a terribly treacherous
one. Any actor who plays it walks a tricky tightrope. One slip on
his part, and the proceedings can tilt into unintentional hilarity.
Yet Hutt remains secure, investing the character with a ravaged
grandeur and a consciousness of destiny all the more horrifying
because it is filtered through the maimed sensibility of a madman.
[*Owen Sound Sun Times,* June 13, 1980]

Nor should we leave *Titus Andronicus* before noticing that "the only
known contemporary drawing of a performance of a Shakespeare play
... shows Tamora pleading with Titus for the lives of her sons." Thomas
Marc Parrott, ed., *Shakespeare: Twenty-three Plays and the Sonnets*
(New York: Charles Scribner's Sons, 1953), plate 14. One curious feature of this drawing is that the man standing, with drawn sword, next
to the kneeling sons is evidently a Moor. (Aaron, it should be remembered, says nothing in this opening scene—or during the long first act
of the play).

See, for still another assessment of the significance of Rome for
Shakespeare, John Alvis, "The Coherence of Shakespeare's Roman
Plays," 40 *Modern Language Quarterly* 115 (1979). Consider, also,
Rabindranath Tagore, *Towards Universal Man* (New York: Asia Publish-
ing House, 1961), pp. 130–31:

There is no place in the universal scheme of things for a man of
ambition to rest forever on the peak of triumph, triumph for himself or for his race. That Alexander failed to bring the world under
the banner of Greece only proves the futility of such designs;
Greece's arrogant ambition has no meaning for us today. The
Roman dream of a world-empire was foiled by the barbarians—
and whoever deplores that blow to Rome's imperial pride? Greece
and Rome have laden the golden boat of Time with the ripe harvests of their culture; that they themselves failed to get into the
boat proved no loss, but rather lightened its load.

II. JOHN MILTON (1608-1674)

83.   See Edward S. Le Comte, ed., *A Milton Dictionary* (New York: Philo-
         sophical Library, 1961), p. 308; Kester Svendsen, "Milton's Sonnet on
         the Massacre in Piedmont," 20 *Shakespeare Association Bulletin* 147,
         155 (1945). See, on the influence of Milton's *Paradise Lost,* the text at
         note 158, below, and the text at note 258, below.

84.   *Wall Street Journal,* March 29, 1978, p. 1. This welcome of Mr. Carter
      was extended by the President of Venezuela.
           "Classical philosophy created the idea of the universal state. Modern
      philosophy, which is the secularized form of Christianity, created the
      idea of the universal and homogeneous state." Leo Strauss, *On Tyranny*
      (New York: Free Press of Glencoe, 1962), p. 221. See the text at note
      197, below. See, also, note 76, above, notes 103 and 238, below.
           Edmund Burke says somewhere that the rights of Englishmen offer
      more security than "the rights of man." See, on Burke and natural right,
      Strauss, *Natural Right and History,* p. 294f. Cf. Anastaplo, *The Consti-
      tutionalist,* p. 801. See, also, the text at note 24, above, notes 95 and
      277, below. See, as well, Appendix F, Sections vi and vii, below.

85.   Marjorie H. Nicolson, *John Milton: A Reader's Guide to His Poetry*
      (New York: Farar, Straus and Giroux, 1963), pp. 173–74.

86.   *Ibid.,* p. 174 (using an occasional spelling different from mine). See, for
      a useful technical discussion of the poem, A.S.P. Woodhouse and Doug-
      las Bush, eds., *A Variorum Commentary on the Poems of John Milton*
      (New York: Columbia University Press, 1972), pp. 435–37.

87.   See Douglas Bush, ed., *John Milton: The Minor Poems in English* (New
      York: Macmillan, 1972), p. 332; Woodhouse and Bush, eds., *A Variorum
      Commentary on the Poems of John Milton,* p. 431.

88.   Woodhouse and Bush, eds., *A Variorum Commentary on the Poems of
      John Milton,* pp. 434, 440.

89.   "Shortly before midnight, Maj. Gen. Rafael Eitan gave a final briefing
      to his commanders, and ordered the attack [on the PLO] to start, quot-
      ing a line from the late Chaim Nahman Bialik, Israel's poet-laureate:
      'The devil himself has not devised fitting revenge for the blood of a
      child.' " *Miami Herald,* March 17, 1978, p. 8-A.
           See, in note 3, above, my comment on line 3 of Muir's "The Animals."

90.   One is reminded of the Amish in the United States. See, on "primitive
      Christians," John Henry Cardinal Newman, *Apologia Pro Vita Sua* (New
      York: Modern Library, 1950), pp. 38, 53, 70, 105–6, 120, 126, 129,
      150–51, 205, 214. Cf. *Wisconsin* v. *Yoder,* 406 U.S., at 247 n. 5 (1972).
           Are not the uses of icons in Christianity almost as old as the Faith
      itself? "The Tradition of the Church is expressed not only through
      words, not only through the actions and gestures used in worship, but

also through art—through the line and colour of the Holy Icons. An icon is not simply a religious picture designed to arouse appropriate emotions in the beholder; it is one of the ways whereby God is revealed to man. Through icons the Orthodox Christian receives a vision of the spiritual world. Because the icon is a part of Tradition, the icon painter is not free to adapt or innovate as he pleases; for his work must reflect, not his own aesthetic sentiments, but the mind of the Church. Artistic inspiration is not excluded, but it is exercised within certain prescribed rules. It is important that an icon painter should be a good artist, but it is even more important that he should be a sincere Christian, living within the spirit of Tradition, preparing himself for his work by means of Confession and Holy Communion." Timothy Ware, *The Orthodox Church* (Baltimore: Penguin Books, 1963), p. 214. See note 226, below.

In a sense, an icon is like a proper name—and hence, in its particularity, it is something of a departure from the "truth so pure of old"? In any event, we notice that the only proper names associated with people in Milton's sonnet are given to the oppressors ("the bloody Piemontese," "the Babylonian woe"). The cherished victims are anonymous: they could be any Christians? Is complete matyrdom thus—in that one is nothing *here* but very much *there* (that is, through eternity)?

91.   See, e.g., Sister Candida Lund, "At home in the Church," in John J. Delaney, ed., *Why Catholic?* (Garden City: Doubleday & Co., 1979), pp. 95, 105–6; Anastaplo, *National Law Journal,* June 18, 1979, p. 33, n. 17; *The Constitutionalist,* pp. 508–9, 515; *Human Being and Citizen,* Essay No. 4; Letter, *National Law Journal,* Dec. 3, 1979, p. 14.

Was not the selection of the canon of scriptures subsequently studied by Milton itself dependent upon, if not a part of, the traditions of interpretation provided by some community? See note 95, below; also, the text at note 106, below. See, as well, Appendix C, Section viii, below; Anastaplo, *The Constitutionalist,* pp. 431–32.

See, for the Puritan view of the Roman Church, Bunyan, *The Pilgrim's Progress,* pp. 99–100, 334–35, 377. See, also, note 248, below.

92.   Woodhouse and Bush, eds., *A Variorum Commentary on the Poems of John Milton,* p. 433.

93.   It does seem that some of the Waldensians had, in violation of an earlier treaty (with the Duke of Savoy), come down from the adjacent mountain valley and settled on the plain of Piedmont. This does not justify what happened to them, of course, but it should at least help one understand

how it had all come to happen when it did. See *ibid.,* p. 431f. See, also, Hugh R. Trevor-Roper, *The Crisis of the Seventeenth Century* (New York: Harper & Row, 1967), p. 102f.

94. See John T. Shawcross, ed., *The Complete Poetry of John Milton* (Garden City: Anchor Books, Doubleday & Co., 1971), p. 242, n. 8. See, also, the text at note 87, above, and the text at note 100, below.

See, on the useful discipline provided by numbers, Plato, *Epinomis* 978A–B; Anastaplo, *The Constitutionalist,* e.g., chap. 9, n. 12 and n. 39; *Human Being and Citizen,* p. 268, n. 1; "American Constitutionalism and the Virtue of Prudence," n. 20; Ronald K.L. Collins, Book Review, 50 *Southern California Law Review* 337, 340, n. 17 (1977). See, also, Epilogue, Section ii, below; note 209, below. Consider note 145, below.

See, on the significance of various numbers, Thomas L. Pangle, *The Laws of Plato* (New York: Basic Books, 1980), p. 527, n. 13, p. 528, nn. 12 and 21; Cicero, *On the Commonwealth,* p. 258, n. 25; *Khandogya-Upanishad,* I, 1, 3; Plutarch, *On Isis and Osiris* 354F, 361A, 363A, 367 C–E, 373F sq., 381E sq., 383E sq.; Strauss, *Thoughts on Machiavelli,* pp. 48–49, 279, 284, 286, 313, 324, 332. Friedrich von Schiller, *The Piccolominis,* 609–31; Anastaplo, "Jacob Klein of St. John's College," *Newsletter,* Politics Department, The University of Dallas, Spring 1979, pp. 1–9; Epilogue, below.

Eleven, in the passage cited from the Schiller play, is considered an evil number. Leopold Bloom's son, in Joyce's *Ulysses,* lived only eleven days, and his father's fantasy can turn him into an idealized eleven-year-old. See the text after note 261 and the text at note 262, below; note 275, below. See, also, note 102, below. See, as well, notes 174 and 202, below.

Various studies are available of precisely how Milton marshals his poetic skills in this sonnet. Consider a summary by one commentator: "Thus the technical elements of the poem, alliteration, assonance, metrical variation, cacophony, and euphony support and signalize the statement of the lines and the force of the images, and are organically responsible for the movement of the poem, for the impression of passion and fluid power in the sweep of the lines held in exquisite control. This consummately conscious artistry enables both poet and reader to preserve aesthetic distance. Perception of these effects enriches the poem for the reader; the precise adjustments of sound and sense, of pattern and variation, lends conviction and a sincerity to the thought and persuades us that the poet does control the experience and does communicate it to the reader. Milton, though powerfully moved by the massacre to a powerful language of righteous anger and religious indignation, is not beside himself; he is beside the reader." Kester Svendsen, "Milton's Sonnet on the Massacre in Piedmont," p. 154. See the text at note 189, below.

See, on expressions which are a kind of force in words, *Roth v. United States*, 354 U.S. 476, 514 (1957); Anastaplo, *The Constitutionalist*, p. 520 ("so closely brigaded with illegal action as to be an inseparable part of it").

95.   See, for the Russian academician, 20 *Shakespeare Association Bulletin* 101 (July 1945). Cf. *Testimony: The Memoirs of Dimitri Shostakovich*, Solomon Volkov, ed. (New York: Harper & Row, 1979), pp. 86–87. Cf., also, note 277, below.

The respect for natural right to which I have several times referred presupposes established institutions and sound thought. Such thought is to be found in the humanities, which have to be studied with care (as we have seen in considering this sonnet). A vital respect for the humanities may be the best protection for human rights in the modern world. The humanities appeal to and shape the best in us all. Their discipline is such as to sponsor contests among us in which there are only winners, no losers. See Appendixes B, C, and G, below. See, also, note 285, below. See, as well, Appendix E, below.

See, on natural right, Anastaplo, *Human Being and Citizen*, Essays No. 4 and 6; Book Review, 41 *Review of Politics* 587 (1979); Book Review, *Chicago Sun-Times, Show/Book Week*, June 26, 1977, p. 8; Book Review, *Chicago Sun-Times, Show/Book Week*, August 19, 1979, p. 8; Book Review, *Modern Age*, Winter, 1981, p. 106. See, also, note 20, above, note 145, below. See, on prayer, Plato, *Laws* 688B.

III. JOHN BUNYAN (1628–1688)

96.   Bernard Shaw, *Dramatic Opinions and Essays* (New York: Brentano's 1913), II, 142–43. "[Shakespeare] would have gained from the classics that virtue in which he and all his contemporaries are so woefully deficient, sobriety." Housman, *Selected Prose*, p. 11. Cf. *ibid.*, p. 189. See note 27, above.

97.   Shaw, *Dramatic Opinions and Essays*, II, 143. See note 28, above. John Sparrow said of Bernard Shaw on another occasion, "Shaw stated, with his usual exactness, the opposite of the truth." *Independent Essays* (London: Faber and Faber, 1963), p. 123. See, also, George Steiner, *Language and Silence* (New York: Atheneum, 1974), p. 200.

See, on Falstaff, James Joyce, *Ulysses*, p. 204.

98.   Consider, for instance, an intricate intersection on a busy highway. It
        is obviously better that everyone does, and can be counted on to do,
        that which is ordained (even though the system ordained is faulty) than
        that everyone should do whatever seems best to each of them. But if
        the ordained system is patently foolish, people will not believe it was
        intended, or they will try to amend it unilaterally—in either case at
        great risk both to themselves and to others. Consider, in this connec-
        tion, Cicero, *The Nature of the Gods,* I, ii, 3: "Piety like any other
        virtue cannot long endure in the guise of a mere convention and pre-
        tence." See note 76, above. Cf. note 145, below.

99.   See the opening passages in Aristotle's *Nicomachean Ethics* and *Politics.*
        See, also, Chapter II, Section vii, above. See, as well, note 175 (end),
        below.

100.   One could even say a "hunder'd-fold" worse. See the text at note 94,
        above.

101.   Our own desire for that which is ours inclines us to recognize in others
        what would be a deprivation in us as well. For a man to take (or to keep)
        that which is known to belong to another suggests that something *is*
        wrong, that his will (that is, his desire?) is bad. Such a man has too high
        a regard for his self. See, on the self, Anastaplo, *Human Being and Citi-
        zen,* Essay No. 7. See, also, note 181, below. Cf. note 175 (end), below.

102.   See, on the status of pilgrimage for the Christian, Augustine, *The City
        of God,* X, 7, XII, 21, XV, 1, 5, XVI, 9, 41, XVII, 13. Cf. *ibid.,* XI, 9.
        See, also, Chaucer, *Canterbury Tales* (Baltimore: Penguin Books, 1959),
        e.g., p. 93: "We are pilgrims passing to and fro. Death is the end of every
        worldly sore." See, as well, Langland, *Piers Plowman,* XI, 247 ("for we
        are pilgrims together"), XX, 370–83 (end of the poem); Cotton Mather,
        On Witchcraft (New York: Bell Publishing Co., 1974), pp. 53 ("in this
        which may too reasonably be called the *Devils World*"), 55–56.
             See, on how flexible one's view of time can be, Chapter XI, Section
        iv (end), below. An archaeologist-neighbor reports that the Egyptians
        have a saying, "A 'day' of the government is a year." See, for the trans-
        formation of days into years in Joyce's *Ulysses,* note 94, above.

103.   See, for reaffirmations of the demands upon us of "ordinary prudence,"
        Anastaplo, "The Occasions of Freedom of Speech," 5 *Political Science
        Reviewer* 382–85, 401–2 (1975); "American Constitutionalism and the
        Virtue of Prudence," pp. 138–39. See, also, Strauss, *Natural Right and
        History,* pp. 13–14, 16, 162, 304 ("prudence, the controlling virtue of

all practice"). See, as well, Chapter I, Part One, above; note 112, below; Appendix B, below.

"How can a positive political philosophy emerge from a [Christian] vision of being which does not seem to take the *polis* seriously, for which the end of man is beyond and above the nature of man?" Joseph J. Carpino, Book Review, 8 *Interpretation* 222 (May 1980). See note 84, above. See, also, note 76, above.

See, on the relation of "justice to an adversary" to "prudence to [oneself]", *The Complete Works of Abraham Lincoln* (New Brunswick: Rutgers University Press, 1953), III, 44. See, on justice as "another's good," Aristotle, *Nicomachean Ethics* 1130a 4-5, 1134b 4-6. See, on what holds cities together, *ibid.* 1132b 34, 1155a 22-28, 1159b 25 sq., 1161a 10. See, also, notes 20, 22, above, 175, below.

104.   Also critical here, of course, is Shakespeare's *Measure for Measure.* Bunyan was preceded by many others, as may be seen in the following lines from an eighth century Irish song, *Rob tu mo bhoile, a Comdi cride (Be Thou My Vision)*—the influence of Bunyan can perhaps be seen in the translation of these lines (by Mary Byrne): "Be thou my buckler, my sword for the fight;/ Be thou my dignity, thou my delight,/ Thou my soul's shelter, thou my high tower;/ Raise thou me heavenward, O power of my power./ . . . High King of heaven, when victory is won/ May I reach heaven's joys, O bright heaven's Sun!" *The Harvard University Hymn Book* (Cambridge: Harvard University Press, 1964), p. 208. ("Only four decades ago, H.L. Mencken defined a Puritan as one obsessed by the haunting, haunting fear that someone, somewhere, might be happy." Thomas Werge, Book Review, 36 *Review of Politics* 316 [1974].) See Strauss, *Natural Right and History,* pp. 60–61.

The Philosopher is likely to differ from the Believer in certain critical respects. Philosophy has few adherents, which means (among other things) that it can be more restrained in public (since it is not a popular movement). Also, philosophy is more self-critical, especially with respect to the earthly consequences of its activities: it is more likely to recognize what it, in fact, does. Finally, philosophy does tend to acknowledge, if not depend more upon, the body, and this with a "clear con- 50, 74f, 81–82, 163; *Anastaplo, Human Being and Citizen*, Essays No. 2 and No. 16; note 145 (end), below. See, also, Appendix E, Section viii, below.

Western Christianity is to be distinguished in some respects from Eastern Orthodoxy. There seems to be in Eastern Orthodoxy more concern for the community, a perhaps closer tie between monasticism and the lives of most men (with less emphasis on extended individual pilgrimage [certainly not (and here a Jew would agree) if one has a family]), and a greater regard for the body (as indicated by the greater reliance upon icons [see note 90, above]). See note 110, below. Consider this episode from the account of the life of the Abbess Etheldreda in Bede's *History of the English Church and People* (IV, 19; p. 235 in the Penguin edition):

> It is said that when she was affected by this tumour and pain in her jaw and neck, she welcomed pain of this kind, and used to say: 'I realize very well that I deserve this wearisome disease in my neck, because I remember that when I was a girl, I used to wear the needless burden of jewellery. And I believe that God in His goodness wishes me to endure this pain in my neck so that I may be absolved from the guilt of my needless vanity. So now I wear a burning red tumour on my neck instead of gold and pearls.'

Both Bunyan's Puritan Christian and Yeats's Roman Catholic Joyce (note 248, below) could "feel" with the abbess. Consider, also, as a rebuke to the Mencken spirit, Dr. Johnson's outburst to a tedious clerk: "Leave off tormenting your neighbors about paper and packthread, while we all live together in a world that is bursting with sin and sorrow." Max Byrd, "Johnson's Spiritual Anxiety," 78 *Modern Philology* 368, 370 (1981).

See, on *Measure for Measure*, Harry V. Jaffa, "Chastity as a Political Principle," in Alvis and West, eds., *Shakespeare as Political Thinker*, p. 181; William T. Braithwaite, "Poetry and the Criminal Law: The Idea of Punishment in Shakespeare's *Measure for Measure*," 13 *Loyola University Law Review* (1982).

105.   See Harry V. Jaffa, *Thomism and Aristotelianism—A Study of the Commentary by Thomas Aquinas on the Nicomachean Ethics* (Chicago: University of Chicago Press, 1952). See note 101, above.

Earthly justice is not to be relied upon, the pilgrim believes. One is always vulnerable. There are no truly good men or secure stations, except as provided by (and in?) heaven. All earthly regimes are flimsy, as is any life or career dependent upon them. An essential equality among men is promoted. See note 108, below.

See, on Christianity and civic virtue, Ernest L. Fortin, "St. Augustine," in Strauss and Cropsey, eds., *History of Political Philosophy*, p. 174f. See note 76, above, note 175 (end), below.

106.   Is reason needed to determine whether the commands one *is* following are indeed those of God? Is it usually assumed by the pious that no spe-

cial effort of the reason is needed, or at least available, to determine *that*? Does the community slip back in here? See note 91, above, and the text at note 110, below; also, note 288, below. See, as well, Fortin, Review of Frederick D. Wilhelmsen, *Christianity and Political Philosophy* (Athens: University of Georgia Press, 1978), 41 *Review of Politics* 578 (1979).

Consider how Venice, if not also her father, ratified for Desdemona the pretenses and attractions of Othello. See Chapter I, Section iv, above.

107. Does this attitude linger on, after religious zeal fades, in the insistence that "values" are but matters of opinion, not subject to rational assessment or determination? See Hobbes, *Leviathan,* I, 8: "For the Thoughts are to the Desires, as Scouts, and Spies, to range abroad, and find the way to the things Desired..." See Franklin, *Autobiography,* pp. 35–36 Cf. Appendix A, below. Cf., also, Plato, *Protagoras* 352B–C; Strauss, *Natural Right and History,* p. 35f. Cf., as well, Aristotle, *De Anima* 435b4–26, *Politics* 1252b26–1253a40.

Not even feeble-mindedness is a hindrance to one's salvation, if one has "accepted" (by chance—or, shall we again say, because of Providence?) the correct guide. Cf. note 20, above. See the text at note 162, below.

See note 98, above.

108. Perhaps, in principle, each man's fate is determined independent of what he may do—independent of what he may choose to do. Are not some Christian sects inclined thus to believe? See Bunyan, *The Pilgrim's Progress,* pp. 8, 58, 103, 112, 156, 376. Compare Chapter VI, Sections v–vi, below.

The "natural" state is, for the Christian, a "wilderness." Compare Shakespeare, *Titus Andronicus,* III, i, 54, where Rome is said to have *become* "a wilderness of tigers." See Chapter I, Part Two, Section iv, above.

See, on the problem of the status of equality, Anastaplo, *Human Being and Citizen,* Essay No. 5; "American Constitutionalism and the Virtue of Prudence," n. 64; Book Review, *Modern Age,* Summer 1979, p. 315. See, also, note 76, above.

109. See Chapter IV, Section iii (end), below. The Adam of Milton's *Paradise Lost,* it should be remembered, ate of the forbidden fruit in order to be able to stay with an already fallen Eve. See note 78, above. See, also, Ramban (Nachmanides), *Commentary on the Torah: Genesis* (New York: Shilo Publishing House, 1971), p. 83: "Our Rabbis have called Adam 'ungrateful' for this remark [in *Genesis* 3: 12]. By this they

mean to explain that the sense of his answer to God was: 'Thou caused me this stumbling for Thou gavest me a woman as a help, and she counseled me to do evil.'"

110.   Even the hermit in the desert takes with him the considerable legacy provided him by civilization. See Anastaplo, *Human Being and Citizen*, Essay No. 16, sec. i; note 106, above. Consider, also, what has been happening to the Mount Athos monasteries (and consequently to the monks and hermits dependent upon them) as their sources for wealth and for recruits have been reduced since the 1920s. See Ware, *The Orthodox Church*, e.g., pp. 140–43.

111.   See Anastaplo, *The Constitutionalist*, p. 658. (It is this passage which was intended to be cited by the reference to chap. 8, n. 107, *ibid.*, p. 794. See note 13, above.) See, also, Mark Twain, *The Adventures of Huckleberry Finn* (New York: Chandler Publishing Co., 1962), p. 137.

112.   I am somehow reminded, by the first part of *The Pilgrim's Progress*, of Shakespeare's Coriolanus—and of the limits of *his* self-assertive pilgrimage. Is there not anticipated here a view of the "self" which is seen in people as diverse (in appearance) as Immanuel Kant and our contemporary existentialists? See note 101, above, note 175, below.

      I am reminded also of the Outcast in *Moby Dick*. See notes 179 and 182, below.

      See, for the reservations some have about prudence, Anastaplo, "American Constitutionalism and the Virtue of Prudence," p. 139; also, the text at note 27, above, Appendix B, below. See, as well, notes 27 and 103, above, and Chapter XI, Section iv (beginning), below.

      See note 145, below.

IV. JANE AUSTEN (1775-1817)

113.   Joseph Conrad, *Heart of Darkness* (New York: New American Library, 1960), pp. 94–95.

114.   Sigmund Freud, *Moses and Monotheism* (New York: Vintage Books, 1939), pp. 66–67.

115.   *Ibid.*, p. 67.

116.   The four novels I draw upon in this chapter are *Sense and Sensibility, Pride and Prejudice, Mansfield Park,* and *Emma.* If there are acts of

violence in these stories, they are not memorable. See, as a civilized substitute for violence, the memorable encounter between Elizabeth Bennett and Lady Catherine in Chapter 56 of *Pride and Prejudice.*

The student of Jane Austen should find of interest Eva Brann, "The Perfections of Jane Austen," *The College,* April 1975, p. 1; Maurine Stein, *Reality Perception and Self Knowledge in Jane Austen: A Study of the Six Novels* (University of Chicago Ph.D. dissertation, 1968); Stuart Tave, *Some Words of Jane Austen* (Chicago: University of Chicago Press, 1973); the introductions by Tony Tanner to the Penguin editions of the novels.

117.   See the text at note 109, above. Compare the *Odyssey,* about the authorship of which an argument *is* possible. See Samuel Butler, *The Authoress of the Odyssey* (Chicago: University of Chicago Press, 1967). See, as well, notes 141 and 274, below.

Although these stories are written from a woman's point of view, it is said that Disraeli read *Pride and Prejudice* seventeen times. See note 82, above.

See, on lyric poetry and the woman's point of view, Anastaplo, "Lyric Poetry and Political Philosophy: Some Glimpses of the Beautiful Sappho," *Proceedings,* 1980 Annual Convention, American Political Science Association.

118.   Cf. note 121, below. She *does* record letters written by one man to another, a kind of conversation between men alone. See *The Complete Novels of Jane Austen,* e.g., pp. 268, 407, 411, 449, 462. But she can witness *these,* that is, read them. Of course, she could have been *told* of what men say to one another—but such reports are less reliable, coming from men, than are the letters to be read. Do her interests and approach require the most intimate acquaintance with her subject? Is eighteenth century courtship (which Austen reported, but evidently did not experience personally) more easily observed by outsiders than is twentieth century courtship?

119.   This proposition is repeatedly examined in the works of Plato and Aristotle. See *The Complete Novels of Jane Austen,* pp. 523–24: "...Julia, whose happy star no longer prevailed, was obliged to keep by the side of Mrs. Rushworth, and restrain her impatient feet to that lady's slow pace... The politeness which she had been brought up to practise as a duty made it impossible for her to escape; while the want of that higher species of self-command, that just consideration of others, that knowledge of her own heart, that principle of right, which had not formed

any essential part of her education, made her miserable under it." See, also, *ibid.*, pp. 18, 31, 33, 51, 119, 155-57. See, on proper and defective training, *ibid.*, pp. 257, 356-57, 369-70, 372-73, 399, 409, 463, 632-33, 682 (cf. p. 634), 753, 851. Cf. the text at note 232, below.

120.   See, *ibid.,* pp. 544f, 552f, 560f, 569f, 581-82, 605, 687, 752. See, also, Vladimir Nabokov, *Lectures on Literature* (New York: Harcourt Brace Jovanovich, 1980), pp. 28-38. Cf. note 17, above. See, on the use of forms, *ibid.,* pp. 702, 706. See, also, Aristotle, *Poetics,* e.g., chap. 26. See, as well, Appendix F, below.

121.   One might even wonder whether indications of the vulnerability of this system are not visible in the attraction an Emma (who is not without serious flaws) is for so sober a product of the regime as George Knightley. (Emma *is* attractive, of course, but then so is Emma Bovary. See Anastaplo, *Human Being and Citizen,* p. 297, n. 20: compare what *she* drank at the end.)

One might even... Austen said, on commencing *Emma,* "I am going to take a heroine whom no one but myself will much like!" Austen, *Emma* (London: Dent; Everyman's Library, 1976), p. ix. Is the similarity such between Austen and Knightley (who, like Austen, *does* like Emma) that she can know *his* private thoughts? See *The Complete Novels of Jane Austen,* pp. 972, 1027-28. Cf. the text at note 118, above.

See Plato, *Republic* 549C sq., on what becomes of a well-ordered regime when husband and wife happen to be of different inclinations. See, also, note 164, below.

122.   Our toleration of television and what it is doing to us, for example, is indicative of a loss of confidence in our right and ability to govern ourselves as a people. See, for an argument for the abolition of broadcast television in this country, Anastaplo, "Self-Government and the Mass Media." See notes 6 and 7, above. See, also, Appendixes A and F, below.

123.   Consider how a respectable lady responds to "a matrimonial fracas," which finds a married woman running off with an unmarried friend of her husband: "Fanny seemed to herself never to have been shocked before. There was no possibility of rest. The evening passed without a pause of misery, the night was totally sleepless. She passed only from feelings of sickness to shudderings of horror; and from hot fits of fever to cold. The event was so shocking that there were moments even when her heart revolted from it as impossible; when she thought it could not be. A woman married only six months ago; a man professing himself

devoted, even *engaged* to another; that other her near relation; the whole family, both families connected as they were by tie upon tie; all friends, all intimate together! It was too horrible a confusion of guilt, too gross a complication of evil, for human nature, not in a state of utter barbarism, to be capable of! Yet her judgment told her it was so." *The Complete Novels of Jane Austen,* pp. 738–39. Cf. note 198, below.

Consider, on the shifts in marriage arrangements and their effect upon the "fairly steady framework provided by the community," Mary Ann Glendon, "Modern Marriage Law and Its Underlying Assumptions: The New Marriage and the New Property," 13 *Family Law Quarterly* 441, 447 (1980):

> Many controversial changes in marriage law reflect the fact that, to varying degrees in different places, family law, employment law and social welfare law all are incorporating a new set of assumptions about the respective roles of work (including work-derived benefits such as pensions), government and the family in furnishing the basis of an individual's economic security against illness, old age, incapacity to work, or family disruption by death or divorce. Other changes in marriage law can be usefully analyzed as part of a long historical process through which an individual's wealth and social status is decreasingly determined by his family and increasingly fixed by his occupation, or (in a negative way) by his dependency relationship with government. Marriage law, indeed family law generally, reflects this movement in that legal ties among family members are becoming attenuated and the legal structure of the family is becoming looser. Employment law, on the other hand, reflects the increased importance of the job, in that the web of relationships that secure an individual's job to him (and, more subtly, tie him to his job) is becoming tighter and more highly structured. Similarly, in social welfare law, support claims against government are made a matter of right...

See, also, *ibid.,* pp. 453–54. Cf. *ibid.,* pp. 457–60. (Similar observations have been made to me by John V. Long, a member of the Washington, D.C., bar, who combines in a highly unusual and instructive way a family law practice with a labor law practice.) Cf., also, Nabokov, *Lectures on Literature,* p. 12n.

Critical to the ability of Sherlock Holmes to be as effective as he is may be the "fairly steady framework" within which he works (without which he could not notice the anomalies he does). This bears as well upon the continuing appeal of the Sherlock Holmes stories: they seem to depict well a remarkably civilized (and hence stable) society.

124.   See Plato, *Republic* 329B sq., 620C–D. See, also, the text at note 5, above.

A narrator observes that "one's happiness must in some measure be always at the mercy of chance." *The Complete Novels of Jane Austen*, p. 148. (See, also, *ibid.*, pp. 754, 990–91.) This is partly because things are not always what they seem. See *ibid.*, 276, 279, 282, 283, 286–87, 318, 355, 366 ("There certainly was some mismanagement in the education of those two young men. One has got all the goodness, and the other all the appearance of it."). See, as well, note 171 (beginning), Plato, *Critias* 112E; note 145 (end), below.

Consider the implications of the observation that in the United States, "love always leads by a direct and easy road to marriage." Tocqueville, *Democracy in America*, p. 493. See note 17, above.

125.   See Epilogue, Section viii, below.

126.   Is she reticent about death for the same reason she does not presume to describe conversations between males? See note 118, above.

See, for some of the oaths and prayers in Austen's work, *The Complete Novels of Jane Austen*, pp. 54, 104, 149, 158, 167, 189, 192, 194, 277, 278, 296, 312, 331, 386, 420, 446, 510, 546, 651, 664, 703, 728, 738, 740, 748, 750, 842, 1004, 1015, 1024, 1026, 1052, 1115. See, for some references to the place of religion in the community, *ibid.*, pp. 61, 266, 272–73, 295, 756.

127.   See Plato, *Apology* (conclusion), *Republic* 386A sq. The city, if its concerns and its sanctions are to be taken "seriously," must regard death quite differently from the way Socrates does. See, also, Anastaplo, *Human Being and Citizen*, Essay No. 17; note 18, above, notes 145 and 175, below.

Nikos Kazantzakis says somewhere in his *Odyssey*, "Death is the salt which gives to life its sting." Deaths in the Austen novels are apt to be events of convenience. (This tends to distinguish comedies from tragedies? Is not this one implication of my discussion of prudence and mortality in Shakespeare's tragedies [Chapter I, Part One, above]? See the text at note 129, below.)

128.   See Epilogue, Section viii, below. Rather, one should do what one can to secure, in life itself, "the happiest, wisest, and most reasonable end!" *The Complete Novels of Jane Austen*, p. 439.

129.   *Horace Walpole's Correspondence with Sir Horace Mann*, W.S. Lewis

et al., eds. (New Haven: Yale University Press, 1967), VII, 387 (March 5, 1772). Walpole continues, "This is the quintessence of all I have learnt in fifty years!" See, also, *ibid.*, pp. 396–97. See, as well, notes 30 and 127 and Chapter X, Section v, Epilogue, Section ii (end), above; and note 222, below.

Consider Hegel's observation, "To him who looks upon the world rationally, the world in its turn presents a rational aspect." *The Philosophy of History*, p. 11. See, also, *ibid.*, p. 338 (where he can refer to certain circumstances as "a most repulsive and consequently a most uninteresting picture").

See, on the inherent political tendencies of tragedy and comedy, Laurence Berns, "Transcendence and Equivocation," in Alvis and West, eds., *Shakespeare as Political Thinker*, pp. 47–49. (This essay includes illuminating comments on *Macbeth, Hamlet, Richard II, The Tempest,* and *Measure for Measure.*)

See, on combining levity and gravity, Strauss, *Thoughts on Machiavelli*, pp. 40, 285, 289–90, 292, 294–295; Strauss and Cropsey, *History of Political Philosophy*, p. 290. See also, note 285, below. See, as well, note 227, below. (An exquisite blend of levity and gravity may be found in *Marbury* v. *Madison*, 1 Cranch 137 [1803]. Consider, also, the work of Jacob Klein. See Anastaplo, "Jacob Klein of St. John's College," which includes my assessment of the work of Robert Maynard Hutchins.)

V. MARY WOLLSTONECRAFT SHELLEY (1797–1851)

130.   Christopher Small, *Mary Shelley's Frankenstein: Tracing the Myth* (Pittsburgh: University of Pittsburgh Press, 1973), p. 20. See, for a much longer summary, *ibid.*, pp. 37–40. See, also, the text at note 142, below.

    "We have noted before that in democracies the springs of poetry are fine but few. They are soon exhausted. Finding no stuff for the ideal in what is real and true, poets, abandoning truth and reality, create monsters." Tocqueville, *Democracy in America*, p. 489. "The writers of our time [such as Byron] ... have not sought to record the actions of an individual, but by exaggeration to illuminate certain dark corners of the human heart. Such are the poems of democracy." *Ibid.*, p. 487. Cf. the text at note 113, above, and note 147, below.

131.   W. H. Lyles, ed., *Mary Shelley: An Annotated Bibliography* (New York: Garland Publishing Inc., 1975), p. 170.

132.   *Ibid.,* p. 97.

133.   *Ibid.,* p. 142. See, also, note 29, above; Chapter XII, Section i, below.
This "tingling" was evident from the beginning, as is reflected in the
complaint that "Jane Austen was being unduly neglected in favor of
more lurid novelists like Mrs. Shelley." *Ibid.,* p. 64. That which is
appealed to by such novelists may be seen as well in ghost stories,
which depend upon a (natural?) grasp of the soul by listeners. That is,
the soul is there recognized by the gifted storyteller in a way that is
superior to the way of modern psychologists. See Anastaplo, *The Constitutionalist,* p. 595. See, also, notes 170 and 246, below. Cf. note 10,
above.

134.   House of Lords, Great Britain, May 16, 1824. *Ibid.,* p. 122. Thus, A.
Conan Doyle was to regard his Sherlock Holmes character as his own
"Frankenstein's monster," whom he tried to kill off. Doyle, *The Hound
of the Baskervilles* (New York: Schocken Books, 1975), p. x. See, also,
Lyles, ed., *Bibliography,* p. 121. See, for recent uses of "Frankenstein"
in public discourse with respect to gene-splicing developments, *Chicago
Tribune,* June 23, 1980, sec. 4, p. 3 (cartoon); *Wall Street Journal,*
June 24, 1980, p. 1, col. 1.
        See, on Sherlock Holmes's continued "life," *Wall Street Journal,*
August 25, 1980, pp. 1, 8.

135.   Is it not likely that this *was* a dream by Mary Shelley, even though
she did not realize she had dozed off? See the epigraph to Chapter
IX, below.
        Consider what Nietzsche says in *The Birth of Tragedy,* sec. 17, about
the sense of primordial being which is at the core of art. See, also,
Chapter XII, below. See, as well, note 163, below.

136.   See Lyles, ed., *Bibliography,* p. 75.

137.   See Noel B. Gerson, *Daughter of Earth and Water: A Biography of
Mary Wollstonecraft Shelley* (New York: William Morrow & Co., 1973),
p. 76. Cf. the text at note 149, below.
        See, on the disturbing effect even a forgotten dream can have,
Bede, *History of the English Church and People,* I, 27. Have we not
all had chance stimuli during the day move us to recall dreams of the
previous night that we had not been conscious of since awaking? If
so, are there not likely to be many other dreams, of perhaps consider-

able hidden influence upon us, that are not thus accidentally stimulated into recollection?

138.   Of course, talent and education (or training) are also needed. Indeed, the lack of serious education can severely confine an artist today, making him depend too much on chance passions and on intellectual fashions, not enough on disciplined thought. This has been an obstacle that Harry Mark Petrakis, the contemporary Greek-American novelist, has had to hurdle. See, also, note 279, below. Cf. Chapter XIII, Part Two, Section ix, below, for a suggestion about the relation of thought to inspiration in James Joyce's *Ulysses.* Joyce's problem may be seen in the poetry of T.S. Eliot as well. A proper balance, on the other hand, may be seen in the poetry of Edwin Muir. See, for example, my analysis of his poem, "The Animals," in note 3, above. See, also, note 191, below. See, as well, Sara Prince Anastaplo, review of Petrakis, *The Hour of the Bell* (Garden City, N.Y.: Doubleday & Co., 1976), in *Chicago Magazine,* November 1976, p. 184. "Greek-American fiction has its ultimate expression in the works of Harry Mark Petrakis." Moskos, *Greek Americans,* p. 101. (T.S. Eliot has been compared to Callimachus. John Ferguson, *Callimachus* [Boston: Twayne Publishers, 1980], p. 170. But, for one thing, Callimachus' poems are much more accessible. See, e.g., Appendix E, below [where I quote several times from the Ferguson book]. See, also, Appendix G, below, for the kind of obscurity that T.S. Eliot has legitimated in our time.)

139.   Elizabeth Nitchie, *Mary Shelley, Author of "Frankenstein"* (New Brunswick: Rutgers University Press, 1953), pp. 200, 181.

140.   See, e.g., Shelley, *Frankenstein,* James Rieger, ed. (Indianapolis: Bobbs-Merrill Co., 1974), p. 138: the monster comes upon young William; or, the monster can easily locate (or be located by) Frankenstein on various occasions. See *ibid.,* pp. 202, 208. Unless otherwise indicated, all citations in these notes to *Frankenstein* are to this edition.

141.   The circumstances of the writing of *Frankenstein* are well known, as are the supposed circumstances of the writing of Samuel Coleridge's *Kubla Khan.* This is consistent with the modern inclination to make much of the personality and life of the artist. See Chapters XII and XIII, below. Cf. Joyce, *A Portrait of the Artist,* p. 215; Nabokov, *Lectures on Literature,* p. 97; Anastaplo, *Human Being and Citizen,* p. 293.

See, on "personality" and art, Chapter IX, Section iv (beginning); Chapter XIII, Part Two, Section vi; Appendix C. Section vii (end); Appendix F, Section ii; Appendix G, Section vi, below. See, also, William Ellery Leonard, *The Locomotive-God* (New York: Century Co., 1927). See, as well, notes 164 and 202, below.

142.   Mary Wollstonecraft Shelley, *Frankenstein*, M.K. Joseph, ed. (London: Oxford University Press, 1969), pp. x–xi.

143.   See Lyles, ed., *Bibliography*, p. 88. Frankenstein's prefatory material is divided into four chapters in one edition, three in another. In the edition I am citing to (note 140, above), there are three such chapters. In that edition, Walton's preliminary letters are at pages 9–25; Franken-stein's full account is at pages 27–206; and Walton's concluding letters are at pages 206–21.

144.   See Lyles, ed., *Bibliography*, pp. 47, 53. See, also, Shelley, *Franken-stein*, p. 228 ("any human endeavour to mock the stupendous mechan-ism of the Creator of the world"). See, as well, note 168, below. The subtitle of *Frankenstein* is *The Modern Prometheus.* See Nietzsche, *The Birth of Tragedy*, p. 69f.

145.   Is what Socrates says about death in the *Apology* (see note 127, above) that which nature suggests to the most thoughtful? Do both the city and biblical revelation incline toward opinions about death radically different from Socrates', partly with a view to utility? See Anastaplo, *Human Being and Citizen,* Essays No. 2 and No. 16; *The Constitution-alist,* p. 702, n. 70.

Is not the artist, too, ultimately rooted in nature, whether or not he knows it? Would it be possible otherwise for us to think much about the wonderful things artists make? Does not nature suggest how works of art are to be understood—and to be used? Thus, both intellectual and moral judgments are called for here, as well as that "aesthetic" judgment which makes much of beauty.

The beauty that artists produce can be plausibly related to the "in-trinsic intelligibility" of things. (See note 7 [end], above; also, Epigraph, Appendix C, below.) That is, the artist aims to present (uncover, dis-cover) truth and goodness by showing how they manifest themselves in particulars. He can even be heard to insist that there is something good (and hence pleasurable) in the very act of *offering up* particulars as they are, and not only because this serves man's desire to know.

Does not the artist, as artist, stand for the virtually sacred "individuality" of each thing, including the individuality of each way of presenting things? It has been said of Virginia Woolf by an intimate of hers (*New Yorker,* August 18, 1980, p. 92):

> I never knew what [she] would talk about or what she would say, but I did know what she would not. She would never make the living into the dead, or the concrete into the abstract. . . . She would not generalise, she would always particularise; never flatten the focus, always heighten the three-dimensional depth of detail.

But can particulars be reliably grasped on their own? Ezra Pound argued, "Art does not avoid universals, it strikes at them all the harder in that it strikes through particulars." *Instigations* (New York: Boni and Liveright, 1920), p. 199. Even so, when the emphasis *is* on particulars, at which the artist intently looks when he "strikes," can the "universals" be seen fully for what they are? Are they not radically dependent upon the particulars? Is not all this still another way of saying that the artist, as artist, may not truly know what he is doing—that he cannot be fully a thinker? (See Strauss, *Natural Right and History,* pp. 89–90; Anastaplo, *The Constitutionalist,* pp. 454, 582–84; note 275, below. Consider, also, Plato, *Theaetetus* 151E sq. Consider, as well, the significance of the "ideas" in the Platonic dialogues and of the "self-evident" in Aristotle's discussions of reasoning. See, also, note 288, below.)

Does not the artist, in his dedicated dependence on the particular, necessarily make more of himself and hence of death than does the thinker (who tends to see himself as substantially the same as every other thinker)? Thus, it is the artist, not the thinker (insofar as these can be distinguished), who can speak in this self-centered way:

> I dare not, must not die: I am the sight
> And hearing of the infinite; in me
> Matter fulfils itself; before me none
> Beheld or heard, imagined, thought or felt;
> And though I make the mystery known to men,
> It may be none hereafter shall achieve
> The perfect purpose of eternity;
> It may be that the Universe attains
> Self-knowledge only once; and when I cease
> To see and hear, imagine, think and feel,
> The end may come, and matter, satisfied,
> Devolve once more through wanton change, and tides
> Of slow relapse, suns, systems, galaxies,

Back to ethereal oblivion, pure
Accomplished darkness, might immaculate
Augmenting everlastingly in space.
Me, therefore, it beseems while life endures,
To haunt my palace in the Milky Way,
And into music change the tumult high
That echoes through the vast, unvaulted courts
Interminable, where the nebulae
Evolving constellations, their spindles whirl;
Me it beseems to take my joy in heaven,
Revealing glory by my soul conceived,
And by my soul begotten, in the rapt
Cohabitation with eternity.

John Davidson, *The Testament of John Davidson,* 2112–2137. See Chapter VIII, below. See, also, Appendix E, below. (It seems that this desperate man [1857–1909] died a suicide, although evidently both in good health physically and well-regarded professionally. Did *his* desire to live fully [that is, forever] kill him?) See, as well, Plato, *Laws* 661B–D.) See, for a more congenial form of solipsism, Harold Skimpole's observations in Charles Dickens's *Bleak House* (Boston: Houghton Mifflin, 1956), pp. 192–193 (chapter 18).

The relation of artist to thinker examined in this book is illustrated by the movement, in the naming of the tenth stained-glass window described in Appendix D, from "Creativity" (that window's original name) to "Works of the Mind" (its present name). This movement was furthered by my contribution, to the development of this window, of what the principal designer has called "intellectual elements." Appendix D, Part Two, below.

Compare Nietzsche, *The Birth of Tragedy,* sec. 12 sq. (including his strictures on the dangers of aesthetic Socratism [with its assumption that for something to be beautiful, it must be intelligible], on Socrates' "audacious reasonableness," on Socrates' collaboration with Euripides, on Socrates' disparagement of the instinctual, and on the lack in Socrates of "any natural awe of death"). See note 251, below.

See on the circumstances and capacities of thoughtful men, Anastaplo, *The Constitutionalist,* p. 581, n. 43; *Human Being and Citizen,* pp. 270–71, nn. 19, 20. See, also, *ibid.,* p. 317, n. 4, for the argument that the thoughtful man recognizes that the more thoughtful he is (that is, the better attuned he is to nature?), the less likely he is to be unique (that is, "individual"). See, as well, *ibid.,* pp. 293–94, n. 13. "The quarrel between the ancients and the moderns concerns eventually, and perhaps even from the beginning, the status of 'individuality.'" Strauss, *Natural Right and History,* p. 323. Does not dedication (or, better still, "commitment") to individuality assume that there is no standard rooted in nature in accordance with which one should shape either oneself or one's art? See *ibid.,* p. 121f. See, also, notes 175 and 181, below. (Compare Heinrich Schenker, *Harmony* [Chicago: University of Chicago Press, 1954, (first published in 1906)], for an attempt to show the special way in which even music is dependent upon nature. See, e.g., *ibid.,* pp. 3–4, 20–32, 41–44, 49–54. See, also, note 7, above.)

Current opinions about the relation of nature to art are affected, of course, by the status of nature. A passage from a talk, "Psychiatry and the Law," which I gave at the University of Chicago, October 12, 1979, speaks to the question of the status of nature today:

> Psychiatry (as a modern intellectual movement) has attacked repressive conventions (that is, traditions, regimes, religions, laws, cultures) in the name of nature. Does not *this* reliance of modernity upon nature, in its condemnation of various long-standing conventions, suggest that I am mistaken to argue that psychiatry has been deprived of the influence upon it of nature?
>
> Curiously enough, the modern attack upon convention in the name of nature—an attack not by psychiatry alone—has had the effect of undermining the status of nature among us. It should be helpful to our inquiry about the relation of psychiatry to the law to review (if only briefly) how it is that the *modern* attack upon conventions, in the name of nature, has undermined the status of nature. This review should also tell us something about modernity and hence about that sense of individuality and of community which influences the relations of law and psychiatry among us.
>
> 1. Conventions (including, of course, rather arbitrary, sometimes even silly, conventions) are needed if men are to be properly trained—if they are to be disciplined, if they are to take *some* standards seriously. (Consider what is resorted to in basic training or in boot camp in the military services.) Thus, conventions seem to be necessary if men are to be able to learn, to be able to learn about nature herself, and to be able to control themselves in accordance with nature. This means, among other things, that conventions can be truly seen for what they are, and in the light of nature, only by someone who has been subjected to conventions and who has, in a sense, graduated from or risen above them. But if conventions are repudiated from the outset, the preliminary

training that the community provides becomes deficient and a later (higher) development becomes difficult if not impossible.

2. Related to the first way by which the modern attack on conventions in the name of nature has undermined the status of nature is this one: it is natural for men to have conventions; to rule out conventions completely, therefore, is to subvert, at least to that extent, the promptings of nature.

3. Furthermore, the modern attack on conventions in the name of nature was made on the basis of an inadequate view of nature. Nature was seen by these moderns to be reflected primarily, if not only, in the *desiring* part of us, not in the rational or moral (or self-restraining) part of us. That is, a certain aspect of nature—seen in the persistent, instinctual, physical desires of men—was legitimated in the struggle against certain (restraining) conventions, but conventions which to some extent reflect the sobriety suggested by nature. This struggle can be said to have gone too far, in that it permitted one aspect of nature to overwhelm other aspects of nature in the human soul.

4. Perhaps critical to the development I am trying to account for here may have been the assumption, for some four or five centuries now, that nature is something to be conquered, to be used, to be exploited. If nature is to be conquered and harnessed, she is difficult to regard as a master or a guide. The conquest, or exploitation, of nature is to be done (again) for the sake of our desires, including whatever peculiar desires we happen to have from time to time (which begin to sound in their variability like conventions). Thus, enduring conventions are attacked in the name of nature, a nature which comes to be understood to be in the service of quite changeable desires.

5. A related consideration here is that nature is more apt to be set aside today because she is easily lost sight of. Thus, manifestations of nature in growing things (whether woods and meadows, whether crops and flowers, to say nothing of all kinds of animals) are largely concealed from view for most of us. [I note in passing that the root of the Greek word for *nature* implies becoming, growing, begetting, shooting up, sprouting and also being.] But it goes further than this. Nature is also concealed from view in modern science. Ordinary experience can no longer be relied upon in our effort to understand the nature of things. Not only that, but the explanations constructed by modern science cannot be put in

terms of everyday observations, even as rough approximations or as crude analogies. Only mathematics can be used to "describe" what scientists (especially the physicists) construct—and these descriptions, however ratified they may be in common opinion by astonishing technological marvels, are simply incomprehensible to most of the community. But it is not only in physics that nature is concealed from view. Ideological considerations have also tended to interfere with our ability to see nature. Thus, for example, the modern emphasis upon equality *can* mean that what would once have been considered obvious distinctions, say between the sexes or between the bright and the dull, can be dismissed as conventional. In this way, too, we lose sight of natural differences and hence of nature herself; in this way, too, we extend the domain (in our theories, at least) of the conventional, and hence of chance.

6. Furthermore, art is no longer seen as an imitation of nature. It is seen, rather, as the free expression of the unencumbered soul. Such free expression is seen as natural. Here, too, we can see that it is a less inhibiting aspect of nature which replaces the older understanding. This means, among other things, that art no longer teaches or reassures us about nature.

7. Finally, the decline in the status of nature can also be traced to the opinion that constant change is good, that there is always something even better that lies ahead, that perpetual progress is vital to the happiness of mankind. The emphasis here is on the process, not on the goal (which can be dismissed as "static"). Thus, there is nothing fixed, no perfection set by or evident in nature, by which we are to take our bearings.

Related to this eclipse of nature is what has happened (at least in the public discourse of intellectuals) to the status of the divine. A useful way of talking about nature once was to talk about the divine. Certainly, the divine, too, provided standards, guidance, and goals; it provided a reliable context within which the arts, including the art of medicine, could work. It was once considered natural, even among most of the more skeptical philosophers, that the divine should be publicly respected. Certainly, a general respect for the divine, as manifested in various religious practices and commandments, can very much affect conduct in most people. But such respect is considered, by all too many intellectuals, as repressive, or as an illusion, or as hypocritical, or as a kind of wish-fulfillment, or as mere fearfulness. Be all this at it may, a respect for nature (in the old-fashioned sense) and a respect for religion pretty much go hand in hand today—whatever tension there may be between students of nature and students of the divine from time to time, and whatever ultimate divergence there may always be between them.

(This talk may be published by Scholarly Resources Press in Lawrence Z. Freedman, ed., *Psychiatry and the Law: Reaching for a Consensus*.) See, also, Strauss, *Natural Right and History*, pp. 31–32, 74–76, 81f, 92, 105, 121, 296–97; Jacob Klein, "On the Nature of Nature," *Independent Journal of Philosophy*, vol. 3 (1979); Laurence Berns, "Francis Bacon and the Conquest of Nature," 7 *Interpretation* 1 (January 1978); Pangle, *The Laws of Plato*, p. 513, n. 12, p. 519, n. 17. See, as well, Appendix C and Appendix G, below; note 76, above, notes 215 and 230, below. (The *Index to Legal Periodicals* may be consulted for my article "Mr. Crosskey, the American Constitution, and the Natures of Things.")

The modern opinion, which sees nature as something to be surpassed, may be evident in Tocqueville: "For me poetry is the search for and representation of the ideal. The poet is one who, by omitting parts of what is there, adding some imaginary touches, and puttings things together actual but not found together, *ennobles nature*. It is, therefore, not the poet's function to portray reality but to beautify it and offer the mind some loftier image." *Democracy in America*, p. 483 (italics added). But what is the source of any standard for genuine beautification, if not nature herself? Or consider the approach of C.S. Lewis in his book, *Miracles:* he disparages nature, and yet must he not depend upon her if he is to exercise the poetic talent upon which he ultimately relies for his effectiveness in making his case for the possibility of miracles? Consider, as well, Edmund Burke, *Works* (London: Oxford University Press, World Classics Series, n. d.), I, 160. See note 2, above.

Closer to the classical position, of course, are Sappho's lines, "To have beauty is to have only that, but to have goodness is to be beautiful too." *The Poems of Sappho*, Suzy Q. Groden, trans. (Indianapolis: Library of Liberal Arts, Bobbs-Merrill Co., 1966), p. 29. See, also, Plato, *Symposium* 216C–217A. Compare *The Works of Robert Louis Stevenson* (New York: P.F. Collier & Son, 1912), VI, 224 ("[Certain powers were] none the less natural to me because they were the expression, and bore the stamp, of lower elements in my soul.").

Still another way of considering the question of the relation of nature to art (with which this note opened) is to consider whether artists are truly wise. Leo Strauss (see Epilogue, below) observed, in the course of a 1961 seminar on Plato's *Republic* at the University of Chicago, that he had once read an article by T. S. Eliot on higher education. He then added something like this:

> I must say I found this article very unintelligent and lacking in wisdom, and yet I hear that Eliot is a great poet.... There may be great poets, for all I know, who are not wise people—that is, who can, as though caught by the Muse, say marvelously wise things but who, if they are on their own feet, can't speak.... I am not satisfied that this is universally true and especially that it is true on the highest level.

(Mr. Strauss had referred to an Eliot article in *Measure*. Perhaps he was recalling that issue of the journal, Spring 1951, in which both Mr. Eliot and he had had articles.) In any event, we should never forget, in assessing the wisdom of poets, that on the occasion of Plato's *Symposium*, with its dedication to love, the tragedian and the comic poet were the ones who came closest to keeping up with Socrates. (See Epigraph, Chapter X, below.) Even so, does not the Aristophanes of the *Symposium* make too much of the body? Thus, he can be temporarily incapacitated by hiccoughs. Compare Socrates' all-engrossing "seizure" at the beginning of the dialogue. See notes 12 and 104, above.

See Strauss and Cropsey, *History of Political Philosophy,* pp. 38–40, 168; Anastaplo, *Human Being and Citizen,* pp. 135–38. See, also, Chapter XIII, Part One, Section ii (end), below; Appendix A, below; Epigraph, Appendix C, below. See, as well, notes 3 (end), 16, 28, 29, and 95, above; notes 164 and 280, below.

See, on the relation of truth, beauty, pleasure, and the good, Plato, *Philebus* 64D sq., 65E sq., 67B; *Phaedrus* 254B; *Protagoras* 309C, 315B; *Greater Hippias* 297B, 303A, 304E; *Euthydemus* 300E–301A; *Republic* 478E–480A, 484C–D, 493E–494A, 507A sq. Cf. Plato, *Sophist* 236A. Cf., also, note 124, above, and note 155, below.

See, on the function of criticism, T. S. Eliot, *Selected Essays, 1917–1932* (New York: Harcourt, Brace & Co., 1932), p. 13:

> I do not deny that art may be affirmed to serve ends beyond itself; but art is not required to be aware of these ends, and indeed performs its function, whatever that may be, according to various theories of value, much better by indifference to them. Criticism, on the other hand, must always profess an end in view, which, roughly speaking, appears to be the elucidation of works of art and the correction of taste.

But may not a critic also be inspired at times? See the last paragraph of the Preface, above.

Be all this as it may, it has been noticed that "the highest art has its roots...in the highest necessity. The perfect book or speech obeys in every respect the pure and merciless laws of what has been called logographic necessity." Strauss, *Thoughts on Machiavelli,* p. 121. See, also, Strauss, *Persecution and the Art of Writing* (Glencoe, Ill.: Free Press, 1952); Strauss, *On Tyranny: A Study of Xenophon's Hiero* (New York: Free Press of Glencoe, 1963).

146.   See, also, Shelley, *Frankenstein,* pp. 143, 145. See, as well, Anastaplo, *Human Being and Citizen,* p. 280, n. 50; "Jacob Klein of St. John's College," *Newsletter,* Politics Department, The University of Dallas, Spring 1979, p. 2. Consider other invocations of God in Shelley, *Frankenstein,* e.g., pp. 40, 56, 67, 75, 131, 216, 217.

147.   One is reminded, by all this, of such things as the passions touched upon by Conrad in *Heart of Darkness.* See the text at note 113, above. See, also, the text at note 201, below.

        See, on the uses of discipline, Nietzsche, *Beyond Good and Evil,* p. 100f; Whitehead, *Aims of Education,* pp. 118–19; Anastaplo, *The Constitutionalist,* p. 736, n. 135, pp. 759–60, nn. 170–71, pp. 786–87, n. 12. See, also, Chapter IV, Sections iv and v, above; the text from note 93 to note 94, above; introduction to Appendix F, below.

148.   Frankenstein invokes for Walton "the manes [family ghosts, demanding vengeance] of William, Justine, Clerval, Elizabeth, my father, and of the wretched Victor," asking Walton to thrust his sword into the monster's heart. Shelley, *Frankenstein,* p. 206.

149.   Frankenstein's father had himself married a daughter-like wife. *Ibid.,* p. 28. Elizabeth's identification of herself as William's sister seems more intense than how one usually regarded one's brother-in-law (who *would* be known as a "brother").

150.   Consider, in Section ix of this chapter, Walton's period of gestation.

151.   See Plato, *Phaedrus* 230a. See, also, Chapter XII, Section ii, below.

152.   *Dictionary of National Biography* (Oxford: Oxford University Press, 1921–22), XVIII, 29. It is also reported that Mary Shelley lamented, after her husband's death, "Alas! having lived day by day with one of the wisest, best, and most affectionate of spirits, how void, bare and drear is the scene of life!" *Ibid.,* XVIII, 30. See note 273, below. It is reported of their six years of marriage (*ibid.,* XVIII, 29):

They were seldom apart, and her devotion to him was complete. Some differences were unavoidable between persons in many respects so diversely organised. Endowed with a remarkably clear, penetrating, and positive intellect, she could not always follow Shelley's flights, and was too honest to affect feelings which she did not really entertain. Possessing in full measure the defects of her qualities, she had not the insight to discern the prophetic character of Shelley's genius ...

See notes 178 and 208, below.

153.   It is well to keep in mind Mark Twain's comment about Mary Shelley, "She was a child in years only. From the day she set her *masculine* grip on Shelley he was to frisk no more." Lyles, ed., *Bibliography*, p. 165 (italics added). Even so, was Mary Shelley able to save her sanity (and assume some control over those around her), in the volatile circumstances in which she found herself, partly because she could work out ("talk through") her feelings in this book? See notes 164 and 202, below.

Horace called Sappho "masculine." *Lyra Graeca* (Loeb Classical Library Edition), I, 167. See note 117, above.

154.   An early stage production of this story used the title, *Presumption; or, The Fate of Frankenstein.* Shelley, *Frankenstein*, p. xxxiii. See note 242, below. See, also, Section iv (end) of this chapter.

155.   Frankenstein is put off by one professor's appearance. *Ibid.*, pp. 41, 45. Consider the "angelic" photograph published in newspapers a few years ago of a twelve-year-old Florida boy who had stabbed to death a younger playmate. See, e.g., *Chicago Tribune,* Dec. 2, 1976, sec. 1, p. 10. Far the more interesting things to study in pornographic photograph-displays of nudes are the faces of the people who can be prevailed upon to exhibit themselves thus. It is primarily to the face one naturally looks for visible signs of character? See Shakespeare, *Twelfth Night*, III, iv, 312–50. See, also, notes 78 and 145 (end), above. See, as well, Appendix A, below. Cf. Plato, *Symposium* 215 A–B, 216E–217A, 221E–222A.

See, on the relation of misery to crime, note 20, above.

156.   There is in this conception something of Rousseau? See note 251, below. In other respects, however, Mary Shelley's doctrines about the impressionability of the mind remind of John Locke. See Burton R. Pollin, "Philosophical and Literary Sources of *Frankenstein*," 17 *Comparative Literature* 97, 107 (1965).

See, on the relation between a people's literature and their sensibilities, T. S. Eliot, *On Poetry and Poets* (New York: Noonday Press, 1961), p. 10. See, also, *ibid.,* p. 15; Housman, *Selected Prose,* p. 169. See, as well, note 145, above, note 279, below; Appendix G, Sections iii and ix, below.

157.   See Small, *Mary Shelley's Frankenstein,* p. 63. See, also, Epigraph, Chapter I, Part One, above.

158.   *Ibid.,* pp. 58f, 67–68. See the text at note 258, below. Do James Joyce's works also provide "models for resentment"?

159.   Nikos Kazantzakis, in *The Sickness of the Age* (1906), refers to Werther as "the sentimental and melancholy suicide." See Kazantzakis, *Serpent and Lily,* trans. Theodora Vasils (Berkeley: University of California Press, 1980), p. 98. See, also, the text at note 12, above.

160.   Consider Machiavelli, as well as Raskolnikov of Dostoyevski's *Crime and Punishment,* on the morality of founders. Is Frankenstein the would-be heir of Machiavelli and Hobbes? See Shelley, *Frankenstein,* p. 42. The monster does "admire peaceable law-givers, Numa, Solon, Lycurgus, in preference to Romulus and Theseus." *Ibid.,* p. 125. It is also familiar with Volney's *Ruins of Empire.* Shelley, *Frankenstein,* p. 144.

161.   Augustine, *The City of God,* XXII, 22 (beginning). Compare Nietzsche's "abyss." See note 251, below.

162.   Augustine, *The City of God,* XXII, 22 (end). See Shelley, *Frankenstein,* p. 41. See, also, Fortin, "St. Augustine," p. 175.

163.   See, on the taming of the terrible, Nietzsche, *The Birth of Tragedy,* sec. 17. See, also, note 251, below. See, as well, Sophocles, *Oedipus at Colonus* 510–12; Lucretius, *On the Nature of Things,* bk. 2 (beginning); note 164 (end), below.
       See, on the faults and merits of other Polar explorers which account for failure and success, Roland Huntford, *Scott and Amundsen* (London: Hodder and Stoughton, 1979). "To adapt Shackleton's saying, Kathleen [Scott] and the country preferred a dead lion to a live donkey.... [T]here was a memorial service at St. Paul's Cathedral [for Robert F. Scott]; all for one of the most inefficient of Polar expeditions, and one of the worst of Polar explorers.... [Roald E.] Amundsen had made the

conquest of the [South] Pole into something between an art and a sport. Scott had turned Polar exploration into an affair of heroism for heroism's sake.... [T]hat Scott was responsible for his companions' deaths was evident." *Ibid.,* p. 559. Do we see here, in the distinction made between Amundsen and Scott, something of the difference between an Odysseus and an Achilles? See, also, *ibid.,* p. 563; note 238, below. See, as a contrast to Walton's sister's sober marriage back in England, *ibid.,* pp. 545–46.

164.   The "justice of our judges" is relied on with respect to Justine. Shelley, *Frankenstein,* p. 76. However, the facts (despite her name?) were against her. *Ibid.,* p. 77. (See note 252, below.) Her case proves a "mockery of justice." *Ibid.,* p. 76. The efficient workings of the system of justice are taken for granted. *Ibid.,* p. 84. Justine cannot believe she has any "enemy on earth." *Ibid.,* p. 79. But, in a sense, Frankenstein is her enemy, just as he is the enemy of everyone intimately connected with him. *Ibid.,* p. 72. Is there a rough justice in what happens to the presumptuous Frankenstein and his circle? *Ibid.,* p. 88. Are all of them somehow vulnerable "projections" of his tormented psyche?

The classic case of "projection" may well be Clytemnestra's lines in Aeschylus, *Eumenides* 110–13. Consider, also, the "Ariadne" poem in the dedication to this book (which poem it would be instructive to consider somewhere in this book and not irrelevant to turn to here). Consider, as well, the sketch quoted at the end of Section vi of the Epilogue, below; Diogenes Laertius, *Lives,* II, 36–37; Aristotle, *Rhetoric,* II, ii–iii; Shakespeare, *Two Gentlemen of Verona,* IV, iv, 164–67.

Is not our Ariadne's passion revealing? Considering what she had done in betraying her family to secure Theseus for herself, she could not be trusted to take second place as a queen. Could she be liked as a wife or as a travelling companion? It must have been difficult even for her to bear the ugliness in the soul which her self-gratifying anger exposes. (See Aristotle, *Nicomachean Ethics* 1166b18.) Notice how appearances, even yet, matter for her, as she prepares for the coming of Dionysus. Such childish people become tiresome: one cannot *discuss* serious matters with them, partly because they invest so much of their personality in whatever position they happen to take, and partly because they cannot discipline themselves to allow for their limitations. (See Anastaplo, "American Constitutionalism and the Virtue of Prudence," pp. 147–48, n. 33. Anger has been identified as "the emotion behind most neuroses." 207 *Science* 1030 [March 7, 1980]. Consider, also, Jessica's heartless betrayal of Shylock in Shakespeare's *Merchant of Venice* and Desdemona's thoughtless betrayal of *her* father in *Othello.*

See Chapter I, Part One, Section iv, above. See, on "personality" and art, note 141, above, note 202, below.)

Or, put another way, did Ariadne "invite" betrayal by Theseus? Is she of the type who imagines the worst in others and thereby provokes (perhaps even requires) the very conduct that is dreaded? But see Anastaplo, *The Constitutionalist,* p. 607, n. 23; also, notes 121 and 152, above, note 273, below. See, as well, Chapter XII, Section ii, below. Is not Ariadne more attuned to ecstatic Dionysus than to the sober goddess of the hearth whom Dionysus is sometimes said to have replaced? See Pangle, *The Laws of Plato,* p. 516, n. 40, p. 525, n. 19, p. 527, n. 21.

That is, does not the ecstasy at the end of the poem we are considering echo the violent passion of the opening lines (which rush pell-mell at the reader)? Ariadne, in her proneness to ecstasy, may have indeed been a fit companion for Dionysus. Is this why she can prophesy his advent? Has she (by nature?) always smoldering within her the passion he depends upon? See, e.g., Euripides, *The Bacchae.* A prudent Theseus (more respectful, as a founder, of the hearth?) should have wanted no part of *that?* (See, on Theseus himself, the epigraph to Appendix G, below. See, also, Sophocles, *Oedipus at Colonus;* Shakespeare, *A Midsummer Night's Dream;* note 29, above. See, as well, note 260, below. There may be reflected in the tradition with respect to Ariadne, a Cretan princess, and her receptivity to Dionysus, a recognition of the consequences of a lack of proper training in wine-drinking among the rigidly abstemious Cretans of antiquity. Is Ariadne, that is, peculiarly vulnerable to the lure of Dionysus once the conventional barriers are down? See Plato, *Laws,* I-II. See, also, Euripides, *Hippolytus,* for another instance of vulnerable abstemiousness? See, as well, Shakespeare, *Measure for Measure,* for the questionable rigidity of Isabella as well as of Angelo.)

Cf. Nietzsche, *Beyond Good and Evil,* pp. 234–35; Karl Reinhardt, "Nietzsche's Lament of Ariadne," 6 *Interpretation* 204 (1977). Cf., also, Plutarch, *Comparison of Theseus and Romulus,* I, 5:

> It is therefore my opinion that the philosophers give an excellent definition of love when they call it "a ministration of the gods for the care and preservation of the young." For Ariadne's love seems to have been, more than anything else, a god's work, and a device whereby Theseus should be saved. And we should not blame her for loving him, but rather wonder that all men and women were not thus affected towards him; and if she alone felt this passion, I should say, for my part, that she was properly worthy of a god's love, since she was fond of virtue, fond of goodness, and a lover of the highest qualities in man.

Be all this as it may, the complicated poet of "Ariadne at Naxos" may be seen here in still another (but calmer [i.e., Northern?]) poem of royal abandonment:

Highland Ballad
Charlie is over the water
   The prince has crossed the sea.
I sit alone on the rocky shore;
   He'll never come back to me.

I look in my children's faces
   And hold my eyes from the sea
For fear I should spy my outgrown love
   Laughing, apart from me.

Consider, by way of "resolution," the following poem from the same mind (a poem in which again the form employed reinforces the content [see note 189, below]):

The Tempest
Come all my passions, and collect
Into a tempest, cold, compact
And continent.

Assault only him and let
Me not to the marriage of minds admit
Impediment.

This poet may be glimpsed as well in Anastaplo, *The Constitutionalist,* p. 767. A longtime admirer of her poems was Malcolm P. Sharp. See, on Mr. Sharp himself, Edmund Wilson, "Conversing with Malcolm Sharp," 33 *University of Chicago Law Review* 198 (1966); Anastaplo, "Malcolm P. Sharp and the Spirit of '76," *University of Chicago Law Alumni Journal,* Summer 1975, p. 18 (reprinted in 121 *Congressional Record* 40241 [December 12, 1975]); Obituary, *New York Times,* August 15, 1980, p. D15.

We are again obliged to wonder: do poets "think out" and recognize what readers find in their work? (See Appendix G, Section iii, below.) The fine things made by poets (Plato, *Apology* 22B–C) do seem to have a life (and hence a rationale) of their own. (Consider such fine things as the fruit produced by the cherry tree, the complicated making of which can be articulated only by astute observers, not by the tree itself.) See note 145, above, note 180, below. See, also, note 141, below.

The most reliable observers of impressive things both human and nonhuman are those among us who can adopt the stance of Athena upon confronting the Furies and the bloodstained Orestes at her altar (Aeschylus, *Eumenides* 405-7):

> I see upon this land a novel company
> which, though it brings no terror to my eyes,
> brings still wonder. Who are you?

See note 289, below.

165. Shelley, *Frankenstein*, pp. xxvi-xxvii, 60. Consider, also, Rousseau on Geneva. See Anastaplo, *The Constitutionalist*, p. 770, n. 192.

166. Consider the significance of the survival of Coriolanus' son, and of his grandmother to inspire *him* also. See Shakespeare, *Coriolanus*, I, iii, 51-65; Chapter I, Section iv, Item 6, above.

  Was it not Volumnia who taught Coriolanus that one's sword must be "lawful" in order to be meaningful? See the text at note 24, above.

167. See, on Socrates' protective *daemon* (as invoked in Plato's *Apology*), Anastaplo, *Human Being and Citizen*, pp. 27-28. (The monster is several times referred to as a daemon by Frankenstein.)

  Consider also Dante's "Odyssey" (*Inferno*, xxvi, 112f): are there not echoes of Ulysses' speech in the speech made by Frankenstein to Walton's men? Shelley, *Frankenstein*, p. 212. See Anastaplo, *Human Being and Citizen*, p. 46f. See, also, Huntford, *Scott and Amundsen*, p. 563: "[Ernest] Shackleton died of heart disease on January 5th, 1922, at the start of his next Antarctic expedition, and was buried in South Georgia. His last words, to a doctor remonstrating with him over his way of life, were: 'What! Do you want me to give up now?'"

  See, on Walton's intense desire for intimate friendship with another man, Shelley, *Frankenstein*, pp. 13-14, 22-23, 209. Is this, too, a substitute for natural sexual relations? See note 230, below.

  Walton gives in to his men's desire to turn back, just as does the leader in Nikos Kazantzakis's *Alexander the Great* (Theodora Vasils, trans.) (Athens: Ohio University Press, 1982).

168. Consider Zeus' production of Athena. See Laurence Berns, "Gratitude, Nature and Piety in *King Lear*," p. 33; Anastaplo, *The Constitutionalist*, p. 791; "American Constitutionalism and the Virtue of Prudence," p. 154, n. 44. See, also, Lyles, ed., *Bibliography*, p. 128; Radu Florescu, *The Secret of Frankenstein* (Boston: New York Graphic Society, 1975), p. 183. See, as well, the text following note 150, above.

Is this story Mary Shelley's way of reconsidering the always burden-some and sometimes risky gestation process that women are subjected to?

See Benardete, "Euripides' *Hippolytus*," p. 25. See, also, note 230, below.

VI. CHARLES DICKENS (1812-1870)

169.   See Eric T. Owen, *The Harmony of Aeschylus* (Toronto: Clarke, Irwin & Co., 1952), p. 102; *Encyclopaedia Britannica, Macropaedia* (15th ed.), vol. 5, p. 706.

See, also, Edmund Wilson, "Dickens: The Two Scrooges," in *The Wound and the Bow* (Cambridge: Houghton Mifflin Co., 1941); George Orwell, "Charles Dickens," in *Inside the Whale, a Book of Essays,* (London: Victor Gollancz Ltd., 1940); Anthony Trollope, *An Autobiography* (Edinburgh: William Blackwood and Sons, 1883), II, 69-72. See, on Dickens's suspicion of statistics, June Goodfield, "Humanity in Science: A Perspective and a Plea," 198 *Science* 580, 582 (Nov. 11, 1977); William Kruskal, Letter, 199 *Science* 1026 (March 11, 1978). Cf. Kruskall, "Statistics," *International Encyclopedia of the Social Sciences,* XV, 217f. See, for a useful collection of comments on Dickens's work, Philip Collins, ed., *Dickens: The Critical Heritage* (London: Routledge and Kegan Paul, 1971).

There has become available to me, since this chapter was originally prepared for *Interpretation* (where it appeared in volume 7, January 1978), *The Annotated Christmas Carol,* Michael Patrick Hearn, ed., (New York: Clarkson N. Potter, 1976), a useful reference work for readers of *A Christmas Carol.* See, e.g., *ibid.,* p. 64 (on the number seven). (The University of Chicago Works of the Mind lecture on which this chapter is based was dedicated on the occasion of its delivery, December 12, 1976, to the memory of a University of Chicago colleague who had died that week, Professor Arthur Heiserman.)

170.   A more obvious use by Dickens of a dream may be seen in his next story of the Christmas season, *The Chimes.* See *The Christmas Books,* Michael Slater, ed. (Baltimore: Penguin Books, 1971), I, 149. (One can be reminded by the way "went to bed" may have been used in *A Christmas Carol* of the two accounts of Creation in *Genesis.* See, also, Hilail Gildin, "Revolution and the Formation of Political Society in the *Social Contract*," 5 *Interpretation* 247, at 248 [1976].)

See, for suggestions about how dreams "work" in other stories, Chapter V, above, Chapters IX, XII, and XIII, below. See, also, Appendix G, Section vi, below. See, as well, Aeschylus, *Eumenides* 104-5: "Eyes illuminate the sleeping brain, but in the daylight man's future cannot be seen."

It is instructive to notice how solidly grounded *A Christmas Carol* is in nature—in the nature of dreams or at least of a dreamlike recollection, in the nature of certain vices, and perhaps even in the "nature" of Providence. This grounding assures us that the story is deeply realistic, not mere "fancy," and hence something worthy of serious study. Thus, Scrooge can sense ("I know it, but I know not how.") when the final episode with the Ghosts is drawing to a close. *The Christmas Books*, I, 123. That is, what happens to him is not arbitrary but rather complete and purposeful. (Scrooge *had* heard stories about the ways of ghosts. *Ibid.*, I, 57. See note 133, above.) See, also, note 174, below. See, as well, note 137, above.

171.   See, on avarice, *New Catholic Encyclopedia*, I, 1122; Plato, *Phaedo* 66C-D, 68B-C. Compare the *Andy Capp* comic strip for June 15, 1977: the importunate hero observes, in response to his long-suffering wife's reminder that "money can't buy 'appiness," "True, pet, true—but it 'elps you to look for it in a lot more places." Compare, also, Plato, *Republic* 591E. (One is reminded of the role assigned by Aristotle to "equipment" in the happy life. See *Nicomachean Ethics* 1097b20, 1099a31 sq., 1101a14 sq., 1110a8 sq., 1117b17-19, 1119b20-1123a31, 1138b1-4, 1153b13 sq., 1155a1 sq., 1176a30 sq., 1178b31 sq., 1180a1 sq., 1179a30 sq. See, also, note 124, above, note 195, below.)

The appeal of avarice is related to why some prefer driving over flying, even though "statistics" indicate they are safer (as passengers in commercial airlines): when they drive, they can more easily believe they are "in control." See, also, *The Spiritual Physick of Rhazes* (London: John Murray, 1950), pp. 64-65; Diogenes Laertius, *Lives*, IV, 50-51; Ronald Kotulak, "Life in America: Dangerous, but we must risk it," *Chicago Tribune*, Sept. 14, 1980, sec. 1, p. 5. See, as well, Lucretius, *On the Nature of Things*, bk. III (opening pages); Raymond L. Weiss and Charles Butterworth, eds., *Ethical Writings of Maimonides* (New York: New York University Press, 1975), pp. 68-69.

That which Tocqueville said about the enterprising Yankee can perhaps be applied to Scrooge as well, "[H]is eagerness to possess things goes beyond the ordinary limits of human cupidity...; there is something wonderful in his resourcefulness and a sort of heroism in his greed for gain." *Democracy in America,* p. 347. Consider, as well, the discussion, which is central to Tocqueville's *Democracy,* of "self-interest properly understood." Also applicable to Scrooge may be that which Malcolm Muggeridge said of Somerset Maugham: "Like all timid, lonely people, money seemed to him a protection. It set up a buffer between him and a largely alien and hostile world. To this end he sought it, first diligently and ardently, and finally as an addiction." *The American Spectator,* August 1980, p. 19. See, also, note 173 (end), below.

Competition for money can be a means also for seeking victory and honor and for otherwise expressing one's "virtue." But in such circumstances, one need not want to *keep* the money or to accumulate it indefinitely: such a man can also compete in philanthropy. See Anastaplo, *The Constitutionalist,* p. 622, n. 115, p. 689, n. 37. See, also, Aristotle, *Nicomachean Ethics,* I, 5, IV, 2, VIII, 2.

In any event, avarice has been recognized, at least since Plutarch's day, as a symptom of the melancholic disposition. See David Sansone, "Lysander and Dionysius (Plut. *Lys.* 2)," 78 *Classical Philology* 202 (1981).

172.   See, on the heroine's self-preservative instincts in Chaucer's "The Franklin's Tale," Anastaplo, *Human Being and Citizen,* p. 293. (Is Scrooge, too, essentially Epicurean? See note 175, below. See, also, note 253, below.)

173.   Scrooge had been told by Marley *(Prodromos?)* that he would be subjected to three nights of visitations. *The Christmas Books,* I, 63. But all three visits were accomplished in one night. *Ibid.,* I, 128. This can be considered a Trinitarian element in a Christmas story in which explicit religious references are (in a rationalistic age) prudently muted (as can be seen even in how far the boy is permitted to go in singing his carol [*ibid.,* I, 53]). See *ibid.,* I, 49, 56, 65, 87, 91, 94, 104, 120, 131. See, for the Trinity in still another form, note 76, above. See, also, note 226, below.

Scrooge, as he looks ahead, carries the carol sung by the boy through to its "logical" conclusion: when he dies in Christmas Yet to Come, it is said by one of his business acquaintances, "Old Scratch [i.e., Satan] has got his own at last, hey?" *The Christmas Books,* I, 112. This tends to confirm the grim alternative indicated in the lines subsequent to those sung by the boy:

Remember Christ our Saviour
Was born on Christmas Day,
To save poor souls from Satan's power
Which had long time gone astray.

Oxford Book of Carols (London: Oxford University Press, 1928), p. 25.

Fragments of the Christmas Eve conversations in Scrooge's counting-house are worked into his nightlong recapitulation of his life. Various episodes in that recapitulation either challenge positions Scrooge has taken or illustrate what has been said to him by others. Scrooge himself comes to recognize that even seemingly trivial details serve his Ghosts' purpose. *The Christmas Books,* I, 113.

Consider the use of "blessing" in the Epigraph to this chapter taken from *Macbeth.*

Also muted, if readers are not to be put permanently "out of humour" with their comic hero, is the ugly evil that an unrepentant Scrooge was capable of. See *The Christmas Books,* I, 41, 110–20. A grimmer version of Scrooge is Uriah Heep of Dickens's *David Copperfield.* In him, avarice irrevocably overreaches itself. (See *The Works of Charles Dickens,* National Edition [London: Chapman and Hall, 1907], vol. 21, p. 364.) Compare, also, the visitations by Scrooge's Ghosts with Steerforth's "nightmare" in *David Copperfield.*

Consider, as well, Willa Cather, *On Writing* (New York: Alfred A. Knopf, 1949), pp. 86–87:

> [Daniel] Defoe seems to have had only one deep interest, and that was in making a living. Read *The Complete British Tradesman* and marvel at how intensely, how acutely, every mean device and petty economy appealed to him; how every stingy trim, every possible twist and sharp practice in shopkeeping and servant-grinding, stirred him and gratified him. All the misers in fiction are sentimental, inexpert, and unresourceful, judged by the standards advocated in this work written for the guidance of Defoe's fellow tradesmen. It is one of the meanest and most sordid books ever written. It makes one ashamed of being human.

(It should be noticed, however, that Trollope called Defoe's *Robinson Crusoe* "the earliest really popular novel which we have in our language." *Autobiography,* II, 26. That is, was the "deep interest...in making a living" that which truly guided Defoe in his art? To the extent it was, did not "personality" and chance get in the way of his artistic thought? See, for an instructive discussion of this artist as thinker,

Thomas S. Schrock, *On the Basis of Defoe's Political Thought: Robinson Crusoe* [University of Chicago Ph.D. dissertation, 1964].)

174.   See note 108, above. On the dramatization of Dickens's work, see Richard P. Fulkerson, *"Oliver Twist* in the Victorian Theatre," 20 *The Dickensian* 83 (May 1974).

Had the inspired Dickens recognized the extent to which Scrooge's experiences took the form of a dream, he might have left us more clues toward the solution of such puzzles as how Scrooge knew (if merely dreaming) about Topper and "the plump sister in the lace tucker" at his nephew's house on Christmas Day. *The Christmas Books,* I, 103, 105. See Plato, *Apology* 22B–C.

It should be noticed, in considering this and other anomalies, that the printed editions (as well as Dickens's original manuscript) do happen to show an extra space before the final two paragraphs of *A Christmas Carol* (and nowhere else in the book). *The Christmas Books,* I, 133. Thus, the ingenious Scrooge *can* be understood to have extended his dream to include his immediate acts of reformation, permitting him to provide the Cratchits a huge turkey for their Christmas dinner, to run into the charitable solicitor, to visit his nephew's home (where he can meet the guests earlier conjured up by him), and to "have" Cratchit come in 18½ minutes late to work (something highly unlikely for the clerk to do?) on the day after the Christmas holiday. (Was Cratchit thrown off schedule because of Scrooge's anonymous turkey gift the day before? Can *18½* be considered a modern magic number? Thus, this was the number of minutes in the controversial gap in the White House Watergate tapes. See note 94, above.)

If Scrooge is understood to have dreamed almost to the very end of the book, it does take care of the problem of how Scrooge could dream events of the following day, for example, Cratchit's dinner (with its *goose*) and the nephew's party (without Scrooge present) which would be proved wrong or decisively changed by what Scrooge himself is reported to have done after "waking" on Christmas Day. (We touch here upon the dilemma of any prophecy? See *Jonah* 4: 1–2.) But it *is* indicated that the scenes depicted are of *tendencies* only.

Certainly, various things seem to happen in the story as if Scrooge had willed them: for example, his glance rests on the bell in his room and *then* it begins to ring; he suggests the Spirits all come in one night, and they do just that; the movement of Marley and the movement of the window are coordinated. *The Christmas Books,* I, 56–57, 63, 64. See, also, note 170, above. See, as well, Chapter IX, Section v, below.

However all this may be, the final two paragraphs of the book do assure us that Scrooge has been permanently reformed by his experience of this fateful Christmas Eve. What more should be expected? That the nephew's prospective child, if a boy, should be named Ebenezer? And that Scrooge will have "the satisfaction of thinking...that he [will] benefit [his nephew's family] with [his wealth]"? *Ibid.*, I, 49, 102–3, 112. See, also, Plato, *Republic* 328C–D, 331D.

Is not the reformation of Scrooge caused more by his pained awareness of what is happening to him than by a selfless dedication to virtue for its own sake? Compare Plato, *Republic* 558E–589C, 591A–E, 619B–D. See Aristotle, *Nicomachean Ethics* 1157b15–19, 1172a20–21. Does not death remain for Scrooge, as for Dickens himself, too great a concern? See note 175, below.

175.   Modern men have allowed themselves to act as if they have discovered death. One need only compare the attitude toward the prospect of death in Tolstoy's popular *Death of Ivan Ilych* to that in Homer's *Iliad* or to that in Plutarch's *Lives* (to say nothing of that in Plato's *Phaedo*) to recognize our decline in this respect. Compare Plato, *Republic* 386C, 516D–C; Anastaplo, *The Constitutionalist,* pp. 278–81.

Or is it that we are to believe that we have somehow become more sensitive than our predecessors to the "situation" of man in the universe? What we certainly do have, I am afraid, is considerably more anxiety than they (despite the considerable concern with death in the mystery religions of antiquity)—as well as considerable hostility toward those who are not anxious or who are otherwise superior. See, on Martin Heidegger, *ibid.,* p. 815. (Self-centeredness [with its relativistic tendencies] can be seen in the contemporary [existentialist?] preference for "authentic" over the old-fashioned "good" or "substance" or "true." Is not this related to the preference for "self" and "emotion" over "soul" and "passion"? See, on "authentic," *New Yorker,* Nov. 5, 1979, p. 216. See, also, note 248, below. [See, for Hector's response to Troilus' "existentialism," Appendix A, Epigraph, below.] The following passage from Chapter 93 of Melville's *Moby Dick,* "The Castaway," suggests how overwhelming the sense of abandonment to one's self can be:

> ...Pip jumped again [from the whale-boat]...and hence, when the whale started to run, Pip was left behind on the sea, like a hurried traveller's trunk....In three minutes, a whole mile of shoreless ocean was between Pip and [the others]. Out from the centre of the sea, poor Pip turned his crisp, curling, black head

to the sun, *another lonely castaway,* though the loftiest and the brightest.

Now, in calm weather, to swim in the open ocean is as easy to the practised swimmer as to ride in a spring-carriage ashore. But the awful lonesomeness is intolerable. The intense concentration of self in the middle of such a heartless immensity, my God! *who can tell it?* Mark, how when sailors in a dead calm bathe in the open sea—mark how closely they hug their ship and only coast along her sides.

. . . Pip's ringed horizon began to expand around him miserably. By the merest chance the ship itself at last rescued him; but from that hour the little negro went about the deck an idiot; such, at least, they said he was. The sea had jeeringly kept his finite body up, but drowned the infinite of his soul. Not drowned entirely, though. Rather carried down alive to wondrous depths, where strange shapes of the unwarped primal world glided to and fro before his passive eyes; and the miser-merman, Wisdom, revealed his hoarded heaps; and among the joyous, heartless, ever-juvenile eternities, Pip saw the multitudinous, God-omnipresent, coral insects, that out of the firmament of waters heaved the colossal orbs. He saw God's foot upon the treadle of the loom, and spoke it; and therefore his shipmates called him mad. So man's insanity is heaven's sense; and wandering from all mortal reason, man comes at last to that celestial thought, which, to reason, is absurd and frantic; and weal or woe, feels then uncompromised, indifferent as his God.

For the rest, blame not [the leader of the whale-boat] too hardly. The thing is common in that fishery; and in the sequel of the narrative, it will then be seen *what like abandonment befell myself.*

Italics have been added here with a view to the discussion in Chapter VII, below.

See, on death itself, the funeral talk reproduced in Section viii of the Epilogue, below. See, also, the essays on death, on the *Apology,* on natural right, on the *Crito,* and on Jacob Klein's *Meno* in Anastaplo, *Human Being and Citizen.* See, as well, the discussion of Edwin Muir's "The Animals" in note 3, above; W. B. Yeats, "Death"; Leo Paul S. de Alvarez, *"Timon of Athens,"* in Alvis and West, eds., *Shakespeare as Political Thinker,* pp. 174–179; notes 18, 30, 78, 145, and 174, above, notes 195 and 237, below; Chapter IV, Section viii, above, Appendix E, below.

One is induced to wonder whether any villain in a Dickens story eats well. *The Christmas Books*, I, 86, 90, 93, 94–96. In any event, Scrooge is shown that he will die *thoroughly* if he continues to pursue the course he has chosen. *Ibid.*, I, 111, 115, 126. "Good deeds," on the other hand, imply "life immortal"? *Ibid.*, I, 118. See note 20, above.

Be all this as it may, it should be remembered (in assessing the self-centeredness of men such as Dickens's Scrooge and Bunyan's Christian) that "it is for himself most of all that each man wishes what is good." Aristotle, *Nicomachean Ethics* 1159a9–13. But it should also be remembered,

> Those, then, who busy themselves in an exceptional degree with noble actions all men approve and praise; and if *all* were to strive towards what is noble and strain every nerve to do the noblest deeds, everything would be as it should be for the common weal, and every one would secure for himself the goods that are greatest, since virtue is the greatest of goods.

Ibid., 1169a6–11. See note 103, above, note 194, below.

VII. HERMAN MELVILLE (1819–1891)

176.   See Chapter I, Part One, above; also, Anastaplo, *The Constitutionalist*, pp. 437–38. Are wars, and hence stories about war, less disciplined and disciplining in this respect? Does chance ordinarily play a significantly greater part in war than in peace? Is this not related to the popular opinion that "there are no atheists in foxholes"?

177.   See Herman Melville, *Moby Dick* (New York: Modern Library, 1926), pp. 315, 488, 433–39, 530–31, 470–71. See, also, Anastaplo, *The Constitutionalist*, pp. 463–64. On each ship the aggregates of men are moved by their leaders—and this we know also from everyday experience. Thus, a Herblock cartoon shows a massive whale, labeled "Nuclear Superiority," virtually overwhelming a small ship with a one-legged captain who is addressed by a crew member, "Cap'n, You Keep Chasing After That Great White Whale, We're All Gonna End Up In Trouble." *Chicago Sun-Times*, May 3, 1962.

Tocqueville could report of the Pequots that they lived "only in men's memories." *Democracy in America*, p. 321.

178.   See Anastaplo, *The Constitutionalist,* pp. 651, 798. See, on Sophocles'
Antigone, Seth Benardete, 4 *Interpretation* 148 (1975), 5 *Interpretation*
1, 148 (1975). See, also, note 12, above. Still, Percy Shelley could say,
"Some of us have loved an Antigone in a previous state of existence,
and can find no full content in any mortal tie." *Dictionary of National
Biography,* XVIII, 29. See, on the noble and the just, Strauss, *Natural
Right and History,* pp. 128, 140. See, also, note 208 (end), below. See,
as well, Section ii of the prologue, above.

Critical to Ahab's view of things is the opinion that there has been
"an eternal war since the world began." Melville, *Moby Dick,* p. 276.
Similarly, the partisans of Parnell (see note 263, below) regard him as
having been "killed"; he did not just "die." Joyce, *A Portrait of the
Artist,* p. 36. (Consider, also, Joyce, *Ulysses,* pp. 7 ["someone killed
her"], 12, 565.) Is there not something Ahabian in Callicles' indignation that a good man can be killed by a bad? See Plato, *Gorgias* 481–
86; Epilogue, Section ii (end), below.

The following exchange between a Capuchin friar and a soldier about
the merits of Wallenstein bear on our effort to understand Ahab (Friedrich von Schiller, *Wallenstein's Camp,* 591–99):

> *Friar:* ... The mischief comes from above!
> As the head does, so the members must,
> And nobody knows in whom *he* puts trust!
>
> *Soldier:* Priest! Us soldiers you can slander,
> But don't you dare rail at our Commander!
>
> *Friar: Ne custodias gregem meam!*
> He is like unto Ahab and Jerobeam,
> Corrupting men's faith and making them bow
> Unto false idols in spite of their vow.

See, also, note 180, below.

179.   Consider, also, the Xenophon of the *Anabasis,* III, i, 11: "And Xenophon was one of their number."

Ishmael can note, at the midpoint of his book, "[S]ome invisible,
gracious agency preserved me." Melville, *Moby Dick,* p. 283. Cf. note
175, above. He had said of Ahab, as we have seen, that he was a "grey-
headed ungodly old man." *Ibid.,* p. 186. See, also, *ibid.,* pp. 80, 92–93,
122, 164–65, 496, 511. See, on Jonah, *ibid.,* pp. 39–48, 364–65, 445,
566.

Consider, in Chapter XI, below, the decisive actions taken (or attitudes displayed) by Alice at the midpoint of her careers in *Wonderland*

and *Looking-Glass.* Cannot Ishmael be considered at the midpoint of the "career" I am tracing of the Artist from Shakespeare to Joyce in the English-language tradition? See note 182, below. See, also, note 280, below.

180. The whole *is* mysterious, subject to misreading, we are warned early in the book—as is evident from the varied responses to the "marvelous painting" hanging in the Spouter-Inn. Melville, *Moby Dick,* pp. 9-12. See, also, *ibid.,* pp. 426-32. "But Melville, though born the same year as Whitman, looked the other way—not forward to the democratic apotheosis but backward to Calvinism and its dark negations." John Updike, *New Yorker,* May 10, 1982, p. 138.

The relation of Ishmael to Ahab is critical to our understanding of that whole which the book attempts to describe. Consider the following comment by Sacvan Bercovitch (in a review of Rowland A. Sherrill, *The Prophetic Melville: Experience, Transcendence, and Tragedy* [Athens: University of Georgia Press, 1979], 60 *Journal of Religion* 342 [1980]):

[Sherrill's] emphasis on Ishmael, for example, tends to blur the importance of Ahab. As Lawrence Thompson (in *Melville's Quarrel with God*) diminished Ishmael by portraying him as Ahab's spokesman, so Sherrill, conversely, diminishes Ahab by portraying him as a mere foil to Ishmael, an emblem of the "incorrigible rule of the self" which the hero overcomes on his way to "self-transcendence."

Pip and Ahab (who form an alliance of sorts) are alternative, extreme (if not mad) responses to the enormity of the world in which man must find himself a place. (See, on Pip as another outcast, note 175, above.) In a way, everyone on the ship is a projection of Ahab's—except for Ishmael, who is somehow different, aloof and *sane.* The story makes some sense for us because of Ishmael. Consider how the story would be presented if it came to us through Ahab's diary or through the mind of Pip (in the fashion, say, of William Faulkner's Benjy).

Ahab is, in some respects, like Abraham: he has a radical dedication to his quest, to his special relation with the One. Is Ishmael the rejected son who is not fully in the tradition the father cherishes? Some readers tend to discount Ishmael, considering what is said in his name to be (especially after the beginning and before the very end) only what Melville himself says. But, we must remind ourselves, Melville could have told the entire story himself, assigning an Ishmael little or no part in the great account. In short, did not Melville know what he was doing to present the story as he did? Was he not *thinking?* See note 280, below.

181.   See Anastaplo, *Human Being and Citizen,* p. 317, n. 4. See, also, *ibid.,*
        p. 87f, p. 281, n. 3; *The Constitutionalist,* pp. 771–72; note 175, above;
        Appendix B, Section ii, below. See, as well, Plato, *Phaedo* (which liter-
        ally takes its point of departure from the *autós*). Cf. Virginia Woolf, *A
        Letter to a Young Poet* (London: Hogarth Press, 1932), e.g., pp. 18–19.

182.   Discipline means, among other things, that a few stand guard (or other-
        wise serve) while many sleep.
            See, on the duties of the artist and of critics, Anastaplo, *Human
        Being and Citizen,* Essay No. 10; "Human Nature and the First Amend-
        ment," p. 745f. Would not artists be better positioned to do their duties
        if they did not believe they had to be outcasts in order to survive? To
        what extent are they, or those who educate them about the nature of
        things, responsible for the awkward position artists consider themselves
        obliged to assume in modern times? See note 251, below. Did not artists
        such as Shakespare, Milton, Austen, and Dickens consider themselves
        very much part of what we call "the Establishment" (albeit a superior
        part)? (It should be noticed that these artists were widely acclaimed in
        their lifetimes. It is a modern myth that the greatest artists are rarely
        appreciated by their contemporaries. Cf. T. S. Eliot, *On Poetry and
        Poets* [New York: Noonday Press, 1961], pp. 10–11.) See note 253,
        below.
            Cannot we see in John Bunyan that "individualism" which became
        so critical in the work of Mary Shelley and Matthew Arnold and many
        of their successors? One can see in Ishmael both a rootedness in the
        "Thou shalts" and the "Thou shalt nots" of the Old (classical as well
        as biblical) and an openness to the "liberated" self-expressiveness of
        the New. (Consider the determined independence of James Joyce's
        Stephen Dedalus as well as of Mark Twain's Huckleberry Finn.) One
        can also see in the restless Leopold Bloom a tamer (far less noble and
        hence far less dangerous, as well as far less interesting?) version of an-
        other great wanderer, Captain Ahab. See Chapter XII, section vii, below.
            But, I remind the reader, the evocation of such patterns among artists
        in this book must be secondary to my obligation to read pretty much on
        its own each work of art I happen to consider. See note 145, above. See,
        also, Appendixes B and C, below.

VIII. MATTHEW ARNOLD (1822–1888)

183.   Norman N. Holland, *The Dynamics of Literary Response* (New York:
        Oxford University Press, 1968), p. 116. It is also said to be "the most

widely explicated" poem in the language. *Ibid.* See, as well, A. Dwight
Culler, *Imaginative Reason: The Poetry of Matthew Arnold* (New Haven:
Yale University Press, 1966), pp. 39–41; Kenneth Allott, ed., *The Poems
of Matthew Arnold* (New York: Barnes & Noble, 1965), p. 239.

"Dover Beach" was the favorite poem of Hans W. Mattick (1920–
1978), a sometimes desperate man who was "the star" in Henry Rago's
humanities class during my first year as a University of Chicago student.
(Among the students in that course that year was George Steiner. It was
in the Rago class that I arranged for the astonishing appearance of Gus
Matzorkis and David S. Halperin as the now legendary Ubangi and his
monkey. I tested thereby certain suggestions Mr. Rago had made to us
about comedy and incongruity. See note 30, above.)

The University of Chicago talk of March 2, 1978, from which this
chapter was developed, was prepared by me as a memorial to Mr. Mattick.
See *Chicago Tribune,* January 27, 1978, sec. 3, p. 9; *Chicago Sun-Times,*
January 27, 1978, p. 72; *Chicago Daily News,* January 27, 1978, pp. 4,
10 (editorial). See, also, Appendix E, below. Cf. John Milton, "Comus,"
410–12:

> Yet where an equall poise of hope and fear
> Does arbitrate th' event, my nature is
> That I encline to hope, rather than fear . . .

See note 285, below.

184. See J. D. Jump, *Matthew Arnold* (London: Longman's, 1960), pp. 81,
      115; Denys Thompson, ed., *Matthew Arnold: Selected Poems and
      Prose* (New York: Barnes & Noble, 1971), p. 239.

185. See, e.g., Thompson, ed., *Matthew Arnold,* p. 8.

186. See Carl Dawson, ed., *Matthew Arnold, The Poetry: The Critical Heri-
      tage* (London: Routledge & Kegan Paul, 1973), p. 401.

187. *Ibid.,* p. 181.

188. See Jump, *Matthew Arnold,* pp. 76–77, 79.

189. See Paull F. Baum, *Ten Studies in the Poetry of Matthew Arnold* (Dur-
      ham: Duke University Press, 1958), pp. 94–96; W. Stacy Johnson, *The
      Voices of Matthew Arnold* (New Haven: Yale University Press, 1961),
      p. 133. See, also, Allott, ed., *The Poems of Matthew Arnold,* p. 240, on
      monosyllables and on the movement in line 4 of "Dover Beach" mim-

icking the observation (see note 164, above, notes 215 and 289, below). See, as well, note 94, above.

190.   See Jump, *Matthew Arnold,* pp. 79–90; Allott, ed., *The Poems of Matthew Arnold,* p. 285.

191.   T.S. Eliot, *The Use of Poetry and the Use of Criticism* (Cambridge: Harvard University Press, 1933), p. 96. I venture to suggest, in passing (and in the safety of a note), that "Dover Beach" is a better poem than the markedly cerebral *The Waste Land,* even though it may not be as "important." See, on Mr. Eliot, notes 138 and 145, above, Appendix E, below. See, also, note 271, below. See, as well, Ian Gregor, "[T.S.] Eliot and Matthew Arnold," in Graham Martin, ed., *Eliot in Perspective* (New York: Humanities Press, 1970); Appendix G, Section vii, below.

192.   There is no problem *here* with the text, except perhaps with the first line. Should there be a period at the end of it? Some editions have a comma there, but I believe a period is better.

193.   Did the "roar" in line 9 induce the "roar" in line 25 and, thereafter, reflections on the state of the Sea of Faith and only then on what Sophocles heard and thought?

194.   To emphasize self-sufficiency need not be the same as to emphasize the self? Was Machiavelli the last of the ancients in this respect, preferring as he did self-sufficiency to love? See *The Prince,* chap. 17. See, also, note 105, above. See, as well, notes 145 and 175, above, notes 251 and 263, below. Cf. note 195, below.

         Appropriately central to the extravagant speeches about love found in *The Song of Songs* is, according to my calculations, that found in verse 9 of chapter 5: "What is thy beloved more than another beloved, O thou fairest among women? What is thy beloved more than another beloved, that thou dost so charge us?" (See, on the series of speakers, *Interpreter's Bible* [New York: Abingdon Press, 1965], vol. 5.) See note 5, above. See, also, note 209, below. (Appropriately central to the speeches in the dialogue recorded in *The Bhagavad Gita* is the response to the critical questions put by Arjuna in VIII, 1–2. See, also, note 248, below.)

195.   See Plato, *Alcibiades II* (on ignorance sometimes being good). Aristotle again and again indicates an awareness of the goodness of existence.

"[F]or perhaps there is some portion of the noble in life even as it is by itself alone, so long as the hardships of life are not too excessive. And it is clear that most men endure much evil suffering, clinging to life, as if in life itself there is a certain serenity and natural sweetness." Aristotle, *Politics* 1278b25–29 (in the Laurence Berns translation). See, also, Homer, *Odyssey*, XI, 203, 487–491; Aristotle, *Nicomachean Ethics* 1161a17, 1166a18 sq., 1168a5, 1169b17, 1170a15–19, 1170a25 sq., 1177b24, 1178b 18–19; Aristotle, *Eudemian Ethics* 1244b29 ("for living must be deemed a mode of knowing"); Aristotle, *Rhetoric*, I, 6; Plato, *Republic* 479C; Benardete, "Euripides' *Hippolytus*," p. 21; Nietzsche, *The Birth of Tragedy*, sec. 17 (end).

See, as well, Thomas Aquinas, *Summa Theologica*, I, Q. 4, A. 1, Rep. Obj. 3; Q. 5, A. 2, Ans.; Q. 5, A. 3, Rep. Obj. 2; Q. 13, A. 11; Q. 16, A. 3; Q. 19, A. 5, Rep. Obj. 3; Q. 20, A. 2.

Cf. Plato, *Republic* 486A–B; Lucretius, *On the Nature of Things*, V, 159f, VI (end); Whitehead, *Science and the Modern World*, p. 192 ("Apart from [the fact of the religious vision], human life is a flash of occasional enjoyments lighting up a mass of pain and misery, a bagatelle of transient experience."). Cf., also, Aristotle, *Eudemian Ethics* 1215b15–1216a28; Montaigne, *Essays*, I, 44; *Khandogya-Upanishad*, VIII, 15, 1; Küng, *Freud and the Problem of God*, pp. 78–79, 109f, 116f. See note 127, above, Appendix E, Epilogue, below.

May not Machiavelli's endorsement of a life dedicated to honor and glory (by any means) reflect a certain morbidity (despite his surface gaiety and robustness)? It is no accident that he chooses to end the *Prince* (with its advocacy of self-confident assertiveness) on the word, "dead." Notice also that his first uses of "death" in that book (in Chapter IV) are in connection with the celebrated conqueror, Alexander the Great. The limits to ambition seem thereby to be tacitly acknowledged. See note 208, below. See, also, note 171, above.

196.   See Anastaplo, "On the Use and Abuse of Old Books," in *Notes on the First Amendment to the Constitution of the United States* (note 24, above), p. 473. See, also, Appendixes B and C, below. See, as well, note 276, below.

197.   In Dante's *Inferno*, the worst sin is not the betrayal of love (whether with respect to one's beloved, family, friends, or guests)—bad as this is— but rather the betrayal of one's ruler or country. Consider, on the control one has over whom one chooses to love, note 5, above.

See note 84, above.

198. "Is not general incivility the very essence of love?" *The Complete Novels of Jane Austen,* p. 316. "Love of *one* is a barbarism . . ." Nietzsche, *Beyond Good and Evil,* Aphorism 67. Cf. note 123, above. This seems to be Giovanni's position. Mozart, *Don Giovanni,* II, 1. Cf. note 228, below.

199. Consider, in Goethe's *Faust,* the challenge Mephistopheles undertakes: to satisfy the seemingly insatiable Faust. Cf. Anastaplo, *The Constitutionalist,* pp. 775–76.

200. See *ibid.,* pp. 784–85. See, also, the text at note 238, below, as well as note 238.

201. One can see how psychoanalysis might work here. See note 164, above, note 207, below. See, also, Chapter V, above, notes 210 and 212, below. Frank Harris spoke of Arnold's "debasing Puritanism." *Contemporary Portraits* (New York: Mitchell Kennerley, 1915), p. 256. See notes 245 and 248, below.

202. See the text at note 4, above. "Personal temperament" can be very much inflenced by chance: thus, *202* became (for me) an auspicious sign in my high-school days because it happened to be the number assigned to me on a couple of occasions when I did well in mathematics and language contests at a nearby university in Southern Illinois. See note 15, above, note 259, below. See, also, note 94, above.

Consider, as shaping one's "personal temperament," the effects of chance childhood experiences. Thus, Mark Twain's recollection of "the shooting down of poor old Smarr" found expression many years later in the shooting down of poor Boggs in *Huckleberry Finn.* See note 220, below. (Notice the odd similarity between "Smarr" and "Boggs": both are one-syllable names; both are undistinguished sounds; both use a double consonant; one begins and the other ends with an *s.*)

The effects of chance may be seen also in the circumstances in which something happens to be written (as is true, for example, of various chapters in *The Artist as Thinker*). It may be virtually impossible, except perhaps for the greatest writers, to remove completely all traces of the origins of a work. (Consider, for example, what it may reveal about an author who is himself a father that he several times indicates concern about what a Desdemona or a Cordelia represents. No doubt, his family circumstances may distort his judgment. Still, this *is* a time when the integrity of the family and hence of oldfashioned piety *should* be vigorously upheld. See, on "reverence for the sources of one's origins," note 76, above. See, also, note 285, below.)

See, further, on the relation between an artist and his "personality," the text at notes 274 and 275, below. (Thus, for example, there may well be "personal" causes [rooted in St. Louis, Athens and Carterville] for my happening to have been drawn over the years to Alexandrian nostalgia. See Appendix E, below. See, also, notes 153 and 164, above.)

See note 145 (end), above. See, also, the Epilogue to Appendix B, below.

203.   It is usually instructive to speculate about what had gone on just before the Platonic dialogue one is interested in began. Cf. Lord Byron, *Don Juan*, I, 6-7.

204.   Is this necessarily an inauspicious sign? Compare how we regard flickering fireflies on a soft summer night. But is the fireflies' light steadier, despite its intermittent character, and hence less troublesome as a portent than what the narrator sees? See, also, the John Davidson poem quoted from in note 145, above. See, as well, Sappho's "Evening Star" lines. *The Poems of Sappho,* p. 51 (*Lyra Graeca* [Loeb Classical Library Edition], I, No. 149; note 117, above).

205.   Is not the narrator English? And the beloved? Consider, also, the Second World War song, "The White Cliffs of Dover." There was something much steadier, and more reassuring, about *that* image. "Don Juan now saw Albion's earliest beauties,—/Thy cliffs, *dear* Dover..." Byron, *Don Juan,* X, 69 ("dear," here, means "expensive").

206.   Most of Arnold's poems do not interest us. Is his scholarship too evident in most of them? (See Chapter XIII, Part Two, Section ix, below.) I find many of his "best" poems tedious. They are mannered, too long, too contrived—so much so that the sentimentality which is perhaps in all of them becomes all too evident. Exceptions, perhaps, are "Growing Old" and "The Last World," as well as "Dover Beach."

207.   See Holland, *The Dynamics of Literary Response,* p. 117. See, also, note 164, above.

208.   Baum, *Ten Studies in the Poetry of Matthew Arnold,* p. 85. Is there not in the relation of the narrator and his beloved something of the relation of Lear and Cordelia? "Come, let's away to prison./ We two will sing like birds i' th' cage." Shakespeare, *King Lear,* V, iii, 8-9. (I am developing here a point suggested to me by Sophie B. Raven of the University of Chicago Laboratory Schools.) It should be noticed that the cliffs at Dover have been known to this day, because of *King Lear,*

as "Shakespeare's Cliffs." It should also be noticed that Lear had had to be stripped in order to be able to come to terms with the world—in order to be able to see himself, to find himself. See, on *King Lear,* Chapter I, Part One, Section iv, above.

A.E. Housman has said, "... Arnold was not merely instructive or charming nor both together: he was what it seems to me no one else is: he was illuminating." *Selected Prose,* p. 198. In any event, cannot "Dover Beach" be regarded as a useful (or, at least, not harmful) poem to occupy the "Melancholy" niche every language should provide for? (See, e.g., Callimachus' "Heraclitus," which is discussed in Appendix E, below.)

Arnold's "pleasing melancholy" reminds of the honey Lucretius places on the rim of the cup of bitter medicine. Both Lucretius and Arnold assume a cycle of ebbings and flowings—even as they prefer to end their respective masterpieces on an ebbing. Both, also, draw on Thucydides for their closing passages, Lucretius for the plague at Athens and Arnold for the night battle. Cf. *The Bhagavad Gita,* V, 4 sq. See note 195, above.

Does Arnold, in what he says about Shelley, speak also of himself as a poet, that he was "a beautiful and ineffectual angel, beating in the void his luminous wings in vain"? *Wall Street Journal,* June 24, 1981, p. 21. See note 178, above.

IX. LEWIS CARROLL (1832-1898)

209.   See Anastaplo, *The Constitutionalist,* pp. 30–32, 787, 806–8. Consider, also, the instructive organization in Boccaccio's *Decameron* of the ten sets of ten stories. Consider, as well, the comments on Homer, Prologue, section ii, above. See notes 7, 94, 100, and 202, above. See, also, notes 179 and 194, above.

210.   Virginia Wexman has observed (in an unpublished paper, The University of Chicago, 1973), "[Once Alice] has learned to control her size by eating the appropriate side of the mushroom, the issue of her identity never again comes up. And from that point onward, her predominant attitude toward the creatures of Wonderland changes from one of timid acquiescence and confusion to a more relaxed assertiveness." Thus, Mrs. Wexman, too, seems to have responded (from another perspective) to my Stage VII as the turning point of the *Wonderland* story.

It is not clear, by the way, that the mushroom can affect anyone else as it does Alice. Is not the Caterpillar satisfied with its size? It seems to be only the child Alice for whom changes in size matter, as is appropriate for creatures who are all too often aware of their disabilities because of their size and who long for the day when they can both know and cope with the adult world (or, rather, the world run by adults—by the adults who matter so much to the young and whom they are destined to replace). See Bruno Bettelheim, *The Uses of Enchantment: The Meaning and Importance of Fairy Tales* (New York: Alfred A. Knopf, 1976), pp. 23-28.

Alice's twelve size changes in *Wonderland* may be found at the following places in Martin Gardner, ed., *The Annotated Alice* (New York: World Publishing Co., 1971), pp. 31, 35, 39, 57, 63, 73, 74, 77, 78, 91, 104, 147-61.

211.   Mr. Gardner observes, "Alice's bewildering changes of size in [*Wonderland*] are replaced [in *Looking-Glass*] by equally bewildering changes of place, occasioned of course by the movements of chess pieces over the board." *The Annotated Alice*, p. 172.

It must suit Carroll just fine that a pawn begins in the second row: he is not interested in infancy; he likes his children mobile and articulate, and of course well mannered. (Alice is seven in *Wonderland*, seven and one-half in *Looking-Glass*. Ruskin's impressions of Alice Liddell as a child are indicated in *The Annotated Alice*, p. 12.) See note 215, below.

Playing cards figure critically in *Wonderland*. Does thirteen (as in the thirteen stages I have conjured up there) come from the number of cards in each suit in a deck of cards? To ask such a question is to assume that dreams *do* make sense? See, e.g., notes 170 and 174, above; also, Section v of this chapter, below.

212.   Alice Liddell was born in 1852. The *Wonderland* story was first told to her and her sisters in 1862; it was published in 1865. *Looking-Glass* was published in 1871.

On May 11, 1865, Dodgson recorded in his diary, "Met Alice and Miss Prickett in the quadrangle: Alice seems changed a good deal, and hardly for the better—probably going through the usual awkward stage of transition." Mr. Gardner notes that although "the majority of Carroll's child-friends broke off contact with him (or he with them) after their adolescence," "the finest tribute ever paid to Carroll are the recollections of him expressed by Alice in her later years." *The Annotated Alice*, p. 173. (Does "the usual awkward stage of transition" referred to by Dodgson include the onset of the menstrual cycle? And is that critical to Carroll's emphasis on the fluid character of things in the cen-

tral stage of *Looking-Glass?* See note 201, above. See, also, Thomas
Aquinas, *Summa Theologica*, II–II, Q. 88, A. 10.) In any event, it is
suggestive that a man of experience is *believed* to be needed in the
Seventh Square to help an egg-laden girl find her way among the trees.

213.   The selfish part of Dodgson-Carroll may be seen in the Red Knight,
whom the White Knight must overcome before Alice can go on to her
destination.

    See, for an indication of Dodgson's psychic limitations, *The Anno-
tated Alice,* p. 251, n. 4. Readers familiar with the theological, political,
and academic controversies of Dodgson's day can no doubt find much
of interest buried in the *Alice* books, as can those with a taste for socio-
logical and psychoanalytical excavations. See the text at note 234, below.

    The three accounts of the old man's life, given (autobiographically?)
by the White Knight, bear looking into. What he describes in the first
account ("I look for butterflies/ That sleep among the wheat;/ I make
them into mutton-pies,/ And sell them in the street.") is both incongruous and attractive. But the old man's first account is not attended
to, and he must give another (more prosaic?) and still another (even
more prosaic?) account. But should not the first account remain the
most haunting and instructive, at least for those who listen properly?
Those pies *are* sold to men—all of us?—"who sail on stormy seas." *The
Annotated Alice,* pp. 307–13.

    A suppressed episode in *Looking-Glass* has become available since I
prepared this chapter for publication in the *University of Chicago Magazine* (Winter 1975). The episode has been reproduced and discussed in
the *Smithsonian Magazine* (December 1977). It describes Alice's encounter with an elderly wasp in a wig, and was originally placed by Carroll just after the parting of the White Knight and Alice and just before
the crossing by Alice over the final brook to queenhood. Thus, this
episode is included within my Stage VI of Alice's journey. It can be
taken to reinforce what I have suggested about the relation of Alice
and Dodgson-Carroll. The bad-tempered (waspish?) insect can be seen
as the other side of the White Knight (even as a revival, of sorts, of the
Red Knight). This (less romantic?) episode suggests what old age will
do to the White Knight (who has neither armor nor hair nor [as a male
wasp] sting).

    Even so, the confident Alice is seen as kind. The suppressed episode
opens with Alice recognizing, upon hearing a deep sign from the woods
behind her, "There's somebody very unhappy there." It concludes,
"Alice tripped down the hill again, quite pleased that she had gone
back and given a few minutes to making the poor old creature comfortable." But whereas Alice had allowed the White Knight to leave her, it

is she who leaves the wasp. This is, however the White Knight preferred to make it seem, the way things really are? And so, the White Knight-Old Wasp can be expected to be "very unhappy." (The episode was suppressed by Carroll in deference [it is said] to his illustrator, John Tenniel, who insisted that "a *wasp* in a *wig* is altogether beyond the appliances of art." Be that as it may, the episode does seem to fit in nicely with my analysis of what happens in Stage VI of the *Looking-Glass* journey. May not Carroll have been willing to be persuaded to suppress the wasp episode because it was so painful in its self-revelation?)

214.   Such bringing together of the two worlds is also done after Alice's dream in *Wonderland*, but there it is done primarily by Alice's older sister.

   The reader with common sense is not likely to be as uncertain, as Carroll tries to have both Alice and the reader be, about whether it is all the Red King's dream or Alice's dream in *Looking-Glass*. Is it not clearly the dream of Carroll's Alice, in that it is Alice's character which determines what happens in this dream? In this respect, Carroll's deep-rooted artistic instincts prevail over his modern "philosophical" opinions.

   The "whose dream?" inquiry Carroll attempts to leave us with may draw upon and reflect the Cartesian influence in modernity. Indeed, one might even say that Lewis Carroll would not have been possible without René Descartes. See Chapter XIII, Part Two, Section ii, below. See, also, note 251, below.

215.   Uses, in the *Alice* books, of some form of "nature" may be found at the following places in *The Annotated Alice*: pp. 26, 45, 55, 87, 90, 139, 198, 211, 232, 263, 287, 335. See, also, *ibid.,* pp. 33 ("what generally happens," "in the common way"), 148 ("grow at a reasonable pace"), 226–27 (on the significance of names), 266 ("one cannot help growing older"). See, on nature and the guidance it provides, Anastaplo, "One Introduction to Confucian Thought," *University of Chicago Magazine,* Summer 1974, p. 21; (this talk was dedicated to the memory of Leo Strauss); *Human Being and Citizen,* Essays No. 4 and No. 6; "Jacob Klein of St. John's College." See, also, note 145, above, Epilogue, below.

   Does Carroll's nominalism undermine "nature" as a standard? And does the modern infatuation with individualism also encourage a depreciation of nature as something in accordance with which individuals should be shaped? Has the modern unnatural enthronement of childhood been prompted by the prevailing concern with individuality and hence with the formative years one happens to have? See Anastaplo, *Human Being and Citizen,* Essays No. 7 and No. 17.

   If Alice's adult career is reflected, as in a mirror image, in *Looking-*

Glass, then she can be expected to sink eventually into a fairly amiable infancy-like old age. See note 211 and the text thereat, above.

The emphasis in *Wonderland* seems to be placed upon Alice's "adventures" and in *Looking-Glass* upon "what Alice *found* there." The former dream may be more concerned with the play of children and with action (and ends, at the trial, with a problem of justice), the latter with a journey of maturation and with one's observations *en route* (and ends with a problem of knowledge: whose dream is it?). Thus, the first story is concerned more with *acting,* the second with *knowing.* Are we not to understand that one must, before one can become a complete adult, come to terms with both of these related, yet quite different, activities of the human soul? See Plato, *Republic* 487B–488A. See, also, Epilogue, Section ii (end), below. Is the decisive human movement, then, from *doing* and *looking* to *being* and its apprehension?

Bearing upon these observations are the concluding remarks of the talk, "One-sixteenth of a Lecture on Alice's Wonderlands," in which I first brought together in a systematic fashion the argument of this chapter (an argument I had developed in a course at The Clearing in August 1974). The talk (given on January 17, 1975, in the Works of the Mind Lecture Series of the Basic Program of Liberal Education for Adults, The University of Chicago) concluded in this fashion:

> Our understanding of human things, which poetry is dedicated to helping us with, cannot depend on these two books alone. How much of the whole is addressed in these books? Only a small part? We still need to learn, for example, about what Alice would be like as a woman. Thus, we have considered only one-half of the story implied here. But to say one-half may be to see more here than there is: for the male side of humanity, both among children and among adults, must be taken account of in any effort to make sense of the whole of things. Thus, we have touched upon no more than one-fourth of human existence—and that is reduced to one-eighth when we recognize that we need (in order really to make sense of the whole) to hear also about the tragic side of life, not only about what is (as in the *Alice* books) essentially comic. [So, nature must be looked to....]
>
> ...When one speaks of nature, one is reminded of still another dimension of human things which would have to be covered in any serious attempt (whether through tragedy or through comedy) to deal with the whole of human existence: one is reminded, that is, of those who discovered nature—the ancients. But the *Alice* books speak from the modern perspective. Thus, we come to the recognition that we have, in what we have said on this occasion

surveyed *not* one-half, *not* one-fourth, not even one-eighth, but only one-sixteenth of the ground to be covered! This is, as Alice says somewhere, "curiouser and curiouser": the further we go in these speculations, the greater our awareness of what there is left to consider—and hence the less of a lecture we have had.

This can be a frightening experience indeed, as still further divisions suggesting reductions to one-thirty-second and one-sixty-fourth) might be considered as the result of adjustments for the sex of the *narrator* of a story and as the result of adjustments depending on whether a story is narrated by an outsider or in the first person. Perhaps we can, by insisting that the narrator does not truly matter in a well-wrought story, make an effort to salvage one-sixteenth of a lecture. Certainly, we can appreciate the observation of the Red Queen in *Looking-Glass*—an observation which seems to apply to our present embarrassment as well, "Now, here, you see, it takes all the running *you* can do, to keep in the same place. If you want to get somewhere else, you must run at least twice as fast as that."

But, alas, I cannot hope to run any faster than I have. And, as you have just seen, I run a grave risk of losing what little ground I may have gained. That is, we are (as we grow in our recognition of how little we have really said on this occasion) back with Alice, in the middle of her original adventures in Wonderland, facing immediate extinction—she as an adventurer, I as a lecturer. It is reported that Alice "felt that there was no time to be lost, as she was shrinking rapidly": she had to move fast and so she made a desperately successful effort to open her mouth and thereby eat some of the mushroom which would save her from vanishing altogether. My effort must be as heroic as hers, and just as immediate. That is, I must at once forego further tasting of the many instructive delights of these two books: I must quit talking while I still have something, if only a little something, of a lecture left to share with you.

At this point, my talk ended. See Sterne, *Tristram Shandy,* p. 207 (IV, xiii). See, also, the end of Appendix C, below. See, as well, Arnhart, *Aristotle on Political Reasoning,* pp. 189–190; Anastaplo, "American Constutionalism and the Virtue of Prudence," pp. 155–156; note 289, below.

X. MARK TWAIN (1835-1910)

216.   Arthur L. Scott, ed., *Mark Twain: Selected Criticism* (Dallas: Southern Methodist University Press, 1967), pp. 44–45.

I have found useful, in thinking about Mark Twain, discussions with Joel Rich, a University of Chicago colleague.

The quotation from Huckleberry Finn among the epigraphs at the front of this book may be found in Mark Twain, *Tom Sawyer, Detective*, chap. 2.

217.   This is to be contrasted to, say, Aristotle, who would make an effort to recognize the merits as well as the defects of each. See, e.g., *Politics*, Book III. Mark Twain sees the aristocrat only as proud and reckless? And he ignores the compassion shown by the people?

Popular compassion may be seen even in the Boggs episode: the artist shows more than he is aware of? Less compassion is shown toward "the drunk" on "the wild horse" in the circus scene. See Section v, of this chapter, below. Is this because the crowd senses what Huck does not, that is *is* a show? Consider, also, the ambivalent response to the threat of smallpox, Twain, *The Adventures of Huckleberry Finn*, pp. 125–27.

218.   Such a sheriff may be found in William Faulkner's work. See Faulkner, *Intruder in the Dust* (New York: Vintage Books, 1972), e.g., pp. 33–35, 40, 43. See, also, Anastaplo, *The Constitutionalist*, pp. 219, 613.

Just as the speech given by Twain to Colonel Sherburn facing the lynch-mob is deeply inappropriate for a man of his character, so is some of the music given by Mozart to the "hero" of *Don Giovanni*. See notes 10 and 198, above, note 263, below.

When one considers various of the songs given to Giovanni—are not the two or three best songs in the opera his?—, one can see what art can do to make a dubious cause plausible. Particularly striking is the famous duet between Giovanni and Zerlina, in which the nobleman seduces the peasant girl, *Là ci darem la mano*. This song is so appealing that anyone of healthy sensibilities should perhaps yearn to give in to it: it would be almost unnatural for a woman to resist such entreaties, such a plea for sharing the most precious things of this world with another of like sensibilities. It is difficult for one not to feel—either as the girl being addressed or as a member of the audience listening—that it must be good to have and to give in to the longing expressed in that lovely song and thereby to relieve "the pangs of an innocent love."

There is something dreamlike about this duet, intensifying the youthful passions and the fantasy that opera is so adept at minstering to, especially when matters of love (or, perhaps to be more accurate, romance) are being dealt with. Certainly, the taste for sensuality is catered to, perhaps even heightened, and in any event legitimated.

But, the moralist will persist, it is not appropriate that exquisitely beautiful music should be used to describe, and in effect to serve and to justify, Giovanni's often dubious and always selfish purposes. Certainly, we find this love song by Giovanni more attractive, more humane and more likely to be something we ourselves will try to hum and sing than, say, Elvira's harsh condemnation of Giovanni which cuts short the seduction of Zerlina or Masetto's angry outburst at a Zerlina who is (at one point) obviously attracted by Giovanni. We can admire the crafts-manship evident in Elvira's fierce music (his lips, she says, are lying, his eyes deceiving): it is music appropriate to the character in her cir-cumstances, a character not altogether free of madness. We may even concede the justice of what she says, especially if we should study in prose what she accuses him of and what Giovanni says to defend himself. But it *is* Giovanni's song to Zerlina that attracts us—and that continues to haunt us long after we have come to know the worst about him.

One is not encouraged, as a spectator, to notice and to think but rather to feel and to respond—and thus one's soul is shaped, or reshaped, in a way that is not properly examined either by the artist or by the audience. And here the moralist, who concedes the haunting beauty of Giovanni's seductive song, might go to a deeper level in his complaint. Other things said by Giovanni in the opera are more reliable expressions of his ugly soul than this song, things such as his exchange with Anna (at the beginning of the opera) when he had tried to rape her. That is to say, it can be argued, no one with the soul evident in the song sung to Zerlina could be the man Giovanni is or could do the things he so callously does in matters of love and in other matters. For an artist to imagine otherwise is to be guilty of a serious error in judgment: it is to imagine a virtual impossibility, and to do so to the detriment of the moral training of his audience. This song is of a kind to be shared by true lovers, preferably as they embark upon, or reaffirm, a genuine mar-riage; it should not be used to pander to something so casual, and so meaningless, as Giovanni's two thousand sixty-sixth seduction.

A similar error in judgment is exhibited by Twain in permitting Colonel Sherburn to speak as he does to the mob.

219.　　Compare the authorities at the end of *The Adventures of Tom Sawyer*: *they* recognize, and extol, Tom's achievements. See, e.g., Jaffa, *The Conditions of Freedom*, pp. 191–92, 218.

　　We see in Huck a curious blend of the detached but observant inno-cence of Ishmael and the instinctive guilefulness of Odysseus.

220.　　*The Complete Essays of Mark Twain,* Charles Neider, ed. (Garden City: Doubleday & Co., 1963), pp. 676–77. See, for the childhood experience on which the death of Boggs is based, Mark Twain, *Autobiography* (New

York: Harper and Bros., 1924), I, 131; Anastaplo, *The Constitutionalist,* p. 612. See, also, note 202, above.

221.   I am reminded of clowns I have seen in a Russian circus. They provide biting, yet privileged, commentaries on the regime. Others have noticed the parallel I comment upon in the text between the Boggs-Sherburn episode and the circus episode; but I do not believe they have put it to the use I have. See Twain, *The Adventures of Huckleberry Finn,* pp. xiv-xv. Consider, also, the parallel between the Grangerford-Shepherdson feud and *Romeo and Juliet. The Adventures of Huckleberry Finn,* pp. xiv, 143–56, 170–71, 177, 180, 194.

The prose in the circus episode is marvelous. (I am somehow reminded of the description of Tom and the church fly in *The Adventures of Tom Sawyer,* chap. V.) Huck enjoys himself hugely at the circus: this makes one wonder, still another time, what the relation is for Mark Twain between one's ignorance and one's humanity. Consider, in the work of Leo Tolstoy, the naïveté of Natasha at the opera (*War and Peace,* VIII, 2) and Gerasim's peasant kindness (*The Death of Ivan Ilytch;* see note 175, above). Cf. Epilogue, Section v (beginning), below.

222.   See, on tragedy, death, and comedy in Mark Twain, Anastaplo, *Human Being and Citizen,* pp. 321–22 (the conclusion of the lecture from which this chapter was developed). See, also, *ibid.,* pp. ix, xiii. See, as well, Epilogue, Section ii (end), below.

Consider, in the chapter immediately after the circus, what the duke and the king do with, and say about, tragedy. See, also, the text at note 236, below. See, as well, Bruno Bettelheim, "Surviving," *New Yorker,* Aug. 2, 1976, p. 31 (on Lina Wertmüller's unfortunate film, *Seven Beauties*). See, for the book form of the Bettelheim review, note 279, below. See, on films generally, Appendix F, below.

See, on the considerable "contributions to civilization" of the American regime, Arthur M. Schlesinger, "America's Influence," *Atlantic Monthly,* March 1959, p. 65.

XI. WILLIAM S. GILBERT (1836-1911) AND ARTHUR SULLIVAN (1842-1900)

223.   James Joyce, *Ulysses,* p. 160.

224.   *Ibid.,* p. 163.

225.   *Ibid.*, p. 165. See, also, *ibid.*, p. 285; Joyce, *A Portrait of the Artist as a Young Man*, pp. 191–92.

226.   *Martyn Green's Treasury of Gilbert & Sullivan* (New York: Simon and Shuster, 1961), p. 564.

   Of course, the Green account does not explain how this song was originally conceived—whether the tune or the lyrics came first—many years before.

   How the words can influence the music may be seen in the rendering of the Nicene Creed in Bach's *Mass in B Minor* (BWV 232). Of the nine divisions which comprise the *Credo*, only one is an aria (one is a duet, all the others are for chorus). This bass aria, the most solemn-sounding passage in the *Credo* music, is reserved by Bach for the seventh division in the *Credo*. It is this passage which includes the *filioque* language which chanced to be so critical in dividing the Western Church from Eastern Orthodoxy. (Orthodoxy's determined rejection of the *filioque* addition by the Western Church, it can be said, compensated for the considerable reliance by the Orthodox upon icons. See note 90, above. In the *filioque* controversy, it can also be said, the Orthodox sided with the more rigorous Judaic monotheistic element in Christendom. See note 173 [beginning], above.)

227.   See, for the British schoolboy's spirit in a sometimes hilarious form, Rudyard Kipling, *Stalky & Co.* (1899).

   Contributing to the proper development of the schoolboy's spirit among us is so civilized a game as baseball, about which I had occasion to write to the *New York Times Book Review,* May 9, 1981: "Daniel Okrent's all-star baseball team drawn from fiction (May 3) has one perhaps happy omission: it lacks that unfortunate modern experiment, the designated hitter. Who else should that be but the ill-fated Casey?" See Anastaplo, *The Constitutionalist,* pp. 660, 683, 792. See, also, note 123, above.

228.   See, for another kind of "framing," the discussion of *The Rape of Lucrece* and of *Titus Andronicus* in Chapter I, Part Two, above. How much, in such cases, *does* the flawed artist grasp of what he is (instinctively?) doing? See note 263, below.

   See, for still another instance of framing, the comments on the side borders (for a stained-glass window) in Appendix D, Part Three, below.

229.   Does all this promote justice? Or does it only make necessarily imperfect attempts at justice less attractive offstage? See note 16, above.

See, on a possible reemergence of Jupiter *et al.,* Sterne, *Tristram Shandy,* pp. 346–47 (VII, vii).

230.   The naturalness of sexual pairings has been strikingly evident whenever I have participated in a "Do-It-Yourself-*Messiah*" sung by thousands of voices in Chicago's Orchestra Hall: Handel guides his basses and tenors to expect and to rely on the quite different women's voices. (See, on the *Messiah* in Leopold Bloom's Dublin, Joyce, *Ulysses,* p. 180.) See, on the related problem of homosexuality, Anastaplo, *The Constitutionalist,* pp. 624–25, 672; *Human Being and Citizen,* pp. 76, 268–70; note 78, above. See, also, Strauss, *Natural Right and History,* p. 300. See, as well, Aristotle, *Nicomachean Ethics* 1162a14 sq. See, on nature, note 145, above. See, also, note 246 (end), below.

See, on nature and convention, the comments on Desdemona, in Chapter I, Part One, above. It is, we are told by Gilbert and Sullivan, natural to have party divisions. See *The Complete Plays of Gilbert and Sullivan* (New York: Modern Library, 1936), e.g., pp. 266–67. See, for other comments on the nature of nature, *ibid.,* pp. 53 ("nature is constantly changing"), 211 ("But Nature [in the form of love], for restraint too mighty far, has burst the bonds of Art"), 272–73, 319, 373 ("Nature is lovely, and rejoices in her loveliness."), 626, 642. See, as well, Dante, *Paradiso,* XXVI, 130f.

231.   Consider *Trial by Jury:* the ruthless judge gets his way again; the plaintiff who gets him gets what *she* deserves; the defendant, who had spoken for the principle of changeableness in matters of love, has the last word as he wonders how enduring is the match just made in the courtroom. *Princess Ida* is anticipated, of course, by Aristophanes' *Lysistrata.* See note 236, below. See, also, Shakespeare, *Love's Labor's Lost,* I, i, 291, IV, iii, 212. See, as well, *ibid.,* IV, iii, 279, V, ii, 441, 746, 784.

We are told that "woman's heart is one with woman's hand." *Complete Plays of Gilbert and Sullivan,* p. 546. Cf. *ibid.,* pp. 512–13. We are also told, "In her first passion woman loves her lover,/In all the others all she loves is love..." Byron, *Don Juan,* III, 3. Cf. Anastaplo, *Human Being and Citizen,* p. 274, n. 36.

232.   Compare Aristotle's *Nicomachean Ethics,* where it is again and again indicated that the good man takes pleasure in, or at least is not pained by, doing what he should. Compare the text at note 240, below. See, also, note 119, above, notes 239 and 244, below. See, as well, Anastaplo, *Human Being and Citizen,* p. 313, n. 1.

233.   Max Beerbohm could say of this ballad, in 1905 (John B. Jones, ed.,

W.S. Gilbert: A Century of Scholarship and Commentary [New York: New York University Press, 1970], p. 65), "The story of the little maid's rescue of her former lover from the headsman's block is a joy for ever." This only goes to show that the Gilbertian temperament was shared by others, perhaps many, many others, as well! See Plato, *Republic* 424C.

See, on the flexibility of one's view of time, note 102, above.

234.   See note 29, above. Cf. note 213, above.

235.   *Martyn Green's Treasury,* p. 424. Consider, in this respect, the uncomfortable implications of Edmund Rostand's *Cyrano de Bergerac.* Consider, also, whether the Olivia of Shakespeare's *Twelfth Night* can be fully satisfied with Sebastian after having been drawn to him through Viola-Cesario. See note 78, above.

236.   Are the more fundamental problems for tragedy to deal with? But see Leo Strauss, *Socrates and Aristophanes* (New York: Basic Books, 1966). See, also, notes 129 and 222, above, Epilogue, Section ii (end), below (quoting from Strauss, *Thoughts on Machiavelli,* p. 292). Cf. note 195, above.

Machiavelli's *Mandragola* is now available in a careful translation by Mera J. Flaumenhaft, published by The Waveland Press.

237.   See Aristotle, *Politics,* I, i. See, also, Plato, *Republic* 376E sq. See, as well, the text at note 165, above, note 288, below.

See, on death, *The Complete Plays of Gilbert and Sullivan,* pp. 27, 285, 539. See, also, notes 18 and 175, above.

238.   See the text at note 200, above, as well as note 200, above. Cf. *The Complete Plays of Gilbert and Sullivan,* pp. 164–66 ("Go, ye heroes, go to glory"). An instructive anticipation of that war may be seen in Paul Valéry's "A Conquest by Method" (first published in 1897) and in Erskine Childers's *Riddle of the Sands* (first published in 1903); an instructive indication of the passions of that war may be seen in John Buchan's novels (such as *The Thirty-Nine Steps,* first published in 1915). Cf. Tagore, *Towards Universal Man,* pp. 270–71: "India's awakening is a part of the awakening of the world. With the Great War the door of a new age has flung open. The peoples of the earth have been drawing closer to one another, almost unawares; but as all humanity feels the stress of war, the fact of their mutual dependence can no longer be denied. All at once the foundations of civilization, western civilization to be precise, seem to quake. It is evident that the tremors are neither

local nor momentary; they are world-wide and will not stop until human relationships, reaching from continent to continent, become based on true harmony." But see note 84, above. The Enlightenment was slow in reaching India?

See, on the somewhat childish desire of the English to be heroes, Huntford, *Scott and Amundsen,* p. 564. See, also, note 163, above. Cf., as a perhaps "natural" reaction to excessive heroic appetites, the state of things described in J. Linn Allen, "Losing Control," *Chicago Reader,* March 13, 1981, p. 51: "Since John Osborne's *Look Back in Anger* in 1956, British dramatists have made an industry of denunciation. In an unrivaled outpouring of absorbing tirades their heroes have excoriated themselves, their lovers, and particularly their rotten society. If plays could kill, England would have been guillotined over and over again, like some particularly galling aristocrat whose death a rebellious mob can't get enough of. As it is, the nation has been gored repeatedly by the adder's teeth of its thankless children. In truth, there is much in these attacks of the child's rage at its parents for being flawed, for being discovered not to measure up to the idealizations of early youth. The invective burns with the violent self-righteousness of disillusioned adolescence. At the same time, the assaults are desperately self-destructive, permeated with the child's need to be controlled, the child's daring (and intense desiring) of its parent to be strong enough to control it." (Homer's Thersites comes to mind. See Anastaplo, "Freedom of Speech and the First Amendment," 42 *University of Detroit Law Review* 55, 56f [1964].) Is not the *political* art needed to heal such wounds? See note 288, below. Cf. John H. Wigmore, 14 *Illinois Law Rev.* 539 (1920).

239.   In any event, Jack Point does counsel:

> For he who'd make his fellow-creatures wise
> Should always gild the philosophic pill.

The Complete Plays of Gilbert and Sullivan, p. 479. See, also, *ibid.,* pp. 122–23, 160, 163, 170, 177, 295, 455–56, 477. See, as well, Anastaplo, *The Constitutionalist,* pp. 260, 766, 793–94; *Human Being and Citizen,* Essay No. 3; note 13, above.

XII. ROBERT LOUIS STEVENSON (1850–1894)

240.   Thus, Henry James said of this story: "Is [it] a work of high philosophic intention, or simply the most ingenious and irresponsible of fictions? ... It deals with the relation of the baser parts of man to his nobler, of

the capacity for evil that exists in the most generous natures ..." *Partial Portraits* (Westport, Conn.: Greenwood Press, 1970), p. 169. See, also, note 244, below. Cf. note 232, above. See, also, on this story, Nabokov, *Lectures on Literature*, p. 179f.

Elsewhere, James observed that "the greater imagination [is] the imagination of the moralist." Quoted by Catherine H. Zuckert, "American Women and Democratic Morals: *The Bostonians*," *Feminist Studies*, Spring/Summer 1976, pp. 31, 48.

See, on the status of the noble today, Anastaplo, *The Constitutionalist*, pp. 670–71.

241.   Mr. Hyde does engage in some rather vague escapades, but nothing like what John Barrymore does in a movie made from the story. See *The Works of Robert Louis Stevenson* (New York: P.F. Collier & Son, 1912), VI, 195, 221, 227–28. There is also, of course, the Carew murder. *Ibid.*, VI, 185f, 232. He indulges in blasphemies as well. *Ibid.*, VI, 212, 238.

242.   Consider the question addressed by Maimonides in *The Guide of the Perplexed*, I, 2. Dr. Jekyll refers to the power of transformation he developed as ethically neutral. *The Works of Robert Louis Stevenson*, VI, 226. See, also, *ibid.*, VI, 183, 230–31, 234. (One is reminded here of Victor Frankenstein's presumptuousness? See Chapter V, Section vii [end], above; also, note 154, above. One can hear echoes from the earlier story in the later. Thus, Mary Shelley takes as her point of departure, "It was on a dreary night of November." See Chapter VI, section iii, above. And Stevenson can have Dr. Jekyll report, "late one accursed night." *Ibid.*, VI, 224.) See Chapter XII, Section vii, below.

Stevenson's Long John Silver (in *Treasure Island*) may be a more interesting (and attractive) version of the kind of man seen in Dr. Jekyll *and* Mr. Hyde (but in one form). Henry James, I should note here, observed: "... I have some difficulty of accepting the business of the powders, which seems to me too explicit and explanatory. The powders constitute the machinery of the transformation [of Dr. Jekyll into Mr. Hyde], and it will probably have struck many readers that this uncanny process would be more conceivable (so far as one may speak of the conceivable in such a case), if the author had not made it so definite." *Partial Portraits*, p. 171. But critical to the effect of the story are the desperate efforts to secure the powders necessary for the vital drug. *The Works of Robert Louis Stevenson*, VI, 205–6, 214–21, 238. Cf. the text at note 230, above.

243.   The murder committed by Mr. Hyde, says Dr. Jekyll, "was not only a

crime, it had been a tragic folly." *The Works of Robert Louis Stevenson*, VI, 233. See Anastaplo, *Human Being and Citizen*, p. 257, n. 46.

244.   We have seen this in *Frankenstein*. We see it again in Gilbert and Sullivan. See, also, the comments on beauty in note 145, above, Chapter XIII, Part One, Section ii, below. See, as well, Appendix A, below.

        Cf. Plato, *Symposium* 215B, 216D–E.

245.   See, e.g., *Romans* 7: 23. Consider, also, Bunyan, *The Pilgrim's Progress*, p. 98:

> I took notice that now poor Christian was so confounded that he did not know his own voice, and thus I perceived it: just when he was come over against the mouth of the burning pit, one of the wicked ones got behind him, and stepped up softly to him, and whisperingly suggested many grievous blasphemies to him which he verily thought had proceeded from his own mind. This put Christian more to it than anything that he met with before, even to think that he should now blaspheme him that he loved so much before; yet could he have helped it, he would not have done it: but he had not the discretion neither to stop his ears, nor to know from whence those blasphemies came.

See Chapter III, Section ii (end), above, note 201, above. See, also, Plato, *Laws* 854A–C.

    Dr. Jekyll can be considered to have had a duplicity of character all his life. See *The Works of Robert Louis Stevenson*, VI, 181, 222–23, 230–31.

246.   The Manson cult comes to mind. See, on human nature and the criminal law, Anastaplo, "Human Nature and the First Amendment," p. 715f.

    Freud seems to have been anticipated in Dr. Jekyll's opinions about the soul. See, e.g., *The Works of Robert Louis Stevenson*, VI, 223–24. See, also, Matthew Arnold, *The Buried Life;* Joyce, *Ulysses*, p. 414; note 245, above.

    Consider Trollope, *An Autobiography*, II, 34–35:

> [I]t becomes to [a novelist] a matter of deep conscience how he shall handle those characters by whose words and doings he hopes to interest his readers. It will very frequently be the case that he will be tempted to sacrifice something for effect, to say a word or two here, or to draw a picture there, for which he feels that he has

the power, and which when spoken or drawn would be alluring. The regions of absolute vice are foul and odious. The savour of them, till custom has hardened the palate and the nose, is disgusting. In these he will hardly tread. But there are outskirts on these regions, on which sweet-smelling flowers seem to grow, and grass to be green. It is in these border-lands that the danger lies. The novelist may not be dull. If he commit that fault he can do neither harm nor good. He must please, and the flowers and the grass in these neutral territories sometimes seem to give him so easy an opportunity of pleasing!

The writer of stories must please, or he will be nothing. And he must teach whether he wish to teach or no. How shall he teach lessons of virtue and at the same time make himself a delight to his readers? That sermons are not in themselves often thought to be agreeable we all know. Nor are disquisitions on moral philosophy supposed to be pleasant reading for our idle hours. But the novelist, if he have a conscience, must preach his sermons with the same purpose as the clergyman, and must have his own system of ethics. . . .

The problem of how to "teach lessons of virtue and at the same time make [oneself] a delight to [one's] readers" is one continually faced by newspaper columnists who specialize in advice to the lovelorn and others. Have not the more successful tended to become moral relativists (if not even risqué) in order to remain interesting? Compare the repeated reaffirmations of the community and of old-fashioned standards evident in the columns of Dorothy Dix, *the* newspaper advisor of the past generation or two. Thus, she answered a young woman "who wrote to protest the way the people in her small town peered at her from behind their blinds, checked on her goings and comings, and then whispered about her," and who asked whether gossip wasn't a terrible thing:

You're wrong. Gossip is an influence for good—an invisible policeman that enforces law and order, and keeps the feet of weak people on the path. We may quiet the voice of conscience, Louise, but not the voice of the neighbors. It is the fear of "they'll say" that often makes us curb our appetites and stick to standards of conduct set up by society. Think what would happen if we could do as we pleased and get away with it. There would be many more philandering husbands and wives, many more neglected children, badly-kept houses, wife-beating husbands and virago wives.

Those who are down on gossip and feel the world should cover up their shortcomings are unreasonable. Why should others be more

careful of your reputation than you are yourself? If you do not
care enough for your good name to protect it, why demand that
service of the general public? There is no chaperone so efficient
as Mrs. Grundy, and the only way to escape being talked about is
to be so exemplary in behavior that you are a dull subject for
conversation.

Harnett T. Kane, *Dear Dorothy Dix: The Story of a Compassionate
Woman* (Garden City: Doubleday & Co., 1952), 289-90. See, also,
Thucydides, *History of the Peloponnesian War,* II, 45 ("On the other
hand, if I must say anything on the subject of female excellence to
those of you who will now be in widowhood, it will all be comprised
in this brief exhortation. Great will be your glory in not falling short
of your natural character; and greatest will be hers who is least talked
of among the men whether for good or for bad."). See, as well, note
230, above. (For women, Pericles seems to say, glory is being remembered for having been forgotten?)

See, on art and novelty, *The Works of the Emperor Julian* (Loeb
Classical Library Edition), I, 7: "As for the poets, their Muse, and the
general belief that it is she who inspires their verse, obviously gives them
unlimited license to invent.... Poets who compose and publish some
legend that no one had thought of before increase their reputation,
because an audience is entertained by the mere fact of novelty." See,
also, Plato, *Laws* 660A–B; Anastaplo, *Human Being and Citizen,*
pp. 137-38; Strauss, *Natural Right and History,* p. 83. See, as well, note
218, above, note 279 (end), below. Cf. Plato, *Laws* 656D sq.

XIII. JAMES JOYCE (1882-1941)

247. *The Letters of W.B. Yeats,* Allan Wade, ed. (New York: Macmillan Co.,
1955), pp. 598-99 (a letter of 1918). See Richard Ellmann, *James
Joyce* (New York: Oxford University Press, 1965), pp. 402-3. See, also,
ibid., pp. 545, 589n, 608n.

The Ellmann book provides a useful guide to both the life and the
work of Joyce. See, *ibid.,* e.g., pp. 5, 309, 729-30. Cf. note 248, below.

248. *Ibid.,* p. 807. See, also, Joyce, *A Portrait of the Artist,* p. 137: "his
soul within him was a living mass of corruption." See, as well, Ellmann,
James Joyce, p. 590; Joyce, *Ulysses,* pp. 245-46; note 245, above.
"For all the vices are seasoned with pride just as the virtues are seasoned
and enlivened by charity." St. Catherine of Siena, *The Dialogue,*
trans. Suzanne Noffkes (New York: Paulist Press, 1980), p. 251.

Is not the "sense of sin" Yeats refers to almost pathological in the compulsive sexuality exhibited by Joyce in his 1909 letters to his wife? See *Selected Letters of James Joyce,* Richard Ellmann, ed. (New York: Viking Press, 1975), e.g., p. 169: "Now, my darling Nora, I want you to read over and over all I have written to you. Some of it is ugly, obscene and bestial, some of it is pure and holy and spiritual: all of it is myself." See, also, Joyce, *Ulysses,* p. 732. See, as well, note 201, above.

See, on whether these letters should have been published, Irving Howe, *New York Times Book Review,* November 23, 1975, p. 3; Richard Ellmann, *American Scholar,* Autumn 1976, p. 582. Mr. Howe has properly questioned "the moral and esthetic appropriateness of publishing letters so utterly *intimate* in character." See the concluding paragraph of Chapter XIII, Part One. See, also, notes 257 and 260, below. See, as well, Anastaplo, *The Constitutionalist,* pp. 546–47; Plato, *Greater Hippias* 298D–299B.

Is it because of the Roman Catholic upbringing of his characters that Joyce can use *soul* where many of his contemporaries would use *self?* (The *soul* which is very much concerned to "express" itself is now known as the *self?*) See notes 175 and 185, above. (See, on that upbringing, sexuality, and the sense of sin, Bede, *History of the English Church and People,* I, 27 [Pope Gregory's eighth response]. See, also, note 104, above.)

See, on rebelliousness, Newman, *Apologia Pro Vita Sua,* pp. 244, 273. See, also, the text at note 158, above. Cf. *Bhagavad Gita,* II, 9, XVIII, 73; *Job* 42: 1–6. See, on Joyce's perversity, Nabokov, *Lectures on Literature,* p. 342. See, on Joyce at his best, *ibid.,* pp. 296–97, 306, 322, 363–64, 370. Cf. *ibid.,* p. 349n.

See, on whether it belongs to God alone to create, Thomas Aquinas, *Summa Theologica,* I, Q. 45, AA. 5–8; Plato, *Timaeus* 41A sq.

249. Cf. W. B. Yeats, "Under Ben Bulben," sec. V (*The Collected Poems of W. B. Yeats* [New York: Macmillan Co., 1956], p. 343). See, on "conscience," Joyce, *A Portrait of the Artist,* p. 128f; note 27, above. See, for a preacher's "poetic" accounts of hell and eternity designed to move the consciences of boys, *ibid.,* pp. 117f, 127f, 132. "He came down the aisle of the chapel, his legs shaking and the scalp of his head trembled as though it had been touched by ghostly fingers." *Ibid.,* p. 124. Is not Dedalus's sensibility excessive? See, e.g., *ibid.,* p. 138. See, also, note 248, above. Cf. Chapter IV, Section iv (end), above, Appendix A, below.

250. If *mine* (or one's own) is so critical, then the conquest of chance becomes vital? Otherwise, one does not truly rule? See Machiavelli, *The Prince,* chap. 25.

If one's own is made so much of, does not that mean that the will is decisive (unless there *is* a best to which one's own happens to conform?)? See Appendixes A, B, and C, below. See, on property, Anastaplo, *The Constitutionalist,* pp. 213–17. See, also, note 123, above.

See, on the relation to one another of past, present, and future, Joyce, *A Portrait of the Artist,* p. 251. See, on chance, notes 7 and 202, above, note 260, below. See, as well, the note at the end of Appendix E, below.

See, for Aquinas's aesthetics, Ellmann, *James Joyce,* pp. 196–97; Plato, *Greater Hippias* 297E–298B, 303C–D. See, also, the Epigraph to Appendix C, below.

251.   See, on Joyce's *Ulysses, The Letters of W. B. Yeats,* pp. 651, 679. It is said of Dedalus, during his first term in college, that "[h]is soul was still disgusted and cast down by the dull phenomenon of Dublin." Joyce, *A Portrait of the Artist,* p. 78. Dedalus considers himself "a priest of eternal imagination, transmuting the daily bread of experience into the radiant body of everliving life." *Ibid.,* p. 221. (Cranly plays John the Baptist to Dedalus's Jesus? *Ibid.,* p. 248. See, also, note 173, above.)

Sean O'Faolain, in 1955, called Joyce "the great literary rebel of our time." *Ibid.,* back cover (paperback edition). ("Credit" *could* be given to Machiavelli or to Rousseau or to Nietzsche as the most rebellious artist in modern times. See, on Machiavelli, Leo Strauss, *Thoughts on Machiavelli.* [The first highly reliable translation of *The Prince* into English has been made by Leo Paul S. de Alvarez and is now available from the University of Dallas Press.] See, on Rousseau, note 273, below. See, on Nietzsche, J. Harvey Lomax, *Nietzsche's New Nobility and the Eternal Return in "Beyond Good and Evil": A Proemium* [University of Chicago Ph.D. dissertation, 1979]; also, note 7, above [the Dannhauser citation]. See note 182, above. See, also note 214, above. "The Straussians, despite their opposition to Nietzsche, seem to have yielded partially to his fascination." E.B.F. Midgeley, "Concerning the Modernist Subversion of Political Philosophy," 53 *New Scholasticism* 168, 189 [1979]. Cf. note 145, above, Epilogue, Section iii [end], below. Cf., also, note 285, below.) See, on the status of *A Portrait of the Artist* as an autobiographical novel, William H. Nolte, "The Incomplete Maugham," *The American Spectator,* August 1980, p. 20.

See, on Joyce and Proust, Ellmann, *James Joyce,* pp. 5, 502, 523–24.

See, on Joyce's pride, *ibid.,* pp. 104, 509, 536. Cf. *ibid.,* pp. 1, 114. See, on Lucifer's pride, Langland, *Piers Plowman,* I, 126, XV, 51, 63f; Dante, *Paradiso,* XIX, 46f. See, also, Anastaplo, *The Constitutionalist,* pp. 771–72, n. 193; Henry Kramer and James Sprenger, *Malleus Maleficarum,* Pt. I, Q. 17.

The complaint is often made that "nothing happens" during Joyce's "one day in one town." See note 279, below, on the interests of "mere readers."

252.   See note 215, above. See, also, note 244, above. See, as well, Anastaplo, "Human Nature and the First Amendment," p. 715f.; note 145, above.

Dedalus "often thought it strange that Vincent Heron had a bird's face as well as a bird's name." Joyce, *A Portrait of the Artist,* p. 76. What does this suggest about the relation of nature to convention? Compare "the world" of *Frankenstein,* in which a Justine is unjustly condemned and executed. See note 164, above. But see note 3, above, on names, naming, and animals. See, also, Plato, *Cratylus, Philebus* 17A sq., *Phaedrus* 252B.

See, on the ancient Daedalus, Plato, *Euthyphro* 11C–D, 15B; Pangle, *The Laws of Plato,* p. 521, n. 2.

253.   Laurence Berns, "Thomas Hobbes," in Strauss and Cropsey, eds., *History of Political Philosophy,* p. 370. See, on one critical problem of materialism, Appendix D, Part Three, below (on the question of the placement of the longest segment in Socrates' divided line). See, also, note 172, above.

Compare Anastaplo, "The Declaration of Independence," pp. 394–98; also, Chapter XIII, Part Two, Sections ix, below; Appendix E, Section viii, below.

An aide to Pope Paul VI reported, "The Pope has faith in artists. He considers them antennas reflecting human thought." *Chicago Tribune,* June 24, 1973, sec. 1, p. 42.

Consider, also, Pope John Paul II, *Laborem Exercens,* Sec. 25 (quoting from *Gaudium et Spes,* Second Vatican Ecumenical Council): "Far from thinking that works produced by man's own talent and energy are in opposition to God's power, and that the rational creature exists as a kind of rival to the creator, Christians are convinced that the triumphs of the human race are a sign of God's greatness and the flowering of his own mysterious design." Consider, also, Plato, *Epinomis* 989A–990B; Michael Platt, "Shakespeare's Wisdom?", in Alvis and West, eds., *Shakespeare as Political Thinker,* pp. 274–275. See note 182, above.

254.   S.L. Goldberg, *Joyce* (New York: Capricorn Books, 1962), p. 94. Thus, also, even so old-fashioned a critic as John Sparrow can assume that *Ulysses* is a masterpiece. See his *Too Much of a Good Thing* (Chicago: University of Chicago Press, 1977), p. 83.

Ulysses ends with the dateline, "Trieste-Zurich-Paris, 1914–1921";

A Portrait of the Artist as a Young Man ends with the dateline, "Dublin, 1904. Trieste, 1914."

255.   Several participants in the James Joyce conference in Zurich, July 1979, confirmed this quotation for Philip W. Kenny (whom I had asked for a source), but none of them knew where precisely the quotation could be found in print. See Ellmann, *James Joyce,* pp. 275–76, 405, 473. But see Joyce, *Ulysses,* p. 210. See, also, the text at note 212, above.

256.   Richard Cobb, *The Times Literary Supplement,* January 21, 1977, p. 66. Mr. Ellmann collects various disparagements of Joyce by eminent contemporaries.

257.   R. Emmett Tyrrell, Jr., *The Alternative: An American Spectator,* December 1976, p. 35. Joyce once wrote to his wife, "As you know, dearest, I never use obscene phrases in speaking. You have never heard me, have you, utter an unfit word before others. When men tell in my presence here filthy or lecherous stories, I hardly smile." *Selected Letters of James Joyce,* p. 182. Cf. note 248, above. (See the conclusion of the introduction to Appendix F, below.)

         See, for indications of Joyce's troubles with the law, Joyce, *Ulysses,* pp. vii–xiv; Ellmann, *James Joyce,* pp. 417, 429, 512, 517f, 678f, 692n. See, also, *ibid.,* p. 410.

258.   Hugh Kenner, *The Alternative: An American Spectator,* December, 1976, p. 22. See, also, Eliot, *On Poetry and Poets,* pp. 161–64; Steiner, *Language and Silence,* pp. 235–36. Cf. the text at note 279, below. See, as well, note 158, above.

         Does not Joyce's *Ulysses* itself "take for granted" Sterne's *Tristram Shandy?* Is there not about both of these ingenious books much that is contrived and arch? (My own first reading of *Tristram Shandy* was after *The Artist as Thinker* had been submitted for publication in December 1979. Had I read it earlier, I would no doubt have made considerable use of it, and perhaps even prepared a chapter or at least some discursive notes on it. See note 259, below.)

259.   Is not the passage I have quoted in keeping with the overblown style of the section of *Ulysses* in which the passage is found? Does not the press tend to make out each episode it reports to be *the* event of the century? (About this, too, inquiries were made at the Zurich conference in July 1979. See note 255, above.) See, for an illustration of the distortions to which its now insatiable appetite for the "dramatic" leads the press, *National Law Journal,* Nov. 5, 1979, p. 35. Cf. *Chicago Daily Law Bul-*

letin, October 25, 1979, p. 1, col. 2 ("application" should read "appreciation"); *National Law Journal,* Dec. 3, 1979, p. 14.

Compare Eric Ambler, *A Coffin for Dimitrios* (New York: Alfred A. Knopf, 1939), pp. 51–52: "The situation in which a person, imagining fondly that he is in charge of his own destiny, is, in fact, the sport of circumstances beyond his control, is always fascinating. It is the essential element in most good theatre from the *Oedipus* of Sophocles to *East Lynne.* When, however, that person is oneself and one is examining the situation in retrospect, the fascination becomes a trifle morbid. Thus, when Latimer used afterwards to look back upon those two days in Smyrna, it was not so much his ignorance of the part he was playing but the bliss which accompanied the ignorance that so appalled him. He had gone into the business believing his eyes to be wide open, whereas, actually they had been tightly shut. That, no doubt, could not have been helped. The galling part was that he had failed for so long to perceive the fact."

See, on the newspaper-office episode, Ellmann, *James Joyce,* pp. 297–98. James Joyce, in his ability to make the trivial seem interesting, reminds one of Laurence Sterne. See Sterne, *Tristram Shandy,* e.g., pp. 4–5, 61, 72, 113, 139, 226, 273. See, also, Ellmann, *James Joyce,* pp. 427, 566. Joyce could insist, "I never met a bore." *Ibid.,* p. 5. See Sterne, *Tristram Shandy,* p. 377 ("In short, by seizing every handle, of what shape or size soever, which chance held out to me on this journey——I turned my *plain* into a *city*——I was always in company, and with great variety too . . ."). (See, on chance, note 7, above.)

See, for another mystery running through the book (the problem of the man in the macintosh, at the Dignam funeral), Joyce, *Ulysses,* pp. 108, 110, 369, 420–21, 632. We are reminded, by this running gag, that life *is* thus, that loose ends are never all tucked in. (This is vital, for example, to a sensible assessment of the many fanciful critics of the official account of the John Kennedy assassination. See Anastaplo, *The Constitutionalist,* pp. 735–36; "Human Nature and the First Amendment," pp. 702–5.) But see Nabokov, *Lectures on Literature,* pp. 316–20. Cf. John Simon, *Times Literary Supplement,* April 24, 1981, p. 457.

The character of loose ends may be seen, for example, in the episode of the virtually worthless throw-rug which disappeared from the Lingles' house when they lived in Herrin some thirty-three years ago. The person they were convinced must have hidden it, as a prank, *knew* he had not—and thus knew also how much of a mystery that disappearance truly was. See Anastaplo, *The Constitutionalist,* p. 798, n. 32; note 275, below. See, also, the first paragraph quoted in the text at note 216, above.

Still another mystery in *Ulysses* has to do with the time at which

Bloom's watch stops. *Ibid.,* pp. 355, 363, 590. "Wristwatches are always going wrong. Wonder is there any magnetic influence between the person because that was about the time he." *Ibid.,* p. 367. What *is* to be understood to be the cause of *that?* Also, *was* Corny Kelleher's Nighttown appearance "highly providential"? *Ibid.,* pp. 588–92, 598. (See, on the nature of dreams, Chapter IX, Section v, above. See, also, note 202, above.)

260. *Selected Letters of James Joyce,* p. 5; Ellmann, *James Joyce,* pp. 161–63, 389–90, 540. Chance and one's own are thus emphasized? See note 250, above. Consider, in this connection, the date (January 28, 1976) of the *Final Report of the Governor's Commission on Individual Liberty and Personal Privacy,* State of Illinois. (See Anastaplo, "The Public Interest in Privacy," p. 767, n. 1.) See, on the relation of privacy to marriage, note 248, above. See, also, note 164, above.

  Copies of the *Report,* which I helped write, may be gotten from the Privacy Commission chairman, Bernard Weisberg, 69 West Washington St., Chicago, Illinois. Also available from Mr. Weisberg is his instructive essay on reading to one's children.

261. See Joyce, *Ulysses,* e.g., pp. 66–67, 69, 74, 91 ("Worst man in Dublin"), 122, 170–71, 172, 173 (even the copulating flies remind Bloom of his circumstances), 177, 180–81, 259–60, 307, 312, 313–14, 318, 363, 427, 550–53, 602–3, 635–36, 714, 716. See, also, *ibid.,* pp. 224–25, 229, 250, 260–65, 272, 363, 723–68.

262. Had Bloom found signs that Boylan had eaten in his bed that day? See *ibid.,* pp. 716, 726. Cf. *ibid.,* p. 88.

  See, on "eight," *ibid.,* p. 732; Plutarch, *Theseus,* xxxvi, 3–4.

  See, on Molly Bloom's monologue, Ellmann, *James Joyce,* pp. 516–17, 536. See, also, Joyce, *A Portrait of the Artist,* p. 169 ("Yes! Yes! Yes!"); *Ulysses,* p. 442. See, as well, Nabokov, *Lectures on Literature,* pp. 363–64, 370.

  See, on "long-suffering and long-suffered," Epilogue, Section vi (end), below. See, also, note 164, above.

263. Parnell had died in 1891, thirteen years before, after having been disgraced upon the exposure of his long-standing affair with the wife of an army officer. See Joyce, *Ulysses,* pp. 35, 111, 162–63, 633f, 639.

  There is about this setting, with its lack of attractive public opportunities for talented young men, something of the atmosphere of Stendahl's *The Red and the Black.* "There are always numerous connections between the social and political condition of a people and the inspiration of its writers. He who knows the one is never completely ignorant of the other." Tocqueville, *Democracy in America*, p. 474. See the conclusion of Appendix G, below.

I assume throughout this book that artists often record things they may not fully recognize the implications of. See notes 145 and 164, above. Be that as it may, the Parnell controversy provokes a fierce family argument in *A Portrait of the Artist* (pp. 31-40). See, also, *ibid.*, pp. 27-28, 203. See, as well, Ellmann, *James Joyce*, pp. 32-33; note 178, above.

It is instructive to recur to the *Don Giovanni* parallel I have drawn upon. See notes 10 and 218, above. How, one may well wonder, did Giovanni get to be the way he is? Or, rather, how was he *permitted* to act this way (for, it may be, there are always people of his inclinations around)? It should be noticed that the tradition, which Mozart accepted, places the story of Don Juan in seventeenth century Spain. And that means, among other things, that the "Golden Century" of Spanish history is over and that Spain is in decline, socially, politically, economically. These are bleak times for Spain. Seville, where the action of the opera is laid, was the city which looked out to the new world. The decline of Spain evidently hit Seville particularly hard: much had been hoped for—and expectations had had to be considerably lowered. Is this spirited nobleman's obsession with "love" compensation for the demoralization of the political order which might have provided his life discipline and meaning? See note 195, above.

264.   Stephen Dedalus has his father's gift of expression. Joyce, *Ulysses*, p. 102. Consider the "crucified shirts" on the clotheslines. *Ibid.*, p. 42. A blasphemy, with respect to the conception of Jesus, follows?

We see in *A Portrait of the Artist* (pp. 216-24) the making of a poem, as well as the materials out of which it is shaped. We can see, in *Ulysses*, how the wanderings of the mind can be portrayed. Thus, five minutes in the life of Bloom's mind outdoors can take ten pages of text; fifteen minutes in the life of Molly's mind indoors can take nine pages. Joyce, *Ulysses*, pp. 151-62, 757-66. Cf. Cather, *On Writing*, pp. 38-42, 96-97.

265.   In any event, there will be no child produced from the June 16 encounter between Boylan and Molly Bloom. See Joyce, *Ulysses*, p. 754. Would Bloom want a son thus provided him?

See, with respect to Bloom's impotence in his marriage, *The Spiritual Physick of Rhazes*, pp. 69-70.

266. Is this book good for the Jews? If it is truly good for the Jews, it may be, for that reason alone, good for everyone, since humanity can be seen to suffer in the modern world when Jews are not treated as they should be. See Anastaplo, *Human Being and Citizen,* Essay No. 13 ("The Case for Supporting Israel"). See, also, Harry James Cargas, "World Literature and the Holocaust," *Christian Century,* November 14, 1979, p. 1125.

   Bloom is the only character in the book who is again and again said to "wonder." See Joyce, *Ulysses,* e.g., pp. 55, 56, 77, 113, 366, 367, 371, 380, 407, 420, 421. Certainly, he does have a considerable intellectual curiosity. He has also a morbid imagination. See *ibid.,* e.g., pp. 112-13, 117, 150. He first comes to view as a man with odd appetites. *Ibid.,* p. 55.

267. Joyce evidently quizzed at length Jews he came to know in Zurich. He does not seem to have been close to any Jews in Dublin. See, e.g., Joyce, *A Portrait of the Artist,* p. 100. See, also, Ellmann, *James Joyce,* pp. 238, 383f, 408, 715, 722, 749-50. See, for attitudes in Dublin toward Jews, Joyce, *Ulysses,* pp. 22, 34-35, 37, 39, 82-83, 107, 180, 198, 202, 215, 240-41, 287, 299, 308, 331, 419. Cf. *ibid.,* pp. 139-41, 203.

   See, on art and exile, Appendix G, below. See, also, Paul Breslin, "How to Read the New Contemporary Poem," 47 *American Scholar* 357 (1978). See, as well, the text at note 182, above.

268. The third sign, that Jews have a sense of shame or modesty, is a problem in Bloom's case? Or is this Joyce's failing, not Bloom's?

   See, on whether Bloom is a Jew, Joyce, *Ulysses,* pp. 79, 117, 121, 123, 149, 157, 169, 336, 372, 627-28, 641-42, 660, 666, 675-76.

   See, as illustrative of Bloom's kindness, *ibid.,* pp. 178-79, 242-43. Molly Bloom, in the course of her monologue, several times indicates Bloom's perverse inclinations. Not that we are surprised from what we have seen of him during our day with him.

269. Cf. Nabokov, *Lectures on Literature,* p. 316. See Anastaplo, "The Rosenberg Case and the Perils of Indignation," *Chicago Lawyer,* June 1979, pp. 19, 20 (col. 4). See, on Israel and attitudes of Jews prior to its establishment as a state, Martin Gilbert, *Exile and Return: The Struggle for a Jewish Homeland* (Philadelphia: J.P. Lippincott, 1978), p. 190f.

270. I am reminded of a rabbi who used to refer to an occasional college student as an atheist with a good Jewish heart. See Anastaplo, "American Constitutionalism and the Virtue of Prudence," p. 170.

"To state that Jesus is a Jew is to insult, distress, annoy, and, indeed, provoke [many people] to the point of contradiction, suspicion, and hatred." Markus Barth, *Jesus the Jew* (Atlanta: John Knox Press, 1978), p. 11.

See, on the altercation in the pub, Ellmann, *James Joyce,* pp. 370, 383. See, on the pacifism of both Bloom and Dedalus, *ibid.,* e.g., p. 379. Molly, too, is pacific. See Joyce, *Ulysses,* pp. 733-34, 763. Bloom is *not* troubled about *not* having put money on the victorious long shot that day. *Ibid.,* p. 660. See Nabokov, *Lectures on Literature,* pp. 312-14.

See Epilogue, Section vii, below. See, also, note 282, below.

271.   The United States is in principle different—and should not be used as an indication of what goes on elsewhere. See David Caplovitz and Fred Sherrow, *The Religious Drop-outs: Apostasy Among College Graduates* (Beverly Hills: Sage Publications, 1977), pp. 59-60, 64, 85, 126, 160-61, 164-65, 186f; John B. McConahay, Book Review, 23 *Contemporary Psychology* 535 (1978); Jack Houston, "Rabbi: U.S. Jews must save identity," *Chicago Tribune,* July 28, 1980, sec. 1, p. 1. See, also, Anastaplo, *The Constitutionalist,* pp. 497-98, n. 111, p. 503, n. 11; Werner J. Dannhauser, *Commentary,* January 1980, pp. 30-31; note 284, below. Cf. Karl Marx, "On the Jewish Question." See, as well, the epigraph to Chapter III, above.

See, for the controversy about T.S. Eliot's opinions respecting Jews, Roger Kojecky, *T.S. Eliot's Social Criticism* (New York: Farrar, Straus and Giroux, 1971), pp. 12-13.

272.   Consider what happens to "love" in the episode immediately following Bloom's encounter with "the citizen": it becomes either sickly romanticism (in Gerty MacDowell) or mere physical self-indulgence (in Bloom). See, on the episode, Ellmann, *James Joyce,* pp. 151, 385, 487; Nabokov, *Lectures on Literature,* p. 342. (The backdrop for this episode is provided by a church service nearby: "Through the open window of the church the fragrant incense was wafted and with it the fragrant names of her who was conceived without stain of original sin..." Joyce, *Ulysses,* p. 350.) I somehow have the impression that "the citizen" and Gerty MacDowell are related by blood. Am I correct? Such connection *would* be fitting. See *N.Y. Times Book Rev.,* Sept. 19, 1982, p. 7.

See, on "the same people living in the same place" in a poem by Robert Pinsky, *Poetry,* August 1980, pp. 302-4.

273.   See, on Rousseau the "solitary dreamer," Strauss, *Natural Right and*

History, pp. 252–94. See, on the considerable merits of Nora Barnacle
Joyce, Ellmann, *James Joyce,* e.g., p. 163. She once rebuked her husband, "Why don't you write sensible books that people can understand?"
Ibid., p. 603. Still, she could say of him in later life, "I don't know
whether my husband is a genius but I'm sure of one thing, there is
nobody like him." *Ibid.,* p. 387n. But such appraisals did not keep her
from commenting upon C.G. Jung's praise of *Ulysses* for what it displayed of "the real psychology of women," "He [Joyce] knows nothing at all about women." Ellmann, *James Joyce,* p. 642. Even so, after
his death she often complained, "Things are very dull now. There was
always something doing when he was about." *Ibid.,* p. 755. See note
152, above.

274.   This is so much so that some serious readers cannot decide whether the
Homer of the *Odyssey* was a man or a woman. See note 117, above. See,
also, note 141, above. See, as well, note 202, above.

275.   Consider Mr. Dedalus's curse, "The devil break the hasp of your back!"
Joyce, *Ulysses,* p. 92. This has been said to refer to a creditor of Joyce's
father. See Ellmann, *James Joyce,* p. 377. See, also, Nabokov, *Lectures
on Literature,* p. 316. See, as well, note 259 (end), above.

   See, on Joyce's use of Dublin, Ellmann, *James Joyce,* pp. 113–14,
706. See, also, Pound, *Instigations,* p. 199: "James Joyce has written
the best novel of my decade, and perhaps the best criticism of it has
come from a Belgian who said, 'All this is as true of my country as of
Ireland.'" See, on the great being reflected in the small, note 94, above
(one day can be transformed into a year), Appendix G, Section viii,
below. See, also, on "particulars" and "universals," note 145, above.
See, as well, Freud, *Introductory Lectures on Psychoanalysis,* p. 186.

   See note 202, above. See, also, Epilogue to Appendix B, below.

276.   Indeed, I doubt that it can be said that Joyce truly read the masterpieces upon which he drew. See Anastaplo, *Human Being and Citizen,*
pp. 55–56. See, also, Appendixes B and C, below. See, as well, notes
95 and 196, above, Epilogue, Sections ii–viii, below.

   The defects of Joyce as a reader of the classics are typical of most
highly talented men and women of our time. See, for example, Albert
Einstein's sloppy reading of Aristotle on slavery, in *Out of My Later
Years* (New York: Philosophical Library, 1950), p. 133. Cf. Strauss,
Natural Right and History, pp. 23, 118, 121, 159; Harry V. Jaffa,
"Aristotle," in Strauss and Cropsey, eds., *History of Political Philoso-*

phy, pp. 74–77; Anastaplo, Book Review, *Modern Age,* Winter 1981, p. 106; Chapter X, above. See, also, note 285, below.

See, on the *Odyssey* as Joyce's inspiration for *Ulysses,* Ellmann, *James Joyce,* p. 430. "Dante was perhaps Joyce's favorite author . . ." *Ibid.,* p. 2. Cf. Nabokov, *Lectures on Literature,* p. 288. (See, on inspiration itself, Appendix G, Section vi, below.)

277.   See the text at note 239, above. In any event, the much-maligned Ireland did produce not only Joyce himself but also one of the finest English-language poets of the twentieth century in W. B. Yeats. See, on Yeats and Joyce; Frank O'Connor, *American Scholar,* Summer 1967, p. 466.

Cannot the same be said of the Norway against which Ibsen inveighed, that *it* produced (or permitted the production of) widely acclaimed artists? Norway produced not only Ibsen himself but also Edvard Munch, who could paint in 1892 *The Artist's Sister* (the portrait of a lovely woman, perhaps with a touch of the sinister in the picture). Cf. Munch's *The Dance of Life,* of 1899–1900 (a grotesque group of dancers). (Both paintings are in the Nasjonalgallerei, Oslo.)

Ours, on the other hand, is an epoch when so-called progressive regimes routinely become merciless "refugee machines" in their operations. See *Chicago Tribune,* editorial, June 26, 1980, sec. 3, p. 2:

> How is it that Marxist regimes can make so much misery in the world? Every continent is now suffering the burden of refugees from these malignant, war-making, people-hating governments as they attempt to impose unwanted ideologies on unwilling populations.

See Strauss, *Natural Right and History,* p. 301f; Anastaplo, *The Constitutionalist,* pp. 639 (the comment on the Alexander Beck novel), 681–82; Tocqueville, *Democracy in America,* p. 396. See, also, notes 20 and 95, above, Appendix G, end note, below. See, as well, Ellmann, *James Joyce,* p. 401:

> [Joyce] was to dismiss all talk of democratic Utopias with the remark that he had never been happier than under the lax rule of the Austro-Hungarian emperor in Trieste. "They called it a ramshackle empire," he said later. . . . "I wish to God there were more such empires."

Cf. the text at note 84, above. See, also, note 24, above.

See, on the requirements of civilization, Anastaplo, "Passion, Magnanimity and the Rule of Law," 50 *Southern California Law Review* 351 (1977). See, also, note 285, below.

278.   See Anastaplo, *Human Being and Citizen,* Essays No. 2, No. 14, and No. 16. See, also, Anastaplo, "Human Nature and the First Amendment," p. 745f. See, as well, Martin Northway, "Getting smart," *Chicago Journal,* June 18, 1980, p. 1.

279.   Plutarch, *Lycurgus,* XV, 2. See Eva T.H. Brann, *Paradoxes of Education in a Republic* (Chicago: University of Chicago Press, 1979), e.g., p. 20f. Joyce would argue, of course, that the great cannot appear today (if it ever could) in anything but the ordinary. See, e.g., Joyce, *Ulysses,* pp. 15 ("Old and secret she [the milk woman] had entered from a morning world, maybe a messenger.... A wandering crone, lowly form of an immortal serving her conqueror ..."), 188 ("A man of genius makes no mistakes. His errors are volitional and are the portals of discovery."), 190 ("Our national epic has yet to be written, Dr. Sigerson says."). See, also, George Steiner, *New Yorker,* Feb. 9, 1981, p. 115: "Joyce's 'Ulysses' shifts the Greek epic and its heroics toward ironic modernity." See, as well, Appendix G, Section iv (end) and Section vii, below.

    "One reason [Philip] Roth's stories are unsatisfactory is that they come out of a thin personal culture." Irving Howe, *Chicago Sun-Times Book Week,* September 9, 1979, p. 11. See, also, the concluding paragraph of Chapter XIII, Part One, above. See, as well, note 138, above. Cf. Bruno Bettelheim, "Portnoy Psychoanalyzed," in *Surviving and Other Essays* (New York: Alfred A. Knopf, 1979), p. 387f.

    Divergent approaches to literary criticism, one American, the other English, have been described by S. L. Goldberg, in "The Deconstruction Gang," *London Review of Books,* 22 May–4 June 1980, pp. 14–16. I do not presume to judge whether his is an adequate account of either approach or whether one is indeed primarily American, the other English. But the differences in two such approaches (as described) can be significant. That which is here labeled the "English" approach seems to me the one I have preferred for some years now in preparing materials for this book. Therefore, it may be useful, now that I have dealt in this book with each of several dozen works of art more or less on its own terms, to remind readers of how literary criticism is often done and discussed today. Three passages from the Goldberg article follow:

    In reviewing a book on literary theory recently, a noted American structuralist, Jonathan Culler, drew a stern line between the sort of assumptions about literature that might do for ordinary "readers" and those that are currently giving "vitality," as he put it, to "literary studies." The point is well taken; and it also casts a certain light... on the general condition (and conditions) of American academic "vitality." What makes "literary studies" alive there [in America], as Dr. Culler reminds us, is the rejection of the simple "reader's" assumptions in favour of more rigourous, more objective concerns: for example, with "the problems of the status of the text and textual patterns, the relevance and accessibility of authorial intentions, the relationship of a work to other texts, their conventions, and the tacit assumptions of a society." Clearly, these are important theoretical problems, and nothing called "literary studies" could avoid them. But it is also clear that any "study" that takes these as its only "vital" issues is not likely to take much account of whatever draws and holds mere "readers" of literature, or the connections between that and other kinds of vitality. As far as "literary studies" are concerned, there is nothing interesting about the mere "reader." He only reads books, after all, not "texts," and he often skips what doesn't engage him.... Although the strong theoretical bent of American "literary studies" is much admired nowadays, not least by its proponents, it is worth noticing that there are bad reasons for it as well as good ones. The cultural and (more especially) the professional conditions of the business exert a constant pressure on its practitioners to turn particular insights about particular literary works instantly into universal generalisations about all literary works....

... Such assumptions as these operate even at the most sophisticated levels of "literary studies" in America, and they silently mould the very conception of what literary theorising is properly *about,* what "criticism" consists in, how its practice properly relates to theory. True, they also prompt an interest in many areas of thought, a concern with some important questions about language, literature and criticism, an admirable intellectual openness, breadth and adventurous curiosity. Yet all too often this genuinely philosophic interest goes with an amazing philosophical gullibility—an inability to distinguish assertions or speculations, especially if they are systematic and pretentious, from demonstrated truth. The result is an over-eager willingness to take some elaborated body of speculative *theory* as a body of established *knowledge,* and therefore as a validating basis for literary theory, and therefore as a programmatic rationale for critical (and pedagogical) practice. The peristaltic movement through the academic mind of psychoanalysis, Marxism, semiotics, iconology, phenomenology, existentialism, McLuhanism, stylistics, hermeneutics, formalism, structuralism, and so on, together with the jargon each of these generates, and their noisy competition for academic prestige and power, can make American "literary studies" seem at once deeply intellectual and highly professional, exciting, "vital," especially beside the contemptibly "humanist," "empirical," tradition-based, "reader"-directed attitudes that still prevail (more or less) in England and whose own vitality, unfortunately, has so rarely been explained or defended by philosophic self-reflection that it can easily seem to go by default. . . .

. . . Another way of putting the difference between the two kinds of assumptions might be to say that the English "close-reader" tends to read texts in those human and moral categories that require some conception of individual persons. He usually does this in terms of the modes and logic of *belief,* in which the specifically personal necessarily mediates the impersonal. The American "close-reader," on the other hand, tends to read them without such "subjective" categories as far as possible, and where it isn't possible, then in terms of the modes and logic of *statement* or *declaration,* in which the personal and the impersonal have a different content and stand in a different relationship. In effect, the American "close-reader" naturally tends to the same conclusion as [the] deconstruction [school] seems to: that the central fact, the ideal text, in English literature is *Finnegans Wake.* . . .

See, with respect to the riddles *Finnegans Wake* poses, James Russell Lowell, *Among My Books,* Second Series (Boston: Houghton, Mifflin, 1886), p. 235: "If a poet resolve to be original, it will end commonly in his being merely peculiar." See, also, Anastaplo, *The Constitutionalist,* p. 772, n. 193; *Human Being and Citizen,* p. 294, n. 14; Jo Brans, "Common Needs, Common Preoccupations: An Interview with Saul Bellow," *Southwest Review,* Winter 1977, pp. 1, 7–8. Compare the observation by a "mere reader" (or rather, in this case, a "mere listener"), in note 17, above, "That Shakespeare is the only poet I've heard who was fed on raw meat." See notes 145 and 280, above.

Socrates noticed long ago that it is the fashion of poets to make riddles. Plato, *Republic* 332C. See Prologue, Sections i and iii, above. Perhaps there should be said about *Finnegans Wake* what has been said about the painting of Pablo Picasso:

Yet the inventions of necessity slowly gave way to the needs of mere performance. Picasso's sculpture retained its intensity almost to the end, but his painting did not, and this became clear after 1950. . . . The Picassian energy is still there, masquerading as inspiration, but too often it ends as a form of visual conjuring. . . . He was the most influential artist of his own time; for many lesser figures a catastrophic influence, and for those who could deal with him . . . an almost indescribably fruitful one.

Robert Hughes, *Time,* May 26, 1980, p. 76. I find something revealing in Pablo Picasso's paraphrases of the art of great masters of the past. One can sometimes see by contrast (when, as in the 1980 Picasso Exhibit at the Museum of Modern Art in New York, photographs of the paraphrased art are displayed along with Picasso's "versions") what genuine art is like. Picasso's work again and again stands revealed as essentially "journalistic," despite his obvious gifts and his occasional "lyricism." See Tocqueville, *Democracy in America,* pp. 484–85, 487. See, also, Robert Conquest, "But What Good Came of It At Last? An Inquest on Modernism," *Intercollegiage Review,* Fall/Winter 1980; Frederick Crews, "Criticism Without Constraint," *Commentary,* Jan. 1982, p. 65; *New Yorker,* April 19, 1982, p. 155 (Walter Allen on the ivory-towered American intellectual).

See, as well, Aristotle, *Parts of Animals,* I, i ("For this is the Reason, and the Reason forms the starting-point, alike in the works of art and in works of reason."); Aristotle, *Metaphysics* 983a5 ("according to the proverb, 'bards tell many a lie'").

Be all this as it may, Picasso's great talent *is* reflected in his matter-of-fact observation, "Other people search. I only find."

See note 246 (end), above.

Epilogue: THE THINKER AS ARTIST

280.   Even so, the work itself (in each case) suggests, at least to the experienced reader, how it should be dealt with. Principles of interpretation are suggested in the Preface, in the Prologue, Section ii, in Chapter I, Part One, above, and in the Appendixes, below. See, also, notes 3, 29, 38, 145, 164, 179, 182, 263, and 279, above. See, as well, Anastaplo, *Human Being and Citizen,* p. 281, n. 52.

I have had occasion (7 *Interpretation* 71 [January 1978]) to collect "indicated interpretations of various literary texts" heretofore, as found in Anastaplo, *The Constitutionalist:* pp. 651, 798–99 *(Antigone),* 30–32, 436–38, 651, 687, 725, 772 *(Hamlet),* 278–81, 552–53, 690, 791–92, 807–8 *(Iliad),* 790–91 *(King Lear),* 581, 707–8, 817 (item 1) *(Little Orphan Annie et al.),* 439, 503, 793 *(Nathan the Wise),* 278–81, 546,

552–53, 612, 690, 719–20, 791–92, 797 *(Odyssey)*, 642, 783, 798–99 *(Oedipus)*, 510, 779, 787 *(Remembrance of Things Past)*.

Consider, as well, the following observation in Kitto, *Sophocles— Dramatist and Philosopher*, p. 1:

> In the end I hope to have persuaded you that Sophocles was not only a superb artist but also a profound thinker. Indeed, I would argue that he could not be the one without also being the other.

281. The article may be found in the *University of Chicago Magazine*, Winter 1974, p. 30. No major changes in the text have been made in the reproduction here of that article. The seven sections of the article, which appear here as Sections ii–viii of the Epilogue, originally had the following titles:

"When we were in our twenties"
Memorabilia
A leave-taking
"Comedies, parodies, and satires"
The Socratic question
Jerusalem, yes; Athens, now and then?
"The sacredness of 'the common'"

The article, which included a fine picture of Mr. Strauss, was written as of the first anniversary of his death. Notes 282, 283, and 284, below, were provided with the original publication of this article. Several citations were provided *in the text* of the original article. They remain in the text here.

The original article had the following dateline:

Hyde Park
Chicago, Illinois
22 Tishrei 5735.

282. Mr. Strauss, I should add, may not have been as conservative as most of his devoted students, not only because he did not care as much as (or in the way) they did about practical matters, but also because he knew better than they that the institutions which conservatives so passionately protect often have questionable radical origins.

His conservatism, I should also add, did not even mean that he dogmatically took the conventional "anti-Communist" position. Thus, he could (in a two-sentence letter of June 22, 1961) write to a student of his who had been turned down in the courts after running afoul of McCarthy era "loyalty proceedings": "This is only to pay you my respects for your brave and just action. If the American Bench and Bar have any sense of shame they must come on their knees to apologize to you." [Original note]

283.   *Interpretation* is the name of the valuable journal, edited at Queens College of the City University of New York, in which Mr. Strauss's influence may be seen. [Original note]

284.   Mr. Strauss himself treated Heidegger's conduct quite differently from Husserl's. Thus, he could instruct certain of his students visiting Germany after the war not to have anything to do socially with Heidegger. (I know also that he refused to have anything further to do personally with a noted scholar, a Jewish friend of his from their youth in Germany, who made his peace with Heidegger.) Even so, he always acknowledged the remarkable talents of Heidegger, considering him "incomparable in our time," especially in the comprehensiveness of his thought.

   Fortunately, the revival of the classics in political science today is saved from serious temptations to, or facile charges of, fascism because someone as important to that revival as Mr. Strauss was obviously and passionately anti-Nazi in his conservatism. [Original note]

285.   One can get some notion of the discipleship Mr. Strauss inspired among some students when one learns that even this eulogy by me has *evidently* not been considered sufficiently laudatory by the more zealous defenders of the faith. The self-crippling as well as ungenerous suspicions of this silent minority can perhaps be traced back to their failure to read carefully enough what I had written—a childish failure to appreciate what I did and did not say. See Plato, *Symposium* 198D sq., *Meno* 95A. On the other hand, no article of mine has received as favorable a response from strangers as has this one—including from a number of people who identified themselves as having studied with Mr. Strauss at one time or another over the years.

   Even so, I apologize to anyone I might have unintentionally offended: I can only hope to deserve some day to be spoken of one-seventh as highly as I have spoken here of Mr. Strauss, perhaps the soundest teacher of our day. See, for my defense of Mr. Strauss's partisans, who *can* at times be provocative in their cliquishness, *Modern Age,* Summer 1979, p. 315. See, also, *National Review,* Jan. 22, 1982, pp. 36–45; note 251, above. See, for an indication of the silly things that can and will be said about Mr. Strauss, Elisabeth Young-Bruehl, *Hannah Arendt: For Love of the World* (New Haven: Yale University Press, 1982), pp.

98, 169; *Newsweek,* May 3, 1982, p. 75. (Mr. Strauss was inclined to dismiss Professor Arendt as a "coffee-house intellectual." Perhaps it suffices to say that she *was* an intellectual. See, e.g., Anastaplo, *Human Being and Citizen,* p. 95; note 288, below.)

One thing should be noticed about the circumstances of my article: Mr. Strauss's standing at the University of Chicago, when he left, was such that a farewell address by him could be conveniently given only at the Downtown Adult Education Center of the University. (This was conceived of and arranged by me.) Special commendation is due to Don Morris, then editor of the *University of Chicago Magazine,* that an article as laudatory as this one is of Mr. Strauss (and as critical implicitly of the University for its shabby and self-destructive treatment of him) could be published at all. See for my long-standing reservations about the then-president of the University, Anastaplo, 9 *Southwestern University Law Review* 977, notes 42 and 62 (1977); *National Law Journal,* June 18, 1979, p. 33. See, also, note 280, above.

The longstanding reservations I have about some of the positions taken by perhaps the most influential politically of Mr. Strauss's students are suggested in the remarks I had occasion to make about the best-known "Straussian" (at Rosary College, on December 4, 1980):

> It is my privilege to introduce on this occasion a friend of a quarter century and a distinguished political scientist, Harry V. Jaffa, of Claremont Men's College and Claremont Graduate School. Professor Jaffa, whose appearance at Rosary College has been made possible by the support of him by the Intercollegiate Studies Institute, is available this afternoon for an extended conversation with us about matters ancient and modern.
>
> Mr. Jaffa is, to my mind, the most instructive political scientist writing in this country today. The things he writes about range from Socrates and Aristotle to Thomas Aquinas and William Shakespeare, from the Founding Fathers to Abraham Lincoln, from Tom Sawyer and Winston Churchill to contemporary politics and the joys of cycling.
>
> I am reminded, when I encounter Mr. Jaffa, of another provocatively influential American, a great woman who died only this past weekend, Dorothy Day of the *Catholic Worker* movement (whom I was privileged to see close-up only once). It was true of Miss Day, as it is true of Mr. Jaffa, that it was virtually impossible for her not to be interesting about whatever she wrote. Intelligence, hard work, and a gift for language no doubt contribute to this capacity to invest every discourse with significance. But funda-

mental to such influence is a certain integrity, even a single-minded moral fervor. Thus, it could be said of Miss Day in her obituary in the *New York Times* on Monday of this week that she had sought "to work so as to bring about the kind of society where it is easier for people to be good." Much the same can be said about Mr. Jaffa. Indeed, Miss Day, in the way she lived her life, in an unrelenting effort to better the lives of the downtrodden, could be said to have put into practice the much-quoted proposition by Mr. Jaffa which was used by Senator Goldwater in his Acceptance Speech upon being nominated for the Presidency by the Republican Party in 1964, "I would remind you that extremism in the defense of liberty is no vice. And let me remind you also that moderation in the pursuit of justice is no virtue."

A little more should be said by me about Mr. Jaffa now, if only to suggest matters that we might want to talk about on this occasion. A few differences between us, of which I was reminded when I heard him speak yesterday at Loyola University, could usefully be indicated.

Mr. Jaffa not only makes far more of exercising than I do—I limit myself to walking whenever possible and to the avoidance of elevators for ascents or descents of less than five floors—but he also is a much more vigorous moralist than I am, both in regulating his own conduct and in judging the conduct of others. I believe that I allow more than he does for good-intentioned errors, for inefficiency on the part of people, and for circumstances which account for, sometimes even justify, what seem from the outside to be moral aberrations. Compassion can be almost as important as moral indignation in these matters, particularly with respect to domestic relations, whether the subjects be abortion, divorce, or homosexuality. Perhaps also I make more than he does of the importance—if only out of respect for the sensibilities of others and for the moral tone of the community—of discretion, if not even of good-natured hypocrisy.

We differ as well with respect to the conduct of foreign relations. We do share an abhorrence of tyranny, whether of the Right or of the Left. But we sometimes part company on assessments of how constitutional government and American republicanism can best be defended abroad. Thus, he was much more hopeful than I could ever be that our involvement in the Vietnam War (however noble in intention that involvement might have been, and *that* it surely was, in some respects)—he was much more hopeful than I was that our Vietnam involvement could do the American *or* the Indo-Chinese people some good. Today we differ as to precisely what kind of a threat the Russians pose to us. I see them as much more vulnerable (both politically and militarily) than does he; and I consider all too many calculations about nuclear war "scenarios" to depend too much on game theories and not enough on political judgment. I believe, for example, that Russian leaders are much more constrained by domestic public opinion (by a pacific, even though patriotic, public opinion) and by other factors than many of us recognize. They have suffered, at home and abroad, a considerable setback in Afghanistan; we can only hope that they, and we, do not suffer an even greater setback by a Russian invasion of Poland. But whatever happens in Poland, it is now evident that the cause of freedom is bound to be in better shape in Eastern Europe than it has been since the Second World War—in part because of what Polish workers have done in showing the world how things really stand there. The only question may be what price the Polish people will have to pay, and this may depend, in part, on their prudence and on ours.

Perhaps at the heart of the differences between Mr. Jaffa and me—whether the differences be as to the status of exercise or as to assessments of the Russians—is with respect to how much one should be concerned with the preservation of one's life. An immoderate cherishing of what happens to be one's own can lead, it seems to me, to psychic paralysis or to undue combativeness: either can undermine that relaxed competence which makes healthy statesmanship more likely. Certainly, Mr. Jaffa responds much more than I do to the apocalyptic as against the comic and somewhat less than I do to "liberty" as against "equality." Obviously, we touch here on questions about the nature of human existence, of virtue, and of happiness.

On the other hand, at the heart of our deep affinities—besides the fact that we were both fortunate enough to share a great teacher in Leo Strauss—is our minority belief that fundamental to sensible political science and to a decent life as a community is a general respect for natural right and what is known as natural law. This means, among other things, that discrimination based on arbitrary racial categories cannot be defended, especially by a people dedicated to the self-evident truth that "all men are created equal." It also means that the family as an institution should be supported.

I mention in passing that we do differ with respect to the Equal Rights Amendment—but here I believe that Mr. Jaffa, even though he puts what he says in terms of nature in his opposition to that amendment, has allowed himself to be unduly influenced by the antics and "principles" of a minority of the proponents of that largely symbolic grace note for our Constitution.

Be all this as it may, an informed study of nature in human things is perhaps the most pressing demand in education today—and for this Mr. Jaffa, with his profound grasp of the classical writers, of Shakespeare's thought, and of the career of Abraham Lincoln, is an invaluable guide.

Permit me to close these introductory remarks by returning to something else that has been said about Dorothy Day, something which (with appropriate adjustments) can be applied to the tireless dedication Mr. Jaffa devotes to his "conservative" creed and to his graduate students. We are reminded by Dorothy Day's *New York Times* obituary that Church officials in New York were "often sorely tempted to rebuke Miss Day—her ardent support of Catholic cemetery strikers a number of years ago especially irked Cardinal Spellman—but they never could catch her in any breach of Church regulations." Besides, the editor of *Commonweal* has observed, one of the bishops she fought with, James Francis McIntyre (who later became a cardinal himself), "was afraid he just might be dealing with a saint." "He was alluding to what has been called Miss Day's 'indiscriminate and uncompromising love of the Mystical Body' as well as to her courage and her care for the poor in hospices she established in New York and elsewhere."

But enough of this canonization of Harry Jaffa, who does remind me in certain ways of St. Augustine. Any effort at canonization, you recall, requires that the devil's advocate have his say also. As you can see, I have had to take on more than one role in introducing to you a gifted colleague whom we are privileged to have with us today.

Some of you must have questions—but first, Mr. Jaffa may have something to say in response to the remarks I have made in an effort to guide the conversation I look forward to in the hours and years ahead.

Mr. Jaffa's immediate response to my remarks was, "Well, thank you very much, Professor Anastaplo. I must say that that is the most remarkable introduction I have ever had or that I am ever likely to have." Two hours later, at the end of the general discussion, he concluded, "Thank you for your introduction, which certainly inspired me, or gave me a

sense of responsibility for something to live up to." Mr. Jaffa has
subsequently spoken well of this introduction to others. The transcript
of this two-hour conversation at Rosary College has been published in
the December 1981 issue of the *Claremont Review of Books,* pp. 5–14.

My discussions of Mr. Jaffa's work over the years may be found in
Human Being and Citizen, especially Essay No. 5; in "American Constitutionalism and the Virtue of Prudence," especially note 64; and in
Modern Age, Summer 1979, p. 315. His considerable influence may be
seen in Anastaplo, "Abraham Lincoln's Emancipation Proclamation."
See, also, *Modern Age,* Winter 1981, p. 106. See, as well, Jaffa, "Invent-
ing the Past," *The St. John's Review,* Autumn 1981, p. 1, Winter 1982,
p. 113. Cf. Anastaplo, "Preliminary Reflections on the Pentagon
Papers," *University of Chicago Magazine,* Jan./Feb., March/April 1972
(reprinted in 118 *Congressional Record* 24990 [July 24, 1972]); "Notes
Toward an 'Apologia Pro Vita Sua': A Response to Mr. Thurow,"
Interpretation, 10/2, 3(1982) (note 13, above).

Still another way of indicating my differences with some of Mr.
Strauss's students is to note that I have been a student as well of Malcolm P. Sharp. See, on Mr. Sharp, note 164, above. See, also, Anastaplo,
"The Rosenberg Case and the Perils of Indignation," *Chicago Lawyer,*
June 1979, p. 19; Sharp, "Crosskey, Anastaplo, and Meiklejohn on the
United States Constitution," 20 *University of Chicago Law School Record* 3 (Spring 1973); Sharp, "The universe has its good and friendly
features" (my intended title), *Bulletin of the Atomic Scientists,* May
1981, p. 1; ("Kuana" should be "Kuaua"); Anastaplo, *Human Being
and Citizen,* Essay No. 4. See, as well, *Daedalus,* Winter 1981; *Nation,*
Jan. 24, 1981.

See the text at note 65, above, notes 95 and 183 (end), above, note
288 and Appendix F, below.

286.   See, for example, Anastaplo, "Jacob Klein of St. John's College"; also,
Book Review, *Modern Age,* Summer 1979, p. 314.

Citations to other eulogies and articles honoring Mr. Strauss may be
found in Emma Brossard, "Leo Strauss," *Academic Reviewer,* Fall–
Winter, 1974, p. 1. See for other discussions bearing on the work of
Leo Strauss: (1) Victor Gourevitch, 22 *Review of Metaphysics* 58, 281
(1968); (2) James Steintrager, 32 *The Thomist* 307 (1968); (3) Henry
S. Kariel, 1 *Political Science Reviewer* 74 (1971); (4) Gerhart Niemeyer,
1 *Political Science Reviewer* 277 (1971); (5) Willmoore Kendall, *Contra
Mundum* (New Rochelle: Arlington House, 1971); (6) Charles N.R.
McCoy, 35 *Review of Politics* 161 (1973); (7) Allan Bloom, 2 *Political
Theory* 372 (1974) (also, Bloom, *The Republic of Plato;* Pangle, *The*

Laws of Plato); (8) Howard B. White, 41 *Social Research* 3 (1974); (9) Werner J. Dannhauser, *American Scholar* (Fall 1974) (reprinted in Epstein, ed., *Masters*); (10) James R. Adams, *Wall Street Journal,* Oct. 18, 1974, p. 14; (11) Harry V. Jaffa, *The Conditions of Freedom* (Baltimore: Johns Hopkins Press, 1975); (12) Eugene Miller, in Anthony de Crespigny and Kenneth Minogue, eds., *Contemporary Political Philosophers* (New York: Dodd, Mead & Co., 1975); (13) Milton Himmelfarb, *Commentary,* August 1974, p. 60, January 1975, p. 14; (14) George N. Nash, *The Conservative Intellectual Movement in America Since 1945* (New York: Basic Books, 1976); (15) Harvey Mansfield, Jr. and J.G.A. Pocock, 3 *Political Theory* 372, 385, 402 (1975); (16) John P. East, *Modern Age,* Winter 1977, p. 2; (17) Ralph Lerner, *American Jewish Year Book,* 1976, p. 92; (18) Harry V. Jaffa, *How to Think About the American Revolution* (Durham: Carolina Academic Press, 1978); (19) John G. Gunnell, 72 *American Political Science Review* 122 (1978); (20) Joseph A. Buijs, 27 *Judaism* 448 (1978); (21) Seth Benardete, 8 *Political Science Reviewer* 1 (1978); (22) Hwa Yol Jung, 9 *Journal of the British Society for Phenomenology* 11 (1978); (23) Hans-Georg Gadamer and Leo Paul de Alvarez, *Newsletter,* Politics Department, The University of Dallas, Spring 1978, p. 4; (24) Laurence Lampert and S. A. Maaranen, *Modern Age,* Winter 1978, pp. 38, 47; (25) Frederick D. Wilhelmsen, *Christianity and Political Philosophy* (Athens: University of Georgia Press, 1978); (26) E.B.F. Midgley, 53 *New Scholasticism* 168 (Spring 1979). See, also, note 215, above.

See, for bibliographies of the writings of Leo Strauss, Joseph Cropsey, 5 *Interpretation* 133 (1975); Hilail Gildin, ed., *Political Philosophy: Six Essays by Leo Strauss* (Indianapolis: Bobbs-Merrill, 1975); David L. Schaefer, *Intercollegiate Review,* Summer 1974, p. 139. See, for various of Mr. Strauss's works, notes 2, 4, 15, 145, 24, 77, and 236, above.

See, for citations to the work of various scholars influenced by Mr. Strauss, J. Harvey Lomax, ed., *A Contemporary Bibliography in Political Philosophy and in Other Areas* (1976) (4215 Glenaire Drive, Dallas, Texas 75229).

See, for an obituary of Leo Strauss, *New York Times,* October 21, 1973, p. 77.

287. See the end of Section iii of this Epilogue, above. The scholar quoted here is David Grene, The Committee on Social Thought, The University of Chicago. See, on Mr. Grene, *National Law Journal,* June 18, 1979, p. 33, n. 17; Strauss, *What is Political Philosophy?,* p. 299.

The Jason Aronson funeral remarks (in Section viii of this Epilogue) were originally published by Dean Maurice F. X. Donahue for the University of Chicago (along with remarks by Thomas McDonald and me). Mr. Aronson was, at the time of his death, an instructor in the Basic Program of Liberal Education for Adults.

Mr. Strauss's "Nietzsche!" story (in Section v of this Epilogue) may now be found also (in a slightly different version) in 7 *Interpretation* 1–2 (September 1978). See, as well, *The College,* St. John's College, January 1979, p. 30.

See, on the relation of poetry and philosophy, Strauss, *Liberalism, Ancient and Modern* (New York: Basic Books, 1968), p. 134. See, also, notes 3 (end) and 145, above.

288. See, on politics as the master art, Aristotle, *Nicomachean Ethics* 1094a18 sq.; note 237, above. See, also, note 3 (end), above.

Consider, for a suggestion that the political art should be used to master the religion-based strife between evolutionists and creationists, my essay, "Science, Repression and Morality," prepared for the annual Clarence Darrow memorial meeting in Chicago, March 13, 1981:

i

Clarence Darrow, a few years after the Scopes evolution trial, explained, "I am an agnostic because I do not believe everything I hear. I believe some things. No person can believe anything unless he is an agnostic about something else.... We are all agnostics. The question is, what are you agnostic about?" Just as we may all be in some sense agnostics, may we not be, in a sense, all deists as well?

It can be useful, therefore, to begin to clarify one's thoughts as to what one is, or must be, agnostic about, and as to what belief in a divinity (or in nature) can mean. A case in point is the current evolutionist-creationist controversy, at the heart of which are doctrinal differences as to what one is entitled to believe about the origins of life on this planet.

ii

For some time now we have been warned against repressive attacks by religious fundamentalists upon Darwinian opinions. Thus, I recall meeting the mild-mannered John Scopes (here in Chicago more than a decade ago) when he was campaigning against such efforts with respect to textbooks. This past fortnight, front page stories in the press reported an effort in court by creationists to change how these matters are taught in California public schools. They insist that evolution should be taught as no more than a "theory" (whatever that may mean to them), not as a dogma. More such efforts are anticipated, especially since we now have a President who is believed to be in sympathy with the creationists.

But lest "right-thinking" people become unduly alarmed, certain obvious facts should be pointed out. The most telling is that there is virtually no chance that creationists will long prevail anywhere in the Western world at this time. They are fighting a rearguard battle. The scientific prejudices of this age, which are remorselessly against them, are growing stronger, not weaker. Indeed, that may have already been true in this country at the time of the Scopes Trial in 1925. This suggests that there is something unrealistic, if not even hysterically unbecoming, about the threats now being publicized by evolutionists, as well as something illusory, if not even shortsightedly provocative, in the challenges now being made by creationists.

Still, it should be recognized by those who ridicule the challenges posed by creationists that evolution theories are themselves critically limited in certain respects. On the one hand, they require, in explaining what has happened in the emergence of animal life on this planet, a fantastic series of minor changes made over a vast time—changes made in "slow motion," so to speak. On the other hand, they require, in explaining the era which saw the formation of the universe in which all this has taken place, cataclysmic reactions (associated with the so-called Big Bang) which happened on a gigantic scale almost instantaneously.

For most of us, then, the complicated accounts given today by science about the sudden origins of the present universe and about the gradual descent of the various species we know are so incredible, if not incomprehensible, as to require at least as much (if not the same kind of) faith as does belief in the accounts given some thirty-three centuries ago in *Genesis*. Of course, both the scientist and the mystic may believe themselves to *know* the things they tell the rest of us about.

Be all this as it may, one of the critical questions remaining for anyone interested in these things is *how* life itself originated, whether from inanimate matter (which matter is assumed by many scientists "always" to have existed) or from nothing (which is assumed by most creationists). (The more sophisticated among the creationists and the evolutionists can now be understood to agree that there may have been stages of development in the emergence of the life we now have—stages recorded, for example, in the ample fossil record. Thus, the six "days" of creation can now be seen as laying down in matter the patterns which were destined to take the forms we know—with the first three or four "days," by the way, not being defined in their duration by any existing sun.) To believe that a divine artist originated life still leaves a considerable mystery, of course, but then so does the belief that the richly varied forms of life we know, which routinely exhibit a sense of purpose as well as a remarkable exuberance, developed more or less accidentally after chance electrical charges (or whatever) animated something in the primordial "soup" once available on this planet. Certainly, the modern biologist in his study of animate things again and again assumes that a purposeful art is naturally involved in the operations of living bodies. (It is also instructive to notice that every science, indeed everything we know, rests upon impressions and premises which are somehow simply grasped as self-evident rather than secured through demonstration. Thus, a kind of trust [*pistis*] or faith, not agnosticism, is naturally relied upon at the foundation of all we believe ourselves to know. See, e.g., Plato, *Epinomis* 974B–C.)

To say all this about the limitations of evolution theory is not to disavow the proposition I have advanced, that the present faith in science, its claims and its accomplishments is apt to grow among us. Perhaps science would come to be generally repudiated if mankind should suffer unprecedented disasters (in war or otherwise) because of the powerful technology, grounded in modern science, which we depend upon. But such repudiation is, in our present circumstances, highly unlikely.

Those, then, who stand with modern science—and this would include, I take it, most of those who continue to honor the memory of Clarence Darrow—should appreciate that they deal from considerable strength. Certainly, such people are not truly vulnerable these days to sustained repression, however much chatter there should be by media intellectuals to that effect. Rather, as people of superior education and standing in the community, they should be particularly tolerant—as well as confident that they will prevail both in the courts and in the academies.

A much more serious question than whether desperate creationists will win a temporary victory here or there is the question of whether the moral foundations of our national community are being subverted, those foundations which depend to a considerable extent upon the traditional religious opinions (particularly with respect to divine providence) which careless scientists do tend to undermine. Unless those foundations are firm, we are not apt to have a community which is confident and sensible enough to resist such genuine threats to our well-being, if not to our very existence, as fearful and hence reckless recourse to nuclear and biological weapons in the coming decades. Do not both scientific research and a productive use of that research, as well as a safe and decent way of life, continue to depend on a community which is rooted in moral assurances and in a political harmony which science is itself *not* the source of?

In short, the more "advanced" members of our community should moderate doctrinal quarrels among us, especially since (for better or for worse) time does seem (at least with respect to the evolution issue) to be on their side. This means, among other things, that they should deal prudently (and hence gently) with creationists, whose moral dedication and good will a healthy community cannot long do without, however troublesome their self-righteousness and intolerance may be at times.

iii

It has been in the spirit of Clarence Darrow that I have suggested that we should not believe everything we hear about the repression we face today.

One danger we do face, and about which privileged intellectuals should not be agnostic, is with respect to the permanent damage that can be done when "right-thinking" people make much in public, without regard to social consequences, of their differences from their seemingly less enlightened fellow citizens. Are not magnanimity and accommodation called for among us in these matters today?

See, as bearing on the subjects of this Clarence Darrow memorial essay, Anastaplo, *The Constitutionalist*, pp. 803–4. *Human Being and Citizen*, Essays No. 7, No. 8, and No. 10. See, also, Franklin, *Autobiography*, pp. 56–57; note 76, above. See, as well, Plato, *Laws* 885B sq.; Epilogue, Section ii, Appendix C, Sections v–vi, xi–xii; Appendix E, Section viii; notes 3 and 145, above.

289.   Xenophon, *Memorabilia*, I, vi, 14. See Anastaplo, *Human Being and Citizen*, p. 8. See, also, note 145, above.

Consider, as well, A. Conan Doyle, *The Adventure of the Norwood Builder,* in which Sherlock Holmes observes of an ingenious culprit who overreached himself in executing his "masterpiece of villainy": "But he had not that supreme gift of the artist, the knowledge of when to stop."

Index